CONNECTIONISM AND THE MIND

For
David E. Rumelhart
a pilgrim mind and master modeler

Connectionism and the Mind

Parallel Processing, Dynamics, and Evolution in Networks

Second edition

William Bechtel and Adele Abrahamsen

BLACKWELL
Publishers

First published 1991
Second edition published 2002

2 4 6 8 10 9 7 5 3 1

Blackwell Publishers Inc.
350 Main Street
Malden, Massachusetts 02148
USA

Blackwell Publishers Ltd
108 Cowley Road
Oxford OX4 1JF
UK

Library of Congress Cataloging-in-Publication Data has been applied for.

ISBN 0–631–20712–0 (hardback); 0–631–20713–9 (paperback)

British Library Cataloguing in Publication Data
A CIP catalogue record for this book is available from the British Library.

Typeset in 10/12pt Imprint
by Graphicraft Ltd, Hong Kong
Printed in Great Britain by MPG Books Ltd, Bodmin, Cornwall

This book is printed on acid-free paper.

CONTENTS

PREFACE

Connectionism is what happened when certain cognitive scientists began using neural networks as a means of modeling cognition. This was probably the first strong indicator that cognitive science is a shape-changer that can endure by repeatedly incorporating new ideas and techniques. In the 1970s cognitive science received its name and a distinct identity as the intellectual home of researchers who produced new symbolic models of cognition by blending key developments of the 1950s and 1960s: the cognitive revolution in psychology, the Chomskian revolution in linguistics, and the heady early days of artificial intelligence. By the 1980s what is now called "classic cognitive science" became more diverse in its disciplinary influences (e.g., certain philosophers, anthropologists, and sociologists became involved), but cognitive scientists continued to find unity in their allegiance to core assumptions of the symbolic approach and their commitment to interdisciplinary work. At the same time, a challenge to this unity was mounted by researchers who reached back to a slightly earlier era (the 1940s and 1950s) in which crosstalk between neuroscience and an emerging science of computation had yielded neurally inspired networks of units which achieved computation by propagating activation. The cognitive scientists who revived them in the early 1980s pressed the case that such networks should be embraced as a subsymbolic alternative to symbolic models of cognition, and referred to them as connectionist, neural network, artificial neural network (ANN), or parallel distributed processing (PDP) models.

The first edition of *Connectionism and the Mind* appeared in 1991, approximately one decade after connectionism made its entrance. Battle for dominance between symbolic and connectionist modeling was at a peak. The first edition provided a primer on the computational basics of networks, then reviewed the battle, and in a final chapter discussed how a variety of disciplines might be affected by the rise of connectionism. Another decade has passed as this second edition goes to press, and the landscape has again been considerably altered. What is now sometimes called "classic connectionism" has become more established within cognitive science and some of its contributing disciplines, but it has faced new external challenges from transdisciplinary trends towards dynamical systems, artificial life research, and cognitive neuroscience. Some network modelers have been inspired to incorporate these trends into their work, resulting in less classic varieties of connectionism to which we give ample attention in this new edition.

Connectionism and the Mind (2002), like its predecessor, is written primarily for those who are curious but not yet knowledgeable about connectionism. For individuals who simply want to know what all the fuss is about and to navigate occasional encounters with networks, this book should serve as a one-stop shopping emporium. We envisage such readers to include advanced undergraduates with above-average interest in cognitive science, graduate students and faculty whose interests intersect those of connectionists, and individuals outside the academic world who have been hooked by a casual encounter with networks and want to know more. We also have kept in mind those graduate students in the cognitive sciences for whom this book may be among their first entry points into a field they intend to explore in much greater depth and perhaps make their career. The boxes and appendices offer them a little more detail than the text alone, and the cross-references to specific modeling software as well as the "Sources and Suggested Readings" at the end of each chapter should help guide their next steps. Finally, large portions of the book are relevant to those who want to update knowledge that is no longer current. We worked especially hard at finding the best avenues of explanation and examples of research for such challenging topics as dynamical systems theory. We hope we came close to meeting the goal that every reader find these topics both accessible and exciting.

Both editions are distinctive in the extent to which they cover conceptual issues and philosophical inquiry into the mind while also introducing the nuts and bolts of connectionist modeling. This new edition of *Connectionism and the Mind* retains and updates the first three chapters of the first edition, in which the stage is set and a variety of connectionist architectures and learning procedures are described (including worked-out examples of basic computations). As before, the next few chapters focus on theoretical claims and counterclaims. Certain well-known network models provided the original context for these arguments, but a number of proposals and models from the 1990s have been added in this new edition. Specifically, chapter 4 (on pattern recognition) combines parts of the original chapters 4 and 5 and adds a new network model of logical derivation. Chapter 5 (on using networks rather than rules to perform such tasks as past-tense acquisition) combines parts of the original chapters 6 and 7 and adds more recent past-tense simulations. Chapter 6 (on issues of representation) combines parts of the original chapter 6 with a variety of new material. The final four chapters are entirely new. Each focuses on a different context in which network research moved beyond classical connectionism in the 1990s: modular networks and feature maps in chapter 7, dynamical systems in chapter 8, artificial life research in chapter 9, and cognitive neuroscience in chapter 10.

The final chapter of the first edition was eliminated. Its predictions of the impact of connectionism on various disciplines now read more like postdictions (or in a few instances, misses) and need not be repeated. However, we regret that limitations of time and space prevented us from retaining and updating that chapter's coverage of enduring issues involving linguistics, philosophy, developmental psychology, ecological psychology, cognitive psychology, AI, and the structure of disciplines (including reductionism and the appropriate level for connectionist accounts). Readers interested in these issues should consult the first edition. (However, the implications of connectionism for developmental theory have more extensive treatments elsewhere now, e.g., Chapter 10 of McLeod, Plunkett, and Rolls, 1998.) Neuroscience is the one topic that was retained and expanded into a separate chapter in the new edition. A few key advances involving the eliminated topics found a place within sections of the new edition: first, the entry of Optimality Theory into linguistics (section 1.5); second, progress on connectionist approaches to concerns in developmental psychology regarding past-tense acquisition (section 5.4), the nativism issue (section 3.3), and maturation (section 6.4); and third, network controllers for robots (sections 9.4–9.6). This last development (embodying interactive networks as the brains of robots) delighted us as an unexpected answer to our concern that in connectionism's first decade, "the network is dynamic, but the input is not." We had noted the potential of networks to model "the functioning of the mental system in dynamic articulation with the environment" and thereby "become increasingly ecological" (Bechtel and Abrahamsen, 1991, p. 267). Network-controlled robots realize that hope, but we must leave to a later time any extended discussion of underlying or explicit relationships to ecological psychology.

There are a few practical matters to address. The only mathematical background assumed for most of the material is basic familiarity with algebra, although more would be required to pursue networks or dynamics beyond the level presented here. To make the equations governing activity and learning in networks as accessible as possible, we use a mnemonic notational system and minimize the amount of detail presented. To provide concrete experience with the functioning of connectionist networks, we provide a step-by-step guided tour of several simulations. These originally were run using the **PDP** software provided with McClelland and Rumelhart's *Explorations in Parallel Distributed Processing: A Handbook of Models, Programs, and Exercises* (1988). However, readers can get hands-on experience with almost all of the simulations by downloading updated software and user manuals from the web: **PDP++** at www.cnbc.cmu.edu/PDP++/PDP++.html and **tlearn** at crl.ucsd.edu/innate/tlearn.html. These simulation software packages also are supplied on disk and discussed at length in certain textbooks, as indicated in the suggested readings for chapter 2 and in the cross-references we supply with each particular simulation.

The PDP books by David Rumelhart and James McClelland are still a touchstone for a wide variety of work on networks and we retain our coverage and conventions for referring to these books. The two 1986 volumes entitled *Parallel Distributed Processing: Explorations in the Microstructure of Cognition* are composed of 26 chapters, each of which was written by some combination of Rumelhart, McClelland, and the members of the PDP Research Group at UCSD. We refer to these chapters by their authors, date of publication (1986), and chapter number. For example, chapter 14 (which happens to be in volume 2) is referred to as Rumelhart, Smolensky, McClelland, and Hinton (1986, in *PDP:14*). The third volume, which is the 1988 book described in the preceding paragraph, is referred to as the *Handbook*. The PDP books use more than one notation, and it is somewhat different from ours. Appendix A compares our notation to that of *PDP:2* and *PDP:8*, and also shows schematically at what point in processing each equation is applied.

Acknowledgments

See the preface to the first edition for specific acknowledgments and appreciation of the roles played by Lawrence W. Barsalou, Richard Billington, Dorrit Billman, James Garson, Geoffrey E. Hinton, David Klahr, Sige-Yuki Kuroda, Henri Madigan, Robert N. McCauley, James L. McClelland, Ulric Neisser, Britten Poulson, Robert C. Richardson, David E. Rumelhart, and Paul R. Thagard, as well as groups of scholars at Georgia State University, Skidmore College, and University of Cincinnati.

The contributions of these individuals provided *Connectionism and the Mind* (2002) with a strong legacy, but it would not exist in its current form without the added involvement of a number of recent students and colleagues. Those who carefully read and commented on early drafts of multiple chapters have our deep gratitude: David Adams, Michael Cortese, Henry Cribbs, Pim Haselager, Brian Keeley, Cees van Leeuwen, Pete Mandik, and Jonathan Waskin. We also benefited from discussions of specific topics with many individuals, particularly István S. N. Berkeley (logic simulations), Rick Grush (DST), Brett Hyde (Optimality Theory), Karalyn Patterson (dyslexia), and Cees van Leeuwen (DST). Joan Straumanis provided feedback from her study group, and Robert Straveler II alerted us to an error in a previous version of figure 2.2.

One of us (Bechtel) was a Visiting Fellow in the Department of Psychology at Free University of Amsterdam in May–August 1995. He is grateful to the participants in his seminar on representation for insightful discussions of issues considered in this book and especially to his host, Huib Looren de Jong. Back home in St. Louis, in spring 1996 he and Andy Clark jointly led a seminar on dynamical systems theory and situated action that helped incubate chapter 8. This was just one of countless ways in which both of us have benefited from the camaraderie and intellectual sparks generated by the faculty, postdoctoral fellows, students and visitors in Washington University's Philosophy–Neuroscience–Psychology program as well as other colleagues in the departments of philosophy and psychology. We also have a valued, longstanding relationship with Blackwell Publishers. We thank Steve Smith for his strong leadership and Beth Remmes for her expert guidance, and both for their patience when other projects (including two other books for Blackwell) often took priority. Valery Rose adroitly shepherded the manuscript into press.

Our greatest debt is to David E. Rumelhart, who was graduate adviser to one of us (Abrahamsen) at the University of California, San Diego, during the period when he worked with semantic networks. Not everyone has the opportunity to follow the work of their dissertation adviser through two different sea changes in one field of inquiry: the cognitive revolution which licensed semantic networks and other symbolic models of mind, and the connectionist commitment to a subsymbolic level of explanation. During the symbolic era, when he was "R" in the LNR research group (along with Peter Lindsay and Donald A. Norman), Abrahamsen benefited from observing his mind in motion almost daily. When she heard from afar of the remarkable innovations of its successor, the PDP research group, she was grateful for the gift of new tools for gaining glimpses of the microstructure of cognition. David Rumelhart's deep curiosity, unparalleled mind for modeling, and skilled but flexible use of research tactics enabled him to make landmark contributions across the entire range of human cognition (from perception to the structure of stories). Sadly, he gradually lost his power to make new contributions to cognitive science when he developed Pick's disease in the 1990s. As we were writing these words we also were reading a book on Galileo, another modeler of dynamical systems who, as his own powers declined, took comfort in the thought that yet more discoveries would emerge from "other pilgrim minds." We hope that among our readers there will be some who will be inspired to further study and, with tenacity and originality approaching that of David Rumelhart, will make discoveries that would have delighted him.

1

NETWORKS VERSUS SYMBOL SYSTEMS: TWO APPROACHES TO MODELING COGNITION

1.1   A Revolution in the Making?

The rise of cognitivism in psychology, which, by the 1970s, had successfully established itself as a successor to behaviorism, has been characterized as a Kuhnian revolution (Baars, 1986). Using Kuhn's (1962/1970) term, the emerging cognitivism offered its own *paradigm*, that is, its research strategies and its way of construing psychological phenomena, both of which clearly distinguished it from behaviorism (for overviews, see Neisser, 1967; Lindsay and Norman, 1972). This change was part of a broader cognitive revolution that not only transformed a number of disciplines such as cognitive and developmental psychology, artificial intelligence, linguistics, and parts of anthropology, philosophy, and neuroscience; it also led to an active cross-disciplinary research cluster known as *cognitive science* (see Bechtel, Abrahamsen, and Graham, 1998). Its domain of inquiry centrally included reasoning, memory, and language but also extended to perception and motor control. As the cognitive paradigm developed, the idea that cognition involved the manipulation of symbols became increasingly central. These symbols could refer to external phenomena and so have a semantics. They were enduring entities which could be stored in and retrieved from memory and transformed according to rules. The rules that specified how symbols could be composed (syntax) and how they could be transformed were taken to govern cognitive performance. Given the centrality of symbols in this approach, we will refer to it as the *symbolic paradigm*.

In the 1980s, however, an alternative framework for understanding cognition emerged in cognitive science, and a case can be made that it is a new Kuhnian paradigm (Schneider, 1987). This new class of models are variously known as *connectionist*, *parallel distributed processing* (*PDP*), or *neural network* models. The "bible" of the connectionist enterprise, Rumelhart and McClelland's two volumes entitled *Parallel Distributed Processing* (1986), sold out its first printing prior to publication and sold 30,000 copies in its first year. The years since have seen a steady stream of additional research as well as a number of textbooks (J. A. Anderson, 1995; Ballard, 1997; Elman et al., 1996; McLeod, Plunkett, and Rolls, 1998; O'Reilly and Munakata, 2000; Quinlan, 1991) and new journals (e.g., *Connection Science*, *Neural Computation*, and *Neural Networks*). Clearly connectionism has continued to attract a great deal of attention.

Connectionism can be distinguished from the traditional symbolic paradigm by the fact that it does not construe cognition as involving symbol manipulation. It offers a radically different conception of the basic processing system of the mind-brain, one inspired by our knowledge of the nervous system. The basic idea is that there is a network of elementary *units* or nodes, each of which has some degree of activation. These units are *connected* to each other so that active units excite or inhibit other units. The network is a *dynamical system* which, once supplied with initial input, spreads excitations and inhibitions among its units. In some types of network, this process does not stop until a *stable state* is achieved.[1] To understand a connectionist system as performing a cognitive task, it is necessary to supply an interpretation. This is typically done by viewing the initial activations supplied to the system as specifying a problem, and the resulting stable configuration as the system's solution to the problem.

Both connectionist and symbolic systems can be viewed as computational systems. But they advance quite different conceptions of what computation involves. In the symbolic approach, computation involves the transformation of symbols according to rules. This is the way we teach computation in arithmetic: we teach rules for performing operations specified by particular symbols (e.g., + and ÷) on other symbols which refer to numbers. When we treat a traditional computer as a symbolic device, we view it as performing symbolic manipulations specified by rules which typically are written in a special data-structure called the *program*. The connectionist view of computation is quite different. It focuses on causal processes by which units excite and inhibit each other and does not provide either for stored symbols or rules that govern their manipulations. (For further discussion of the notion of *computation*, and whether it extends to the type of processing exhibited by connectionist networks, see B. C. Smith, 1996; van Gelder, 1995; and chapter 8, below.)

While connectionism has achieved widespread attention only since the 1980s, it is not a newcomer. The predecessors of contemporary connectionist models were developed in the mid-twentieth century and were still being widely discussed during the early years of the cognitive revolution in the 1960s. The establishment of the symbolic paradigm as virtually synonymous with cognitive science (at least for researchers in artificial intelligence and computational modeling in psychology) only occurred at the end of the 1960s, when the symbolic approach promised great success in accounting for cognition and the predecessors of connectionism seemed inadequate to the task. A brief recounting of this early history of network models will provide an introduction to the connectionist approach and to the difficulties which it is thought to encounter. The issues that figured in this early controversy still loom large in contemporary discussions of connectionism and will be discussed extensively in subsequent chapters. For additional detail see Cowan and Sharp (1988), from which we have largely drawn our historical account, and Anderson and Rosenfeld (1988) and Anderson, Pellionisz, and Rosenfeld (1990), which gather together many of the seminal papers and offer illuminating commentary.

1.2   Forerunners of Connectionism: Pandemonium and Perceptrons

The initial impetus for developing network models of cognitive performance was the recognition that the brain is a network. Obviously, given the complexity of the brain and the limited knowledge available then or now of actual brain functioning, the goal was not to model brain activity in complete detail. Rather, it was to model cognitive phenomena in systems that exhibited some of the same basic properties as networks of neurons in the brain. The foundation was laid by Warren McCulloch and Walter Pitts in a paper published in 1943. They proposed a simple model of neuron-like computational units and then demonstrated how these units could perform logical computations. Their "formal neurons" were binary units (i.e., they could either be on or off). Each unit would receive excitatory and inhibitory inputs from certain other units. If a unit received just one inhibitory input, it was forced into the *off* position. If there were no inhibitory inputs, the unit would turn *on* if the sum of the excitatory inputs exceeded its threshold. McCulloch and Pitts showed how configurations of these units could perform the logical operations of *and*, *or*, and *not*. McCulloch and Pitts further demonstrated that any process that could be performed with a finite number of these logical operations could be performed by a network of such units, and that, if provided with indefinitely large memory capacity, such networks would have the same power as a universal Turing machine.

The idea captured by McCulloch–Pitts neurons was elaborated in a variety of research endeavors in succeeding decades. John von Neumann (1956) showed how networks of such units could be made more reliable by significantly increasing the number of inputs to each particular unit and determining each unit's activation from the statistical pattern of activations over its input units (for example, by having a unit turn on if more than half of its inputs were active). In von Neumann's networks each individual unit could be unreliable without sacrificing the reliability of the overall system. Building such redundancy into a network seems to require vastly increasing the number of units, but Winograd and Cowan (1963) developed a procedure whereby a given unit would contribute to the activation decision of several units as well as being affected by several units. This constitutes an early version of what is now referred to as "distributed representation" (see section 2.2.4).

In addition to formal characterizations of the behavior of these networks, research was also directed to the potential applications of these networks for performing cognitive functions. The first paper by McCulloch and Pitts was devoted to determining the logical power of networks, but a subsequent paper (Pitts and McCulloch, 1947) explored how a network could perform pattern recognition tasks. They were intrigued by the ability of animals and humans to recognize different versions of the same entity even when quite different in appearance. They construed this task as requiring multiple transformations of the input image until a canonical representation was produced, and they proposed two networks that could perform some of the required transformations. Each network received as input a pattern of activation on some of its units. The first network was designed to identify invariant properties of a pattern (properties possessed by a pattern no matter how it was presented), while the second transformed a variant into a standard representation. Because their inspiration came from knowledge of the brain, they presented evidence that the first type of network captured properties of the auditory and visual cortex, while the second captured properties of the superior colliculus in controlling eye movements.

Frank Rosenblatt was one of the major researchers to pursue the problem of pattern recognition in networks. In his *elementary perceptron*, a single layer of McCulloch–Pitts units (shown as triangles in figure 1.1) received input from sensory units. Each McCulloch–Pitts unit was influenced in its own way by the input activations, as determined by a modifiable connection with each input that could range from strongly inhibitory to strongly excitatory. Whether the resulting activation was sufficient for the McCulloch–Pitts unit to fire depended upon its threshold (t). In this example,

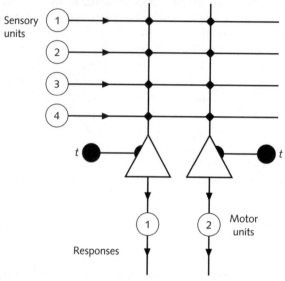

Figure 1.1 An elementary perceptron, as investigated by Rosenblatt (1958). Inputs are supplied on the four sensory units on the left and outputs are produced on the two motor units at the bottom. The network's computational units are the two McCulloch–Pitts neurons (large triangles), each of which has an inhibitory connection to a threshold unit (small dark circles). Each intersection between horizontal and vertical lines represents the synapse of one sensory unit on one of the McCulloch–Pitts neurons. This way of diagramming a network arranges the synapses such that, if their modifiable weights were shown, they would be in tabular format. Reprinted with permission from J. D. Cowan and D. H. Sharp (1988) Neural nets and artificial intelligence, *Daedalus*, 117, p. 90.

the output was sent to a motor unit (not an essential part of the architecture). Rosenblatt also explored networks with multiple layers of McCulloch–Pitts units, including some in which later layers might send excitations or inhibitions back to earlier layers.

Rosenblatt differed from McCulloch and Pitts in making the strengths (commonly referred to as the *weights*) of the connections continuous rather than binary and in introducing procedures for changing these weights so that perceptrons could learn. For elementary perceptrons, Rosenblatt's procedure was to have the network generate, using existing weights, an output for a given input pattern. The weights on connections feeding into any unit that gave what was judged to be an *incorrect* response were changed; those feeding into units giving the correct response were not. If the unit was off when it should have been on, the weight on the connection from each active input unit was increased. Conversely, if the unit was on when it should have been off, the weight from each active input unit was reduced. Rosenblatt offered a proof of his important Perceptron Convergence Theorem with respect to this training procedure. The theorem holds that if a set of weights existed that would produce the correct responses to a set of patterns, then through a finite number of repetitions of this training procedure the network would in fact learn to respond correctly (Rosenblatt, 1961; see also Block, 1962).

Rosenblatt emphasized how the perceptron differed from a symbolic processing system. Like von Neumann, he focused on statistical patterns over multiple units (e.g., the proportion of units activated by an input), and viewed noise and variation as essential. He contended that by building a system on statistical rather than logical (Boolean) principles, he had achieved a new type of information processing system:

> It seems clear that the class C' perceptron introduces a new kind of information process-
> ing automaton: For the first time, we have a machine which is capable of having ori-
> ginal ideas. As an analogue of the biological brain, the perceptron, more precisely, the
> theory of statistical separability, seems to come closer to meeting the requirements of a
> functional explanation of the nervous system than any system previously proposed. . . .
> As a concept, it would seem that the perceptron has established, beyond doubt, the
> feasibility and principle of non-human systems which may embody human cognitive
> functions at a level far beyond that which can be achieved through present day automatons.
> The future of information processing devices which operate on statistical, rather than
> logical principles seems to be clearly indicated.   (Rosenblatt, 1958, p. 449; quoted in
> Rumelhart and Zipser, 1986, in *PDP:5*, pp. 156–7)

Oliver Selfridge (1959) was another of the early investigators of the pattern recognition capabilities of network models. Unlike Rosenblatt, he assigned a particular interpretation to each of the units in his network. One of the pattern recognition tasks he explored was recognition of letters, a task that is made difficult by the fact that different people write their letters differently. He called his model *pandemonium*, capturing its reliance upon *cognitive demons* that performed computations in parallel without attention to one another, each of them "shouting out" its judgment of what letter had been presented (figure 1.2). These cognitive demons each specialized in gathering evidence for one particular letter; the greater the evidence the louder they shouted. The *decision demon* then made the identification of the letter on the basis of which unit shouted the loudest. The evidence gathered by each cognitive demon was supplied by a lower layer of *feature demons*. Each feature demon responded if its feature (e.g., a horizontal bar) was present in the image. The feature demon was connected to just those cognitive demons whose letters contained its feature. Thus, a cognitive demon would respond most loudly if all of its features were present in the image, and less loudly if some but not all of its features were present. One of the virtues of this type of network is that it would still make a correct or plausible judgment about a letter even if some of its features were missing or atypical (see Selfridge, 1959; Selfridge and Neisser, 1960).

Early researchers recognized that, in addition to modeling pattern recognition, networks might be useful as models of how memories were established. In particular, researchers were attracted to the problem of how networks might store associations between different patterns. An extremely influential proposal was developed by Donald Hebb (1949), who suggested that when two neurons in the brain were jointly active, the strength of the connection might be increased. This idea was further developed by Wilfrid Taylor (1956), who explored networks of analog units that took activations within a continuous range (e.g., − 1 to + 1). In the network he proposed, a single set of motor units was connected to two different sets of sensory units (which we will call the *base units* and the *learning units*). The network was set up such that each pattern on the base units was associated with a pattern on the motor units. A different set of patterns was defined for the learning units. No associations to the motor units were specified, but each learning unit pattern was assigned an association with one base unit pattern. When the network was run, the associated sensory patterns were activated at the same time. The eventual outcome

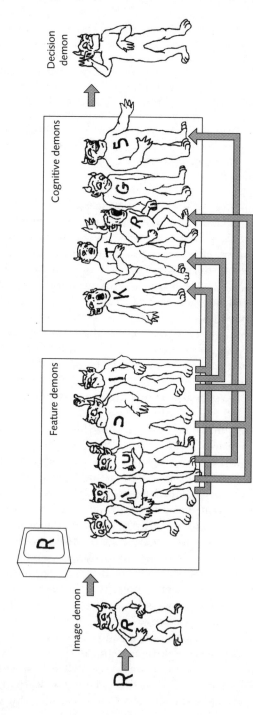

Figure 1.2 Selfridge's (1959), pandemonium model. The "demons" at each level beyond the image demon (which merely records the incoming image) extract information from the preceding level. Thus, a given feature demon responds positively when it detects evidence of its feature in the image, and a cognitive demon responds to the degree that the appropriate feature demons for its letter are active. Finally, the decision demon selects the letter whose cognitive demon is most active. Figure drawn by Jesse Prinz.

was that the learning units acquired the ability to generate the same motor patterns as the base units with which they were associated.

Another researcher who pursued this type of associative memory network was David Marr (1969), who proposed that the cerebellum is such a network which can be trained by the cerebrum to control voluntary movements. The cerebellum consists of five different kinds of cell or unit, with the modifiable connections lying between the granule cells and Purkinje cells. The other cell types serve to set the firing thresholds on these two cell types. The development of connections between the granule cells and Purkinje cells, he proposed, underlay the learning of sequences of voluntary movements in activities like playing the piano. Marr subsequently proposed models for the operation of the hippocampus (Marr, 1971) and neocortex (Marr, 1970).

The early history of network models we have summarized in this section indicates that there was an active research program devoted to exploring the *cognitive* significance of such networks. It is important to emphasize that while some of this research was explicitly directed at modeling the brain, for Rosenblatt and some other researchers the goal was to understand cognitive performance more generally. The relative prominence of research devoted to network models diminished in the late 1960s and early 1970s, as the alternative approach of symbolic modeling became dominant. In section 1.3 we will examine what made the symbolic approach so attractive to cognitive researchers, and in section 1.4 we will see that interest in networks declined until revived by connectionism in the 1980s. Finally, in section 1.5 we will get an overview of connectionism's continued development in the 1990s via alliances with other new approaches to cognition and end by raising the prospect of a *rapprochement* with the symbolic approach.

1.3   The Allure of Symbol Manipulation

1.3.1   From logic to artificial intelligence

The symbol manipulation view of cognition has several roots. One of these lies in philosophy, in the study of logic. A logical system consists of procedures for manipulating symbols. In propositional logic the symbols are taken to represent propositions (i.e., sentences) and connectives (e.g., *and, or, if–then*). Generally there is a clear goal in such manipulation. For example, in *deductive logic* we seek a set of rules that will enable us to generate only true propositions as long as we start with true propositions. A system of such rules is spoken of as *truth preserving*. The simple inference rule *modus ponens* is an example of a truth-preserving rule. From one proposition of the form *If p, then q* and another of the form *p*, we can infer a proposition of the form *q* (where *p* and *q* are placeholders for specific propositions, e.g., "If I think, then I exist").

We have actually adopted two perspectives in the previous paragraph, and it is the relation between them that makes logic, and systems designed to implement logic, so powerful. From one perspective, we treat the symbols for propositions as representational devices. For example, we conceive of a proposition as depicting a state of affairs that might or might not hold in the world. From this perspective, we speak of a proposition as either *true* (if the proposition corresponds to the way the world is) or *false* (if it does not correspond). This perspective is generally known in logic as a *model theoretic* perspective. We think of a model as a set of entities and properties and identify those propositions as *true* whose ascriptions correspond to the properties that the entities in the model actually possess. Within this framework we can evaluate whether a pattern of inference is such that for any model in which the premises are true, the conclusion will also be true. The second perspective, known as the *proof theoretic* perspective, focuses not on the relations between the propositions and the entities they represent, but simply on the relations among the propositions themselves, construed as formal entities. When we specify inference rules in a logical system, we focus only on the syntax of the symbols and disregard what they refer to. What gives logic its power is, in part, the possibility of integrating these two perspectives by designing proof procedures that are complete, that is, that will enable us to derive any proposition that will be true in all models in which the premises are true.

The relation between proof theory and model theory gives rise to a very powerful idea. If intelligence depended only upon logical reasoning, for which the goal was truth preservation, then it would be possible to set up formal proof procedures which will achieve intelligent performance. However, intelligence does not depend solely on being able to make truth-preserving inferences. Sometimes we need to make judgments as to what is probably (but not necessarily) true. This is the domain of *inductive logic*. The goal of inductive logic is to establish formal rules, analogous to the proof theoretic procedures of deductive logic, that lead from propositions that are true to those that are likely to be true. If such rules can be identified, then we may still be able to set up formal inference procedures that produce intelligent performance.

The crucial assumption in both deductive and inductive logic is that in making inferences involving a symbolic expression, we consider only its form. We can disregard the expression's representational function, that is, whether it is true or not, and if true, what state of affairs it describes. For example, the form of the expression (*p and* (*q or r*)) is that of a particular connective (*and*) with two arguments; one is a proposition (*p*) and the other is composed from another connective (*or*) with two propositional arguments (*q, r*). Based just on the form of the expression, without knowing anything about *p* or the other propositions, we infer *p*. If (*p and* (*q or r*)) is in fact true this is a sound inference, but if it is false then *p* may or may not be true and inferring it risks error. Thus, it is important to take care that the initial expressions (premises) are true before undertaking inference in a formal system. One advantage gained is the efficiency of attending only to form; another is that the symbols may be reinterpreted (i.e., assigned new representational roles) without affecting the validity of the inferences made using them.

The idea that intelligent cognitive processes are essentially processes of logical reasoning has a long history, captured in the long-held view that the rules of logic constitute rules of thought. It is found in authors such as Hobbes, who treated reasoning as itself comparable to mathematical computation and suggested that thinking was simply a process of formal computation:

> When a man *reasoneth*, he does nothing else but conceive a sum total, from *addition* of parcels; or conceive a remainder, from *subtraction* of one sum from another; which, if it be done by words, is conceiving of the consequence of the names of all the parts, to the name of the whole; or from the names of the whole and one part, to the name of the other part. . . . These operations are not incident to numbers only, but to all manner of things that can be added together, and taken from one out of another. For as arithmeti-

cians teach to add and subtract in *numbers*; so the geometricians teach the same in *lines*, *figures*, solid and superficial, *angles, proportions, times*, degrees of *swiftness, force, power*, and the like; the logicians teach the same in *consequences of words*; adding together two *names* to make an *affirmation*, and two *affirmations* to make a *syllogism*; and *many syllogisms* to make a *demonstration*; and from the *sum* or *conclusion* of a *syllogism*, they subtract one *proposition* to find the other.   (Hobbes [1651], 1962, p. 41)

The idea of thinking as logical manipulation of symbols was further developed in the works of rationalists such as Descartes and Leibniz and empiricists such Locke and Hume, all of whom conceived of the symbols as ideas, and formulated rules for properly putting together or taking apart ideas.

With the development of automata theory and physical computers in the mid-twentieth century, there was a burgeoning of more subtle and varied views of symbols and symbol manipulation. From one perspective (well characterized in Haugeland, 1981), the digital computer is simply a device for implementing formal logical systems. Symbols are stored in memory registers (these symbols may simply be sequences of 1s and 0s, implemented by *on* and *off* settings of switches). The basic operations of the computer allow recall of the symbols from memory and execution of changes in the symbols according to rules. In the earliest computers, the rules for transforming symbols had to be specially wired into the machine, but one of the major breakthroughs in early computer science was the development of the stored program. The stored program is simply a sequence of symbols that directly determines what operations the computer will perform on other symbols. The relation between the stored program and those other symbols is much like the relation between the formally written rule *modus ponens* and the symbol strings to which it can be applied. Like the formal rules of logic, the rules in the computer program do not consider the semantics of the symbols being manipulated, but only their form. This perspective has been given a variety of renderings by such theorists as Dennett (1978), Fodor (1980), and Pylyshyn (1984).

An alternative way to construe the semantics of computational systems was offered by Newell and Simon (1981). For them, a computer is a *physical symbol system* consisting of symbols (physical patterns), expressions (symbol structures obtained by placing symbol tokens in a physical relation such as adjacency), and processes that operate on expressions. They pointed out that there is a semantics (designation and interpretation) within the system itself; specifically, expressions in stored list-processing programs designate locations in computer memory, and these expressions can be interpreted by accessing those locations. They regarded this internal semantics as a major advance over formal symbol systems such as those of logic, and argued that intelligence cannot be attained without it:

> *The Physical Symbol System Hypothesis.* A physical symbol system has the necessary and sufficient means for general intelligent action.
>
> By "necessary" we mean that any system that exhibits general intelligence will prove upon analysis to be a physical symbol system. By "sufficient" we mean that any physical symbol system of sufficient size can be organized further to exhibit general intelligence.   (Newell and Simon, 1981, p. 41)

Newell and Simon thus disagreed with those cognitive scientists who, in emphasizing the continuity between computers and formal logic, retained the assumption that syntax should be autonomous from semantics. They saw computers as providing an advantageous dovetailing of syntax and semantics that was not available within abstract formal logic. A similar difference in perspective arose with respect to what work the computer is regarded as carrying out. From a continuity perspective, computers are powerful devices for implementing logical operations: programs can be written to serve the same function as inference rules in a logical system. From the alternative perspective (Simon, 1967), it took work in artificial intelligence to show us that *heuristics* (procedures that *might* obtain the desired result, often by means of an intelligent shortcut such as pruning unpromising search paths) are often more useful than *algorithms* (procedures that are guaranteed to succeed in a finite number of steps but may be inefficient in a large system).

Hence, work in artificial intelligence is rooted in formal logic, but has achieved distinctive perspectives by pursuing the idea that computers are devices for symbol manipulation more generally. AI programs have replaced formal logic as the closest external approximation to human cognition; programs exist, for example, not only for proving logical theorems or performing logical inference, but also for playing chess at a grandmaster's level and diagnosing diseases. The (partial) success of these programs has suggested to many researchers that human cognitive performance also consists in symbol manipulation. Indeed, until recently this analogy provided a locus of unity among cognitive scientists.

1.3.2   From linguistics to information processing

Yet another root of the symbolic approach is found in Noam Chomsky's program in linguistics. In his review of B. F. Skinner's *Verbal Behavior*, Chomsky (1959) argued that a behavioristic account was inadequate to account for the ability of humans to learn and use languages. Part of his argument focused on the creativity of language: Chomsky contended that any natural language has an infinite number of syntactically well-formed sentences, and that its speakers can understand and produce sentences that they had not previously encountered (Chomsky, 1957, 1968). This ability did not seem explicable in terms of learned associations between environmental stimuli and linguistic responses, even if these were augmented by such processes as generalization and analogy. In Chomsky's view, Skinner had not succeeded in adapting the constructs of behaviorism to the precise requirements of a linguistic account, and a quite different approach was needed.

In particular, Chomsky developed the notion of *generative grammar*: to write a grammar was to specify an automaton that could generate sentences (which could comprise an infinite set if at least one recursive rule was included). One way to evaluate such a grammar was to ask whether it could generate all of the well-formed sentences of the target language, and only those sentences. Chomsky described and evaluated several different classes of generative grammars with respect to natural languages. Of particular importance, he argued that finite state grammars (those most consistent with a behaviorist account) were too weak even when they included recursive rules. They could generate an infinite set of sentences, but not the *correct* set. Specifically, they were unable to handle dependencies across indefinitely long strings (e.g., the dependency between *if* and *then* in sentences of the form "If A, then B" where A is indefinitely long). To handle such dependencies, at least a phrase structure grammar (and preferably a transformational grammar) was required. These grammars produce phrase structure trees by applying a succession of rewrite rules

(rules which expand one symbol into a string of subordinate symbols, each of which can itself be expanded, and so forth). Indefinitely long constituents can be embedded within such a tree without affecting the surrounding dependencies. Transformational rules (rules that modify one phrase structure tree to obtain a related, or transformed, tree) provide additional power, but the most important and enduring part of Chomsky's argument is the rejection of finite state grammars.

Chomsky viewed generative grammar as a model of linguistic *competence*; that is, a model of the knowledge of their language that speakers actually possess in their minds. Although he pioneered the use of (abstract) automata for specifying grammars, he did not intend to model linguistic *performance* (the expression of competence in specific, real-time acts such as the production and comprehension of utterances), nor did he implement his grammars on physical computers. Hence, his version of cognitivism is somewhat more abstract than that of information-processing psychology. Nevertheless, many psychologists were influenced by Chomsky as they moved from behaviorism to information processing because his grammars suggested ways to model human knowledge using linguistic-style rules (that is, formally specified operations on strings of symbols).

Although Chomsky focused on linguistic competence, he did make some general, controversial claims about linguistic performance. One of these claims, that a process of hypothesis testing is involved in language acquisition, bore implications that were fruitfully developed by Jerry Fodor (1975). Before we can test a hypothesis, such as that the word *dog* refers to dogs, we must be able to state it. Fodor reasoned that this requires a language-like medium, which he called the *language of thought*. Further, since there is no way for a child to learn this language, it must be innate. Thus, Fodor contended that procedures for formal symbol manipulation must be part of our native cognitive apparatus. Fodor's argument represents a minority position within psychology, but virtually all researchers in the majority tradition of information processing assume some weaker version of a symbolic approach to cognition.

1.3.3 Using artificial intelligence to simulate human information processing

We have briefly reviewed two strands of the symbolic approach: a strand leading from formal logic to artificial intelligence, in which computers came to be viewed as symbol manipulation devices, and a strand leading from linguistics to psychology, in which human cognition came to be viewed likewise as consisting in symbol manipulation. In cognitive science, these two strands are often brought together in a cooperative enterprise: the design of computer programs to serve as models or simulations of human cognition. This raises a number of interesting issues that we can only briefly mention here (a number of penetrating discussions are available, e.g., Haugeland, 1985). Does a successful computer simulation closely approximate mental symbol processing at some appropriate level of abstraction, so that both the human and the computer are properly construed as symbol processors? Or should true symbol manipulation be attributed to only one of the two types of system; and if so, to the human or the computer? On one view, the human is the true symbol manipulator (because, for example, the human's symbols are meaningful), and the computer is merely a large calculator or scratchpad that can facilitate the process of deriving predictions from models of human performance (similar to the meteorolo-gist's use of computers to calculate equations that describe the fluid dynamics of the atmosphere, for example). A contrasting view holds that the computer is the true symbol manipulator, and that human cognition is carried out quite differently (in less brittle fashion, as might be modeled in a network, for example). These issues, which have been troublesome for some time, gained increased salience with the reemergence of network models in the 1980s. We turn now to a brief history of networks as an alternative to the symbolic tradition.

1.4   The Decline and Re-emergence of Network Models

1.4.1   Problems with perceptrons

By the 1960s substantial progress had been made with both network and symbolic approaches to machine intelligence. But this parity was soon lost. Seymour Papert provided a whimsical account:

> Once upon a time two daughter sciences were born to the new science of cybernetics. One sister was natural, with features inherited from the study of the brain, from the way nature does things. The other was artificial, related from the beginning to the use of computers. Each of the sister sciences tried to build models of intelligence, but from very different materials. The natural sister built models (called neural networks) out of mathematically purified neurones. The artificial sister built her models out of computer programs.
>
> In their first bloom of youth the two were equally successful and equally pursued by suitors from other fields of knowledge. They got on very well together. Their relation-ship changed in the early sixties when a new monarch appeared, one with the largest coffers ever seen in the kingdom of the sciences: Lord DARPA, the Defense Depart-ment's Advanced Research Projects Agency. The artificial sister grew jealous and was determined to keep for herself the access to Lord DARPA's research funds. The natural sister would have to be slain.
>
> The bloody work was attempted by two staunch followers of the artificial sister, Marvin Minsky and Seymour Papert, cast in the role of the huntsman sent to slay Snow White and bring back her heart as proof of the deed. Their weapon was not the dagger but the mightier pen, from which came a book – *Perceptrons*. . . .   (1988, p. 3)

Clearly the publication of *Perceptrons* in 1969 represented a watershed. Thereafter research on network models, such as perceptrons and pandemonium, no longer progressed apace with work on symbolic models. Some researchers did continue to pursue and develop network models and in fact established some important prin-ciples governing network systems (see J. A. Anderson, 1972; Kohonen, 1972; Grossberg, 1976). But their work attracted only limited attention and funding. What is less clear is whether Minsky and Papert's book precipitated the decline, or whether it was only a symptom.

Minsky and Papert's objective in *Perceptrons* was to study both the potential and limitations of network models. They used the tool of mathematics to analyze what kinds of computation could or could not be performed with an elementary perceptron (one in which input units are connected to a single layer of McCulloch–Pitts units). The centerpiece of their critique was their demonstration that there are functions, such as those determining whether a figure is connected or whether the number of elements is odd or even, which cannot be evaluated by such a network. An example is the logical connective *exclusive or* (usually abbreviated as "XOR"). The expression p *XOR* q is defined as true if p is true and q is not, or q is true and p is not. In order for a perceptron to compute XOR, it is necessary to include an additional layer of McCulloch–Pitts units (now known as *hidden units*) between the input units and the original layer of McCulloch–Pitts units (now known as *output units*). While Minsky and Papert recognized that XOR could be computed by such a multi-layered network, they raised an additional problem: there were no training procedures for multi-layered networks that could be shown to converge on a solution. As we will discuss in section 3.2.2, an adaptation of Rosenblatt's training procedure for two-layer networks has now been developed for multi-layered networks. But Minsky and Papert raised further doubts about the usefulness of network models. Even if the problem were overcome, would it be possible to increase the size of networks to handle larger problems? In more technical terms, this is a question as to whether networks will *scale* well. Minsky and Papert offered the intuitive judgment that research on multi-layered networks would be "sterile."

The inability of networks to solve particular problems was, for many investigators, only symptomatic of a more fundamental problem: the only kind of cognitive processes of which networks seemed capable were those involving associations. Within limits, a network could be trained to produce a desired output from a given input, but that merely meant that it had developed procedures for associating that input with the desired output. Associationism was exactly what many of the founders of modern cognitivism were crusading against. Chomsky contended, for example, that finite automata or simple associationistic mechanisms were inadequate to generate all the well-formed sentences of the language. One needed a more powerful automaton capable of recursive operations for generating trees and manipulating them. The identification of network models with associationism thus undercut their credibility and supported the pursuit of symbolic programs as the major research strategy in cognitive science. As we will see in chapters 5 and 6, many advocates of the symbolic tradition continue to fault modern connectionism on precisely this ground.

1.4.2 Re-emergence: The new connectionism

In the early 1980s the type of network research pioneered by Rosenblatt began once again to attract attention and to gain adherents within what had now become known as cognitive science. Geoffrey Hinton and James A. Anderson's (1981) *Parallel Models of Associative Memory* was a harbinger, based on a 1979 conference that brought together UCSD's core group of cognitive scientists (especially David Rumelhart and Donald Norman) with some key researchers who had never abandoned networks (e.g., Anderson, Hinton, Teuvo Kohonen, and David Willshaw) and others who were newly attracted to them (e.g., Terrence Sejnowski from computational neuroscience and Jerome Feldman from artificial intelligence). Papers that employed networks to model various cognitive performances began to appear in cognitive journals. At the 1984 meeting of the Cognitive Science Society, two symposia presented the network approach and debated its role in cognitive science. One, entitled "Connectionism versus Rules: The Nature of Theory on Cognitive Science," featured David Rumelhart and Geoffrey Hinton advocating network modeling (connectionism) and

Zenon Pylyshyn and Kurt Van Lehn arguing that networks were inadequate devices for achieving cognitive performance. Debate at that session and others during the conference occasionally became acrimonious as these "new connectionists"[2] began to press their alternative and challenged the supremacy of the symbolic approach. Connectionist research increased dramatically across the 1980s and became part of the established order in the 1990s, as departments hired young connectionists and many senior researchers added connectionist modeling techniques to their repertoire as tools to be employed for at least some purposes.

An intriguing question is why connectionism should have re-emerged so strongly when it did. Probably there was a confluence of factors. First, powerful new approaches to network modeling were developed around the early 1980s, including new architectures, new techniques for training multi-layered networks, and advances in the mathematical description of the behavior of nonlinear systems. Many of these innovations could be applied directly to the task of modeling cognitive processes. Second, the credibility and persuasiveness of some of the key innovators helped their message to get a hearing within cognitive science. For example, in chapters 2 and 3 we discuss an important mathematical insight into network behavior that was proposed by John Hopfield, a distinguished physicist. Anderson and Rosenfeld commented:

> John Hopfield is a distinguished physicist. When he talks, people listen. Theory in his hands becomes respectable. Neural networks became instantly legitimate, whereas before, most developments in networks had been in the province of somewhat suspect psychologists and neurobiologists, or by those removed from the hot centers of scientific activity.   (1988, p. 457)

Third, a related factor that was probably not essential but helped jump-start the new developments was that certain people were in the right place at the right time (e.g., Hinton and Anderson were visitors at UCSD, a leading center of symbolic cognitive science that became a leading center of network modeling, especially parallel distributed processing). Fourth, cognitive science had remained, either intentionally or unintentionally, somewhat isolated from neuroscience through the 1970s. In large part this was because there was no clear framework to suggest how work in the neurosciences might bear on cognitive models. But by the 1980s cognitive scientists began to see advantages in the neural-like architecture of connectionist models. Fifth, this attraction to networks was one reflection of a more general interest in finding a fundamental explanation for the character of cognition. Rule systems, as they became more adequate, also became more complex. The desire for parsimony, which earlier had characterized behaviorism, re-emerged. Sixth, a number of investigators began to confront the limitations of symbolic models. While initially the task of writing rule systems capable of accounting for human behavior seemed tractable, intense pursuit of the endeavor raised doubts. Rule systems were hampered by their "brittleness," inflexibility, difficulty in learning from experience, inadequate generalization, domain specificity, and inefficiencies due to serial search. Human cognition, which the rule systems were supposed to be modeling, seemed to be relatively free of such limitations.

Cognitive scientists who were motivated by several of these factors became connectionists, and quite a battle ensued with advocates of the classic symbolic approach beginning in the mid-1980s. At the same time, though, developments within both symbolic and network approaches often had the effect of softening the boundary between them. Some symbolic modelers, focusing on the fifth and sixth factors listed above, sought unified frameworks for cognitive modeling that shared some attributes with network models. ACT-R (John R. Anderson, 1993; Anderson and Lebière, 1998) uses a localist network architecture for its long-term memory and a production system architecture for operating on what is retrieved. The *Soar* architecture (Laird, Newell, and Rosenbloom, 1987) makes a production system do both jobs. However, as described in Newell's (1990) master work, *Unified Theories of Cognition*, it seems to approximate the spirit of connectionist models in its simplicity (e.g., fine-grained rules compete in parallel with no conflict resolution attempted).

On the connectionist side, some designers made *hybrid models* by implementing specific rule-based accounts in connectionist architectures so as to gain advantages of both approaches (e.g., Touretzky and Hinton, 1988; see section 6.2.1, below). Connectionists also found more general inspiration in certain approaches that emerged from the symbolic tradition shortly before connectionism itself emerged, and never fully resided in either the symbolic or connectionist camp; examples include schema theory and story grammars (Rumelhart, 1975), probabilistic feature models (Smith and Medin, 1981), symbol-based semantic networks with spreading activation (J. R. Anderson, 1983), prototype theory (Rosch, 1975), and scripts (Schank and Abelson, 1977). Some of these can be given a connectionist implementation, arguably superior to the original theory. For example, schemata should be flexible and easy to modify, but this is much harder to achieve in a symbolic than in a connectionist implementation (Rumelhart, Smolensky, McClelland, and Hinton, 1986, in *PDP:14*). Also, a major effort to implement scripts in networks is the focus of chapter 7. Work that combined aspects of the symbolic and connectionist approaches helped lay the groundwork for the more pluralistic, if not always less contentious, cognitive science that opened the twenty-first century.

1.5 New Alliances and Unfinished Business

The big story of recent years, however, is not the softening of the boundary between symbolic and connectionist approaches. It is the new alliances that specialized subgroups of connectionists have formed with other emerging frameworks for understanding cognitive and sensorimotor abilities. In this second edition we examine three such alliances.

- *Dynamical approaches* to cognition give long-overdue priority to the dimension of time, and the mathematical and visual tools of dynamical systems theory illuminate how certain types of connectionist networks achieve their success.
- *Embodied cognition* is the idea that mind cannot be understood only by modeling internal activity; it is crucial to extend inquiry outwards to the mind's interactive couplings with the body and environment. Creating network controllers for robots provides a way of pursuing this idea, and using simulated evolution as the method makes them especially relevant to a new research field called "artificial life."
- *Cognitive neuroscience* is a field that has thrived recently due to the availability of new ways to measure and form images of the activity of the brain during cognitive activity. Network modelers increasingly are moving their focus down into

the brain, tailoring the architecture and tasks performed by networks to knowledge about particular brain areas that has been gained not only from neuroimaging but also from such traditional methods as lesion studies, ERP, and single-cell recording in animals.

These new alliances will produce some of the most exciting work of the first decade of the twenty-first century. Whatever their success, though, they will leave some unfinished business. For reasons that we still do not understand, systems with enough parallel, distributed, dynamical, embodied and neurally grounded activity to do just about anything – perhaps even achieving Turing equivalence – repeatedly find themselves in the same grooves. That is, they behave in ways that can be closely approximated by symbolic models, and for many purposes it is the symbolic models that are most convenient to use. This is especially clear in the case of language: network models of the brain's activities in processing language, however good they get, will not displace linguistics. The real challenge for connectionists will not be to defeat symbolic theorists, but rather to come to terms with the ongoing relevance of the symbolic level of analysis. That is, the ultimate new alliance may be as simple, and as difficult, as forming a new relationship with the long-time opponent.

In most circles this idea currently has little priority and few adherents. If the future of connectionism lies in yet another alliance – one with the symbolic approach it has been opposing vigorously for years – a glimpse of that future is available now in Optimality Theory (OT; see Prince and Smolensky, 1993). This new linguistic framework originated in an alliance between two people: Paul Smolensky, who was a major contributor to connectionism in the 1980s, and Alan Prince, who was a major opponent during that same period. They found common ground in the discovery that various phonological phenomena can be described using a universal set of soft constraints to select the optimal output among a large number of candidates. A given language has its own rigid rank ordering of these constraints, which settles the numerous conflicts between them.

As a very simple example (see Tesar, Grimshaw, and Prince, 1999, for the five-constraint version from which this is drawn), the constraint NoCODA is violated by any syllable ending in a consonant (the coda) and the constraint NoINSV is violated if a vowel is inserted in the process of forming syllables (the output) from a phoneme string (the input). If these were the only two constraints to consider (in fact there always are more), the input string /apot/ would be syllabified as .a.pot. in a language that ranks NoINSV higher (e.g., English), but as .a.po.to. or some other vowel-final form in a language that ranks NoCODA higher (e.g., Japanese). Working with talented collaborators, Smolensky and Prince developed Optimality Theory into such an elegant account that in just a few years it came to dominate work in phonology.

One unfinished task for optimality theorists is to achieve an equally compelling OT account of syntax. Another is to achieve a well-motivated interface between OT and the network-like level that is assumed to be its substrate (see Prince and Smolensky, 1997, for the recent status of this effort). As we will see in chapter 2, networks can be viewed as devices for constraint satisfaction and hence should provide a fairly natural implementation of OT. In Smolensky's harmonic grammar, for example, weighted connections can be used to optimally satisfy a set of linguistic constraints (in accord with Smolensky's more general Harmony Theory; see Smolensky, 1986, in *PDP:6*). The problem is that the networks of harmonic grammar engage in competition quantitatively – various input patterns and the weights of various connections can yield many different outcomes – but a strict ranking of constraints always emerges at the higher level of description provided by OT. Why? Nobody knows. Until that problem is solved, the network level of description is of limited explanatory utility with respect to OT. But the solution, when and if it is found, may create a *rapprochement* between network models and symbolic accounts that triggers an era of dramatic progress in which alignments are found and used all the way from the neural level to the cognitive/linguistic level.

We mention this future possibility in order to now put it aside. Classic connectionism and its battle with the classic symbolic approach fill the next six chapters of this book, and the alliances that are currently most influential within connectionism are the focus of the last three chapters. Specifically, we introduce network architectures in chapter 2 and learning procedures in chapter 3. Then some specific network models are presented in the context of philosophical positions: some that are concordant with connectionism in chapter 4, followed by battles over rules in chapter 5, and battles over representations in chapter 6. A modular network implementation of a quasi-symbolic framework, scripts, is presented in some detail in chapter 7. We then move to alliances with the dynamical approach in chapter 8 (a prickly alliance, it will be seen), artificial life and embodied cognition in chapter 9, and cognitive neuroscience in chapter 10. It will become increasingly apparent in these later chapters that classic connectionism is just one way of "doing networks" and that an era of pluralism is already well under way.

NOTES

1   If one were trying to model the ongoing life of the mind, as opposed to its response to a specific input, one might not want the network to really stabilize but only to achieve temporarily stable states, which might then be disrupted by new inputs or other internal processes.
2   The earliest connectionists were not neural network modelers of the mid-twentieth century like Rosenblatt, but associationists who viewed higher-order competencies as arising from connections among simpler elements. For Wernicke in the late nineteenth century the elements were neurally realized sensory and motor encodings; for Thorndike in the early twentieth century they were stimuli and responses. Each called his approach "connectionism."

SOURCES AND SUGGESTED READINGS

Anderson, J. A. and Rosenfeld, E. (1998) *Talking Nets: An Oral History of Neural Networks*. Cambridge, MA: MIT Press.

Anderson, J. A. and Rosenfeld, E. (eds) (1988) *Neurocomputing: Foundations of Research*. Cambridge, MA: MIT Press.

Anderson, J. A., Pellionisz, A., and Rosenfeld, E. (1990) *Neurocomputing 2: Directions for Research*. Cambridge, MA: MIT Press.

Churchland, P. M. (1995) *The Engine of Reason, the Seat of the Soul*. Cambridge, MA: MIT Press.

Clark, A. (1989) *Microcognition: Philosophy, Cognitive Science, and Parallel Distributed Processing*. Cambridge, MA: MIT Press.

Clark, A. (1993) *Associative Engines: Connectionism, Concepts, and Representational Change.* Cambridge, MA: MIT Press.

Cowan, J. D. and Sharp, D. H. (1988) Neural nets and artificial intelligence. *Daedalus,* 117, 85–121.

Cummins, R. and Cummins, D. D. (eds) (2000) *Minds, Brains, and Computers: The Foundations of Cognitive Science: An Anthology.* Oxford: Blackwell.

Franklin, S. (1995) *Artificial Minds.* Cambridge, MA: MIT Press.

Grossberg, S. (1982) *Studies of Mind and Brain: Neural Principles of Learning, Perception, Development, Cognition, and Motor Control.* Dordrecht: Reidel.

Rutgers Optimality Archive (ROA): electronic repository of papers on Optimality Theory at *http://ruccs.rutgers.edu/roa.html.*

2

CONNECTIONIST ARCHITECTURES

Connectionist networks are intricate systems of simple units which dynamically adapt to their environments. Some have thousands of units, but even those with only a few units can behave with surprising complexity and subtlety. This is because processing is occurring in parallel and interactively, in marked contrast with the serial processing to which we are accustomed. To appreciate the character of these networks it is necessary to observe them in operation. Thus, in the first section of this chapter we will describe a simple network that illustrates several features of connectionist processing. In the second section we will examine in some detail the various design principles that are employed in developing networks. In the final section we will discuss several appealing properties of networks that have rekindled interest in using them for cognitive modeling: their neural plausibility, satisfaction of "soft constraints," graceful degradation, content-addressable memory, and capacity to learn from experience. Connectionists maintain that the investment in a new architecture is amply rewarded by these gains but, as we will also note, they must overcome some serious challenges.

2.1 The Flavor of Connectionist Processing: A Simulation of Memory Retrieval

We will begin by describing a connectionist model which McClelland (1981) designed for the purpose of illustrating how a network can function as a content-addressable memory system. Its simple architecture conveys the flavor of connectionist processing in an intuitive manner. The information to be encoded concerns the members of two gangs, the Jets and the Sharks, and some of their demographic characteristics (figure 2.1). Figure 2.2 shows how this information is represented in a network, focusing on just five of the 27 gang members for readability. These figures are redrawn (including corrections) from McClelland and Rumelhart's *Handbook* (1988, pp. 39, 41), which uses the gang database for several exercises; there is related discussion by Rumelhart, Hinton, and McClelland (1986) in *PDP:2* (pp. 25–31). In this section we present the results of several different runs which we performed on the Jets and Sharks network using the **iac** (interactive activation and competition) program in chapter 2 of the *Handbook*. It will be seen that this simple network could retrieve names of individuals from properties, retrieve properties from names, generalize, and produce typicality effects.

The Jets and the Sharks

Name	Gang	Age	Education	Marital status	Occupation
Art	Jets	40s	J.H.	Sing.	Pusher
Al	Jets	30s	J.H.	Mar.	Burglar
Sam	Jets	20s	COL.	Sing.	Bookie
Clyde	Jets	40s	J.H.	Sing.	Bookie
Mike	Jets	30s	J.H.	Sing.	Bookie
Jim	Jets	20s	J.H.	Div.	Burglar
Greg	Jets	20s	H.S.	Mar.	Pusher
John	Jets	20s	J.H.	Mar.	Burglar
Doug	Jets	30s	H.S.	Sing.	Bookie
Lance	Jets	20s	J.H.	Mar.	Burglar
George	Jets	20s	J.H.	Div.	Burglar
Pete	Jets	20s	H.S.	Sing.	Bookie
Fred	Jets	20s	H.S.	Sing.	Pusher
Gene	Jets	20s	COL.	Sing.	Pusher
Ralph	Jets	30s	J.H.	Sing.	Pusher
Phil	Sharks	30s	COL.	Mar.	Pusher
Ike	Sharks	30s	J.H.	Sing.	Bookie
Nick	Sharks	30s	H.S.	Sing.	Pusher
Don	Sharks	30s	COL.	Mar.	Burglar
Ned	Sharks	30s	COL.	Mar.	Bookie
Karl	Sharks	40s	H.S.	Mar.	Bookie
Ken	Sharks	20s	H.S.	Sing.	Burglar
Earl	Sharks	40s	H.S.	Mar.	Burglar
Rick	Sharks	30s	H.S.	Div.	Burglar
Ol	Sharks	30s	COL.	Mar.	Pusher
Neal	Sharks	30s	H.S.	Sing.	Bookie
Dave	Sharks	30s	H.S.	Div.	Pusher

Figure 2.1 Information about members of two gangs, the Jets and Sharks. Reprinted by permission of author from J. L. McClelland (1981) Retrieving general and specific knowledge from stored knowledge of specifics, *Proceedings of the Third Annual Conference of the Cognitive Science Society*. Copyright 1981 by J. L. McClelland.

2.1.1 Components of the model

The most salient components of a connectionist architecture are: (a) simple elements called *units*; (b) equations that determine an *activation* value for each unit at each point in time; (c) weighted *connections* between units which permit the activity of one unit to influence the activity of other units; and (d) *learning rules* which change the network's behavior by changing the weights of its connections. The Jets and Sharks model exhibits components (a)–(c); we defer the important topic of learning until later.

(a) *The units* There are 68 units in the complete model: a unit for each gang member (27 units); a unit for each gang member's name (27 units); and a unit for each of the properties members can exhibit (14 units). The units are grouped into seven clusters (the "clouds" in figure 2.2); within each cluster the units are mutually exclusive.[1] In addition to two clusters for the members and their names, there are five clusters for properties that distinguish the members (age, occupation, marital

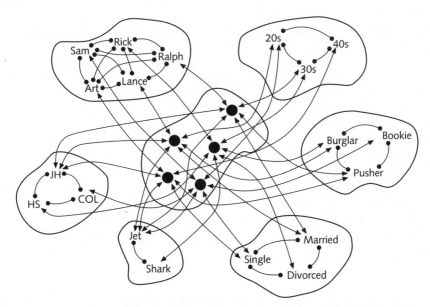

Figure 2.2 McClelland's (1981) Jets and Sharks network. Each gang member is represented by one person unit (center) that is connected to the appropriate name and property units. Only 5 of the 27 individuals from figure 2.1 are included in this illustration. Adapted (with corrections) from J. L. McClelland (1981) Retrieving general and specific knowledge from stored knowledge of specifics, *Proceedings of the Third Annual Conference of the Cognitive Science Society.* Copyright 1981 by J. L. McClelland.

status, educational level, and gang membership). Note that the names are regarded as a special kind of property; the name cluster is just one cluster among others around the periphery. Each individual gang member is represented, not by his name, but by a person unit in the center cluster that is connected to the appropriate name and property units. As a notational convention in the equations that follow, any of these units can be referenced by the variables u (the *unit* of interest) and i (a unit that provides *input* to u).

(b) *Activations* Associated with each unit is an activation value, $activation_u$. Initially each unit is set at a "resting activation" of -0.10. When a simulation is run, the activations vary dynamically between the values -0.20 and $+1.00$, reflecting the effects of external input, the propagation of activation from other units in the system, and decay over time. External input is the activation of certain units by the environment (in practice, the investigator, who wishes to observe the effects). It is only the property and name units, however, that can receive external input; for this reason they are referred to as the *visible* units. The person units cannot be directly accessed from outside the network, and are therefore referred to as *invisible* or *hidden* units. Their only source of change in activation, besides decay, is the propagation of activation from other units to which they are connected.

(c) *Weighted connections* In this particular network, all connections are bidirectional and are assigned a binary weight. Wherever there is a connection from unit i to unit u with $weight_{ui}$, there is a converse connection from unit u to unit i with $weight_{iu}$ of the same value. (Conventionally, the order of subscripts is the reverse of the direction of propagation of activation.) Specifically, for each person unit there is a two-way excitatory connection (with weight + 1) with that person's name and with each of his properties (one property unit per cluster). Hence, a person unit propagates activation to all of its property units, and a property unit propagates activation to all of the units for persons who exhibit that property. Weights of − 1 are used to form inhibitory connections among units within a cluster; hence, activation of one property tends to suppress the activity of other properties in its cluster. (However, we deleted the inhibitory connections between name units to obtain certain generalizations across names.) For example, if the property **divorced** is activated, the immediate effects are that the property units **single** and **married** will become less active (due to their inhibitory connections with **divorced**) at the same time that the person units **JIM, GEORGE, RICK**, and **DAVE** will become more active (due to their excitatory connections with **divorced**). Note that person units like **RICK** (which are hidden units) are indicated by upper case, and name units like "**Rick**" (which are visible units) by lower case in quotes.

2.1.2   Dynamics of the model

The Jets and Sharks model exhibits a variety of interesting behaviors when it performs memory retrieval tasks. To understand the dynamics, it is important to work through the equations that govern the propagation of activation through the network. In this section we introduce the general task of memory retrieval and then describe the equations that are involved in carrying it out. In the final section, we illustrate the operation of the network by tracking its performance across several specific memory retrieval tasks.

2.1.2.1   Memory retrieval in the Jets and Sharks network   To simulate a memory retrieval task, we supply an external input to one or more of the visible units and observe the effects. For example, to simulate using Art's name to retrieve his properties, we can increase the input into "**Art**" (Art's name unit). The excitatory connections in the network will propagate this activation first to the person unit **ART**, and from there to the units for Art's properties. This is only the beginning, however; the increased activation will continue to reverberate through the network across numerous cycles of processing, during which Art's property units will become increasingly active (in addition to other, less direct effects). At the same time, each active unit will send inhibitions to other units in its cluster. Every change in activation produces additional changes in other units, and the process of dynamically changing activation values can be repeated many times. For tractability, it is useful to set up discrete processing cycles; once per cycle, the fixed amount of external input is again supplied, and each unit sends and receives excitations and inhibitions and updates its own activation. After a number of cycles, the system will stabilize so that the input to each unit will be precisely that which enables it to retain its current activation. (In the language of dynamical systems, discussed in section 8.2.1, the network has settled into a *point attractor*.) At this time, only a subset of the units will have high activation values. In our "**Art**" example, the units that would stabilize at high activations include **ART, Jets, single, pusher, 40s**, and **junior high**. Thus, by querying the network with a name, we recovered the person's other properties.

2.1.2.2 The equations To explain how these effects are produced, we will present some of the relevant equations. We have made every effort to make this material accessible even to those with some degree of math anxiety. To enhance readability, we use English-like labels for variables and constants; most are similar to those in McClelland and Rumelhart's (1988) *Handbook*. The subscripts that we use to index units are mnemonic (and therefore idiosyncratic). It is fairly straightforward to translate our equations into the *Handbook*'s relatively accessible notation. To aid with transfer to the somewhat less accessible notation in Rumelhart and McClelland's (1986) *PDP* volumes, we provide translations of important equations in Appendix A (p. 349). Notation varies widely in connectionist modeling, and we leave it as an exercise for the reader to carry out any additional translations when reading primary sources.

Most of the equations can be viewed as focusing on a particular unit, for example, a unit whose activation is being calculated. We refer to this unit as u. (Actually, in its usual use as a subscript, u is an index that ranges over all of the units to which the equation will be applied.) Often the equation refers as well to another unit (or units) that is feeding into u; we refer to such a unit as i. (This notation is not particularly mnemonic here, but it will be later when we discuss feedforward networks.) To propagate activation, each unit i sends an excitatory or inhibitory output to every unit u to which it is connected. In the simplest case, the output sent by a unit would be identical to its activation. In practice, a variety of output functions have been explored. For the Jets and Sharks model as implemented in the *Handbook*, the output is identical to the activation if it is above a threshold of zero, and is set at zero otherwise. That is:

$$output_i = activation_i \text{ if } activation_i > 0 \text{ and } output_i = 0 \text{ otherwise.} \tag{1}$$

When i's output value is multiplied by the *weight* of its connection with u, the resulting value serves as an *input* to u:

$$input_{ui} = weight_{ui}\, output_i \tag{2}$$

For the Jets and Sharks network, in which weights are either $+1$ or -1, the weight simply determines the sign of the input (whether it is excitatory or inhibitory). In most models, the weight varies within a continuous range, such as $+1$ to -1, and therefore affects the magnitude of the input as well.

Next, the concept of *net input* is needed. Unit u receives input from all of the units to which it is connected. Usually these inputs are simply added together, and the total multiplied by a strength parameter, to obtain the net input to u. (The strength parameter is simply a number that is selected to scale down the input to a desired degree; the lower its value, the more gradual are the changes in activation values.) However, if u is in contact with the environment (as are the property and name units in Jets and Sharks), it might also receive an external input. In this model any external input is supplied at a value determined by the modeler, which is then scaled by its own strength parameter. The two strength parameters allow for adjusting the relative influence of internal input versus external input; we have used the *Handbook*'s default values of 0.1 (internal) and 0.4 (external). (There is an option of setting different internal strength parameters for excitatory versus inhibitory inputs; for simplicity we omit that distinction here.) Therefore, for the options we have taken, the equation for calculating the net input is:

$$netinput_u = 0.1 \sum_i weight_{ui} \; output_i + 0.4 \; extinput_u \qquad (3)$$

The term in this equation that begins with a summation sign (Σ) with an index i tells us that the input to u from each unit i is calculated as in equation (2) above, and that the inputs from all of the i units are then added together for inclusion in the *netinput*. On the basis of the net input, the unit will now either increase or decrease its activation according to a fairly simple activation rule, as shown in equations (4) and (5) below. We will use a_u to represent the current *activation$_u$*, and Δa_u to represent the net change to be made to *activation$_u$*. There are two terms in the equation. The first calculates the change that is due to the net input (an increase for positive net input, a decrease for negative net input). The second term is a decay term that decreases activation, even in the absence of net input. (One effect of this is that external input has its greatest effect when it is first presented to a unit.) Because the first term depends on the sign of the input, there are two versions of the equation. If the net input is positive (greater than 0), then the change in the activation is given by:

$$\Delta a_u = (max - a_u)\,(netinput_u) - (decayrate)\,(a_u - rest) \qquad (4)$$

Here *max* represents the maximum activation value that a unit can take (1 in this case). Hence, the first term says that if we have a positive net input, we scale it by a multiplier that depends upon how far the current activation is from the maximum activation, and then increase the activation by that amount. Thus, the greater the net input and the lower the current activation, the more we increase the activation. The decay term, which is subtracted from that amount, is determined by the decay rate (which is set at 0.1) and the difference between the current activation and the unit's resting activation (which is set at -0.1). Thus, the lower the current activation, the less we adjust for decay.

If the net input is less than or equal to 0, the change in activation is given by:

$$\Delta a_u = (a_u - min)\,(netinput_u) - (decayrate)\,(a_u - rest) \qquad (5)$$

The decay term is the same as above. If the net input is 0, the unit will simply decay by that amount. When the net input is negative, on the other hand, we will determine how much further to decrease the activation by multiplying the net input by the difference between the current activation and the minimum activation (which is set here at -0.2). Hence, the greater the current activation, the greater is the effect of negative input in decreasing that activation.

2.1.3 Illustrations of the dynamics of the model

With the basic machinery in place, we now can work through what happens in the network when it performs memory retrieval tasks. By varying the queries that we present to the Jets and Sharks network, we can observe it perform several different tasks: retrieving properties from a name, retrieving a name from properties, categorization, prototype formation, and utilizing regularities.

2.1.3.1 Retrieving properties from a name This is the task that we briefly described above. The investigator activates the "**Art**" unit (by supplying it with external input), and consequently Art's properties become activated. On cycle 1, every unit's current activation is equal to the resting activation of -0.10. Equation (1) specifies that any unit with an activation below the threshold of zero (0.0) produces an output of 0.0; since this is the case for all units, their net inputs to other units are also 0.0. The name unit "**Art**" is supplied with an external input of 1.00, with the result that it is the only unit with a non-zero net input. By equation (3):

$$netinput_{\text{"Art"}} = (0.10)\ (0.0) + (0.40)\ (1.00) = 0.40$$

This strong net input causes the activation of "**Art**" to increase. By equation (4):

$$\Delta a_{\text{"Art"}} = (1.00 - (-0.10))\ (0.40) - (0.10)\ (-0.10 - (-0.10))$$
$$= (1.00 + 0.10)\ (0.40) - (0.10)\ (0.00) = 0.44 - 0.0 = 0.44$$

While all other units, including the hidden (person) units, remain unchanged at the resting activation value:

$$\Delta a = (-0.10 - (-0.10))\ (0.0) - (0.10)\ (-0.10 - (-0.10))$$
$$= 0.0 - 0.0 = 0.0$$

Because the current activation of "**Art**" for cycle 1 is -0.10, adding 0.44 yields a new activation of 0.34. For all other units, adding 0.0 to -0.10 yields a new activation that is the same as the current activation, -0.10. These new activations are used as the current activations for cycle 2.

Beginning on cycle 2 the activation of "**Art**," which now is positive, sends excitatory (positive) input to **ART**, the person unit for Art. By cycle 4, **ART** has climbed to a positive activation. At the same time "**Art**" continues to grow in activation. This is partly due to the continued presentation of external input on each cycle, and partly (beginning in cycle 4) from the input it begins to receive from **ART**. After **ART** becomes positively activated, it begins to send excitatory inputs to the units for Art's properties. Thus, on cycle 5 the units **Jets, 40s**, etc., start to become less negative and eventually become positive (on cycle 12). Once Art's properties become positive, the competing properties in their clusters, such as **Sharks, 20s**, and **30s**, become slightly more negative. The reason is that the units for **Jets** and **40s** send inhibitory inputs to their competitors, thus driving them below the resting activation. These changes in activation are illustrated for the age property cluster in figure 2.3.

Hence, the person unit **ART** becomes active during the early cycles of processing, and by propagating activity to the property units to which it is connected, enables the retrieval of Art's properties. Beginning with cycle 18, though, some other activities begin to appear in the network. The person units **CLYDE** (and also **RALPH**, not shown), and subsequently **MIKE** (and also **FRED** and **GENE**, not shown) become less negative, and on cycle 25 **CLYDE** becomes positive. The reason for this is that the units for Art's properties begin to send positive activations to the units for persons who share properties with Art. Clyde, in fact, shares all of Art's properties except for occupation (he is a bookie whereas Art is a pusher). Mike shares three of five properties with Art, and so his person unit also begins to rise in value, but not sufficiently to achieve a positive activation.[2] Eventually the activation on **CLYDE** becomes high enough that it sends a positive input to the name unit "**Clyde**," and it too becomes active. The result is that by accessing the system through "**Art**," we not only get back Art's properties, but also the names of people similar to Art. One way to interpret this process intuitively is to note that thinking about a person's properties may tend to remind us of people who are very similar to that person.

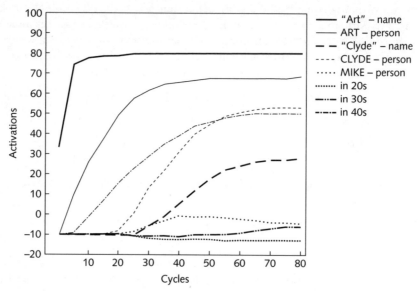

Figure 2.3   The activation values across cycles of some of the units in the Jets and Sharks network after the name unit "**Art**" is activated by an external input.

2.1.3.2   Retrieving a name from other properties   The network is even more versatile than this, however. Suppose we access it by supplying external inputs simultaneously to several units, namely, the units for Art's demographic properties (**40s, junior high, single, pusher**). These will activate **ART**, which will activate "**Art**," and in this way Art's name will pop out. This is the clearest illustration of what is meant by a *content-addressable memory*: the name is retrieved by supplying contents (see the discussion of content-addressable memory in section 2.3.4). Generalization comes free along with this capability; that is, names of persons with similar properties will pop out also at a lower degree of activation.

2.1.3.3   Categorization and prototype formation   The same memory retrieval processes can produce less obvious phenomena, which have been observed in human categorization performance. First, the network can recover category instances. If we supply external input to **Sharks**, for example, that unit will activate the person units for the individual Sharks. Second, as processing continues these individuals become graded according to how well they exemplify the category (analogous to the human ability to judge the relative typicality of various category members; see Rosch, 1975). Figure 2.4 shows the activation across cycles for three of the person units and three of the name units after we activated **Sharks**. Some names clearly acquire more activation than others. For example, after 70 cycles of processing, "**Phil**" is most active, "**Don**" is less active, and "**Dave**," after being initially activated, has dropped almost to its resting level. What causes this emergence of grading by typicality? The third capability, the extraction of prototypes, provides a key part of the mechanism (and is exhibited by humans as well; see Posner and Keele, 1968). Activating **Sharks** results in the activation of the person units for the Sharks, which results in the activation of the property units to which they are connected. The most widely shared properties become the most active. Thus, in figure 2.5 we see that the **30s**

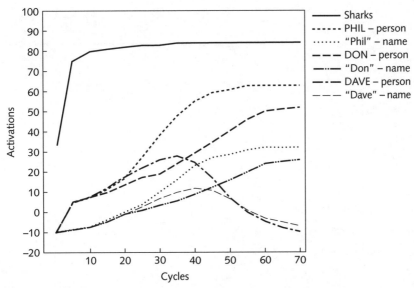

Figure 2.4   The activation values across cycles for name and person units of various members of the Sharks after the property unit **Shark** is activated by an external input. The name units become less active than the person units, because the name units receive activation only via the person units.

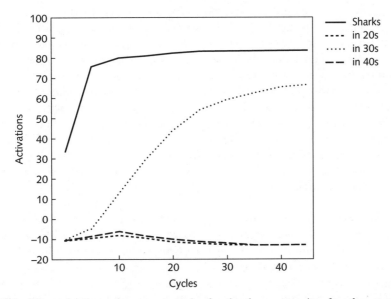

Figure 2.5   The activation values across cycles for the three age units after the property unit **Shark** is activated by an external input.

unit becomes quite active, while the **20s** and **40s** units never rise much above their resting level. This is due to the fact that nine of the twelve Sharks are in their **30s**. These activations are then forwarded to those person units that exhibit the most frequent properties, thus creating a positive feedback loop which further sharpens

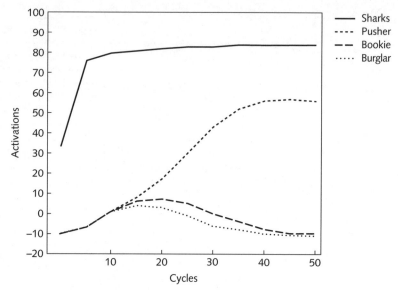

Figure 2.6 The activation values across cycles for the three occupation units when the property unit **Shark** is activated by an external input.

the prototype. The name units are too individual to regard them as part of the prototype, but they change by the same process as the other properties, and their activations come to reflect the extent to which each individual displays the prototypical properties (hence displaying the second capability mentioned just above).

An interesting twist can be observed for the occupation properties in figure 2.6. Initially the units for all three occupations rise in activation. This is because the gang members are equally distributed in their chosen careers. Nevertheless, subsequently the unit for **pusher** continues to grow in activation, while those for **burglar** and **bookie** drop back below zero. This is due to the fact that those individuals who provide the best match on those properties that are not equally distributed grow in their activations, and so provide increased activation to pusher, and it, in turn, inhibits both of the other occupation units.

2.1.3.4 Utilizing regularities As a final example of the variety of ways in which the memory can be queried, we can activate two properties, such as **20s** and **pusher**, and discover which individuals are most likely to fit that scenario. The network will initially produce higher activations in the person units for all individuals who possess any one of these properties, with those sharing both properties (**GREG, FRED**, and **GENE**) getting the highest activations. As person units become active, they not only activate name units, but also other property units. The units for the most widely shared properties (**Jet, single**, and **high school**) also became more active than other units in their cluster. This leads to Pete's person and name units receiving significant activation even though Pete did not fit the original description, since he is a bookie, not a pusher. Thus, the network not only identified which individuals shared the initial pair of properties, but what their other properties were likely to be, and who amongst those not possessing the initial pair show the best fit with those who did satisfy the initial pair of properties. Making inferences from known properties to other properties is a kind of behavior that is familiar to social psychologists working in attribution theory.

2.2   The Design Features of a Connectionist Architecture

In the Jets and Sharks simulation we have presented one particular network architecture that has some very nice characteristics for modeling recall of information from memory and for illustrating some of the capabilities of connectionist networks. However, this design is not suitable for most purposes, and work has proceeded using a variety of other designs. In fact, connectionism as a research paradigm is still in its infancy, and investigators are still in the process of exploring different kinds of connectionist systems. Many of the design features are rather complex, and require considerable mathematics to characterize. In order to provide a general overview of the various types of systems, we will bypass material that is foundational but complex. (For example, we make no direct use of vector notation[3] or matrix algebra.) Also, in this chapter and the next, we limit ourselves to those architectures that are emphasized in Rumelhart and McClelland's (1986) *PDP* volumes, which can be consulted for more depth. For other technical treatments of these or other architectures see, in particular, J. A. Anderson (1995), Ballard (1997), Grossberg (1982, 1988), Kohonen (1988), Levine (1991), and Wasserman (1989). We can characterize the distinctions between different connectionist architectures by considering four issues: (a) how the units are connected to one another; (b) how the activations of individual units are determined; (c) the nature of the learning procedures which change the connections between units; and (d) the ways in which such systems are interpreted semantically. We use a mnemonic notation in these sections; see Appendix A for a translation into two different notations used by Rumelhart and McClelland in the *PDP* volumes.

2.2.1   Patterns of connectivity

The first decision in setting up a connectionist network is to determine which units are connected to one another, that is, the pattern of connectivity. There are two major classes of patterns: (a) *feedforward networks* have unidirectional connections (inputs are fed into the bottom layer, and outputs are generated at the top layer as a result of the forward propagation of activation); (b) *interactive networks* have bidirectional connections. The Jets and Sharks exercises illustrate how interactive networks change state gradually over a large number of processing cycles, as dynamically changing activations are passed back and forth over the two-way connections. We will discuss each of these classes in turn.

2.2.1.1   Feedforward networks   In feedforward networks, units are organized into separate layers, with units in one layer feeding their activations forward to the units in the next layer until the final layer is reached. The simplest such configuration consists of only two layers of units: *input units* and *output units*. There is a weighted connection from each input unit to each output unit. When the weights (connection strengths) are properly set, this type of network can respond to each of a variety of input patterns with its own distinctive output pattern; therefore, it is sometimes referred to as a *pattern associator*.

For example, consider a network with four input units ($i_1 - i_4$), each of which is connected unidirectionally to each of four output units ($u_1 - u_4$), with output activations allowed to range over a continuous domain (figure 2.7). Several input patterns are constructed, each of which consists of a series of four binary values ($+ 1$ and $- 1$). When a pattern is presented to the input layer, each of its binary values is the external input to one input unit, which takes that value as its activation. In presenting the input pattern $+ 1 - 1 - 1 + 1$, for example, an external input of $- 1$ is supplied to the second input unit (i_2), so its activation becomes $- 1$. The activations of the input units are then propagated to the output units by an activation rule that can supply a different weighted sum of the various input activations to each output unit. Therefore, each output unit achieves an activation value that reflects the activity of some input units more than others (see the following section for details). The activation patterns across the input and output units are, in mathematical terms, *vectors*. We will refer to them using the more familiar term *patterns*.

It is informative to compare figure 2.7 with figure 1.1 in the previous chapter. These figures illustrate the two approaches that are taken to diagramming two-layer networks. In figure 1.1, the sensory layer is drawn vertically and the motor layer horizontally. As a result, each connection must be drawn with a change of direction from horizontal to vertical, and its weight can be placed at the junction. The advantage is that the layout of the nodes for the weights is the same as in a weight matrix (cf. the matrix for Case A or B below). In figure 2.7, the layers are parallel and the connections are indicated by straight lines; each connection has a weight associated with it. The weights are not included in either illustration. This latter format has the advantage, though, that it can be adapted to more complex networks (see below).

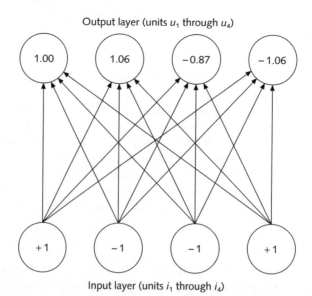

Output layer (units u_1 through u_4)

Input layer (units i_1 through i_4)

Figure 2.7   Pattern recognition network with two layers of units. Activations for the input layer are all set at $+ 1$ or $- 1$; they are multiplied by the weight on each connection and summed to obtain the activations for the output layer. All connections are shown; each has a numerical weight that is not shown.

The paradigmatic task for a pattern associator is paired-associate learning in which the input–output pairings are arbitrary (e.g., supplying names for objects). However, with appropriate weights it could instead be used to reproduce each input pattern on the output layer, in which case it would be a type of *auto-associator*. Or, the output layer could be used to represent a small number of categories into which a larger number of input patterns would be sorted or classified. We will often use the term *pattern associator* generically for these varieties of two-layer networks.

Pattern associators have many useful applications, and we discuss several simulations that make use of them in subsequent chapters. There are, however, problems for which a two-layer network is inadequate, as we will discuss in section 3.2.1. A well-known example is the Boolean function of *exclusive or* (XOR), which is a special case of parity detection. To overcome the limitations of two-layer networks, it is necessary to add *hidden units* to the system. These are units which serve neither as input nor output units, but facilitate the processing of information through the system. We have already encountered hidden units in the Jets and Sharks network (in that network, however, there was no distinction between input and output units; all non-hidden units could serve both functions). In section 3.2.2 we illustrate how the XOR problem can be solved by a network with two input units, two hidden units, and one output unit. Most tasks for which multi-layered networks are used, however, require considerably more units in each layer. For examples, see the discussion of NETtalk in section 3.2.2 and the logic network in section 4.3.2.

As a point of terminology, note that investigators frequently refer to a network that has three layers of units as a *two-layer network*; in that case, it is the number of layers of *connections* that is being referenced. In this book we reference the number of layers of *units*, but reserve the term *multi-layered network* for networks with hidden units (i.e., three or more layers of units).

A number of variations can be made on two-layer and multi-layered architectures. One variation is to allow units in the same layer to send inhibitions and excitations to each other as well as to units in the next layer. A more interesting variation is the *recurrent network*, which can receive input sequentially and alter its response appropriately depending upon what information was received at previous steps in the sequence. It does this by feeding a pattern achieved on a higher layer back into a lower layer, where it functions as a type of input (Elman, 1990; see also the sequential networks of Jordan, 1986). We will discuss such networks in section 6.4. Finally, Rumelhart, Hinton, and McClelland (1986, *PDP:2*) discuss the interesting idea that multi-layered feedforward networks could be used for top-down rather than bottom-up processing, by reversing the direction of the connections without changing the units and patterns at each level. All of these variations soften the design constraint that activations be propagated exclusively in one forward pass. In the next section, we discuss a type of network that departs more dramatically from the basic feedforward design.

2.2.1.2 Interactive networks For interactive networks, at least some connections are bidirectional and the processing of any single input occurs dynamically across a large number of cycles. Such networks may or may not be organized into layers; when they are, processing occurs backwards as well as forwards. A major exemplar of an interactive network is the *Hopfield net*, developed by the physicist John Hopfield (1982) by analogy with a physical system known as a *spin glass*. In their review, Cowan and Sharp (1988) characterized a spin glass as consisting of a matrix of atoms which may be spinning either pointing up or pointing down. Each atom, moreover, exerts a force on its neighbor, leading it to spin in the same or in the opposite direction. A spin glass is actually an instantiation of a matrix or lattice system which is capable of storing a variety of different spin patterns. In the analogous network that Hopfield proposed, the atoms are represented by units and the spin is represented by binary activation values that units might exhibit (0 or 1). The influence of units on their neighbors is represented by means of bidirectional connections; any unit can be (but need not be) connected to any other unit (except itself). As with any interactive network, activations are updated across multiple cycles of processing in accord with an activation rule (see section 2.2.2).

Hopfield (1984) has also experimented with networks taking continuous activation values. Other examples of interactive networks include *Boltzmann machines* (Hinton and Sejnowski, 1986, in *PDP:7*) and *harmony theory* (Smolensky, 1986, in *PDP:6*). As in the original Hopfield nets, the units take binary activation values. We will not discuss harmony theory further, but it uses a probabilistic activation rule and a *simulated annealing* technique very similar to those of the Boltzmann machine (see section 3.2.3).

2.2.2   Activation rules for units

Networks differ not only in their pattern of connectivity, but also in the activation rules that determine the activation values of their units after processing. We have already encountered the major classes of possible activation values. (a) Discrete activations are typically binary, taking values of 0 and 1 (as in Boltzmann machines and harmony theory) or -1 and $+1$. (b) Continuous activations can be unbounded or bounded. As examples of bounded ranges, -0.2 to $+1.0$ was stipulated for the Jets and Sharks network, and a range of -1 to $+1$ is a common choice. In figure 2.7, we used binary input activations and continuous unbounded output activations.

Even greater variation is found in activation rules, which specify how to calculate the level of activation for each unit at a given time. In the following sections we present some of these rules, first for feedforward networks and then for interactive networks. Often the rules for the two types of networks are quite similar, and we will find a rule used in the interactive Jets and Sharks network useful as a framework for introducing our first feedforward activation rule.

First, though, a note of clarification. You may find it odd that the very investigators who reject rules and representations talk about *activation rules* and *learning rules*. These are not rules in the sense intended by symbolic theorists; rather, they refer to mathematical manipulations and often are referred to using the alternative terms *activation functions* and *learning functions*.

2.2.2.1   Feedforward networks   Recall that for the Jets and Sharks network, the activation rule for unit u made use of the net input to that unit:

$$netinput_u = 0.1 \sum_i weight_{ui} \, output_i + 0.4 \, extinput_u \qquad (3)$$

Note that the net input has two components: the effects of activity in other units to which u is connected, and the effects of external input.[4] In a pattern associator (a two-layer feedforward network), the functions served by these two components are divided between specialized sets of units. As shown in figure 2.7 above, units in the input layer (i) are specialized to receive external input, and take the values of the input patterns as their activations. The input unit's activation depends only on the external input, and therefore does not need to be determined by an activation rule. Based on that activation, the input unit then sends an output along each of its connections. In the simplest case, $output_i = activation_i$, but other functions are possible.

Units in the output layer (u) are specialized to receive activation from other units in the network (rather than receiving external input). The terminology now gets a bit confusing, because "input" and "output" are used to refer to the transmission of values as well as to types of units. Each input unit (i) sends output towards each output unit (u). To convert the input unit's output into the output unit's input, $output_i$ is multiplied by the weight of the connection: $input_{ui} = weight_{ui} \, output_i$. Adding these together for every unit i in the input layer yields the net input to u ($netinput_u$). The equation describing this is one component of equation (3), which was used for the Jets and Sharks network:

$$netinput_u = \sum_i weight_{ui} \, output_i \qquad (6)$$

Optionally, a term $bias_u$ can be added to equation (6) in order to adjust the responsiveness of each output unit individually; it can be thought of as a fixed input supplied by a special unit that is not affected by what is happening in the rest of the system. If the value of the bias is low or negative, the output unit will respond conservatively to activation sent from the input units; if it is high, the output unit will behave "impulsively." We consider this version of equation (6) in section 3.2.2.

Finally, an activation rule is applied which makes use of the net input to determine the activation of each unit u. We will refer to $activation_u$ simply as a_u. In the simplest case, the *linear activation rule*, $a_u = netinput_u$ (producing a straight-line, or linear, function). This rule is very useful when two-layer networks are provided with patterns that meet certain constraints (see section 3.2.1). The additional power needed to violate those constraints can be obtained by adding one or more layers of hidden units, but only if the activation rule is also changed to a nonlinear function. Typically the function chosen is a continuous, monotonically increasing (or at least nondecreasing) function of the input for which a derivative exists. In particular, the *logistic function* has been widely used (in two-layer as well as multi-layered networks):

$$a_u = \frac{1}{1 + e^{-(netinput_u - \theta_u)/T}} \qquad (7)$$

This function is sigmoidal in form (as figure 2.8 illustrates for the stochastic version of this function in the section on Boltzmann machines below). Within the exponent, θ_u is a threshold that is subtracted from the net input; it has the same effect on the activation value as adding a bias to the net input equation (6) if $\theta_u = -bias_u$. (In their 1988 *Handbook* McClelland and Rumelhart uniformly used a bias term, whereas in their 1986 *PDP* volumes they usually subtracted a threshold from net input instead.) T is a parameter which determines how flat the curve is across the range of net input values. (When the number of input units that feed into each output unit is large, the range of net input values also tends to be large. A higher value of T stretches the function so that it will cover this range.)

Each of these activation rules can be adapted to obtain discrete rather than continuous activation values, typically for use in networks in which both input and output units are binary (on or off). For the linear activation rule, the adaptation is to compare the net input to a threshold value. If net input exceeds the threshold, the output unit's activation is set to 1 (on); otherwise it is set to 0 (off). With a zero threshold, for example, positive net input turns the output unit on and negative net input turns it off. A unit that uses a threshold in this way is called a *linear threshold unit*. A network with an output layer of linear threshold units and an input layer of binary units is an *elementary perceptron* (Rosenblatt, 1959). Linear threshold units can also be used in the hidden and output layers of multi-layered feedforward networks and in interactive networks.

For the logistic activation rule, discrete activations can be achieved by using a stochastic version of equation (7); this is presented as equation (9) in the discussion of Boltzmann machines in the next section. When equation (9) is used in a feedforward network of binary units, presenting the same input pattern on different trials will not always have the same effect on a given output unit; that is, the relation between its net input and its activation becomes probabilistic. The equation determines the relative frequency with which the unit will turn on versus turn off. An example of a feedforward network with a stochastic activation function is discussed in section 5.2.2 (Rumelhart and McClelland's 1986 past tense model).

2.2.2.2 *Interactive networks: Hopfield networks and Boltzmann machines* The equations that govern the propagation of activation in feedforward networks can be used in interactive networks as well. A parameter t for time (or in some notations, n for cycle number) must be included, however, because activations are updated many times on the same unit as the system works towards settling into a solution to a particular input. (For readability, we show t in our equations only when it is necessary to distinguish it from $t + 1$.) Interactive networks may use a *synchronous* update procedure, in which every unit's activation is updated once per timing cycle, or an *asynchronous* update procedure, in which there is no common sequence of cycles, but rather a random determination of the times at which each unit separately is updated. Each update requires a separate application of the activation rule. (In contrast, in a feedforward network there is just one forward sweep of activation changes; the activation rule is applied just once to each unit.)

In the original Hopfield nets (Hopfield, 1982), each unit is a linear threshold unit. That is, the activation rule is the same as that of Rosenblatt's perceptron (but it is applied many times to each unit). On each update, if a unit receives net input that is above its threshold, it acquires an activation of 1. Otherwise, its activation is 0. (Alternatively, values of $+1$ and -1 can be used if the threshold is adjusted appropriately.) Hopfield employed an *asynchronous* update procedure in which each unit at its own randomly determined times would update its activation depending upon the net input it received at that time. (This helps to prevent the network from falling into unstable oscillations.) Processing is initiated in a Hopfield net by providing an initial input pattern to a subset of units (i.e., each unit receives an activation value of 1 or 0). Then, all units will randomly update their activations until a state is achieved in which no unit will receive a net input that would lead it to change its activation. If that occurs, the network is then said to have *stabilized* or reached a state of *equilibrium*. The particular stable configuration into which the network settles constitutes the system's identification of the initial input. (Some networks, however, never stabilize; rather: they behave as chaotic systems that oscillate between different configurations.)

Hopfield's analogy between this sort of network and a physical system paid an important dividend when he showed that one could calculate a very useful measure of the overall state of the network (*energy*, or E)[5] that was equivalent to the measure of energy in a physical system (Hopfield, 1982). A Hopfield net tends to move towards a state of equilibrium that is mathematically equivalent to a state of lowest energy in a thermodynamic system. Using the update rule described in the previous paragraph, each change in activation of any unit will result in an overall lower (or same) energy state for the system. In our notation, the global energy measure E is given by:

$$E = - \sum_{u<1} weight_{ui}\, a_u\, a_i + \sum_u \theta_u\, a_u \tag{8}$$

To see how the update rule lowers the value of E, consider one example that focuses on just two units in a network of binary units taking activations of 0 and 1. If at the outset $a_u = 0$, $a_i = 1$, $weight_{ui} = 1$ and $\theta_u = 0.5$, then the contribution to E of these two units is: $-(1)(0)(1) + (0.5)(0) = 0$. Now assume that unit u has been randomly selected to have its activation updated. The input to unit u from unit i equals $weight_{ui}$ $a_i = (1)(1) = 1$. Since this exceeds the threshold of 0.5, unit u changes its activation from 0 to 1. We now evaluate E for this part of the network as: $-(1)(1)(1) + (0.5)(1)$ $= -0.5$. Therefore, the network has moved to a state with a lower value for E. (Note that in actual practice, we must apply the update rule by considering all inputs to a_u not just that from a single a_i. This insures that we would change a_u only if it would contribute to an overall lower value for E.) Rumelhart, Smolensky, McClelland, and Hinton (1986, *PDP:14*) emphasized that E indicates how well the network satisfies the constraints that are implicit in the pattern of weights and the input to the network. They therefore adapted Hopfield's energy measure to obtain G, a measure of the *goodness of fit* of the state achieved by the network to the constraints. G is the negative of E and may also include a separate term for input if the input is continuously supplied during processing (a procedure that is referred to as *clamping* the relevant subset of units to a constant activation value).

Hopfield nets are useful for solving a variety of optimization problems. The connections literally constrain the possible stable configurations into which the network can settle. If we regard the initial pattern of activation supplied to such a network as specifying a problem and the stable state as a solution, then the connections will represent conceptual constraints on the solution and the stable state should be the state of the network that best satisfies these constraints. The traveling salesperson problem is one type of constraint satisfaction problem which has traditionally been used as a challenging case for developing optimization procedures. The salesperson needs to visit a number of cities and desires to travel the shortest distance. Hopfield and Tank (1985; see also Durbin and Willshaw, 1987) developed a modified Hopfield net which offers quite good solutions to this problem. Although it does not find the absolutely shortest route, its performance is comparable to that of a (nonnetwork) computational procedure for constrained optimization problems developed by Lin and Kernighan (1973).

One of the difficulties confronted by the Hopfield net is that it can settle into local minima (see section 3.2.1.3), in particular, situations in which there would not be sufficient net input to any given unit to get it to change its value, but in which the

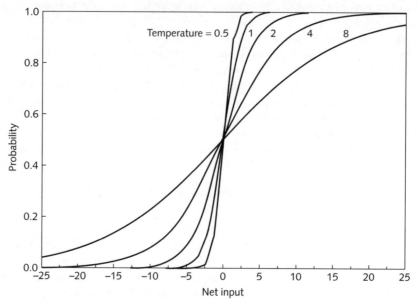

Figure 2.8 Probability that a unit takes an activation value of one as a function of net input at five different values of T (temperature). Note that θ (threshold) is zero. Reprinted with permission from D. E. Rumelhart, G. E., Hinton, and J. L. McClelland (1986) A general framework for parallel distributed processing. In D. E. Rumelhart, J. L. McClelland, and the PDP Research Group (1986) *Parallel Distributed Processing: Explorations in the Microstructure of Cognition*, vol 1: *Foundations*. Cambridge, MA: MIT Press, p. 69.

system would still not have reached the optimal overall solution given the constraints imposed by the weights in the network. That is, the stable state is not the state that would yield the lowest possible value of E (the global energy minimum). This may result when different parts of the network have settled into incompatible solution patterns, each part of which is stable and unable to be altered by the other partial solutions. The Boltzmann machine is an adaptation of the Hopfield net which reduces this tendency.

The Boltzmann machine was proposed by Hinton and Sejnowski (1983, 1986; see also Ackley, Hinton, and Sejnowski, 1985). Like the Hopfield net, it updates its binary units by means of an asynchronous update procedure. However, it employs a *stochastic activation function* rather than a deterministic one. Specifically, it is a probabilistic version of the logistic function in equation (7). On each update of a particular unit u, the probability that it becomes active is a function of its net input:

$$probability \, (a_u = 1) = \frac{1}{1 + e^{-(netinput_u - \theta_u)/T}} \tag{9}$$

The effect of T is to alter the slope of the probability curve, as illustrated in figure 2.8 (with $\theta = 0$). When T is close to zero, the curve approaches a discontinuous step function that jumps from 0 to 1 when $netinput_u$ crosses the value 0.0 (i.e., it approximates a linear threshold unit). When T becomes very large, the curve flattens, so there is more variability in the unit's response to a given net input value across updates. At high values of T the network will jump quickly into a solution to a new input (that is, it will require relatively few updates) but the solution is unlikely to be optimal.[6]

Equation (9) works best when a procedure called *simulated annealing* is used to vary the temperature parameter during the processing of a single input pattern. The procedure is based on an analogy from physics. Something comparable to local minima occurs in formation of crystals when incompatible sets of bonds begin to form in different parts of the crystal. If these bonds become fixed, the crystal will have a fault in it. The common way to avoid such faults is referred to as *annealing*. In this process, a material is heated, thereby weakening the bonds and allowing the atoms to reorient, and then cooled very slowly so that there is a maximal chance that as the bonds reform the atoms will orient appropriately with each other. If the cooling is carried out slowly enough around certain critical temperatures, the alignment emerging in one part of the structure has the greatest opportunity to affect that emerging elsewhere in the structure so as to develop one cohesive structure. The idea is carried over to networks by treating the patterns of activation in different parts of the network as comparable to the alignment of atoms. Raising the temperature value T has the effect of increasing the probability that activations of units in the network will shift. Reducing T very slowly at critical junctures allows time for patterns of activation developing in one part of the network to affect the patterns developing elsewhere so that one coherent pattern emerges as the network settles into a solution.

Note that the equations just presented make no reference to the prior state of activation of the unit. In contrast, the Jets and Sharks network computed a change in activation (Δa_u) which was added to u's current activation ($a_{u,t}$) to obtain u's new activation ($a_{u,t+1}$):

$$a_{u,t+1} = a_{u,t} + \Delta a_u \tag{10}$$

We left this equation implicit in the Jets and Sharks discussion, but did present two equations for Δa_u. In that case, the change in activation of a unit depended upon its current activation $a_{u,t}$ (relative to the discrepancy with its maximum or minimum activation), its net input, and the rate of decay with time. If the net input was sufficient to overcome the decay, the activation increased; otherwise it decreased. A simpler rule for capturing the same idea is:

$$\Delta a_u = k \; netinput_u - decay \tag{11}$$

where k is a constant determined by the network designer, $netinput_u$ represents the net input to the unit of interest, and *decay* represents a function that specifies an amount by which the activation of each unit will be decremented on each processing cycle. Note that this simple linear rule will not keep activations within a bounded range unless special care is taken in crafting the decay function.

2.2.2.3 Spreading activation vs. interactive connectionist models J. R. Anderson's ACT and ACT* versions of spreading activation in (nondistributed) semantic networks (Anderson, 1976, 1983; see also Anderson and Lebière, 1998) utilized nonlinear activation functions that, as in the PDP tradition, could incorporate decay and interactivity. Anderson's models could account for a variety of empirical findings, including fact retrieval (Anderson, 1974) and priming effects (e.g., McKoon and Ratcliff, 1979). An important difference, however, is that Anderson's network was used in the service of a production system; it enabled a degree of parallel processing within the production system architecture by making a number of productions simultaneously active so as to compete with one another, and allowed a partially matching production to fire if there was no stronger competitor (see also Thibadeau, Just, and Carpenter, 1982). This is similar to the notion of *soft constraints* that is discussed in section 2.3.2 below.

Hence, the parallel propagation of activation is an idea that was used to good effect immediately prior to and into the current era of connectionist research, by J. R. Anderson and other spreading activation modelers. At least three differences distinguish spreading activation from connectionist models, however. First, Anderson retained a control structure (by means of a production system utilizing his network), whereas connectionists usually try to limit the network to its own highly decentralized local control. Second, some of the most interesting connectionist models use distinctive types of distributed representation such as coarse coding (discussed in section 2.2.4). Third, there are differences in the equations that govern the propagation of activation.

As this sketch makes clear, network designers have a variety of options available in determining both the types of activation a unit might take and how that activation is determined. The common element to all of these functions is that the new activation of a unit will be dependent in some degree on the net input a unit receives from other units. This net input is determined in part by the weights on the connections. These can be hand-tailored, but much of the interest in connectionist networks arises from their ability to modify their own weights adaptively, that is, to learn. In the next section we consider the basic idea of learning in such networks and introduce one quite simple learning procedure. Active research in this area has generated a large number of different learning procedures, however, and we will devote chapter 3 to a more detailed discussion.

2.2.3   Learning principles

For a connectionist system, learning is accomplished not by adding or modifying propositions, but rather by changing the connection weights between the simple units. Since the weights of these connections partly determine the state a network reaches as a result of its processing, these changes in weights result in changing the overall characteristics of the system. The basic goal is to provide a way of changing weights that increases the ability of the network to achieve a desired output in the future. The challenge is to have the network figure out the appropriate changes in weights without the aid of an external programmer or an internal executive in the network. Thus, the control over weight change should be entirely *local*. The information that is generally available locally to any weight is the current value of that weight and the activations of the units to which it is connected. If other information is to be employed, it must be provided to the units involved so that it is just as available as the current activations of the units.

One of the simplest such learning procedures for two-layer networks draws upon an idea proposed by Donald Hebb (1949), who suggested that learning might occur in the nervous system by strengthening the connections between two neurons whenever they fired at the same time. Expanding on this idea for connectionist networks, the strength of the connection between two units (the weight) can be increased or decreased in proportion to the product of their activations. What is now referred to as the *Hebbian learning rule* specifies this function:

$$\Delta weight_{ui} = lrate \; a_u \, a_i \tag{12}$$

where *lrate* is a constant specifying the rate of learning, a_u is the activation of the output unit, and a_i is the activation of the input unit. Thus, whenever both units have the *same* sign (positive or negative), the connection between them is *increased* proportionally to the product of the two activations. But when the activations of the two units have *different* signs, the weight of the connection is *decreased* proportionally to the product of their activations.

To see how the Hebbian procedure can enable a network to learn, let us consider a two-layer network that is using the Hebbian rule. Assume that the activations of the output units *u* are determined by the simplest linear rule; that is, the output of each input unit *i* is identical to its activation, the activation of each output unit *u* is identical to its net input, and the net input to a given output unit *u* can therefore be obtained by simply summing the products of each *i* unit's activation by the weight of its connection to *u*:

$$a_u = \sum_i weight_{ui} \; a_i \tag{13}$$

To train the weights using the Hebbian learning rule, we supply the network with the paired input and output patterns that it is supposed to learn (we will refer to each such pair as a *case*). If the learning rate (*lrate*) is set to $1/n$, where *n* is the number of input units, the system will exhibit "one trial learning." That is, if it is presented with the same input again on the next trial, its weights will already be adequate to generate the appropriate output. To illustrate, suppose that a simple network with four input and four output units is presented with case A, that is, input pattern A (+ 1 + 1 − 1 − 1) paired with desired output pattern A (+ 1 − 1 − 1 + 1). If it is allowed to set its own weights according to the Hebbian principle, it will create the following matrix of 16 weights:

CASE A

Input unit	Input activation	Output unit			
		e	f	g	h
a	+ 1	0.25	− 0.25	− 0.25	0.25
b	+ 1	0.25	− 0.25	− 0.25	0.25
c	− 1	− 0.25	0.25	0.25	− 0.25
d	− 1	− 0.25	0.25	0.25	− 0.25
Desired output activation		1.00	− 1.00	− 1.00	1.00

For example, the value of the upper left cell in the matrix was obtained by multiplying the learning rate (1/4 = 0.25) by the input value for unit **a** (1) and the output value for unit **e** (1), yielding 0.25. We can readily see that this weight matrix will enable the network to reproduce the same output pattern if we now test it with the same input pattern. To obtain the value 1 on unit **e**, for example, the input values on **a** and **b** are each multiplied by 0.25, the input values on **c** and **d** are each multiplied by − 0.25, and the four resulting values are added together. (Note that when we train the network, the input and output activations are fixed and the weights are calculated. When we then test the network, the input activations and weights are fixed, and the output activations are calculated. Case A, above, is illustrated in training mode; the label "desired output activation" indicates that this is a fixed output pattern supplied to the network. Though shown to two decimal places, all such values are +1 or −1.)

This same network can in fact learn to produce specified output patterns for several different inputs without decreasing its performance on those it has already learned. It can do this as long as the new inputs are not correlated with those it has already learned. (Unfortunately, this is a highly constraining assumption that is difficult to satisfy in real life.) Consider input pattern B: $(+1 -1 -1 +1)$. We can verify that input pattern B is uncorrelated with input pattern A by calculating that, with the current weights, presenting input pattern B would cause the network to produce the output $(0\,0\,0\,0)$. This tells us that we could now *train* it to produce some designated output pattern B; let us specify $(+1 +1 -1 -1)$. This training would result in the following modified weight matrix:

CASE B

Input unit	Input activation	Output unit e	f	g	h
a	+ 1	0.50	0.00	− 0.50	0.00
b	− 1	0.00	− 0.50	0.00	0.50
c	− 1	− 0.50	0.00	0.50	0.00
d	+ 1	0.00	0.50	0.00	− 0.50
Desired output activation		1.00	1.00	− 1.00	− 1.00

With these weights, the network will still respond correctly if presented with case A again (because the new weights are an alternate solution to that problem), but now it also will respond correctly to case B.

While the Hebbian rule produces impressive results, and is often preferred by computational neuroscientists who like its biological plausibility, we will see that there are serious limits to what it can accomplish (in feedforward networks). Thus, in chapter 3 we will explore a variety of different learning procedures that are now employed in connectionist networks. The idea that links the simplest procedures (section 3.2.1) is that learning involves changing weights in a network and that this is to be accomplished using only information that is available locally, that is, at the units linked by the connection on which the weight is placed. We will also discuss the backpropagation procedure (section 3.2.2), which gains computational power by finding a way to apportion weight changes nonlocally through multiple layers.

2.2.4   Semantic interpretation of connectionist systems

In designing a connectionist network to function as a model of human performance in a particular domain, attention must be given to the question of how the concepts relevant to that domain will be represented in the network. There are two approaches: in *localist* networks each concept is assigned to one unit; in *distributed* networks the representation of each concept is distributed across multiple units. (The use of the term *local* here should not be confused with that in the preceding paragraph.)

2.2.4.1 Localist networks The Jets and Sharks network exemplifies the localist approach. Each concept (being a burglar, having the name "Art," etc.) is represented by one individual unit of the network. The semantic networks of the 1970s were also clearly localist, and when these have been augmented by equations that specify *spreading activation*, the resulting models (particularly the network portion of J. R. Anderson's 1983 ACT* theory) have been similar in many respects to localist connectionist networks. Localist networks, from whatever research tradition, share the advantage that units can be labeled in the investigator's own language to facilitate keeping tabs on what the network is doing. This carries a danger: it is easy to forget that the label conveys meaning to the investigator, but not to the network itself. The correspondence between unit and concept relies on an external process of semantic interpretation, which must be performed with care. When the network is being used as a model of a particular domain, its success will be limited by the designer's intuitions of what concepts in that domain should be encoded (i.e., associated with a unit in the network) and by his or her skill in setting up connections appropriate to that encoding.

Despite these demands on the designer, it is generally even more difficult to set up a distributed network. Therefore, a localist network may be preferred when the task does not require the distinct advantages of distributed encoding (which are discussed below). The task of *multiple constraint satisfaction*, for example, can be adequately performed by an interactive localist network. Units represent concepts, and positive or negative connections between pairs of units represent constraints between those concepts. A positive connection between two units puts a constraint on the entire network to favor states (overall activation patterns) in which the two units have the same activation (e.g., both *on* or both *off*); a negative connection favors states in which the two units have opposite activity. To run this procedure, each unit is given a baseline activation value (often zero), and each connection weight is fixed as positive or negative. External input is optional, and acts as an additional source of constraint. The network then runs interactively until it settles into a stable state (pattern of activation values); if a global energy minimum is attained, that state will be the state that best satisfies the constraints. One of the important features of this procedure is that these are *soft* constraints. Even if there is a negative constraint between two units, if other constraints involving those units favor their having the same state, the most stable solution may have both units *on* or both units *off* (violating that one particular constraint but satisfying a number of other constraints).

2.2.4.2 Distributed networks In a distributed network, each concept is represented by a pattern of activation across an ensemble or set of units; by design, no single unit can convey that concept on its own. To convert the Jets' and Sharks' three occupations to distributed representations, for example, we might continue to use three units, but arbitrarily associate each occupation with a different pattern of activation values across those units as follows:

$$+1 + 1 + 1 = \text{Burglar} \qquad -1 - 1 + 1 = \text{Bookie} \qquad +1 - 1 - 1 = \text{Pusher}$$

In this example individual units do not have a semantic interpretation. Rather, each semantic interpretation is distributed over three units (rather than assigned to one localist unit), and each unit is involved in three different semantic interpretations.

An alternative way to achieve a distributed representation of a concept is to carry out a featural analysis of the concept, and encode that analysis across an appropriate

number of units. Featural representation is widely used in the psychological literature on concepts and categories, for example in exemplar models (Medin and
Schaffer, 1978). What is new here is to situate the featural representation in a
network architecture. The idea that this constitutes a distributed representation is
often difficult to grasp, because the features themselves are typically encoded on
individual units. That is, there is a localist representation of the features (one unit
per feature), and a distributed representation of the target concept. In illustration,
suppose that a large number of occupations are the objects to be represented. The
network designer might craft a set of 50 units in which each unit is interpreted as
corresponding to some feature that is salient to occupations, and represent each
occupation as a pattern across those units. Those occupations chosen by the Jets and
Sharks would all share the feature **illegal**, for example, but only the pusher occupation (like the pharmacist occupation) would have the feature **involves drugs**.

How does one obtain a featural analysis of a domain in order to build these
representations? One method is to let an existing theory guide this work; for example, a particular linguistic account might be used as a basis for representing words
as patterns over phonemic units. In the connectionist research program the interest
lies, not so much in the particular features and assignments, but rather in how the
system makes use of its distributed representation once it has been built. We might,
for example, explore generalization or associative learning under the conditions
offered by such a representation. A second method is to let the system perform its
own analysis of the domain. When a multi-layered network is run in a learning
paradigm (as described in section 3.2.2), the network designer specifies the interpretations only of the input and output units; the input–output cases used for training
are selected with respect to this interpretation. The designer does not know what
aspects of the input–output cases each hidden unit will become sensitive to; the
learning process is in part a process of feature extraction, and observing this is one of
the most intriguing aspects of connectionist research. Usually the hidden units do
not arrive at a simple, localist representation of the most obvious regularities (features) in the input. Rather, each hidden unit is sensitive to complex, often subtle,
regularities that connectionists call *microfeatures*. Each layer of hidden units can be
regarded as providing a particular distributed encoding of the input pattern (that is,
an encoding in terms of a pattern of microfeatures).

One virtue of distributed representation is that part of the representation can be
missing without substantially hurting performance. Using the arbitrary distributed
representations of three occupations displayed at the beginning of this section, for
example, we might specify an input only for the first two units and leave the third
questionable (+ 1 + 1 ?). Nevertheless, the network will treat this pattern similarly to
a complete burglar input (+ 1 + 1 + 1), since this is the pattern to which the partial
input is most similar. The point is even clearer in networks with more units. Consider, for example, a pattern associator network with two layers of 16 units each.
Each of the units in the input will be connected to all of the units in the output layer,
and depending upon the size of the weights, will contribute either a little or a lot of
the information needed to determine the value of the output unit. Each output unit
will be receiving inputs from 16 different input units. If there is no input from a
given input unit, or the wrong input, the activity on the other input lines generally
will compensate. The point here is that once we distribute information as a pattern
across units, we also distribute the resources used to process it. Thus, a distributed
system becomes more resilient to damage. Beyond this, we make it possible for the

system to learn new information without sacrificing existing information. For example, without adding new units, we can teach the network to respond to a new input that is different from any it has learned so far. It often is sufficient to make slight changes to a variety of weights, which do not significantly alter the way the network responds to existing patterns. (There are limits to this capacity, however; in some circumstances teaching a new input disrupts previous learning to an unacceptable degree. For a demonstration of *catastrophic interference*, see McCloskey and Cohen (1989); for connectionist responses, see Hetherington and Seidenberg (1989), and French (1992). In subsequent chapters we identify a number of contexts in which catastrophic interference seems to arise, and a number of connectionist attempts to overcome the problem.)

For a final virtue of distributed networks, consider a distributed network that has encoded a structured domain of knowledge, in which there are regularities in the input–output pairings. If the network is presented with a new input pattern, a reasonable response should appear on the output units. Humans often exhibit a similar capacity when provided with only partial information about a new entity. Generally, we infer some of the other properties the entity might have, based on its similarity to entities we already know. In their discussion of distributed representations, Hinton, McClelland, and Rumelhart (1986, *PDP:3*) provide the following example: if we are told that chimpanzees like onions, we will probably revise our expectations about whether gorillas like onions as well. This reflects a general tendency of organisms to make *generalizations* (and specifically exemplifies what Shipley (1988) calls an *over-hypothesis*). Distributed representations are well suited to producing and investigating generalization.

There is one additional approach to achieving distributed representations that is counterintuitive in many respects, but is ingenious and exhibits some very useful properties. This is a technique known as *coarse coding*. The basic idea is that, rather than deploying units so that each unit represents information as precisely as possible, we design each individual unit (called a *receptor* in this context) to be sensitive to many different inputs (which constitute its *receptive field*). Each unit is sensitive to (activated by) a different set of inputs, and each input has a number of units that are sensitive to it. In this architecture, the fact that a particular unit is active is not very informative; but if a high percentage of the units that are sensitive to a particular input are active, the presence of that input can be inferred with high confidence.

To consider a concrete example, coarse coding was used by Touretzky and Hinton (1988) in a connectionist system that they constructed to implement a production system. One of their purposes was to show that connectionist systems can indeed represent and use explicit rules; for discussion of this aspect of their paper, see section 6.2. Their other purpose was to illustrate certain advantages of coarse coding. The production system that they implemented was designed to follow rules involving meaningless triples composed from a 25-letter vocabulary. The triples themselves were not directly encoded in the network; rather, each coarse-coded triple was presented by turning on all of the units (28 on average) that were designated as its receptors in the *working memory* network that was one component of the system. Each such unit was a receptor for a large number of different triples. For example, one of the units that was a receptor for the triple (F A B) was also a receptor for any other triple that could be formed from the following receptive field by selecting one letter from each column in the order shown:

Position 1	Position 2	Position 3
C	A	B
F	E	D
M	H	J
Q	K	M
S	T	P
W	Y	R

Hence that particular receptor unit was turned on (became active) if (F A B) was to be presented; but the same unit would be turned on if (C A B) or (S H M) or any one of 216 (6^3) different triples was to be presented. The particular sets of letters were determined randomly and were different for each unit. For example, another of the receptor units for (F A B) might have had the following receptive field:

Position 1	Position 2	Position 3
F	A	B
I	C	D
K	H	E
P	K	J
S	R	M
V	W	U

From the perspective of the triple itself, those two receptor units and their distinctive receptive fields were only two of the approximately 28 different units that would be activated as the means of presenting (F A B) to the working memory network. From the perspective of a single receptor unit, it might have been turned on as a means of presenting any one of the 216 different triples in its receptive field. To know which triple was actually being presented, one would need to know the particular combination of 28 activated units and to consult the external listing of their receptive fields (which would reveal that they had in common only that F was one of the six letters in position 1, A was one of the six letters in position 2, and B was one of the six letters in position 3).

This may seem like a very strange way to design a memory, but Touretzky and Hinton pointed out several advantageous or human-like properties gained from coarse coding. First, the number of units needed to store all possible triples is minimized. There are 15,625 possible triples, about half a dozen of which are present in working memory at any given time. But the working memory is composed of only about 2,000 different units. Second, the memory is tolerant of noise (i.e., a few units can be in the wrong state without materially affecting performance). Third, the memory does not have a rigid, fixed capacity; rather, its ability to distinguish triples will gradually decline as the number of stored items increases. Fourth, active triples will gradually decay as new triples are stored. Fifth, a degree of generalization is exhibited: if two of the triples that have been presented to the memory network both happen to have F as their initial letter, more than the usual number of receptors will be active for other F-initial triples.

Coarse coding is one of the most distinctive, nonobvious techniques made possible by the use of distributed (rather than localist) representations. Hinton, McClelland, and Rumelhart (1986, *PDP:3*) provide further discussion of coarse coding, including design considerations that must be attended to (e.g., a tradeoff between resolution and accuracy in setting the size of the receptive fields). They also make the following intriguing suggestion, with which we will close this section:

Units that respond to complex features in retinotopic maps in visual cortex often have fairly large receptive fields. This is often interpreted as the first step on the way to a translation invariant representation. However, it may be that the function of the large fields is not to achieve translation invariance but to pinpoint accurately where the feature is! (1986, *PDP:3*, p. 92)

2.3   The Allure of the Connectionist Approach

One reason many people are attracted to network models of cognition is that they seem to exhibit many properties found in human cognition that are not generally found in symbolic models. In this section we will review, without much critical discussion, some of the properties that have been cited.

2.3.1   Neural plausibility

Certainly one of the major features that has attracted researchers to network models is that they seem more compatible than symbolic models with what we know of the nervous system. This is not surprising: network models are *neurally inspired*. Pitts and McCulloch, for example, built their models using a simplified conception of how neurons work. Hence, the state of activation of a unit (especially of units that only acquire discrete activations, 0 and 1) was intended to correspond to a neuron either resting or firing. The connections between units were conceived on the model of the axons and dendrites of neurons. Thus, the propagation of activation within a network is, at least on this very general level, similar to the kinds of processing that we observe in the nervous system.

Of course, connectionist networks do not capture all features of neural architecture and processing in the brain. For example, little attention is paid to trying to model the particular pattern of connectivity of neurons in the brain. Nor is there any attempt to simulate the differences between various neurotransmitters, or the very intricate way in which excitations to neurons are compounded to determine whether the neuron will actually fire. Thus, networks only capture aspects of the coarse architecture of the brain. Conversely, there are aspects of connectionist networks that do not clearly map on to what is known about the nervous system; the back-propagation procedure for learning (section 3.2.2) is a particularly important example.

These differences present no difficulty, and in fact may be desirable, if one focuses on connectionist models as cognitive (rather than biological) models. Some investigators, however, prefer to push the neural analogy as far as possible. For example, it is known that neural systems carry out basic processing (e.g., recognizing a word) very quickly, that is, within a few hundred milliseconds. Since it takes each neuron several milliseconds to fire, it has been argued that basic cognitive tasks cannot require more than a hundred steps of sequential processing (Feldman and Ballard, 1982). This, it is claimed, poses a serious problem for traditional symbolic architectures, since to model even simple tasks often requires programs embodying several thousand instructions. But since network processing relies on performing many different operations in parallel, it seems much easier for networks to satisfy the 100-step constraint. For example, the network described in section 2.1 could identify a gang member on the basis of some of his properties and then determine the remainder of those properties, well within 100 processing steps (assuming it were implemented on appropriate, parallel hardware).

Neural plausibility is most obviously advantageous if one is concerned with the interface between psychology and neuroscience (see chapter 10), and least advantageous if "mere implementation" is regarded as outside the domain of concern for psychologists (see section 6.1). A middle position is to view the neural metaphor as a source of ideas that may or may not pan out, with its biological underpinnings favoring but not determining that it will succeed. Other useful metaphors might come from such remote areas as physics (e.g., the hologram theory of memory). On this view the neural metaphor is superior to the extent that it inspires models that deal nicely with particular problems or phenomena, such as generalization. The further idea that the models work well *because* they use neurally inspired concepts (i.e., that there is a causal relation) is speculative, but points the way to a potentially attractive bonus that is not shared by most other metaphors, including the currently dominant von Neumann computer metaphor. (See chapter 10 for further discussion of the relation between connectionist models and actual neural systems.)

2.3.2 Satisfaction of soft constraints

The existence of a connection between two units in a network constitutes a constraint on the processing of that network. If that connection is excitatory (has a positive weight), then, if the first unit is active, the second unit is constrained to be active as well. Rules in a symbolic system likewise serve as a constraint. If the antecedent of a production system rule is satisfied so that the rule fires, then the consequent action is constrained to occur. In this sense connections serve the same function as rules: they determine the future action of the system. But there is an important difference. Rules are deterministic so that if a rule fires, its action is certain to occur. In a network, on the other hand, a given unit receives input from many other units. If one unit delivers an excitatory constraint while two others deliver inhibitory constraints of greater total magnitude, the overall effect will be inhibitory (using the simplest activation function). The unit finds the best overall solution to the multiple constraints, and that solution may not be compatible with all of the individual constraints. Thus, the constraints imposed by the connections are often spoken of as *soft constraints*.

Note that this is not an absolute distinction; there are degrees of softness in constraints. Some rule systems allow for competition between rules whose antecedents are equally satisfied, and even allow the resolution of this competition to be probabilistic (MacWhinney and Bates, 1989). These systems exhibit some, but not all, of the advantages of networks. As for networks, it is possible to design networks that (like rules) exhibit relatively hard constraints; the trained XOR network in section 3.2.2 provides an example. Hence, although connectionist networks offer a particularly natural way to achieve soft constraints, the association is not exclusive or inevitable.

There are many tasks or domains in which cognition seems to be better modeled by soft constraints than by hard constraints. For example, in decision making a person is often confronted with conflicting desiderata and must choose among them. The most realistic preconnectionist decision-making models have been mathematical rather than purely propositional. They have been limited, however, by their reliance on linear functions. A localist interactive network, in contrast, can be designed as a nonlinear dynamic system. Each possible desideratum may be modeled as a soft constraint between one of the units representing different aspects of the situation and one of the units representing possible actions. When a new situation is presented, we can allow the network to settle into a stable state which represents the best satisfaction of these constraints. Not all desiderata will be satisfied, but the network will have efficiently identified the best outcome. The use of soft constraints enables connectionist systems to account for the competition between competing desiderata without having to specify rules that arbitrate the competition, and without the limitations of linear models.

Soft constraints are also beneficial in designing systems to deal with new situations that have not been envisaged in advance. If a new input is provided to a connectionist network, for example, it will respond with no special effort using the connections it has already developed. If the situation is like one on which the network had previously been trained, it will generate a similar response. If the new situation shows weaker similarities to a variety of old situations, the network will use the connections developed in the old cases to construct a plausible new response. Designers of rule systems have also shown increased interest in developing strategies for flexible response to new situations; the next few years should bring some vigorous discussion of the relative merits of different approaches.

The naturalness with which connectionist networks implement soft constraints is part of what enables connectionist networks to overcome a common problem that confronts researchers in the symbolic tradition. The problem is that rules tend to have exceptions. This is seen particularly clearly in attempts to formalize principles of language, where in fact we see two different kinds of exception. First, there are the exceptions to generally applicable rules that nevertheless are recognized as proper uses of the language. For example, many irregular verbs violate the general rules for forming the past tense, but these irregular forms are the correct forms for those verbs. To handle these cases, symbolic theorists may write more complex sets of rules in which the exceptions themselves are specified by rules of limited application. The more exceptions there are, the less satisfactory is this approach. (See Lakoff, 1970, for a consideration of the problems posed by exceptions.) Second, there are the mistakes people make in actually speaking the language, which result in sentences that are more or less ungrammatical. Chomsky's *competence/performance* distinction has frequently been invoked as a way of construing these cases. A speaker is assumed to have a system of rules, which constitutes his or her linguistic competence. Additional factors become involved when this competence is expressed in specific linguistic acts, all of which create variations (e.g., in the timing of pauses in sentence production) among which are grammatical errors. Preferably, the errors would be accounted for within the same mechanistic explanation that accounts for how we produce sentences at all.

Connectionists, in fact, have some hope of accounting for both rule-like and exceptional behavior by means of a single mechanism. In each case, it is the set of connections in the network that determines the response of the system. The particular set of constraints found in a network may enable it to perform consistently with a general rule in some contexts, but to select the appropriate exceptional response in other contexts. Sometimes when we analyze a network we can find connections that can be interpreted as serving the same function that a rule might serve in a symbolic system. But even when we find such an interpretable connection, it is only a soft constraint that the system as a whole might override. Hence, connectionism attempts to avoid some of the problems posed by exceptions to rules by using a system of *soft* constraints rather than *hard* rules. The goal is to account for exceptions as well as regularities within the same system. (See chapter 5 for opposing views of the success of one such attempt.)

2.3.3   Graceful degradation

One of the notable features of the human brain is that it seems to be an extremely reliable device. Like any mechanism, though, it has its limits. It can be overloaded with too many demands or too much information, or it can be impaired by physical damage. But when its limits are exceeded, generally it does not crash. It simply begins to perform sub-optimally. When confronting a task that makes too many demands, it begins to ignore some of the demands or some of the information. The more it is overloaded, or the more it is impaired, the less well it functions. The same gradation of effect is found when some components are destroyed. In a very few situations, a clearly delineated behavioral deficit will arise. For example, the classical work on aphasia correlated particular lesions (e.g., in Broca's area) with particular behavioral deficits (inability to produce articulate speech). But in general the brain is rather resilient in the face of damage. Nerve cells die every day, but generally this does not leave a trace in terms of specific impairment of performance. Loss of even large numbers of neurons may lead not to specific losses but to a nonspecific gradual impairment of function. For example, we do not forget how to divide 12 by 2 and yet remember the rest of the division tables; rather, we gradually become more limited in our numeric abilities. This characteristic of gradually failing performance is generally referred to as *graceful degradation*.

A traditional symbolic system does not exhibit graceful degradation. If any of its elements are lost, the information they encode is no longer available to the system. This is particularly clear if we consider what happens if a rule is eliminated. The system is simply not able to respond to any of the situations in which that rule was needed. It is possible to develop implementations of symbolic systems that are more resistant to damage, for example, by storing information at redundant locations or using error-checking techniques to recover from damage. Such an implementation still may fail to exhibit the more subtle phenomenon of graceful degradation.

A connectionist network, on the other hand, does exhibit graceful degradation. Destruction of a few connections or even of a few units (except in networks which only have a few units to begin with) generally does not significantly impair the activity of the system. In a localist system, destroying a unit will destroy a particular piece of that system's information, with possibly serious consequences, but destroying connections instead will result in graceful degradation. For example, using the Jets and Sharks network which employs a localist encoding, we destroyed at random 53 of the 1,062 connections in the network (5 percent of the total) and then explored its performance on the same tasks that we discussed at the beginning of this chapter. On two of the tasks its performance was qualitatively the same: it still correctly identified Art's properties and it still correctly identified the individuals that met the specification of being in their twenties and being pushers. It did perform differently when queried about Sharks. It still responded by activating particular Sharks, but it offered different judgments as to who were the most prototypical Sharks (Nick, Neal, and Dave). The reason the network was still able to identify Art's properties was that none of the connections between Art's person unit and his properties happened to be broken. But as an additional experiment we broke one of these connections (between **ART** and **junior high** education). The network now answered incorrectly that Art had a **high school** education. What is interesting is how it arrived at this answer: those individuals who were most similar to Art in other respects tended to activate the unit for high school education. Thus, even when disabled, the network still offered plausible judgments. It did not crash.

In systems using distributed representation, we can eliminate a number of units in the system and the system will still behave in only a slightly distorted fashion. For example, if an input normally consists of a distributed representation over eight units, and one of these is disabled, the system will still respond normally to most input patterns. With more damage, the system will increasingly make errors; however, even these will not be random, but rather be associated with closely related patterns to which the distorted input is now more similar. Hence, a connectionist cognitive system inherently displays graceful degradation as a consequence of its own architecture. It will display that property whether it is implemented in a nervous system, on a parallel machine, or even on a serial computer.

2.3.4 Content-addressable memory

The human ability to remember information is quite remarkable. Frequently information that we need comes to mind spontaneously. We identify a book that we need, and we remember that we loaned it to a student. Sometimes, though, we need to work at recalling information: we remember we loaned the book to a student, but now have to work at trying to recall who the student was. This may involve retrieving cues that will help us identify the person. Typically, we can retrieve the same piece of information from a variety of different cues that constitute part of the contents of the memory itself. Since such memory is accessed through its content, it is generally termed *content-addressable memory*. Designing this type of memory access into a symbolic system is a challenge, and requires maneuvering around the architecture of the system rather than taking advantage of it.

A common model for a symbolic memory is a filing system: we store information on paper, place the paper in a file folder, and position the folder in a cabinet sorted according to some procedure we take to be reasonable. If each folder is positioned by an arbitrary index, or by the serial order of its creation, there is no content addressability in the filing system. More frequently, each folder will be positioned in accord with one or at most two aspects of its content. For example, suppose that we keep track of students in our classes by placing information about them in file folders arranged alphabetically. Sometimes this works very well. If we want information on a particular student, we can rapidly access the file with that student's name. If, however, we seek to recover the information by taking a different route, the task is more difficult. Suppose that the information we want to access about a student is her name, and the cues we start with are what class she took and what grade she got. Now we face a serious problem: since the information is not organized in this manner, the only way to retrieve the student's name is to go through each folder until we find a student who took the class in question and received the specified grade. If we had known in advance that there might be different ways in which we would want to access the information in our filing cabinet, we could have developed an indexing system that would have told us where information satisfying certain descriptions would be found. For example, we might have constructed an index identifying by name the students in each class. But then it is necessary to identify in advance all the ways we might want to access the file. Furthermore, if we make errors in recalling the contents that are indexed (e.g., confusing our course on research methods with our course on statistics), the index is of little or no use.

The disadvantages of the filing cabinet system are exhibited in a variety of memory systems. In computer systems, for example, information is stored at register locations, and the only way to access information directly is by means of the address of the location. Symbolic systems that are implemented on such computers often (although not necessarily) make some of the same assumptions about storage and retrieval. Serial search through separate items therefore figures prominently in memory retrieval. Some such systems attain superior performance by means of intelligent search procedures that mitigate this difficulty.

Connectionist networks offer a relatively natural alternative means of achieving content-addressable, fault-tolerant memory. The Jets and Sharks network provides a simple illustration. Properties could be retrieved from names, names from properties, and so forth. We might even make a mistake on one property and still retrieve the right person. For example, we gave the network the task of remembering George's name and we described him as a Jet, in his thirties, junior high educated, and divorced. As an experiment, we deliberately made a mistake about one of George's properties (he is in fact still in his twenties). No one, in fact, precisely fits this description. But, since the connections only constitute soft constraints, the network proceeds to find the best match. The units for Jim and George become most active (0.31 after 70 cycles), while Al is slightly less active (0.30). Jim and George actually have identical properties and match on three out of four cued properties, while Al has different properties, but also matches on three out of four. Thus, even with erroneous cues, the network has recalled the persons who best match what cues were given.

The advantages of content-addressable memory are particularly evident in systems employing distributed representations; in such systems it is often possible, given part of a pattern, to reconstruct the whole pattern. A question arises, however, as to how we should characterize this sort of memory. Within symbolic systems remembering is a process of retrieving a symbol that has been stored away. But in connectionist networks, remembering is carried out by the same means as making inferences; the system fills in missing pieces of information. As far as the system's processing is concerned, there is no difference between reconstructing a previous state, and constructing a totally new state (confabulating):

> One way of thinking about distributed memories is in terms of a very large set of plausible inference rules. Each active unit represents a "microfeature" of an item, and the connection strengths stand for plausible "microinferences" between microfeatures. Any particular pattern of activity of the units will satisfy some of the microinferences and violate others. A stable pattern of activity is one that violates the plausible microinferences less than any of the neighboring patterns. A new stable pattern can be created by changing the inference rules so that the new pattern violates them less than its neighbors. This view of memory makes it clear that there is no sharp distinction between genuine memory and plausible reconstruction. A genuine memory is a pattern

that is stable because the inference rules were modified when it occurred before. A "confabulation" is a pattern that is stable because of the way the inference rules have been modified to store several different previous patterns. So far as the subject is concerned, this may be indistinguishable from the real thing.   (Hinton, McClelland, and Rumelhart, 1986, *PDP:3*, pp. 80–1)

2.3.5   Capacity to learn from experience and generalize

A final feature of networks that makes them attractive is their capacity to learn from experience by changing the weights of connections. In addition to the Hebbian approach introduced in section 2.2.3, network researchers have developed a variety of procedures for gradually adjusting the weights of a network so that, if an adequate set of weights exists, the network will find them. One advantage of these approaches is that they generally allow networks to generalize beyond the training sets to give correct responses to new inputs. These learning procedures are the focus of the next chapter. They give connectionism a resource that may enable it to explain such things as learning a language or learning to do arithmetic, kinds of learning which are awkward to model symbolically.

2.4   Challenges Facing Connectionist Networks

In the previous section we have examined some of the touted advantages of connectionist networks. But there are, as well, some well-known challenges facing connectionist researchers. Some of these, such as catastrophic interference, we have already noted. Others, such as accounting for the productivity and systematicity of thought, are discussed in detail in subsequent chapters. A few others, though, should be noted here. One is that there are a large number of parameters connectionist researchers can manipulate, explicitly or implicitly, in setting up their networks. These reflect numerous decisions involving the architecture of the network, the activation and learning functions, and the means of encoding tasks to be performed. While manipulating this range of parameters may enable connectionist modelers to account for a wide diversity of cognitive performances, it also represents a potential weakness of connectionist modeling. If a given simulation succeeds in accounting for behavior with a fortuitous set of parameters, this may not be very informative as to how humans generate the behavior.

Of particular note in this respect is the manner in which researchers encode the inputs and desired outputs for their simulations. By carefully crafting these, a researcher may simplify the challenge to the network and the resulting simulation may not significantly advance our understanding of human performance. Even if the simulation accurately characterized human performance, our explanation of the performance would then require us to determine how it is that the inputs and desired outputs for the cognitive system came to have that form. A greater risk is that the encoding used by humans is very different from that supplied by the researcher to the network and as a result the simulation does not correspond to the way humans perform the task.

A final challenge facing connectionism concerns learning. As we will see in the next chapter, to overcome the limitations with Hebbian learning, connectionists frequently adopt a form of gradient descent learning in which a repetitive process of changing weights ultimately enables networks to perform their task. But not all learning is so gradual. At least in the case of human beings, some information can be learned rapidly in one or two encounters. Also, some information is encoded in relative isolation rather than as part of a highly connected system. In illustration of both of these points, suppose that I am told verbally, "To make this thing work, push a candy bar through the slot in the center." I am highly likely to remember that rather bizarre instruction. This kind of learning is relatively easy to model in symbolic models, since it only requires encoding a new rule, but not in networks that learn by gradient descent. The Hebbian procedure we introduced in this chapter provides one way networks can achieve one-trial acquisition of idiosyncratic responses. There are other approaches to connectionist learning, such as Kohonen's procedure for self-organizing feature maps which we discuss in section 7.5, that enable one-trial learning of distinctive information. However, it is not obvious how to integrate these approaches with the more frequent use of gradual learning. Since humans are capable of both sorts of learning, one would hope that a unified account will eventually be attained.

2.5   Summary

In this chapter we have presented a simple connectionist network (the Jets and Sharks network), and examined some of the basic architectural features that can be employed in connectionist networks more generally. We have also examined some of the features of connectionist systems that have served to attract interest in them. In the next chapter we will examine in more detail the ability of connectionist systems to learn; then in chapter 4 we will turn to a cognitive task, pattern recognition, for which connectionist networks appear particularly adept.

NOTES

1   Usually the word "cluster" is used for sets of items that are similar in some way, whereas here the items in each cluster form a contrast set.
2   In fact, as processing continues, the activation of the person unit **MIKE** begins to drop again. The reason is that as **ART** and the person units for gang members most similar to Art grow in activation, they send increasingly inhibitory inputs to **MIKE**.
3   The activation pattern across a layer of n units can be treated as a vector (directed line segment) in an n-dimensional space.
4   The hidden units did not receive external input, so that term would always have a zero value for those units.
5   Hopfield's E should not be confused with the measure of mean squared error that is used in deriving the delta rule. In boxes 1 and 2 of chapter 3 we call this measure *Error*, but it is often called E.
6   When equation (9) is applied to a feedforward network, temperature does not affect the time to reach a solution (because each output unit's activation is calculated just one time). If a learning rule is also being applied, however, high variability of response across different presentations of the same input will make learning slower (which often is desirable).

Sources and Recommended Readings

Anderson, J. A. (1995) *An Introduction to Neural Networks*. Cambridge, MA: MIT Press

Ballard, D. H. (1997) *An Introduction to Natural Computation*. Cambridge, MA: MIT Press.

Ellis, R. and Humphreys, G. (1999) *Connectionist Psychology: A Text with Readings*. East Sussex: Psychology Press.

Levine, D. S. (1991) *Introduction to Neural and Cognitive Modeling*. Hillsdale, NJ: Erlbaum.

McClelland, J. L. and Rumelhart, D. E. (1988) *Explorations in Parallel Distributed Processing: A Handbook of Models, Programs, and Exercises*. Cambridge, MA: MIT Press. (Includes **PDP** simulation software on disk.)

McClelland, J. L., Rumelhart, D. E. and the PDP Research Group (1986) *Parallel Distributed Processing: Explorations in the Microstructure of Cognition*, vol. 2: *Psychological and Biological Models*. Cambridge, MA: MIT Press.

McLeod, P., Plunkett, K. and Rolls, E. (1998) *Introduction to Connectionist Modelling of Cognitive Processes*. Oxford: Oxford University Press. (Includes **tlearn** simulation software on disk; also downloadable from crl.ucsd.edu/innate/tlearn.html.)

O'Reilly, R. C. and Munakata, Y. (2000) *Computational Explorations in Cognitive Neuroscience: Understanding the Mind by Simulating the Brain*. Cambridge, MA: MIT Press. (Keyed to **PDP++** simulation software, downloadable from www.cnbc.cmv.edu/PDP++/PDP++.html.)

Plunkett, K. and Elman, J. L. (1997) *Exercises in Rethinking Innateness*. Cambridge, MA: MIT Press. (Includes **tlearn** simulation software on disk; also downloadable from crl.ucsd.edu/innate/tlearn.html.)

Rumelhart, D. E., McClelland, J. L. and the PDP Research Group (1986) *Parallel Distributed Processing: Explorations in the Microstructure of Cognition*, vol. 1: *Foundations*. Cambridge, MA: MIT Press.

3

LEARNING

One of the features of connectionist systems that has been most attractive to researchers is the capacity of these systems to learn. In this chapter we first discuss alternative approaches to learning that were developed earlier than, and compete with, connectionism. Second, we describe and illustrate some of the principal learning strategies that have been developed for connectionist networks. Third, we discuss two essentially philosophical issues that are raised by connectionist learning strategies.

3.1 Traditional and Contemporary Approaches to Learning

Treatments of learning generally divide along a major philosophical distinction, that between empiricism and rationalism. Empiricism and rationalism represent two major intellectual traditions that can be traced back at least to Plato and Aristotle. They were developed most systematically in the wake of the Scientific Revolution in the seventeenth century, which overthrew the then current Aristotelian theories of the natural world (according to which objects behaved in accord with their natural forms or essences) and of the human capacity for knowledge (which involved internalizing the forms of objects). The distinctive claims of these two traditions have continued to divide contemporary disciplines such as psychology and linguistics.

3.1.1 Empiricism

The tradition of philosophical empiricism emerged in Britain and is associated with such theorists as Bacon, Locke, Berkeley, and Hume. The empiricists faulted the Aristotelian tradition for excessive dependence on established principles of reasoning and for insufficient attention to our sensory experience of the world. For the empiricists, such sensory experience provided the only authority that we could employ if we sought truth. The empiricists' primary concern was thus epistemological: knowledge must be grounded in sensory experience. Also incorporated within their framework, however, was an account of psychological processes that became known as *associationism*. In this account, sensory experience gave rise to simple ideas (e.g., *red*, *round*), which then became composed into more complex ideas (e.g., *apple*). In this example, it is spatial contiguity that produces the association. For

Hume and others, temporal contiguity was also important, because it was viewed as giving rise to our idea of causation. Once associated, the idea of a cause could elicit the idea of its effect. Similarity was an additional principle governing the formation of associations in most treatments. The associationist approach was further developed by psychological theorists such as David Hartley in the eighteenth century and James Mill, John Stuart Mill, Alexander Bain, and Herbert Spencer in the nineteenth century. J. R. Anderson and Bower (1973) offers a useful review that suggests four defining features of associationism: the notion that mental elements become associated through experience; that complex ideas can be reduced to a set of simple ideas; that the simple ideas are sensations; and that simple additive rules are sufficient to predict properties of complex ideas from simple ideas.

A kind of associationism found expression in the behaviorist models of classical and operant conditioning, which were developed in the United States in the twentieth century. Here, the strategy was to limit the entities involved in the posited associations to what could be observed by an investigator: environmental events (stimuli, reinforcements) and the behavioral responses of the organism. During the era when behaviorism dominated psychology, learning was the central topic of concern. Researchers actively investigated the efficacy of different ways of arranging the environment (by varying the timing and degree of reinforcement, punishment, contiguity, and the like). Some used the tool of mathematical modeling to develop general theories of learning. Learning was operationally defined as changes in the frequency of a particular response. The major limitation of this work was the lack of an adequate means of modeling what occurred *inside* the system as it learned. In fact, this limitation was regarded as a virtue: learning theorists preferred to regard the organism as a black box. Some investigators developed notions of mediated learning that referred to internal stimuli and responses, but had no way of actually building models of the internal events. They were intrigued, for example, by the ability of older children (but not younger children or animals) quickly to reverse the responses made to two kinds of stimuli when the experimenter suddenly reversed the contingencies. "Reversal learning" was regarded as a phenomenon that presented a challenge for learning theory. Although no solution was directly forthcoming, the limitations of behaviorism made some of its practitioners receptive to the information-processing approach that emerged in the 1960s. Hence, behaviorism has lost its pre-eminence but endures as a research tradition within psychology.

3.1.2   Rationalism

The other major intellectual tradition that the cognitive sciences have inherited is rationalism, represented by philosophers on the European continent such as Descartes, Spinoza, and Leibniz. Rationalism rejected empiricism's strong reliance on sensory experience and offered a different diagnosis of the problems with Aristotelianism (in particular, the fact that it had not achieved true knowledge). Rationalists did not seek to restrict ideas to those grounded in experience. Ideas, for the rationalist, were innate; what was critical in arriving at true beliefs was the way we reasoned using these ideas. Rationalists did not reject reliance on sensory experience altogether. They proposed that it could tell us which of several possible coherent arrangements of ideas were actually instantiated in this world. But they insisted that far more basic than experience was careful reasoning using our native ideas.

The rationalist tradition has had its major contemporary impact in the discipline of linguistics. As discussed in section 1.3, Noam Chomsky (1957, 1965) moved away from the behaviorist foundations of structural linguistics and came to view his own generative grammars as essentially cognitive theories – models of human linguistic *competence*. The crucial core of that competence, Universal Grammar, is innate. Chomsky took a distinctly rationalist position with respect to learning as well. As early as his review of B. F. Skinner's *Verbal Behavior*, Chomsky (1959) countered Skinner's claim that a behaviorist theory could account for language learning, and by the time he presented the Beckman lectures at Berkeley (Chomsky, 1968), he had developed a mentalistic account grounded in Descartes' seventeenth-century rationalism. One of Chomsky's main arguments, which came to be known as the *poverty of the stimulus* argument, contended that the sentences in a child's environment provide too impoverished a database to make it credible that ordinary learning can account for the child's competence; instead, the innate Universal Grammar must guide the child's inductions from input.

In fact, two issues are combined in Chomsky's attack on behaviorist models of language acquisition. First, what role is played by innate knowledge in language acquisition? Second, for those aspects of a language that must be learned (e.g., particulars of the inflectional system), by what process does that learning occur? Language acquisition researchers within the Chomskian tradition initially put forward the *little linguist* model: that the child formulates hypotheses and tests them against data (typically not consciously). With changes in linguistic theory, this became refined into the claim that the child is born with parameters that can be set to one of a small number of predetermined values; the incoming data are used to determine which setting is appropriate. In one version, the parameters are initially set to unmarked (default) values that can be reset on the basis of experience. For example, *pro drop* specifies that subject pronouns can be omitted, and is assumed unless the child encounters disconfirming evidence (as in English; see Hyams, 1986). There has been an ongoing tension in developmental psychology between those adopting the Chomskian approach, and those preferring an empiricist framework. Neither group has been able to offer a detailed model of the mechanisms involved in language acquisition.

3.1.3 Contemporary cognitive science

Chomskian linguists have continued into the 1990s as the contemporary representatives of a rationalist view of learning. Cognitive psychologists and artificial intelligence researchers, in contrast, initially tended to ignore learning. In formulating an alternative to behaviorism, they addressed questions on which immediate progress could be made using rule-based symbolic models: how information is represented in the mind, what kinds of memory systems are involved, and what processes operate on mental representations. Several factors resulted in increased attention to learning beginning in the 1980s; prominent among these was the rise of connectionist approaches to learning. Some researchers in the symbolic tradition also exhibited a new interest in learning, but expressed that interest by designing rule-based systems that can learn. For instance, by the 1980s there was new work on learning by analogy and inductive procedures (e.g., J. R. Anderson, 1981; Holland, Holyoak, Nisbett, and Thagard, 1986).

Within artificial intelligence, an active research area known as *machine learning* has emerged, which pursues strategies for getting machines to learn from experience (see Mitchell, 1997, and Thagard, 1998, for overviews). Since rules are the major determinant of behavior in symbolic systems, the strategies focus on modifying or adding rules. One of the factors that makes this work challenging is that altering rules can have fairly global effects on behavior; hence, a rule modification designed to deal with one circumstance may inadvertently result in new, incorrect behavior in certain other circumstances. A more general problem is that modifying or adding rules can be too crude a technique to capture the gradualness and subtlety of learning. As research has proceeded, techniques have emerged to make much finer adjustments to rule systems that overcome these difficulties and result in performance that is more human-like (see, for example, Holland et al., 1986).

Hence, a researcher interested in learning has a choice of approaches. The empiricist branch of the symbolic approach (e.g., cognitive psychology and AI) offers increasingly sophisticated methods for modifying rules and symbolic representations. The rationalist branch of the symbolic approach (e.g., linguistics and Chomskian language-acquisition research) offers new interpretations of how adjustments are made to an innate grammar in order to acquire a specific language. And connectionism offers powerful learning algorithms that have revived interest in subsymbolic network architectures as a vehicle for an essentially empiricist program. We turn now to a more detailed consideration of how connectionist networks learn.

3.2   Connectionist Models of Learning

In section 2.2.3 we have already provided an introduction to learning in connectionist systems. Learning consists in changing the weights of connections between units, so as to alter the way in which the network will process inputs on subsequent occasions. When a network is run in training mode, both activations and weights change on each learning trial; after training, the network can be tested by presenting inputs and observing their effect on the activations alone. It is important to understand that although both weights and activations can change in response to inputs, their roles are distinct. Activation values are the vehicle for temporary state changes in a network that should tell us which one of a set of possible input patterns has just been processed. Weights are the vehicle for more enduring changes in a network that make it capable of processing all of the various input patterns on which it has been trained. In fact, some training procedures make the weight changes only after the entire batch of input patterns has been processed rather than on every trial; in the end, the results are very similar. In contrast, it would not make any sense to change activations less frequently than every trial (that is, every presentation of an input pattern).

One similarity between activations and weights is that their changes are determined locally; that is, they are based solely on information that is directly available to a particular unit or connection. In the case of a weight change, the outputs (which are often simply the activations) of each of the two units between which the connection is being adjusted count as local. Any units other than those indexed in the weight's subscripts are remote, not local. In a multi-layered or interactive network these remote units can affect the activation of the local units by means of unit-to-unit (local) propagation of activity through the network; hence they can affect the changes in weights as well. However, the effects must come only via the series of local changes; it is somewhat like playing a game of rumor (A whispers to B, B whispers to C) rather than A simply talking to everyone at once.

A variety of learning procedures is now employed in connectionist networks. The precise procedure chosen depends in part upon the architecture of the network that is to learn. In this chapter we will describe some of the most commonly used learning procedures. In order to make clear the basic principles, we have chosen to provide a detailed treatment of representative examples of learning in one class of networks (feedforward networks). Recall that in such networks, a pattern of activation is provided across the units of the input layer, and the network is supposed to produce an appropriate pattern of activation across the units of the output layer. We will begin with learning procedures for two-layer feedforward networks (pattern associators) and then move on to multi-layered feedforward networks. We must be briefer in our treatment of other learning procedures, including those for the Boltzmann machine (as an exemplar of interactive networks), competitive learning, and reinforcement learning. Note that learning procedures are often classified as exemplifying *supervised learning* versus *unsupervised learning*. In supervised learning, the network is explicitly told what output was desired for a particular input (and must compare that to its actual output). In unsupervised learning, the network classifies a set of inputs without feedback. This distinction seems clear enough, but considerable controversy has emerged regarding the proper application of these terms; we will refer to it only for the clearest cases.

3.2.1　Learning procedures for two-layer feedforward networks

3.2.1.1　Training and testing a network　The goal of the learning procedure is to develop weights that enable a network to respond appropriately to a set of cases. Each case is composed of a pattern of activations across the units of the input layer (the *input pattern*) and a pattern of activations across the units of the output layer (the *output pattern*). These patterns technically can be treated as n-dimensional *vectors*, where n is the number of units; however, we will simply refer to them as *patterns*. Typically, the network's ability to learn is determined by running it in two different modes: a training mode, in which entire cases are presented (input patterns with their associated output patterns) and a test mode, in which only the input patterns are presented. During training, the weights increasingly accommodate the constraints in the set of cases. Minimally, every case would be presented once in the training mode (so that the number of training trials would equal the number of cases); this is referred to as one *epoch* of training. Depending upon the learning procedure used and the difficulty of the set of cases, a large number of epochs may be required to achieve satisfactory performance. If the training has been sufficient, when the network is tested with the input patterns, it will respond with the appropriate output pattern on its own.[1]

We will consider two different learning rules that are variations on this general scheme: the *Hebbian rule* (which we have already introduced) and a more powerful variation known as the *delta rule*.

3.2.1.2　The Hebbian rule　When a two-layer feedforward network incorporates a linear activation rule, and applies the Hebbian rule to a set of input–output cases, the result is a learning device called a *linear associator*. In training mode, as described in section 2.2.3, a linear associator is presented with each input pattern together with its associated output pattern. (Since the Hebbian rule treats them identically, however, the input–output distinction is not really relevant until test mode.) The Hebbian rule tells the network how to change the weight of each of its connections after each such presentation:

$$\Delta weight_{ui} = lrate\ a_u\ a_i \qquad\qquad (1)$$

That is, the weight change is obtained by multiplying the activations of the two connected units along with a constant (the learning rate). If the two units have similar activations (e.g., both positive or both negative), the current weight will be incremented by the amount given by equation (1). If the activations are dissimilar (e.g., one positive and one negative), the value of equation (1) will be negative and the current weight will be reduced. The efficacy of the weight change can be evaluated by running the revised network in test mode (that is, presenting the input pattern alone and observing what output is obtained).

The Hebbian rule works well as long as all the input patterns are uncorrelated.[2] However, it fails if we try to use it to teach patterns that are correlated. Consider what happens if we try to train the network described in section 2.2.3 using an additional case C, after it had already learned to respond to cases A and B. Case C's input pattern is $(+1 +1 -1 +1)$ and desired output pattern is $(+1 +1 +1 -1)$. Because its input pattern is positively correlated with the input patterns in cases A $(+1 +1 -1 -1)$ and B $(+1 -1 -1 +1)$, learning case C disrupts the ability of the network to respond properly to cases A and B. For example, after one learning epoch in which the three patterns were presented in the order A–B–C, the weight matrix would look like this:

Case C

Input unit	Input activation	Output unit e	f	g	h
a	$+1$	0.75	0.25	-0.25	-0.25
b	$+1$	0.25	-0.25	0.25	0.25
c	-1	-0.75	-0.25	0.25	0.25
d	$+1$	0.25	0.75	0.25	-0.75
Desired output activation		1.00	1.00	1.00	-1.00

To evaluate the success of these weights, we can run the network in test mode. On input pattern C, it will produce the erroneous output pattern $(+2 +1\ 0 -1)$. Moreover, its performance on inputs A and B is also diminished. For A it will now produce output pattern $(+1.5 -0.5 -0.5 +0.5)$ instead of $(+1 -1 -1 +1)$, and for B it will now produce $(+1.5 +1.5 -0.5 -1.5)$ instead of $(+1 +1 -1 -1)$. Furthermore, additional training on the three patterns will not improve matters; the added trials will only increase the size of the weights and hence the size of the output values, without increasing accuracy.

The requirement that all input patterns be uncorrelated with one another, in fact, imposes a serious limitation on what can be taught to a linear associator. There are sets of cases (with correlated inputs) for which a two-layer network can *produce* the correct responses on a test, if the weights have been manually set (or have been determined by means of a more powerful procedure than the Hebbian rule). However, when the Hebbian rule is applied to make the two-layer network a linear associator (a learning device), there is no guarantee that it can learn to respond to the same sets of cases.

3.2.1.3   The delta rule   A far more powerful learning rule is the least mean squares (LMS) or Widrow–Hoff rule (see Widrow and Hoff, 1960). Rumelhart and McClelland (1986), who called this the *delta rule*, regarded it as a variant of the Hebbian rule, because it maintains the basic intuition that each change in weight should depend upon what is happening at the relevant input unit and at the relevant output unit. The delta rule is more powerful than the simple Hebbian rule, however, because it directly utilizes the discrepancy between the *desired output pattern* and an *actual output pattern* to improve its weights during the training phase. Specifically, the network receives an input pattern, generates an actual output pattern using the existing weights (a step that is omitted in Hebbian learning), compares that to the desired output pattern, and changes each weight based upon the difference at each output unit (referred to as the unit's *error* or *discrepancy*). Thus, this procedure is an *error correction procedure*, and it is regarded as a prototypical example of supervised learning.

The error for the entire output pattern is referred to as *pss* (*pattern sum of squares*) in McClelland and Rumelhart's (1988) *Handbook*. It is computed as follows: for each output unit u, compute the difference (discrepancy) between the desired output of u (d_u) and the actual output of u (a_u); square each of the differences; and add together the squared differences over all of the output units:

$$pss = \sum_u (d_u - a_u)^2 \tag{2}$$

By summing the *pss* values across all of the input–output cases being learned by the system, we can obtain the value of *tss* (*total sum of squares*). This is a useful indicator of how much room for improvement remains to achieve perfect performance on the entire set of input–output cases.

Five points should be noted. First, it is the use of the *differences* ($d_u - a_u$) that motivates calling this the *delta* rule (Rumelhart, Hinton, and McClelland, 1986, in *PDP:2*, p. 53). Second, both d_u and a_u are activation values (a desired and actual activation on output unit u, respectively). Third, section 2.2.2 made a different distinction that we will be able to ignore here: the *output* of a unit was sometimes, but not always, identical to its *activation*. In the learning procedures reviewed here, the identity function $output_u = activation_u$ always holds; we can therefore simplify matters by referring directly to activations. Fourth, most presentations use an error measure, $Error_p$, which is the same as *pss* except that the sum of squares is divided by 2. Using $Error_p$ simplifies the derivation of the delta rule (see below); for all other purposes in this chapter we find *pss* more convenient. Fifth, a more careful rendering of most of the equations in this chapter would include a subscript p on most variables, indicating that the equation applies to each output pattern (or input–output case). For the sake of readability, we omit this index here and in the equations that follow.

The delta rule requires that each weight in the network be changed according to the following equation:

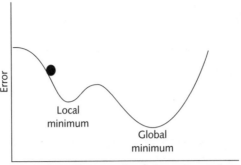

Weight on the connection between two units

Figure 3.1   Illustration of the principle of gradient descent in a one-dimensional landscape. Imagine that someone has put sand between two plates of glass to make a child's ant farm, and has inserted a ball bearing inside that rolls down the hill on the left and stops in the higher of the two valleys or, if rolled from the right, stops in the deeper valley. Applied to gradient descent in networks, the hilly landscape is a curve that represents the value of the error measure as a function of the value of the connection weight. The ball bearing represents the amount of error associated with the current weight. A gradient descent algorithm is a way of getting the weight to change such that the ball moves downhill until a minimum is reached. There are two minima on the curve, a local minimum and a global minimum. If the initial weight happens to be low (towards the left), the network will become trapped in a local minimum. If it happens to be high (towards the right), the network will settle in the global minimum.

$$\Delta weight_{ui} \doteq lrate\,(d_u - a_u)\,a_i \qquad\qquad (3)$$

The underlying strategy is to change each weight in the network so as to reduce the total error (as revealed in a test or during the next epoch of training). If a particular unit produced the desired output, then $(d_u - a_u)$ equals 0 and so none of the weights feeding in to it is changed. If there is an error on the output unit, we still do not change the weight if the input unit for that connection had 0 activation, since that weight could not have been contributing to the error. When there is an error and the input was not zero, this equation causes a change in the weight in the direction that would reduce the error.

A deeper understanding of this informal characterization can be obtained by working through a derivation of the delta rule. Rumelhart and McClelland (1986) noted that there are a variety of ways of deriving the delta rule. They selected one that shows that the delta rule (which changes weights) indeed achieves this minimization of total squared discrepancies (which is the error measure). They did this by showing that the derivative of the error measure with respect to each weight is (negatively) proportional to the amount of change in the weights that results from applying the delta rule. They further interpreted this as an implementation of *gradient descent* in *weight space*, which can be visualized as seeking the lowest point on a landscape of error values across possible weights; see figure 3.1 for an illustration using possible values of just one weight. We recapitulate their derivation in box 3.1, translated into our notation and with some differences in exposition. (This relatively technical material can be bypassed without loss of continuity. For an excellent presentation of error reduction methods and gradient descent, see chapter 9 of J. A. Anderson, 1995; also see the discussion in section 2.2.2 of local vs. global minima in Hopfield nets.)

Box 3.1   Derivation of the delta rule

The general strategy underlying the delta rule is to start with a measure of *Error* in the output

$$Error = \tfrac{1}{2} \sum_u (d_u - a_u)^2$$

and then to modify the weights in a way that decreases error. An initial difficulty we face is that the error measure is calculated for the whole pattern so that information about it is not available locally at each weight. What we actually need in order to know how to change the weights, however, is not the *Error* itself, but the partial derivative of *Error* with respect to the activation of each output unit so that we can determine how *Error* will change with change in that activation. This partial derivative can be evaluated locally. In fact, it is simply the difference between the desired and actual output activations (with appropriate sign):

$$\frac{\partial Error}{\partial a_u} = -(d_u - a_u)$$

This tells us how much the activation of each output unit must change in order to reduce to zero that unit's contribution to *Error*. Now we work backwards, because the relevant way to change the output unit's activation is to change the weight of each of its connections with an input unit. (The irrelevant way would be to change the input activations.) Therefore, the problem has become one of specifying how to change the connection weights so as to reduce *Error*. This requires that we determine the partial derivative of *Error* with respect to the weights. Here we appeal to the chain rule:

$$\frac{\partial error}{\partial weight_{ui}} = \frac{\partial Error}{\partial a_u} \frac{\partial a_u}{\partial weight_{ui}}$$

We need now to evaluate the partial derivative of the activation with respect to the weight. If we are using the linear activation function,

$$a_u = \sum_i weight_{ui}\, a_i$$

then this partial derivative is simply the activation of the input unit:

$$\frac{\partial a_u}{\partial weight_{ui}} = a_i$$

Hence, the partial derivative of the error with respect to each weight (with negative sign) can be computed by simply multiplying the discrepancy by the activation of the input unit:

$$\frac{\partial Error}{\partial weight_{ui}} = -(d_u - a_u) a_i$$

The delta rule now multiplies the negative of this derivative by the learning rate to determine the change in the weight between units i and u:

$$\Delta weight_{ui} = lrate (d_u - a_u) a_i$$

If weights are changed after the presentation of each case c, error is calculated separately for each case. Alternatively, error can be summed across cases to obtain an overall measure of error, on the basis of which weights can be changed just once per epoch:

$$\Delta weight_{ui} = \sum_c lrate (d_{cu} - a_{cu}) a_{ci}$$

The latter method achieves true gradient descent with respect to the overall error measure; however, weight changes made after each case yield a very similar result if *lrate* is sufficiently small.

The increased power obtained by using the delta rule can be illustrated empirically by returning to the problem of learning input–output cases A, B, and C. Recall that all three could not be learned by a linear associator, which uses a simple Hebbian rule, because input pattern C is correlated with input patterns A and B. To see how the delta rule overcomes this limitation, let the network begin with all weights = 0 and *lrate* = 0.25. Case A specifies that input pattern $(+ 1 + 1 - 1 - 1)$ should elicit the desired output pattern $(+ 1 - 1 - 1 + 1)$. When input pattern A is first presented to the network, since all weights are 0, all four output units will take activation values of 0. (See section 2.2.2 to review how each input activation is multiplied by each weight, with the four resulting quantities for each output unit summed at the bottom of the column.) Hence, the actual output pattern will be (0 0 0 0). The error (discrepancy) for output unit e is obtained by taking $1 - 0 = 1$; for unit f, the error is obtained by taking $- 1 - 0 = - 1$; and so forth, resulting in errors on the four output units of $(+ 1 - 1 - 1 + 1)$. The squared errors are therefore $(+ 1 + 1 + 1 + 1)$; summing these would yield a *pss* of 4 for case A.

Case A, Training trial 1

Input unit	Input activation	Output unit			
		e	f	g	h
a	+ 1	0.00	0.00	0.00	0.00
b	+ 1	0.00	0.00	0.00	0.00
c	− 1	0.00	0.00	0.00	0.00
d	− 1	0.00	0.00	0.00	0.00
Desired output activation		1.00	− 1.00	− 1.00	1.00
Actual output activation		0.00	0.00	0.00	0.00
Error (discrepancy)		1.00	− 1.00	− 1.00	1.00

The delta rule is now applied to each of the 16 weights. To see how this is done, consider just the upper left cell (the weight for the connection between input unit a and output unit e). The change in the weight is obtained from equation (3), that is, by multiplying the learning rate (0.25) by e's error (1) by a's activation (1):

$$\Delta weight_{ui} = lrate\,(d_u - a_u)\,a_i, \text{ so } \Delta weight_{ea} = (0.25)\,(1 - 0)\,(1) = 0.25$$

This weight change ($\Delta weight_{ea} = 0.25$) is added to the current weight (0) to obtain the new weight (0.25). By applying the delta rule to each of the 16 weights in the matrix, a new weight matrix is obtained. Although a test mode trial would not ordinarily be inserted at this point, we do so in order to observe the consequences of these new weights:

Case A, Test trial 1

Input unit	Input activation	Output unit e	f	g	h
a	+ 1	0.25	− 0.25	− 0.25	0.25
b	+ 1	0.25	− 0.25	− 0.25	0.25
c	− 1	− 0.25	0.25	0.25	− 0.25
d	− 1	− 0.25	0.25	0.25	− 0.25
Desired output activation		1.00	− 1.00	− 1.00	1.00
Actual output activation		1.00	− 1.00	− 1.00	1.00
Error (discrepancy)		0.00	0.00	0.00	0.00

This new weight matrix, and therefore the output activations, are the same as those produced by the linear associator with its simple Hebbian rule (although by a different computational path; see section 2.2.3). Furthermore, the network will behave in the same way as the linear associator did when we now present input–output case B in training mode. Specifically, the network will again produce 0 on all output units (and would do the same for any input pattern that was uncorrelated with input pattern A):

Case B, Training trial 1

Input unit	Input activation	Output unit e	f	g	h
a	+ 1	0.25	− 0.25	− 0.25	0.25
b	− 1	0.25	− 0.25	− 0.25	0.25
c	− 1	− 0.25	0.25	0.25	− 0.25
d	+ 1	− 0.25	0.25	0.25	− 0.25
Desired output activation		1.00	1.00	− 1.00	− 1.00
Actual output activation		0.00	0.00	0.00	0.00
Error (discrepancy)		1.00	1.00	− 1.00	− 1.00

Applying the delta rule to obtain new weights that will work well for case B (while not losing the ability to handle case A), we again obtain the same new weight matrix as we did previously using the Hebbian rule. Again inserting a test trial we exhibit the new weights and their consequences:

Case B, Test trial 1

Input unit	Input activation	Output unit e	f	g	h
a	+ 1	0.50	0.00	− 0.50	0.00
b	− 1	0.00	− 0.50	0.00	0.50
c	− 1	− 0.50	0.00	0.50	0.00
d	+ 1	0.00	0.50	0.00	− 0.50
Desired output activation		1.00	1.00	− 1.00	− 1.00
Actual output activation		1.00	1.00	− 1.00	− 1.00
Error (discrepancy)		0.00	0.00	0.00	0.00

The difference in power between the two learning rules becomes apparent only when we present input–output case C to the network:

Case C, Training trial 1

Input unit	Input activation	Output unit e	f	g	h
a	+ 1	0.50	0.00	− 0.50	0.00
b	+ 1	0.00	− 0.50	0.00	0.50
c	− 1	− 0.50	0.00	0.50	0.00
d	+ 1	0.00	0.50	0.00	− 0.50
Desired output activation		1.00	1.00	1.00	− 1.00
Actual output activation		1.00	0.00	− 1.00	0.00
Error (discrepancy)		0.00	1.00	2.00	− 1.00

Again applying the delta rule and running a test trial on the new weights, we obtain the following:

Case C, Test trial 1

Input unit	Input activation	Output unit e	f	g	h
a	+ 1	0.50	0.25	0.00	− 0.25
b	+ 1	0.00	− 0.25	0.50	0.25
c	− 1	− 0.50	− 0.25	0.00	0.25
d	+ 1	0.00	0.75	0.50	− 0.75
Desired output activation		1.00	1.00	1.00	− 1.00
Actual output activation		1.00	1.00	1.00	− 1.00
Error (discrepancy)		0.00	0.00	0.00	0.00

For the first time, the weights are different from those obtained using the Hebbian rule. Those feeding into output unit *e* are unchanged from the preceding weights (after case B), because there is no discrepancy between the actual activation of *e* and the desired activation; the Hebbian rule, working only with the desired output

Table 3.1   Two learning rules contrasted

Epoch	Output pattern A	Output pattern B	Output pattern C
		Desired pattern	
NA	1.00 − 1.00 − 1.00 1.00	1.00 1.00 − 1.00 − 1.00	1.00 1.00 1.00 − 1.00
		Learning with the Hebbian rule	
1	0.00 0.00 0.00 0.00	0.00 0.00 0.00 0.00	1.00 1.00 1.00 − 1.00
2	1.00 − 0.50 − 0.50 0.50	1.50 1.50 − 0.50 − 0.50	3.00 1.00 − 1.00 − 1.00
3	3.00 − 1.00 − 1.00 1.00	3.00 3.00 − 1.00 − 3.00	5.00 2.00 − 1.00 − 2.00
4	4.50 − 1.50 − 1.50 1.50	4.50 4.50 − 1.50 − 4.50	7.00 3.00 − 1.00 − 3.00
		Learning with the delta rule	
1	0.00 0.00 0.00 0.00	0.00 0.00 0.00 0.00	1.00 0.00 1.00 0.00
2	1.00 − 0.50 0.00 0.50	1.00 1.50 0.00 − 1.50	1.00 0.50 0.00 − 0.50
3	1.00 − 0.75 − 0.50 0.75	1.00 1.25 − 0.50 − 1.25	1.00 0.75 0.50 − 0.75
4	1.00 − 0.87 − 0.75 0.87	1.00 1.12 − 0.75 − 1.12	1.00 0.87 0.75 − 0.87
5	1.00 − 0.93 − 0.87 0.93	1.00 1.06 − 0.87 − 1.06	1.00 0.93 0.87 − 0.93
6	1.00 − 0.96 − 0.93 0.96	1.00 1.03 − 0.93 − 1.03	1.00 0.96 0.93 − 0.96
7	1.00 − 0.98 − 0.96 0.98	1.00 1.01 − 0.96 − 1.01	1.00 0.98 0.96 − 0.98
8	1.00 − 0.99 − 0.98 0.99	1.00 1.00 − 0.98 − 1.00	1.00 0.99 0.98 − 0.99
9	1.00 − 0.99 − 0.99 0.99	1.00 1.00 − 0.99 − 1.00	1.00 0.99 0.99 − 0.99

activations, produced a quite different set of weights for this unit. The weights feeding into output unit g do reflect changes to the previous weights, but the changes are different from those produced by the Hebbian rule. Finally, the weights feeding into output units f and h happen to be the same as those produced by the Hebbian rule at this point in training. Over all 16 weights, therefore, half are the same and half are different from those produced by the Hebbian rule.

As for the pattern of activations on the output units, the 16 weights produced by the delta rule have generated the correct output for case C, an outcome not achieved by the Hebbian rule. As with the Hebbian rule, however, trying to learn case C has disrupted the ability of the network to generate the correct output for cases A and B. Running these cases once again in test mode, the actual output patterns are now $(+ 1.0 − 0.5 \ 0.0 + 0.5)$ instead of $(+ 1 − 1 − 1 + 1)$ for A and $(+ 1.0 + 1.5 + 1.0 − 1.5)$ instead of $(+ 1 + 1 − 1 − 1)$ for B. Fortunately, the discrepancies are not as serious as those produced by the Hebbian rule, and additional training epochs will gradually bring further improvement in the ability of the network to respond to all three patterns. Table 3.1 contrasts the course of learning across epochs for the Hebbian rule (which shows no improvement) and the delta rule (which learns the patterns virtually perfectly by epoch 9). Hence, our examination of cases A, B, and C illustrates that the delta rule, unlike the simple Hebbian rule, need not be restricted to sets of input patterns that are uncorrelated (orthogonal).

Note that the results shown in table 3.1 were obtained using the **pa** (pattern associator) program in McClelland and Rumelhart's (1988) *Handbook*, chapter 4. The simulators packaged with several of the other textbooks recommended on p. 53 (or downloaded from the web sites listed there) can also be used for pattern association projects. In O'Reilly and Munakata (2000), see sections 4.3 through 5.2 for variations on Hebbian learning and 5.3 through 5.5 for the delta rule. Pattern association via the delta rule (but not the Hebbian rule) can also be explored using **tlearn**: see the **pa** project in McLeod, Plunkett, and Rolls, 1998, pp. 65–71, or set up the project outlined in Plunkett and Elman, 1997, chapter 3.

3.2.1.4   Comparing the Hebbian and delta rules   Having observed these differences in performance between the Hebbian and delta rules, it is worth considering how the rules themselves compare. The two rules have in common that they use only information that is locally available at each connection as a basis for changing the weight of the connection. Hence, there is no need to posit an executive; learning is under local control. Also, both rules make use of desired pairings of input and output patterns that are determined by the trainer. With the Hebbian training procedure, however, the desired output patterns are imposed on the output units. The network is not free to generate its own actual output, and therefore cannot use the discrepancy between desired and actual outputs to guide its learning. In test mode we can observe the network generating an actual output, and as observers we can note how discrepant it is from the desired output, but we have no way of telling the network about this discrepancy. The innovation in the delta rule is that it offers a way for the network to compute and utilize the discrepancies. The discrepancy can be regarded as a transformation of the desired output pattern (obtained by subtracting from it the actual output pattern) that is more informative than the desired output pattern itself. The delta rule is identical to the Hebbian rule except that this transformation is carried out before multiplying the output value by the input value. Hence, the delta rule can use the discrepancies to improve its weights, whereas in Hebbian learning the discrepancies can be obtained only while in test mode and are used to evaluate, but not change, the weights.

3.2.1.5   Limitations of the delta rule: The XOR problem   Exactly how powerful is a two-layer network that is using the delta rule? That is, how weak are the constraints that limit the sets of cases that it can learn? The network is guaranteed to converge on a weight matrix that is capable of producing the desired outputs as long as such a weight matrix exists. The weight matrix will exist, however, only under certain conditions. First, if you want the network to learn an arbitrary output for each input pattern, you will have to construct the input patterns in such a way that they form a *linearly independent* set. That is, none of the input patterns can be derived as a linear combination of the other patterns (e.g., by adding patterns together; see McClelland and Rumelhart's (1988) *Handbook*, pp. 95–6). For example, suppose that you have a network with just two input units. If you choose 1 0 as one input pattern, then you can also use the pattern 0 1 since neither pattern can be derived from the other. But now you cannot introduce the pattern 1 1 and teach an arbitrary output, since this input pattern is the sum of the other two. Furthermore, the number of patterns you desire to teach places a constraint on the size of the network that is required. (In general, encoding n linearly independent patterns requires n units; see Jordan, 1986, in *PDP:9*, pp. 370–3.)

What if you ignore the first constraint, and design a set of input–output cases for which the input patterns are *not* linearly independent? Whether the network can learn the proper output patterns will then depend upon whether the input–output pairs are *linearly separable*. To meet that requirement, there must exist at least one set of weights such that the same weights can be used to generate the desired output pattern for every input pattern. If such a set exists, the delta rule will find it. (This is automatic when the inputs are linearly independent, but must be determined when they are not.) For a simple example, suppose we try to teach the following function to a network with two input units and one output unit:

Case	Input unit I1	Input unit I2	Desired output
A	0	0	0
B	0	1	1
C	1	0	1
D	1	1	1

This function is equivalent to the truth table for the logical connective *inclusive or* (OR), which is false (0) when both disjuncts are false and is true (1) otherwise. The network can compute it without error if there are sufficiently high positive weights on the connections and the activation function for the output unit is a threshold function. Even though input pattern D is a linear combination of patterns B and C, the weights that generate the desired output for B and C happen to generate the desired output for D as well. But consider what would happen if we changed the desired output for D; that is, suppose we sought to teach the following function:

Case	Input unit I1	Input unit I2	Desired output
A	0	0	0
B	0	1	1
C	1	0	1
D′	1	1	0

This revised function is equivalent to the truth table for the logical connective *exclusive or* (XOR), which is true only when exactly one of the disjuncts is true. The XOR function exemplifies the more general problem of parity detection that was one focus of Minsky and Papert's (1969) argument against perceptrons. This sort of problem cannot be solved by a network with two inputs and one output, because the input–output pairs are not linearly separable.[3] Just as for the OR function, to handle input patterns B and C we need positive weights on both connections between the input units and the output units. But that means there is no way to obtain a zero output when the inputs are both 1, as required for pattern D′. A graphical interpretation is provided below. The output value for each combination of input values is placed at their intersection. In the first diagram a straight diagonal line can be drawn which will separate the three output values of 1 from the single output value of 0. But in the second diagram no straight line can be drawn to separate the 1s from the 0s.

OR

```
        1 |  1          1

Input unit I2

        0 |  0          1
          |_____
             0          1

           Input unit I1
```

XOR

```
        1 |  1          0

Input unit I2

        0 |  0          1
          |_____
             0          1

           Input unit I1
```

What happens if we persist in teaching a set of input–output patterns which are not linearly separable? In this case there will be no set of weights that can generate the correct outputs, and so the delta rule cannot solve the problem exactly. But, unlike the simple Hebbian rule, the delta rule will do the best job possible: it will converge on a set of weights that minimizes total squared error (*tss*). Furthermore, its sensitivity to dependencies (regularities) in the patterns can be useful. In real life, patterns tend to cluster together, and similar input patterns tend to be associated with similar output patterns. If presented with cases that show this kind of structure, rather than cases exhibiting linear independence and arbitrary association, the delta rule will do a good job of learning the cases and will (as a free bonus) generalize to new input patterns on the basis of their similarities to the training patterns. You are not guaranteed that every input pattern will elicit exactly the correct output pattern, but typically, output patterns will be similar (if not identical) to the correct pattern. As Rumelhart, Hinton, and Williams (1986a) pointed out in *PDP:8* (p. 318), this kind of learning is a task for which two-layer networks are well suited. For illustrations, see our discussion in sections 5.2.1 and 5.2.3 of two simulations from Rumelhart and McClelland (1986) in *PDP:18* (English past-tense acquisition and the rule of 78).

Even in the 1960s it was known that adding one or more layers of hidden units was a means of overcoming the constraint of linear separability. Unfortunately, there was no known learning algorithm for setting the weights in these more complex networks. It was left to researchers in the 1980s to devise procedures for training hidden units, and by any reckoning the discovery of these procedures was a major advance for connectionism. One of the most widely used procedures, *backpropagation*, makes use of a more powerful generalization of the delta rule. It was independently discovered by Rumelhart, Hinton, and Williams (1986a, 1986b), who called it the *generalized delta rule* (producing immediate influence on other researchers), by Le Cun (1986), Parker (1985), and, unfortunately relatively unnoticed at the time, by Werbos (1974).

3.2.2 The backpropagation learning procedure for multi-layered networks

3.2.2.1   Introducing hidden units and backpropagation learning   In the previous section we noted that two-layer networks cannot be guaranteed to learn sets of input–output cases when neither of the following constraints is met: (1) linear independence of the input patterns; (2) linear separability of the input–output assignments. We have already cited XOR as one problem that violates these constraints, and other violations are ubiquitous in the tasks that organisms must carry out daily. Hinton (1989) made this point nicely with respect to the task of viewing an object (encoded in an intensity array, as on a monochromatic television screen) and producing its name as the desired output:

> Consider, for example, the task of identifying an object when the input vector is an intensity array and the output vector has a separate component for each possible name. If a given type of object can be either black or white, the intensity of an individual pixel (which is what an input unit encodes) cannot provide any direct evidence for the presence or absence of an object of that type. So the object cannot be identified by using weights on direct connections from input to output units. Obviously it is necessary to

explicitly extract relationships among intensity values (such as edges) before trying to identify the object. Actually, extracting edges is just a small part of the problem. If recognition is to have the generative capacity to handle novel images of familiar objects the network must somehow encode the systematic effects of variations in lighting and viewpoint, partial occlusion by other objects, and deformations of the object itself. There is a tremendous gap between these complex regularities and the regularities that can be captured by an associative net that lacks hidden units.   (Hinton, 1989, pp. 5–6)

In order to solve problems like this, it is necessary to insert hidden units between the input and output units that can preprocess the information to obtain the pieces that are needed for the final solution of the overall problem. This produces a more complex flow of information in which intermediate results (such as the identification of an edge) are obtained by combining input activations in certain ways, it is then the final set of intermediate results that is used by the output units.

The introduction of hidden units raises several questions that the network designer must answer. First, how many hidden units should be used, and in how many layers should they be arranged? There is no easy recipe to follow to assure optimal performance. Second, should connections be made only between adjacent layers, or should additional connections be allowed (e.g., connect all hidden units to the output layer as well as to the next hidden layer)? Third, what activation rule should be used? Multi-layered networks are more powerful than two-layer networks only if a nonlinear activation rule is used.[4] The logistic activation function is a common choice, and is assumed throughout the remainder of this chapter. In its simplest form it is:

$$a_u = \frac{1}{1 + e^{-netinput_u}} \tag{4}$$

The final, and most interesting, challenge is to devise a learning procedure that can be applied to hidden units. The original delta rule is inappropriate, for example, because it can be applied only to connections that feed directly into output units for which an error measure can be calculated. The *generalized delta rule* bypasses this limitation by propagating the error measure that is calculated at the output units back through the network (i.e., by *backpropagation*). Hence, on a given training trial, activations propagate forward from the input units through the hidden units to the output units, and then error and the resulting adjustments to the weights propagate in the reverse direction back through the hidden units to the input units. This must be done in a way that solves the credit assignment problem. That is, for each lower layer it must be determined how each of its units contributed to error on the output layer, and the weights must be adjusted accordingly.

The equations used to change the weights are more complex in the backpropagation rule than in the delta rule; this is due to the use of a different activation function and to the addition of hidden layers. For purposes of exposition, we will assume a network with just one hidden layer, and use i, h, and u to refer to units in the input, hidden, and output layers respectively. (For networks with additional layers, the mnemonic value of our subscripts breaks down, and a more general notation referring to arbitrary layers would be needed.) The equation for changing weights that feed into the output units is the simplest one, since that is the layer at which error is computed. First, *delta_u* is computed by multiplying the error $(d_u - a_u)$ by the derivative of the logistic activation function (see box 3.2):

Box 3.2   Derivation of the backpropagation learning rule

The strategy underlying the backpropagation learning rule is much the same as that for the delta rule. We begin with the same error measure:

$$Error = \frac{1}{2} \sum_u (d_u - a_u)^2$$

Our goal is to determine the partial derivatives with respect both to weights feeding into the output units and to those feeding into the hidden units, and to adjust each set of weights accordingly. We shall determine each of these separately.

Changing weights feeding into output units

We begin by taking the partial derivative of the error measure with respect to the activation of the output unit:

$$\frac{\partial Error}{\partial a_u} = -(d_u - a_u)$$

The next step is to determine $\partial a_u/\partial weight_{uh}$ so that we can then use the chain rule to determine the $\partial Error/\partial weight_{uh}$. But this is a more complex task than in the case of the delta rule since we are employing a nonlinear activation function (the logistic function):

$$a_u = \frac{1}{1 + e^{-netinput_u}}$$

Since the logistic activation function is specified in terms of net input to u, we shall work in stages. Let us first determine:

$$\frac{\partial a_u}{\partial netinput_u} = a_u(1 - a_u)$$

From this we can now use the chain rule to evaluate $\partial Error/\partial netinput_u$ the negative of which is often referred to as $delta_u$:

$$\frac{\partial Error}{\partial netinput_u} = -delta_u = \frac{\partial Error}{\partial a_u} \frac{\partial a_u}{\partial netinput_u} = -(d_u - a_u) a_u(1 - a_u)$$

We now need to determine $\partial netinput_u/\partial weight_{uh}$, for then we shall be able to employ the chain rule to determine $\partial Error/\partial weight_{uh}$. Since we are employing the logistic activation function:

$$netinput_u = \sum_h weight_{uh} a_h,$$

then:

$$\frac{\partial netinput_u}{\partial weight_{uh}} = a_h$$

Now we employ the chain rule once again:

$$\frac{\partial Error}{\partial weight_i} = -delta_u \frac{\partial netinput_u}{\partial weight_i} = -(d_u - a_u) a_u (1 - a_u) a_h$$

As with the delta rule, we shall now change weights leading to output units proportionately to the negative of this partial derivative:

$$\Delta weight_{uh} = lrate\, delta_u\, a_h = lrate\, (d_u - a_u) a_u (1 - a_u) a_h$$

Changing weights deeper in the network

The major challenge at this point is to allocate *Error* among the units in the system. For this we need to employ a recursive procedure. For expository purposes, however, we shall assume that we are dealing with a three-layer network and shall use the subscript h to refer to hidden units and i to refer to input units; the same procedure could be iterated if there were additional layers of hidden units (with h now referring to the previous i, and i to the next layer down). What we need first is to determine the derivative of *Error* with respect to the activation of units in the hidden layer. We shall do this by distributing the *delta*$_u$ that we have already calculated. Let us focus on a particular unit h and its connection to a particular output unit u. We now determine what portion of the *Error* assigned to u to allocate to h. We again use the chain rule:

$$\frac{\partial Error}{\partial a_h} = -delta_u \frac{\partial netinput_u}{\partial a_h}$$

Since

$$netinput_u = \sum_h weight_{uh}\, a_h,$$

then

$$\frac{\partial netinput_u}{\partial a_h} = weight_{uh}$$

Thus, the part of $\partial Error/\partial a_h$ contributed by *weight*$_{uh}$ is simply $(-delta_u\, weight_{uh})$. We now sum over all the connections from h to the output level to determine

$$\frac{\partial Error}{\partial a_h} = \sum_u -delta_u\, weight_{uh}$$

With the value for $\partial Error/\partial a_h$ in hand, we now proceed as before to determine $-delta_h$, which equals the partial derivative of the error with respect to the netinput to h:

$$-delta_h = \frac{\partial Error}{\partial netinput_u} = \frac{\partial Error}{\partial a_h} \frac{\partial a_h}{\partial netinput}$$

$$= a_h\,(1 - a_h) \sum_h -delta_u\,weight_{uh}$$

The partial derivative of the error with respect to $weight_{hi}$ is now readily determined:

$$\frac{\partial Error}{\partial weight_{hi}} = -delta_h\,\frac{\partial netinput_h}{\partial weight_{hi}} = -delta_h\,a_i$$

and the weight of the connection from i to h is changed in proportion to the negative of this partial derivative:

$$\Delta weight_{hi} = lrate\;delta_h\,a_i = lrate\;a_h\,(1 - a_h) \sum_u (delta_u\,weight_{uh})\,a_i$$

If we needed to apply this procedure to yet another layer, we would start with $delta_h$ and distribute the error to the units in our current i level. Thus, we have a recursive procedure for figuring the delta value for units at each layer in the network and we can use this to determine the change of all connections coming into these units.

$$delta_u = (d_u - a_u)\,a_u\,(1 - da_u) \tag{5a}$$

This more complex delta value is then inserted in the otherwise familiar equation for changing weights (here, the weight on the connection from hidden unit h to output unit u):

$$\Delta weight_{uh} = lrate\;delta_u\,a_h \tag{6a}$$

Multiplying by a_h has the effect of changing the weight on a particular connection only to the degree that the hidden unit on that connection is active; thus the weights are changed most on those connections that contribute most to the error.

Additional machinery is needed to change the weights that lie deeper in the network; in the case of our three-layer network those are simply the weights that feed from the input units to the hidden units. We do this by first apportioning to each hidden unit its contribution to the overall error, yielding the value of a new function, $delta_h$:

$$delta_h = a_h\,(1 - a) \sum_u delta_u\,weight_{uh} \tag{5b}$$

Once $delta_h$ is obtained, the hard work has been done; we insert it into the familiar equation for changing weights, this time for $weight_{hi}$:

$$\Delta weight_{hi} = lrate\;delta_h\,a_i \tag{6b}$$

It should be clear that values of delta can be computed recursively for networks of any depth. For a derivation of the generalized delta rule, which is adapted from the derivation in Rumelhart, Hinton, and Williams (1986a) in *PDP:8*, see box 3.2.

3.2.2.2   Using backpropagation to solve the XOR problem   It is useful to work through an example of how a multi-layered network learns by means of backpropagation. Most such networks are too large to follow the learning events in detail. However, McClelland and Rumelhart's (1988) *Handbook* includes an exercise on learning the XOR function by means of backpropagation (pp. 145–52; also see pp. 123–6).

The simulation used a very compact three-layer network (figure 3.2). It requires just two input units (**I1** and **I2**), two hidden units (**H1** and **H2**), and a single output unit (**U**), and has a total of six weights to be adjusted as the four input–output cases are repeatedly encountered across training epochs. We ran this exercise using their **bp** (backpropagation) program, and report it here in order to illustrate this learning procedure. (The simulators packaged with several of the other textbooks recommended on p. 53, or downloadable from the web sites listed there, could also be used for this exercise. For discussion and guidance in running it with **tlearn**, see McLeod, Plunkett, and Rolls, 1998, pp. 117–126, or Plunkett and Elman, 1997, chapters 3 and 4 and pp. 119–21.)

Included in the net input to each of the hidden units and the output unit is an additional source of incoming activation known as *bias*. Each unit has its own bias, which has the effect of increasing or decreasing the activation value that is computed on each trial. As noted in section 2.2.2, it plays essentially the same role as a threshold; together with the logistic activation function, it introduces nonlinearity into the system. For purposes of computation, it may help to think of the bias as coming in from an extra unit that is connected only to the unit that it biases (and therefore not directly influenced by input patterns). The hypothetical extra unit (square in figure 3.2) is assumed to have a constant activation of 1. The weight on the connection from the hypothetical unit can, however, be adjusted by learning; when we speak of the bias on the unit, we are referring to that weight.

The simulation begins by initializing the weights with a random set of weight assignments,[5] which is shown in figure 3.2. We specify a learning rate of 0.50. Table 3.2 shows the activations that result when we send each of the four input patterns through the network as a test prior to training (that is, the activations at epoch 0).

We will calculate the activation values for the first row of this table manually to make it clear how the network operates. Since both of the input units are given the value 0, each of the hidden units receives input of 0 from these units. The net input is not 0, however, because the bias supplies an activation of −0.27 to Hidden Unit 1 (**H1**) and of −0.40 to Hidden Unit 2 (**H2**). Applying the logistic activation function (equation (4)), we obtain the activations for the two hidden units that are shown in table 3.2. The activation of **H1** is now multiplied by the weight on its connection to the output unit (0.27) while the activation of **H2** is multiplied by its corresponding weight (0.08). These are summed (0.12 + 0.03 = 0.15) and then are added to the bias on the output unit (0.27) to generate a net input to the output unit of 0.42. When the logistic activation function is applied, an output unit activation of 0.60 is obtained (rightmost column of table 3.2).

With the activations computed for input–output case A ("Neither"), each of the weights can be altered in accord with the version of the generalized delta rule that is appropriate to its layer (or this could be done at the end of epoch 1, that is, after all

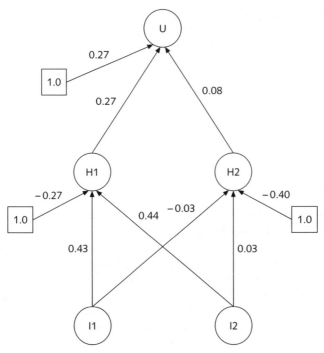

Figure 3.2   Initial state of the network that learns to compute the XOR function. Each of the three layers has one or two units (circles). Except for the input layer, each unit has a bias which is shown here as the weight on the connection from an additional unit with a fixed activation of 1 (squares).

Table 3.2   Results of testing the initial network with each input–output case

	Trainer-defined values			Actual activation values		
Case	*Input* *Unit I1*	*Input* *Unit I2*	*Desired* *Output*	*Hidden* *Unit H1*	*Hidden* *Unit H2*	*Output* *Unit*
Neither	0	0	0	0.43	0.40	0.60
Unit I1	1	0	1	0.53	0.39	0.61
Unit I2	0	1	1	0.54	0.40	0.61
Both	1	1	0	0.64	0.40	0.61

four patterns have been presented). To continue with the example, we will compute two of the weight changes now. This requires first calculating delta for certain units. For the output unit, equation (5a) yields a *delta*$_u$ of – 0.14, calculated by multiplying (– 0.60) (0.60) (0.40). The *delta*$_h$ values for each of the hidden units can now be calculated recursively from *delta*$_u$ using equation (5b): multiply *delta*$_u$ by the weight of the connection, and then multiply the result by the $a_h (1 – a_h)$ term for that hidden unit. This yields a *delta*$_h$ of – 0.09 for **H1** and of – 0.02 for **H2.** Next, the delta values are entered into the Δ*weight* equation, and Δ*weight* is added to the current weight to

Table 3.3   Weight on each connection at four points in learning

Connection	Epoch 0	Epoch 90	Epoch 210	Epoch 289
Inputs to H1	0.43	0.45	2.17	5.72
H1 to output	0.27	0.12	1.71	6.40
Bias of H1	− 0.27	− 0.28	0.10	− 2.16
Inputs to H2	0.00	− 0.04	0.06	3.18
H2 to output	0.08	− 0.04	− 0.44	− 6.96
Bias of H2	− 0.40	− 0.48	− 0.43	− 4.82
Bias of output	0.27	− 0.05	− 1.17	− 2.82

obtain the new weight of the connection. For example, for the connection from **H1** to the output unit **U**, equation (6a) specifies that the learning rate (0.50) is multiplied by the relevant delta (− 0.14) and by the activation of the incoming unit (0.43) to obtain $\Delta weight_{UH1}$ (− 0.03); this is added to 0.27 (obtained from figure 3.2) to yield a new weight of 0.24. For the connection from **I1** to **H1**, the calculation for $\Delta weight_{H1I1}$ from equation (6b) is (0.50) (− 0.09) (0) = 0. Thus, the new value for $weight_{H1I1}$ is 0.43 + 0 = 0.43. That is, there is no weight change for this connection.

The network's progress in learning the XOR problem is displayed in table 3.3 (the changes in the weights and biases) and table 3.4 (the changes in the output activation values). At first it learns very slowly. By epoch 90 it has seen each of the four input–output cases once per epoch, for a total of 90 learning trials per case. The resulting changes in the weights have not improved the network's ability to discriminate among the inputs; the output unit produces an activation of 0.50 regardless of which input is supplied. During this period most of the change is concentrated in the upper part of the network (the output unit bias and the weights between the hidden units and the output unit all *decrease* somewhat). In effect, the system is temporarily learning to ignore the input. The reason for this is that it is following a gradient descent, seeking the most efficient way to reduce its error. By simply reducing its output activation from 0.61 to 0.50 on each unit, it has indeed reduced its *tss* (total squared error across input–output cases) from 1.0507 to 1.0000. This still leaves a good deal of error, so the network must adopt a different "strategy" to continue reducing error. Specifically, it begins gradually to increase the weights from both input units to **H1** (averaged in table 3.3 because these weights are very similar), and from **H1** to the output unit. Simultaneously, the bias on the output unit becomes increasingly negative (in effect, raising its response threshold so that it will require a fairly high net input to reach a high activation value itself). After 210 epochs of training it is clear that **H1** is becoming an OR detector: it is serving to excite the output unit when either of the input units is active, and especially when both are active. When neither input unit is active, **H1** propagates only its own small bias to the output unit; combined with the negative bias of the output unit itself this results in a negative net input to the output unit. Applying the logistic activation function has the result that any net input is scaled to a value between 0 and 1; for this particular case, the output unit's activation ends up as a somewhat low 0.38 (compared to values above 0.50 for the other inputs).

With **H1** moderately well established as an OR detector by epoch 210, **H2** now starts to become an AND detector. This will permit "subtracting" the AND cases

Table 3.4   Activation of the output unit at four points in learning

Input pattern		Epoch 0	Epoch 90	Epoch 210	Epoch 289
Neither	0 0	0.61	0.50	0.38	0.09
Unit I1	1 0	0.61	0.50	0.54	0.90
Unit I2	0 1	0.61	0.50	0.54	0.90
Both	1 1	0.61	0.50	0.57	0.10

(1 1) from the OR cases (1 0), (0 1), (1 1) at the level of the output unit, so that it can function as an XOR detector (1 0), (0 1). Specifically, the weights from the input units to **H2** become increasingly positive, while the bias on **H2** becomes so negative that it will become active only if both inputs are active. (Hence, **H2** is now an AND detector.) Meanwhile, the weight from **H2** to the output unit becomes increasingly negative (so that when **H2** detects AND, the excitation of the output unit from **H1** will be countered by inhibition from **H2**). Hence, **H2** becomes active only when both input units are active, and when it does become active, it inhibits the activity of the output unit. This specialization of **H2**'s function occurs fairly rapidly once it begins around epoch 210, so that by epoch 289 the network has essentially learned the XOR function.

The learning sequence exhibited in this simple network is quite characteristic of backpropagation generally. The first stage of learning sets the weights in the network in such a way that the output units adopt the mean of the various training states. Over subsequent training epochs, the various hidden units begin to specialize; the output units receive and coordinate the hidden units' analysis of the input, and therefore can respond differentially to different input patterns. In more complex networks it is often difficult to determine precisely what information each hidden unit is responding to, but analysis often does reveal that individual units are identifying particular information in the input that is germane to solving the problem.

3.2.2.3   Using backpropagation to train a network to pronounce words   Backpropagation provides a powerful training technique for networks with hidden units. One particularly impressive example of a network trained by backpropagation is Sejnowski and Rosenberg's (1987) NETtalk model, a three-layer network which was trained to read English text. The text (either separate words or connected discourse) was presented letter by letter to the input layer, and a succession of phonemes was produced by the network on its output layer and submitted to a speech synthesizer. More specifically, what was supplied to the input layer was a localist encoding of the target letter, plus the three preceding and three following letters. Since spaces and punctuation were encoded by three special characters in addition to the 26 English alphabet characters, 7×29 input units were required. These units fed connections to a single layer of 80 hidden units, which then fed into 26 output units. These output units provided a localist encoding of 23 articulatory features and 3 features for stress and syllable boundaries. Each phoneme was represented by a distributed pattern across these 26 units.

In one simulation, the network was trained through repeated exposures to a continuous speech corpus of 1,024 words, with desired outputs determined by phonetic transcription of the speech of a child. After 10,000 training trials (approximately ten presentations of each word) the network's "best guess" (most active phonemic representation) was correct 80 percent of the time. After 50,000 words it achieved 95 percent accuracy. It was then tested on a 439-word continuation of the text, and achieved 78 percent accuracy (Sejnowski and Rosenberg, 1986). When the output was actually supplied to a voice synthesizer, it produced recognizable speech, albeit with a few errors. Subsequently, Sejnowski and Rosenberg (1987) analyzed the behavior of the hidden units by first determining the activation patterns across those units for each of the 79 grapheme–phoneme correspondences in English and then performing a cluster analysis. The analysis revealed that the hidden units differentiated vowels from consonants, and produced grapheme–phoneme clusterings similar to those in standard analyses of English, demonstrating that the hidden units had become sensitive to theoretically relevant features of language. These sensitivities of the hidden units, it is important to recognize, were not directly determined by the network builder, but rather were the product of training through backpropagation and constituted the network's construal of the regularities involved in pronouncing English text.

3.2.2.4   Some drawbacks of using backpropagation   Despite the power and versatility of the backpropagation learning procedure, there are drawbacks. First, backpropagation can be an extremely slow learning procedure. The XOR network, with only six connections to train, required 289 epochs. Learning time increases exponentially with the size of the network; NETtalk required 5,000 training epochs, consuming approximately 12 hours of CPU time on the VAX that was a fast laboratory computer for its era (the mid-1980s). Hinton (1989) offered the estimate that the learning time in a network simulated on a serial machine will be roughly proportional to c^3, where c is the number of connections in the network. In response, it can be noted that much of human learning occurs in domains for which the amount of input over time is massive; to model this learning we may want a network that requires large numbers of learning trials. Once this learning has occurred, however, humans clearly have some very efficient means of reutilizing its results in new domains or tasks (for example, learning by analogy, by verbal instruction, and by coordinating the functioning of previously independent schemata). If connectionists wish to offer a general account of human learning, they will have to learn how to incorporate these means in connectionist models. Slow adaptive learning algorithms such as backpropagation either will play no role in reutilization of already trained networks, or will operate in a way that permits very rapid convergence in the new network. A second response to this point is to agree that backpropagation is computation-intensive, but that hardware is on an inexorable rise to faster speeds and that the use of parallel processors is advancing as well. (Hinton estimated a learning time for parallel machines roughly proportional to c^2.) Nonetheless, 15 years after NETtalk, a major connectionist theory of reading aloud still has not been fully implemented because laboratory computers would require months to learn tasks involving the coupling of just three interactive networks of three layers each (see section 10.2.3.2).

   A second drawback, for those whose attraction to connectionism is based on its plausibility at the biological level, is that backpropagation does not map directly on to any known biological processes. There is no evidence that information is passed backwards through the nervous system in a manner that precisely adjusts the forward performance of the system. The most straightforward response to this objection is to make a clear distinction between levels of analysis, placing backpropagation

at the psychological level (i.e., at Marr's algorithmic level). On this view, backpropagation is simply one mechanism by which multi-layered networks can implement
gradient descent, that is, learning by reducing the error in output. Backpropagation constituted a breakthrough for psychological modeling since it overcame the
restriction of gradient descent learning to two-layer networks and so opened up the
investigation of networks with hidden layers. The question of how this sort of learning is implemented at the biological level cannot easily be addressed at this time. We
return to this issue in section 10.3.

A third drawback is that, in contrast to two-layer networks, multi-layer networks
have complex error surfaces. Gradient descent learning procedures can get caught in
local minima on such an error surface, usually finding a good solution but not
necessarily the best one. On the other hand, the best solution may be too good: if
learning is allowed to proceed until error is mimimized, the network may have done
such a good job of capturing the quirks in the specific training set that it does not
generalize well to new cases in the domain. The bottom line is that there is no free
lunch. Fully benefiting from backpropagation's power requires ongoing attention to
its potential pitfalls.

3.2.3   Boltzmann learning procedures for non-layered networks

In addition to feedforward networks, there are interactive networks such as Hopfield
nets and Boltzmann machines that have their own distinctive architectures. As we
noted in section 2.2.1, one presentation of an input pattern results in multiple cycles
of processing in these networks; across the cycles, the activations dynamically interact until the network settles into a stable state. These cycles should not be confused
with learning epochs; they involve computation of activations, not modification of
weights. They yield a response (or solution) to a single input pattern, just as a single
pass through a feedforward network yields its response to an input pattern. We also
noted in section 2.2.2 that one problem faced by interactive networks is the tendency
to land in local minima, that is, states that are stable but do not represent the best
solution to the constraints. We described the technique of simulated annealing,
which the Boltzmann machine can employ to avoid these local minima. This involves slowly decreasing the temperature parameter (T) in the stochastic activation
function:

$$probability\,(a_u = 1) = \frac{1}{1 + e^{-(netinput_u - \theta_u)/T}} \tag{7}$$

which has the effect of reducing the probability of the network settling into a local
minimum.

In *PDP*:7 Hinton and Sejnowski (1986) showed that Boltzmann machines can
be trained using a variation on Hebbian learning that is conceptually similar to
backpropagation. Here we adapt Hinton's (1989) exposition. Each unit is designated
as either an *input unit, output unit,* or *hidden unit.* In test mode, problems are posed
by clamping certain input units so as to force them to maintain an activation of
either 1 or 0; the network's solution is the stable pattern of activation that is reached
on the output units.

In training mode, there are two stages. In stage one, each input–output case is
imposed on the network by clamping both the input units and output units in the

designated patterns. The units of the network are selected in random order to update their activations using the stochastic activation function in equation (7). As this processing is occurring the temperature parameter T is gradually reduced to 1. Processing stops when the network reaches a thermal equilibrium, that is, a state in which units' activations continue to change, but the probability of finding the network in a given global state (pattern of activation across units) remains constant and the most probable states are the ones that best satisfy the constraints. While at equilibrium, each input–output case is processed for a designated period of time. For each pair of connected units, the proportion of that time that both are active is measured. The proportions are averaged across cases to obtain the expected probability $<a_i\,a_j>^+$ that both units are active together under these conditions. (Note that these are non-mnemonic subscripts; the equations refer to any pairing of units, e.g., input–input, output–hidden, input–output.)

In stage two, only the input units are clamped, and the network determines its own output ("runs free," as in test mode). Except for this variation, the process used in stage one is repeated. This time the expected probability of joint activity is written as $<a_i\,a_j>^-$. The size of the discrepancy between stages one and two determines how much to change the weight of the connection:

$$\Delta weight_{ij} = lrate\,(<a_i\,a_j>^+ - <a_i\,a_j>^-) \tag{8}$$

Ackley, Hinton, and Sejnowski (1985) showed that as long as the learning rate is set slow enough, this procedure will result in weights that minimize the error on the output units (that is, the difference in their behavior when they are clamped versus running freely).

The intuition underlying the Boltzmann procedure is similar to that of the delta rule and generalized delta rule; discrepancies between desired (clamped) and actual (free-running) outputs are used to guide changes in weights. If two connected units are jointly active more frequently when the network is running with the desired output clamped than when it is running free, the joint activity needs to be increased by increasing the weight of the connection. Conversely, if they are jointly active more frequently when running free than when the desired output is clamped, the joint activity needs to be decreased by decreasing the weight on that connection. As Hinton pointed out, the Boltzmann machine faces several difficulties. Due to the time it takes the network to reach equilibrium after being presented with each pattern, learning occurs very slowly. Moreover, if not enough cases of $<a_i\,a_j>^+$ and $<a_i\,a_j>^-$ are sampled, the information used for weight change will be very noisy. This architecture has not often been chosen for cognitive modeling, but the behavior of already-trained Boltzman machines can be explored using the **cs** (constraint satisfaction) program in McClelland and Rumelhart's (1988) *Handbook*, chapter 3.

3.2.4   Competitive learning

We now turn to a quite different learning procedure, competitive learning, in which no trainer is involved (hence, a form of unsupervised learning). In competitive learning, a network is presented with a series of input patterns and must discover regularities in those patterns that can be used to divide them into clusters of similar patterns. In the simplest case, there is one layer above the input layer, and each of its units is connected to every input unit. It is like a hidden layer in that its task is to detect

regularities despite receiving no direct feedback from a trainer regarding the appropriateness of its activity. It is like an output layer in that the activity of its units
constitutes the response of the system to the input patterns. We will simply call it
the *detection layer* (not a standard term). The number of clusters that this network
detects is determined by the network designer when the number of detector units is
set. If there are three units, for example, the best way of partitioning the input
patterns into three clusters will be sought (and, in at least some versions, will be
attained by gradient descent). The activation rule is set up to assure that on a given
trial just one unit will "win": the activation of the unit with the greatest net input
will go to 1, and the other units' activations go to 0. (That is, the winning unit inhibits
the others.) Learning now ensues. Each detector unit has a fixed total of incoming
weights. The learning rule reallocates the weights of the winning unit, such that the
weights on its connections from active input units are incremented, while those from
connections with inactive input units are decremented by an amount that keeps the
total of the weights constant. The connections to the losing units do not change.

The effect of this is a positive contribution to the likelihood that the same detector
unit will become active the next time the same input pattern is presented. (Of
course, intervening patterns will have their own effects on the rates which may
themselves raise or lower that likelihood.) Furthermore, there is a negative impact
on the likelihood that it will become active for input patterns significantly different
from it. This increases the likelihood that different detector units will win the
competition on these significantly different patterns.

Competitive learning is a clear case of unsupervised learning, because the designer
has determined only the number of detector units; there are no desired patterns of
activation across those units of which they are informed. (Of course, if the designer
constructed the input patterns with forethought, she or he might be aware of the
optimal clustering. But the network must figure it out just by observing the input
patterns.)

The designer can produce more complex behavior by including more than one set
of mutually competing units in the detector layer. In particular, if these sets have
different numbers of units, each set will partition the input patterns into a different
number of clusters. Another option is to incorporate additional layers that can learn
to detect higher-order regularities (by applying the same learning rule to the weights
between each pair of layers). For variations on competitive learning, see von der
Malsburg (1973), Rumelhart and Zipser (1985; reprinted in *PDP:5*), Hertz, Krogh,
and Palmer (1991, chapter 5), Kohonen (1982), Rolls and Treves (1998, chapter 4),
and a variety of papers in the journal *Biological Cybernetics* (e.g., Fukushima, 1980;
Grossberg, 1976; Amari, 1983).

3.2.5 Reinforcement learning

One final learning paradigm, reinforcement learning, deserves at least a brief characterization. In reinforcement learning, the network is told whether or not its output
pattern was close to the desired output pattern, but is not told what the desired
output actually was. Thus, only global information on performance is available as a
guide to changing weights. Against the context of backpropagation this withholding
of information may appear unnecessarily penurious; however, it corresponds to
the commonsense notion that reward and punishment are the primary means of

changing behavior. This is also the basic strategy used in operant conditioning, although with considerable sophistication in the timing of reinforcement which increases its effectiveness.

Essentially, what the network does is carry out an experiment with a large number of trials. Various combinations of weights might be tried, for example, and notice taken of what global reinforcement was delivered on each attempt. On each trial, each connection will be informed of that reinforcement. Those values of weights that tend to result in greater reinforcement become favored and are tried more often on succeeding trials. Eventually, the weight matrix tends towards values that will maximize reinforcement. (For an interesting simulation that utilized reinforcement learning, see Barto and Anandan, 1985; see also Sutton and Barto, 1998.)

Hinton (1989) pointed out that in one respect, reinforcement learning is much simpler than backpropagation, since it does not require computing the error derivatives for each weight. On the other hand, it can take many trials for each weight to assess the effects of its possible values on the reinforcement. This becomes especially problematic with large networks. Hinton graphically illustrated the problem: "It is as if each person in the United States tried to decide whether he or she had done a useful day's work by observing the gross national product on a day by day basis" (1989, p. 22). Nevertheless, the literature on reinforcement learning suggests points of contact between traditional learning theory and network modeling that could help to bring together typically unconnected groups of researchers. In this regard, it is interesting to note that the International Neural Network Society lists among its cooperating societies both the Society for the Experimental Analysis of Behavior and the Cognitive Science Society.

3.3   Some Issues Regarding Learning

3.3.1   Are connectionist systems associationist?

We have now surveyed several of the best-known connectionist learning procedures, although we have not yet observed their application in large-scale models intended to simulate aspects of human cognition. It is appropriate to make a short excursion here to address one of the broad criticisms that has been raised against connectionism (Fodor and Pylyshyn, 1988). The critics object that connectionism is a return to associationism, and that to accept its construal of cognition is to give back territory that was won by diligent effort in the cognitive revolution. According to the critics, it has already been shown that an adequate model of cognition must employ the resources of a recursive system with symbols, variables, and related devices for encoding and manipulating information. Learning must therefore consist in manipulating symbols; depending on the particular theoretical approach, this might involve testing hypotheses, setting parameters, making analogies, or some other means of arriving at improved rules and representations. In chapters 5 and 6 we will discuss a variety of limitations that the symbolic theorists impute to connectionism as a result of its eschewment of such resources. Here we will focus just on the question of whether connectionism represents a return to associationism.

Our short answer is that connectionism is an *elaboration* of associationism that has benefited from and can contribute to many of the goals of the cognitivism of the 1980s to the present. It is not a *return* to associationism; it is not *mere* associationism;

but its most obvious ancestor is indeed associationism. (Its less obvious ancestor is cognitivism; connectionism has been informed in many ways by the computational and conceptual advances achieved within that tradition.)

Classical associationism offered a vision of how knowledge might be built up on the basis of contiguity and other principles. It provided a sketch of the form of mental representations and of the learning processes that produce them (later given more specific interpretations, such as Hebbian learning as one framework for explaining classical conditioning); however, it lacked the technology and more differentiated constructs to go further. Connectionism can be regarded as the outcome of returning to the original vision of the associationists, adopting their powerful idea that contiguities breed connections, and applying that idea with an unprecedented degree of sophistication. Among the elaborations that were not even conceived of within classical associationism are: distributed representation (particularly coarse coding), hidden units (which function to encode microfeatures and enable complex computations on inputs), nonlinear activation rules, mathematical models of the dynamics of associationist learning, supervised learning (in which error reduction replaces simple Hebbian learning), backpropagation, and simulated annealing within a self-organizing dynamic network.

In classical associationism, the elemental units were ideas. A localist connectionist network using the Hebbian learning rule is essentially an implementation of classical associationist learning: the learning rule serves to increase or decrease the strength of association between ideas based on their contiguity (i.e., their pairing in the same input–output case). If the network is multi-layered, less obvious but more powerful variations on associationism can be attained. For example, hidden units can fractionate and recombine ideas into microfeatures, a degree of reduction not conceived of within associationism. Furthermore, ideas or microfeatures can achieve "contiguity" (joint activation) by means of the propagation of activity within the network, not just by occurring together in immediate experience (e.g., within the same sensory-level input pattern). This might be viewed as an implementation of the two ways in which ideas can be experienced together in classical associationism (reflective thought as well as sensation).

From a more contemporary perspective, connectionist networks can function as causal models of how rule-like behavior (as well as exceptional behavior) can be produced by a mechanism that makes no use of explicit rules. Hence, connectionism exemplifies the preference in psychology for relatively uniform mechanisms that operate at a fine grain, but it also can benefit from cognitivism's higher-level descriptions of what it is the mechanism is accomplishing. Furthermore, connectionist models of learning provided a fresh approach in the 1980s to the question of how concepts and cognitive skills are acquired. Traditional symbolic modeling had not been well prepared to deal with exceptions and learning, but connectionists promised plausible, powerful learning mechanisms and a unified explanation of rule-like behavior and the handling of exceptions. Any success in these enterprises (see chapter 5) provides further rebuttal to the charge of mere associationism, and enhances the status of connectionism as an integration of associationism and cognitivism that has a broader domain of applicability than either of its predecessors. However, it should be noted that traditional symbolic modelers have greatly improved some of their rule-based models and, more important, have given much more attention to learning than in the past. So even if connectionists have gotten free of the associationist label, the larger battle is in a stalemate as the two sides continue to talk past each other.

3.3.2 Possible roles for innate knowledge

3.3.2.1 Networks and the rationalist–empiricist continuum   In discussing Chomsky's criticism of Skinner's account of language learning in section 3.1, we noted that one of Chomsky's major arguments, the argument from the poverty of the stimulus, was directed against the ability of the organism to learn everything it needed from experience. It is now time to return to this question of nativism. There is no doubt that, historically, nativism has been more closely connected with the rationalist view of learning than with the empiricist approach that is generally assumed to characterize connectionists. But, as many have noted, empiricists need not be entirely opposed to nativism. In fact, if associations are to be based on similarity, empiricism requires some criterion for similarity that precedes learning. Thus, contemporary empiricists like Quine (1969a) postulate innate quality spaces as a basis for subsequent associationist learning. (Quality spaces are multi-dimensional spaces in which sensory inputs can be located so as to be able to compare them.) Since all learning theorists require some pre-existing structure within which learning is to occur, the nativism controversy should not be construed as a conflict over whether anything is innate, in the sense of being present in the organism before the organism has sensory experiences. Rather, the conflict concerns what is native. In the symbolic approach, since the operations performed by the system all involve manipulating symbols, it seems that at least some symbols and initial ways to manipulate symbols must be innate (and possibly compositions of symbols, such as rules, as well). For approaches that do not rely on symbol manipulation, the capacities that are taken to be native can be specified in other ways.

In the 1980s most connectionists did not view the nativism issue as highly salient. To the extent that connectionism is a descendant of associationism, this represented a considerable shift in focus away from that issue. Possible reasons include: (1) research in genetics and developmental neurophysiology had revealed a very complex picture that does not easily reduce to empiricism or nativism in their original forms (see Wimsatt, 1986); and (2) for most connectionists in the 1980s, the interesting problems were computational and mathematical; many were in academic fields, such as computer science, in which nativism has not been a focal issue. Nonetheless, there were a few published discussions of this issue in the 1980s and an entire book in 1996, which we will discuss in turn.

First, Rumelhart and McClelland (1986) devoted a few pages of their discussion of general issues in *PDP:4* to the question of nativism versus empiricism. It strikes us as a very sensible discussion; they suggested that either extreme position could be implemented within a connectionist model but they focus on integrating the positions. For example, they posited an organism whose initial state is determined by genetics, but for which all connections are modifiable by experience. Two such organisms provided with similar genetics and environments would show similar trajectories through a space of possible networks as they develop.

A more extensive treatment of this question was provided by Shepard (1989). He conjectured that "in systems that have evolved through natural selection, the features of the world that are both biologically significant and absolutely invariant in the world have tended to become genetically internalized" (p. 104). That is, the species has evolved internal structures that are adapted to these features of the world, so individual members of the species need not learn them. How might such adaptations be incorporated in the initial connectivity of a network, providing a base from which learning may proceed to add its own contributions? Shepard suggested that evolution does not supply individuals with innate knowledge of which features characterize specific objects and events. Rather, it supplies knowledge of the structure of the features themselves. For example, the psychological space for colors is three-dimensional (hue, lightness, saturation) and is approximately Euclidean. Generally, psychological spaces incorporate abstract constraints that are not arbitrary but rather reflect evolutionary accommodation to the environment in which we live. For example, a rigid object moving in three-dimensional literal space has exactly six degrees of freedom of position (three of location and three of orientation); these constraints may be incorporated in the initial structure of the mental system that is responsible for recognizing objects regardless of their position in space. If so, translation invariance need not be learned.

3.3.2.2 Rethinking innateness: Connectionism and emergence We alluded above to the complexity of contemporary thought and findings relevant to the nativism issue. Articulating a connectionist perspective on this issue required an entire book, published in 1996: *Rethinking Innateness: A Connectionist Perspective on Development*. In an unusual international collaboration, Jeffrey Elman, Elizabeth Bates, Mark H. Johnson, Annette Karmiloff-Smith, Domenico Parisi, and Kim Plunkett worked out an account that was both connectionist and interactionist. They emphasized *emergence* – the idea that it is the *dynamic interaction* of an organism's genetic endowment and encounters with an environment that produces the adult organism. From this perspective, one cannot simply parcel out its features as due to nature or nurture.

At any given stage of development, as a result of the organism's genetic constitution and what has already occurred in the development of the organism, there are only a limited number of steps that can be taken next. The biologist C. H. Waddington (1975) introduced the notion of an *epigenetic landscape* to characterize the range of possibilities for an organism and the path it would take. In diagramming an epigenetic landscape, Waddington used a three-dimensional surface to portray the possibilities for an organism. The possible paths for development are those leading downhill from where the organism is currently situated. In *Rethinking Innateness*, it was noted that Waddington's epigenetic landscape is similar to a typical connectionist representation of an error surface in weight space and that his developmental paths are comparable to gradient descent learning. Figure 3.3 shows such an error surface for two weights, which is a simplification relative to the number of weights in a real network but much more complex than the plot of error against the possible values of a single weight in figure 3.1. The line from *a* to *d* is a path of gradient descent that a hypothetical network might follow as it adjusts its weights. The authors then suggested that connectionist implementations of gradient descent and tools for analysis of gradient descent learning could contribute to the understanding of development in this context.

Despite the view that features of the adult cannot be parceled out between nature and nurture, nascent organisms are assumed to have a native constitution that can be characterized by developmental theorists. *Rethinking Innateness* identified three different classes of constraints which theorists sometimes claim are native: representations, architecture, and timing. Traditional nativists such as Chomsky and Fodor have emphasized innate representations. The representations of a connectionist network, in contrast, are generated from its connection weights, and these are the least

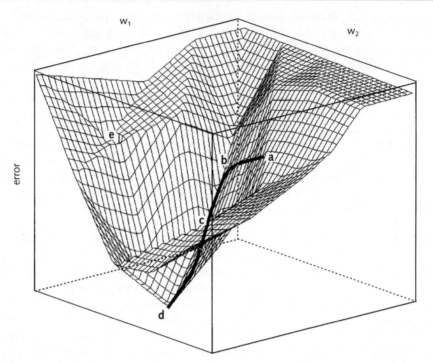

w_1

w_2

error

Figure 3.3   A hypothetical error surface for a neural network with two weights which represents gradient descent as downward paths on the error surface. The line from **a** to **d** shows one path of gradient descent to the global minimum, **d**. There is also a local minimum at **e**. Reprinted with permission from Elman (1993).

likely aspect of a network to be innately fixed. The authors of *Rethinking Innateness* emphasized recent discoveries of neural plasticity (the ability of the brain to develop alternative wiring patterns when one pattern is disrupted) as evidence against detailed microcircuitry as a genetic endowment.

A more plausible locus of innate specification is the architectural level. The basic types of neurons in an organism seem to be fixed. At a slightly higher level, one can focus on such characteristics as the type of connectivity (excitatory versus inhibitory) and the nature of the interconnectivity (e.g., how much fan-in or fan-out there is from a given unit). At an even higher level, there is the question of how specific networks are connected to one another. Most connectionist simulations have assumed that the architecture is fixed at all of these levels, and have focused on the development of representations within that fixed architecture. However, in chapter 9 we will examine research programs that allow some aspects of the architecture to develop as a consequence of individual experience or of simulated evolution. Such work gives connectionists a framework for exploring how native endowment and experience may dynamically interact.

The third class of constraints, those having to do with timing, are perhaps the most intriguing in the *Rethinking Innateness* taxonomy. Learning in networks may provide a useful modeling medium for such phenomena as critical periods and developmental stages. Even the simple XOR network discussed in section 3.2.2 developed its solution over several stages. Of greater interest, in section 6.4 we will discuss two methods suggested by Elman (1993) by which "starting small" can enable networks to eventually solve large problems. In his second method (illustrated in section 6.4 using the work of Christiansen, 1994) simulating maturational change – by increasing working memory capacity – has the effect that a network will achieve success with dependencies between adjacent elements (e.g., subject–verb agreement) when the span is low and then can build on that to master dependencies between nonadjacent elements (e.g., subject–verb agreement when an embedded clause intervenes) when span becomes greater. Starting out with a large span forces the system to pay attention to the more complex sentences before it is ready, and it fails ever to develop adequate weights.

It is not always necessary to manipulate memory span in order to obtain stage-like developmental trajectories. Connectionist models have been constructed which, in the course of repeated training on a corpus and with no changes in the network itself, exhibit stages roughly similar to those observed by developmental psychologists. In particular, Mareschal, Plunkett, and Harris (1995) simulated two stages of object permanence that differ in the conditions under which an infant will reach for an object (visible objects versus both visible and occluded objects). McClelland (1989) simulated stages of performance in a task in which objects are placed on the two ends of a balance beam (attending only to weight; attending to distance if weight is equal; coordinating weight and distance). In both cases, interpretation is difficult. Stages emerged despite no changes in the structure of the network, contrary to Piaget's interactionist claims. But that structure, built into the network before the first training trial, already encoded some key aspects of the task. Such simulations are an early step towards using networks to grapple with controversies that have resisted resolution for years.

In summary, although connectionism has roots in associationism, it is not inherently anti-nativist. Perspectives as rationalist as Shepard's can be incorporated at least as readily as empiricist perspectives, and a rich set of possibilities for an interactionist connectionism were opened up in *Rethinking Innateness*. By providing a flexible but powerful framework for exploring the interaction between native endowment and experience, connectionism may significantly contribute to overcoming the classical dichotomy of nature versus nurture. However, any connectionist who chooses a purer empiricism or rationalism will find that connectionism provides a language and tools to pursue those positions as well.

NOTES

1   If the weights are updated at every trial, on a given trial both the activations and the weights would be changed. Alternatively, weights may be updated at the end of each epoch. During testing, only the activations change in order to evaluate the weights; on each trial the weights are applied to the input pattern to obtain an actual output pattern.

2   A simple way to determine if two patterns are correlated is to compare the two patterns position by position, and score $+ 1$ every time the two patterns have the same value in a position, and $- 1$ every time they differ. If the total score after comparing all positions is 0, the patterns are uncorrelated (orthogonal); if not, the patterns are correlated (nonorthogonal). In the example which follows, there are four positions. The score for case A versus case B is 0 (the sum of $+ 1, - 1, + 1, - 1$ obtained by comparing the four positions), but the score for case A versus case C is 2 (the sum of $+ 1, + 1, + 1, - 1$).

3   A two-layer network can compute the XOR function if the input patterns are recoded across an enlarged input layer so as to yield linearly separable inputs. The problem itself has then been altered, however; the relation between the two sets of values is no longer an XOR relation.

4   If a linear rule is used for both hidden and output layers, then one can construct from the sets of weights used in the multi-layered network a set that will work for a two-layer network. Thus, a multi-layered network with linear activations cannot overcome the limitations of a two-layer network.

5   The initialization procedure utilizes a pseudo-random number generator. The particular set of initial weights used for the XOR exercise happened to be rather favorable to learning XOR. Starting with the same weights and training the network on *if and only if* (IFF), the negation of XOR, required 540 training epochs, almost twice as many as required to teach the network XOR. This is the case even though the solutions the network generated to the two problems are essentially isomorphic.

Sources and Suggested Readings

Note: Most of the readings listed for chapter 2 include sections on learning.

Chauvin, Y. and Rumelhart, D. E. (1995) *Backpropagation: Theory, Architecture, and Applications*. Hillsdale, NJ: Erlbaum.

Elman, J. L., Bates, E. A., Johnson, M. H., Karmiloff-Smith, A., Parisi, D. and Plunkett, K. (1996) *Rethinking Innateness: A Connectionist Perspective on Development*. Cambridge, MA: MIT Press.

Haykin, S. (1994) *Neural Networks*. New York: Macmillan.

Hinton, G. and Sejnowski, T. J. (1999) *Unsupervised Learning*. Cambridge, MA: MIT Press.

4

PATTERN RECOGNITION
AND COGNITION

This book has three general groupings of chapters, and we are now at the transition from the first group to the second. The previous three chapters provided an overview of connectionist systems and their capacity to learn. We worked through the operations of one interactive and one feedforward network step by step in order to get an initial grasp of the nuts and bolts of connectionism. We also initiated discussion of some interpretive and philosophical issues. In the next group of chapters we pursue these two inquiries jointly and in greater depth. For each of four issues, discussion of the issue is advanced by considering one or more connectionist models of human performance in some detail. These chapters need not be read in order; you may wish to be guided by which issues or models most interest you. The four issues are:

- Chapter 4: Is pattern recognition, a core capability of networks, adequate to the whole range of cognitive as well as perceptual abilities?
- Chapter 5: Or, as classicists claim, are rules needed to account for such phenomena as children's stage-like acquisition of the past tense?
- Chapter 6: What about the corresponding classicist claim that syntactically structured representations must be produced within the system in order to support processing (e.g., of embedded sentences)?
- Chapter 7: Can networks successfully simulate higher cognitive capabilities, such as paraphrasing stories and answering questions?

In the last three chapters we discuss the intersection between connectionism and certain other intellectual streams that captured attention during in the 1990s: dynamical systems theory, artificial life research, and cognitive neuroscience.

Turning now to the current chapter, we have seen that networks are devices for mapping one class of patterns on to another class of patterns, and that they do so by encoding statistical regularities in weighted connections that can be modified in accord with experience. This has led to a claim that connectionist networks are a highly suitable medium for modeling human cognition. Since what networks do is map patterns, this claim would entail that (a) pattern mapping is fundamental to a variety of human capabilities; and (b) connectionist networks perform pattern mapping in a particularly advantageous manner.

Pattern mapping is actually a very broad concept, and it is useful to distinguish among types of mappings. *Pattern recognition* is the mapping of specific patterns on to a more general pattern (that is, the identification of individuals as exemplars of a class). *Pattern completion* is the mapping of an incomplete pattern on to a completed version of the same pattern. *Pattern transformation* is the mapping of one pattern on to a different, related pattern (for example, a verb stem such as *come* can be transformed into a past tense form such as *came*). *Pattern association* is the arbitrary mapping of one pattern on to another, unrelated pattern (as in the paired-associate task that was a mainstay of the traditional psychology of learning). Finally, *auto-association* is the mapping of a pattern on to itself.

All five types of pattern mapping have proven useful in connectionist models of human cognitive performance, but in this chapter we will focus on pattern recognition. In humans, the most obvious venue in which pattern recognition plays a major role is sensation and perception. When you look at a scene, the pattern of light is encoded on the retina and then re-encoded in various ways in the nervous system. In the simplest cases, you might see a vertical line or a square: you have recognized (perceived) a form. In a slightly more complex case, the square may be connected to four vertical lines, one extending down from each corner; combining these along with color, texture, and size, you see an oak table: you have recognized (perceived) a table. But this already brings you beyond perception to a more cognitive level of concepts and categories, and from there it is a short additional step to label the visually recognized table linguistically as a "table." Advancing yet further, you can compare this table to the one you remember from your last apartment, make deductive inferences involving it, and even spin a story about it.

In the first section of this chapter we illustrate how connectionist networks operate as pattern recognition devices by describing the performance of two networks in some detail and then focusing on their ability to generalize to new cases. Then we address the cases that go beyond perception. Specifically, in section 4.2 we discuss a proposal by Margolis (1987) that higher-level cognition may simply consist in sequences of acts of pattern recognition, and in section 4.3 we show that networks implementing this idea can perform certain tasks of formal logic. Finally, in section 4.4 we ask whether networks must be made to exhibit additional capabilities to account for what is known about how people develop and learn.

4.1   Networks as Pattern Recognition Devices

4.1.1   Pattern recognition in two-layer networks

To credit a system with pattern recognition, it must be observed to respond with the appropriate pattern for each instance it encounters. For example, a system that recognizes letters of the English alphabet should respond to each of the hundreds of elements in a page of text with one of 26 patterns. This is exactly what a two-layer, feedforward network can do quite well (if the patterns meet certain constraints already discussed). Moreover, adding a learning procedure enables the network itself to arrive at an appropriate set of weights for a particular task. To illustrate, we will employ a network like the one displayed in chapter 2 as figure 2.7 but with eight rather than four input units and output units. Each input unit has a modifiable connection to each output unit. We set up this network to run under the **pa** (pattern

Table 4.1 Input and output patterns for the two-layer pattern recognition network

Case	Prototypical input pattern	Desired output pattern
A	− 1 − 1 − 1 − 1 + 1 + 1 − 1 − 1	− 1 − 1 − 1 − 1 − 1 − 1 − 1 − 1
B	− 1 − 1 + 1 + 1 + 1 − 1 − 1 − 1	− 1 − 1 − 1 − 1 + 1 + 1 + 1 + 1
C	− 1 + 1 + 1 + 1 − 1 + 1 − 1 + 1	− 1 + 1 − 1 + 1 − 1 + 1 − 1 + 1
D	+ 1 + 1 + 1 + 1 + 1 + 1 + 1 + 1	+ 1 + 1 + 1 + 1 + 1 + 1 + 1 + 1

associator) program in the *Handbook* (McClelland and Rumelhart, 1988, chapter 4); to run it as a new project using **PDP++** see sections 5.3 through 5.5 and part III of O'Reilly and Munakata (2000), or using **tlearn** see chapter 3 of Plunkett and Elman (1997) or appendix 3 (and chapters 3 and 4; see the footnote on page 74) of McLeod, Plunkett, and Rolls (1998); or download a simulator and its manual and experiment with it (web sites are listed on p. 53). In specifying the program options in **pa** we selected the delta rule with a learning rate of 0.0125 and the linear activation rule:

$$a_u = netinput_u = \sum_i weight_{ui}\, a_i$$

For this illustration, we specified four input–output cases using binary values of + 1 and − 1 (although the network itself will take continuous activation values). For example, table 4.1 shows that the input pattern for case A is (− 1 − 1 − 1 − 1 + 1 + 1 − 1 − 1), and the desired output pattern is (− 1 − 1 − 1 − 1 − 1 − 1 − 1 − 1). (For convenience, we will often refer to these simple as *input A* or *output A*, or in context as the *input* and *output*.) To make the illustration concrete, we can loosely think of each input as a distributed representation for a prototypical exemplar of each of four categories (e.g., a prototypical table) and of each output as a distributed representation of a conventional name for each category (e.g., the spoken word "table").[1]

In the simplest possible simulation, we could train the network by presenting it with each of the four input–output cases repeatedly across a number of training epochs. On each trial the network would produce an actual output for the input, compare it to the desired output, and adjust its weights according to the delta rule. Eventually it would learn to produce the appropriate output for each input. As a bonus, by this time it would also do a good job of generalizing. That is, if we presented it with the following input that it had never seen before

$$- 1 - 1 - 1 - 1 + 1 - 1 - 1 - 1 - 1$$

(which differs from the standard input A in position 6), it would produce an output closely resembling output A. Thus, without any additional training, the network would recognize a new pattern as similar to the one on which it was trained. But this is a somewhat unrealistic model of how we learn to identify the categories to which exemplars belong. Typically, our exposure is not limited to ideal or prototypical exemplars. Rather, we confront a variety of exemplars that more or less resemble each other. Likewise, when we hear the names, they will be pronounced somewhat differently each time. We simulated this situation by distorting each input and (desired) output pattern: a randomly chosen quantity in the range 0.5 and − 0.5 was generated independently for each unit and added to its original value. Thus, instead of the original input A (which we will refer to as the *prototype*) on a given trial we presented the network with a *distorted* input A′ such as:

$$-0.76 \quad -0.89 \quad -1.21 \quad -1.01 \quad 1.33 \quad 0.99 \quad -0.65 \quad -0.92$$

Similar distortions were imposed on the desired output so that the network's actual output would now be compared with a *distorted* output A′.

The network was trained with randomly distorted input–output cases across 50 epochs; during each epoch it received a new randomly distorted version of each of the four inputs and a new randomly distorted version of each corresponding output. After just a few epochs the network responded in a qualitatively correct manner: by epoch 4 the activations of all output units were on the correct side of 0 (i.e., positive or negative as appropriate). The additional training was required to refine the outputs across epochs (bringing them closer to -1 or $+1$, i.e., the base values from which the distorted values were obtained).

After training, the network was tested on three different types of input for each case; these test inputs and the actual outputs that the network produced are shown in table 4.2. First, when presented with the *prototype* (which had never been encountered during training), the network produced an actual activation value for each output unit that was within 0.2 of the desired value. Second, when presented with a new exemplar obtained by *randomly distorting* the prototype in the way described above, the actual values on the output units were all within 0.5 of the desired values. Third, even when presented with a new exemplar obtained by *reversing the sign* of one of the prototype's input units (making the pattern in that respect closer to the prototype of a different category),[2] the network produced outputs that were usually within 0.5 of the target. All except one of these output values (boldface) were on the correct side of 0.

The fact that there is variability in the output may be disconcerting. Can we really say that the network has recognized the pattern on the basis of this kind of outcome? If this is thought to be a problem, however, it is one that is easily remedied. Instead of using a linear activation function for the output units, we could employ a threshold function that would make the value of the output unit $+1$ if the net input to it was greater than 0, and make it -1 otherwise. In many contexts this sort of digitalization is useful. One advantage is that the activations on the output units would have more of the character of symbolic representations (that is, a given class of output could always have the same representation; e.g., "table" could always be $-1 \ -1 \ -1 \ -1 \ -1 \ -1 \ -1 \ -1$). However, for some purposes the variability produced by a continuous activation function may be preferable. For example, if a distorted input produces a distorted output, other processing components that utilize that output will be able to compute the degree of distortion. Having that information available may be useful, e.g., in suggesting a degree of uncertainty which may be due to context effects or other factors.

Even though this is a very simple network, it does a credible job of learning to recognize several categories of input patterns. It is worth emphasizing the fact that the network can handle distorted patterns and readily classifies new patterns that are similar to the training inputs. Hence, it can deal in a natural way with some of the variability that is encountered in the real world (e.g., people identify various tables as "table"). On the other hand, there are definite limitations to this capability for two-layer networks, as we discussed in section 3.2.1. Overcoming these limitations requires multi-layered networks, whose pattern recognition capacities we consider next.

Table 4.2   Activation of units in the two-layer pattern recognition network after 50 training epochs

Case	Layer	Units 1–8 in input or output layer							
		1	2	3	4	5	6	7	8
(A)	**Tested with prototypes of four categories as inputs**								
A	Input	− 1.00	− 1.00	− 1.00	− 1.00	1.00	1.00	− 1.00	− 1.00
	Output	− 1.12	− 0.98	− 1.02	− 0.92	− 1.10	− 0.84	− 0.94	− 1.06
B	Input	− 1.00	− 1.00	1.00	1.00	1.00	− 1.00	− 1.00	− 1.00
	Output	− 0.99	− 1.06	− 0.98	− 0.96	0.91	0.94	0.99	0.88
C	Input	− 1.00	1.00	1.00	1.00	− 1.00	1.00	− 1.00	1.00
	Output	− 0.91	0.96	− 0.87	1.05	− 0.84	1.06	− 0.90	0.92
D	Input	1.00	1.00	1.00	1.00	1.00	1.00	1.00	1.00
	Output	0.99	0.94	1.05	1.07	0.93	1.03	0.92	1.15
(B)	**Tested with distorted instances of four categories as inputs**								
A′	Input	− 0.76	− 0.51	− 0.82	− 1.11	1.47	0.82	− 0.83	− 0.90
	Output	− 0.81	− 0.90	− 0.71	− 0.83	− 0.77	− 0.72	− 0.62	− 0.89
B′	Input	− 1.00	− 0.54	1.34	0.63	0.98	− 0.59	− 1.24	− 0.81
	Output	− 1.06	− 0.81	− 1.03	− 0.68	0.63	1.00	0.70	0.88
C′	Input	− 1.18	0.62	1.20	0.87	− 1.21	1.38	− 1.02	1.48
	Output	− 1.07	1.11	− 1.01	1.22	− 1.12	1.10	− 1.18	0.92
D′	Input	1.42	1.44	0.64	1.31	0.72	1.24	1.03	1.19
	Output	1.20	1.28	1.25	1.39	0.81	1.00	0.77	1.15
(C)	**Tested with one of the input features (italics) of a prototype replaced by a feature of reverse sign. One output response has the wrong sign (boldface)**								
A″	Input	− 1.00	− 1.00	− 1.00	− 1.00	1.00	− *1.00*	− 1.00	− 1.00
	Output	− 0.86	− 1.39	− 0.85	− 1.41	− 0.26	− 0.78	− 0.16	− 0.89
B″	Input	− 1.00	− 1.00	− *1.00*	1.00	1.00	− 1.00	− 1.00	− 1.00
	Output	− 0.98	− 1.24	− 0.96	− 1.22	0.30	0.06	0.39	**− 0.03**
C″	Input	− 1.00	− *1.00*	1.00	1.00	− 1.00	1 .00	− 1.00	1.00
	Output	− 1.20	0.38	− 1.14	0.49	− 0.74	0.87	− 0.75	0.68
D″	Input	− *1.00*	1.00	1.00	1.00	1.00	1.00	1.00	1.00
	Output	0.13	0.75	0.21	0.85	0.38	1.18	0.41	1.15

4.1.2   Pattern recognition in multi-layered networks

4.1.2.1   McClelland and Rumelhart's interactive activation model of word recognition
To recognize some patterns it is not sufficient to map input patterns directly on to output patterns. Rather, one or more intermediate layers of units are needed to extract information that is then passed to units in higher layers. McClelland and Rumelhart (1981) and Rumelhart and McClelland (1982) offered an interactive activation model that illustrates how a multi-layered network can recognize visual patterns, specific-ally, four-letter words presented in a particular font. They constructed an interact-ive network with an input layer of feature units (e.g., top horizontal bar), a middle

layer of letter units (e.g., E), and an output layer of units for four-letter words (e.g., *HELD, BOTH*). Interactivity was achieved by including connections in both directions between the middle and output layers. This multi-layered network differs from later ones in that its middle layer of units is not actually a hidden layer: (a) the connection weights and interpretations of its units were specified by the designers rather than learned by the network; (b) the activation patterns on the middle layer (as well as the top layer) are "visible." That is, when the network recognizes a word (top layer), it also recognizes letters (middle layer) and can report either level depending upon the task. Note that there would be little reason to report the middle layer if it were actually a hidden layer, because individual hidden units generally are interpretable only as complex microfeatures that are not easily labeled.

All of the units and connection weights in the word recognition network were hand-crafted around 1980 – before the backpropagation learning procedure was available – and it is best regarded as a transitional type of multi-layered network. Nevertheless, it produces human-like responses under a variety of conditions, including low contrast (dim lighting) and missing features (as would occur if ink blots were spilled across the word). It is able to exhibit fault-tolerant processing because, like any interactive network, it operates to satisfy multiple soft constraints.

There are some more subtle phenomena of human pattern recognition that were also addressed by McClelland and Rumelhart. In particular, they were able to simulate the *word superiority effect*. The basic effect is that very briefly displayed letters are better recognized when they are presented in the context of a word (or a pronounceable nonword). Helpful effects of context are ubiquitous in human information processing; that is, doing more often costs less effort. It might be thought that this is because context narrows the possibilities, but Reicher (1969) showed that there is more to the effect than that (see also Wheeler, 1970). Reicher constructed pairs of words that differed in just one letter position, e.g., *TOLD/COLD*. On each trial he briefly presented one word from the pair (e.g., *TOLD*), then a masking stimulus to stop visual processing, and then a test display that had the correct letter (T) above or below the letter from the contrasting word (C), with dashes placed in the positions of the three shared letters to orient the choices. Subjects' ability to choose the correct letter was better in this word context condition than in control conditions of scrambled strings of letters or isolated letters. Since either test letter would produce a word, something must occur in the course of processing that makes use of the actual word that is displayed. Exactly *what* occurs is the question that has challenged researchers; the McClelland and Rumelhart model opens up one good avenue for answering that challenge. We will not discuss McClelland and Rumelhart's full simulation of the word superiority effect (which involves presentation of a word, then of a mask, and then a forced choice response), but rather we will discuss only the critical part of the model in which recognition of words affects the recognition of component letters.

As noted above, the network is built from three kinds of units, which encode features of letters (14 units),[3] letters (26 units), and words (1,179 units). The system is designed to handle words of four letters using separate ensembles of units for each letter; so four copies of the feature and letter units are provided (one copy for the first letter of the word, one for the second letter, etc.; this is known as *positional encoding*). Each of the feature units is positively connected to units for letters that possess the feature and negatively connected to units for letters that do not. Similarly, the letter units are positively connected to units for words that contain the letter in the appropriate position, and negatively connected to words that do not. Importantly, there are also top-down connections: the word units are positively connected to the units for the letters they contain. Finally, word units and letter units are each negatively connected to all competitors within the same ensemble. Figure 4.1 shows all of the features and letters, and a few of the words and connections. Simulations can be run with this network under a variety of conditions and parameter values using the **ia** (interactive activation) program in McClelland and Rumelhart's *Handbook* (1988, chapter 7).

An input is provided to this network by activating the appropriate features in each of the four letter positions. For a word with an E in position 2, five of the units in the second ensemble of feature units will be activated. Figure 4.2 shows how an E is constructed in the Rumelhart–Siple font that was used in this study (Rumelhart and Siple, 1974). The features that are activated are: top horizontal bar, bottom horizontal bar, top left vertical bar, bottom left vertical bar, and leftmost center horizontal bar. (Note that the use of a fixed set of straight-line features has the result that a few letters look somewhat odd, e.g., B and V, but this is of no consequence for the simulation. Also note that sets of features can be supplied that do not correspond to actual letters, or that are incomplete and therefore ambiguous; e.g., the top and bottom horizontal bars and bottom left vertical bar alone are consistent with C, E, G, O, and Q.) Each of the active feature units then sends activation to all of the letter units in the second ensemble of letter units with which it is consistent. For example, the top horizontal bar sends activation to such letters as C, E, and F; the bottom horizontal bar sends activation to such letters as C, E, and J; and so forth. Almost every letter will receive some activation in this manner, but E will receive the most because it is consistent with all of the activated features. Finally, as the letter units become active, they in turn excite those word units with which they are consistent. These word units will then send further excitations back in the reverse direction to those same letter units. (Note that the backward connections are unrelated to backpropagation, which is a *learning* procedure for *feedforward* networks; here we have an activation route in an interactive network that is not set up for learning.) Because this is an interactive network, the propagation of activation will continue across a large number of processing cycles, during which a winner gradually emerges within each ensemble of letters (e.g., E in the second ensemble) and *HELD* simultaneously builds activation as the winner at the word level. The equations used for the output from units, the net input to units, and the change in activation are very similar to those for the Jets and Sharks simulation discussed in section 2.1. For letter and word units the only differences are in the values used for parameters such as connection strength and decay (and that they lack external input); feature units, however, receive *only* external input (in the form of binary values).

The fact that information flows both from letter units to word units and from word units to letter units is critical in determining the behavior of this network. The letter units receive top-down input from the word units, and bottom-up input from the feature units. If the feature units do not correspond to an actual word, the word unit that is most consistent with those features can override some of the featural detail by strengthening the activations of its letters (i.e., the letters that should be favored because they form a word). To illustrate the override capacity, we presented McClelland and Rumelhart's **ia** network with the features corresponding to *BOTJ* instead of *BOTH*, and obtained the results shown in table 4.3. Despite the misspelling, the word unit *BOTH* quickly reached a high activation value. At the letter level,

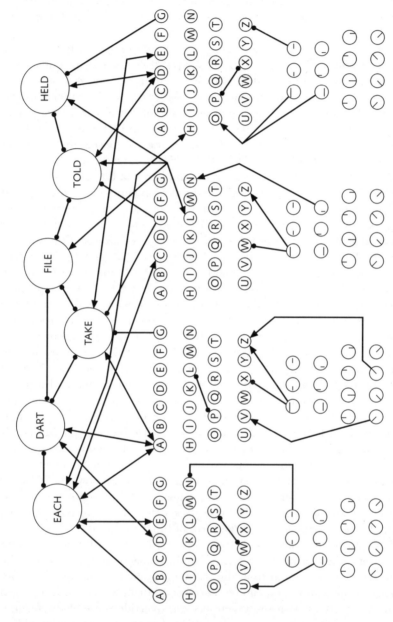

Figure 4.1 Basic interactive activation architecture of McClelland and Rumelhart's (1981) word recognition network. Connections may be excitatory (arrow) or inhibitory (filled circle). All of the feature and letter units that are used for each of the four letter positions in a four-letter word are shown; however, only a few connections and a few word units are shown.

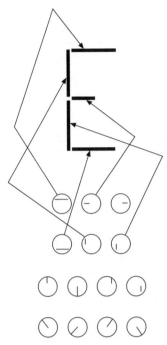

Figure 4.2   The featural encoding of the letter E in the Rumelhart–Siple font used by McClelland and Rumelhart's (1981) word recognition network.

Table 4.3   Activations of output units in the word recognition network when presented with BOTJ

	Processing cycle			
Unit	10	20	30	40
B	0.51	0.75	0.79	0.79
O	0.51	0.75	0.79	0.79
T	0.51	0.75	0.79	0.79
J	0.38	0.47	0.49	0.49
BOTH	0.29	0.60	0.66	0.67

Activation for unit H never reached zero.

the letters B, O, and T quickly became more active than J. Hence, the higher-level (word) unit was able to respond and override the lower-level (letter J) unit in order to arrive at an actual four-letter word.

Given that the input served to activate the fourth-position J unit and to inhibit any other response, the top-down response from the word unit $BOTH$ was not able to suppress the J unit completely and activate the H unit. But in another simulation, in which the input was simply the features for $BOT\blacksquare$ (that is, the fourth letter position was left blank), the H unit became almost as active as the units for the letters that were actually presented (table 4.4). What is of particular interest is that

Table 4.4   Activations of letter and word units when the word recognition network is presented with BOT■

Unit	Processing cycle											
	1	2	3	4	5	6	7	8	9	10	20	30
Letter units in four positions (LPI–LP4)												
LPI: B	6	13	18	24	30	35	41	45	50	55	78	80
LP2: O	6	13	18	24	30	35	41	46	51	55	78	80
LP3: T	6	13	18	23	29	34	39	44	49	53	78	80
LP4: B, D					0	0	0	0	0	0	0	0
E				0	0	1	1	1	1	1	0	0
H			0	1	3	5	8	13	18	24	69	76
L					0	0	0	0	0	0	0	0
N,T				0	0	0	0	0	0	0	0	0
K,Y				0	0	0	1	1	1	1	0	0
Word units												
BOMB				0	0							
BOND				0	0	0						
BATH, BONE				0								
BORE, BOWL				0								
BOAT, VOTE			0	0	0	0	0					
BORN, NOTE			0	0	0	0	0	0				
BOOK			0	1	0	1	0	0	0			
BODY			0	1	1	1	1	0	0			
BOTH		0	3	6	9	13	18	23	29	35	71	75

Blanks should not be confused with 0s. A blank indicates that the activation was below zero.

along the way the system partially activated several other word units (e.g., *BOOK* and *BODY*). As a result, several letter units other than *H* were brought above zero (e.g., *K* and *Y*). Note that the partially activated words agreed with the input in only two positions, whereas *BOTH* was consistent in all three of the positions that had input. Hence *BOOK* and *BODY* were suppressed eventually by *BOTH*. Its activation in turn had the effect of activating the fourth-position *H* unit, and interactive processing further strengthened these units: after *BOTH* activated *H*, *H* activated *BOTH*, and so it went back and forth across cycles. This mutual buildup in excitation continued until a stable state was achieved, in which both units were nearly as active as they would have been if *BOTH* had been presented to the system to begin with.

In the case just described only one four-letter word was consistent with the input in the first three positions. The behavior of the system becomes even more interesting when more than one match is available. In a final simulation, we presented the system with the features for:

DIS⊢

In the Rumelhart–Siple font, the partial letter in the fourth position was compatible with an *A*, *F*, *H*, *K*, *P*, or *R*. Initially the units for all six letters became equally

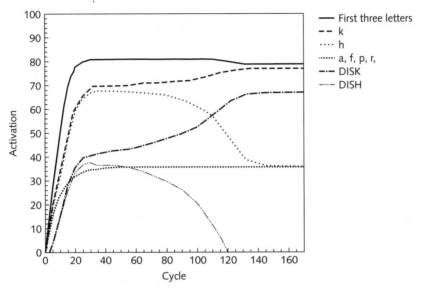

Figure 4.3 Change in activation across cycles of the most active units in McClelland and Rumelhart's (1981) word recognition network when presented with DISʰ.

active (through cycle 5). As shown in figure 4.3, in cycle 3 the units *DISH* and *DISK* both started to become active. As these word activations increased across cycles, *H* and *K* became most active, although the other candidates for the fourth letter position continued to grow in activation at a slower rate. Through cycle 30 the units for both words grew in activation at roughly equal rates, pushing the *H* and *K* units to much higher activation levels than the other four letters. After cycle 30 *DISH* gradually lost out to *DISK* until it dropped below 0 activation after cycle 120. As a result, *H* began to lose activation after cycle 50, eventually settling back to the same level of activation as the other four letter units. The reason for this is that *DISK* is more frequent in English than *DISH*, and this fact was incorporated in the simulation by assigning a higher resting activation to its unit. As a result, the activation was always slightly greater for *DISK* than *DISH*, and so it was able to exert a greater inhibitory effect on its competitor, as well as a greater excitatory input to its fourth-position letter unit (*K*). Here, then, is an example in which higher-level information about which word is more likely in English influences the behavior of the lower-level letter units. Clearly, this effect could be extended. For example, an even higher level could be added for relating words in a context. If the context were a discussion of food, that might be sufficient to override the overall frequency difference and therefore to activate *DISH* over *DISK* and *H* over *K*.

This last simulation illustrated two important characteristics of networks. In addition to *recognizing* patterns, they can also *complete* patterns by filling in what was not present in the input. This capacity is a general feature of connectionist networks. In addition, this simulation showed how higher levels of information (e.g., information about what four-letter words exist in English and their relative frequency) can affect the recognition of lower-level entities (e.g., the letters that comprise the words). It is relatively easy to see, in principle, how one might employ a model of this sort to simulate theory-laden perception wherein higher-level knowledge, such as knowledge of scientific theories, was construed by philosophers of science such as Kuhn (1962/1970) and Hanson (1958) as influencing what scientists would observe. The higher-level units would encode the information that constitutes the "theory," and could influence the responsiveness of lower-level perceptual units that recognize objects. If a learning procedure were incorporated into such a network, it would be possible for the higher-level units to serve as training units, leading to the revision of weights at the lower level, and subsequently generating different recognition behavior at the lower level.

4.1.2.2   Evaluating the interactive activation model of word recognition   Though designed around 1980, McClelland and Rumelhart's word recognition network provides a still-impressive demonstration. It can handle distorted sensory information and makes reasonable inferences about what it is seeing. It does this without using rules to manipulate symbols, employing instead a set of weights and an activation function. However, this network has some nontrivial limitations. First, it cannot learn. Later in the 1980s, this limitation was overcome by the development of new learning procedures (such as backpropagation) that enable multi-layered networks to use their intermediate layers to extract microfeatures. Examples of tasks for which such networks have been designed include forming compressed representations of gray-scale images of visual scenes (Cottrell, Munro, and Zipser, 1989); sonar detection of rocks versus mines (Gorman and Sejnowski, 1988); identification of phonemes (Hampshire and Waibel, 1989); recognition of complex objects (e.g., houses) from digitalized television images (Honavar and Uhr, 1988); and recognition of handwritten characters (Skrzypek and Hoffman, 1989).

Second, in the real world letters can appear in different parts of the visual field and in different fonts, and may undergo orientation transformations in two or three dimensions. The invariants of shape that determine that a letter is R rather than S must somehow be recovered, for example, even if the R is rotated counterclockwise 90 degrees to obtain a logo for the "Lazy R Ranch" or is spun on its axis to make a cute name for a toy store. For a limited domain such as letters, a traditional approach is to pre-process sensory input to obtain standardized letters in canonical orientation. The McClelland and Rumelhart simulations set aside the problem of getting a network to do this by letting the investigator activate the appropriate features for each letter. Recognition of complex invariants under three-dimensional transformations of objects in real environments (Gibson, 1966) poses even more of a challenge and has been addressed by only a few investigators; see Hinton (1987); Zemel, Mozer, and Hinton (1988); Hummel and Biederman (1992); and Biederman (1995).

Third, the word recognition network is limited to four-letter words. Each letter position has its own dedicated ensemble of feature and letter units; there are four positions and hence four ensembles of units. There is literally no place to put a fifth letter. One can imagine constructing separate networks for each word length, starting with one-ensemble networks for the article *a* and pronoun *I* and moving on up to a 28-ensemble network for *antidisestablishmentarianism*. Understandably, no one has taken that path. Other potential solutions include Wickelfeatures (see section 5.2.1) and recurrent networks (see section 6.4), but Wickelfeatures have been largely abandoned (for reasons noted in section 10.2.3.3) and recurrent networks are best suited to tasks other than pattern recognition. Hence, word recognition models in the 1990s still generally made the simplifying assumption of a fixed word length (e.g., Hinton and Shallice, 1991; Plaut, McClelland, Seidenberg, and Patterson, 1996).

4.1.3   Generalization and similarity

Before leaving our general discussion of how networks perform pattern recognition and completion tasks, we need to note that one of the important characteristics of a pattern recognition network is its capacity to generalize. We have seen evidence of this capacity already: once our networks were trained to classify input patterns into particular classes, they responded to novel patterns in a way that took advantage of that training.[4] The ability of a network to generalize is rooted in its sensitivity to similarities between the inputs on which it has been trained and the new inputs. This, however, raises a fundamental question: what is the basis for determining similarity? Similarity poses a notorious philosophical problem. One commonsense approach is to state that object A is more similar to B than C if it shares more properties with B than with C. But this only forces us to individuate properties, and in attempting this we encounter the sorts of difficulty identified by Nelson Goodman (1955). He argued that any two objects are alike in an infinite number of respects. For example, you share with a pine tree the properties of being less that 2,000 feet tall, being approximately 93,000,000 miles from the sun, etc. This suggests that assessing similarity in terms of numbers of properties held in common is inadequate unless we can provide a plausible restriction on what counts as a property or what properties are relevant.

Despite these philosophical difficulties, we all make judgments about similarity. Moreover, there is a fairly clear sense in which connectionist networks are making similarity judgments: the similarity structure of the inputs is implicit in the weight matrix. The weights are the means of treating similar inputs similarly. One question that arises is whether this approach to similarity is sufficient. Often we assume that similarity is a matter of fact, and that it has an objective basis. When we develop a network that generalizes in the way we do, we tend to be pleased and think it has found the correct solution to the task we posed. When the network is tested and generalizes in a different manner, there is a sense in which we have failed. But we might do well to remember Wittgenstein's (1953) example of extrapolation and rule-following in which he imagines a student who has learned, by following the teacher's example, to write a series of numbers by incrementing by two. The teacher is pleased as the student gets as far as 996, 998, 1,000, but then is puzzled to see the student write 1,004, 1,008, 1,012. When queried, the student claims to have gone on in the same way. Wittgenstein comments:

> In such a case we might say, perhaps: It comes natural to this person to understand our order with our explanations as *we* should understand the order: "Add 2 up to 1000, 4 up to 2000, 6 up to 3000 and so on."
>
> Such a case would present similarities with one in which a person naturally reacted to the gesture of pointing with the hand by looking in the direction of the line from finger-tip to wrist, not from wrist to finger-tip.   (Wittgenstein, 1953, §185)

Wittgenstein's point seems to be that the only framework for evaluating the correct way to follow a rule, such as adding by twos, is the practice of a group and that someone who behaves differently is simply following a different practice. There is no independent criterion for correct performance. Likewise, the network that generalizes as we do may recognize similarity as we do, and one that does so differently may simply have a different way of determining similarity.

What is necessary to get a network to determine similarities as humans do and so generalize in the same way? In part, this may require having much the same architecture as humans. In so far as the architecture of current networks is very simple and general compared to the mind-brain, then it should not be surprising if current networks will frequently generalize in different ways from humans. But we also need to consider the fact that how a network generalizes is partly determined by the particular set of input–output cases on which it is trained, as has been demonstrated for human generalization. For example, Nelson and Bonvillian (1978) showed that children at age $2\frac{1}{2}$ years produce (and comprehend) invented names for unfamiliar objects much more successfully if they have been exposed to two or four different exemplars, rather than just one exemplar, during informal teaching sessions. Moreover, our experience does not consist simply in processing discrete pieces of information. We live in a body, interact with an environment, and play roles in various social structures. Dreyfus and Dreyfus (1986) have argued that these factors may all figure importantly in determining human cognition. This may mean that networks cannot completely share our sense of similarity and generalize as we do unless they share these other features of human existence as well.

Overall, then, one of the attractive characteristics of networks is that they generalize by means of the same mechanism that recognizes explicitly trained patterns; generalization comes "for free." Important questions remain, however. Exactly how well do networks generalize? Specifically, how does network generalization compare to that of the best rule-based models, particularly those that implement (in their own way) such properties as satisfaction of soft constraints? A different question is whether their generalization is similar to that of humans. Pavel, Gluck, and Henkle (1988) raised the concern that if a network does not show the same profile of relative difficulty across different kinds of generalizations as humans, its status as a model of human performance is compromised. Gluck and Bower (1988) found that networks mirrored the human difficulty with multidimensional categories like BLACK TRIANGLE OR WHITE SQUARE only after they added configural features like **black & triangle** to the input patterns. Other attempts to make rigorous comparisons among people, networks, and rule-based models will be discussed in section 6.6.

4.2   Extending Pattern Recognition to Higher Cognition

Having demonstrated how networks carry out pattern recognition, we now turn to questions concerning the broader role of pattern recognition in human cognition. Within a connectionist framework, pattern recognition plays a fundamental role at all levels of processing, from sensation through reasoning. This was not obvious at the outset: networks in the mid-twentieth century were originally conceived as simple devices for connecting sensory patterns to motor patterns. Network modelers became more ambitious and capable over time, however, and the connectionists of the 1980s were especially quick to use networks to model linguistic, conceptual, and other higher cognitive processes. This contrasts with the classic symbolic framework, which expanded its reach in the opposite direction. Information-processing psychologists, artificial-intelligence researchers, and other symbolic modelers had in common the use of rules operating on representations. It was most natural to build such models for higher cognitive processes; early examples can be found in Norman (1970) for memory models, Minsky (1968) for semantics and question answering, and Newell and Simon (1972) for problem solving. However, rules and representations also were extended to accounts of sensory and perceptual processes (e.g., Marr, 1982), where it became most evident how they could achieve an alternative implementation of pattern recognition. In this section we will mostly leave aside the question of how pattern recognition is specifically implemented, and focus on the fundamental question of what it might mean to view cognition as pattern recognition. Then in section 4.3 we will describe an initial assessment of the feasibility of such a construal by reporting two network models for tasks in formal logic.

4.2.1   Smolensky's proposal: Reasoning in harmony networks

The basic strategy of generalizing pattern recognition to account for higher cognitive capacities was suggested by Smolensky in *PDP:6* when he spoke of "an abstraction of the task of perception":

> This abstraction includes many cognitive tasks that are customarily regarded as much "higher level" than perception (e.g., intuiting answers to physics problems). . . . The abstract task I analyze captures a common part of the tasks of passing from an intensity pattern to a set of objects in three-dimensional space, from a sound pattern to a sequence of words, from a sequence of words to a semantic description, from a set of patient symptoms to a set of disease states, from a set of givens in a physics problem to a set of unknowns. Each of these processes is viewed as *completing an internal representation of a static state of an external world.* By suitably abstracting the task of interpreting a static *sensory* input, we can arrive at a theory of interpretation of static input *generally* . . . that applies to many cognitive phenomena in the gulf between perception and logical reasoning.   (Smolensky, 1986, pp. 197–8)

Smolensky also developed a more detailed model of how pattern recognition might suffice for reasoning. He used the connection weights in a *harmony network* (an interactive network that behaves in many respects like a Boltzmann machine) to encode basic laws relating voltage, resistance, and current in electrical circuits (specifically, Ohm's Law and Kirchoff's Law). He then presented problems to the network by activating units to partially specify a situation, for example, that one resistance in the circuit increases and the voltage and other resistance remain the same. The network must determine what happens to the remaining variables, in this example by specifying the current and the two voltage drops. The process is one of completing a pattern. Smolensky's simulation generated the correct answer 93 percent of the time. Thus, he was able to demonstrate high levels of performance on physics problems when these problems were treated as pattern recognition problems in a network rather than as logical reasoning problems in a symbolic system.

4.2.2   Margolis's proposal: Cognition as sequential pattern recognition

One apparent shortcoming of the suggestion that cognitive tasks such as reasoning might actually be achieved by means of pattern recognition is that pattern recognition seems to be a one-step process – the system receives a static pattern as input and delivers an identification as output. Reasoning, on the other hand, seems to involve multiple steps. Howard Margolis (1987) suggested a solution: reasoning might simply consist in a sequence of acts of pattern recognition. In his theory, the recognition of one pattern constitutes an internal cue which, together with the external cues available from outside the system, facilitates yet another recognition. Thus, we work our way through a complex problem by recognizing something, and with the help of that result, recognizing something further, and so on until it the problem is solved.

Margolis contended that even in unfamiliar contexts we function by pattern recognition, invoking the pattern template that best matches the situation until we are able to generate a better one. Learning then involves modification of the template to better accommodate the new scenario. In Margolis's account, a few species are capable not only of recognizing that something is the case, but also of *reasoning why* they have made that judgment. Reasoning why does not involve introspection into the process of recognition, but rather is itself a process of pattern recognition – one that proceeds through smaller steps to justify the judgment. Reasoning why also facilitates a kind of critical evaluation, which can challenge the more global pattern recognition response and lead to a second kind of learning, a revision of basic pattern recognition tendencies on the basis of the critical review.

To support the view that higher-level cognition is fundamentally pattern recognition, Margolis offered two major types of evidence. First, he advanced an account of some of the striking results of research on human reasoning that have been used to suggest that people have limited logical and statistical acumen. For example, he offered the following analysis of Tversky and Kahneman's (1982) "Linda" problem (Margolis, 1987, p. 163):

> Linda is 31 years old, outspoken, and very bright. She majored in philosophy. As a student, she was active in civil rights and in the environmental movement. Which is more probable:
> (a)   Linda is a bank teller.
> (b)   Linda is a bank teller and is active in the feminist movement?

Approximately 90 percent of subjects select (b), although according to the laws of probability, the probability of a conjunct is never greater than the probability of one of its parts. One obvious source of difficulty is that subjects may understand option (a) as "Linda is a bank teller and is not active in the feminist movement." Even when the directions are clarified to avoid this ambiguity, however, a majority still answer in a manner that Tversky and Kahneman took to be incorrect. Margolis proposed that what happens is that this problem triggers a different scenario than the one the researchers intended: people understand the word *probable* as meaning *plausible* rather than *statistically likely*. If this were a problem in statistical probabilities, then the subjects would be making an error. However, if they understand the task as one of recognizing plausible construals, then they are performing that task correctly. Hence, according to Margolis, the difficulty has to do with what kind of pattern recognition the problem elicits, not with a failure of logical acumen.

Subsequently, Margolis's approach to the problem received support from the investigations of Gigerenzer, Hell, and Blank (1988; see also Gigerenzer, 1991). They contended that if probability is understood as relative frequency (known as the *frequentist* position), a question about a single event cannot be treated as a question about probability. To answer, subjects must supply some other construal of the problem, such as Margolis's suggestion that pattern recognition procedures are used to determine which outcome seems most plausible. To encourage subjects to construe the Linda question as a probability question, Gigerenzer et al. recast it in terms of frequency: "Out of 100 people who fit Linda's description, how many are: (a) bank tellers (b) bank tellers and active in the feminist movement?" As expected, many more subjects construed this as a question about probability and answered correctly.

Margolis's other main strategy was to analyze developments in the history of science in terms of pattern recognition. In particular, he focused on major transformations in science, such as those Kuhn termed *scientific revolutions*, and sought to explain the difference between those practitioners of the science who succeeded in developing and using a new paradigm and those who resisted the new perspective (sometimes bitterly). Developing and learning a new paradigm involves, on Margolis's analysis, learning to recognize new patterns and guide behavior accordingly. Those who fail to understand the new paradigm are those who do not learn the new patterns. Often this results from dependency on old pattern recognition capacities, which cannot be surrendered without temporarily undergoing significant deterioration in performance.

Margolis filled out this account in part by examining the endeavors of scientists – including Darwin and Copernicus – who accomplished major revolutions. In the case of Darwin, most pre-Darwinian biologists regarded each species as having its own essence, and therefore sharply distinguished from other species. Hence, they lacked the concept of gradual transition between species that was needed to grasp the notion of transmutation from one species to another. Darwin, as a result of being trained by Lyell to recognize gradual transitions in geology, was cued by his observations on the voyage of the *Beagle* to recognize gradual change in life-forms as well. This pattern was at odds, however, with biology's pattern of recognizing species as distinct. The tension between an old pattern and a new one requires the expenditure of cognitive energy. Gradual change is effected in one's pattern recognition system until the new pattern is seen as the one that clearly fits. For Darwin, this effort involved, in part, recalling the Malthusian pattern from economics and recognizing its applicability to the transmutation of species in the form of natural selection. After the new pattern recognition capacity was clearly developed, on Margolis's account, Darwin returned to the *reasoning why* mode. By filling in constituent steps of pattern recognition, he could build up in other individuals the ability to recognize the new overall pattern.

Margolis did not ground his view that cognition consists solely in different forms of pattern recognition on any underlying theory of how pattern recognition is accomplished, although he briefly noted that connectionism provides one possible mechanism. Nor did he offer a precise, verifiable account; he deliberately painted a general view of cognition with a broad brush. To pursue the question of how Margolis's ideas might be actualized, one might begin with one of the existing cognitive science theories that incorporates pattern matching.

The localist network component of J. R. Anderson's (1993) ACT-R theory does pattern matching as a means of selecting rules to be used in the production component. Other uses of pattern matching are discussed in Holland, Holyoak, Nisbett, and Thagard (1986) and Schank (1982). However, connectionism suggests a more radical possibility: that recognizing patterns (matching current patterns to the cognitive residue of previous patterns) is not only a broadly applicable process, but is one that is carried out without the use of symbols as such. Hence, connectionism provides one avenue for empirically exploring Margolis's argument that pattern recognition is the fundamental cognitive capacity.

A connectionist implementation of Margolis's sequential pattern recognition might involve designing linked networks in which the product of one network's pattern recognition activity could serve as the input to another network's pattern recognition activity. That is, the output units that have been activated in recognizing a pattern would themselves send activations and inhibitions to the input layer of a network to which it is linked (see chapter 7 for an extended example). Or the same layer may serve both output and input functions, as is routine for the hidden layers of a multi-layer network. Yet a further idea is to recycle the output of a network as input to the same network in subsequent epochs. The network for developing logical derivations in section 4.3.4 employs this strategy. All of these proposals have in common that they provide a way to build complex sequences of pattern recognition activity, so that what look to be steps of reasoning might consist ultimately in pattern elicitations organized across time.

Setting up networks to perform sequential pattern recognition has implications beyond Margolis's proposal. As we will discuss in section 10.2.2, many cognitive scientists make a major distinction between procedural and declarative knowledge (Cohen and Squire, 1980). Definitions of procedural knowledge vary, but basically it involves skills rather than facts or episodic memories. A precursor is the distinction between *knowing how* and *knowing that* that was proposed by philosopher Gilbert Ryle (1949). Procedural knowledge (e.g., *knowing how* to cook a frittata) generally involves multiple steps; for example, steps in cooking a frittata include boiling, peeling, and slicing the potatoes; cutting other vegetables, stirring while heating them in a pan; cracking open, beating, and adding the eggs; and cooking until done. Sequential pattern recognition by networks arguably provides a new way of thinking about procedural knowledge. The important innovation is not in the sequential aspect (all construals of procedures involve steps taken across time) but rather in the nature of the elementary acts that comprise the sequences: the propagation of activity through a network so as to move from one pattern to another in a way that honors statistical regularities in the network's experience. In the next section we explore the possibility that logical inference (both simple and sequential) can be construed as pattern recognition in networks.

4.3　Logical Inference as Pattern Recognition

Logical inference is often taken as a prime exemplar of high-level reasoning. If pattern recognition is to account for higher-level reasoning, then it needs to be able to account for logical inference. But there is another reason to focus on logical inference: it has constituted a forte of classical, symbolic approaches. The first running AI program was called Logic Theorist (Newell and Simon, 1956). If connectionist pattern recognition systems, including ones configured to implement Margolis's suggestion of sequential pattern recognition, can succeed in this domain, there is reason to be optimistic as to their ability to compete successfully with symbolic approaches even with respect to higher-level cognition.

4.3.1　What is it to learn logic?

One reason that higher-level reasoning has been relatively easy to model in a symbolic system is that the ability to make logical inferences is taken to be a primitive cognitive ability. Rules for manipulating symbols have been developed by logicians, and adapted by cognitive scientists. For example, the logical inference rule of *modus ponens*,

$$\text{If } p, \text{ then } q$$
$$\underline{p}$$
$$\therefore q,$$

is the basis for the format of rules in a production system. A production (If p, then q) fires when the antecedent (p) is satisfied, with the result that the specified action (q) is carried out. If our minds are symbolic systems, then when we learn *modus ponens* in a logic class, we are learning to express and apply consciously a principle that our mind already has encoded within it, albeit in a different format. (Sometimes this is referred to as *explicit* versus *tacit* knowledge.) According to this account, when we learn rules our mind may not yet have encoded, such as the *alternative syllogism*:

$$p \text{ or } q$$
$$\underline{\text{Not } p}$$
$$\therefore q,$$

these rules are encoded into the symbolic reasoning system as new productions that may fire when their conditions are satisfied.

The question is whether this is a really plausible account of how we learn formal logic. One of us (Bechtel) has considerable experience teaching both informal and formal logic, and reflection on that experience is quite revealing. Consider first informal logic, where the goal is to teach students not to prove theorems, but only to evaluate and construct arguments in natural language using basic valid forms such as the sentential forms noted above. To do this, instructors typically begin by presenting students with valid argument forms and demonstrating that these forms are indeed valid (e.g., using truth tables). We contrast these valid forms with invalid forms such as *affirming the consequent*:

$$\text{If } p, \text{ then } q$$
$$\underline{q}$$
$$\therefore p,$$

which we demonstrate to be invalid. The next step is to present students with a set of problems consisting of arguments presented either in abstract symbols (as above) or in natural language, and to ask them to identify which form is used and judge whether or not the argument is valid. As experienced instructors recognize, at this point students require practice, usually in the form of homework. Homework performed after having simply read the material in a textbook, or heard it in lectures, often contains numerous errors; but after the instructor points these out, many students come to perform quite well. They seem to have learned the rules governing basic logical forms and know how to apply them.

But what have the students really learned? Have they simply entered additional rules into their inventory of rules, so that they can now employ them in various tasks? If so, why is the process of learning so gradual and error-prone? Moreover, most students do not ever achieve flawless levels of performance; even on fairly straightforward tests, error rates of 25 percent are not unusual.

Why is this? A symbolic approach, in which students posit mental rules to accord with the external rules, offers at least two avenues of explanation. First, some of the posited rules may have been partly incorrect. For example, the difference between *modus ponens* and *affirming the consequent* is a subtle one, and it is plausible that students had collapsed them into a more general mental rule that would later be split into two correct rules. Siegler's (1976) rule-assessment technique for characterizing cognitive development in children is an elegant, well-developed example of this kind of account. Second, the same problem might elicit the use of different mental rules on different occasions. For example, the overly general rule that was just mentioned may still be utilized on some proportion of trials during a transition period towards replacement by the correct rules. Siegler's more recent work emphasizes variation and adaptive selection of rules (Siegler, 1996). Also, several older models have attached quantitative parameters to rules which determine their probability of being utilized. Examples include the fixed probabilities of Suppes (1970), and the experience-sensitive strength parameters used in Anderson's (1983) ACT* model and in models proposed by Holland (1975) and Thagard (1988). In these last three models, learning is accomplished most simply by functions that change the strength parameters, but additional mechanisms are also explored. These include knowledge compilation and production tuning (Anderson, 1983) as well as algorithms for positing and evaluating new rules, as described in Holland et al. (1986) and in Anderson and Thompson (1989). Do any of these models provide the best way to understand what is happening with the logic students? Perhaps; but further observation of the students has led us to view logic learning as an appropriate domain in which to explore the connectionist alternative that emphasizes pattern recognition.

We made these further observations as we pursued the goal of enhancing students' learning rather than settling for 70 percent or 80 percent accuracy. One of our first steps was to allow students to correct their homework answers during class review, and then still collect and grade the homework (with their self-corrected answers counting for their grade) to make sure that students recognized their errors and could learn from them. We were greatly surprised to note that many students who made errors did not realize that they had done so when the correct answer was presented in class, and that sometimes students changed correct answers to incorrect ones. (Typically, these errors were between similar forms such as *modus ponens* and *affirming the consequent*.) Clearly, these students had failed to recognize what made an answer correct when it was discussed in class. To try to draw their attention to what distinguished the various forms, we then introduced computer-aided instruction, in which students were informed immediately when they had an incorrect answer and could not proceed until they had corrected it. For a given type of problem, the instructional logic program continued to provide new instances until the student met a criterion, such as 14 out of the last 15 correct.

The use of the instructional program did generate substantial improvement on subsequent tests, but it also provided an opportunity to observe students in the process of learning. The observations revealed that some students were quite surprised when the computer told them that their answer was incorrect after they thought they had mastered the material from reading. They now had to look more carefully to determine what was expected in a correct answer. After a short time, many of the students who were having difficulty would copy out a template for each of the forms on which they were working, and then explicitly compare the form of the questions to the templates. (When students worked in pairs at a terminal, one would often point out to the other where a particular form deviated from a template.) Even

Table 4.5   Twelve argument forms

Name and abbreviation	Valid forms	Invalid forms
Modus ponens (MP)	If p, then q p $\therefore q$	If p, then q q $\therefore p$
Modus tollens (MT)	If p, then q not q $\therefore$ not p	If p, then q not p $\therefore$ not q
Alternative syllogism (AS)	p or q not p $\therefore q$	p or q p $\therefore$ not q
	p or q not q $\therefore p$	p or q q $\therefore$ not p
Disjunctive syllogism (DS)	Not both p and q p $\therefore$ not q	Not both p and q not p $\therefore q$
	Not both p and q q $\therefore$ not p	Not both p and q not q $\therefore p$

then some errors were made, but over time, performance improved and students came to rely less on their templates.

The experiences related above strongly suggested to us that students were learning to recognize patterns of inference. As we noted earlier, many rule-based models have been designed in a way that incorporates pattern recognition or matching, including those of Anderson, Holland, Newell, Schank, and Thagard. Here we raise the possibility that the rules can be eliminated entirely in the modeling medium, letting networks do all the work. Specifically, we report our initial attempts to build connectionist networks that would learn to respond to valid and invalid logical forms as patterns to be recognized. (We report here only on this pattern recognition task, but we also simulated pattern completion; see Bechtel and Abrahamsen, 1991.)

4.3.2   A network for evaluating validity of arguments

For this exercise we developed 12 argument forms from the variables p and q and the connectives *if, then, or,* and *not both*; six of the forms were valid and six were invalid, as shown in table 4.5. (Note that we encoded arguments that affirm the consequent as invalid instances of *modus ponens* and arguments that deny the antecedent as invalid instances of *modus tollens*. This is somewhat arbitrary in that these assignments could have been reversed.) Specific problems were generated by substituting any two of the atomic sentences A, B, C, and D for the variables p and q; either order

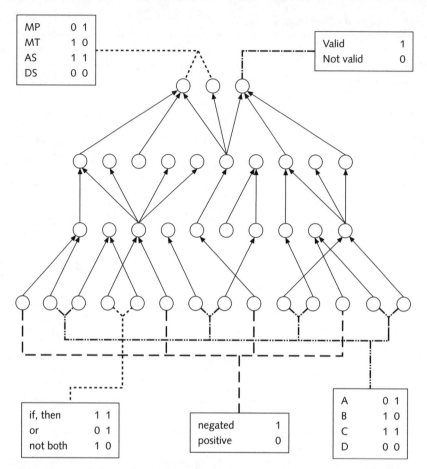

Figure 4.4   A network for evaluating simple argument forms from sentential logic. The interpretation of each unit in the input and output layers is shown in one of the boxes. The network includes full sets of connections between adjoining layers; only some of these are shown.

could be used (e.g., p = A and q = B, or p = B and q = A); and each atomic sentence could be either negated or positive. Altogether, this generated a problem set of 576 different arguments. The network was presented with a complete argument; its task was to identify the argument form employed and to evaluate the validity of the argument.

In developing a simulation model to solve such a problem one of the challenges is to identify what features are employed in recognizing the various argument forms. Since we did not have a well-developed theory as to what information students were actually using to recognize argument forms, we could not engineer a network specifically to simulate student performance. Rather, we proceeded simply by constructing a network that we thought might be able to perform the task. As shown in figure 4.4, it is composed of 14 input units (which encode the two premises and the conclusion), three output units (which give the network's judgment of which argument form was used and whether or not it was valid), and two layers of ten hidden units each. (The number of units in the input and output layers was the minimum number adequate to encode the problem and the answer; the number of hidden units was determined experimentally.) By way of example, consider this invalid *modus ponens* problem:

$$\frac{\text{If A, then not C}}{\text{Not C}}$$
$$\therefore A$$

As shown at the bottom of figure 4.4 and more specifically just below, this problem is encoded on the 14 input units as follows: the first eight units encode Premise 1 (if A, then not C, sometimes written as A ⊃ ~ C); the next three units encode Premise 2 (not C); and the final three units encode the conclusion (A). Within each premise, an atomic sentence (A, B, C, or D) requires two units and the negation indicator requires one unit (1 if negative; 0 if positive). In Premise 1 there is an additional atomic sentence and a connective that requires two units (*if, then; or; or not both*). Hence, the input encoding for this problem is:

Premise 1					Premise 2		Conclusion	
((Negl Propl)		Conn	(Neg2	Prop2))	(Neg3	Prop2)	(Neg4	Propl)
+	A	⊃	~	C	~	C	+	A
0	0 1	1 1	1	1 1	1	1 1	0	0 1

At the top of figure 4.4, it can be seen that the first two units of the output layer indicate which of the four argument forms is instantiated in the input pattern, and the third unit indicates whether it is the valid or invalid version of that form; altogether, the three units distinguish the eight forms shown in table 4.5. Our example problem should be labeled *modus ponens, invalid*:

MP	INV
1 1	0

To teach the network to make accurate judgments of this kind, we trained it using the **bp** (backpropagation) program discussed in chapter 5 of McClelland and Rumelhart's (1988) *Handbook*. (Alternatively, **tlearn** uses backpropagation when any multi-layer network is specified as a new learning project; for guidance in setting up a network such as the one shown in figure 4.4, see chapter 3 in Plunkett and Elman, 1997, or appendix 3 in McLeod, Plunkett, and Rolls, 1998.) Activation values were constrained to range between 0 and 1 by using the logistic activation function, and weights tended to fall in the range − 10 to + 10 after training. We divided the 576 problems into three sets of 192 problems by a method that ensured that each set would contain at least one valid and one invalid example of each basic problem type (e.g., would have at least one *modus ponens* argument with A or not-A as the antecedent of the conditional, and B or not-B as the consequent). Set 1 was used for the initial training period, which consisted of 3,000 epochs. An epoch consisted of 192 trials, during which each problem was presented once in random order. When tested on the training set (Set 1), the network answered all problems correctly. Its ability to generalize was then tested by presenting the 192 patterns of Set 2 in test mode. Since activations on output units could range from 0 to 1, an answer was judged to be correct if the value on all three output units was on the correct side of the neutral value 0.5.[5] On this test the network was correct on 139 patterns (that is, 76 percent of the test trials, where chance would be 12.5 percent). Thus, the network had generalized to a substantial extent, but there remained a good deal of room for improvement. We then trained the network for 5,000 epochs on the 384 problems produced by combining Set 1 and Set 2, after which it was correct on all but four of the training problems.[6] Finally, the network's ability to generalize was tested using Set 3. The network was correct on 161 patterns in Set 3 (84 percent of the trials).

The network did a credible job of learning to recognize argument forms and evaluate the validity of arguments. This is not a trivial accomplishment, since there were many features of the input that the network had to check in order to generate the correct answer on the output units. Without a detailed analysis of the activities of the hidden units (which we have not performed), we cannot determine exactly how the network solved this problem. But clearly the network exhibited one of the prominent characteristics of student performance: it required a good deal of practice and error correction before it could solve most of the problems. By the end of training, its overall performance was similar to that of our average students.

4.3.3   Analyzing how a network evaluates arguments

While we did not attempt an analysis of the hidden units of our network, Berkeley et al. (1995; see also Dawson, Medler, and Berkeley, 1997) ran the same simulations in a different architecture that lent itself more readily to such analysis. The key difference was their use of *value units*, which employ a Gaussian instead of a sigmoidal activation function. A Gaussian activation function is bell-shaped so that the activation will be greatest for a specific net input value, and will be less both for lower and higher net input values. Using a nonmonotonic activation function enables the network to get by with fewer hidden units. Accordingly, Berkeley et al. used only a single layer of 10 hidden units.

A more important consequence of using value units in the hidden layer is that training tends to result in each unit taking activations in just a few discontinuous ranges (*bands*). For example, the values taken by their hidden unit 7 eventually became clustered in narrow bands around 0.06, 0.54, and 0.99 and did not take values elsewhere in the 0.00 to 1.00 range. The particular band into which activation fell on a given test trial depended on characteristics of the problem. Thus, the full set of problems could be divided into three subsets in accord with unit 7's activation on each problem, and the subsets could be examined to determine those characteristics. For example, the activation of unit 7 was in the band around:

- 0.06 when the connective was *not both* and/or the second proposition was negated;
- 0.99 when the connective was *not both* and/or the second proposition was positive;
- 0.54 when the connective was *if, then* or the connective was *or*.

This was the only unit that was sensitive to the negation value of the second proposition, but eight of the ten units were sensitive to which connective was presented. (The activation bands of the other two units were uninterpretable.)

Taking advantage of the fact that the activation bands are discrete and most are interpretable, Berkeley et al. viewed their network as using rules. Among the rules they identified, some turned out to be classical rules of logic, but others were novel default rules (e.g., "if the connective is *or* and there are no other salient features, the argument is a valid alternative syllogism"). Dawson, Medler, and Berkeley (1997) construed this ability to analyze the network in terms of rules as reducing the difference between classical symbolic accounts and connectionist approaches. However, what is most distinctive and quite useful in their network is the relative transparency of the sensitivity profiles of its units. Its actual performance, like that of many other networks, exemplifies the idea that networks can approximate rules but generally do so in an advantageous fashion. Among the advantages are:

- the network encodings are less brittle than rules;
- the network could discover nonstandard rules (even Dawson et al. found this noteworthy);
- the uninterpretable activity bands may have promoted successful performance in ways too nuanced to capture in a few simple rules.

There is some justification for regarding the more interpretable aspects of the knowledge encoded in the network as rules. However, the network implementation of such rules is not itself symbolic or propositional. Like hidden units in other simulations, each hidden unit here tends to be sensitive to multiple aspects of the input, and multiple hidden units tend to be sensitive to each aspect of the input. This many–many mapping is typical of the propagation of activation in networks; it may (in part) be viewed as implementing rules but is not itself a set of rules. Finally, it should be noted that the activation bands were induced by the use of the Gaussian activation function; how to relate the results to those from networks with more traditional sigmoidal activation functions remains to be determined. Further work on both types of networks and how to relate and interpret their results should be of considerable interest in a variety of problem domains.

The larger question is how to relate the performance of the networks to that of humans. While the networks did well, there are obviously substantial differences between networks and humans in the way they achieve success. Clearly the large number of training cycles is a major difference, since even quite slow humans learn to identify argument forms correctly with only a few hundred practice trials, not the 576,000 trials which were used to train our network on Set 1. Why might this be? First, humans do not confront a problem like this as a *tabula rasa*. They already possess a great deal of information, such as the distinction between sentences and connectives, and have some idea of what each connective means in ordinary speech. Moreover, it is likely that humans do not treat the whole problem as a single undifferentiated string, but rather use their prior knowledge to partition the input patterns into meaningful parts (e.g., the conclusion). The network, in contrast, must make the effort to discover these partitionings. However, the point of developing these simple models is not to attain a precise simulation of human performance. Rather, it is to show that logic problems, when viewed as tasks of pattern recognition, can be solved by networks which, like humans, seem to be capable of learning from errors and tuning their performance.

The finding that networks can perform pattern recognition on logical argument forms, and thereby evaluate the validity of arguments, buttresses the suggestion that human competency in formal reasoning might be based on processes of pattern recognition that are learned gradually as by a network. This ability to apply pattern recognition to linguistic symbol strings may be an extremely useful capacity for organisms that encounter linguistic symbols in their environment and need to manipulate them in a truth-preserving manner (see section 6.5) The crucial suggestion that emanates from a connectionist perspective is that the ability to manipulate

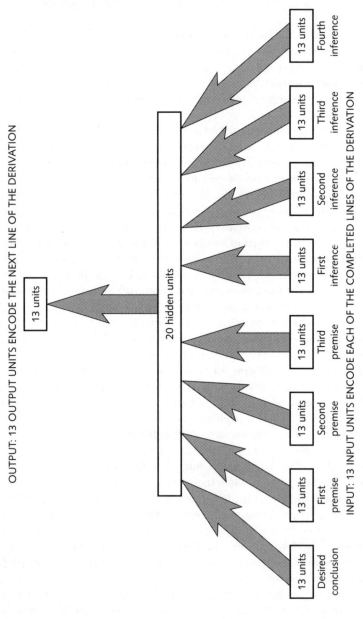

Figure 4.5 A network for proof construction. The desired conclusion, the premises, and whatever inferential steps have been completed so far are supplied on the input units; the network learns to generate the next inferential step on the output units.

external symbols in accordance with the principles of logic need not depend upon a mental mechanism that itself manipulates *internal* symbols. In the next section the plausibility of this idea is exhibited in the context of a more challenging task in logic: the construction of proofs.

4.3.4 A network for constructing derivations

Consider what is involved in teaching students in a symbolic logic course to develop proofs in a natural deduction system. The task in constructing a proof is to proceed from initial premises to the conclusion, proceeding only by licensed steps. Valid argument forms such as those we have considered so far are rules of natural deduction (*external* symbol strings) that license adding new statements to a sequence of premises and already-established statements. After teaching the rules, instructors typically do some model proofs; then students are sent off to construct proofs of their own. What they need to discover are the conditions under which it is useful to apply the various rules of natural deduction; that is, they must develop their pattern recognition capabilities. This generally requires practice.[7]

Frequently, as students are trying to master this procedure, the instructor will continue to do model proofs in front of the students and explain why one step was taken rather than another. When the one of us who teaches symbolic logic (Bechtel) offers such explanations, however, he often has the uncomfortable feeling that he is confabulating. It is simply obvious, when one has done enough proofs, what steps are useful in which circumstances. The explanations seem to be developed after the fact. This is revealed most clearly when, after giving a reason that seems plausible in the context of a particular problem, one does another problem that presents a similar situation, but where another step seems more appropriate. A particularly attentive student may notice this fact and ask: "Why?" Again, one can usually come up with a reason, but it is not at all clear that these reasons capture what actually governed the behavior. What seems more plausible is that after much practice more complex pattern-recognizing capacities have developed. Instead of simply recognizing the steps licensed by the basic argument forms, one recognizes situations in which application of particular rules of natural deduction should be useful.

A natural way of describing what happens when someone who knows logic constructs proofs is that he or she simply *recognizes* or *sees* what to do in particular situations. The expert solves a problem by recognizing what to do on the basis of extensive experience. If connectionists are able to provide accounts of how these patterns are recognized, as seems quite plausible, then we will not have to try to formulate logical expertise in terms of a set of mental rules; rather, we can treat it as involving mental activity that is more akin to pattern recognition than to rule application. Since the procedures used in constructing logical proofs are a means of manipulating formal symbols, this raises the prospect that the very ability to engage in formal symbol manipulation may not be a basic cognitive capacity; rather, we may develop and *learn how* to use nonsymbolic internal procedures that are effective at dealing with external symbols and tasks (a point developed below and in section 6.5).

As a first test of the feasibility of this approach, Bechtel (1994b) designed a network to construct simple formal proofs. As shown in figure 4.5, it was designed so that at each step the desired conclusion and the inferences that had already been completed were presented on the input units, and the network's task was to generate the next inference on the output units. By the final step, all except the last inference had to fit within the eight ensembles of input units. Thus, the derivation of each proof was limited to the desired conclusion, three premises, and the four inferential steps preceding the final one (which should match the desired conclusion). Some arguments had four premises and hence were limited to one less inferential step.

The network was initially trained on proofs that exemplified 14 different derivational patterns, which were constructed using a pool of five different inference rules (*or*-introduction, *or*-elimination, *and*-introduction, *and*-elimination, and conditional-elimination). Employing common symbols for logical connectives (&: *and*; ∨: *or*; ~: *not*; and ⊃: *if, then*), one of the derivational patterns was as follows:

To derive s & q:

1.	p & q	:premise
2.	$p \supset {\sim}r$	:premise
3.	$r \vee s$	:premise
4.	p	:1, &-elimination
5.	${\sim}r$	:2,4 ⊃-elimination
6.	s	:3,5 ∨-elimination
7.	q	:1, &-elimination
8.	s & q	:6,7 &-introduction

Twenty-four actual exemplars were constructed from each of the 14 derivation patterns by different substitutions of the constants A, B, C, and D for the variables p, q, etc., and by varying the order of the first three premises; the resulting 1,008 derivations provided ample variety for an initial feasibility simulation of natural deduction. The justifications in the right-hand column were not explicitly encoded, but the expression on the left in each line of the derivation was given a localist encoding on one of the input ensembles (requiring 13 units, in contrast to the maximum of 8 units per premise for the distributed encodings in figure 4.4 above). For example, if the second premise (line 2) was instantiated as C ⊃ ~A, it was encoded on the third ensemble as follows: five units for the first argument (the C unit turned on, and the units for negation, A, B, and D turned off), three units for the connective (⊃ unit turned on; & unit and ∨ unit turned off); and five units for the second argument (the negation and A units turned on, and the units for B, C, and D turned off). The first inference (line 4) required just one unit to be turned on (the first C unit in the fifth ensemble). Three-fourths of the derivations were selected for the training set; the rest were withheld for testing generalization.

An epoch of training consisted of one complete pass through each of the 756 derivations in the training set. The network began to get most of the steps correct after only a few epochs of training (again by backpropagation using the **bp** program). By epoch 500 it had mastered the training set. The 252 derivations reserved for testing generalization involved a total of 936 inferences; the network was judged to have made these correctly if all units that had target values of 1 had activations greater than 0.5 and all units that had target activations of 0 had activations less than 0.5. The network was correct on 767 of these inferences (81.9 percent). Some of the errors involved either no unit or two units encoding propositions having an activation above 0.5. If a competitive activation procedure had been incorporated to ensure that one unit would become active (A, B, C, or D), performance would have risen to 90.5 percent correct. The errors generally were not random but systematic:

if the network got a step wrong on one problem, it tended to make an error on the same step in similar problems.

A significant question is whether the network has learned how to construct natural deductions, or only ones that conform to the 14 derivational patterns. This question was partially answered by developing 6 new derivational patterns, from which 72 exemplars were constructed, yielding 252 inferences on which to test for generalization. The network was correct on 198 (78.6 percent). Again, the errors were mostly systematic. (For additional details, reports of other tests with this network, and discussion of how this approach to logical inference compares with more traditional psychological models of natural deduction such as those of Braine, Reiser, and Rumain, 1984, and Rips, 1994, see Bechtel, 1994b.)

While these networks are clearly limited to dealing with only a subset of formal logic, they do offer some support for the hypothesis advanced above that logical reasoning relies on pattern recognition, and that more sophisticated reasoning, such as constructing proofs in a natural deduction system, can be realized by sequences of pattern recognition steps. A key element in achieving this sort of success is that the network always has access on its input units to the premises, the target conclusion, and the steps completed so far. This is comparable in many ways to a human having this information written on paper, and only having to fill in one piece at a time. By storing all the propositional structures on paper, the person only has to *recognize* the next step in the inference, not build up representations of the propositional structures. Accordingly, one can speak of the person or network working with *external symbols*. We pursue the implications of this idea in section 6.5.

4.4   Beyond Pattern Recognition

In this chapter we have examined one kind of cognitive performance at which connectionist networks seem to excel: pattern recognition. After illustrating this ability in simple networks, we asked how important it is to human cognition. We suggested that higher-level cognitive tasks, which would seem to require reasoning about propositionally encoded knowledge, might instead be achievable by pattern recognition. We then explored this idea by presenting network simulations of two logical inference tasks: evaluation of logical forms (which was within the capabilities of a multi-layered feedforward network) and simple natural deduction (which could be performed by a network configured for recurrent acts of pattern recognition).

Although this approach seems very promising, we conclude by introducing a caveat: connectionists may find it necessary to learn how to make networks carry out other processes in addition to pattern recognition (albeit with pattern recognition as an elementary process by which more elaborate processes are carried out). For example, humans do not have to learn each new task *de novo*. Often they can make use of their knowledge in an analogous domain to help deal with a current domain. Perhaps that knowledge is copied and used as an initial sketch for the new task, so that weights need only be tuned rather than constructed from an initially random matrix. In fact, the *tabula rasa* approach to learning that is currently adopted in most connectionist models may be quite rare or even nonexistent in actual development and knowledge acquisition. (Cf. Piaget's developmental theory, in which all development germinates outward from a few initial schemes, such as sucking, and the processes of accommodation and assimilation that operate on them.) Exploring alternatives within a connectionist framework may require the incorporation of new mechanisms that go beyond the existing, basic capabilities for constraint satisfaction and generalization which currently enable simple pattern recognition. Examples include: the mechanism (just mentioned) of copying and adapting an existing network for new uses; mechanisms for coordinating multiple networks in a semi-modular architecture; and mechanisms by which existing relevant networks are identified, copied, combined, and expanded upon to carry out new tasks.[8]

Some interesting suggestions along these lines have been offered by Karmiloff-Smith (1992; see also Clark and Karmiloff-Smith, 1993, and Abrahamsen, 1993). She proposes, for example, that networks must be enhanced so as to enable them to re-represent the knowledge they have encoded in their weights; the knowledge could then be further manipulated and applied to other problems. If current versions of connectionism must be extended, one challenge is to figure out a way of getting a network to generate such mechanisms itself and, more generally, to exhibit such pervasive attributes of human thought as creativity and initiative. That is, can a network that readily accomplishes pattern recognition develop emergent capabilities? Can it learn not just new patterns, but more complex procedures, as an outcome of applying its current capabilities to increasingly challenging tasks? If not, the same jumble of *ad hoc* mechanisms, which have too frequently characterized symbolic modeling, will need to be brought in. This would compromise the simplicity of the basic connectionist mechanisms of propagating activations and modifying weights; it would be so much more interesting to find that networks can truly behave adaptively instead. (For a related view, see Gluck and Bower, 1988.)

NOTES

1   Note that a full-scale simulation of the task of naming the categories of exemplars would use a more principled way of representing the input and output; typically, the binary values would encode features based on a systematic characterization of the domain. For example, the input units might encode visual and other features that specify exemplars of basic-level categories, and the output units might provide a phonemic or articulatory encoding of category names such as "table." Specifying encodings of this sort presents some difficulties that we need not address; for our illustration, arbitrarily chosen strings of eight values are adequate. Furthermore, most investigators would want separate layers or networks for encoding the category as a mental concept and for generating a conventional name in a language such as English. Again, we can ignore this source of added complexity in carrying out our illustration.

2   This models the situation in which an instance of one category (e.g., a hat) has a feature (e.g., a strap that looks rather like a handle on a bucket) that makes the hat, in that respect, look more like a bucket than a typical hat.

3   Actually, for each feature there is one unit that is activated when the feature is present, and a different unit that is activated when it is absent, making a total of 28 units; absence can therefore be distinguished from lack of information. For simplicity, we do not discuss the units that encode absence.

4   If the new cases are intermediate with respect to those on which it has been trained, then the generalization is a form of *interpolation*. If, on the other hand, the new cases are outside that range, the generalization may have the form of extrapolation – for example, applying the same procedure or rule to new cases. *Extrapolation* is significantly more difficult than interpolation, but, as we will show in discussing networks that have learned

to produce the English past tense in chapter 5, an ability that is at least partially within the range of connectionist networks.

5   When errors were made, they were usually large errors (e.g., when 0 was the target, the output would be 0.98). Conversely, correct answers were typically very close to the target (e.g., when 1 was the target, the output would be 0.98). Thus, the very relaxed criterion for correctness played only a small role in determining the overall level of correct answers.

6   The error that remained at this point could not be eliminated by further training with backpropagation. The reason has to do with a peculiarity of the backpropagation algorithm. If the network generates an answer that is completely reversed from the target (e.g., a 1 instead of a 0), the delta value becomes 0 since the equation for determining the delta value includes the product $a_u (1 - a_u)$. Since the weight change equation involves multiplying by delta, there will be no change to weights in such a situation and the network will continue to produce the error.

7   At a given step of the proof, there often are rules that are licensed (locally) but do not contribute to the proof (globally). To select an appropriate rule, the student must attend to the larger pattern that is formed by the premises, conclusion, and steps already taken. Although this larger pattern is produced by a serial process (e.g., working backwards from the conclusion), the whole pattern (or parts of it) must be available at each step. It takes a good deal of experience to become aware of these patterns and to become efficient at recognizing them.

8   Symbolic approaches have not reached this point of sophistication yet, either. For interim, partial solutions see Schank's (1982) armory of MOPS, TOPS, and other high-level devices for dealing with the complexity of cognition, J. R. Anderson and Thompson's (1989) analogy-based PUPS system (see also J. R. Anderson, 1989), and Newell's (1989) chunking in the SOAR system.

Sources and Suggested Readings

Bechtel, W. (1994) Natural deduction in connectionist systems. *Synthese*, 101, 433–63.

Dreyfus, H. L. and Dreyfus, S. E. (1986) *Mind over Machine: The Power of Human Intuition and Expertise in the Era of the Computer*. New York: Free Press.

Margolis, H. (1987) *Patterns, Thinking, and Cognition: A Theory of Judgment*. Chicago: University of Chicago Press.

McClelland, J. L. and Rumelhart, D. E. (1981) An interactive activation model of context effects in letter perception: Part 1. An account of basic findings, *Psychological Review*, 88, 375–407.

5

ARE RULES REQUIRED TO PROCESS REPRESENTATIONS?

5.1   Is Language Use Governed by Rules?

Classical systems are often characterized as systems of rules and representations. Both are composed of (possibly structured) sequences of symbols, the difference being that rules specify operations upon representations (possibly referencing them with variables) and representations get operated upon by rules. Some instantiations of the contrast are program vs. data in a computer system, production rule vs. expression in production systems, and phrase-structure rule vs. symbol string in linguistics. Operations can include creating a representation, moving it into working memory, transforming it into another representation, and so forth. Representations can be simple symbol strings, but the symbols in classical cognitive models are hierarchically structured. An important way in which connectionist systems are often distinguished from classical systems is that they do away with rules and structured symbolic representations. We examine the arguments regarding rules in this chapter and those regarding structured representations in chapter 6. Both chapters emphasize arguments and simulations developed during connectionism's first decade, when controversy was strongest. The last part of each chapter gives a sampling of more recent work, and disagreements about rules and representations punctuate the work discussed in chapters 7–10 as well.

Findings suggesting that rules are needed to account for cognitive processes played a major role in directing many psychologists away from behaviorism and toward a cognitive approach in the 1960s . Most connectionists are not behaviorists, but they have reopened the debate by seeking to model some of the same phenomena as classical cognitivists by means of networks rather than rule systems.[1] To the extent that these attempts are successful, the plausibility of connectionism is enhanced and the choice between the traditional and connectionist approaches must be made on other grounds.

The domain of language provides a good context in which to examine the role that rules might play in a cognitive model.[2] A central task of linguistics is to provide a systematic description of languages. Grammars generally include recursive rules that are capable of generating any of an infinite number of grammatical sentences in a natural language such as English (Chomsky, 1957). Some psychologists have been attracted to the view that people produce and comprehend sentences by utilizing a mental grammar. Within this psycholinguistic tradition, two assumptions are often made regarding how these rules could be acquired: (a) children possess innate knowledge of Universal Grammar, which constrains the possible rules that can be employed in language; and (b) in learning a specific language children create hypotheses about which of these rules apply to it, and then test these hypotheses against their linguistic experiences. In contemporary versions, Universal Grammar includes parameters with a limited set of values that constrain which rules may occur in that language. For example, Italian allows the subject of some sentences to be omitted; English does not. From experience hearing the language, children can set the parameters to their appropriate values. Whether rules are constrained by parameters or in some other way, the important assumption here is that a system of rules is represented in people's minds. Often this is referred to as *tacit* knowledge, because people are presumed to mentally represent and use the rules without being able to state them.

One particular linguistic activity, the formation of the past tense in English, has become the focus of an intense, ongoing debate between those connectionists who would like to eliminate rules and classicists who insist that such attempts would be either unsuccessful or vacuous. The linguistic facts are not in dispute. For regular verbs, the past tense can be formed by adding an inflectional morpheme (which we will write as -*ed*) to the basic verb form (the stem); examples of this regular stem + *ed* form are *looked* and *needed*. There are, however, a number of irregular verbs which constitute exceptions, such as *give* → *gave*, and many of these occur frequently in daily conversation. Thus, most classical accounts of past-tense formation identify both a general rule for the regular cases, and a set of exceptions which are stated separately. Rumelhart and McClelland (1986a; *PDP:18*) developed a connectionist model which challenged both the need for separate treatment of regular and irregular verbs and the claim that rules are involved. They proposed that

> lawful behavior and judgments may be produced by a mechanism in which there is no explicit representation of the rule. Instead, we suggest that the mechanisms that process language and make judgments of grammaticality are constructed in such a way that their performance is characterizable by rules, but that the rules themselves are not written in explicit form anywhere in the mechanism.   (1986a, p. 217)

In addition to their claim that a single network was sufficient to form the past tense of both regular and irregular verbs, Rumelhart and McClelland proposed that training such a network would replicate aspects of children's emerging mastery. The available data indicated that there are three (overlapping) stages of acquisition, as summarized in Brown (1973) and Kuczaj (1977). In stage 1 (ages 1–2 years), children tend to use the same basic verb form, the stem, whether talking about present or past events. However, for a handful of verbs they know and sometimes use the correct past-tense form instead; most of these are irregulars such as *came*, *got*, and *went*, but regulars such as *looked* are possible as well. In stage 2 (ages 2–5 years), children know the past-tense forms of a much larger number of irregular verbs and show evidence of acquiring a general rule for forming the past tense of regular verbs – informally stated, add -*ed* to the verb stem. They quickly overgeneralize this rule to some of the irregular verbs for which they had previously used the stem alone and, more interesting, some of those for which they knew the correct irregular form in stage 1 (Ervin, 1964). Usage is often inconsistent as this lengthy stage unfolds. For example, a child who starts overregularizing *come* as *comed* might also continue to use the correct irregular form *came* on other occasions and (especially later in stage 2) sometimes blend the two forms to get *camed* (Kuczaj, 1977). By about age 5 children can often add *-ed* to nonsense verbs such as *rick* on request (Berko, 1958), but now almost always refrain from overgeneralizing this suffix to familiar irregular verbs. Children of this age have traversed most of the slow transition to stage 3, in which the correct forms are generally produced for both regular and irregular verbs. The most eye-catching aspect of this developmental course is the *U-shaped* function exhibited by some of the earliest irregular verbs: correct, then often regularized inappropriately, then correct again. This suggested to pioneering symbolic theorists in the 1960s (against the prevailing behaviorism) that stage 1 children have memorized a few past-tense forms, stage 2 children have also acquired a rule, and stage 3 children have learned the exceptions to the rule. On one account, these stage 3 children (and adults) use the rule for regular verbs and look up memorized forms in a lexicon for irregular verbs.[3]

Rumelhart and McClelland wanted to demonstrate that mental rules (augmented by lexical look-up for exceptions) did not necessarily provide the best interpretation of this evidence. They did this by showing that a connectionist network could exhibit many of the same learning phenomena as children: the three stages of acquisition, the gradual transition between stages, and error patterns that are distinctive to certain phonology-based subclasses. They did not attempt to show how past-tense formation would be carried out as part of an overall language production system, and they set limits on the extent to which they tried to capture the many details in empirical data sets or in theoretical linguistic accounts of the English past tense. Their model and accompanying claims elicited a storm of controversy that has still not abated. We begin by presenting their model and then explore more fully the ensuing controversy and alternatives.

5.2   Rumelhart and McClelland's Model of Past-tense Acquisition

5.2.1   A pattern associator with Wickelfeature encodings

Rumelhart and McClelland were able to substantially accomplish their goal using a model with a rather simple structure, as shown in figure 5.1. The heart of their model is a two-layer pattern associator network in which the input units represent a verb stem in terms of context-sensitive phonological features called *Wickelfeatures* (defined below) and the output units represent the past-tense form of the same verb, again in terms of Wickelfeatures. Superficially it appears that these two Wickelfeature layers are the hidden layers in a four-layer network, but this is not the case. Figure 5.1 actually collapses the representation of three separate networks, each of which passes information from its input layer to its output layer in a different way. The encoding network at the front end uses a fixed (nonstatistical) procedure to translate a phonological representation of the stem into the Wickelfeature representation used by the pattern associator. The decoding/binding network at the back end, which translates the Wickelfeature outputs into a phonological representation of the past-tense form, is more complex. Roughly described, it is a dynamic network in which phonological representations on the output layer compete to account for incoming Wickelfeatures. When processing is terminated, each phonological representation has attained a different level of activation, and this is used to determine the model's response.

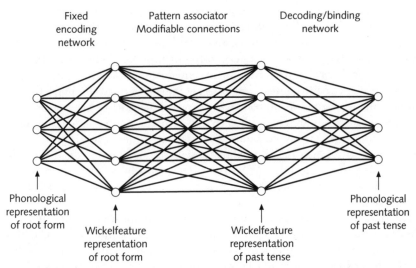

Fixed
encoding
network

Pattern associator
Modifiable connections

Decoding/binding
network

Phonological
representation
of root form

Wickelfeature
representation
of root form

Wickelfeature
representation
of past tense

Phonological
representation
of past tense

Figure 5.1 The basic structure of Rumelhart and McClelland's model for past-tense formation. Reprinted with permission from D. E. Rumelhart and J. L. McClelland (1986a) On learning the past tense of English verbs. In J. L. McClelland, D. E. Rumelhart, and the PDP Research Group, *Parallel Distributed Processing: Explorations in the Microstructure of Cognition*, volume 2: *Psychological and Biological Models*. Cambridge, MA: MIT Press/Bradford Books, p. 222.

The pattern associator in between the encoding and decoding networks was the part of the model emphasized by Rumelhart and McClelland. Its task was to transform the Wickelfeature encoding of the sound pattern of each verb stem (which they called the *base form*) on its input layer into the appropriate past-tense form on its output layer. The units in both layers were binary, activations were propagated using the stochastic version of the logistic activation function (equation (9) in chapter 2), and it learned by using the delta rule to adjust its weights.

We will see below that Wickelfeature encodings are no longer in use. Nonetheless, they are not a mere historical curiosity. Wickelfeatures provided an innovative solution to a problem that still has not been adequately addressed: networks cannot directly encode order information. In linguistics – a quintessentially symbolic science – the phonemic representation of a verb stem is composed of an ordered sequence (*string*) of phonemes. For example, the past-tense form *came* can be represented as /kAm/ (using Rumelhart and McClelland's notation, in which upper vs. lower case matters: /kam/ is the first syllable of *camcorder* in contrast to /kAm/ for *came*). If this string is presented to a network, unless special measures are taken, the order of the phonemes will be lost. For example, consider a localist network in which one input unit encodes each possible phoneme, with unit 1 designated for /A/, unit 2 for /k/, unit 3 for /m/, and so forth. Presenting the string /kAm/ will activate unit 2, unit 1, and unit 3. But it does not matter whether they are activated in sequence or simultaneously; the resulting activation pattern (units 1–3 active and the rest inactive) is indistinguishable from that of /mAk/ or /Akm/. The input layer and its representations can be thought of as having one rigid order (unit 1, then 2, then 3, etc.), but the numbers are arbitrary labels. It is perhaps more appropriate to think of the input layer as an unordered collection of units that are distinct due to what they encode (as reflected in their different weight matrices).

Connectionists have devised only a few special measures to make networks preserve order information. We will see in section 6.4 that simple recurrent networks provide a solution that is appropriate to certain tasks and is in common use today. Rumelhart and McClelland took a very different approach. Their starting point was a type of phonological representation invented by Wickelgren (1969), in which phoneme units are made context-sensitive by indicating the phonemes that precede and follow the phoneme of interest (which we will call the *target phoneme*). Hence, each representational element is sensitive to a target phoneme and its immediate context. Using # to mark word boundaries, the verb *came* would be encoded using three elements: $_{\#}k_A$, $_k A_m$, $_A m_{\#}$. Rumelhart and McClelland called these *Wickelphones*. It is generally possible to reconstruct the *sequence* of phonemes in a word from the unordered *collection* of Wickelphones; hence a distinctive representation of *came* can be obtained using three Wickelphones.

Wickelphones carry a high cost, however: an enormous number of units would be needed to handle a full set of sounds. Specifically, the number of Wickelphones is the cube of the number of phonemes (about 35 in English) plus the number of units that include word boundary markers. Rumelhart and McClelland calculated that more than 42,000 units would be needed for their set of phonemes, only three of which would be active for a three-phoneme word (an uneconomical use of units). Also, this representation is so specific that special steps would be needed to obtain generalization to words with similar phonemes (e.g., generalizing from *sing/sang* to *ring/rang* and, to a lesser extext, to *drink/drank*). Rumelhart and McClelland's solution was to obtain a coarse coding (a concept that we introduced in section 2.2.4) of the Wickelphones across the pattern associator layers by making each unit correspond to a Wickelfeature. Wickelfeatures were generated by analyzing the target and context phonemes in the Wickelphone according to four featural dimensions. (For example, /A/ is a *Low Long Vowel* that has a *Front* place of articulation.) Two dimensions were binary and two trinary, yielding ten different features plus an additional feature (#) to indicate word boundaries. A particular Wickelfeature consisted of an ordered triplet of features, one each from the preceding context phoneme, the target phoneme, and the following context phoneme. Altogether there is a pool of 1,210 different Wickelfeatures ($11 \times 10 \times 11$). A given Wickelphone for a target phoneme that is not at a word boundary corresponds to 64 different Wickelfeatures ($4 \times 4 \times 4$). By disregarding Wickelfeatures for which the two context features are from different dimensions, these figures can be reduced to a pool of 460 Wickelfeatures, with 16 different Wickelfeatures per Wickelphone. This makes the number of units quite manageable, and reduces unneeded redundancy.

By way of example, the Wickelphone $_k A_m$ (targeting the vowel in *came*) has the Wickelfeatures (Interrupted, Low, Interrupted), (Back, Low, Front), (Stop, Low, Nasal), (Unvoiced, Low, Voiced), plus 12 other Wickelfeatures obtained by substituting for Low, in turn, the three other features of the target phoneme: Long, Vowel, and Front. Only that particular Wickelphone has that particular set of 16 Wickelfeatures, but each individual Wickelfeature is associated with a number of different Wickelphones. For example, (Interrupted, Low, Interrupted) is a Wickelfeature for $_p e_t$, $_b I_k$, and a number of other Wickelphones. Generalization is fostered by this arrangement. To use an example from the preceding paragraph, the first Wickelphone for the verb *sing*, phonemically /siN/, is $_{\#}s_i$; that for *ring*, phonemically /riN/, is $_{\#}r_i$. Since the target phonemes /s/ and /r/ differ in two of their four features, and the context phonemes are identical, half of the Wickelfeatures for the first

Wickelphone in each word are the same. Since the same phonemes are context phonemes for the second Wickelphone (and the other two phonemes are identical), half of the Wickelfeatures are identical for the second Wickelphone as well. Finally, the third Wickelphone is identical for the two words ($_iN_\#$), so all 16 Wickelfeatures are identical. Because the degree of overlap for each of the three Wickelphones is considerable, the network will show a relatively high degree of generalization across the verbs *sing* and *ring*.

The result of these choices concerning representation is that the input and output layers of the pattern associator part of the network each have identical sets of 460 units, one for each Wickelfeature. A verb stem is presented to the network by simultaneously activating all of the input units that correspond to its Wickelfeatures. To present the stem *come* (/kum/), for example, 16 Wickelfeatures would be activated for each its three phonemes, yielding a total of 48 activated Wickelfeatures. These would be propagated across the weighted connections, resulting in a somewhat different pattern of activation on the output units which, for a network at learning stage 3, should be translatable by the decoding/binding network into the past-tense form *came* (/kAm/). Note that neither layer has any direct way of keeping track of which Wickelfeatures correspond to which target phonemes; also, in longer words there typically would be some overlap in Wickelfeatures from different phonemes (to that extent, fewer units than 16 times the number of phonemes would be activated).

It turned out that this novel approach works surprisingly well. The representations are distinctive enough that different words can be distinguished, but they overlap enough to support generalization on the basis of the similarity structure of the verb stems. Hence, the network can usually generate the correct past-tense forms for verbs on which it has not been trained by generalizing from the verbs on which it has been trained. Having learned that *sing* produces *sang*, for example, the network can be presented with *ring* and produce *rang* (retaining the distinctive first consonant and the shared final consonant, and appropriately changing the vowel). Knowing *sing* would not be as helpful for generalizing to a less similar new verb, such as *say*. (Of course, the network is not operating on the verb pairs as such, but rather on their distributed encoding across the Wickelfeature units; these encodings overlap quite a bit for *sing* and *ring* and much less for *sing* and *say*.)

The same weight matrix that enables the network to form the past tense of regulars is also used to determine which verbs require a regular past tense. There are three variants of the regular past tense morpheme *-ed*, based upon the phonological characteristics of the stem. Specifically, /əd/ (also written as /^d/ or /id/) is added to stems that end in alveolar stops /d/ or /t/; otherwise, /d/ is added to stems that end in a voiced obstruent, and /t/ is added to stems that end in a voiceless obstruent. By stage 3 the network does a good job of using a regular past-tense form where required and of using the correct variant. It can even generalize fairly well to untrained stems, as discussed later in section 5.2.5.

To encourage generalization, Rumelhart and McClelland used an additional strategy for increasing the coarseness, or "blurring," of the representations across the Wickelfeature units. When a particular Wickelfeature was activated, they also activated a subset of similar Wickelfeatures (specifically, 90 percent of the Wickelfeatures that were identical except for one of the two context features).

The goal of the Wickelfeature encoding is thus to capture the phonological similarity among verbs for which a similar past tense is required so that the network could make the generalization. Rumelhart and McClelland made this point explicit in explaining their use of Wickelphones, from which Wickelfeatures are derived:

> One nice property of Wickelphones is that they capture enough of the context in which a phoneme occurs to provide a sufficient basis for differentiating between the different cases of the past tense rule and for characterizing the contextual variables that determine the subregularities among the irregular past-tense verbs. For example, [it is] the word-final phoneme that determines whether we should add /d/, /t/, or /^d/ in forming the regular past. And it is the sequence $_iN_\#$ which is transformed to $_aN_\#$ in the ing → ang pattern found in words like *sing*.   (1986a, p. 234)

The encoding of inputs and outputs in terms of Wickelfeatures has been one of the most criticized aspects of Rumelhart and McClelland's simulation. One criticism exemplifies a generic objection that the performance of connectionist models is dependent upon particular ways of encoding inputs which are borrowed from other theories, usually symbolic theories. As applied here (see Lachter and Bever, 1988), the objection is that much of the model's work is actually accomplished by the Wickelfeature representation, which is a context-sensitive adaptation of standard linguistic featural analyses, leaving in doubt the contribution of the network's architecture as such. The usual connectionist response is that much processing remains to be done once an encoding scheme is decided upon, and the connectionist contribution is in offering a non-rule-based means of accounting for this processing.

More specific criticisms of Wickelfeature encodings were raised in Pinker and Prince's (1988) critique, as discussed in section 5.3.2. Ultimately, though, Wickelfeatures were abandoned because connectionists themselves had problems getting adequate generalization using them in a network model of reading aloud (Seidenberg and McClelland, 1989) – a task which involves more arbitrary associations than modifying a verb to get its past-tense form. Current connectionist models of past-tense acquisition (section 5.4.3) and reading aloud (sections 8.3.2.2 and 10.2.3.3) retain the idea of distributed encodings of phonemes but no longer use coarse coding across context-sensitive features to implement it; instead they rely on an interim strategy of position-specific ensembles of units. We still do not know how the human mind itself solves the long-vexing "problem of serial order in behavior" (Lashley, 1951) nor how the networks of ten or twenty years hence will do so.

5.2.2   Activation function and learning procedure

Other aspects of the model also exemplify the early excitement of experimenting with parallel distributed processing as an approach to cognitive modeling prior to the discovery of backpropagation. To run their simulations, Rumelhart and McClelland presented the Wickelfeature encoding of each verb stem as an input pattern to the pattern associator, which is a two-layer feedforward network. The network would then compute the past-tense form by applying the stochastic version of the logistic activation function (presented in the context of Boltzmann machines as equation (9) in section 2.2.2.2):

$$probability\,(a_u = 1) = \frac{1}{1 + e^{-(netinput_u - \theta_u)/T}}$$

The parameter θ_u is a threshold that is individualized for each unit during training. Input and output units are *binary* (active or inactive); whether or not a particular output unit is active on a particular trial is stochastically determined. As the equation shows, the probability of activation is a continuous function of the extent to which the net input from the input units exceeds the output unit's threshold. A stochastic function was chosen for two reasons: it enabled the network to give different responses on different occasions without change in the weights (the degree of variability being determined by the temperature parameter T), and it slowed the learning, allowing the effects of overregularization to endure for some time. (Contemporary connectionists still use the logistic function to obtain nonlinear behavior, but usually prefer the efficiency of the nonstochastic version.)

Once a pattern of activation had been obtained on the output layer by means of the stochastic function, the network could learn by means of an error correction procedure. That is, the obtained pattern was compared to the target output pattern (the correct Wickelfeature encoding of the past-tense form). For any output unit that had an activation of 0 when its target value was 1, the weights feeding into it were decreased by a small amount and the threshold was increased by the same amount. If the activation was 1 when the target value was 0, weights were increased and the threshold decreased. Note that this is simply the *perceptron convergence procedure* (Rosenblatt, 1962), a discrete version of the delta rule that is suitable for stochastic as well as nonstochastic units. Although Minsky and Papert (1969) demonstrated that there are serious limitations on what input–output functions can be computed and learned by perceptrons, Rumelhart and McClelland (p. 226) noted that those functions that *can* be learned by a perceptron can also be learned (to an arbitrarily low probability of error) by a stochastic variation such as their past-tense network. In fact, their particular input–output pairs were learned rather well.

5.2.3 Overregularization in a simpler network: The rule of 78

Rumelhart and McClelland's pattern associator network was large by any standard, and the coarse coding scheme made it even more difficult to examine the detailed behavior of the network. These characteristics followed from their desire to show that past-tense formation could be substantially carried out by a network (rather than a rule system) utilizing distributed representations at the phonological level. Another objective, however, was to simulate the stage-like sequence by which exceptional forms are correct, then overregularized, and finally correct again. They were able to illustrate this particular phenomenon by teaching a simple, invented rule and exceptions to that rule to a much simpler network. The number of weights was small enough to inspect them individually to see how the stage-like behavior emerged. This simulation could therefore be used to clarify what was happening in the more complex past-tense simulation.

The *rule of 78* specifies a transformation that applies to certain binary patterns. Rumelhart and McClelland wrote the rule and used it to construct a set of input–output cases which were presented as teaching patterns to a pattern associator network with eight units per layer. If the network learned to transform the input sequences into the appropriate output sequences, it could be said to have learned to behave in accordance with (but not by means of) the rule. In the more interesting condition, one of the cases was distorted by changing its transformation into one that violated the rule. To handle that condition, the network had to learn a rule with an exception.

Specifically, the rule first specifies input patterns in which one of the first three, one of the second three, and one of the last two units must be *on* (1) and all other units must be *off* (0). Thus,

$$0\ 1\ 0\ 0\ 1\ 0\ 0\ 1$$

is a permissible input pattern, but

$$1\ 1\ 1\ 0\ 0\ 0\ 0\ 0$$

is not. It is convenient to refer to these patterns by identifying which of the units 1–8 are active. Thus, the first pattern above is (258). The rule specifies a mapping from the permissible input patterns to output patterns according to which units 1–6 are identical and units 7 and 8 reverse their activation values (hence, the name *rule of 78*). For example, the output for (258) is (257):

$$0\ 1\ 0\ 0\ 1\ 0\ 1\ 0$$

Any other output for this pattern would be an exception to the rule. There are 18 input–output cases that exemplify the rule.

Rumelhart and McClelland taught the rule of 78 to the network using the same kind of binary stochastic units, activation rule, and learning rule as they used for the past-tense simulation (however, θ_u was set at zero, and T had a lower value). The first thing to notice is that the set of 18 input patterns is considerably larger than the number of linearly independent patterns for which the network could learn an arbitrary mapping to outputs (which is equal to the number of input units, here, eight). The fact that the mappings between input and output patterns are in fact not arbitrary, but rather are completely systematic, allowed the network to achieve perfect performance in learning these 18 cases.

McClelland and Rumelhart (1988, pp. 114–19) made this rule of 78 problem available as an exercise for the **pa** (pattern associator) program in their *Handbook*. To run it as a new project using **PDP++** see sections 5.3 through 5.5 and part III of O'Reilly and Munakata (2000) or using **tlearn** see chapter 3 of Plunkett and Elman (1997) or appendix 3 (and chapters 3 and 4; see the footnote on page 74) of McLeod, Plunkett, and Rolls (1998).

We trained the 18 pairs of patterns that exemplify the rule of 78 for 30 epochs using **pa**. At this point the network was making sporadic errors, generally attributable to the fact that a stochastic unit has a small probability of firing even when net input is negative. An examination of the weight matrix for this network shows the exact mechanism by which the network behaves in accord with the rule of 78. The three outlined boxes in table 5.1 indicate the regions with the largest weights (recall that each weight specifies the strength of the connection between the two indicated units). The weights in the upper left box ensure that whichever unit is active among units 1–3, the corresponding output unit will get the greatest net input. Specifically, the connection from an input unit to the corresponding output unit has a positive weight whereas the noncorresponding connections have negative weights. Hence, the states of input units 1, 2, and 3 will be replicated on the corresponding output units. The weights in the central box do the same job for units 4, 5, and 6. The weights in the lower right box, however, are reversed in sign: if input unit 7 is active, the positive connection to output unit 8 will ensure that it becomes active as well,

Table 5.1 Network weights for the rule of 78 with no exceptions

Input unit	*Output unit*							
	1	*2*	*3*	*4*	*5*	*6*	*7*	*8*
1	58	– 36	– 38	– 4	– 6	– 10	– 2	2
2	– 34	62	– 38	– 2	– 6	– 8	4	– 2
3	– 40	– 44	54	– 6	– 4	– 4	0	– 2
4	– 6	– 4	– 4	62	– 34	– 44	2	6
5	0	– 6	– 6	– 36	60	– 36	4	– 4
6	– 10	– 8	– 12	– 38	– 42	58	– 4	– 4
7	– 6	– 16	– 10	– 10	– 6	– 14	– 60	52
8	– 10	– 2	– 12	– 2	– 10	– 8	62	– 54

and the same holds for the connection from 8 to 7.[4] By means of its weights, the network has encoded information necessary to perform in accord with the rule of 78 without ever explicitly encoding it.

The important question is: what happens when some specific instances do not follow the general rule? Rumelhart and McClelland wished to see if they could simulate the three learning stages described for the past tense. To do this, they converted one of the 18 cases into an exception. The exceptional case was (147) → (147), in place of (147) → (148). Since, for children, a substantial percentage of the earliest-learned verbs are irregular, Rumelhart and McClelland started the network with just the exceptional case and one regular case, (258) → (257). After 20 epochs of training, the network showed good item-specific learning, but it had no way of extracting a rule from just two inputs (stage 1). When the remaining 16 rule-generated cases were added, the network quickly exhibited rule-based learning with over-regularization of the exception (stage 2), and then slowly learned to incorporate the exception across hundreds of trials before achieving excellent performance (stage 3).

To observe this ourselves, we again ran the rule of 78 exercise in the *Handbook*, this time using the version that included the exceptional case, (147) → (147). As expected, after 20 epochs of training on the first two cases, the network had learned these as separate cases. We then added the remaining 16 (rule-following) input–output cases. During the next ten epochs of training, the network essentially learned the regularity that is expressed in the rule of 78. In the process, though, it began to produce substantially more errors on the exceptional case. At this point the probability that input pattern (147) would activate output unit 7 was only 0.28, while the probability of activating unit 8 was 0.60. Thus, there was a tendency to overregularize and produce (148). Forty epochs later this tendency was still in evidence but reduced: the probability for unit 7 was now 0.50 and for unit 8 was 0.53.[5] Across a great many more training epochs, however, the weights gradually adjusted until the network almost always dealt correctly with the exceptional case. Table 5.2 shows the weights after epoch 520. From this it can be calculated that the probability of activation given input (147) was 0.92 for unit 7 and 0.08 for unit 8, making the network fairly reliable at producing the exceptional mapping (147) → (147).[6] Rumelhart and McClelland (p. 233) characterized this result as follows:

Table 5.2   Network weights for the rule of 78 with one exception

Input unit	Output unit 1	2	3	4	5	6	7	8
1	108	− 66	− 74	− 08	− 14	− 14	**68**	− 76
2	− 72	112	− 70	− 10	− 06	− 08	− 20	34
3	− 66	− 68	116	− 12	− 06	− 08	− 24	22
4	− 14	− 08	− 08	116	− 70	− 74	**70**	− 68
5	− 10	− 04	− 08	− 78	110	− 72	− 24	24
6	− 06	− 10	− 12	− 68	− 66	116	− 22	24
7	− 08	− 12	− 10	− 18	− 16	− 16	**− 100**	108
8	− 22	− 10	− 18	− 12	− 10	− 14	**124**	− 128

Weights shown in boldface provide the mechanism for producing the correct output for the exceptional case 147. In that case, the net input to unit 7 is 68 + 70 + (− 100) = 38, giving unit 7 a probability of 0.926 of becoming active.

if there is a predominant regularity in a set of patterns, this can swamp exceptional patterns until the set of connections has been acquired that captures the predominant regularity. Then further, gradual tuning can occur that adjusts these connections to accommodate both the regular patterns and the exception. These basic properties of the pattern associator model lie at the heart of the three-stage acquisition process, and account for the gradualness of the transition from Stage 2 to Stage 3.

5.2.4   Modeling U-shaped learning

For the actual simulation of English past-tense acquisition, Rumelhart and McClelland selected 506 English verbs, which they divided into three sets: ten high-frequency verbs (eight of which were irregular), 410 medium-frequency verbs (76 irregular), and 86 low-frequency verbs (14 irregular). The verbs in the high-frequency set, for example, included the regular verbs *live* and *look* and the irregular verbs *come, get, give, make, take, go, have* and *feel*. The simulation began by training the network only on the ten high-frequency verbs, with each verb presented once per epoch. By epoch 10, the network had learned a good deal about how to produce the proper past-tense forms from the stems for both the two regular and eight irregular verbs (between 80 and 85 percent of Wickelfeatures were correct). At this juncture the medium-frequency verbs were added to the training set and 190 more training epochs ensued. Figure 5.2 (from *PDP:18*) shows that early in this period the network exhibited the dip in performance on irregular verbs that is characteristic of children's stage 2. Thus, immediately after the additional verbs were added on epoch 11 (referred to as trial 11 in this figure), the percentage of features correct on the high-frequency irregular verbs dropped approximately 10 percent, whereas progress on the high-frequency regular verbs was hardly affected. After the initial drop, however, the irregular verbs began to improve again by epoch 20, gradually increasing to approximately 95 percent of features correct by epoch 160. The drop in accuracy was due to interference from learning the regular pattern; once that pattern was established, the weights could be fine-tuned so that the irregular verbs could be

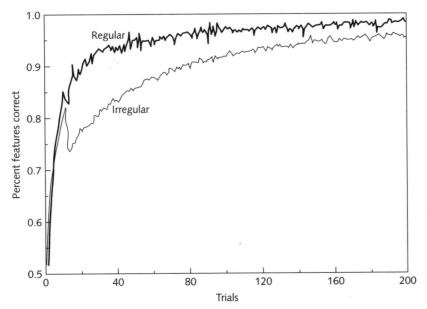

Figure 5.2 Performance of Rumelhart and McClelland's (1986) model for past-tense
formation: percentage of features correct across epochs (which they called "trials")
for regular and irregular high-frequency verbs. Reprinted with permission from D. E.
Rumelhart and J. L. McClelland (1986a) On learning the past tense of English verbs.
In J. L. McClelland, D. E. Rumelhart, and the PDP Research Group, *Parallel Distributed
Processing: Explorations in the Microstructure of Cognition*, volume 2: *Psychological and
Biological Models*. Cambridge, MA: MIT Press/Bradford Books, p. 242.

relearned as exceptional cases, as in children's stage 3. Finally, it should be noted
that performance on the medium-frequency verbs became at least as good as performance on the original set of ten high-frequency verbs within a few epochs of their
introduction on epoch 11 (not shown in figure 5.2); in fact, performance was a bit
better for the new irregular verbs because on average they happened to involve
easier transformations (few were as arbitrary as *go/went*).

Through further analysis, Rumelhart and McClelland were able to show that during the period when the network was making errors on the irregular verbs, most errors
were of the expected type; that is, in the direction of overregularization. For example,
for the stem *come*, the correct (irregular) past-tense form is *came*; errors that reflect
overregularization are stem + *ed* (*comed*) and past + *ed* (*camed*). Note that the past + *ed*
error is actually a blend that combines the correct and incorrect way to form the past
tense; it was counted as an overregularization error since that is the only aspect of
the form that is in error. (For most verbs, the past + *ed* form was relatively infrequent.)

To examine the relative frequency of overregularization, Rumelhart and
McClelland had to consider how the decoding/binding network would operate on
the Wickelfeature representation of the past tense to generate a phonological representation. This would most easily be done by initially decoding the Wickelfeature
representation into Wickelphones, from which context-free phoneme strings and
hence words could be recovered. Even this would be a daunting task computationally,
however, so what they actually did was to set up a competition between pre-defined

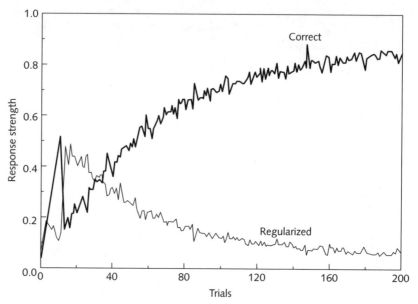

Figure 5.3   Performance of Rumelhart and McClelland's (1986) model for past-tense formation: response strengths across epochs (which they called "trials") for the high-frequency irregular verbs. The response strengths for the correct responses increased, while those for the regularized (incorrect) alternatives decreased. Reprinted with permission from D. E. Rumelhart and J. L. McClelland (1986a) On learning the past tense of English verbs. In J. L. McClelland, D. E. Rumelhart, and the PDP Research Group, *Parallel Distributed Processing: Explorations in the Microstructure of Cognition*, volume 2: *Psychological and Biological Models*. Cambridge, MA: MIT Press/Bradford Books, p. 243.

alternative forms. In the case of *come*, the alternatives were the phoneme strings corresponding to *came, comed, camed*, and *come*. *Come* is the error of making no change to the stem, which was the only type of error explicitly considered in addition to overregularization. A response strength was calculated for each of these four alternatives by having them compete to account for the particular set of Wickelfeatures that were active; essentially, the response strength of an alternative reflected the proportion of Wickelfeatures that it could account for but the other alternatives could not. The response strength calculated in this way roughly captures the propensity to produce one form rather than the others. Adding the strengths of all four alternatives together, the maximum sum would be one. (The sum would be less than one to the extent that some features are not accounted for by any of the alternatives.) It should be noted that this procedure is sensitive to which alternatives are in competition. For example, if *camt* were added to the alternatives (as a phonologically impermissible way to regularize *come*), *camed* would presumably lose strength since the final phonemes share many features. Also, the sum of response strengths would be larger since those Wickelfeatures unique to /t/ would now be accounted for.

Figure 5.3 shows how the error of overregularization dominated during stage 2 (approximately epoch 11, when the mid-frequency verbs were introduced, through epoch 30) and then declined during a gradual transition to the reliably correct performance of stage 3. It does not, however, show what other forms might have had nontrivial response strengths had they been included; since the sum of the response strengths tended to fall into the 0.65–0.75 range during stage 2 and the early transition, it would be of interest to know whether anything systematic was happening in the 0.25–0.35 gap. Nevertheless, the ability to simulate the overregularization of the past tense without positing rules is a striking result of this study.

5.2.5 Modeling differences between different verb classes

Having simulated the stage-like aspect of children's acquisition data, Rumelhart and McClelland went on to consider more detailed aspects. In particular, within each of the two major types of verbs – regular and irregular – there are subtypes that exhibit distinctive patterns of past-tense formation. Bybee and Slobin (1982), for example, described the distinctive course of acquisition for each of nine different classes of irregular verbs. Rumelhart and McClelland found that many of these class differences showed up in the simulation results. For example, one class of irregular verbs ends in a final /t/ and is left unchanged in the past tense (e.g., *hit*). In human acquisition, this irregular form tends to be overextended to certain verbs in other classes that also end in /t/ (or /d/). Also, children perform well on this class in a grammaticality judgment task (Kuczaj, 1978). As described in the next two paragraphs, the simulation results were consistent with these findings (and even went beyond them to make a new prediction).

Seven of Bybee and Slobin's classes involved a vowel change; they found that these classes differed dramatically in their propensity for overregularization in preschoolers' spontaneous speech, from a low of 10 percent for class IV (e.g., *bring*/ *brought*) to a high of 80 percent for class VIII (e.g., *fly*/*flew*). When Rumelhart and McClelland determined their network's propensity for overregularization errors in these classes, they found less dramatic differences, but a similar ranking of the classes. However, class VI verbs were overregularized relatively less often than expected, and class VII verbs more often than expected. Rumelhart and McClelland noted that their simulation did not incorporate more subtle word-frequency differences within the medium-frequency verb class, and that this may have been responsible for the discrepancies. As for those aspects of the ranking that were replicated in the simulation, they made special note of the fact that Bybee and Slobin's own explanations focused on factors that were irrelevant in the simulation. They suggested that the actual explanations may have to do with other factors (ones that were incorporated in the simulation). For example, Bybee and Slobin had proposed that for certain classes of verbs (e.g., *fly*/*flew*) children have trouble matching up the present-tense form with its past-tense form. However, the two forms were always explicitly paired when presented to the network, and it made the same errors as the children. Rumelhart and McClelland focused their alternative explanation on the degree of similarity of the irregular past tense to the form stem + *ed* (the form obtained by overregularizing). Here is a case, then, in which the model suggests a hypothesis that conceivably would provide a superior account of the human data. Finally, Rumelhart and McClelland considered the time-course of the two types of overregularization errors: stem + *ed* (e.g., *comed*, *singed*) and past + *ed* (e.g., *camed*, *sanged*). Kuczaj's (1977) study of 15 children (2 at each six-month interval from 2 years 6 months to 5 years 6 months, plus 1 longitudinal) found that the latter error was most frequent in older children, and the model showed this effect as well. Early in stage 2 (epoch 11 on), the response strength for stem + *ed* was much greater than for past + *ed*. The response strength for stem + *ed* showed the steepest decline, however, so that in later epochs the error past + *ed* became strongest. In examining their data in further detail, Rumelhart and McClelland also noted that the response strength for past + *ed* errors differed across the various classes of irregular verbs. Thus, they made a prediction, which had not yet been tested, that a similar result would be found in human learning of the past tense.

As their last simulation, Rumelhart and McClelland tested the model on 86 low-frequency verbs on which it had not been trained in order to assess its ability to generalize. Overall, presenting these items to the input units resulted in activation of 92 percent of the appropriate Wickelfeatures on the output units for regular verbs, and 84 percent for irregular verbs. Rumelhart and McClelland wondered to what extent this good performance on Wickelfeatures could be carried through to Wickelphone representations and thence to production of the correct word (phoneme string). Therefore, on these items they tried out a version of their decoding/binding network which would freely generate responses. Instead of a competition among designated words, there was a competition among all relevant Wickelphones. To encourage production of actual words, pairs of Wickelphones that could be pieced together into phoneme strings received extra excitation from one another. (This procedure consumed considerable processing time, especially since it was run on computers of the early 1980s, and this was cited as the reason for not using it earlier. Wickelphones not needed for any of the verbs were excluded for the same reason.) Translating the Wickelphone representations into phoneme strings, it was then possible to calculate the response strength of each phoneme string generated. Rumelhart and McClelland adopted as a rule of thumb that only response strengths above 0.2 be regarded as relevant. Six of the 86 new low-frequency verbs generated no phoneme string that exceeded this level. The level was exceeded by exactly one string for 64 verbs, and by more than one string for an additional 13 verbs. Examining the 14 irregular verbs separately, in just one case was the past tense correctly produced and in two cases the correct form was one of two phoneme sequences achieving threshold. The rest of these verbs were either regularized or unchanged from the present tense. As for the 72 regular verbs, the correct response was generated to 48, and the correct response was one of two or three generated in 12 others. While this generalization is far from perfect, Rumelhart and McClelland took it as evidence that the basic principles for generating the past tense had been learned by the network. They noted that in a study with 5- and 6-year-olds, Berko (1958) found that they too were correct in generating the past tense of novel verbs 51 percent of the time and commented: "Thus, we see little reason to believe that our model's 'deficiencies' are significantly greater than those of native speakers of comparable experience" (Rumelhart and McClelland, 1986a, pp. 265–6).

On the basis of these experiments with their model, Rumelhart and McClelland contended that with a rather simple network and no explicit encoding of rules it is possible to simulate the important characteristics of the behavior of human children learning the English past tense, and that this network shows both that rules are not needed and that separate procedures are not required for the regular and irregular cases:

> We have, we believe, provided a distinct alternative to the view that children learn the rules of English past-tense formation in any explicit sense. We have shown that a reasonable account of the acquisition of past tense can be provided without recourse to the notion of a "rule" as anything more than a *description* of the language. We have

shown that, for this case, there is no *induction problem*. The child need not figure out what the rules are, nor even that there are rules. The child need not decide whether a verb is regular or irregular. There is no question as to whether the inflected form should be stored directly in the lexicon or derived from more general principles. There isn't even a question (as far as generating the past-tense form is concerned) as to whether a verb form is one encountered many times or one that is being generated for the first time. A uniform procedure is applied for producing the past-tense form in every case. The base form is supplied as input to the past-tense network and the resulting pattern of activation is interpreted as a phonological representation of the past form of that verb. This is the procedure whether the verb is regular or irregular, familiar or novel. (1986a, p. 267)

5.3 Pinker and Prince's Arguments for Rules

5.3.1 Overview of the critique of Rumelhart and McClelland's model

Steven Pinker and Alan Prince (1988) mounted an extensive critique of Rumelhart and McClelland's claims. They analyzed the past-tense model in detail "to determine whether the RM [Rumelhart and McClelland] model is viable as a theory of human language acquisition – there is no question that it is a valuable demonstration of some of the surprising things that PDP models are capable of, but our concern is whether it is an accurate model of children" (1988, p. 81). They concluded that it is not, and that rules indeed are necessary to give an adequate account of language and its acquisition.

Pinker and Prince's critique is long and multifaceted. It deserves to be read in its entirety for at least two reasons. First, it is an outstanding exemplar of its genre (that is, defense of the symbolic approach against the challenge of connectionism). Second, Pinker and Prince marshaled and organized an impressively broad array of linguistic analyses and acquisition data on past-tense formation in order to provide a framework for criticism of the Rumelhart and McClelland model. Their own summary of their objections is as follows:

- Rumelhart and McClelland's actual explanation of children's stages of regularization of the past tense morpheme is demonstrably incorrect.
- Their explanation for one striking type of childhood speech error is also incorrect.
- Their other apparent successes in accounting for developmental phenomena either have nothing to do with the model's parallel distributed processing architecture, and can easily be duplicated by symbolic models, or involve major confounds and hence do not provide clear support for the model.
- The model is incapable of representing certain kinds of words.
- It is incapable of explaining patterns of psychological similarity among words.
- It easily models many kinds of rules that are not found in any human language.
- It fails to capture central generalizations about English sound patterns.
- It makes false predictions about derivational morphology, compounding, and novel words.
- It cannot handle the elementary problem of homophony.
- It makes errors in computing the past tense forms of a large percentage of the words it is tested on.
- It fails to generate any past tense form at all for certain words.

- It makes incorrect predictions about the reality of the distinction between regular rules and exceptions in children and in languages.

(1988, p. 81)

Connectionists conceded many of the specific shortcomings identified by Pinker and Prince and addressed some of them in later models (see section 5.4). To get their demonstration under way, Rumelhart and McClelland had made certain simplifications and heuristic decisions which, while reasonable, were not immutable. As well, effective learning algorithms existed only for two-layer networks at the time they designed the model. The number of developmental phenomena that they squeezed out of this architecture provided an impressive demonstration that rules are not the only viable avenue of explanation. They did not account for everything, and Pinker and Prince identified many of the gaps.

Rumelhart and McClelland's original model and Pinker and Prince's critique have provided an enduring foundation for further work on past-tense acquisition. Each team in its own way raised the bar as to what would count as a successful model, and offered systematic accounts of past-tense formation that were unprecedented at the time in their scope and detail. What ensued was a highly polarized debate that has lasted longer, dug deeper, and ranged wider than anyone would have predicted at the outset.

We cannot discuss all of Pinker and Prince's objections and analyses here nor follow the entire debate. In the remainder of section 5.3 we provide a brief portrayal of three dimensions of their argument and some of the ways connectionists could respond. We focus first on their argument that Rumelhart and McClelland failed to do justice to important linguistic facts, and second on their argument that the network's behavior failed to adequately simulate human behavior. Third, we consider their claim that the shortcomings of the past-tense network are not fixable, but rather are generic failures that reflect intrinsic limitations of parallel distributed processing networks. (Particularly at the end of the paper they clarified that this gloomy assessment was limited to two-layer networks.) In section 5.4 we discuss recent models of past-tense acquisition, especially with respect to the issue of U-shaped learning and the role of input.

5.3.2　Putative linguistic inadequacies

In developing their contention that Rumelhart and McClelland failed to do justice to important aspects of linguistic analysis, Pinker and Prince began by noting the justification for positing rules in linguistic explanations:

> rules are generally invoked in linguistic explanations in order to factor a complex phenomenon into simpler components that feed representations into one another. Different types of rules apply to these intermediate representations, forming a cascade of structures and rule components. Rules are individuated not only because they *compete* and mandate different transformations of the same input structure (such as *break–breaked/broke*), but because they apply to different *kinds* of structures, and thus impose a factoring of a phenomenon into distinct components, rather than generating the phenomena in a single step mapping inputs to outputs. (1988, p. 84)

We should point out that the strategy of factoring complex phenomena into their components is not limited to linguistic theory or to rule-based theories in general.

Many advances in science, for example, have involved working out a particular decomposition, separately analyzing each component, and then figuring out how the components are assembled together into a functioning system. (Bechtel and Richardson, 1993, provided an extensive discussion of mechanistic models of biological systems obtained in this way.) Within the domain of language, both linguistic theories and connectionist theories specify a decomposition but, by design, these decompositions are quite different. For example, the connectionist decomposition is intended to be mechanistic in the sense just described, whereas a linguistic decomposition is abstract. The fundamental question is not whether to decompose, but rather what sort of decomposition is needed for particular purposes.

Many of Pinker and Prince's criticisms can be interpreted as arguments that Rumelhart and McClelland invoked the wrong decomposition. To begin with, Rumelhart and McClelland treated past-tense formation as though it were autonomous, whereas the same principles governing past-tense formation also figure in formation of the past perfect participle and the verbal adjective. Although there are different exceptions in each case, the similarities are sufficient to warrant a unified account. Moreover, there is a strong parallel between the three variants of the regular past tense (/əd/) after stems ending in alveolar stops /d/ or /t/, and elsewhere /d/ after a voiced obstruent, and /t/ after a voiceless one) and the three regular ways of forming plurals, third person singulars, and possessives (/əz/ after stems ending in sibilants like /s/ and /z/, elsewhere /z/ after voiced obstruents and /s/ after voiceless ones). Pinker and Prince maintained that the similarity is due to general phonetic factors, a consideration that is lost when one develops a separate network to handle past-tense formation. Hence, in their view Rumelhart and McClelland made the wrong sort of decomposition of linguistic knowledge.

Pinker and Prince argued that further linguistic injustice was perpetrated by the use of Wickelphones and Wickelfeatures. The first problem is that they work imperfectly; specifically, they fail to give an unambiguous encoding of all phoneme sequences, they miss generalizations such as the similarity of *slit* and *silt*, and they do not exclude phonological rules that are alien to human languages (e.g., inverting the order of the phonemes in the verb). Pinker and Prince acknowledged that Rumelhart and McClelland had themselves noted that their coding scheme was adequate to their purpose, but imperfect; however, Pinker and Prince regarded this research strategy as somewhat alien from their own, more linguistic perspective.[7]

> The Wickelfeature structure is not some kind of approximation that can easily be sharpened and refined; it is categorically the wrong kind of thing for the jobs assigned to it. At the same time, the Wickelphone or something similar is demanded by the most radically distributed forms of distributed representations, which resolve order relations (like concatenation) into unordered sets of features. Without the Wickelphone, Rumelhart and McClelland have no account about how phonological strings are to be analyzed for significant patterning.   (1988, p. 101)

Pinker and Prince also pointed out a second problem with Wickelphones: these units are limited to encoding phonemic information, whereas the past-tense system must utilize syntactic, semantic, and morphological information as well. One particularly interesting example involves verbs that are derived from the nominalization of an existing verb (see Kim, Pinker, Prince, and Prasada, 1991). For example, the verb *fly out* as used in baseball is derived from the noun *fly ball* which in turn is derived from the irregular verb *fly*. Because of the intermediate nominal form, *fly out* functions like other verbs derived from nouns in that it takes a regular past tense. Thus, just as we say he *righted* the boat, we say he *flied out*, not he *flew out* (although in performance errors do occur). Pinker and Prince maintained that this is a regular feature of English grammar and thus that formation of the proper past tense requires knowledge of the lexical item, not just a phonemic representation. Moreover, the regularity itself must be expressed by a rule; they claimed that only via rules can we keep different bodies of information separate, and yet bring them to bear on one another when required. Rumelhart and McClelland's connectionist model is limited to encoding patterns of association between input and output representations, and therefore cannot utilize and coordinate the various kinds of abstract information that are necessary to account for linguistic competence.

They cited a third failure to respect linguistic facts: the same network is used to learn variations within both the regular and the irregular past-tense forms, but linguistically these are quite different. The choice among the three forms of the regular past tense is based upon phonological principles, is predictable, and therefore can be expressed in general rules. The varieties of irregular stems, in contrast, exhibit a family resemblance structure at best. Their mappings on to past-tense forms are not sufficiently predictable to avoid having to memorize them. The Rumelhart and McClelland model, however, makes no such principled distinction; it applies a single mechanism to both regular and irregular verbs.

To these specific linguistic objections, a connectionist might respond as follows. (1) The past tense was isolated because it was premature to include related phenomena in the same model. (Also, it is not obvious which linguistic generalizations should, or should not, be accounted for within the same psychological mechanism or component.) (2) The decision to focus on phonological representations (at the levels of Wickelfeatures and Wickelphones) exemplified the subsymbolic approach to modeling: phenomena at one level (e.g., acquisition of past-tense morphology) are best understood in terms of mechanistic models at a lower level (here, phonological features). The addition of lexical, syntactic, and other higher-level constraints might improve accuracy somewhat in a later model but is of secondary importance. (3) The particular kind of phonological representation that was chosen (context-sensitive Wickelfeatures) was a clever solution to the problem of representing order in a network, but more general solutions will need to be found if the connectionist program is to advance. As already noted, coarse coding across those features worked well enough to achieve appropriate generalization in the past-tense task but not in a reading-aloud task. (4) The fact that regular and irregular past-tense formation were carried out by a single mechanism is at the heart of Rumelhart and McClelland's project. Instead of strictly dividing verbs into regular and irregular classes that get treated quite differently in the grammar (but the same within each class), their network extracts whatever regularities are in its training set. These lie on a somewhat lumpy continuum, ranging from those of broadest applicability (the three variations on adding -*ed*) through subregularities of various scope, to micro-subregularities, to a very small number of unique mappings like *go* → *went*. Linguistic accounts serve somewhat different purposes than mechanistic (processing) accounts, and each must be judged on criteria relevant to its purposes. Even assuming that a decomposition into two classes is most appropriate at the linguistic level, that should not be taken as an instruction to build two dissimilar mechanisms into a model at the processing level. The connectionist model must be judged on such grounds as whether it generates behavior that is sufficiently similar to human data on acquisition or processing. We now turn to Pinker and Prince's second line of criticism, which addressed that question.

5.3.3 Putative behavioral inadequacies

Pinker and Prince's second line of criticism involved examining in detail the operation of the Rumelhart and McClelland model and arguing that at just those crucial points where the model is thought to capture important elements of human behavior, it either fails or it succeeds for the wrong reason. One example is Rumelhart and McClelland's success in simulating a U-shaped acquisition function, in which verbs with correct past-tense forms during stage 1 were sometimes overregularized during stage 2. Pinker and Prince attributed this result to characteristics of the input (in particular, discontinuities between stages 1 and 2) rather than the connectionist architecture. We will return to this point in the discussion of U-shaped learning functions in section 5.4.

Another example emerged when Pinker and Prince assessed the ability of the model to generalize to new cases, that is, the 72 test verbs that Rumelhart and McClelland presented to the model after it completed training on the initial set of 420 verbs. They interpreted the poor performance on some of these test cases as indicating the basic inadequacy of connectionist models. First, they focused on the fact that the network offered no above-threshold response to six verbs (*jump, pump, soak, warm, trail,* and *glare*), attributing this to the fact that the network had not been trained on any sufficiently similar verbs from which it could generalize. They argued that to generalize to any new verb, not just ones similar to the training set, requires a system of rules. Roughly, morphological rules would add the past-tense morpheme to the verb stem, and phonological rules would then determine which of the three phonetic variants was appropriate to the context. Second, they examined cases in which the network offered the incorrect past tense (although 91 percent of the verbs with at least one above-threshold response had the correct past-tense form as one response or the only response). They emphasized that a few of the errors were bizarre (e.g., *tour/toureder, mail/membled,* and *brown/brawned*). Pinker and Prince contended that a human, treating irregulars as specially learned exceptions, would initially form regular past tenses for all new cases, regular or irregular, and thus would not make these errors. But the Rumelhart and McClelland network seemed to be trying to use some of the regularities discovered in the already-learned exceptions to handle new cases as well. Thus, Pinker and Prince commented,

> Well before it has mastered the richly exemplified regular rule, the pattern-associator appears to have gained considerable confidence in certain incorrectly-grasped, sparsely exemplified patterns of feature-change among the vowels. This implies that a major "induction problem" – latching on to the productive patterns and bypassing the spurious ones – is not being solved successfully. . . .
>
> What we have here is not a model of the mature system. (1988, p. 125)

Returning to their task of contrasting the model's behavior to that of children, Pinker and Prince also worked through the model's performance on subregularities (such as different classes of irregular verbs) and its simulation of children's blends (the past + *ed* error, which blends a correct vowel change with a suffix added via overregularization, e.g., *come/camed*). The discussion is too detailed to summarize here, but the general theme is the same: rather than focusing on the considerable extent to which the model reproduces phenomena observed in children, they focused on the discrepancies that were duly reported by Rumelhart and McClelland as points to consider if an improved version of the model were to be designed.

5.3.4   Do the inadequacies reflect inherent limitations of PDP networks?

Pinker and Prince argued that, although some of the specific discrepancies between predicted and observed performance might be eliminated by tinkering with the existing past-tense network, for the most part they are due to inherent limitations of PDP networks (by which they meant two-layer networks for parallel distributed processing). Connectionists would agree that the work Pinker and Prince wanted the model to do, such as incorporating lexical constraints, would require a more elaborate architecture than the one that was available to Rumelhart and McClelland.

Connectionist modeling was advancing rapidly around the time that Rumelhart and McClelland's past-tense model was published, yielding a variety of elaborations within 5 or 10 years. Most important, connectionists were quick to take advantage of the additional computational power of hidden layers when the backpropagation learning procedure became available (Rumelhart, Hinton, and Williams, 1986a, 1986b). These additional layers can be viewed as imposing particular factorings (decompositions) and transformations of the information in the input layer. Also, modular architectures offer subnetworks for specialized processing and pathways for combining their outputs, an approach we will illustrate in chapters 7 and 10. In principle, this would be a good way to incorporate nonphonological sources of constraint in past-tense formation. The newer past-tense models discussed in section 5.4.3 incorporate hidden layers and backpropagation but not modular architecture.

Other advances have had no direct connection to network architectures. For example, it is important to know the actual input to the child's past-tense system, taking into account possible roles for comprehension and filtering mechanisms. Early in the debate about the past tense no one had enough information to do this properly (including Pinker and Prince, who relied solely on observed frequencies of production in formulating claims about input to the past-tense system). One benefit of the intense debate over past-tense acquisition is that more adequate information about the input to children has been gathered.

In the end, Pinker and Prince acknowledged that more powerful connectionist architectures might be adequate to produce a model that meets all of their criteria. However, they noted that no one had yet built such a model, so its success was hypothetical. Also, they echoed Fodor and Pylyshyn (1988) in asserting that if someone did build the model, it "may be nothing more than an implementation of a symbolic rule-based account" (1988, p. 182). They expressed doubt that the model would diverge enough from mere implementation of standard grammars to "call for a revised understanding of language" (1988, p. 183), and exhibited little curiosity as to whether they were correct in this negative assessment.

In the 1980s, this difference in curiosity and excitement about networks was probably what most fundamentally divided connectionists from their critics. Connectionists were drawn by a promising unknown territory, whereas symbolic theorists focused on the often elegant ways in which traditional theories had already addressed a considerable body of existing knowledge. In the 1990s debate continued, but some symbolic theorists made limited room for networks within their overall accounts. As noted in section 1.5, Prince became more open to the idea that networks would provide a useful level of analysis as implementations of symbolic accounts (eliminating the "mere" from Fodor and Pylyshyn's "mere implementation" characterization). Also, Pinker decided that associative mechanisms like networks provided a better account of the behavioral data on exceptions than did lexical look-up (section 5.4.1 and footnote 3). Coltheart, Rastle, Perry, Langdon, and Ziegler (2001) made a similar modification to their dual-route model for tasks like reading aloud (section 10.2.3.4). For their part, connectionists moved to less exotic architectures (eliminating Wickelfeatures and coarse coding but adding backpropagation). They used these new models to address criticisms regarding the role of input in producing a U-shaped developmental function for some irregular verbs. We now turn to this issue, which took center stage as the debate over past-tense formation continued into the 1990s and beyond.

5.4   Accounting for the U-shaped Learning Function

In presenting their past-tense model, Rumelhart and McClelland (1986a) acknowledged certain respects in which their training procedure departed from children's experience with verbs. First, the stem and the past-tense form were paired during training, whereas it might be expected that a child usually hears just one form of the verb at a time. Second, the transition from stage 1 to stage 2 was somewhat artificially created by presenting the network first with a small number of verbs, mostly irregular, and then a much larger set of verbs, mostly regular. Rumelhart and McClelland tried to justify this last procedure by arguing that children learn the past tense of those verbs for which they have already mastered the present tense, and that the progression from a small set of verbs to a much larger set roughly corresponds in timing to the overall vocabulary growth spurt that is a typical developmental milestone. They commented that "the actual transition in a child's vocabulary of verbs would appear quite abrupt on a time-scale of years so that our assumptions about abruptness of onset may not be too far off the mark" (p. 241).

In their critique, Pinker and Prince (1988) argued that the model's U-shaped acquisition curve for irregular verbs should be attributed to the discontinuity in its input, not to any intrinsic characteristic of learning in connectionist networks. The uncontested part of their argument is that the model's entry into stage 2 (in which irregulars are sometimes overregularized) was precipitated by the addition of the 410 mediumfrequency verbs (82 percent of which were *regular*) to the original training set of ten high-frequency verbs (80 percent of which were *irregular*). The controversial part is what to make of this. Two separate issues are involved. First, are the input conditions under which children exhibit U-shaped learning so different as to undercut the usefulness of the existing simulation (section 5.4.1)? Second, under what range of input conditions can networks exhibit a U-shaped acquisition curve (sections 5.4.2 and 5.4.3)?

5.4.1 The role of input for children

The onset of stage 2 is marked by several discontinuities (relatively sudden changes) in children's production of past-tense forms. The onset of overregularization errors on previously correct irregulars (the downwards part of the U-shaped function) is part of a new tendency towards marking the past tense when required; hence, correct formation of the past tense for both irregular and regular verbs is increasing as well. The question is whether this package of discontinuities in past-tense formation is precipitated by discontinuities in the input to the past-tense mechanism, for example, the number of new verb stems or the proportion that are regular. Both adult and child corpora can be examined for discontinuities, with the caveat that it is unclear which of these best approximates the actual input getting submitted to the child's internal past-tense mechanism at a given point in time.

There is considerably more quantitative information now than in 1986, but Pinker and Prince (1988, pp. 139–42) compiled what was known at the time. One key measure is the percentage of verbs in a corpus that are regular versus irregular. Slobin (1971) made this count for adult speech to children (the initial input to the overall language-acquisition mechanism), and Pinker and Prince themselves made a count for children's own speech (since this roughly indicates what part of the adult verb vocabulary has survived the child's filtering for salience, pronounceability, etc.). Both child and adult measures were obtained prior to and during overregularization using transcripts of Adam, Eve, and Sarah from Roger Brown (1973) and his collaborators. Counting vocabulary items (number of different verbs in a speech sample, sometimes called *verb types*), the percentage of verbs that were regular was very close to 50 percent throughout the period examined. However, individual regular verbs tend to be used less frequently than irregular verbs. Hence, when the count was made using *verb tokens* (each occurrence of any regular or irregular verb in a speech sample), far fewer than 50 percent were regular.

Marcus, Ullman, Pinker, Hollander, Rosen, and Xu (1992) provided an extensive review and new calculations on transcripts that had been entered into the ChiLDES electronic database (longitudinal corpora for Adam, Eve, Sarah, and seven other children within an approximate age range of 2–5 years plus samples from each of 15 children at 4 years 6 months to 5 years and aggregate data from 58 additional children in the range 1 year 6 months to 6 years 6 months). One point they made was that the proportion of children's verbs that were regular had been underestimated by Pinker and Prince's procedure of making direct counts on small samples. When a statistical technique used in biology to estimate population sizes from multiple samples was applied by Marcus et al. to the corpora from Adam and Sarah, once cumulative vocabulary reached about 150 verbs (at roughly 30 months), estimated regular verb types began to outnumber estimated irregular verb types, reaching about two-thirds regular within the next 12–18 months. (Eve showed a less dramatic increase beginning as early as 22 months.) Using cumulative verbs as a more direct (but more liberal) measure, the percentage of regulars grew to 73 (Adam) or 74 percent (Sarah) at 62 months and was still increasing. There was no sudden spurt in this percentage nor in cumulative verb vocabulary preceding the onset of overregularization, however, nor was there any systematic change in the percentage of tokens that were regular (between 20 and 45 percent in most sessions, averaging 31 percent before and 32 percent after overregularization for Adam and Sarah).[8]

Marcus et al. also calculated this last measure for parents and other adults speaking with Adam, Eve, and Sarah and found it to be quite stable: 25–30 percent in most sessions. Having found no discontinuities in any of these measures (the best available approximations of the input to the past-tense mechanism), Marcus et al. inferred that input discontinuities cannot be what precipitate overregularization and other stage 2 changes in children. Therefore, they concluded, Rumelhart and McClelland's discontinuous input to their network model was an inappropriate way to achieve its U-shaped learning curve for irregular verbs.

What, then, triggers stage 2? Within the symbolic tradition, the abruptness of the onset of regularization is explained by positing that a rule has been induced. Given the lack of corresponding abrupt changes in input, along with the fact that the past-tense form of some irregular verbs is learned prior to stage 2, Pinker and Prince suggested that the mechanism that induces the rule is turned off during stage 1 and works efficiently enough to quickly trigger stage 2 once it is turned on. The memory system that learns individual forms would already be functioning during stage 1 and would continue to be responsible for correct irregular forms after stage 2 begins. To explain the quick onset of overregularization errors in stage 2, affecting even some of the previously correct irregular verbs (the downward part of the U-shaped function), Marcus et al. suggested that memory retrieval of an irregular past-tense form blocks application of the rule, but that retrieval sometimes fails. The frequency with which retrieval failed for different words was ascribed to properties of associative retrieval from a network-like memory, replacing the earlier notion of a simple lexical look-up.

The retrieval failure explanation receives some of its support from the fact that overregularizations are rare for high-frequency verbs, which presumably have the strongest memory encodings. Other support comes from Marcus et al.'s claim that overregularization continues for years at a low overall rate of occurrence. An often-cited figure from their study is that less than 5 percent of irregular tokens get regularized overall. Specifically, they averaged the individual overregularization rates of 25 children, obtaining a mean of 4.2 percent and median of 2.5 percent. Even individual sessions rarely exceeded 30 percent. However, when certain questionable data were excluded (e.g., children with less than 100 past-tense tokens, sessions at the ends of the age range or pre-overregularization, and the verbs *have*, *be*, *do*, and *get*), the mean increased to 10 percent and the median to 9 percent (range 3.6 to 24.0 percent, $N = 6$). The child with an overregularization rate of 24 percent, Abe, was from a larger study by Kuczaj (1977) for which the methodology apparently contributed to higher overregularization rates than other studies (e.g., parents rather than researchers made the recordings and sometimes sought to encourage use of past-tense forms).

One problem is that these two sources of support for the retrieval failure hypothesis are confounded. High-frequency verbs have disproportionate influence when overregularization rates are computed on tokens, but it is exactly those verbs that exhibit the lowest rates. For example, Adam's 7 highest-frequency irregular verbs (of 55 total) were each used correctly more than 100 times but overregularized only 1.3 times on average. Hence, to judge the prevalence of overregularization it is important to count the number of different vocabulary items that get overregularized in addition to calculating overregularization rates on tokens. Marcus et al. discussed some of the methodological issues involved and (in appendix tables A5–A9) tabulated correct and overregularized tokens for each verb separately for Adam, Eve, Sarah, and Abe, and provided summary data for the other 21 children. However, they focused their own analysis of these data on verbs with 10 or more tokens (histograms showing the number of these verbs at each overregularization rate are on pp. 48–9). Marchman and Bates (1994), in contrast, used all of the verbs in tables A5–A9 to calculate that on average 17 percent of a child's irregular verbs were regularized at least once.

This figure is more suggestive of the scope of overregularization than the histograms or 4.2 percent figure based on tokens from Marcus et al. – but even it underestimates the role of overregularization during the prime preschool years. We have recalculated from the same appendix that for the 6 children remaining after exclusions, the average was 43 percent (or 34 percent if Abe is also excluded), in contrast to Marcus et al.'s average of 10 percent for these 6 children based on tokens. The average calculated by Marchman and Bates across 25 children was only 17 percent because the 19 children excluded from our calculation overregularized very few of their verbs: 15 percent for the 4 youngest children (whose ages at the last session were in the range 2 years 8 months to 3 years 1 month) and 7 percent for the 15 children at 4 years 6 months to 5 years.

Among these overregularized verbs, our calculations indicated that mixed use was typical: approximately 70 percent were correct sometimes and overregularized at other times (across a median of about six tokens per verb for the six key children). Of the remaining 30 percent, most had just one token (and none more than four), so the lack of correct responses could reflect either limited opportunity or lack of knowledge. Information on whether use was mixed within sessions or across certain age ranges could not be obtained from the appendix.

Marchman and Bates (1994) filled in some remaining gaps in the data and also contested some of Marcus et al.'s claims. Most important, they contributed their own new estimates based on cross-sectional parental report data from the *MacArthur Communicative Development Inventory (CDI)*. Advantages of this method include parental access to much larger samples of the child's speech than in a taping session and a lower age range that extended from early stage 1 through early stage 2 (16–30 months, with 51–261 children per month totalling 1,130 children). However, only vocabulary items (not tokens) could be tabulated, and these were limited to the 57 regular and 46 irregular verbs on the vocabulary checklist. More detailed responses on past-tense formation were requested for only 16 of the 46 irregular verbs and even these were subject to imperfect recall by parents. Despite these limitations, when they focused on the ages that overlapped between the two studies (27–30 months), Marchman and Bates got results similar to those of Marcus et al. Specifically, they obtained a similar percentage of verbs currently in the child's vocabulary that were regular (53–56 percent) and of irregular verb types that were overregularized (somewhere between 17 and 21 percent, based on their figure 3, which is consistent with the four youngest children in Marcus et al.'s study).[9] Thus, using parent report data permitted an independent confirmation of these two results from naturalistic data.

However, Marchman and Bates were more interested in the nonlinearity of changes in the number of forms: beginning around 24 months the number of stem-only irregular verbs leveled off and declined while the number marked for past tense accelerated. They attributed this to attainment of a critical mass of verb types (approximately 70 verbs). Using data from their full age range (16–30 months) to plot past-tense form as a function of total number of verbs – a measure which itself increases linearly – they found that both correct and overgeneralized irregulars increased slowly at vocabulary sizes of about 10–69 verbs and then more rapidly. This nonlinearity was important to their argument for a single-mechanism connectionist account (section 5.4.3). They also confirmed the general developmental trend of stem-only followed by gradual attainment of correct irregulars and (at some delay for most children) a smaller number of overgeneralized irregulars.

Marchman and Bates also helped to fill an important gap in previous reports by showing that vocabulary tallies look different for children in early stage 1. Regular verbs were just 38 percent of the verbs reported for 16-month-olds and gradually increased until they leveled off around 50 percent at 22 months; they did not rise above 50 percent until 27 months. The findings were even clearer when broken down by number of verbs rather than age: regular verbs were 38 percent of the verbs for children with fewer than 10 verbs, 48 percent at 10–19 verbs, 52 percent at 20–59 verbs, and rose slowly thereafter to 55 percent (the ceiling using this checklist). Thus, at the time they learn their earliest verbs, children are especially attentive to irregulars, presumably due to a coalition of factors including high token frequency in adult speech, semantic salience, and phonological simplicity. This is generally consistent with our own calculation on a limited amount of published naturalistic data (Bechtel and Abrahamsen, 1991, p. 196): less than 50 percent of the verbs in their vocabularies were regular for (a) three of the four single-word speakers for whom Nelson (1973) reported 50-word vocabularies that included at least five verbs; and (b) both of the early multi-word speakers for whom Bloom (1970) listed vocabularies that included fewer than 60 verbs. (These were Allison and Peter, two of the four children excluded from Marcus et al.'s follow-up analysis and our calculation due to their young ages; they used 14 and 34 of the verb types included in appendix A9, respectively.) However, Bloom's third child already had 93 verbs, and consistent with Marchman and Bates, more than 50 percent were regular.

If the mechanism that learns stem–past tense mappings has been turned on already during stage 1 (contrary to Marcus et al.'s suggestion), and if it attends primarily to pairs for which the child already produces the stem (or rarely, just the past-tense form), then the above results indicate that irregular verbs initially predominate in its input. In this scenario, the mechanism would not yet be involved in controlling the production of verbs; its learning would initially be receptive and perhaps Hebbian. That is, some other mechanism would control the child's production of verbs. Some of the child's verbs could then serve as input to the mechanism (as could parental utterances of those verbs) on just those occasions when they are paired with the outputs needed for Hebbian learning. For example, if a child says "Dog eat bone" and the parent responds "Oh, it ate the bone!" the child's past-tense network may accept the pair and adjust its weights without producing any observable past-tense form. (See Bohannon and Stanowicz, 1988, for evidence that children frequently get these kinds of pairings within a child–parent exchange and Hirsh-Pasek and Golinkoff, 1996, for evidence that children can use grammatical devices in comprehension that they do not yet produce, including sensitivity to certain functors by 23–28 months.) Initially the stem–past tense pairs would be learned receptively as arbitrary mappings, but as larger numbers of regular verbs are included in the input during late stage 1 the network might begin to generalize the regular mappings. During this period, the child's overt verb productions increasingly would include regular verb stems. Because these would be uninflected forms, it would be clear that they were not yet under the control of the past-tense mechanism.

Again we meet the question of what pushes the child into stage 2. Within our speculative account, the maturing past-tense mechanism must now become involved in controlling verb production. What might cause this shift? Several developmental theorists have emphasized the idea that certain developmental advances involve the coordination of competencies that had previously developed separately (e.g., Acredolo and Goodwyn, 1990; Bates, Bretherton, and Snyder, 1988). This insight is readily applied to our problem. Producing past-tense forms in appropriate contexts would seem to require at least: (1) a variety of mechanisms for planning and producing utterances more generally; among these may be mechanisms for recruiting knowledge that was gained receptively; (2) receptive knowledge of past-tense formation for some number of verbs; (3) ability to distinguish between past and present time; and (4) knowledge of the semantics and pragmatics of the past tense. All of these would be incomplete and imperfect at the onset of stage 2.

The available data do not tell us whether stage 2 awaits only the coordination of the imperfect parts, or whether the coordination itself is awaiting minimal attainment of one or more of those parts. The data do tell us, however, that the child's acquisition of additional verbs is rapidly progressing, and that regular verbs overtake irregular verbs before the onset of stage 2. Hence, Rumelhart and McClelland's claim that changes in these two factors determine the forms used for the past tense at each stage remains quite plausible. The stronger claim that these changes (and their effects on a single network) are the primary *cause* of transition from stage 1 to stage 2 is harder to evaluate. Rumelhart and McClelland's training regimen may best be viewed as a convenient way to set up initially correct performance on a few irregular verbs, so that a reversal could then be observed in stage 2. Their simplification would be justified by lack of knowledge about what really was happening, and by the inadvisability of building a more complete model at such an early stage of network research. More detailed analysis of child acquisition data is one avenue for assessing the alternatives; exploring the behavior of networks under a variety of input conditions is another. In particular, Pinker and Prince's critique of the discontinuity (abrupt change) in Rumelhart and McClelland's input has been evaluated by providing networks with continuous input and observing the outcome. The next two sections describe explorations of this type.

5.4.2   The role of input for networks: The rule of 78 revisited

McClelland and Rumelhart (1988, p. 118) suggested that the rule of 78 simulation set up for their **pa** (pattern associator) program could easily be modified to provide an exploratory look at input conditions under which U-shaped learning curves can be obtained. In particular, learning curves for continuous input could be examined by presenting cases (pairs of input–output patterns) on an incremental schedule. We did this as follows. We began by training the network on just two cases (subset A), then added two more cases (subset B) so that training continued on four cases, then added two more cases (subset C), then four more cases (subset D), and finally eight more cases (subset E). By this last interval, all 18 patterns were in the training schedule. For each subset, half of the cases were left unaltered (so that they followed the rule of 78) and half were transformed into exceptions by altering two or three of the eight binary digits. As is evident in table 5.3, the exceptions were quite varied.

Table 5.3   Regular and exceptional patterns added after certain epochs

Subset	Epoch	Case[a]	Input Pattern	Desired Output[b]
A	0	*P147	10010010	10010010
		P258	01001001	01001010
B	20	*P357	00101010	01001001
		P368	00100101	00100110
C	40	*P248	01010001	01001110
		P148	10010001	10010010
D	60	*P158	10001001	10001101
		*P367	00100110	00110001
		P347	00110010	00110001
		P157	10001010	10001001
E	100	*P167	10000110	00100101
		*P247	01010010	01001001
		*P267	01000110	01000110
		*P348	00110001	10010010
		P168	10000101	10000110
		P257	01001010	01001001
		P268	01000101	01000110
		P358	00101001	00101010

[a] Irregular patterns noted with asterisk.
[b] Irregularities are underlined.

The weight matrices after learning subsets A–C (six cases) are shown in the top half of table 5.4. It can be seen that there was no systematic structure in the weights that would directly show that the regularities imposed by the rule had been extracted; yet the network performed quite well on all six cases. This illustrates that when there are few enough cases relative to the size of the network, each case can be learned separately as though it were an arbitrary mapping. The percentage of rule-following versus exceptional cases has no real impact, because the network is able to minimize error without extracting the regularities that the rule imposes. The behavior of the network at this point in training is comparable to that of the past-tense network during stage 1 (when it was learning to form the past tense for just eight irregular and two regular verbs). It is the small number of cases that matters, not the percentage that are exceptional.

After subset D had been learned as well (making a total of five regular and five irregular patterns), the weights began to show evidence of systematic structure similar to that in the earlier simulation (cf. table 5.2). As can be seen by examining the weights, this structure became even clearer after all 18 patterns had been made available for learning. At this stage (epoch 140) the network also showed a strong tendency to overregularize. Rather than examining actual outputs, which were determined by a stochastic function, we focused on the tendency of an output unit to be active as indicated by the net input to the unit. We classified as an error any case in which at least one output unit had a net input that would result in a probability of error greater than 0.40. Of the nine regular patterns, three had errors; just one had a probability greater than 0.50. All nine of the irregular patterns, however, produced errors; eight were overregularization errors. (Of these, the probability of error was

Table 5.4 Rule of 78 network trained with exceptions

	Input unit			Output unit				
	1	*2*	*3*	*4*	*5*	*6*	*7*	*8*
(A)	**Weights after 60 epochs**							
1	32	− 22	− 24	22	− 28	− 8	2	− 16
2	− 20	26	4	− 8	32	− 14	2	8
3	− 14	− 20	10	− 20	− 24	20	− 24	0
4	28	− 26	− 20	16	− 26	− 8	4	− 22
5	− 26	36	− 10	− 12	40	− 28	− 2	2
6	− 24	− 2	10	0	− 34	18	− 22	6
7	26	18	− 12	26	− 10	16	− 2	34
8	− 22	− 26	16	− 22	4	− 14	8	− 40
(B)	**Weights after 140 epochs**							
	1	*2*	*3*	*4*	*5*	*6*	*7*	*8*
1	64	− 62	− 28	28	− 10	− 44	− 30	4
2	− 58	72	− 24	− 14	24	− 20	10	− 20
3	− 20	− 52	42	− 32	− 26	28	− 2	− 28
4	2	− 68	30	52	− 66	− 22	− 8	− 28
5	− 26	34	− 16	− 12	80	− 76	− 4	− 4
6	14	12	− 44	− 34	− 30	46	− 36	18
7	8	12	− 8	28	− 42	26	− 36	48
8	− 4	− 14	8	− 28	36	− 18	32	− 42

greater than 0.50 for five patterns.) Thus, the network's tendency to extract and overgeneralize a rule to exceptional cases seems to be robust, even when only half of the cases fully exhibit the rule. This suggests that the past-tense network might have learned the regular past tense and overgeneralized it to irregulars in stage 2 even without an abrupt change in its input. Conclusive evidence could be obtained only by experimenting with the past-tense network itself, of course. Plunkett and Marchman targeted this goal by experimenting with a different past tense network, as discussed in the next section. (It is placed in the broader context of connectionist approaches to language acquisition by Plunkett, 1995, and McLeod, Plunkett, and Rolls, 1998, chapter 9.)

5.4.3 Plunkett and Marchman's simulations of past-tense acquisition

Plunkett and Marchman (1991) carried out an extensive series of simulations of past-tense acquisition in which they presented a complete set of training cases across all 50 epochs of training (rather than "priming" the network with a high proportion of irregulars in the first few epochs). Hence, not only was there no abrupt change in the input, there was no change at all, creating less favorable input conditions for U-shaped learning than in fact are offered to children. Nevertheless, they obtained

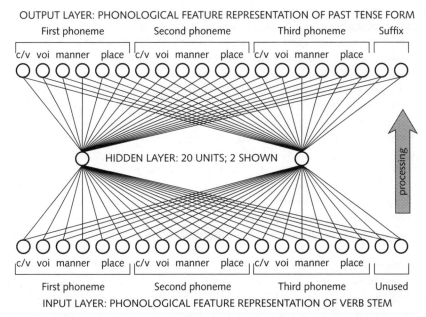

OUTPUT LAYER: PHONOLOGICAL FEATURE REPRESENTATION OF PAST TENSE FORM

First phoneme   Second phoneme   Third phoneme   Suffix

c/v voi manner place c/v voi manner place c/v voi manner place

HIDDEN LAYER: 20 UNITS; 2 SHOWN

processing

c/v voi manner place c/v voi manner place c/v voi manner place

First phoneme   Second phoneme   Third phoneme   Unused

INPUT LAYER: PHONOLOGICAL FEATURE REPRESENTATION OF VERB STEM

Figure 5.4 Plunkett and Marchman's (1991) network for forming the past tense of artificial verb stems. The three phonemes in each stem are encoded using position-specific phonological feature representations. Irregular verbs undergo an arbitrary, identity, or vowel change transformation, and regular verbs get a suffix added on output units 19–20. Layers of units are fully connected with each other, but only 2 of the 20 hidden units and their connections are shown.

U-shaped learning curves for individual verbs and for three classes of irregular verbs. (These more localized *micro U-shaped* areas of the learning curve occurred at multiple times and at different points in training for each class, so when results for all verbs were averaged no global U-shaped curve emerged.)

All of Plunkett and Marchman's simulations used a backpropagation learning procedure in a three-layer network of 20 units per layer, as shown in figure 5.4. It was trained on artificial "verb stems" that were three phonemes in length (two consonants and one vowel). All were phonologically possible in English and could have the vowel in any position (e.g., /erk/); some also happened to correspond to actual English verb stems (e.g., /mEt/). A phonological feature encoding of each stem was provided using six binary input units per phoneme: one for consonant/vowel, one for voiced/unvoiced, two for manner of articulation, and two for place of articulation. This required 18 units on the input layer, so the two leftover units were clamped off. The output layer was similarly arranged, except that units 19 and 20 were used for a nonphonological encoding of the three forms of the regular past-tense suffix. Hence, on units 1 through 18 there was a distributed encoding of the symbols (artificial verbs) across subsymbols (phonological features). This encoding was considerably less distributed than the coarse coding across Wickelfeatures used by Rumelhart and McClelland, but a hidden layer allowed for re-encoding the input patterns (an option not available to Rumelhart and McClelland, who built and trained their pattern associator model before the development of backpropagation). Hence, they obtained good generalization with a much smaller network; this enabled them to run a large number of simulations in order to compare the consequences of various input conditions.

In almost all of Plunkett and Marchman's simulations, four different types of input–output cases were intermixed in training. They were designed to emulate classes of regular and irregular English verbs, and can be illustrated using English examples. The first type was the regular past tense (appropriate suffix is added to stem based on three classes of stem-final phonemes, as in *add/added, play/played,* and *walk/walked*). The irregular types were: arbitrary mapping (unrelated stem and past-tense form, as in *go/went* or *am/was*); identity mapping (past tense is identical to stem, as in *hit/hit*); and vowel change (vowel of stem is changed according to one of eleven patterns, as in *blow/blew, meet/met, rise/rose,* etc.).

What differentiated among the large number of simulations was the type and token frequencies of each of the four classes of training cases. As a simplification, Rumelhart and McClelland had assumed a type-to-token ratio of one. This decision has been criticized, because the type-to-token ratio is generally lower for irregular than for regular verbs. That is, each irregular vocabulary item (type) is used frequently (yields many tokens, so the type-to-token ratio is much lower than one), whereas many regular vocabulary items in a corpus appear just once (a type-to-token ratio of one). Bever (1991) speculated that the network would have learned only the irregulars if more realistic type-to-token ratios had been used, and Pinker and Prince wondered whether more extended training on the initial ten verbs would have "burned in the 8 irregulars so strongly that they would never be overregularized in Phase 2" (1988, p. 142). Plunkett and Marchman (1991) sought to reply to these critics by providing their network with a steady diet of verbs, varying the type-to-token ratios in that diet across a large number of simulations but not within the same simulation. (Hence, no single simulation had a realistic change in amount and composition of input across time, as would a child's past-tense network.)

Plunkett and Marchman's results are not easily summarized. In simulations for which 74 percent or more of the tokens were *irregular*, approximating stage 1 input, regular verbs were overwhelmed and not learned. (Performance on irregular verbs depended upon the type-to-token ratio that was used – few types with many tokens was best – and on whether phonologically marked subclasses were included.) In simulations for which 74 percent or more of the tokens were *regular*, regulars were learned well; now it was irregulars that were overwhelmed and not learned. Children are never exposed to this kind of input. However, the two sets of simulations together demonstrate that networks are sensitive to their training regimens. If dissimilar responses (e.g., irregular vowel change versus regular suffixization) are required to rather similar input patterns (stems), the network will minimize error by learning the more frequent response.

In several simulations (in what they called their *Parent* series), approximately 45 to 50 percent of the tokens (but only 18 percent of the types) were irregular, a situation that better approximates the input to children's past-tense learning mechanisms during stage 2 (but the 410 regular verbs each had just one token; it would be even more realistic to have more tokens of fewer regular types). In these simulations the class of arbitrary irregular verbs needed 15 or 20 tokens per type and the identity and vowel-change classes needed five tokens per type to obtain learning outcomes of 75 percent correct or better. Regular verbs suffered somewhat but were always at least 50 percent correct. Errors included blends (vowel change plus regular suffix), no change to stem, and (for irregulars) overregularization; relative frequencies of error types varied according to verb class and type-to-token ratio. Learning curves that averaged together all items of a type were noisy but generally negatively accelerated (i.e., most improvement came early in training). The lack of an overall U-shaped learning curve is not surprising, because input conditions that would produce good initial learning of a small number of items were not included. Plunkett and Marchman emphasized, however, that the various classes of irregular verbs each exhibited their own micro U-shaped learning curves. They also stressed that these micro U-shaped curves were obtained without the use of any discontinuity in the training set and simply as a consequence of the conflict between regular and irregular verbs.

One feature of children's acquisition that Plunkett and Marchman's (1991) procedure could not simulate is the tendency for children to be inconsistent on some verbs for a period of time; for example, a child might bounce between stem-only and the regular past-tense form for some of her regular verbs, or between overregularization and the correct vowel change for some of her irregular verbs. Although stochastic units can be used to make networks perform probabilistically, they preferred to focus their next simulations on capturing other aspects of children's performance. In particular, Plunkett and Marchman (1993) sought to simulate the acquisition of a few correct irregular past-tense forms in stage 1 prior to the onset of overregularization (along with additional correct forms) in stage 2. They employed an incremental training regime for 500 artificial verbs using a network like that in figure 5.4 but with 30 hidden units. Rather than introduce all of the verbs at once, varying only the proportion of regular and irregular tokens, they first trained the network on a set of 10 regular and 10 irregular verbs (based on MacArthur CDI results reported by Fenson et al., 1994, and consistent with those of Marchman and Bates for 22-month-olds). Then they added verbs one at a time with an 80 percent likelihood that each additional verb would be regular. New verbs were added once every 5 epochs until vocabulary size reached 100; subsequently, they were added once per epoch until all 500 verbs had been included. Comparing their network's learning curves with Marcus et al.'s reanalysis of child data, Plunkett and Marchman concluded that they were similar: the network initially made no errors on irregular verbs, began to make a few overregularization errors after 100 verbs had been learned, and stopped making overregularization errors after the last irregular verb had been learned. Also, high-frequency irregular verbs were rarely regularized.

Marcus (1995), however, criticized Plunkett and Marchman (1993) on a number of grounds, including the manner in which performance was graphed, the presence of discontinuities in the training regime, and the nature of the errors made. Plunkett and Marchman (1996) addressed all of these points, but here we will focus just on the question of the effect of discontinuity in the training regime. Marcus's concern was that overregularization in the network began after 100 verbs had been learned, which was also the point of the changeover from adding a new verb every five epochs to every epoch. Plunkett and Marchman responded first by calling attention to their 1991 study showing that U-shaped learning can be found even when vocabulary size is held constant. Second, they reported new simulations that either introduced a new verb once every five epochs throughout training, or made the switchover to one verb per epoch earlier (following acquisition of the fiftieth verb). In each case, there was a wide range in the timing of the onset of overregularization, and the patterns were roughly comparable. While Plunkett and Marchman acknowledged that discontinuities in the training set may be a factor influencing the pattern of overregularization, they denied that it is either necessary or sufficient to induce overregularization.

On their view, the main cause of overregularization is the competition between regular and irregular ways of forming a past tense. This raised the question of whether regular verbs must make up a majority of the training set for the network to properly learn regularization. In the Arabic plural system, for example, the default procedure applies to only a minority of forms in the lexicon. Nonetheless, Plunkett and Nakisa (1997) developed a network model that succeeded in learning Arabic plurals; they argued that it performed better than an optimized dual-mechanism account that employed a rule to handle the default cases. There were also specific claims about the English plural (Marcus, 1995) to which Marchman, Plunkett, and Goodman (1997) replied by arguing that new tallies using the MacArthur CDI were consistent with how a network would learn plurals vs. past tense.

To close this discussion with a very different approach than network modeling, Jaeger, Lockwood, Kemmerer, Van Valin, Murphy, and Khalak (1996) brought the methods of neuroscience to bear on the issue of whether a single mechanism produces both regular and irregular forms. They used *positron emission tomography (PET)* to determine which brain areas were most active as adults performed several related tasks involving five lists, each composed of 46 verb stems with no overlap between lists: (1) reading aloud a list of verb stems; (2) reading aloud a list of nonsense (artificial) stems; (3) producing the past-tense forms for regular verb stems; (4) producing the past-tense forms for irregular verb stems; (5) producing past-tense forms for non-sense stems. They found distinctive patterns of cortical activation, in particular for the regular versus irregular past-tense formation tasks (relative to a resting state or to simply reading the stems). They interpreted their results as supporting a linguistically-based account in which regular items and exceptions are handled differently. Other interpretations cannot yet be ruled out, however. To cite just one methodological concern, we do not normally form the past tense of long lists of isolated verbs; something like this version of the task was necessary given the requirements of PET, but it may conceivably have skewed the results.[10] As additional neuroimaging studies of language tasks become available, taking advantage of the greater design flexibility of fMRI, the debate no doubt will continue in this new venue. Jaeger et al.'s publication had one immediate distinction, however: we believe it was the first paper in the premier linguistics journal, *Language*, that included color plates.

5.5 Conclusion

Rumelhart and McClelland offered a new proposal in 1986 about the kind of mental mechanism that produces linguistic performance. On their view, the linkage between regular verb stems and their past-tense forms can be *described* using just a few general rules, but is *governed* by a mechanism that does not use explicit rules. Rather, it distributes knowledge of how to form the past tense across connection weights in a network. Furthermore, this mechanism is unified: the more complex linkages between irregular verb stems and their exceptional past-tense forms are encoded in the same set of connection weights as for regular stems. (In a rule-based account, by contrast, each exception must be listed separately.) In moving towards this end-state, the network exhibits learning stages that are similar in important respects to those of human children.

Perhaps because this model was so explicitly set forth as a direct challenge to rule-based accounts, it became a prime target of critics of connectionism. The most extensive discussion was that of Pinker and Prince (1988), which we examined in some detail. We then focused on two issues. First, to what extent did the input to the network approximate the input to children's past-tense learning mechanism? We pointed to data which, combined with certain assumptions about when and how past-tense learning occurs, suggested that the network's input may indeed be predominantly irregular early in the learning process. Second, under what range of input conditions can stages like those of children be obtained in networks? Plunkett and Marchman's simulations indicated that regularization, overregularization, blends, and other stage 2 phenomena can be exhibited by networks even when the higher token frequency of irregular verbs is taken into account. Furthermore, the transition to stage 3 was partly captured in the improvements in performance across training epochs. Their simulations had more limited applicability to stage 1 and the transition to stage 2, but they did show that individual items (and classes of items) can exhibit U-shaped learning under constant input conditions involving a large number of items. The final rule of 78 simulation which we carried out indicated, however, that global stages of U-shaped learning can be observed in a very simple network if it is fed a small (but increasingly large) training set in which exceptions are kept at a constant percentage of 50 percent. Hence, abrupt changes in the input are not the only way to attain U-shaped learning curves.

Rumelhart and McClelland's past-tense model was an early feasibility study that presented complicated, innovative representations to a very simple kind of network (the pattern associator). It is certainly appropriate to probe at its limitations in pursuit of improved models, and the methodological points raised by critics have been a useful part of this process. The development of multi-layered networks has permitted more adequate simulations, but critics have kept the focus on whether systems without rules can really capture the behavior for which rule-based models have been introduced in cognitive science. Although dated in some respects, Rumelhart and McClelland's (1986) paper made it impossible to ignore their radical proposal: networks without reliance on rule structures can account for both the regular behavior which inspired the positing of rules and the exceptions that seemed to require rote memorization. This issue has implications far beyond the question of how to generate the English past tense, and we will grapple with it again in chapter 10: first in the context of dual-route theories of reading (section 10.2.3) and then by suggesting how the cognitive science of the future might advance beyond it (at the end of section 10.3.2).

NOTES

1   Any connectionist system includes an activation rule that operates on activation values and weights to transform input patterns into output patterns. In a broad sense such a system is computational and rule-based. When connectionists challenge (and classicists defend) the need for rules, what is in question is a particular notion of rule captured by the term "symbol manipulation." The activation rule in a network, in contrast, performs quantitative operations on numeric vectors at what is sometimes called the subsymbolic level.

2   Pinker and Prince remarked: "Language has been the domain most demanding of articulated symbol structures governed by rules and principles and it is also the domain where such structures have been explored in the greatest depth and sophistication, within a

range of theoretical frameworks and architectures, attaining a wide variety of significant empirical results. Any alternative model that either eschews symbolic mechanisms altogether, or that is strongly shaped by the restrictive nature of available elementary information processes and unresponsive to the demands of high-level functions being computed, starts off at a seeming disadvantage. Many observers thus feel that connectionism, as a radical restructuring of cognitive theory, will stand or fall depending on its ability to account for human language" (1988, p. 78).

3   Note, however, that the exceptional forms are not arbitrary: the exceptional verbs can be classified on the basis of phonological similarities, and verbs in the same class tend to form their past tense similarly. Some of the errors that children make can be interpreted in terms of these *subregularities*. For this reason, some rule theorists now ascribe the retrieval of irregulars to an associative process (as in a network) rather than lexical look-up; see Marcus et al. (1992).

4   Learning to reverse the values of units 7 and 8 is no more difficult for the network than keeping them in correspondence, for two reasons. First, although we number the units for convenience of reference, the network begins its learning with no particular alignment between input and output units: every unit in one layer is connected to every unit in the other layer. Learning the input–output pairs gradually imposes a kind of alignment. Second, it is no harder to train any output unit to take the opposite value of a given input unit than to make it take the same value. Humans manipulating external patterns do align them and do find reversals more difficult, but presumably our internal micromechanisms have characteristics more like those of networks.

5   Note that it was possible for units 7 and 8 to both become active or both become inactive on a given trial. Also, there was considerable variability in the probabilities observed over different runs of the simulation. What was common across the runs that we performed was that the probability of activation for units 7 and 8 varied around 0.50 for a considerable number of epochs. During this period, when exactly one of the two output units became active, it was about equally likely that it would be unit 7 (the correct output for this exception case) or unit 8 (overgeneralization of the rule).

6   Note that the results we report are quite similar to those reported on p. 231 of *PDP:18*, but not identical. This is because *PDP:18* used only an approximation to the logistic function that was used in the *Handbook* exercise, and because using any function stochastically yields slightly different results on every run.

7   Generally, linguists strive to account for *all* of the relevant *linguistic* facts, and a single counterexample can lead to rejection of a theory. Psychologists, in contrast, are accustomed to accounting for only a *portion* of the variability in a *psychological* data set; it is the failure to predict the central tendency or pattern of results that leads to rejection of a theory.

8   Of the 25 children whose transcripts were their primary data for examining overregularization, Marcus et al. calculated type and token percentages of regular verbs only for Adam, Eve, and Sarah. However, they noted that Adam and Sarah's results were consistent with summary data from two previous studies. One found that 79 percent of verb types and 33 percent of verb tokens were regular in a group of first-graders (mean age 6 years 9 months). A much larger study of kindergarteners found that 23 percent of verb tokens were regular. (In Eve's more limited data, 50 percent of tokens were regular before the period of overregularization, but later transcripts yielded a more typical 27 percent.)

9   Most of the percentages in this section were read from graphs in the published reports and should be accurate within 1 percent unless noted as approximate. Usually ranges indicate variation across monthly age groups, but in this instance we provide a range because Marchman and Bates did not state how many of the overregularized verbs were also reported as correct (as would occur if a parent had picked up on their child's inconsistency in past-tense form for certain verbs). We therefore calculated this percentage once for no overlap and once for complete overlap.

10　This concern actually can be extended further. Past-tense forms are generated from stems in linguists' grammars, and this entire debate rests on the assumption that people do likewise. But Marcus et al. (p. 66) contrasted elicited production studies in which the stem is provided to children with "naturalistic settings in which children produce a past form for an irregular in response to a mental representation of the verb's meaning plus the feature for past tense; the phonetic form of the stem need never be activated." Conceivably this would be true of regular verbs as well, affecting more verbs for a longer period than would be expected on grounds of parsimony. If so, the most appropriate connectionist model of development might start with a network mapping (a) verb meanings on to verb stems, and then add pathways mapping (b) verb meanings + pastness on to past-tense forms and (c) verb stems on to past-tense forms. How these pathways would unfold in time and the nature of any interactions between them would need to be addressed.

SOURCES AND SUGGESTED READINGS

Marcus, G. F., Pinker, S., Ullman, M., Hollander, M., Rosen, T. J., and Xu, F. (1992) Overregularization in language acquisition. *Monographs of the Society for Research in Child Development*, 57 (4, Serial no. 228).

Pinker, S. (1999) *Words and Rules: The Ingredients of Language*. New York: Basic Books.

Pinker, S. and Prince, A. (1988) On language and connectionism: Analysis of a parallel distributed processing model of language acquisition. *Cognition*, 28, 73–193.

Plunkett, K. and Marchman, V. (1991) U-shaped learning and frequency effects in a multi-layered perceptron: Implications for child language acquisition. *Cognition*, 38, 43–102.

Plunkett, K. and Marchman, V. A. (1993) From rote learning to system building: Acquiring verb morphology in children and connectionist nets. *Cognition*, 48, 21–69.

Plunkett, K. and Marchman, V. A. (1996) Learning from a connectionist model of the acquisition of the English past tense. *Cognition*, 61, 299–308.

Rumelhart, D. E. and McClelland, J. L. (1986) On learning the past tense of English verbs. In J. L. McClelland, D. E. Rumelhart, and the PDP Research Group, *Parallel Distributed Processing: Explorations in the Microstructure of Cognition*, vol. 2: *Psychological and Biological Models*. Cambridge, MA: MIT Press, 216–71.

6

ARE SYNTACTICALLY STRUCTURED REPRESENTATIONS NEEDED?

In a classic symbolic model, rules operate on representations. Chapter 5 presented the connectionist case for dispensing with rules and some classicist objections; now in chapter 6 we move the debate forward to the related issue of the status of representations. Linguistic analysis of a sentence like *Joan loves the florist* yields a syntactically structured representation in which the sentence is seen to be constructed from constituents: *loves* is composed with *the florist* into a larger constituent (a verb phrase), which in turn is composed with *Joan* into a sentence. But connectionist models of language processing use distributed encodings. Most connectionists have no qualms about calling these encodings "representations" in the broad sense that they model the mental states that refer to and make sense of the world, as long as the term is not taken to imply sequences of elements with explicit syntactic structure. Their critics also view this as a crucial distinction. One of the first, and most discussed, critiques of connectionism was put forward by Jerry Fodor and Zenon Pylyshyn (1988), who argued that connectionist models whose representations fail to exhibit syntactic structure cannot account for major facts about cognition.

This chapter examines Fodor and Pylyshyn's critique as well as three lines of response offered by connectionists. The first two connectionist responses accept the assumption that cognitive systems can operate on their environments only insofar as they internalize structured representations of this environment, but differ on the nature of the structure that is required. The last response rejects this assumption, and proposes internalizing only the knowledge of how to interact with external representations. Coupled with this last line of response is an appeal to structured external symbol systems, such as natural languages, to account for the features of cognition emphasized in Fodor and Pylyshyn's critique. These responses thus progress from relatively conservative to fairly radical.

6.1 Fodor and Pylyshyn's Critique: The Need for Symbolic Representations with Constituent Structure

6.1.1 The need for compositional syntax and semantics

Fodor and Pylyshyn (1988) began their critique of connectionism by distinguishing between *representationalist* and *eliminativist* approaches to theorizing about cognition.

Representationalists claim that the internal states of the cognitive system are "representational (or 'intentional' or 'semantic') states" that "encode states of the world"; eliminativists "dispense with such semantic notions as representation" (Fodor and Pylyshyn, 1988, p. 7).[1] After offering the distinction, Fodor and Pylyshyn placed connectionism on the representationalist side, citing both textual evidence from connectionist publications and the fact that connectionists typically provide semantic interpretations of the activities of either single units or ensembles of units. This assignment then became the foundation of their argument against connectionism, because it was constructed to show that connectionist systems are inadequate as *representational systems* in ways that classical systems are not.

Although the two kinds of systems differ in their level of representation – subsymbolic vs. symbolic – the critical difference for Fodor and Pylyshyn was the character of those representations. For more than two decades, Fodor has advocated the *language of thought* hypothesis, according to which cognitive activities require a language-like representational medium (see Fodor, 1975). In particular, symbolic representations have a *combinatorial syntax and semantics*. This means that representations are composed of constituents, which may themselves be composed of smaller constituents, and so forth. Unpacking the structure eventually yields atomic symbols (the elements of representation). The rule-governed processes that operate on representations are syntactic; that is, they are applied with respect to form, not meaning, and can apply at any level of the constituent structure that satisfies a specified structural description. When the time comes to provide a semantic interpretation, however, it is compositional in a way that mirrors the syntax: the semantics of the whole depends upon that of the parts. In section 1.3.1 we noted that proof procedures that are complete provide an interface between proof theory (which derives propositions from other propositions syntactically) and model theory (which focuses on whether the propositions are true, that is, on their semantics). In Dennett's (1978) terminology, the *syntactic* engine mimics a *semantic* engine.

For example, the operation that applies to P & Q to get P is licensed for any representation that has the form P & Q. It is a syntactic operation, but is useful because it interfaces with semantics so as to permit the truth of P to be inferred from the truth of P & Q. In the simplest case (atomic constituents), *red & round* can be operated upon to get *red*. (Since we are discussing the language of thought, not the language of English, it is best to think of these words as convenient symbols for common human concepts.) P and Q could be molecular rather than atomic constituents, though. For example, the same operation could have applied to (*red & round*) & (*green* v *square*) to get *red & round* before it applied to *red & round* to get *red*.

Fodor and Pylyshyn charged that connectionist systems lack a combinatorial syntax and semantics. Although individual units or coalitions of units in a connectionist system may be interpreted semantically, they cannot be built into linguistic expressions and manipulated in accord with syntactic rules. Because they are not compositional syntactically, they are not compositional semantically either.

The crux of Fodor and Pylyshyn's argument, then, is that only a system with symbolic representations possessing constituent structure can adequately model cognitive processes. The language of thought exhibits three properties that require a combinatorial syntax and semantics – features that are also exhibited by conventional human languages and were first recognized in that more accessible medium:

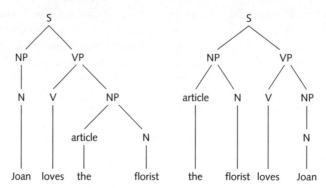

Figure 6.1   Tree diagrams of the constituent structure of two sentences.

- The *productivity* of thought refers to the capacity to understand and produce indefinitely many propositions. This capability for unbounded expression is achieved by using finite resources, particularly recursive operations, which entails a combinatorial syntax of thought.
- The *systematicity* of thought results from an intrinsic connection between the ability to comprehend or think one thought and the ability to comprehend or think certain other thoughts. It is claimed, for example,[2] that anyone who can think *Joan loves the florist* can also think *the florist loves Joan*. For this to be so, "the two mental representations, like the two sentences, *must be made of the same parts*" (p. 39). Figure 6.1 illustrates this point by displaying a simplified constituent structure for the two sentences. The second sentence has the same parts and the same structure as the first sentence; the only difference is that the two noun phrases have been switched between the subject and object positions in the tree. Someone who has mastery of this structure should be equally able to process either sentence.
- The coherence of inference involves the ability to make syntactically and semantically plausible inferences. For example, one can infer from *x is a brown cow* that *x is a cow*, or from a true conjunction (A & B) that both conjuncts are true (A is true and B is true).

6.1.2   Connectionist representations lack compositionality

Fodor and Pylyshyn contended that connectionist systems have no way of composing simple representations into more complex representations, and therefore lack these three essential properties. Part of their argument goes as follows. First, consider connectionist networks that have a *localist* semantic interpretation. Each representational unit is atomic, and there is just one way the units relate to one another: by means of pairwise causal connections. Thus, if **A & B** and **A** are two nodes in a network, the weight of the connection from **A & B** to **A** can be set such that activating **A & B** results in (causes) the activation of **A**. This could be viewed as a kind of inference, but the network's representation of the thought *A* is not in any way part of its representation of the thought *A & B*. Any two nodes could be wired to have the same pattern of influence; for example, node **A & B** might excite node **Z**. Clearly, then, the connection is not compositional in nature, and the inference does not go through in virtue of the syntactic relation between the nodes. One unpleasant outcome, in their view, is that the inference must be built in separately for each instance of conjunction rather than by means of a rule that utilizes variables to specify the syntactic relation of inclusion. For example, the unit **B & C** must be specifically linked to unit **B** if the inference from *B & C* to *B* is to be made, just as **A & B** had to be linked to unit **A**. On this basis, Fodor and Pylyshyn concluded that localist connectionist systems lack the requisite resources for cognition.

Might *distributed* networks be more suitable than localist networks as cognitive systems? In some networks using distributed representations, the units that are active in a particular representation encode features (or microfeatures) of the entity that is being represented. Smolensky (1987) specifically criticized Fodor and Pylyshyn's **A & B** analysis as too simplistic and not relevant to distributed representations. By way of illustration, he adapted Pylyshyn's own example (presented at a 1984 Cognitive Science Society meeting) involving a set of *ad hoc* features for *cup of coffee*. Smolensky noted that they could be viewed as falling into three subsets with respect to questions of combinatorial structure. The first set has features that apply to *cup* alone; if a unit is designated to encode each feature, the activation pattern across the units provides a distributed representation of *cup* (e.g., two such features might be **porcelain curved surface** and **upright container with a handle**). The second set applies to *coffee* alone (e.g., **brown liquid** and **burnt odor**). The third set applies only to *cup* and *coffee* as they interact (e.g., **brown liquid contacting porcelain**). An activation vector for *cup of coffee* will include the vectors for *cup* and for *coffee*, a relation that plays much the same role in processing as the compositionality of symbolic representations. However, it will be approximate rather than exact (because activation values can vary), and the third set of features will be activated only for the particular combination *cup of coffee*. Thus, the network representation offers a sufficiently close approximation to compositionality plus the bonus of context-dependence.

Fodor and Pylyshyn (1988, pp. 19ff) responded that this is the wrong kind of composition for the purpose they have in mind. The way in which a microfeature is part of a representation of an object is not the same as the way in which one syntactic unit (e.g., a noun phrase) is part of a larger syntactic unit (e.g., a verb phrase). Thus, in a symbolic representation of the proposition *Joan loves the florist*, the unit representing *Joan* stands in a particular syntactic relationship to the rest of the proposition, such that the proposition is not confused with *the florist loves Joan*. This is not true of a distributed representation. For example, a (minimally) distributed representation of the proposition *Joan loves the florist* could be achieved in a network whose units corresponded to such concepts as *Joan*, *loves*, and *the florist* by activating those three units. However, Fodor and Pylyshyn argued, it would be indistinguishable from the representation of *the florist loves Joan*. It would not help to add units for relationships, such as a unit for subject, for there is no straightforward way to capture the fact that it is Joan who is the subject and not the florist (that is, to compose the units hierarchically). The units are just bundled together in a relation of co-occurrence, without the structure that syntax would provide. Fodor and Pylyshyn concluded that connectionist networks, whether localist or distributed, forfeit the benefits offered by a combinatorial syntax and semantics.

One interpretation of this point in shown in figure 6.2: the activation of certain units in the input layer of a simple network is adequate to distinguish *Joan loves the florist* from *Terry leaves the baker* but not from *the florist loves Joan*. The subject and

baker   florist   Terry   Joan   loves   leaves   Subject   Object   Verb

Figure 6.2   An attempt to represent constituent structure on one layer of a connectionist network that is too simple to work. With the units for *Joan*, *loves*, *florist*, *subject*, *object*, and *verb* all active, there is no indication that *Joan* is the *subject* and *florist* is the *object* rather than the reverse. Some way of binding words to grammatical roles is needed.

object roles are activated, but are not bound to the person units so as to distinguish which person is in which role – this is a simple case of the notorious *binding problem*. In contrast, the trees in figure 6.1 have hierarchical structure obtained by applying rules of composition. Although the same components and the same rules of composition are involved in both trees, the positions of the components in each tree clearly distinguish which is subject and which is object. According to Fodor and Pylyshyn, these resources are distinctive to symbolic theories, and such a theory

> will have to go out of its way to explain a linguistic competence which embraces one sentence but not the other. And similarly, if a theory says that the mental representation that corresponds to the thought that *P & Q & R* has the same (conjunctive) syntax as the mental representation that corresponds to the thought that *P & Q* and that mental processes of drawing inferences subsume mental representations in virtue of their syntax, it will have to go out of its way to explain inferential capacities which embrace the one thought but not the other. Such a competence would be, at best, an embarrassment for the theory, and at worst a refutation.
>
> By contrast, since the Connectionist architecture recognizes no combinatorial structure in mental representations, gaps in cognitive competence should proliferate arbitrarily. It's not just that you'd expect to get them from time to time; it's that, on the "no-structure" story, *gaps are the unmarked case*. It's the *systematic* competence that the theory is required to treat as an embarrassment. But, as a matter of fact, inferential competences are *blatantly* systematic. So there must be something deeply wrong with Connectionist architecture.   (p. 49)

6.1.3   Connectionism as providing *mere implementation*

Following these and other arguments that an adequate representational system must be symbolic rather than connectionist, Fodor and Pylyshyn did acknowledge that the nervous system in which our symbolic representations are implemented may be a connectionist system. This might seem to be an admission that connectionism has a role to play in modeling cognition. *But Fodor and Pylyshyn maintained that only the analysis at the level of symbolic processing is relevant to cognitive theorizing, and that this level is nonconnectionist.* Connectionism is *merely* an account of the medium within which the symbolic representational system is implemented, and as such is not pertinent to theorizing about cognition itself. This aspect of their critique is grounded in a notion of levels of analysis of nature. There is a causal story to be told about interactions *within* each level (e.g., a story about molecules, a story about stones, a story about galaxies), but "the story that scientists tell about the causal structure that the world has at any one of these levels may be quite different from the story that they tell about its causal structure at the next level up or down" (Fodor and Pylyshyn, 1988, p. 9). Moreover, Fodor has argued elsewhere (Fodor, 1974) that a single function may be implemented in any one of a number of lower-level mechanisms and that a single lower-level mechanism may figure in many functions. For example, money can be physically realized in paper, metal, stones, or clams. Each of these physical entities has its own causal story and properties (e.g., paper is made from trees and can be crumpled), but these are not relevant to the functions they might serve at the monetary level, which has its own story. Likewise, cognitive functioning has its own story which is minimally constrained, if at all, by scientific accounts of the neural substrate.

The causal story that is relevant to cognitive science, for Fodor and Pylyshyn, is a story about actions performed on structured symbolic representations. Since connectionism *per se* cannot provide an adequate story about actions performed on such representations, but the symbolic account does, then connectionism is not a candidate theory of cognition. At best, it is a story about another level, but as such it is no more relevant to theories of cognition than are stories about molecular processes in the brain.

What about the level of implementation itself? In the course of responding to some of the arguments commonly made on behalf of connectionism (such as those discussed in section 2.3), Fodor and Pylyshyn gave some attention to this question. On their view, most of the advantages connectionist models seem to have over symbolic models are due entirely to the fact that symbolic models are currently implemented on von Neumann computers. When symbolic models are implemented in more neural-like hardware, they will exhibit the same virtues as connectionist models. Moreover, the fact that these characteristics stem from the mode of implementation shows that they are not cognitive characteristics at all, but merely features of the implementation. For example, Fodor and Pylyshyn maintain that the time consumed by a particular cognitive process is a matter of implementation, and does not inform us as to the nature of the architecture itself:

> the absolute speed of a process is a property *par excellence* of its implementation. . . .
> Thus, the fact that individual neurons require tens of miliseconds [*sic*] to fire can have
> no bearing on the predicted speed at which an algorithm will run *unless there is at least
> a partial, independently motivated, theory of how the operations of the functional architec-
> ture are implemented in neurons*. Since, in the case of the brain, it is not even certain that
> the firing of neurons is invariably the relevant implementation property (at least for
> higher level cognitive processes like learning and memory) the 100 step "constraint"
> excludes nothing.   (1988, p. 55)

In particular, Fodor and Pylyshyn pointed out that nothing prohibits operations on symbols from being implemented in a parallel architecture and hence being performed much more rapidly than in a von Neumann computer. They applied similar arguments to other purported virtues of connectionist systems (e.g., resistance to noise and damage and use of soft constraints).

It should be noted that Fodor and Pylyshyn's *mere implementation* argument relies on some very particular assumptions about how levels of nature, and the disciplines that study them, relate to one another. Specifically, they place information-processing accounts of cognition and language at the same level as abstract accounts, such as those provided in logic or linguistic theory. The gap we left in the quote above was the following parenthetical comment: "(By contrast, the *relative* speed with which a system responds to different inputs is often diagnostic of distinct processes; but this has always been a prime empirical basis for deciding among alternative algorithms in information processing psychology)" (p. 55). Information-processing accounts are not a matter of mere implementation for Fodor and Pylyshyn, but rather are closely associated with the linguistic theory itself. This exemplifies a desire on the part of Chomskian linguistics to cover some of the traditional territory of cognitive psychology as well as linguistics. In contrast, many psychologists (e.g., McNeill, 1975; Marr, 1982; Rumelhart and McClelland, 1985) have emphasized the distinction between abstract accounts of language as a static product (which make no reference to the real-time processes that produce it) and processing accounts of linguistic behavior.

In our view (see Abrahamsen, 1987, 1991), abstract accounts are the tasks of disciplines such as linguistics and logic. Both information-processing and connectionist models occupy a lower level of analysis and are the tasks of such processing-oriented disciplines as cognitive psychology and artificial intelligence.[3] Computational neuroscience is at a third, yet lower level of biological inquiry. The neural account might be regarded as implementing the processing account, and the processing account as implementing the abstract (linguistic) account. In a multi-level account such as this, one can envisage different levels causally constraining each other without endorsing a strong reductionism (Bechtel, 1988, chapter 6; Bechtel, 1994a); in this way the gap between abstract and neural accounts can be bridged. In contrast, since Fodor and Pylyshyn do not strongly distinguish the abstract linguistic account from the processing account, they have no place to locate connectionist models except at the neural level. The processing accounts that they find acceptable are at the same level as abstract accounts (the symbolic level), and must achieve their combinatorial syntax and semantics in a system of operations on symbol strings.

The connectionist gambit is to develop processing accounts using means other than operations on symbol strings. Connectionists generally agree that their alternative means must account for data that are suggestive of combinatorial structure in language. Furthermore, connectionists themselves have recognized the importance of the *variable binding problem* (a more developed version of the binding problem that was illustrated in figure 6.2 above). Rules usually employ variables as a compact way of indicating that they can apply to any member of a class. In a given application, all occurrences of the same variable must be instantiated by the same individual. (For example, *x loves x* might be instantiated as *Joan loves herself.*) The challenge for connectionists is to make networks do the work that in symbolic theories is performed by means of structured representations which include variables. Unlike Fodor and Pylyshyn, connectionists do not assume that symbolic representations are the only adequate means for doing this work; they are just the most obvious means. Nor do they agree that success at the difficult task of finding alternative means can only be regarded as "mere implementation" of the symbolic account. The connectionist goal is to achieve models that give an account of phenomena that are handled rather well by rules but also, without additional mechanisms, give an elegant account of other phenomena as well (e.g., learning, generalization, and variation). If connectionist accounts did nothing more than implement what traditional rules already do well, they probably would not be worth the effort involved in constructing them.

Fodor and Pylyshyn's critique has been taken seriously by a number of connectionists. They have not, however, agreed on how it should be answered. In the remainder of this chapter, we consider three kinds of global responses that connectionists have made to the claim that structured symbols are required for cognition and to the collateral claim that there must be structure-sensitive rules operating on these symbols. Before presenting these responses, though, we should note that one response open to connectionists is to contest the ubiquity of productivity and systematicity in actual cognitive performance (Christiansen, 1992; Waskan and Bechtel, 1997). We will not develop this issue further here, but clearly it is relevant to evaluating the success of connectionist models – and of symbolic models as well.

6.2 First Connectionist Response: Explicitly Implementing Rules and Representations

Some connectionists agree with Fodor and Pylyshyn's contention that humans carry out explicit symbol processing – at least for such activities as problem solving and reasoning – and hence have directed their efforts to implementing systems of rules and representations in networks. What is distinctive of this approach, and renders it closest to the symbolic tradition, is that it works from the top down, beginning with a rule-based account and designing a network that will implement those rules. In order to ensure that the network employs the desired rules, modelers have tended to engineer their own designs rather than allowing the network to construct its own solutions. But those who adopt this approach deny that they are engaged in *mere* implementation; rather, they contend that by implementing rules and representations in a network they are able to take advantage of many of the crucial benefits that accrue as a result of the connectionist implementation. Dyer (1991, p. 45) well describes the appeal of pursuing this approach:

> What we currently appear to have is a situation in which subsymbolic, distributed processing models exhibit massive parallelism, graceful error degradation, robust fault tolerance, and general adaptive learning capabilities, while symbol/rule based systems exhibit powerful reasoning, structural and inferential capabilities. If we could embed symbol representations and structure-manipulating operations within a distributed, subsymbolic architecture, then very powerful, massively parallel, fault tolerant high-level reasoning/planning systems could be created.

6.2.1 Implementing a production system in a network

Fahlman (1979) and Touretzky and Hinton (1988) offered two early attempts to implement rules and symbolic representations in connectionist networks. In particular, Touretzky and Hinton created a Distributed Connectionist Production System (DCPS), as described in some detail in section 2.2.4.2. In a production system, symbolic expressions are manipulated by production rules (often referred to as *productions*). Each rule has the form *If A then B* where *A* is a condition and *B* is an action, and there is a *working memory* used like a blackboard to drive the selection of rules and record their results. Just one kind of rule was implemented in DCPS: the condition specifies what expressions must be in working memory in order for the rule to fire, the action specifies expressions to be moved in (or out) of working memory, and the expressions are meaningless triples of letters. For example:

$$(\textbf{FAB}) \ (\textbf{FCD}) \longrightarrow + (\textbf{GAB}) + (\textbf{PDQ}) - (\textbf{FCD})$$

This specifies that if (**FAB**) and (**FCD**) are both in working memory, then (**GAB**) and (**PDQ**) should be added and (**FCD**) should be deleted.

Viewed just as a production system, this is pretty uninteresting. In more realistic production systems the symbolic expressions are meaningful: some are goals and subgoals, which direct the activity of the system towards accomplishing a task, and others are more directly task-related (e.g., numerals if the task is multiplication). Touretzky and Hinton used a simple, homogeneous set of rules because their purpose was not to simulate human performance but rather to demonstrate that a rule system can advantageously be implemented in a distributed connectionist architecture. Their implementation was complex and ingenious (they stated that it was one of the largest connectionist systems yet constructed). Even the seemingly straightforward matter of getting the triples into working memory was taken as an opportunity to explore highly distributed encoding – 216 triples were coarse-coded on 2,000 binary receptor units, as described in section 2.2.4.2. Their first system, DCPS1, used distributed or semi-distributed encodings in several components: (a) the working memory, (b) an area where rules were encoded, and (c) two areas used for matching the expressions on the condition side of a rule. For the most part DCPS1 operated as a Boltzmann machine (a type of interactive network that asymmetrically iterates its computations until an energy minimum is reached; see section 2.2.2.2), but a gating mechanism was added to control access to working memory.

The actual structure and operation of DCPS1 is too complex to even summarize here; there is a six-page overview in Bechtel and Abrahamsen (1991), but many details of its impressive engineering can be found only in the original paper. What is important here is that, first, Touretzky and Hinton seemed to have achieved a reasonably successful implementation of a simple production system; although they did not provide detailed performance data, they did cite one test run using a six-rule loop in which 1,000 successive rule firings were carried out without error. Second, by giving the production system a connectionist implementation, it inherited the appealing properties of networks that were introduced in section 2.3, including (a) "best-fit" matches between the expressions in working memory and in a rule's condition side without having to specify in advance all the parameters on which fit might be evaluated; (b) resistance to damage; (c) the capacity to generalize. Touretzky and Hinton themselves noted that they had not fully realized the potential of these characteristics and looked to future work to complete the promissory note of going beyond mere implementation. Also, DCPS1 had at least one disadvantage: slow operation (McDermott, as reported in Dyer, 1991, p. 45, dubbed this the *Touretzky tarpit* problem). Finally, it lacked the ability to learn or to handle rules that included variables. Touretzky and Hinton provided their next system, DCPS2, with a limited capacity to deal with a single variable. However, even quite ordinary human reasoning tasks require multiple variables. In the next section we use one simple inference to illustrate why many theorists think variables are needed and therefore binding them is needed as well.

6.2.2   The variable binding problem

From *John gave Mary Book1* it can be inferred that *Mary owns Book1*. The relevant rule of inference can be stated using a quintessential symbolic system, first-order predicate calculus. In the simplified notation used in an example from Shastri and Ajjanagadde (1993), it is represented as:

$$\forall x, y, z \, [give(x,y,z) \Rightarrow own(y,z)]$$

Elaborating a bit beyond a bare-bones logical treatment of *give* as a three-place predicate (one that takes three ordered arguments), Shastri and Ajjanagadde labeled its three arguments in terms of three semantic roles that are distinctive to that predicate: the *giver*, the *recipient*, and the *give-object*. Similarly, the two-place predicate *own* has two semantic roles: the *owner* and the *own-object*. The variables in the inference rule tell us that whoever is the *recipient* (in a particular act of giving) must also be the *owner* (in a particular relation of ownership that results from the act of giving); this is indicated by the use of the same variable name, y, for the second argument of *give* and the first argument of *own*. (If instead the first expression were *give*(y,x,z) then the inference rule would tell us, mistakenly, that the giver was still the owner after the act of giving.) Similarly, the two appearances of variable z tell us that the object that comes to be owned by the recipient is the same object that was given by the giver to the recipient.

In order to apply this general rule to the case of John and Mary, the *variable binding problem* must be solved. The first step is easy: from the sentence provided, *John gave Mary Book1*, it is easy to bind three specific entities to the three argument positions of the predicate *give* (which makes *John*, *Mary*, and *Book1* the fillers of the roles corresponding to these argument positions). The second step is a bit harder, but this is where the system attains its power: noting the shared variables between *give* and *own* in the inference rule, *Mary* and *Book1* must be additionally bound to the argument positions of *own*. The result is:

$$give(John,Mary,Object1) \Rightarrow own(Mary,Object1)$$

By appropriately binding multiple instances of multiple variables, we have succeeding in inferring that Mary now owns the object that was given to her.

Symbolic theorists like Fodor and Pylyshyn claim that the cognitive system must use structured representations to carry off this kind of reasoning – if not exactly first-order predicate calculus, then some other rule system that is at least as powerful. They are uninterested in its "mere implementation" in a connectionist model or other brain-like architecture. But those connectionists who have actually tried to implement variable binding have gotten a close-up look at how challenging this is. In their 1988 DCPS2 system, Touretzky and Hinton needed to add so much connectivity to handle just one variable in restricted positions that the feasibility of scaling up their approach to handle multiple variables was in question. Smolensky (1990) proposed a more computationally efficient way to achieve binding using tensor product representations. A third approach was originally proposed as a solution to the brain's own version of the binding problem (von der Malsburg, 1981) and was incorporated in a connectionist model by Shastri and Ajjanagadde (1993). This third approach has attracted the most attention and its core idea can be conveyed visually, which we do in the next section. These appealing characteristics do not necessarily make it the best approach, and we suggest that readers interested in drawing their own conclusions start with the three cited papers in exploring this issue further.

6.2.3 Shastri and Ajjanagadde's connectionist model of variable binding

The binding problem became salient in neuroscience as evidence accumulated that a great many different brain areas are involved in processing a visual scene, with analyses of location, shape, color, and so forth parceled out to specialized areas. This gave rise to the question of how the results of these analyses are tracked and put back together into unified percepts. That is, how does the system bind each location, shape, and color analysis to the correct object in a multi-object display? (The problem only gets worse if the analyses of other sensory and higher-order brain areas get considered as well.) A hypothesis put forward by von der Malsburg (1981), now supported by evidence at least from low-level visual areas (Gray and Singer, 1989; Engel, König and Singer, 1991; Singer, 1994), is that the brain uses temporal synchrony: cells that analyze different features of the same object emit bursts of firing in phase with one another. Lokendra Shastri and Verkat Ajjanagadde used this idea in the system they designed in 1993 for making inferences like that of the John and Mary example. It is one of the largest-scale efforts to implement rule-based reasoning over structured representations in connectionist networks, so we will give just a glimpse of it by describing a small part schematically.

Shastri and Ajjanagadde's key innovation was to have units in a network turn on and off in a rhythmic pattern across time, and to use the fact that the appropriate units turn on and off in synchrony to bind names of individuals (*Mary*) to roles (*recipient* and *owner*). Units for a different individual (*Book1*) and its roles (*give-object, own-object*) turn on and off in their own synchronous pattern, offset from the first one, to indicate that they are bound together as well. Shastri and Ajjanagadde referred to these as *dynamic bindings*.

Consider how a technique like this can be used to implement inferences involving just two rules:

1. $\forall x, y, z \ [give(x,y,z) \Rightarrow own(y,z)]$
2. $\forall u,v \ [own(u,v) \Rightarrow can\text{-}sell(u,v)]$.

Rules 1 and 2 employ three predicates, *give*, *own*, and *can-sell*, as illustrated in figure 6.3. Each predicate is represented by the joint activity of its arguments, each of which conveys a predicate-specific role like *giver*. For example, the predicate *give* is represented by the joint activity of units for *giver*, *recipient*, and *give-object* (indicated by the three circles enclosed in an oval). Of the five available individuals (represented by the units to the side labeled *John, Susan, Mary, Book1*, and *Ball1*), three are bound to argument units by firing in phase with them. This is very roughly indicated by showing each unit as patterned (e.g., *Mary* and the arguments to which it is bound have diagonal stripes). When a rule fires, its roles become bound. This can be thought of as happening in the next time cycle, though the temporal dynamics are actually more complex. The downward arrows represent connections that implement constraints on the bindings: there is one such arrow whenever the same variable appears on both the left and right side of a rule. Any two ovals along

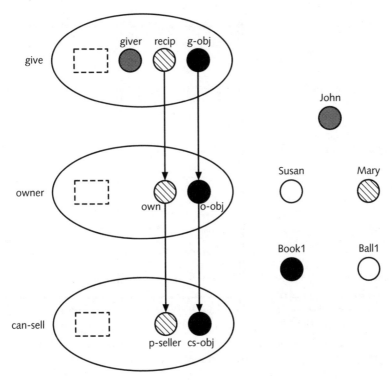

Figure 6.3 A schematic rendering of rules 1 and 2 in Shastri and Ajjanagadde's (1993) structured network implementation of rule-based reasoning. See text for exposition.

with the downward arrows between some or all of those arguments correspond to one rule. (In the actual system, each circle in figure 6.3 is an ensemble of units and each arrow is a set of many-to-many connections. The rectangular boxes within the ovals represent a complex mechanism that determines whether the conditions are satisfied for each rule to fire.)

Figure 6.4 shows how activation is propagated through the network as a result of an initial encoding of the proposition *John gave Mary Book1*. During the first time-step, the ensembles for *John* and *giver* are the first to start turning on and off in phase. The ensembles for *Mary* and *recipient* turn on slightly later but in phase with each other, and likewise for *Book1* and *given-object*. Thus, temporal synchrony is used to encode the argument bindings. Activity across network connections brings rule 1 into play, so approximately one time-step later (the other side of the first double bar in figure 6.4), the ensemble for *owner* synchronizes with those for *Mary* and *recipient*, and the ensemble for *owned-object* synchronizes with those for *given-object* and *Book1*. This pattern of activation brings rule 2 into play, so after one more time-step the ensemble for *can-sell-object* begins turning on and off in synchrony with the already-active ensembles for *owned-object*, *given-object*, and *Book1*. Similarly, the ensemble for *potential-seller* becomes synchronized with the ensembles for *owner*, *recipient*, and *Mary*. These inferences can be made very rapidly even in a large network using this design.

Shastri and Ajjanagadde's system is clearly an impressive piece of engineering and it is capable of carrying out a significant amount of logical reasoning. But it does

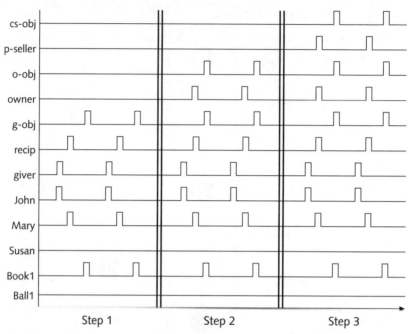

Figure 6.4   Changes in activation over three time-steps in Shastri and Ajjanagadde's (1993) network. The units active simultaneously at step 1 bind each individual to a role in the initial proposition, *John gave Mary Book1*. *Mary* and *Book1* are bound to additional roles as a consequence of applying rule 1 in step 2 and rule 2 in step 3. (In the actual implementation, activity involves ensembles rather than single units and time is not discrete.)

raise a number of questions. The first concerns neurobiological plausibility and is especially germane to this particular connectionist model since it was inspired in part by the neurological synchrony hypothesis. At present (see Singer, 1994), the strongest evidence for temporal binding in the brain is for binding between different columns in primary visual cortex. (V1 is laid out topographically, so object encodings extend over several columns; synchronous firing seems to occur in V1 when different columns are coding for different features of the same object.) The question of whether synchrony is used more widely by the brain to achieve binding is not yet answered. A second concern is the highly detailed architecture that is needed in this model to carry out reasoning: specific ensembles of units have to be connected with just the right other ensembles. Neural connectivity seems to be far less precise. Even if one does not consider this model to be a brain-level model, there is the question of how this connectivity pattern could be laid down. It is far more intricate than could be accounted for by existing connectionist learning principles. Finally, there is the question of what is gained by the connectionist implementation. Currently it employs one important connectionist idea, that of massively parallel propagation of activation (within each time step). As in the case of Touretzky and Hinton's model, this should bring such advantages as soft constraint satisfaction and graceful degradation, but there was no systematic assessment of the extent to which these advantages were achieved and of how they might be exploited.

Michael Dyer (1991) developed a perspective on the relation between connectionist and symbolic accounts that in fact suggests an important possible role for models like that of Shastri and Ajjanagadde. He suggests thinking in terms of a hierarchy of levels of research (p. 50):

> *MIND*
> KNOWLEDGE ENGINEERING (KE)
> LOCALIST CONNECTIONIST NETWORKS (LCN)
> PARALLEL DISTRIBUTED PROCESSING (PDP)
> ARTIFICIAL NEURAL SYSTEMS DYNAMICS (ANSD)
> *BRAIN*

He proposed that these different levels occupy "distinct 'niches' in what might be termed an abstract processing 'ecology.' That is, what subsymbolic/PDP models do well, purely symbolic systems do poorly, *and vice versa*" (36). All too often, inquiries at different levels are carried out in isolation from each other. But the goal, as Dyer sees it, is to allow resources at different levels to complement each other. Discussing the mappings between models at different levels is a crucial step towards achieving a synthesis. For example, the knowledge engineering level is the level of symbolic AI; it is well suited to stating the content and structure of a domain and supporting such tasks as goal/plan analysis. Beneath this is the level exemplified by Shastri and Ajjanagadde's simulation, that of localist networks. At this level dynamical principles such as the propagation of activation come into play. Having such multiple levels available enables choices that may produce better models. For example, in their work on analogical problem solving, Holyoak and Thagard (1989, 1995) faced the task of identifying the best analog to each problem situation, where there are many dimensions on which the situations can be compared and no perfect matches exist. To handle this task, they plugged in a localist connectionist program which was well suited to identify best matches with multiple constraints. For other tasks, they did traditional AI programming. Dyer (1991) also suggested that such techniques as the use of synchrony to implement role bindings may help to bridge these levels.

Designing networks to encode and utilize specifically designated rules is a fruitful endeavor in its own right that extends our understanding of how cognitive functions might be realized in a network. Additionally, though, this approach offers one strategy (a relatively conservative one) for showing that network models can display Fodor and Pylyshyn's three properties. Considering just the two systems described above:

- Both appear capable of displaying *productivity*, by applying their rules indefinitely many times to the output of previously applied rules.
- Their use of coarse coding yields a less crisp version of *systematicity* that should add generalization capabilities "for free" – arguably an improvement over the systematicity of classic systems.
- They exhibit *coherence of inference* to an extent. Of all the items in Touretzky and Hinton's working memory at a given time, any subset of them could be "inferred" to be present. And after Shastri and Ajjanagadde's system has inferred that *Mary* is both *recipient* and *owner* of *Object1*, it should be straightforward to pull out from the full set of in-phase units the simpler information that *Mary* is

the *recipient* of *Object1*. That is, the representation of her various roles is compositional, albeit in a flat (rather than hierarchical) encoding.

Assume for the moment that convincing evidence and arguments had been achieved for all three properties. This would leave untouched the main sticking point: for Fodor and Pylyshyn, even a fully successful network of this kind would *merely* implement a symbolic system, and it is at the level of the symbolic system that the properties of productivity, systematicity, and coherence of inference would reside. Moreover, such networks only partially exploit the resources that make connectionism a serious alternative to the classic symbolic approach. Hence, we turn now to more radical connectionist responses, in which syntactically structured symbols are incorporated only implicitly (the second connectionist response) or are abandoned entirely (the third connectionist response).

6.3   Second Connectionist Response: Implementing Functionally Compositional Representations

6.3.1   Functional vs. concatenative compositionality

Connectionists adopting the second approach grant Fodor and Pylyshyn's claim that, at least for some purposes such as processing sentences, it is necessary that the cognitive system create compositionally structured representations. However, they prefer the compositional structure to be implicit rather than explicit. For example, Timothy van Gelder (1990) distinguished between *functional* and *concatenative compositionality*. He noted that the classic device for representing the compositional structure of a compound (nonatomic) expression, such as a sentence, is *concatenation*: "*linking* or *ordering* successive constituents without altering them in any way" (p. 360). The crucial notion here is that the representation "must preserve tokens of an expression's constituents (and the sequential relations among tokens)" (p. 360). But such explicit incorporation of constituents is not essential for representing a compound expression; it is sufficient to have a representation from which the components can be recovered by some operation. Recognizing this is what opens up the possibility of *functional compositionality*.

The challenge for connectionism in offering an account of representations that are compositional but nonetheless not classical is to show how they exhibit only functional compositionality and yet accomplish the ends for which compositional representations are posited – explaining behavior that depends upon the compositional character of the representation. Van Gelder offered three examples which at least suggest how networks can create functionally compositional representations: Pollack's (1990) recursive auto-associative memory (RAAM) networks, Hinton's (1990) reduced descriptions of levels in hierarchical trees, and Smolensky's (1990) tensor product representations of binding relations. We will focus on RAAM networks because they are grounded in an ordinary feedforward connectionist architecture, whereas the other proposals are more specialized. Pollack and others have shown not only that training RAAM networks on explicitly compositional trees yields distributed representations from which the trees can be recovered, but also that those representations can be utilized by additional networks to carry out inferences requiring sensitivity to constituent structure. These findings are suggestive of functional compositionality.

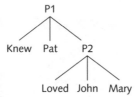

Figure 6.5   A tree diagram of sentence 1, *Pat knew John loved Mary*. It includes proposition 1 (P1) and the embedded proposition 2 (P2).

6.3.2   Developing compressed representations using Pollack's RAAM networks

Pollack set out to solve a different problem than that of creating representations that avoid concatenation. His main goal was to represent recursive structures of variable length (such as linguistic trees) using representations of fixed length (a layer of units in a network). In one study, he obtained trees by recasting 13 sentences into a nested predicate-first propositional format. For example, the sentences "Pat knew John loved Mary," "John loved Pat," and "Pat thought John knew Mary loved John" were recast into nested propositions as follows:

1   (*Knew Pat* (*Loved John Mary*))
2   (*Loved John Pat*)
3   (*Thought Pat* (*Knew John* (*Loved Mary John*)))

In addition to *loved*, *knew*, and *thought*, other propositions included such predicates as *saw*, *ate*, *hit*, *hoped*, *is*, *with*, and *on*. The constituent structure of trees is most clearly displayed in a tree diagram, as shown for sentence 1 in figure 6.5. Its constituents are propositions 1 and 2 (labeled P1 and P2) and the three parts of each proposition. Proposition 2 is composed of the words *Loved*, *John*, and *Mary*. Proposition 1 is composed of the words *Knew* and *Pat* and proposition 2. That is, P2 is nested (embedded) within P1; P2 is a subtree and P1 is the whole tree. In the entire set of 14 trees (one sentence was ambiguous, resulting in two trees), the number of propositions ranged between one and four, and all propositions were triples (a predicate and two arguments). By recasting the sentences as trees, the investigator (not a network) did the initial work of determining each sentence's constituent structure. The interest is in how he got his network to represent and use that structure.

Pollack's solution – the recursive auto-associative memory (RAAM) network – is shown schematically in figure 6.6. It is *auto-associative* in that it can recreate on its output layer any pattern provided to its input layer (from a set of patterns on which it has been trained). It is *recursive* in that its hidden layer incorporates and reincorporates information about a tree when each constituent is presented in turn to its input layer, beginning with the most deeply embedded one. By the time it reaches the top of the tree, it has encoded the entire tree in a *compressed representation* on just 16 units. The fact that the original tree can then be reconstructed by the decoding part of the network is evidence that the compressed representation is functionally compositional. It has no explicit symbols (no words; no parentheses or node

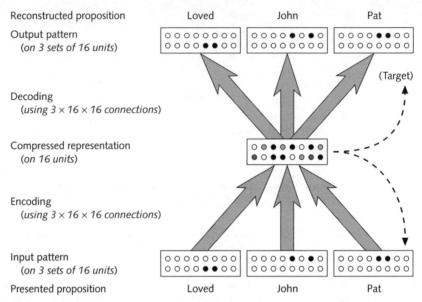

Figure 6.6 Pollack's (1990) recurrent auto-associative memory (RAAM) network. Each large arrow represents a full set of connections. The dashed arrows are not relevant for the simple proposition in this example, (*Loved John Pat*). If it had been embedded within another proposition, its hidden layer pattern would have been copied on to one set of input units (downwards arrow) and become the target pattern for the corresponding set of output units (upwards arrow) as part of processing the higher proposition; see figure 6.7.

labels) and in fact has smeared together the words and their constituent structure in an undifferentiated numeric activation pattern (vector). Yet a 3- or 4-proposition tree can be reproduced, one proposition at a time, on the output layer.

To explain how Pollack's RAAM does this, we will follow the network's activity for a proposition (*Loved John Pat*) which does not involve recursion. As shown in figure 6.6, it is presented to the input layer using a minimally distributed binary representation for each word. (Although all units in the network are capable of taking any value between 0 and 1, Pollack decided to use only 0 and 1 in the word patterns.) Semantically similar words are assigned similar patterns. For example, the four possible words denoting a person result in a value of 1 on unit 5, a different pair of values for each person on units 6–7, and a value of 0 on the rest of the 16 units. Verbs get a value of 1 on unit 13 and on some or all of units 14–16. It takes 48 units in all to represent the three-word proposition. Second, the encoding part of the network compresses the 48-unit activation pattern on to 16 hidden units, smearing together the three words. (That is, each unit in the hidden layer will take a value between 0 and 1; because it receives input from all three sets of input units – via a total of 48 connections – its value can be influenced by all three words.) Third, the decoding part of the network tries to get back the original activation pattern; if it succeeds, the output pattern will have values close to 1 on the units that correspond to (*Loved John Pat*). (Of course, the network cannot perform like this for even the simplest propositions until after it has undergone training, as indicated by the arrow pointing upwards to a target pattern. The downwards arrow, not relevant in this simple example, is equivalent to the arrow between steps (a) and (b) in figure 6.7.)

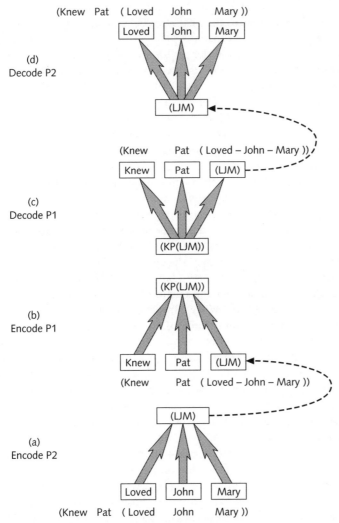

Figure 6.7 Pollack's (1996) RAAM network, separated into an encoder network (steps (a) and (b)) and a decoder network (steps (c) and (d)) in order to reconstruct the propositional encoding of the sentence *Pat knew John loved Mary*. See text for exposition.

Embedded propositions require more steps and compress more information on the hidden layer. They also require a separation of the network into an encoder network and a decoder network; all of the propositions in a tree must be encoded before decoding can begin. Figure 6.7 shows major steps in the processing of the tree in figure 6.5: (*Knew Pat* (*Loved John Mary*)). Figure 6.7 has less pictorial detail than figure 6.6, with labels such as *Knew* and (*LJM*) used to indicate activation patterns across sets of units, and showing only the encoder or decoder network as relevant. Beginning at the bottom of the figure, diagram (a) shows the encoder network's first step: the embedded proposition (*Loved John Mary*) is presented to the input units, holding aside *Knew Pat* until the next step. A compressed representation of those three words is achieved on the hidden layer; we can label this using the acronym (*LJM*). Instead of passing immediately to the output layer (which is not shown), the compressed representation gets copied on to one set of input units, as indicated by the dotted arrow, bringing us to the next step. As shown in diagram (b), the original input patterns are replaced by those for the next proposition – that is, those for the two words that had been held aside along with the compressed encoding of the original pattern. This 48-unit pattern is now itself compressed on to the 16-unit hidden layer (using the same connection weights as in the first step, but with a different result because the input is different). For the network the result is simply a numeric pattern, but for us the label ($KP\,(LJM)$) helps us keep track of what information has been compressed in this recursive encoding procedure.

There are no remaining words, so we can move on to decoding. (Now it is the input layer that need not be shown.) In diagram (c), the fully compressed representation is partly decompressed on to the output units. If all goes well, two sets of units will get activation patterns that approximate those for *Knew* and *Pat*, and the other set will have a pattern that does not approximate any word. Because this pattern is unknown, it must be a compressed representation of an embedded proposition. Therefore, as shown in diagram (d), it is copied on to the hidden layer (replacing the earlier pattern there) and run back over the decoding connections for further uncompressing. A pattern that approximates (*Loved John Mary*) is achieved. Assuming some extra mechanism for storing and nesting the results of multiple steps, the proposition (*Knew Pat (Loved John Mary*)) has been reconstructed.

This procedure of recursive encoding followed by recursive decoding works fairly well, but some caveats and limitations should be mentioned. First, a procedure must be specified for deciding whether an output pattern corresponds to a word or requires a further cycle of decompression. Pollack pointed out that getting this to work in practice may present a problem for scaling up RAAM networks. Second, although the network handled trees with as many as four levels of embedding, its recursive operations can be expected to suffer from capacity limitations; at some point performance should degrade as more information is compressed on to the hidden layer. Explicit symbolic representations do not share this characteristic – levels simply get added to a tree – but a mechanism for handling such trees might be designed so as to exhibit similar performance limitations. (If the system is intended as a cognitive model, such limitations should correspond to those of humans.) Third, the fact that input patterns were binary whereas hidden layer units took real-numbered values means that the opposite problem obtains for single propositions; as Pollack recognized, an "unbounded number of bits can be trivially compressed into a real number" (p. 96). Hence, the hidden-layer patterns can meaningfully be described as compressed only in the case of propositions that include at least one (preferably more) embedded propositions. (For each embedded proposition one 16-unit pattern of real numbers is fed back through the input layer to the 16-unit hidden layer. Hence, a tree with three levels of embedding like tree 3 above would require the compression of 32 units of real numbers plus 7 bit patterns on the 16-unit hidden layer.)

Leaving these technical concerns aside, the key to the successful operation of the encoding and decoding networks is finding appropriate weights for their connections. Thus, training must come first, and this is done using the *auto-associative network* in which the encoding and decoding networks are combined as shown in figure 6.6. In the case of the 14 trees we have been discussing, training is organized into epochs comprised of one training trial for each tree and subtree. On each trial, the network tries immediately to reproduce on its output layer the pattern presented on its input layer, compares the result to the target pattern for that tree (as indicated by the upwards arrow), and adjusts the weights so as to decrease the discrepancy the next time it encounters that tree. As usual, a large number of epochs will be needed to adequately train the weights.

Again using as an example the tree (*Knew Pat (Loved John Mary)*), we begin by presenting to the input units the appropriate binary patterns for the words in the embedded proposition (*Loved John Mary*). The same binary patterns are also designated as the target output. The network, using random initial weights, generates a pattern of activation on the output units that does not even come close to the target. To help remedy this failure to duplicate the input pattern, backpropagation is used to revise both layers of weights in the network so as to reduce error (the discrepancy between the actual output and the target output).

The tree (figure 6.5) has one more proposition, which is presented next so that the weights will be adjusted towards its needs as well. Just as for a trained network, the input units are supplied with the binary patterns for the words *Knew* and *Pat* and with the compressed representation of the embedded proposition. The compressed representation is obtained by copying the pattern that is on the hidden units at the end of the previous step (as indicated by the downwards dotted arrow in figure 6.6, which corresponds to the arrow extending from figure 6.7(a) to 6.7(b). The upwards dotted arrow indicates that the same compressed representation is supplied to the training procedure to use as the target output; it will be compared with the actual output that is obtained by running this second proposition through the network. In this example there are no further propositions, but the procedure can be repeated as many times as necessary to handle more levels of embedding (up to four in the 14 trees of this study).

An interesting problem in training the weights results from the fact that compressed representations are run back through the input layer and, since this is an auto-associative network, also are used as target outputs. The compressed representations are not prespecified, but rather are the products of the network's own activity. Since the weights get adjusted every time a proposition is presented for training, the compressed representation will be different for the same proposition the next time it is presented (i.e., in the next epoch). Thus, during training the network is "chasing a moving target." In early epochs the compressed representations make very poor target patterns for guiding weight changes via backpropagation. Repeated applications of the training procedure bring improved representations and weights, with almost perfect auto-association eventually achieved. The two parts of the network can then be detached and used as encoder and decoder networks in the manner described above.

6.3.3   Functional compositionality of compressed representations

After training, Pollack's encoder network was able to produce compressed representations from which the decoder network could reconstruct all 14 trees. In light of this success, two questions arise. First, how did the networks achieve this performance? Second, what can be done with the compressed representations besides simply decoding them? It turns out that these two questions have related answers, which have to do with the nature of the compressed representations.

The compressed representations exhibit several properties that play a role in the success of the networks. First, they do (implicitly) represent the compositional structure of complex expressions. Using a RAAM network trained on another set of trees (syntactic phrase structure trees), Pollack performed a cluster analysis on the post-training numeric patterns on the hidden layer. The result indicated that the network had made structure-relevant generalizations; for example, verb phrases formed one cluster and prepositional phrases another. It did not do this by concatenating explicit grammatical symbols like V and NP, but neither had it merely memorized a set of unrelated mappings. Generalizations about constituent structure were captured in the network's weights. However, this is only a partial answer to the question of how RAAM networks perform their tasks. A more complete answer – showing that the networks exhibit productivity and systematicity – would also answer some of Fodor and Pylyshyn's objections to networks.

Pollack assessed productivity by encoding and then decoding new patterns of the same kind as those used in training. The network trained on syntactic phrase structure trees was able to generalize its knowledge to a number of additional well-formed patterns, but stopped short of full productivity. The network trained on propositions was less successful; often its encoding of a new proposition was decoded into one of the original training propositions by mistake. Pollack gave just one example: when presented with the new proposition (*Thought John (Knew Pat (Loved Mary John)))* the network returned (*Thought Pat (Knew John (Loved Mary John)))*, which is tree 3 above. He explained the error as due to the fact that "the input patterns are *too* similar; i.e., the Hamming distance between JOHN and PAT is only one bit" (pp. 94–5). This would likely become a more serious problem in trying to scale up the network to handle larger, more realistic corpora. Pollack suggested (p. 96) that the solution might be to use distributed representations for words comparable to those the network constructs for embedded propositions. Critics of Pollack may see in this problem an indication that one of the reasons for the success of the network, the fact that the vocabulary was constructed to make words of a category more similar (a feature that the network clearly picked up on in its generalizations), may actually spell its downfall (see Haselager and van Rappard, 1998). However, it is possible to make a more positive interpretation by arguing that this network error is precisely the sort we expect from humans as well (for example, you might have had to go back to reread the sentence to notice the difference).

Pollack also took a preliminary look at the capacity of the proposition network to exhibit systematicity. Since four names were available in the lexicon used to construct the trees, 16 simple propositions were possible. However, only four of them actually occurred in the 14 trees on which the network had been trained: those in trees 1–3 above plus (*Loved Pat Mary*). Pollack put the 12 untrained propositions through the trained RAAM, and found that its auto-associative abilities generalized well: all 12 propositions could be encoded and decoded with no further training. Recalling the sort of examples Fodor and Pylyshyn offered as illustrative of systematicity, the network would seem to have exhibited this property to some degree. (To know to what degree, further assessments using multi-proposition trees and additional predicates would be needed.)

So the answer to the first question above – how do the networks achieve their success? – has to do with their ability to arrive at connection weights sufficient to encode and decode explicitly compositional trees using compressed representations that are functionally compositional. Evidence for their functional compositionality is preliminary but diverse: the cluster analysis suggested that the networks make generalizations about structure, and the generalization studies indicated some degree of productivity and systematicity. All of this is relevant to answering the second question above – what can be done with the compressed representations besides simply decoding them? To the extent that they are functionally compositional, they should not need to be decoded in order to be useful in performing a variety of interesting tasks that require sensitivity to constituent structure.

6.3.4 Performing operations on compressed representations

As a preliminary demonstration of additional uses for compressed representations, Pollack trained a separate 16–8–16 feedforward network to make a simple kind of inference (unfortunately untrue in real life): (*Loved X Y*) implies (*Loved Y X*). He constructed its training and test cases by using the RAAM network to obtain compressed representations of the 16 simple propositions and from these formed 16 implicational pairs. For example, one pair was (*Loved Pat Mary*) ⇒ (*Loved Mary Pat*); another was (*Loved Mary Pat*) ⇒ (*Loved Pat Mary*). Then he used backpropagation to train the feedforward network on 12 of the pairs. When supplied with a compressed representation of a proposition of the form (*Loved X Y*), its task was to produce on its output layer the compressed representation of (*Loved Y X*). As evidence of generalization, Pollack further showed that it could handle the four untrained pairs as well. However, too much should not be made of this demonstration. As discussed above, Pollack's hidden-layer representations of simple propositions involve something more like recoding than compression, and there is no embedding to keep track of. Further, associating these input–output pairs should not be much of a challenge for a 16–8–16 feedforward network; it is the number of patterns and their statistical structure that determine difficulty, not the fact that they were produced as compressed representations by another network.

The point concerning compression (but not the one concerning embedding) was addressed by Blank, Meeden, and Marshall (1992). Using a procedural variation in which word-by-word presentation produced compressed representations of simple propositions, they succeeded in making and generalizing inferences such as *X chase Y* ⇒ *Y flee X*. As a bonus, another network achieved 85–88 percent accuracy when it was trained to detect categories such as *noun-aggressive* in the compressed representations.

The points concerning both compression and embedding were addressed in the results of Chalmers (1990). His method was similar to Pollack's, but because he used more complex trees as the output targets we can assume that (a) their representations would be more compressed; and (b) the ability to produce and then decode them would indicate some degree of sensitivity to constituent structure. Trees for active sentences, such as (*John Love Michael*), were paired with trees for the corresponding passive sentence, such as (*Michael (Is Love NIL) (By John NIL)*). (To stay with Pollack's triadic format, Chalmers used NIL as a dummy element.) There were five names and five predicates, making 125 possible active sentences. Chalmers first trained a RAAM network to construct compressed representations of 80 trees (40 active and 40 passive), and then obtained an additional 80 compressed representations as a byproduct of testing its ability to generalize. He next trained a feedforward Transformation Network using the first 80 compressed representations, appropriately paired as input and target patterns. When provided with any of the 40 compressed actives the trained network produced the corresponding compressed passive, and when that was presented to the RAAM's decoder network the correct tree was recovered. To test generalization, the extra 40 (untrained) compressed actives from above were presented to the Transformation Network. Only 65 percent of the resulting patterns on its output layer were adequate to produce the correct tree when run through the RAAM's decoder network. Yet, all but one of the errors involved substitutions of words within the same category, revealing that even the errors demonstrated a respect for the systematicity of the uncompressed representational system.

Do RAAM networks perform systematically enough to credit them with solving the variable binding problem? No, if one emphasizes that nouns were sometimes confused when generalization was tested using untrained propositions (especially for Chalmers and for Pollack's embedded propositions). A tentative yes (pending more simulations), if one emphasizes that the confusions were limited to nouns with similar encodings and that the capabilities tested amounted to variable binding (though performed without explicit variables). To the extent that the networks exhibited these capabilities, they did it by making use of positional encodings, that is, encodings on a separate ensemble of units for each position in a sequence. When Pollack trained a network on simple propositions, for example, the first ensemble of 16 units was dedicated to encoding the predicate, the second ensemble to the noun that was the predicate's first argument, and the third ensemble to the noun that was the predicate's second argument. There was no ambiguity of the kind described by Fodor and Pylyshyn when multiple nouns, each in a different syntactic role, are encoded on a single ensemble of units (figure 6.2). Positional encoding was also used in the logic networks in section 4.3 (each proposition and connective had its own small ensemble of units), Plunkett and Marchman's (1991, 1993) past-tense networks (there were separate, though identical, ensembles of units for encoding the first, second, and third phonemes comprising a verb stem), and in many of the networks in chapters 7–10.

Pollack viewed the representations developed by his RAAM network as "a very new kind of representation, a recursive, distributed representation" (p. 102). His method for combining recursive operation with distributed representations was indeed novel, and the initial demonstrations of functional compositionality were encouraging though incomplete. The compressed representations have the potential to be directly usable by a variety of cognitive operations, and to this extent Fodor and Pylyshyn's notion of a cognitive system with explicitly compositional syntax and semantics may be effectively countered. One question that remains is how well RAAM networks might scale up to perform realistic cognitive tasks; for a negative assessment, see Hadley (1994a) and Haselager and van Rappard (1998). A related question is whether they will make the transition from serving to make a theoretical point to becoming a part of modelers' toolkits. It appears that RAAM networks as such will not, but some of the design principles they incorporate (positional encodings, recursive encodings) have found widespread application.

6.4   Third Connectionist Response: Employing Procedural Knowledge with External Symbols

The first two responses to Fodor and Pylyshyn followed the common strategy in cognitive science of building internal representations of the external items with which a system must deal, and then performing internal operations on them. These respondents took classical rule systems and the compositional structure of natural language as starting points, trying to achieve the same ends as classicists but by connectionist means (in part because they expected these new means to confer some distinctive advantages). The systems we reviewed in sections 6.2 and 6.3 had in common the use of distributed representations: in those exemplifying the first connectionist response, the investigator explicitly hand-crafted the representations so as to implement rules, and in those exemplifying the second connectionist response, the networks invented their own representations such that information about compositional structure was implicit and recoverable. Whether explicitly or implicitly, external structure was internalized. This fits with a perspective on cognitive theorizing in which the structure of natural language is taken to be a reflection of the structure of the internal representations we employ in our mental processes, and is a point of similarity between classicists and most connectionists.

A very different approach is to think of external representational systems, such as natural languages, not as reflections of something else, but as comprising their own structured representational systems. On this view, our cognitive system must have the procedural ability to utilize this compositionally structured representational system, *but it need not build up a complete compositional internal representation* of what it is processing. In what follows, we will first explore how connectionist networks might acquire and possess such procedural knowledge. Then we will explore the implications of this external symbols approach for answering Fodor and Pylyshyn.

6.4.1 Temporal dependencies in processing language

Two significant characteristics of sentences are: (1) they are processed sequentially in time; (2) they exhibit long-distance dependencies, that is, the form of one word (or larger constituent) may depend on another that is located at an indeterminate distance. For example, verbs must agree with their subjects, but a relative clause or other constituent can intervene between the subject and the verb. In order for a network to produce or interpret sentences, it must be able to retain information relevant to such relationships. The challenge here is to design networks that can do this without building explicit representations of complete linguistic structures.

A standard feedforward network is incapable of retaining information about specific previous inputs; essentially, the slate is wiped clean when a new input pattern is presented, and the new hidden and output patterns depend just on that input. The only information carried over from past processing is any updating of the weights that occurred if the network was in training mode. The weights provide long-term encoding of information about how to respond to all inputs of the types on which the network is being trained – in human terms, a long-term semantic memory but no long-term episodic memory and no short-term memory. At a given point in time a feedforward network has access only to this limited long-term memory and to the patterns generated by its current input.

We have already seen in section 6.3 that feedforward networks can be modified to remedy their lack of short-term memory, specifically, by adding recurrent connections for copying encodings from one set of units to another. In RAAM networks one set of input units sometimes receives a copy of the hidden unit pattern rather than an externally supplied input. This serves as a short-term memory for already-processed parts of a sentence, allowing fairly complex sentences to be presented on

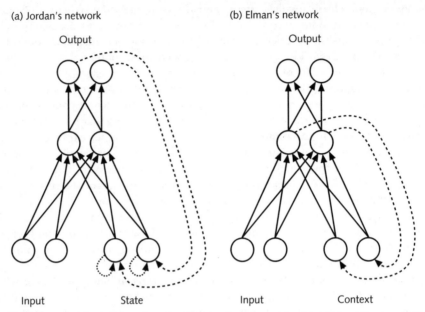

Figure 6.8 Simple recurrent networks (SRNs) as proposed by (a) Michael Jordan (1986) and (b) Jeffrey Elman (1990). The solid arrows represent feedforward connections which connect every unit in one layer with every unit in the next layer. The dashed arrows indicate the recurrent connections used to copy the activation value of specific output or hidden units to special input units (and, in Jordan's proposal, individual input units to themselves).

just three sets of units. In the current section the same basic innovation (copying patterns across recurrent connections) is adapted to the goal of achieving procedural processing of sentences. Simple Recurrent Networks receive sentences one word at a time and use their short-term memory capability to retain whatever information is most useful for predicting the next word or word class. Unlike RAAM networks, they do not necessarily retain the complete constituent structure of the sentences presented to them.

6.4.2 Achieving short-term memory with simple recurrent networks

The basic innovation that gave rise to Simple Recurrent Networks (SRNs) was offered by Michael Jordan (1986b). He added recurrent connections for copying the pattern on the *output units* on to a special set of input units he called *state units*. When the next item in the sequence is presented to the regular input units, both that pattern and the pattern on the state units are fed through the network (figure 6.8(a)). Thus, the network can utilize a trace of the decision it reached on the previous processing cycle. This is made recursive by feeding the previous pattern on the state units back to those units along with the previous output pattern and sending their combined influence to the hidden units. Jeffrey Elman (1990) developed a variation on this design in which it is the values of the hidden units, not the output units, that are copied back on to special input units; he called them *context units* (figure 6.8(b)).

The motivation for this change is that the activation pattern on the hidden units is the network's internal representation of the input. Sending this representation back through the network makes the network's activity sensitive to its own construal of the immediately preceding input.[4] Elman's SRN is similar to a RAAM network in that the copy comes from the hidden layer, but different in sending it to a reserved set of context units. As we will see, SRNs also are distinctive in how they use this architecture to implement procedural processing of externally structured material.

The sort of memory that SRNs provide of past processing differs dramatically from that of traditional cognitive models. This is best seen by considering how an Elman-style SRN uses recursion (in a variation on Jordan's method) to achieve sensitivity to information presented more than one cycle previously. It receives no explicit representation of that input. But it does receive as input the copy of the activations of hidden units on the immediately previous cycle. This pattern was itself the product of the input on that cycle and the activations on the hidden units the cycle before that. So the current pattern on the context units has been influenced not just by the previous input, but also by the one before that. This recursive activity can extend through many cycles, although the further back the cycle, the more degraded is the information in the context pattern and the less it contributes to current activity.

In summary, SRNs process sentences word by word, but use their context units to incorporate information about previous words. This is accomplished not by explicit representations of those words, but rather by a pattern of activation that retains (decreasingly over cycles) a record of the results of processing them. Hence, recurrent networks clearly provide one way to address the first characteristic of sentences mentioned above: they process sentences sequentially in time. They do this in a way that provides some memory function, but is this nontraditional memory adequate to handle the second characteristic of sentences, the dependencies between nonadjacent words?

6.4.3   Elman's first study: Learning grammatical categories

To determine how well an SRN could learn dependencies between words, Elman (1990) trained one to keep predicting the next word in a linguistic corpus. It had 31 units each in its input and output layers, and 150 units each in its hidden layer and context layer. In order to assure that the input patterns were orthogonal, he used a nondistributed binary encoding of a 29-word vocabulary. (For each word, one of the 31 input units was turned on and the rest were off; the other two units were reserved for later simulations). From these he constructed 10,000 simple two- and three-word sentences by filling 15 different sentence templates with words randomly selected from the appropriate set for each position. Three of the templates were:

NOUN-HUMAN VERB-INTRANSITIVE
NOUN-ANIMATE VERB-TRANSITIVE NOUN-ANIMATE
NOUN-HUMAN VERB-EAT NOUN-FOOD

Note that some templates used more inclusive categories than others. The third template could generate just 12 sentences, including *woman eat cookie* and *boy eat bread*. The second template could generate these and several thousand more. Having obtained 10,000 sentence tokens, Elman concatenated them into a single corpus 27,354 words in length (with no indication of the beginning or end of individual sentences). Within a sentence, the possibilities for the second word depend upon the first word, and the possibilities for the third word depend upon the first two words. For example, *woman eat* can be followed only by *sandwich, cookie,* or *bread,* whereas *dragon eat* can be followed by *woman, man, girl, boy, cat, mouse, dog, monster, lion,* or *dragon* as well as *sandwich, cookie,* or *bread.*

The corpus was presented to the SRN one word at a time. On each cycle the network tried to predict the next word in the sequence, compared its output to the target word, and then adjusted its weights. After only six training passes through the entire corpus, the network's predictions closely approximated the actual probabilities of subsequent words in the training corpus. (During training the target output was the actual next word in the corpus, but for testing the output was compared to a composite pattern in which each word's activation level was equal to the proportion of times it was the next word given the preceding words in the sentence. Attaining that composite would be the best the network could do, since it has no way of knowing precisely which sentence is being presented.)

What interested Elman was not just that a network could do this, but how it did it. What representation of the input sentences had been formed on the hidden layer to enable good performance on this task? The statistical technique of cluster analysis is often used to answer this type of question (e.g., for RAAM networks in the preceding section). In a cluster analysis, the similarity between each pair of hidden unit patterns is calculated, and a hierarchical tree structure is generated that displays the similarity structure of the patterns. Hence, input patterns that produced very similar hidden layer patterns will be tightly clustered together at one of the lower branches of the tree, whereas less similar patterns will be more remotely connected through a higher branch of the tree.

Elman performed a cluster analysis on the trained network, which is shown in figure 6.9 (displayed sideways, such that higher branch points are at the left). At the highest level, nouns and verbs formed separate branches of the tree. That is, the patterns of activation across the hidden units distinguished nouns from verbs; the network had been sensitive to the distributional differences between nouns and verbs in the training sentences. Within these broad classes, narrower linguistic classes branched from nodes midway through the tree (e.g., verbs for which a direct object is obligatory vs. optional vs. absent; animate vs. inanimate nouns), and the narrowest classes were clustered at the bottom (e.g., domestic animals vs. aggressive animals).

It is important to note that the pattern of activation produced on the hidden units was determined not just by the input pattern, but by the pattern on the context units as well. Elman demonstrated this effect by substituting a word not previously in the corpus for all tokens of the word *man,* and presenting this revised corpus to the network without any additional training. The patterns generated on the hidden units for this new word were very similar to those that had been generated for *man,* and only the context units could have been responsible for this.

The performance of the SRN is quite impressive, especially when it is recalled that it achieved it without any knowledge of semantics. For example, the network learned to group the encodings for animate objects together only because they were distributed similarly in the training corpus. Elman cited Jay McClelland's characterization of this task as comparable to trying to learn a language by listening to the

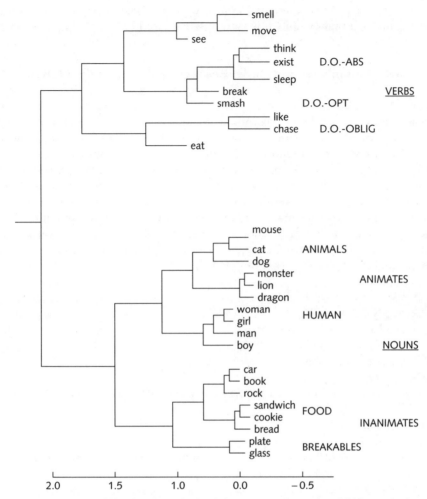

Figure 6.9 Elman's (1990) cluster analysis of the patterns formed on hidden units in a simple recurrent network when the network was trained to predict the next word in a corpus of 10,000 two- and three-word sentences. The cluster analysis reveals how the network has categorized the various words in its corpus by giving items within a category similar activation patterns. For example, the patterns for nouns are generally more similar to each other than to those for verbs, but greater degrees of similarity identify smaller clusters within these broad clusters. This diagram was kindly supplied by Jeffrey Elman.

radio. It turns out, however, that this is not as farfetched as it sounds. In a study published in *Science* that received considerable attention, Saffran, Aslin, and Newport (1996) showed that 8-month-olds exposed to four different three-syllable nonsense words in a continuous stream of randomly ordered tokens for just two minutes picked up enough statistical information about the sequential distribution of the syllables that they became sensitive to the word boundaries. (We cannot pursue the exchanges triggered by this article. In particular, Marcus, Vijayan, Bandi Rao, and Vishton, 1999, responded with their own version of the task and a rule-based "algebraic" explanation that is at odds both with the original article and with models that support an explanation in terms of sensitivity to the statistics of input. For example,

Christiansen, Allen, and Seidenberg, 1998, offered a connectionist model of the word segmentation task that exhibits this kind of sensitivity.)

6.4.4 Elman's second study: Respecting dependency relations

Elman's (1990) study showed that a network exposed to a corpus of sentences one word at a time could gradually incorporate its statistical dependencies into its weights so as to perform the task of predicting which words were possible next. However, the corpus was limited to monoclausal sentences generated from 15 templates. The sentences of any natural language show far greater diversity and require at least recursive rules (not merely templates) for their generation. Elman (1991) employed a significantly more complex stimulus set. Its sentences were constructed from the following phrase structure grammar, in which parentheses indicate optional constituents; vertical bars indicate a choice among alternatives; PropN indicates Proper Noun; RC indicates Relative Clause; and *who* is used rather than the more formal *whom* for object relative clauses (*who* NP VP):

S → NP VP "."
NP → PropN | N | N RC
VP → V (NP)
RC → *who* NP VP | *who* VP (NP)
N → boy | girl | cat | dog | boys | girls | cats | dogs
PropN → *John* | *Mary*
V → chase | feed | see | hear | walk | live | chases | feeds | sees | hears | walks | lives

Additional restrictions

- number agreement between N and V within a clause, and (where appropriate) between head N and subordinate V
- verb class (number of arguments):
    walk, live: verb intransitive (preclude a direct object)
    chase, feed: verb transitive (require a direct object)
    see, hear: verb either (optionally allow a direct object)

Elman noted that the sentences constructed with this grammar exhibit a number of important features of natural language. First, they require agreement between subjects and verbs and adherence to restrictions on verbs and their argument structures. Second, agreement and argument structure must be preserved even when relative clauses intervene. Further, there is the potential for recursive embedding of relative clauses. Finally, many sentences have several different points at which the sentence might end or continue. While still just a small fragment of English, the corpus provides a more challenging test of the SRN's abilities.

In this study Elman used an SRN with more layers than that of Study 1; there were two 10-unit hidden layers above and below a main hidden layer of 70 units. The 70 context units fed directly into the main hidden layer, bypassing the first 10-unit layer. Inputs were encoded in the same localist fashion on 26 input units (that is, a different unit was turned on for each of the 23 words in the vocabulary or for the "." used as an end-of-sentence marker; two units were reserved for later tests).[5]

As before, the network was trained to predict the next item in the string on its 26 output units.

An extremely interesting finding was that when Elman presented the whole corpus at once, the network failed to learn. Rather, it had to be trained in phases – one of two effective methods for achieving what Elman (1993) dubbed "starting small."[6] During the first phase, it was trained on a corpus of 10,000 simple sentences (sentences constructed without relative clauses), which were concatenated as in study 1 except this time the sentence boundaries were marked by a period ("."). The corpus, with a mean sentence length of 3.46, was presented to the network five times. In the second phase, 25 percent of the corpus consisted of complex sentences (sentences with one or more relative clauses) and 75 percent simple sentences; mean sentence length was 3.92 words. In the third phase the percentage of complex sentences was increased to 50 percent, resulting in a mean sentence length of 4.38 words. In the final phase of training, the percentage of complex sentences was 75 percent and the mean sentence length was 6.02.

After the final training phase, generalization was tested on a novel data set constructed in the same manner as that used in the final phase of training (75 percent complex sentences). The network was evaluated in terms of how well its predictions of the next word approximated the probabilities of particular words occurring next, which was a measure of whether it could predict the proper word class according to the grammar. This was done by determining the context-dependent vectors for each word in every sentence in the corpus, which represented the probability of occurrence of each word in such a context. The error produced was quite low (the mean cosine of the angle between the vectors was 0.852 with sd = 0.259).

A more detailed evaluation could be made by examining the network's response to individual sentences during testing. Consider first simple monoclausal sentences (figure 6.10). After it was given the input *boy* the network responded by activating roughly equally the word *who* and each of the three classes of singular verbs. If the input was the plural *boys*, in contrast, the network activated *who* and each of the three classes of plural verbs. (The length of the bar for each verb class was obtained by simply summing the activations for the two verbs in the class.) If the singular *boy* was followed by the verb *lives*, which cannot take a direct object, the network's prediction after this second word was simply ".". If, on the other hand, it was followed by *sees*, for which a direct object is optional, it activated not just "." but also proper name, plural noun, and singular noun. If, instead, the initial word *boy* was followed by the word *chases*, which requires a direct object, the network activated proper name, plural noun, and singular noun but not ".".

The network was also able to handle more complex sentences with relative clauses. Some of the requirements which the network satisfied are rather subtle. For example, following *boys who Mary*, the network predicted that the verb would be one that required a direct object. This was correct, since the direct object (*boys*) had already occurred. Thus, the network is sensitive to direct objects whether they occur after the verb, as in simple sentences, or before the verb, as they might in relative clauses. Sometimes the dependencies it respects are rather long-range. After being presented the sequence *boys who Mary chases* the network correctly predicts that the next word will be in one of the three classes of plural verbs, thus maintaining agreement with *boys*. Note that if the network were not sensitive to long-distance dependencies, and were only relying on the immediate context of *Mary chases*, it presumably would predict a noun.

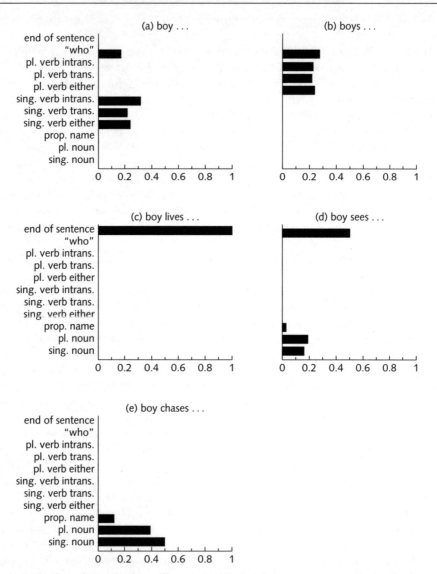

Figure 6.10   Sample results from Elman's (1990) simple recurrent network. Depending on what words have just been encountered, the output units for the words that might come next become active. The activations for all words in the same class (e.g., plural verb intransitive) are summed, as indicated by the length of the bar. (The absence of a bar means that class was not predicted to occur next.)

   Elman claimed that because the grammar he used in his simulation allows recursive embedding of relative clauses, it is the sort of grammar that Chomsky (1957) argued could not be reasonably modeled by a finite state automaton and Miller and Chomsky (1963) argued could not be handled by statistical inference. He interpreted his SRN's success as a demonstration that connectionist networks exceed the limitations of finite state machines and statistical inference engines (Elman, 1993). Nonetheless, the computational requirements in Elman's grammar are far less demanding than those of a natural language such as English (there are no movement

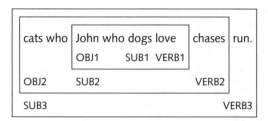

Figure 6.11   The double center-embedded sentence used in Christiansen's (1994) study. The subjects, objects, and verbs each are labeled as belonging to clause 1, 2, or 3.

transformations, for example). Moreover, as a general strategy in investigating any computational model, we should seek to find its limitations and compare them to those of humans. Accordingly, it is interesting to consider briefly Morten Christiansen's (1994) experiments using SRNs for the same task devised by Elman, but using more complicated grammars.

6.4.5   Christiansen's extension: Pushing the limits of SRNs

Christiansen (1994) constructed two grammars that generate some of the more complex structures found in natural languages, including multiple center embeddings and cross-dependencies. (Cross-dependency is a rare structure, found in only a few languages such as Dutch, in which verb complements of each noun phrase occur in the order in which the corresponding noun phrases occur.[7] We will focus on his results with a grammar that permitted recursive center embeddings but not cross-dependencies.) In a center-embedded structure, a complete clause (NP VP) is interposed between the NP and VP of a higher clause. Here is a simple example of a center-embedded sentence: *the cake that Pat baked crumbled.* An example with the same structure, but harder to process is: *cats who John chases run.* Such sentences get much more difficult when there are multiple embeddings, as in: *cats whom John whom dogs love chases run.* As shown in figure 6.11, such a sentence requires noun–verb agreement and linking of a direct object to its transitive verb to extend over one or more intervening relative. (Center embeddings were permitted in Elman's grammar as well, but he did not report any examples of the network's performance on sentences involving multiple center embeddings.)

Christiansen's grammar also allows a variety of sentence structures not permitted in Elman's grammar: prepositional modification of noun phrases, genitives, conjoined noun phrases, and sentential complements for propositional attitude verbs. Moreover, each of these can be employed recursively. The following is the complete grammar Christiansen used for his experiments. Note that V(i) is intransitive, V(t) is transitive, V(o) is optional, and V(c) takes a sentential complement; gen indicates a genitive construction; and other notation is consistent with Elman's:

S → NP VP "."
NP → PropN | N | N rel | N PP | gen N | N *and* NP
VP → V(i) | V(t) NP | V(o) (NP) | V(c) *that* S
rel → *who* NP V(t|o) | *who* VP
PP → prep prepN

gen → N + "s" | gen N + "s"
N → *boy* | *girl* | *man* | *boys* | *girls* | *men* | *cats* | *dogs*
PropN → *John* | *Mary*
V(i) → *jumps* | *jump* | *runs* | *run*
V(t) → *loves* | *love* | *chase* | *chases*
V(o) → *sees* | *see*
V(c) → *thinks* | *think* | *says* | *say* | *knows* | *know*
prep → *near* | *from* | *in*
prepN → *town* | *lake* | *city*

Christiansen offered the following as examples of sentences permitted by this grammar (except that it would not recognize the possessive punctuation in sentence 1):

Mary knows that John's boys' cats see dogs.
boy loves girl from city near lake.
man who chases girls in town thinks that Mary jumps.
John says that cats and dogs run.
Mary who loves John thinks that men say that girls chase boys.
girl who men chase loves cats.
cats who John who dogs love chases run.

Christiansen used a network with 42 input and 42 output units to provide a localist encoding of the 38 vocabulary items (four units were left unused); there were 150 hidden units. Following the same procedure as Elman, he trained the network in five phases with 10,000 sentences per phase. Instead of restricting the training materials in the early epochs to simple sentences with no embedding, he used Elman's alternative technique of limiting the length of recurrent memory available and gradually increasing it as training progresses (see note 6). Overall, the network performed only a little worse than Elman's despite confronting a considerably more difficult corpus (mean cosine: 0.7904; sd: 0.2702).

Whereas Elman emphasized sentences on which the network could make correct predictions, Christiansen focused on the extremely challenging cases for which errors start to appear. We will examine just one of the sentences on which Christiansen tested his network, the doubly center-embedded sentence in figure 6.11: *cats who John who dogs love chases run*. Christiansen stated that the network had little or no difficulty on sentences with a single center-embedded clause, but it did make errors on this doubly center-embedded sentence. Figure 6.12 shows the activations for various classes of words on the output layer as each word was presented to the input layer. The network performed flawlessly as it was fed the first few words of the sentence. For example, panel (b) in figure 6.12 shows that it predicted either a noun, a genitive, or a singular verb following word 4 (*who*).

The network made its first error when it reached the word *love* (d). It should have predicted a singular transitive verb to agree with the subject *John*. It did activate the output unit for this category (dark bar), but also activated intransitive and propositional attitude singular verbs, plural verbs, and especially the end-of-sentence marker (striped bars). It also made too many predictions in the next step (e), but then when supplied with *run* (f), it correctly predicted that the sentence was complete.

That the errors cropped up where they did in this sentence might be viewed as indicating human-like performance, for it is at these points in such sentences that

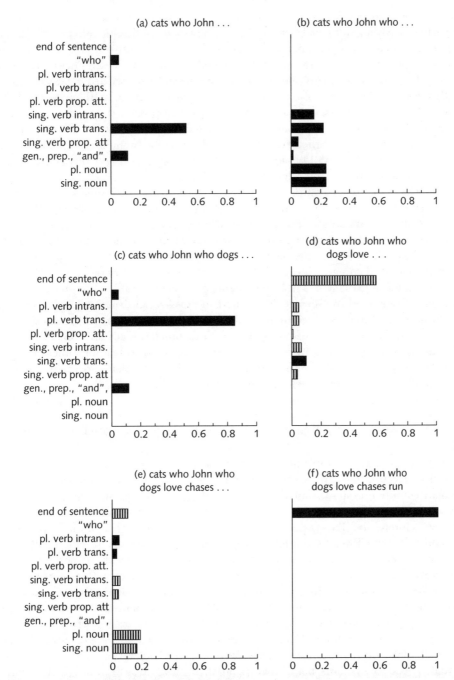

Figure 6.12 The predictions of Christiansen's (1994) network at different points in processing the sentence in figure 6.11. Activation levels are calculated as in figure 6.10, except that the dark bars indicate correct predictions of the next word class by the network and the striped bars indicate erroneous predictions (those not allowed by the grammar).

humans tend to get confused. In this regard, Christiansen cited studies of recall reported by Miller and Isard (1964), of comprehension by Larkin and Burns (1977), and of grammaticality judgments by Marks (1968). The network also showed patterns of sporadic error in the most deeply embedded parts of sentences with prenominal genitives with three levels of recursion, right-embedded relative clauses with two levels of recursion, and prepositional modifications with three levels of embedding. In most cases the network continued to predict the correct continuations, but would also predict grammatically illegal continuations. On the other hand, the network showed no difficulty handling multiple right-branching sentential complements, as in *Mary says that men think that John knows that cats run*, and humans find this kind of embedding relatively easy as well.

To make more precise comparisons between the network and humans, Christiansen and Chater (1999) developed a measure of grammatical prediction error (GPE) that allowed the network's output to be mapped on to common psycholinguistic measures. GPE is computed on the output for each word in a sentence, reflecting the processing difficulties that the network is experiencing at each point, and these can then be averaged to get a mean GPE for each sentence. Christiansen and Chater found that mean GPE scores fit human data on the considerable difficulty of center-embedded sentences in German (compared to cross-serial dependencies in Dutch, for example). Moreover, McDonald and Christiansen (in press) fit human data on the differential processing of singly center-embedded subject and object relative clauses by mapping single-word GPE scores directly on to reading times. Results like these suggest that SRNs can play a role in modeling human performance across a range that includes incompetencies as well as competencies.

6.5   Using External Symbols to Provide Exact Symbol Processing

The assumptions and implications of the third connectionist reply to Fodor and Pylyshyn (section 6.4) are worth exploring a bit further. The core idea is that the human cognitive system might have acquired procedural knowledge for working with structured representations without forming the same kinds of structured representations internally. This suggests a different explanation for the origin of productive and systematic thought: it might be a consequence of humans developing *external* symbol systems, such as those of natural language, which exhibit compositional structure. Consider language as the quintessential symbol system. Part of its interest lies in its dual role as an internal tool (e.g., for mental problem solving) and as an external tool (e.g., for written or verbal problem solving and for communication). This duality is emphasized in Vygotsky's (1962) characterization of problem solving as carried out externally early in development (by means of *egocentric speech*) and internally later on (by means of *inner speech*). It is in the external mode that we can actually observe symbols being manipulated, somewhat as they might be manipulated in a formal symbol system. In the externalist approach to symbol processing, the focus is turned from symbols in their mental roles to symbols in their external roles. (For development of a related approach to religious symbols and religious systems see Lawson and McCauley, 1990.)

Smolensky (1988) discussed the cultural practice of formulating knowledge in external symbols that can be used to communicate that knowledge (e.g., in a textbook or lecture). He viewed these external symbolic formulations as being internalized and utilized by a *conscious rule interpreter* that is distinct from the inherently sub-conceptual *intuitive processor*. Although his interest was directed primarily towards the latter processor, which is the one that requires a connectionist account, he noted three properties of the linguistic encoding of knowledge that are important not just for individuals but also for such cultural goals as the advancement of science:

- *Public access*: the knowledge is accessible to many people.
- *Reliability*: different people (or the same person at different times) can reliably check whether conclusions have been validly reached.
- *Formality, bootstrapping, universality*: the inferential operations require very little experience with the domain to which the symbols refer.

(1988, p. 4)

The pre-connectionist assumption had been that in order for people to operate as conscious rule interpreters they must make use of internal rules and structured representations. It may be fruitful to approach this from another angle, however. Each human is born into a community which makes extensive use of external symbols, and these symbols and the regularities in their relation to one another (and in their relation to the world and to the child's own mental states) are part of the environment in which the infant develops. The novice human acquires the ability to interact with the external symbols by means of lower-level processes (such as connectionist pattern recognition) that do not themselves involve a direct inter-nalization of these symbols. That is, the infant *learns how to use* external symbols. Although an individual's ability to think and reason appears to be aided by eventu-ally internalizing the use of symbols in some sense, this internalization comes later and is incomplete. Even in mature individuals, difficult problems elicit the use of external symbols. Also, it is quite unclear *in what sense* symbols are internalized. The connectionist program includes the goal of uncovering the causal mechanisms that occur at the subsymbolic level in carrying out what is identified at a higher level as *symbolic processing*. Until the program has been actualized to a much greater extent, there is no way of knowing whether additional causal mechanisms at the higher, symbolic level will also be needed to *account for* those regularities that are most efficiently *described at* that level. Alternatively, connectionist processes such as pattern recognition may suffice to account for the ability to use symbols. Or there may be other specialized processes, not themselves symbolic, that generate activity in the system comparable to that occasioned by particular external symbols. If a connectionist wishes to examine symbol processing at this time, networks' use of external symbols may be the most appropriate place to begin; coming to understand what it means to internalize them will be more of a challenge.

The suggestion we are developing here is rather different from the approach of directly designing networks to perform symbolic processing. Rather than trying to implement a rule system, we are proposing to teach a network to *use* a system (language) in which information, including rules, can be encoded symbolically. In encountering these symbols, however, the network behaves in the same basic man-ner as it always does: it recognizes patterns and responds to them as it has been trained. (For a relatively simple simulation of how a network might learn to use language in this way, see Allen, 1988). If the external symbols are in an enduring modality (e.g., handwriting), the external storage will enable the network to perform tasks that it cannot solve on the basis of a single act of pattern recognition. Rumelhart,

Smolensky, McClelland, and Hinton (1986) in *PDP:14* illustrated this by constructing a scenario for solving a three-digit multiplication problem:

> We are good at "perceiving" answers to problems. . . . However, . . . few (if any) of us
> can look at a three-digit multiplication problem (such as 343 times 822) and see the
> answer. Solving such problems cannot be done by our pattern-matching apparatus,
> parallel processing alone will not do the trick; we need a kind of serial processing mech-
> anism to solve such a problem. Here is where our ability to manipulate our environ-
> ment becomes critical. We can, quite readily, learn to write down the two numbers in a
> certain format when given such a problem.
>
> 343
822
>
> Moreover, we can learn to see the first step of such a multiplication problem. (Namely,
> we can see that we should enter a 6 below the 3 and 2.)
>
> 343
822
6
>
> We can then use our ability to pattern match again to see what to do next. Each cycle
> of this operation involves first creating a representation through manipulation of the
> environment, then a processing of this (actual physical) representation by means of
> our well-tuned perceptual apparatus leading to a further modification of this rep-
> resentation.   (Rumelhart, Smolensky, McClelland, and Hinton, 1986, p. 45)[8]

They went on to suggest that this kind of iterative operation using external symbols
is what allows difficult problems, as in logic and science, to be solved:

> These dual skills of manipulating the environment and processing the environment we
> have created allow us to reduce very complex problems to a series of very simple
> ones. . . . This is *real* symbol processing and, we are beginning to think, the primary
> symbol processing that we are able to do.   (p. 46)

Our discussion of formal logical abilities (section 4.3) can be viewed from this
perspective. A person or a network that confronts external symbols that are configured
in accord with rules of logic might learn to process those symbols in the appropriate
logical manner (e.g., detecting what steps to include next in a derivation).

Rumelhart et al. took the additional step of considering how this use of external
symbols might to some extent be internalized. Their basic idea is that a mental
model of the external symbolic environment is constructed, and the procedures that
would ordinarily operate on external symbols operate instead on the mental model.
By using the output of the mental model as the input to the next mental operation of
pattern-matching, and the output of that operation as an input to the mental model,
a loop is obtained that can sustain a series of mental operations. A mental operation
itself is viewed as the network's process of settling or "relaxing" into an interpretation of a symbolic expression. They suggest that the resulting stable state endures
long enough (approximately half a second) to be conscious, but that the rapid cycles
of computation involved in settling are not conscious. (Cf. Dennett's, 1978, analysis
of one aspect of consciousness in terms of a specialized speech module that provides
a means of reporting the results of cognitive processing.) Rumelhart et al.'s speculative, but intriguing, development of this idea can be consulted on pp. 38–48 of

PDP:14. Although they do not specifically discuss the status of the internalized symbols, it is clear from their discussion that the symbols are simply patterns in a network. Stable states of the network are the "symbols"; but this is achieved by a subsymbolic, dynamic encoding that is quite distinct from the construal of symbols in the symbolic tradition.

Processing loops of the type used in the multiplication example would be one way to support recursion computationally, providing a connectionist mechanism for obtaining Fodor and Pylyshyn's properties of productivity, systematicity, and inferential coherence. Fodor and Pylyshyn would not be satisfied by this, because the connectionist mechanism is not one that guarantees the systematicity that they attribute to all thought. They may be wrong, however, to insist on the ubiquity of systematicity. The capacity for recursion arises rather late in development, and therefore should not be a part of a model of nascent cognition. That is, children do not initially construct models and use them to produce the processing loops that may support recursion. This may partly account for the fact that young children's language does not fully exhibit Fodor and Pylyshyn's properties of productivity, systematicity, and inferential coherence. Children's language (and thought) is particularly dependent upon the eliciting conditions and feedback provided by the external environment (symbolic or otherwise). A close analysis of the development of language from a connectionist perspective would pay high dividends as a way of grappling with questions concerning the properties of language and how the cognitive system functions so as to exhibit them.

Smolensky's (1988) distinction between a *conscious rule interpreter* and an *intuitive processor* pursued a somewhat different approach to the internalization question. Here, Smolensky was willing to accept symbolic models as providing an adequate account of the internal encoding and use of linguistically communicated rules. A chess novice would rely heavily on rules, for example, before she had developed sufficient experience to build a good intuitive processor that could often *see* which move to make (see section 4.2). Smolensky did suggest that there are advantages to performing a subsymbolic encoding even of rules (in particular, this would simplify interaction with the intuitive processor, which is a nontrivial problem for his approach); but still he pressed hardest on the idea that two distinct levels are involved at least with respect to explanatory adequacy.

Although we find most of Smolensky's ideas in this paper quite appealing, we are uncomfortable with the sharpness of this distinction. A somewhat different way of thinking about rules (which he touched on but did not apply to this issue) is to regard them as encodings that are unusually isolated from other encodings, and in particular are relatively context-invariant. (Either the rule is elicited in only one context, or is accessible from any relevant context but with rigid form.) This approach would predict a fair degree of continuity in the process of acquiring expert knowledge, and would view rule-like versus non-rule-like knowledge representation more as a continuum than as a dichotomy. At all points on this continuum, the same subsymbolic network approach to encoding would be used. Higher levels would simply be more abstract levels of description of certain regularities displayed in the network; within the network there would be additional nuances that may be useful for some purposes.

Leaving behind the issue of levels, we will note one last idea in Smolensky (1988): his vision of what could be achieved by coordination between a *rule interpreter* and *intuitive processor*. He wrote:

> An integrated subsymbolic rule interpreter/intuitive processor in principle offers the advantages of both kinds of processing. Imagine such a system creating a mathematical proof. The intuitive processor would generate goals and steps, and the rule interpreter would verify their validity. The serial search through the space of possible steps, which is necessary in a purely symbolic approach, is replaced by the intuitive generation of possibilities. Yet the precise adherence to strict inference rules that is demanded by the task can be enforced by the rule interpreter; the creativity of intuition can be exploited while its unreliability can be controlled.   (Smolensky, 1988, p. 13)

It is interesting to note that in many cases of actual mathematical proofs, the rule-checking function is only incompletely performed. The mathematician will say, following Laplace, "It is easily seen that . . . ," when in fact many steps remain to be filled in and sometimes it turns out that the steps cannot be filled in since the move is invalid (Cipra, 1989).

The proposals summarized in this section represent the most speculative of the connectionist perspectives on symbols that we have considered. They treat symbol manipulation as a learned capacity that is initially carried out on symbols in the external environment. On this view, symbols are primarily human artifacts such as linguistic and mathematic expressions, but they may eventually be internalized in the same format as nonsymbolic information.

6.6   Clarifying the Standard: Systematicity and Degree of Generalizability

In addition to these connectionist attempts to explain systematicity, there have been a number of attempts by both symbolic theorists and connectionists to clarify just what systematicity requires. We will briefly consider two such proposals, one focusing on the nomic nature of systematicity, and the other on the relation between systematicity and generalization.

In response to some of the early attempts of connectionists such as Smolensky to demonstrate systematicity in networks, Fodor and McLaughlin (1990; see also McLaughlin, 1993) argued that the issue is not whether one can make a connectionist network exhibit systematicity, but whether one could make it *fail* to do so:

> the problem that systematicity poses for connectionists . . . is not to show that system-atic cognitive capacities are *possible* given the assumptions of a connectionist architecture, but to explain how systematicity could be *necessary* – how it could be a *law* that cognitive capacities are systematic – given those assumptions.
>
> No doubt it is possible for Smolensky to wire a network so that it supports a vector that represents aRb if and only if it supports a vector that represents bRa; and perhaps it is possible for him to do that without making the imaginary units explicit. . . . The trouble is that, although the architecture permits this, it equally permits Smolensky to wire a network so that it supports a vector that represents aRb if and only if it supports a vector that represents zSq; or, for that matter, if and only if it supports a vector that represents The Last of The Mohicans. The architecture would appear to be absolutely indifferent as among these options. Whereas, as we keep saying, in the Classical architecture, if you meet the conditions for being able to represent aRb, YOU CANNOT BUT MEET THE CONDITIONS FOR BEING ABLE TO REPRESENT bRa; . . . So then: it is *built into* the Classical picture that you can't think aRb unless you are able to think bRa, but the Connectionist picture is *neutral* on whether you can think

aRb even if you can't think bRa. But it is a law of nature that you can't think aRb if can't think bRa. So the Classical picture explains systematicity and the Connectionist picture doesn't. So the Classical picture wins. (Fodor and McLaughlin, 1990, pp. 348–9)

One aspect of Fodor and McLaughlin's complaint against Smolensky seems right on target: to the degree that one accepts that cognition is systematic, one wants an explanation for it. Simply showing that a specific connectionist network exhibits systematicity does not provide an explanation. One would also want to know that such a network could emerge reliably under naturalistic conditions (e.g., under variable training conditions such as those experienced by different children) and have an account (e.g., an evolutionary account) showing why such a network would have developed. But the standard they have held aloft – that as a matter of scientific law, connectionist networks should exhibit systematicity – is far too strong, as a number of critics have pointed out. Aizawa (1997), for example, identified possible compositional systems that nonetheless do not exhibit systematicity, thereby demonstrating that compositionality does not, as a matter of law, establish systematicity. In a related manner, Hadley (1997) argued that symbolic representations only acquire systematicity when they are coupled with the appropriate processing mechanism, and no natural laws ensure such coupling. Matthews (1997) pointed out a further limitation of the symbolic approach: merely showing that a syntactic structure can be represented in the cognitive system does not suffice to show that it can be thought (i.e., understood). You might perform the transformation between aRb and bRa and discover that you have come up with a symbol string that is expressible but not thinkable: "I can think the thought that x is the sole member of the singleton set {x}, but I am quite certain that I cannot think the thought that the singleton set {x} is the sole member of x. I have no idea what proposition, if any, the sentence *the singleton set {x} is the sole member of x* expresses" (p. 162).

Turning now to the issue of generalization, one construal of Fodor and Pylyshyn's argument for productivity and systematicity is that these are core characteristics displayed by real cognitive systems when they generalize to new cases. It has been standard fare for connectionists to examine the capacity of their networks to generalize from training cases to new cases. But does the generalization exhibited by networks achieve the level or kind of generalization that inherently characterizes cognitive systems? Hadley (1994a) set out to analyze the sort of generalizability reported in studies of connectionist networks and proposed three degrees of systematicity.

A network exhibits the lowest degree of systematicity, *weak systematicity*, if it is merely "capable of successfully processing (by recognizing or interpreting) novel test sentences, once [it] has been trained on a corpus of sentences which are *representative*" (p. 6). The training corpus is representative if every word that appears in the training corpus appears in each of its permissible positions (if all positions were permissible, this could be accomplished by borrowing the Latin squares used to counterbalance sequences of conditions in an experiment). Thus, in weak systematicity, the sentences to which the network can generalize merely have new combinations of old words in their old positions.

To obtain higher degrees of systematicity the network must process words appearing in positions in which they did not appear in the training set. If its processing of new complex sentences (those with embedded clauses) has certain limitations, the network is said to exhibit *quasi-systematicity*. Specifically, the particular sentence forms must have been experienced during training, and for each word "in an embed-ded sentence (e.g., 'Bob knows that Mary saw *Tom*') there exists some *simple* sentence in the training corpus which contains that word in the same syntactic position as it occurs in the embedded sentence (e.g., 'Jane saw Tom')" (pp. 6–7).

To exhibit *strong systematicity*, for Hadley, a network must "correctly process a variety of novel *simple* sentences and novel *embedded* sentences containing previously learned words in positions where they *do not appear* in the training corpus (i.e., the word within the novel sentence does *not appear in the same syntactic position within any simple or embedded* sentence in the training corpus" (p. 7). Using this criterion, Hadley argues that connectionist models of language processing, including those by Pollack (1990), Chalmers (1990), and Elman (1990) discussed in this chapter, fail to exhibit strong systematicity.

Hadley himself (Hadley and Hayward, 1997) created a connectionist network which he claims does exhibit strong systematicity. As it processes sentences it de-velops bindings between concepts and case roles (both given a localist encoding); as a result, it employs explicitly compositional representations and in this respect ex-hibits affinities with symbolic approaches. It employs a version of Hebbian learning to create these bindings. (In illustration, this would be like adding special binding units and connections to figure 6.2 so that the network is able to pair up Joan-Subject, loves-Verb, florist-Object, or more accurately, completely wiring up the units but then training the resulting network so that only bindings that respect the grammar can be established during actual processing.) During training, Hadley and Hayward withheld a large number of sentences which had some of the nouns in novel positions (e.g., subject or object). When later tested on these, the network could process them correctly.

Although it seemed to have satisfied Hadley's criterion for strong systematicity, the network was designed to handle a very minimal grammar. All sentences had the form NP Verb NP, in which each NP consisted of a single noun or a noun followed by a relative clause (i.e., an embedded sentence of the form NP Verb NP). The network achieved systematicity by creating bindings between localist representa-tions, and so implemented a kind of compositional syntax. It is thus in the spirit of our first connectionist response, explicitly implementing rules and representations. But to accommodate even a minimal grammar, and despite its use of relatively simple localist encodings, it required detailed wiring and activation procedures for each relationship. It is not obvious how one could scale up such a system to handle something like a natural language.

Christiansen and Chater (1994) used Christiansen's network, discussed above, to find out whether a connectionist network that developed its own weights and rep-resentations (rather than being hard-wired to implement a rule system) could satisfy Hadley's strong systematicity condition. They established two tests of strong system-aticity. In one test, during training neither *girl* nor *girls* was permitted in a genitive context either as the possessor or the possessed. In the other test, during training neither *boy* nor *boys* was permitted in noun phrase conjunctions. Thus, in the test sentences the words were appearing in novel syntactic roles. When the network that was trained on the cross-dependency grammar was presented with the test sen-tence *Mary's girls run*, it correctly predicted that *girls* would be followed either by a plural verb or a plural genitive marker. Moreover, when the next word in fact was the plural verb *run*, the network correctly predicted the end-of-sentence marker. The other test sentence was *Mary says that John and boy from town see*. This is perhaps an unnecessarily tough test of strong generalizability: not only is *boy* occurring in a novel syntactic role, but a prepositional phrase is interposed before the verb. Nonetheless, when the recurrent network reached the word *boy* in processing this sentence, it correctly predicted that the next word would be a plural verb, a preposition, a singular genitive marker, or *who*. (It also incorrectly partially activated the singular verbs, but it also did so on a comparison sentence on which it had been trained.) After the prepositional phrase, the network again predicted a plural verb or a preposition, but also erroneously activated to a lesser degree the singular verb and the end-of-sentence marker. (Christiansen and Chater also reported on tests with the center-embedded network. In that case, the genitive test with *girl* and *girls* did not produce positive results; and the other test, with *boy* and *boys* in conjunctions, produced less error than in this case.) Although these are only limited tests of the ability of the network to meet Hadley's criterion of strong systematicity, they are suggestive that connectionist networks might be able to satisfy that standard (but see Hadley, 1994b, and Haselager and van Rappard, 1998, for a pessimistic assessment).

6.7 Conclusion

Classical symbol systems, ones that use concatenation so that constituents are actually encoded in syntactically composed structures, are clearly powerful devices for reasoning. They readily permit (although it is doubtful that they necessitate) the sort of productivity, systematicity, and inferential coherence to which Fodor and Pylyshyn directed attention in their critique of connectionism. Moreover, they make it much easier to achieve the sort of generalization to which Hadley drew attention: working with discrete symbols and syntactic rules, it is easy to handle novel sentences in which the same symbols are placed differently in the same rule-generated structures.

Since connectionist networks do not employ these resources, the challenge for connectionists is to achieve these benefits in some other way. The first approach we considered was top-down: designing networks specifically to encode symbols and implement syntactically specified relations. The second approach was bottom-up: having the network itself develop encodings of symbolic structures which sacrificed concatenation but were still able to perform the functions for which symbolic theorists have employed concatenated structures. Finally, we considered a more radical option, in which networks might conform themselves to the structures found in external symbol systems such as natural language (manifested, for example, in their ability to predict the legal next symbols in the symbol string) without representing the whole string internally, either in a concatenated fashion or functionally. In simple recurrent networks, slightly different activation patterns on hidden units serve to distinguish cases presented on previous cycles which the network must keep track of in order to solve specific problems. It is still too early to decide whether any of these approaches is able to capture whatever level of productivity and systematicity is found in human cognition (investigators differ even on that question), but they represent promising strategies for connectionists to pursue. As for Fodor and McLaughlin's requirement that they capture these properties necessarily, it is an interesting question that cannot be answered as easily as they suggest. It may be that only certain connectionist or post-connectionist architectures with certain types of corpora would be necessarily productive, systematic, and coherent. If so, it would be important to identify these types and why only they behave in that way.

While connectionists and symbolic theorists have devoted considerable effort to arguing for their respective positions and against the alternative, these debates are not likely to settle the dispute. It is our impression that they do not address the actual reasons for one researcher's choice of connectionism or another's preference for symbol processing. In large measure, attraction to connectionism has depended on dissatisfaction with symbolic models. Hence, it is a quite varied assortment of researchers, many not sharing common objectives, who have turned to connectionism. The degree of dissatisfaction depends in part upon what a researcher takes as the data to be explained. Those who are most impressed with the abstract regularities in behavior – as captured in linguistic competence theories, for example – have tended to remain satisfied with symbolic theories. Many of those who are concerned with variations in actual performance, on the other hand, have found it difficult to incorporate those phenomena into symbolic theories and have either pursued connectionist alternatives or have developed less traditional symbolic theories. In a strong sense, this initial difference in basic objectives leads the theorists for the two sides to talk past one another.

NOTES

1   Fodor and Pylyshyn cited John Watson's (1930) behaviorism, Patricia Churchland's (1986) neuroscience eliminativism, and Stephen Stich's (1983) syntactic eliminativism as examples of eliminativism in their sense. However, Churchland, while indeed a strong proponent of eliminativism, accepts the idea that neural states may serve a representational role; her quarrel is with the sentential or propositional approach to representation. Similarly, most connectionists regard networks as representational, but emphasize their distinctness from traditional symbolic representations. Since Fodor and Pylyshyn's paper, though, a number of advocates of dynamical systems approaches to modeling cognition, whom we will discuss in chapter 8, have explicitly argued for doing away with representations. However, as Clark and Toribio (1994; see also Clark, 1997b) point out, most dynamical modeling has been focused at lower-level systems using sensory information to guide spatial navigation. They note that it is higher-level tasks such as long-term planning that are "representation hungry," and propose that when dynamicists confront these tasks they too will need to reintroduce representations.

2   As our small contribution to reducing the gender-typing prevalent in linguistic examples, we have adapted their actual base example, *John loves the girl*, to one with a female grammatical subject and gender-neutral grammatical object.

3   Although connectionist models use finer-grained units (subsymbols) to account for a given phenomenon than do most information-processing models, this is irrelevant to determining whether they occupy the abstract or processing level of analysis. The size and nature of the units reflect choices made within that level, e.g., how deeply one must go into that level's part–whole hierarchy in order to achieve the best account of the phenomenon. As discussed in Abrahamsen (1987), each level has its own part–whole hierarchy of units of analysis appropriate to that level.

4   An alternative to using recurrent networks is to present the context in the input. For example, in modeling language comprehension, one might provide as input not just the target word, but three words on either side. The problem is that one thereby limits what counts as context to the three words on either side. Often the required context is much broader. For example, a language user must be able to supply the proper verb form for its subject even when dependent clauses intervene (e.g., *The dog at whom the gardener in the*

neighbor's yard threw the rock was barking). If the length of the dependency becomes too long, of course, we may fail to remember what the proper verb form should have been. But there is a broad range in which humans are highly accurate and it is simply not reasonable to provide such a range in the input.

5 Because this approach gives each word an independent encoding, a plural noun is not constructed from the corresponding singular form plus a plural inflection. Thus, *girl*, *girls*, and *cats* have equally dissimilar encodings. The network learns from distributional constraints to treat *girls*, *cats*, and the other two plural nouns similarly, but there is no information in this particular corpus that would lead it to treat *girl* as more similar to *girls* than to *cats*.

6 If, instead of this phased training, the network were trained on the whole corpus at once, it would never master the corpus. It would also show a surprising pattern of error: it might get long-range dependencies correct, but fail on short-range dependencies within a relative clause (e.g., producing "The boys who the girl *chase see the dog"). Human children, as Elman noted, master simple sentences before complex ones. Children, though, are exposed to the whole adult corpus from the beginning. Elman (1993) demonstrated that he could achieve the same effect by limiting the number of preceding words for which recurrent connections could provide information. In the earliest epochs the context units were reset every 2 or 3 words; this interval was gradually increased to every 6–7 words and then dropped entirely. (The procedure was meant to mimic children's gradually increasing short-term memory.) Elman's discovery with networks coheres with an earlier empirical discovery and theoretical proposal of Elissa Newport. She showed that late learners of a language (often learners of a second language, as in Johnson and Newport, 1989) never exhibit the same performance as early learners. Late learners tend to make extensive use of fixed forms and show insensitivity to the variability in the internal morphology of these structures. Early learners, on the other hand, tend to learn the components, and their errors often involve omission of components. Newport's proposal is that earlier learners actually benefit from reduced memory which forces them to focus on shorter structures which incorporate the relationships (e.g., subject–verb agreement) that are put together compositionally in the adult language. She called her proposal the "less is more hypothesis."

7 An example from Dutch is "de mannen hebben Hans Jeanine de paarden helpen leren voeren" which, preserving the Dutch word order, becomes in English: "the men have Hans Jeanine the horses help teach feed," which can be translated into English word order as "the men have helped Hans teach Jeanine to feed the horses."

8 Another approach is to use recurrent networks to carry out the sequential operations required in arithmetic. For example, Cottrell and Tsung (1989) have developed simulations of addition of two multi-digit numbers that use a recurrent network to store partial results for later stages of processing.

SOURCES AND SUGGESTED READINGS

Christiansen, M. H., Chater, N., and Seidenberg, M. S. (1999) Connectionist natural language processing: The state of the art. *Cognitive Science*, 23, 417–37.

Fodor, J. A. and Pylyshyn, Z. W. (1988) Connectionism and cognitive architecture: A critical analysis. *Cognition*, 28, 3–71.

Pollack, J. (1990) Recursive distributed representations. *Artificial Intelligence*, 46, 77–105.

Ramsey, W., Stich, S. P., and Rumelhart, D. E. (eds) (1991) *Philosophy and Connectionist Theory*. Hillsdale, NJ: Erlbaum.

Shastri, L. and Ajjanagadde, V. (1993) From simple associations to systematic reasoning: A connectionist representation of rules, variables, and dynamic bindings using temporal synchrony. *Behavioral and Brain Sciences*, 16, 417–94.

7

SIMULATING HIGHER COGNITION: A MODULAR ARCHITECTURE FOR PROCESSING SCRIPTS

Most of the connectionist simulations we have discussed up to this point have been demonstrations of discrete cognitive abilities such as generating the past tense of a verb or predicting the next word in a language corpus. Not infrequently, observers of such demonstrations ask "But what kinds of *interesting* things can these systems do? Can they carry out whole tasks of the kind that characterize daily life for humans?" In this chapter we will describe an ambitious connectionist model designed by Risto Miikkulainen (1993) to read stories about different topics, represent and keep track of them, retell them, and answer questions about them. Miikkulainen took as his starting points (a) an influential approach from traditional cognitive science, Schank and Abelson's (1977) *scripts*; and (b) networks that use backpropagation to learn. But simple networks were not adequate to achieve the variety of script-related activities which Miikkulainen had targeted; with considerable ingenuity, he arrived at a modular connectionist architecture that went beyond what had been previously possible both in connectionist modeling and in the implementation of scripts.

7.1   Overview of Scripts

Scripts are knowledge representations that specify the typical structure of events in such routines as going to a restaurant or giving a birthday party. They have their roots in work on natural language understanding by artificial intelligence researchers in the 1970s, particularly Roger Schank. He began by developing what he called a *conceptual dependency* framework for displaying causal and other links between events (Schank, 1972), and identified 11 primitive acts that provided a simplified means of representing those events (Schank, 1975). Examples of primitive acts are **PTRANS** (the transfer of the physical location of an object, as in *go* or *put*), **MTRANS** (the transfer of mental information within or between subjects, as in *see* and *tell*), **ATRANS** (the transfer of an abstract relationship such as possession of an object, as in *give* and *sell*), and **INGEST** (as in *eat* and *smoke*). Each primitive act is the core of an event that may involve an actor, object, direction of transfer, and instrument (e.g., Babe Ruth would often **PTRANS** a baseball to the outfield with a bat). States could also be represented (e.g., a person's *hunger*). Schank's group wrote a program, MARGIE, that could build a conceptual dependency representation of a sentence, make inferences, and generate a paraphrase incorporating the inferences. Given the sentence *Babe Ruth hit a baseball*, for example, the instrument slot could be inferred and appropriately filled, so that *with a bat* might be included in the paraphrase.

It soon became clear that additional sources of inference and constraint had to be considered in handling longer stretches of text. Hence, Schank and Abelson (1977) proposed the notion of scripts, and implemented them by chaining Schank's primitive acts together into structures that captured human knowledge of familiar situations. A renowned example is their restaurant script, which describes the sequence of events that transpire in a restaurant from the perspective of a customer. Heading the script are lists of props (e.g., money and a menu), entry conditions (e.g., the customer is hungry), and results (e.g., the customer is not hungry). Several roles (e.g., customer, waiter) help glue together the script by appearing repeatedly in the various component events. A script may be divided into scenes (e.g., entering, ordering, eating, and exiting). Since the sequence of events depends upon the kind of restaurant, the restaurant script contains different tracks for fast-food restaurant, cafeteria, coffee shop, fancy restaurant, etc. The coffee shop track includes more than 30 events. Half of these are in the ordering scene, which begins when the customer (S) requests a menu from the waiter (W). The first four of the ordering events will suffice to convey the flavor of the script:

S **MTRANS** signal **to** W
W **PTRANS** W **to** table
S **MTRANS** "need menu" **to** W
W **PTRANS** W **to** menu

When someone *instantiates* the script by telling a story about a particular person ordering a meal in a particular restaurant, typically only a few of the events in the script will be explicitly mentioned. Schank and Abelson proposed that readers invoke their own knowledge of scripts in understanding stories, which enables them to infer the unmentioned events. This would explain people's ability to answer questions that require such inferences and the fact that events not mentioned in a story often get included when people paraphrase it.

Schank and Abelson described an AI program, SAM, that surpassed MARGIE by including script-based inferences and omitting inferences that were correct but less salient. They also began exploring more flexible sources of inference (goals and plans), and their students contributed a crop of additional programs and implementations for representing text, answering questions, and paraphrasing. Later Schank added representations at a higher level than scripts (e.g., MOPs) and proposed replacing inflexible tracks with dynamic access of specific memories (Schank, 1982). However, it is the original notion of a script as a fairly rigid event structure that has endured as one of the showpieces of classic symbolic AI and has been most influential in the wider academic arena.

7.2   Overview of Miikkulainen's DISCERN System

If connectionism is to offer a convincing alternative (or extension) to the symbolic approach used by Schank and other AI researchers, it is important to show that connectionist systems can perform the sorts of behavior – for example, paraphrasing and answering questions about stories – for which scripts have been invoked.

Miikkulainen (1993) designed DISCERN (DIstributed SCript processing and Epis-odic memoRy Network) to provide such a demonstration and to explore the more complex architectures required to perform more complex tasks. He trained his system to handle stories involving three different scripts: going to restaurants, traveling, and shopping. There were three tracks for each script, and a number of specific stories for each track. For example (p. 3), here are shortened versions of three stories with the script and track shown for each:

1   John went to MaMaison. John asked the waiter for lobster. John left a big tip. [Restaurant: fancy]
2   John went to LAX. John checked in for a flight to JFK. The plane landed at JFK.   [Travel: by plane]
3   John went to RadioShack. John asked the staff questions about CD-players. John chose the best CD-player.   [Shopping: electronics]

Since it had already been trained on complete versions of numerous stories like these, DISCERN could generate its own expanded paraphrases of the short ver-sions. For example (pp. 29–30), when presented with story (1) above, it produced the following complete story:

4   John went to MaMaison. The waiter seated John. John asked the waiter for lobster. John ate a good lobster. John paid the waiter. John left a big tip. John left MaMaison.

Notice that DISCERN filled in many details absent in story (1), such as the waiter seating John and John paying the waiter. That is, it behaved as though it knew the restaurant script. But it had never seen the script – rather, the stories on which it had been trained provided a variety of instantiations of each track of the script. The stories differed in the specific participants filling the roles and in the choice of which events were explicitly mentioned. From these DISCERN put together the restaur-ant script, distinguishing among its three tracks and capturing in its weights such statistical regularities as the tendency for food to be good in fancy restaurants, bad in fast-food restaurants, and unpredictable in coffee shops. In fact, three different scripts with three tracks each were simultaneously abstracted, since the restaurant stories were mixed with others. DISCERN also could apply the results of its train-ing to the task of giving plausible answers to queries. It did this by using the query as a cue for retrieving its encoding of the most relevant story and assuming that it contained the answer. For example (pp. 4, 30), queries for which stories (1)–(3) provided plausible answers were:

Q: What did John eat at MaMaison? / A: John ate a good lobster.
Q: Where did John take a plane to? / A: John took a plane to JFK.
Q: What did John buy at RadioShack? / A: John bought a CD-player at RadioShack.

Since Miikkulainen's system is one of the first attempts to produce a network system to carry out cognitive activities on such a large scale, it is worth examining in some detail how it operates. One key characteristic of DISCERN is that it does not consist of a single network; its work is segmented into subtasks accomplished in sequence by the eight modules shown in figure 7.1. There are two memory modules: a lexicon

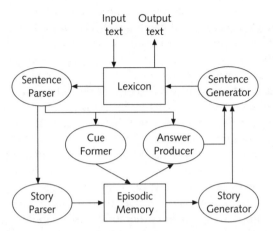

Figure 7.1   Miikkulainen's (1993) DISCERN system. The Lexicon and Episodic Memory are memory modules that utilize Kohonen's self-organizing feature map architecture. The other six modules are processing modules that utilize the FGREP or recurrent FGREP architecture.

which translates written words into meaningful internal representations and an episodic memory which keeps track of the stories presented to the system. These support the work of six processing modules: two for parsing material at the sentence and story levels (to obtain representations of stories), two for generating material at the sentence and story levels (to paraphrase those stories), and two for encoding and answering questions about stories. In the trained system, as shown in figure 7.1, the modules are used sequentially across one of two pathways (paraphrasing or question-answering). However, another key characteristic of DISCERN is that the processing modules have a distinctive architecture (called FGREP) that requires them to interact cooperatively with the lexicon during training, yielding representations that are adapted to the needs of all six modules.

   In what follows, we will first consider the motivations and benefits of modular design; then describe the FGREP architecture in the simplest possible system (a single processing module with a single set of lexical representations); then describe the various modules of the complete DISCERN system and follow the flow of processing through it; and finally present examples of the whole system's performance and provide a brief evaluation of the system.

7.3   Modular Connectionist Architectures

In attempting to explain systems in nature, scientists generally begin with a working assumption that they are composed of subsystems. This is especially evident among biologists, for whom a primary research strategy is to decompose the task performed by a system into subtasks and make a corresponding decomposition of the physical system, localizing each subtask in one of the specialized components. For example, the overall task of a cell is to serve as the basic unit of life. A few of the subtasks carried out by cell components are control of access to and from the cell interior (by the membrane), energy transfer (by the mitochondria), and synthesis of proteins

(by the ribosomes). As research progresses, a hierarchy of finer-grained decompositions and localizations emerges (see Bechtel and Richardson, 1993). A division of labor
into two or more specialized components is the weakest sense in which a system may
be said to be *modular*.

Within the cognitive sciences, the idea of modular organization has played an
especially prominent role in neuropsychology. When a patient exhibits a deficit in a
particular function (e.g., language production), it is assumed to result from damage
to a brain area responsible for performing that function. If the organization of the
brain is essentially modular, deficits in other functions should be indicative of brain
damage in other areas. To obtain better evidence that two different brain areas
qualify as modules subserving different functions, researchers often seek a *double
dissociation*: patients with damage to one brain area should exhibit a deficit in function
1 but not function 2 (e.g., language production but not language comprehension),
whereas patients with damage to the other brain area should exhibit the opposite
pattern. This research strategy has proven so useful that neuropsychologists have
continued to rely upon it heuristically despite concerns. One problem is that it relies
upon two additional assumptions about modules: that they operate independently
and, therefore, that the effects of damage to a module will remain localized within it.
Farah (1994) argued that a better account of double dissociations can be obtained by
abandoning this *locality assumption* and building distributed, graded, interactive
models such as connectionist networks. Shallice (1988) recommended a moderate
stance, in which damage to a module is viewed as primarily affecting that module
but also may have a lesser impact on modules that interact with it. Double dissociations in degree of damage can then be used to identify these non-independent
but distinct modules. Another problem is that even double dissociations do not
guarantee an optimal modular account; further work may result in new decompositions of tasks or new assignments of tasks to brain areas. For example, Zurif (1980)
proposed that the brain area originally thought to serve as a language production
module actually functions as a syntax module in both production and comprehension tasks, and Grodzinsky (2000) narrowed this to just two aspects of syntax (one
affected in production and the other in comprehension).

Connectionists are sometimes construed as anti-modular for yet another reason:
they have often proposed to handle in a single network tasks that other cognitive
scientists divide between two different subsystems (modules). In section 5.2 we
discussed at length the best-known example: Rumelhart and McClelland (1986a)
demonstrated that a single network is sufficient to form the past tense of both
regular and irregular verbs, thereby challenging the claim that two different sorts of
processing are required (one rule-based and one memory-based). In section 10.2.3
we will encounter similar connectionist challenges against dual-route accounts
of reading (a context in which Shallice developed even more nuanced ways of interpreting double dissociations).

But what are these fights really about? They are not targeted on the use of modular architectures, in the weak sense of building a system out of specialized subsystems.
Connectionists share with other cognitive modelers a distaste for holism: they assume not only that different networks exist in humans for performing such disparate
tasks as producing sentences, identifying objects, and traversing a maze, but also
that these networks may be composed from subnetworks which perform different
subtasks. Modular designs have a general appeal because they help make the task
performed by a system theoretically tractable. This is a major concern in scientific

theorizing generally (see Simon's 1969 discussion of decomposable and nearly decomposable systems), and underlies decomposition and localization as research strategies
in many scientific fields (as in the example of cell biology above).

So there is broad agreement in cognitive science that systems can best be built by
composing them from modules. The disagreement has to do with the character of
those modules. Connectionists have a profound preference for general-purpose
designs that can master any number of tasks in a variety of domains. For example,
a feedforward network with three layers of units can form the past tense of verbs
(Plunkett and Marchman, 1991), pronounce written text (Sejnowski and Rosenberg,
1987), or use sonar echo data to discriminate rocks from mines (Gorman and
Sejnowski, 1988). During training the network captures the constraints implicit in
the encodings presented to it, whatever the domain. When connectionists compose
multiple networks into a modular system to perform more complex tasks, not infrequently the modules are of the same general design (but trained on a different part of
the task).

An alternative view is that modules have task-specific architectures. Dual-route
theorists propose different mechanisms (i.e., rule-based or memory-based processing) for regular versus exceptional forms within the same domain. Evolutionary
psychologists scale up this modest task-specificity to a sweeping domain-specificity,
viewing the entire mind-brain as a collection of specialized modules honed by evolution to perform specialized tasks. And a singularly provocative proposal has been
advanced by philosopher Jerry Fodor (1983), who divides the mind-brain into a set
of innately specified modules for processing specific types of inputs (e.g., colors,
shapes, faces, melodies, utterances) and a nonmodular, holistic central system responsible for reasoning and beliefs. The modules are hardwired, special-purpose,
bottom-up processors that work fast in part because they are informationally encapsulated (sharing only inputs and outputs with other modules and otherwise operating autonomously). That is, within-module processing is not influenced by other
modules or by beliefs from the central system.

This thoroughgoing embrace of the independence assumption, along with the
emphasis on task-specific architectures and other strong assumptions, puts Fodorian
modularity generally at odds with systems of interactive modules (called "integrated
systems" by Bechtel and Richardson, 1993), including interactive network designs.
However, McClelland (1987, 1996) arrived at the interesting idea that propagation
of activation across a layer of connections is informationally encapsulated, but that
the pattern of activation across a layer of units often benefits from having multiple
influences (including top-down connections from "later" layers of units). For example, we saw in chapter 4.1.2 that the letter units in McClelland and Rumelhart's
(1981) interactive activation model of word recognition were influenced not only by
feedforward connections from feature units but also by feedbackward connections
from word units. McClelland reinterpreted two human data sets that have been cited
as supporting Fodorian bottom-up modules as actually more consistent with interactive networks. Specifically, he argued that the timecourse of disambiguation both
for word meanings and for phonemes is suggestive of top-down feedback effects.
Whether such effects are bounded within a module (and hence less of a problem for
Fodor) or suggest an ongoing sharing of information between modules is not always
easily decided. At the very least McClelland's analysis suggests that interactive
networks must be among the candidate architectures for implementing modules. To
greater effect, it points to system designs in which backward connections allow

"late" modules specializing in higher-order or integrative processing to influence the operation of "early" modules that perform more localized computations. As we will see in chapter 10, there is growing evidence that this is how the brain itself is organized.

Such lofty debates can be sidestepped in examining Miikkulainen's DISCERN system, because his design has no backward connections between modules. In collaboration with Dyer, he deferred this issue in order to focus on the tasks involved in building any modular network system: analyzing a task into components, deciding which of a small number of general architectures to use for each subtask, deciding how to connect the modules into a system and coordinate their activity and information flow – and not least, implementing and evaluating all of these decisions. The result was a system in which modules are used in sequence and some are usable for more than one task. When the task is to paraphrase a story, information flows into the Lexicon and from there in sequence to the Sentence Parser, Story Parser, Episodic Memory, Story Generator, Sentence Generator, and finally back out through the Lexicon. When the task is to answer a question, the same sequence is traversed except that the Cue Former and Answer Producer replace the Story Parser and Story Generator. Each module completes its subtask via its own internal operations, and the result is copied from its output units on to the next module's input units. The modules differ in how much material they need to complete their subtasks (a word, sentence, or entire story). They also differ in which of three network architectures Miikkulainen chose as most suitable. Two of the architectures are interactive (simple recurrent networks and Kohonen feature maps), but their interactivity is self-contained and not used to implement top-down influences.

During training the modules are hooked up quite differently. The processing modules are detached from each other but connected bidirectionally to the Lexicon, through which each of them is trained simultaneously on the same corpus. One outcome of each training trial is a modified representation of each word involved in the trial (as explained in the next section), and the modified representation is immediately posted to the shared Lexicon. The next module that encounters that word in a training trial will be using a word representation that was most recently altered by a different module. That is, though each module is performing its task autonomously during each of its training trials, across trials and modules (via the Lexicon) there is a flow of shared information about how words should be represented.

7.4   FGREP: An Architecture that Allows the System to Devise Its Own Representations

7.4.1   Why FGREP?

Why does DISCERN change its own lexical representations? In part, this is a response to an objection raised against some early connectionist networks. Critics noted that some of their success could be attributed to the use of nonarbitrary input encodings, taken from a predetermined analysis of the domain. For example, McClelland and Kawamoto (1986) designed a network with hundreds of input and output units (but no hidden layer) to generate case-role representations of sentences – the same task performed by DISCERN's Sentence Parser module. They created a set of semantic dimensions, each with 2 to 7 values (e.g., softness: soft vs. hard), assigned values to words, and from these derived hundreds of conjunctive features which were used to encode each word of a sentence input. For example, *potato* was presented on the 263 units reserved for the direct object by turning on the unit for **soft&food**, turning off units for **hard&tool** and **large&animate**, and so forth. The word *pasta* differed from *potato* on only one dimension (form), so their pre-determined encodings were sufficient to assure that they would get similar case assignments. The encodings amount to a theory about what is salient in the task – here, that lexical semantics is important in assigning case and more particularly that conjunctions of particular dimensions are important. Those who object to such theory-laden encodings have raised the same objection to the Wickelfeature encodings employed by Rumelhart and McClelland (1986a) in their past-tense network (their theory being that verb stems are represented by coarse-coded context-dependent phonological features), and would apply as well to Plunkett and Marchman's (1991) localist encodings (which were based on the related theory that verb stems have a localist encoding using position-specific, context-independent phonological features).

One strategy for answering this charge has been to use input patterns that are arbitrary, rather than crafted by the investigator, and let their task-related structure be discovered on one or more hidden layers during training. In arbitrary encodings the individual input units have no featural or other interpretation, and they can be constructed such that all patterns are equally dissimilar. Hence, whatever internal representations emerge on the hidden layers during training cannot be attributed to explicit packets of information in the input patterns. One example is Hinton's (1986) network for answering questions about relationships in family trees. Each of 24 persons was represented by turning on a single binary unit in an 24-unit array, and each relation (such as parent, sibling) had the same kind of arbitrary encoding in a separate, 12-unit array. Each array fed into a separate set of hidden units, which then fed into two layers of common hidden units and finally into a set of output units that designated the second person in the relationship. After training on such items as the input *Carolyn has-mother* and the target output *Victoria*, the network seemed to have achieved a featural encoding on its hidden units that happened to be fairly localized. For example, in the first set of hidden units there seemed to be units for Italian kin, English kin, first-generation kin, second-generation kin, and so forth.

These nonarbitrary internal representations emerge from the network's activity as it gradually discovers the structure implicit in the particular pairings of inputs with outputs in the corpus of training items. Even though both the input and output patterns are themselves arbitrarily coded, the learning procedure adjusts the weights into the hidden units so that a task-relevant re-encoding of the inputs will be achieved on the hidden units. In the above example, *Carolyn*'s arbitrary input pattern is re-encoded on the hidden layer so as to specify that she is English, is first-generation, and so forth. The re-encodings are calculated on the fly and are replaced on each new trial, but the knowledge used to produce them is retained (in distributed form) in the connection weights.

For Miikkulainen's modular system a more elaborate solution to the problem was needed, because the task-relevant re-encodings had to be equally relevant to the needs of six different processing modules. The work of re-encoding the words in each input pattern and retaining the results could not be contained within the internal operations of any single module. What was needed was a common lexicon that could store the re-encodings in an accessible format both during and after training, and a training procedure that would leave this sort of trace of its activity. Miikkulainen and Dyer (1991) found an elegant solution which they implemented, initially, in a single processing module with a single set of lexical representations. It is in the same spirit as Hinton's reliance on changing the weights of connections into hidden units, but extends backpropagation an additional step so that it changes not only the weights but also the activation patterns on the input units (which initially are arbitrary). The most recent activation pattern for a word is retained in the lexicon, making possible many cycles of retrieval and adaptive modification. Hence, the network gradually arrives at task-relevant re-encodings that are easily accessible from the lexicon, rather than appearing only temporarily on the hidden units.

Miikkulainen and Dyer referred to the architecture of this modified feedforward system as FGREP (Forming Global Representations in Extended back-Propagation). In FGREP, each time a pattern is presented on the input units, the network generates a response on the output units, the error is evaluated, and an error signal is sent back through the network to change each layer of weights and then the input pattern itself. This last, novel step is achieved by changing the activation value of each input unit by the product of the error value at that unit and the learning rate, constrained by the proviso that the value cannot fall below a minimum or exceed a maximum value. (To the backpropagation algorithm, each input pattern is equivalent to an additional set of weights, which can be regarded as weights on connections from an additional set of binary units that feed into the original input units.) The revised word representations achieved on the input layer through this procedure are then stored in the lexicon.

7.4.2   Exploring FGREP in a simple sentence parser

To illustrate the utility of the FGREP architecture, Miikkulainen and Dyer designed a preliminary version of the Sentence Parser module. As shown in figure 7.2 (from Miikkulainen, 1993, p. 54), when provided with a sentence this module assigns its words to case roles. It amounts to a connectionist simulation of a Schankian computer program for translating a sentence into a simple conceptual dependency representation, although its flat structure treats acts as equivalent to case roles (losing both the centrality and abstractness of Schank's primitive acts). In the full DISCERN system (figure 7.1), the Sentence Parser gets its inputs via the Lexicon and sends its output to either the Story Parser or the Cue Former, but in this initial version the only connection was with a simplified lexicon. Miikkulainen and Dyer used the same corpus of 1,475 three- and four-word sentences and case assignments as McClelland and Kawamoto (1986), but replaced the semantic feature representations of each word with arbitrary ones (since the main point of FGREP was to develop its own encodings). Extended backpropagation gradually reshaped these encodings to incorporate the semantic and syntactic structure implicit in the corpus. These FGREP encodings were called *lexical representations*, *semantic representations*, or simply *patterns*.

The input layer of this version of the sentence parser was divided into four assemblies of units, each of which was reserved for a particular grammatical role. A sentence was presented to the network by copying the current encoding of each word from the lexicon to the appropriate assembly of input units: the first set of

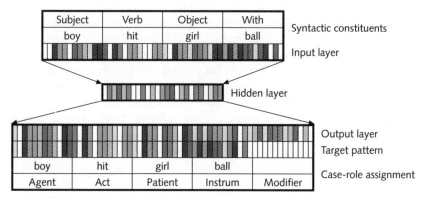

Figure 7.2   Miikkulainen and Dyer's (1991) sentence parser, a single FGREP module that cooperates with a simplified lexicon so that word representations and network weights both become increasingly adapted to the task of determining each word's case role. Reprinted with permission from R. Miikkulainen (1993) *Subsymbolic Natural Language Processing: An Integrated Model of Scripts, Lexicon, and Memory.* Cambridge, MA: MIT Press, p. 54.

twelve units encoded the subject, the next set the verb, the third set the direct object, and the fourth set the with-NP (the noun following the preposition *with*; as a simplification, the determiner *the* is not explicitly represented). The network's task was to channel each word from its syntactic role assembly to the appropriate case role assembly on the output units. There were five assemblies of output units (three or four of which should be filled on each trial): agent, act, patient, instrument, and modifier. Each grammatical role (except verb) can be used to convey more than one case role, but in a particular sentence the arrangement of words across syntactic roles usually adds sufficient constraint that just one way of filling the case roles is appropriate. For example, although the with-NP often identifies an instrument of the action, as in (1), it could instead modify the patient, as in (2):

(1)   The boy ate the pasta with a fork.
(2)   The boy ate the pasta with the cheese.

In this example, the fact that cheese is a food favors its assignment as a modifier of the object of *ate*. (Like the act slot, the modifier slot is defined in relation to case roles but is not a case role; in the simplified flat structure used here, for convenience they are called case roles.) Similarly, the subject of the sentence typically identifies the agent of the action (3), but when non-animate it can instead identify the instrument (4) or the patient (5):

(3)   The girl broke the window with the ball.
(4)   The rock broke the window.
(5)   The window broke.

The network indicated its analysis by channeling the pattern for each word to the appropriate set of output units (as well as it could given its current weights). If there were no word in the sentence that could fill a particular case role, the target output on each unit in that case-role assembly would be set as 0.5 (the null pattern). Thus, for the input sentence *The girl broke the window with the ball* (presented as the sequence *girl broke window ball*), the target on each training trial was to place the current pattern for *girl* on the output units for agent, the pattern for *broke* on the units for act, the pattern for *window* on the units for patient, the pattern for *ball* on the units for instrument, and the null pattern on the units for modifier. (Note that several different terms for such patterns are used in this chapter: in addition to *lexical* or *semantic representation*, the more general terms *encoding, vector, filler*, and *activation pattern* are used interchangeably with *pattern* in various contexts.)

As the network was being trained to perform this task, the FGREP procedure gradually changed both the weights in the network and the patterns used to represent various words. On the trial captured in figure 7.2, the network did a good job of reproducing all except one word on the appropriate case-role assembly. It was uncertain whether to channel the current pattern for *ball* to instrument or modifier, and therefore spread reduced levels of activation across the 12 units in both assemblies. Almost every instrument unit had too little activation, and an error signal based on each discrepancy was passed back to guide changes in the weights on the connections with each of the 25 hidden units. Conversely, almost every modifier unit had too much activation, and their hidden unit connections got weight changes as well. Next the weights between the hidden units and input units were changed, and finally (the step that makes this an FGREP procedure) the activation patterns on the input layer were changed. Although the pattern for *ball* was the most obvious candidate for change, all of the words adjusted to each other in context. For example, the pattern for *broke* changed so as to increase the likelihood that the next time it followed *girl* (or a word with a similar representation, such as *boy*), and preceded *window ball* (or words with similar representations, such as *vase rock*), the with-NP representation (i.e., *ball*) would be channeled to the output's instrument assembly.

With the altered representations replacing the current ones in the lexicon, the next time a sentence with *ball* as the with-NP was scheduled for a training trial, the most recent *ball* representation would supply the activation pattern for the with-assembly and the target pattern for the instrument assembly. The adjustment from the preceding trial would not be sufficient to produce a correct response, but this time more of the activation in the *ball* pattern should get channeled to the instrument assembly and less to the modifier assembly. The remaining discrepancy with the target would produce another round of adjustment, and so on for all the words. (This procedure illustrates the "chasing a moving target" strategy also illustrated in Pollack's RAAM networks discussed in section 6.3.)

7.4.3 Exploring representations for words in categories

The changes brought about in the representations made them sensitive to how they functioned in the corpus. Across the sentences of the corpus a given word might fill several different case roles depending on its grammatical role, what words filled other roles, and which of 12 semantic categories it had been assigned to. Although implicit in the corpus as experienced by the network, regularities involving these categories had been explicitly built into the corpus by McClelland and Kawamoto. Each sentence was generated from one of 19 sentence templates; for example, "The girl broke the window with the ball" was generated from THE HUMAN BROKE THE

FRAGILEOBJ WITH THE BREAKER by replacing THE HUMAN with one of the nouns in the human category (*man, woman, boy, girl*), THE FRAGILEOBJ with one of the nouns in the fragileobj category (*plate, window, vase*), and THE BREAKER with one of the nouns in the breaker category (*bat, ball, hatchet, hammer, paperweight, rock*).

One reason for the uncertainty about the case assignment of *ball* was that it belongs to the possession category (*bat, ball, hatchet, hammer, vase, dog, doll*) as well as the breaker category and could therefore be the with-NP in a sentence generated from another template: THE HUMAN HIT THE HUMAN WITH THE POSSESSION. Though the two templates have the same sequence of syntactic roles and make the same case-role assignments for the first three lexical items, they differ on the last one: THE BREAKER maps to the instrument role and THE POSSESSION maps to the modifier role. Because it belongs to three such subcategories of objects (and to a broader object category as well), the final representation of *ball* should blend influences from each of these categories and the templates using them. By processing *ball* in context as it appears in various sentences, the trained system should be able to channel it to the appropriate case-role assembly on each trial.

As a somewhat more extreme example of the compromise necessitated by limiting each word to one representation, *chicken* is a member of the food and animal categories (and the subcategory prey). Its final representation is intermediate between those of other foods and other animals (and *chicken* exerted its own influence in pulling foods and animals closer together than they otherwise would have been). As with *ball*, sentence context made it clear which template had been used and hence which category and case role were required for *chicken*.

In a few cases ambiguities are inherent in the corpus and no amount of training will eliminate the kind of smearing of activation across two case-role assemblies that is illustrated for the partially trained *ball* in figure 7.2. For example, *bat* belongs to the same object categories as *ball* but also is an animal. The category is clear in most sentences, but there are three (*The bat broke the plate/window/vase*) which could have been obtained from either of two templates:

- THE ANIMAL BROKE THE FRAGILEOBJ (agent–act–patient)
- THE BREAKER BROKE THE FRAGILEOBJ (instrument–act–patient)

Even after training, these sentences produce activation across both the agent and instrument assemblies. This outcome does signal that an unresolvable ambiguity has occurred, but does not provide clear representations of the two alternatives.

Words that are identical in their category memberships suffer from a different problem in forming the patterns that are supposed to distinguish them in the lexicon. In the most extreme case, *girl, boy, woman,* and *man* initially were quite different (each arbitrary), but by the end of FGREP training were virtually identical. As members of just one category (human), these words had identical privileges of occurrence in the corpus. This produced excellent generalization, but at the cost of discrimination. Miikkulainen and Dyer proposed two ways out of this difficulty. The first is that in real world discourse there will be different things people say about girls, boys, women, and men, and this will enable the network to maintain distinct encodings. But a second alternative they offered is to keep part of the representation of each word (which they term the *ID*) fixed so that it does not change with experience like the rest of the encoding (the *content*). They suggested that while arbitrary in the simulation, "the ID + content technique can be thought of as an approximation of sensory grounding" (Miikkulainen and Dyer, 1991, p. 366; Miikkulainen, 1993, p. 72); for example, the ID units might capture sensory qualities of the word's referent while the content units capture its semantics.

7.4.4 Moving to multiple modules: The DISCERN system

Following this preliminary exploration of FGREP, Miikkulainen and Dyer (1991) created a variant design (recurrent FGREP) and used it in a five-module system, DISPAR. With its additional modules, DISPAR could both parse and paraphrase stories. Variations in the stories were easily produced by using the ID + content technique in the lexicon (e.g., some stories had *Mary* as the customer and others had *John*; their content units became almost identical but their ID units remained fixed and distinct). DISPAR was a predecessor to Miikkulainen's (1993) DISCERN system. Besides adding two question-answering modules to DISCERN (making a total of six processing modules), Miikkulainen upgraded the Lexicon and added an Episodic Memory (making a total of two memory modules). In the remainder of this chapter we will examine DISCERN, beginning with methods for storing, organizing, and retrieving information in its Lexicon.

7.5 A Self-organizing Lexicon Using Kohonen Feature Maps

7.5.1 Innovations in lexical design

In giving greater attention to the Lexicon in DISCERN, Miikkulainen (1993) took as his starting point the two innovations reported in Miikkulainen and Dyer (1991):

- enabling the system to gradually form its own meaningful, task-adapted representations by means of extended backpropagation (FGREP);
- mixing fixed and adaptive units (ID + content) within each of these semantic representations.

His first new move was to build a more realistic lexicon – one that was not limited to semantic representations but had more than one kind of information about the words used in the stories. Specifically, he added a set of crude, but adequate, orthographic representations: each letter of a word was bitmapped, and the number of pixels that were dark rather than light determined an activation value which represented that letter in a representation vector for the written word. During training the orthographic representations and the two ID units in each semantic representation remained stable, whereas the content units were transformed from arbitrary encodings to semantic ones by adapting themselves to the needs of all six processing modules. A separate training procedure then organized the orthographic and semantic representations (more than 100 of each) and created connections between them so the system could carry out the storage and switchboard functions expected of a lexicon. We will distinguish the two kinds of representations by using italicized upper case for orthographic representations (e.g., *FRIES*) and continuing to use italicized lower case for the semantic representations that previously were the only kind of lexical representation (e.g., *fries*).

This last task is much more easily said than done: maintaining a set of representations is the kind of memory function for which simple feedforward networks have long been known to be ill-suited. A network's memory is not representation-like (its connection weights normally store only highly distributed knowledge about converting one representation into another), and a network's representations are not remembered (they are activation patterns on multiple layers, all of which change each time a new pattern is presented on the input layer). Those representations that are used as input patterns typically are maintained in a corpus that is external to the network itself, circumventing the question of how they might be incorporated in the inner workings of a more comprehensive model.

7.5.2 Using Kohonen feature maps in DISCERN's lexicon

Miikkulainen found that he could solve the storage problem, and get some bonuses as well, by using Kohonen's (1981, 1989, 2001) self-organizing feature maps to implement orthographic and semantic memories in DISCERN's Lexicon. This specialized network architecture maps a set of high-dimensional vectors (here, the orthographic or semantic representations) to a lower-dimensional space (the feature map). By means of an unsupervised learning procedure, each vector gradually gets mapped to a unit of the feature map such that units for similar vectors tend to be neighbors (that is, the map self-organizes). For example, in the orthographic map the units corresponding to *FRIES* and *TRIED* are close together, whereas in the semantic map the units corresponding to *fries* and *hamburger* are close together.

Figure 7.3 displays the units encoding the high-dimensional vectors (7 for orthographic and 12 for semantic representations), a portion of each map (less than one-fourth of each 20 × 20 grid of units), and a few of the bidirectional connections between units (with those most involved in translating *MARY* into *Mary* highlighted as dark arrows). Regarding terminology: (a) Miikkulainen calls the first map a "lexical map," but we use the term "orthographic map" instead; (b) Miikkulainen calls the second map a "semantic map," we retain that term for lack of a better alternative, but note that such maps reflect syntactic as well as semantic distributional constraints. DISCERN can use these maps to translate between orthographic and semantic representations in either direction, but we will start at the top and work our way down.

7.5.2.1 Orthography: From high-dimensional vector representations to map units A word enters the DISCERN system when an external agent (Miikkulainen, or a computer program acting for him) copies its orthographic representation on to the 7-unit orthographic assembly (here functioning as an input buffer), as is shown for *MARY* at the top of figure 7.3. In this respect, DISCERN has the same reliance on an external corpus as other connectionist models. But the weights on the connections from the assembly to the map units play a special role in this architecture. As illustrated for 3 (of the 7 total) connections into the Mary map unit, one outcome of self-organization is that the weight vector is identical to the input vector for Mary. In fact, for every input vector there is an identical weight vector that can be regarded as the system's way of storing an enduring orthographic representation. When *MARY* is presented to the system, the input vector is compared to each map unit's weight vector, and the degree of similarity determines the responsiveness of each unit. As depicted by the degree of shading of the map units in figure 7.3, presenting *MARY* produces the highest activity in the Mary map unit, some activity in

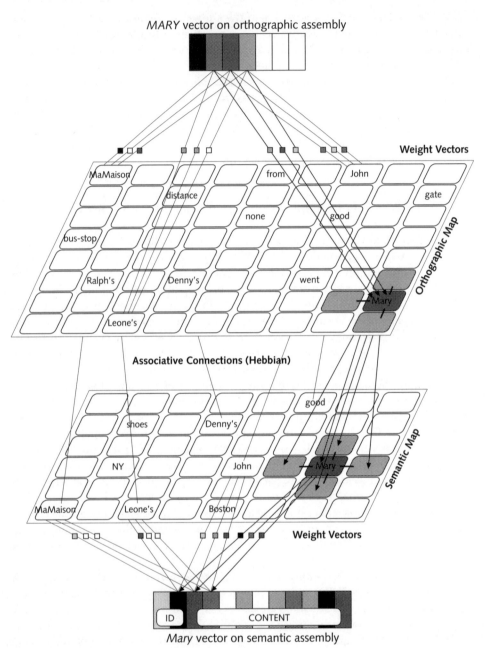

Figure 7.3 The operation of the Lexicon in DISCERN. The pattern for the written word *MARY* is presented on the orthographic ensemble. Since that activation pattern most closely corresponds to the weight vector leading to the Mary unit in the orthographic map, that unit and its neighbors are activated. Associative connections with the Mary unit in the semantic map activate that unit. It then creates a pattern on the semantic assembly that corresponds to its weight vector. In this example, the result is the correct semantic representation, *Mary*.

neighboring units, and essentially no activation in more remote units. Activity bubbles of this kind are a hallmark of self-organized maps. To understand why, a little more detail is needed:

(a) *The map units.* Of the 104 words in the corpus, 13 are mapped to one of the 72 units in the portion of the orthographic space shown in figure 7.3. That is, each of the 13 units that is labeled with a word is the maximally responsive unit for that word, and has a weight vector that has become identical to that word's orthographic representation. The other 59 units do not represent words so directly, but their weight vectors support processing by their similarity to those of the neighboring word-mapped units. Thus, unlabeled units on the right will tend to contribute to activity bubbles for 4-letter words, those in the lower left for 6-letter words with an apostrophe, and those in the upper left for 8-letter words. Unlabeled units can also represent intermediate vectors when appropriate; for example, if the typo *WENT'S* were presented, the maximally responding unit would probably be the one to the right of Denny's.

(b) *The vertical connections and weight vectors.* Each unit of the orthographic assembly is connected to each unit on the orthographic map, making 12×72 connections into the 72 units shown (and 12×400 into the entire map). Just a few of these vertical connections are shown in figure 7.3: those from units 2, 3, and 4 of the orthographic assembly to the maximally responsive units for the two customers (Mary and John) and the two fancy restaurants (MaMaison and Leone's). The weights on these connections are indicated by small shaded squares, and the different gray-scale patterns give a sampling of how weight vectors (and hence the orthographic representations they encode) differ across words.

(c) *The lateral connections.* In a biologically plausible conception of the Lexicon, the units within each feature map have lateral connections whose weights are preset to focus activation around the maximally responding unit by means of lateral excitation (nearby) and inhibition (elsewhere). Figure 7.3 shows the excitatory connections from Mary to her three neighbors; not shown are the excitatory connections around every other unit or the more numerous inhibitory connections between all remaining pairs of units. Presenting *MARY* as input initially produces diffuse activation around the Mary unit, but interactive processing across the lateral connections leads the map to gradually settle into the tight activity bubble shown in figure 7.3. Unfortunately, the settling process is very computation-intensive when simulated on a digital computer. Miikkulainen therefore replaced it with a more efficient computation in which neighborhood size was set by the designer rather than achieved by lateral excitation and inhibition.

(d) *Self-organization.* The weight vectors are the product of an extended period of self-organization (unsupervised adaptation) in which simultaneously the weight vectors became more similar to the input vectors (giving the system a memory) and neighboring weight vectors became more similar to each other (giving the system a topological organization). For example, although the weight vectors for Mary's neighbors are not shown in figure 7.3, they are similar to Mary's weight vector (and hence also similar to her input vector). The organizing process is complex, but each round has these steps: (1) an input vector is presented; (2) the map's resulting pattern of activation is determined; (3) the weight vectors of the active units are adjusted (to varying degrees) towards the input vector. The process works best if neighborhood size is set large at the outset and then decreases. The map in figure 7.3 has completed the organizing process; inputs produce changes in activation but not in weights.

7.5.2.2   Associative connections: From the orthographic map to the semantic map   Once an activity bubble forms around the Mary unit on the orthographic map, associative connections between the two maps are used to create a similar bubble around the Mary unit on the semantic map. The weights needed to achieve the appropriate associations were obtained in Hebbian supervised learning (which occurred during the same period the maps themselves were self-organizing without supervision). The two maps are fully interconnected in both directions, but only a few of the strongest connections are shown (in most detail for Mary, and more sketchily for the other five words appearing on both submaps; not shown are connections from Mary's neighboring units on the orthographic map to a region around the Mary unit on the semantic map, which play a supporting role). These connections provide the key step in retrieving the semantic representation *Mary* from the orthographic representation *MARY*.

7.5.2.3   Semantics: From map unit to high-dimensional vector representations   The final step is to traverse the last set of vertical connections, which connect the semantic map with the 12-unit semantic assembly. Analogous to the orthographic end of the lexicon, the weight vector from the Mary unit is identical to the semantic vector *Mary* and is the system's way of permanently storing that pattern. When the Mary unit becomes active on the semantic map, its weight vector will assure that the full semantic vector representation *Mary* gets placed (temporarily) on the semantic assembly, which here is functioning as an output buffer.

7.5.2.4   Reversing direction: From semantic to orthographic representations   If the Lexicon is hooked up to DISCERN's processing modules, the *Mary* vector is sent to the Sentence Parser and from there is passed along to other processing modules. The output of the last processing module in the loop, the Sentence Generator, kicks the Lexicon into using its connections in reverse: receiving the *Mary* vector on its semantic assembly (now functioning as an input assembly), the Lexicon uses the bottom set of connections to activate the Mary unit (and its neighbors) on the semantic map. Via upwards-directed associative connections (not shown), the corresponding Mary unit (and its neighbors) are activated on the orthographic map, and via the top set of connections (used in reverse) the *MARY* vector appears on the orthographic assembly (now functioning as an output buffer displaying the system's public response).[1]

7.5.3   Advantages of Kohonen feature maps

That completes the tour of figure 7.3. In considering the implications of building a lexicon from feature maps, it is important to realize that this design decision was biologically motivated. In low-level vision, Miikkulainen points out, there has been ample documentation of retinotopic maps and of lateral connections arranged to produce excitation nearby and inhibition elsewhere. In primary visual cortex, feature-detecting cells are laid out topologically such that neighboring cells are responsive to neighboring areas of the retina, and in subareas neurons responsive to a dimension such as line orientation may be systematically laid out according to the values they detect (e.g., Hubel and Wiesel, 1968). Similar arrangements have been found within so many sensory and motor areas of cortex that topological mapping appears to be an important part of the brain's toolkit. Though direct neurophysiological evidence is not yet available to show that this strategy is used for more abstract domains such as semantics, Miikkulainen cites as indirect evidence the category-specific deficits found in some brain lesion patients (e.g., loss of access to the names of fruits and vegetables, as reported by Hart, Berndt, and Caramazza, 1985). In fact, he reviews a variety of aphasic impairments and suggests how they could be produced by different kinds of damage to a lexicon like that of DISCERN (but trained on a richer corpus).

In addition to their possible biological reality, feature maps provide other advantages: weight vectors provide long-term storage of each item; map units provide discrete locations for long-term storage of a less detailed representation of each item; some (though not all) of the structure of the domain is displayed accessibly in two dimensions; map units make associative mapping between orthographic and semantics representations computationally efficient; many-to-many mapping is possible (e.g., the word *bat* could map on to two different semantic map units, whereas a pair of synonyms could map on to one semantic unit); and the particulars of the mapping can adapt as representations are added or fall into disuse. Also, though not discussed above, areas of the N-dimensional space that are especially dense with items get mapped on to disproportionately large portions of the feature space. It is viewed as more important that items get spread out evenly (with minimal overlap) than that Euclidean distance relations get preserved. (See box 7.1 in section 7.7.3 for the equation governing the response to an input in a biologically plausible feature map.)

There is one other memory module in DISCERN, the Episodic Memory, which makes good use of a more elaborate version of the feature map architecture. Before describing this, we will look at how the six processing modules understand and respond to the sequence of words passed to them by the Lexicon in such a way that they can be credited with some degree of knowledge of scripts.

7.6   Encoding and Decoding Stories as Scripts

7.6.1   Using recurrent FGREP modules in DISCERN

DISCERN's six processing modules have in common their utilization of the FGREP architecture. The key attributes of that architecture were exhibited in the preliminary version of the sentence parser (figure 7.2). In DISCERN, though, recurrent connections were added to the hidden layer within four of these modules. They are the type used in Elman's simple recurrent networks (section 6.4); that is, the hidden layer pattern is copied to a special set of input units. This design provides degraded retention of previously processed material, with retention becoming more degraded as the number of cycles back increases. This permits the input (for the parser modules) or the output (for the generator modules) to be pushed word by word through a single set of units rather than represented simultaneously across assemblies of units. In theory this makes for a more flexible system that might handle material of indefinite length. In practice, the sentences and stories that were used in these simulations were short and similar enough that nonrecurrent FGREP modules would presumably have performed adequately – indeed, the success of the preliminary, nonrecurrent sentence parser showed this to be the case. However, including recurrent connections is consistent with Miikkulainen's strong orientation towards simulation of the human system: they provide a kind of working memory for word-by-word processing that is more realistic than presenting a sentence across several assemblies of units simultaneously. (They do not provide long-term memory, since the patterns they retain are replaced when the system begins processing another sentence or story.)

7.6.2   Using the Sentence Parser and Story Parser to encode stories

The four recurrent modules (plus the Lexicon) can work together to encode and paraphrase stories. To begin the encoding process, the first sentence of the story is presented orthographically one word at a time to the Lexicon, which translates each word into its associated semantic representation (as was illustrated for Mary in figure 7.3 above). Each resulting activation pattern is passed along to the Sentence Parser's input units (a single, word-length assembly) and from there it should be channeled to the appropriate assembly of output units (the assembly, of the six available, which corresponds to the correct case role for that word in that position in that sentence). When the Sentence Parser has completed its work on the first sentence, the result is passed along to the Story Parser. This process repeats until the Sentence Parser has encoded each sentence and the Story Parser has used those results to arrive at an overall encoding of the story.

   The operation of the two parser modules is illustrated in figure 7.4 (from p. 86 of Miikkulainen, 1993), where *JOHN WENT TO MAMAISON* has just been processed as the first sentence of story (1). Before the Story Parser could begin its work, the Sentence Parser had to complete the following steps in coordination with the Lexicon:

1   The Lexicon receives *JOHN* (orthographic representation) and outputs *John* (semantic representation).
2   The Sentence Parser receives *John* and propagates activation through its hidden layer such that *John* reappears on the output units for the agent role. (The appropriateness of the agent role reflects the contents of the semantic representation as well as *John*'s implicit syntactic role – in this simple corpus the first noun presented to the parser is always the subject.)
3   Because this is a recurrent network, the activation pattern produced on the hidden layer in channeling *John* to the agent assembly is copied to another set of units, called the "previous-hidden-layer assembly" by Miikkulainen but "context units" here.
4   Next, the Lexicon translates *WENT* and sends *went* to the Sentence Parser. This time the hidden-layer pattern is influenced not only by the current word (*went*) but also by the previous-hidden-layer encoding of *John* on the context units – both patterns serve as inputs to the hidden units, which channel *went* to the act units. (Note that the parser has only implicit knowledge that *went* is in the syntactic role of verb; explicitly it is simply making use of the encoding of the first word that is being supplied via the context units. This context alone should be sufficient to classify *went* as an act, but the contents of the semantic representation point this way as well.)
5   The next word (*TO → to*) does not fill a case role, but after its processing the context units have a pattern reflecting the passage of all three words through the

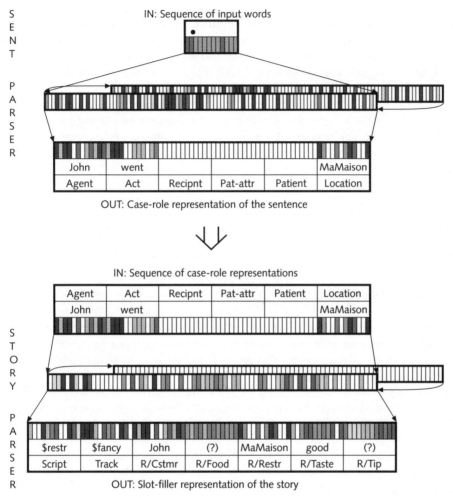

Figure 7.4 The Sentence Parser and Story Parser just after processing the first sentence in story (1), *John went to MaMaison*. Reprinted with permission from R. Miikkulainen (1993) *Subsymbolic Natural Language Processing: An Integrated Model of Scripts, Lexicon, and Memory*. Cambridge, MA: MIT Press, p. 86.

hidden layer assembly (giving greatest emphasis to the most recent word, which helps with the next step).

6　When the last word (*MAMAISON → MaMaison*) is processed, its own semantic representation combines with that of the preceding context to channel it to the location role.

7　Finally, the period ending the sentence is encoded like a word, but signals that the case-role representation should now be regarded as complete. (The Sentence Parser module in figure 7.4 has reached this point in its processing; the period will remain in the input assembly until the next sentence begins.)

The Sentence Parser output – a case-role representation of the sentence – now is used as the source of input to the Story Parser. For each case role in turn, the activation pattern corresponding to the semantic representation of the word filling that role is supplied to the Story Parser's input assembly. If a case role is unfilled in the current sentence, a null pattern is supplied. (The spatial layout of case roles in figure 7.4 makes it appear that the entire representation is supplied at once, but the phrase "Sequence of case-role representations" clarifies that in fact it is supplied one word at a time to a single assembly of 12 input units; that is, the Story Parser's architecture is almost identical to that of the Sentence Parser.)

From the burst of words that comes its way each time the Sentence Parser completes a sentence, the Story Parser creates and refines a script-based representation of the whole story on its output layer. As each story unfolds, it becomes categorized by script and track and its sentences gradually provide the words needed to fill the roles appropriate to that script:

Script	Tracks	Roles in the script
Restaurant	Fancy, coffee-shop, fast-food	Customer, food, restaurant, taste, tip
Travel	Plane, train, bus	Passenger, origin, destination, distance
Shopping	Clothing, electronics, grocery	Customer, item, store

Specifically, a slot-filler representation of the story is gradually formed across seven assemblies of output units: one assembly for script name, one for track name, and five for the roles in that script. The Story Parser fills the slots (a) by binding each word to its role in the script (i.e., channeling each word's activation pattern – its semantic representation – from the input assembly to the appropriate assembly of output units); and also (b) by letting each word influence which patterns appear on the other output assemblies, especially those for script and track. (The names for scripts and tracks within DISCERN are handled just like any other words by the two modules for which they are part of the input: during training these modules alter each such pattern adaptively across trials, using the Lexicon to store the interim and final representations.)

Unlike the Sentence Parser, which achieves a complete output each time one sentence has been processed, the Story Parser may not achieve a complete output until several sentences have passed through the system. One consequence is that the representations on the context units in this module become increasingly compressed as the words of several sentences pass through. On the other hand, as illustrated in figure 7.4, the Story Parser may form a complete output from a fraction of the full story due to its automatic inferencing. For example, when *MaMaison* is encountered as the location while processing the first sentence (which the Story Parser "knows" by combining the *MaMaison* pattern on its input assembly with the context pattern), the Story Parser (a) channels it to the script's fifth slot, which indicates the particular restaurant if this is the restaurant script; (b) decides (at least tentatively) that the script is the restaurant script and the track is fancy; and (c) most interesting, infers that the food tasted good. (*BurgerKing* would have led it to infer that the food tasted bad).

In its usual operation, once DISCERN has finished encoding a story it sends the script representation to the Episodic Memory module for storage. Since that module is itself rather complex, here we will consider a reduced system in which paraphrasing is immediate rather than memory-mediated. That is, the Story Parser's output is copied directly to the input assemblies of the Story Generator.

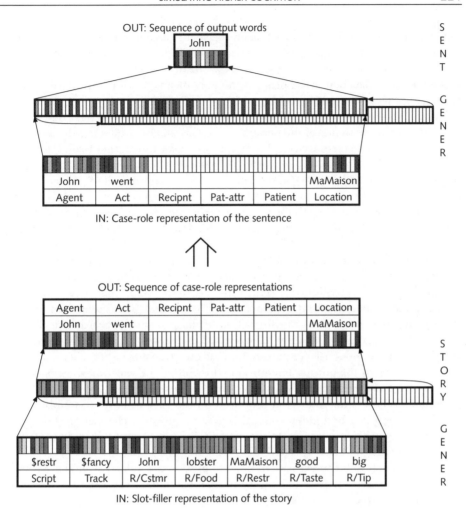

Figure 7.5   The Story Generator and the Sentence Generator in the midst of generating the first sentence in story (1), *John went to MaMaison*. Reprinted with permission from R. Miikkulainen (1993) *Subsymbolic Natural Language Processing: An Integrated Model of Scripts, Lexicon, and Memory*. Cambridge, MA: MIT Press, p. 88.

7.6.3   Using the Story Generator and Sentence Generator to paraphrase stories

In figure 7.5 (from p. 88 of Miikkulainen, 1993), the Story Generator has received a complete script-based representation from the Story Parser, which has finished processing every sentence in story (1). The task of the Story Generator is the reverse of parsing: it must produce (one word at a time) a case-role representation of each sentence that is to comprise the paraphrase. To do this, the Story Generator uses a recurrent architecture that has the same components as the Story Parser, but run in reverse. This actually makes it a quite different architecture: since processing in figure 7.5 begins at the bottom and works its way up, the script representation (laid out simultaneously across seven assemblies of input units) is now a fixed input pattern and the words (pushed sequentially through a single assembly of 12 units) are now the output. As with the Story Parser, the spatial layout of these words according to their case roles in the figure is somewhat misleading; it should be kept in mind that the word patterns are produced serially on one assembly at the top of the Story Generator and that their serial order is the only means by which they are bound to the fixed sequence of case roles.

Figure 7.5 shows the Story Generator at the point at which it has completed its work on the first sentence of the paraphrase. It did this by producing the pattern for *John* on its output assembly (implicitly binding *John* to the agent role), then *went* (the act), then null patterns for words 3–5 (which would have been the recipient, patient-attribute, and patient), and finally *MaMaison* (the location). What drove the changing series of words was the changing series of activation patterns on the context units in combination with the constant script representation. In more detail, the following steps were involved in producing the first few words of the first sentence:

1   The previous-hidden-layer assembly initially encoded a null pattern, and that pattern was sent via one set of weighted connections to the hidden units while the script representation was sent from the input assemblies via another set of weighted connections to the same hidden units. (Here "sent" refers not to simple copying, but rather to a transformation of the pattern in accord with the story knowledge that was gradually incorporated in the weights during training.)

2   The resulting hidden-layer pattern (and its own transformation via the weighted connections to the output assembly) had the effect of selecting the customer in the script representation as agent of the first sentence. As applied in this example, *John* was the first word produced on the 12-unit output assembly.

3   The pattern on the hidden units that was involved in channeling *John* to the output assembly was copied to the context units in order to provide context for the next step.

4   With this non-null context pattern now supplied to the hidden layer along with the unchanging script representation, the Story Generator selected *went* as the second word to be produced on its output assembly.

5   The pattern on the hidden units that was involved in channeling *went* to the output assembly was copied to the context units.

6   This new pattern incorporated information about both of the first two steps and, along with the unchanging script representation, influenced the Story Generator to produce a null pattern as its third output (so that the first sentence would not include a recipient).

This process continued until the entire series of word patterns (including three null patterns) had been produced. As each word was pushed out of the Story Generator, it was retained by copying it on to the appropriate case-role assembly of the next module, the Sentence Generator. At the same time, the hidden-layer pattern involved in its production was copied on to the context units, from which it could help with selection of the next word. In figure 7.5, *MaMaison* has been produced as the last case-role filler of the first sentence. This kicks off a round of processing in the Sentence Generator, but the Story Generator itself does not get reset at this point; it continues compressing additional history on to its context units as it generates the words of the second sentence, third sentence, and so forth until a complete story has been produced.

The Sentence Generator module in figure 7.5, having received a complete case-role representation of the first sentence, has begun converting it into the sequence of words that will comprise the first sentence of the paraphrase. Like the Story Generator, this module has a recurrent architecture that resembles that of the corresponding parser but operates in the reverse direction to produce a series of words on a single output assembly. As each word (semantic representation) emerges, it is passed through the Lexicon so that the first sentence of the paraphrase will appear in public (orthographic) form. In figure 7.5, the Sentence Generator has just produced *John* (the first word of the sentence, and hence implicitly its subject), which can then be translated to the orthographic representation, *JOHN*, by the Lexicon (not shown). The second sentence is generated by a similar process (Story Generator to Sentence Generator to Lexicon), and so forth until the paraphrase is complete. Note that no creativity is involved: during training the generator modules learned the canonical sequence of sentences for each script and how to bind the words in a specific story to the generic roles. What is meant to be impressive is the fact that a complete paraphrase usually will be generated even if the parser modules received only a subset of the sentences forming the complete story.

7.6.4   Using the Cue Former and Answer Producer
to answer questions

Missing from figures 7.4 and 7.5 (though included in figure 7.1) are the two processing modules used to answer questions about previously processed stories. When a question is received, it is processed by the Sentence Parser like any sentence in a story. But the network recognizes it as a question, and so passes it to the Cue Former network rather than the Story Parser. The Cue Former constructs a script-based representation of the information in the sentence. It attempts to fill every slot – those whose fillers are not explicitly mentioned in the sentence as well as those mentioned (and most saliently, the slot for the script role being queried). The output from the Cue Former is then used as a probe to the Episodic Memory, which in this task retrieves the trace of a similar story that had been stored previously (we will see how in the next section). If the cue fails to elicit any memory, there is no response. If it succeeds, though, both the question and the script representation of the memory are supplied to the Answer Producer, which constructs a case-role representation of the answer and sends that to the Sentence Generator. The Cue Former and the Answer Producer were not designed to handle input or output sequentially; each is a non-recurrent FGREP network.

7.7   A Connectionist Episodic Memory

7.7.1   Making Kohonen feature maps hierarchical

In the complete DISCERN system, once the Story Parser has finished constructing a script-based representation of a story this result is stored in the Episodic Memory. This module has a special design that enables it to assign a unique memory location to each story and to keep track of which stories have been presented most recently. This is a very different type of task than confronts most connectionist networks, which generally require many epochs of training to encode new information, encode it in distributed fashion rather than distinctively, and have no way to distinguish new from old information. The basic architecture that enables the Episodic Memory

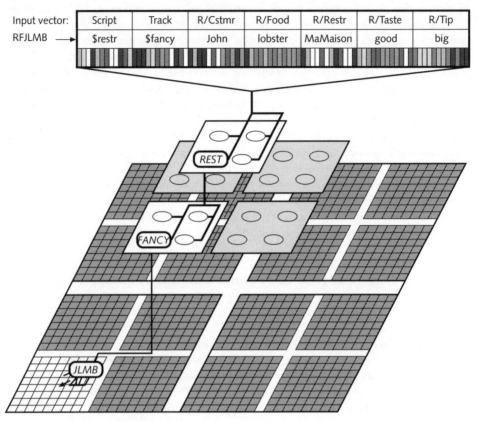

Input vector:	Script	Track	R/Cstmr	R/Food	R/Restr	R/Taste	R/Tip
RFJLMB →	$restr	$fancy	John	lobster	MaMaison	good	big

Figure 7.6   The hierarchy of self-organizing feature maps that constitutes the Episodic Memory of DISCERN. When the Story Parser sends the completed slot-filler representation of story (1) to the Episodic Memory, these units become active in this order: the restaurant unit in the script map, the fancy unit in the track map, and the JLMB unit in the role-binding map (John, Lobster, MaMaison, and Big are the key bindings in this story). Also shown, very sketchily, is the episodic memory trace created around the JLMB unit. Reprinted with permission from R. Miikkulainen (1993) *Subsymbolic Natural Language Processing: An Integrated Model of Scripts, Lexicon, and Memory.* Cambridge, MA: MIT Press, p. 156.

to accomplish its task is that of Kohonen's (1989) self-organizing feature maps. As discussed in the Lexicon section above, this architecture maps high-dimensional vectors to a lower-dimensional (usually two-dimensional) space that self-organizes such that similar items tend to be located near each other.

The Episodic Memory module is used to store script representations of stories, so here the high-dimensional vector is an activation pattern across seven assemblies of units (script, track, and slots for five script roles). Implicit in this representation is a hierarchy; for example, the MaMaison story is one way of filling the slots (bottom level) for the fancy track (middle level) of the restaurant script (top level). Miikkulainen decided to make this explicit by creating a hierarchy of self-organized feature maps, as shown in figure 7.6. At the top level, stories become positioned on a 2 × 2 map that distinguishes them by **script**. During the self-organizing phase, the four weight vectors into that map adapt until one unit reliably becomes most active for restaurant stories, another for shopping stories, and a third for travel stories (the fourth unit is excess here, but would be used if there were four scripts rather than three). Each of these units has its own 2 × 2 map at the next level, which further categorizes the stories by **track** (e.g., fancy, fast-food, and coffee-shop tracks for restaurant stories). Finally, the active unit on the track map passes just the story-specific parts of the input vector to an 8 × 8 **role-binding** map, which organizes the stories according to how their slots are filled. For example, the unit labeled JLMB in figure 7.6 is the maximally responding unit to the fancy-restaurant story in which the customer is John (not Mary), the food is Lobster (not Steak), the restaurant is MaMaison (not Leone's) and the tip is Big (not Small). (The taste is always Good in a fancy restaurant, so this role-binding was mapped at the track level.)

7.7.2   How role-binding maps become self-organized

The script and track maps are unusually small (4 units each) and dense (3 of the 4 units are used), but at first glance the role-binding maps are similar to the lexical maps in DISCERN. There are 16 different stories per track (e.g., for fancy restaurants there are 2 customers × 2 foods × 2 restaurants × 2 tips) and 64 role-binding units (8 × 8). Hence, the density of a role-binding map is similar to that of the lexical maps: for approximately 25 percent of the units there is a story that the unit represents (it is the maximally responsive unit to that story), and the remaining units support processing via lateral connections in both directions between each pair of units. As in the Lexicon, the maps self-organize by adapting their weight vectors to the input vectors (and to each other) during a period of unsupervised learning. The 8 × 8 grid that will become the role-binding map is prepared for learning by setting its lateral weights to be excitatory for neighbors and inhibitory otherwise. As in the Lexicon, this produces a focused activity bubble around the most active unit as the map settles and the vertical weights are adjusted to enhance this response the next time. For fancy restaurants, the result is a map in which (with one exception) lobster stories are in the upper two-thirds and steak stories in the lower two-thirds, small tips on the left and big tips on the right, and customer and restaurant vary in more localized, discontinuous patches (a result of squeezing four orthogonal dimensions on to a two-dimensional space; this patchiness can be seen in figure 7.7 below).

7.7.3   How role-binding maps become trace feature maps

In addition to the use of hierarchical maps and the high densities of the 2 × 2 maps, there is one further innovation that sets the Episodic Memory module apart from the Lexicon module: following self-organization, its maps are reconfigured as *trace feature maps*. This provides them with a mechanism for laying down a memory trace each time a story is processed, so that recently presented stories can be favored during retrieval. The mechanism involves a new use of the lateral connections within the role-binding maps. During self-organization the lateral connections were preset and did not change (except to reduce neighborhood size); the interesting action was in the adaptation of the weight vectors linking the maps to the input vectors (story representations). But once the maps are organized, they can be turned into trace feature maps by reversing which kinds of weights are the ones that change. Presented with a story, the system lays down a memory trace by making large, localized weight changes on the appropriate lateral connections, and the trace gets its

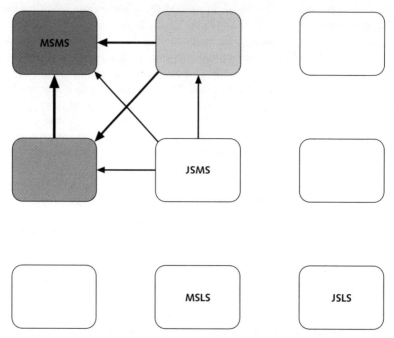

Figure 7.7   The creation of a role-binding map in DISCERN's Episodic Memory for a
story in which Mary ate steak at MaMaison and left a small tip (MSMS). The darkness of
each unit in the bubble around the unit representing the story (upper left unit) represents
the degree of its activation, and the width of the arrows indicates the strength of the
resulting excitatory connections.

meaning from the now-stable weight vectors on the vertical connections. The
excitatory lateral connections shown sketchily around the JLMB unit in figure 7.6
are a trace indicating that the story with those role bindings was recently presented.

The system needs just one presentation to lay down a trace, in contrast to the
gradual weight changes by which standard networks learn a task. How this works is
illustrated in figure 7.7, which displays the lower left corner of the fancy-restaurant
role-binding map just after presentation of the story in which the customer is Mary,
the food is Steak, the restaurant is MaMaison, and the tip is Small. For illustration
purposes we will stipulate a small activity bubble and trace around the MSMS unit
(an actual response would be larger and more symmetrical). There are no pre-
existing traces in the vicinity, so all lateral connections initially are inhibitory. For
each pair of units in this bubble, their level of activity is compared. If $unit_{ij}$ is more
active than $unit_{uv}$, the lateral weight from $unit_{ij}$ to $unit_{uv}$ is increased (usually enough
to change it from negative to positive) and the weight on the reciprocal connection is
decreased (usually a change within the negative range). The changes are greatest
from the more active units.

If only the excitatory connections (positive weights) are displayed, the result of
this process is a circle (or square) of excitatory connections all pointing towards the
maximally responding unit, with the degree of excitation decreasing with distance
from that unit. In the square activity bubble of figure 7.7, for example, JSMS was
less active than the other three units; the resulting weight increases on its outbound
connections were enough to turn them positive (while its inbound connections, not

shown, became more negative). The next most active unit (above JSMS) got positively connected to MSMS and to the third most active unit (next to JSMS), and
that unit in turn got positively connected to the most active unit (MSMS). Stronger
positive weights are indicated by thicker arrows. Connections involving inactive
units remain inhibitory, and reciprocals to the excitatory connections become more
strongly inhibitory.

The trace (the constellation of positive and negative weight changes) creates a
basin of attraction that is "switched off" (at least partly) during any subsequent
storage trials but plays an important role in processing retrieval cues (that is, inputs
for which traces are allowed to influence processing). If a cue activates any unit in
the basin of attraction, the network will settle into an activity bubble with the most-
pointed-at unit giving the maximal response. This enables the system to retrieve a
recently presented story from noisy or partial cues, if they are sufficiently close to
activate a unit within the basin. In our example, a partial cue (the encoding of the
question *WHO ATE STEAK AT MAMAISON?*) might come down through the
vertical connections of the hierarchical Episodic Memory and produce an initial
activity bubble around JSMS. As the lateral connections forming the basin of attraction come into play, however, activity shifts towards MSMS (as it should, since
that story had recently been presented), and the appropriate slot-filler representation of the story gets returned to the system.[2] (The equation governing this retrieval
process is provided in box 7.1.)

If the network is required to store a memory of a new event which is encoded in a
different region of the feature map, it simply creates an additional attractor basin.
However, if the new event must be stored near an existing trace, it "steals" for its
attractor basin some of the units that were in the existing attractor basin. This

---

Box 7.1 Equation governing the output η_{ij} at time $(t + 1)$ of any unit (i, j)
on a trace feature map

$$\eta_{ij}(t + 1) = \sigma\left([1 - \theta]\left[1 - \frac{\|\mathbf{x} - \mathbf{m}_{ij}\|}{d_{max}}\right] + \theta \sum \gamma_{uv,ij}\, \eta_{uv}(t) \right)$$

$\mathbf{x}$ is the external input vector

$\mathbf{m}_{ij}$ is the unit's weight vector

d_{max} is the maximum distance of two vectors in the input space ($\sqrt{2}$ in the 2-D
        unit square $0 \le x, y \le 1$)

$\gamma_{uv,ij}$ is the lateral connection weight on the connection from unit (u,v) to unit
        (i,j)

θ is a parameter that determines the relative contribution of external versus
        lateral activation

σ is the standard sigmoidal function:

$$\sigma(z) = \frac{1}{1 + e^{\beta[\delta - z]}}$$

β determines the slope of the sigmoid

δ determines the displacement of the sigmoid from the origin means that a cue which primarily activates stolen units will now retrieve the more recent memory. As additional stories create additional traces, only the closest cues will retrieve the first story; when all of the units in its original basin have been stolen, there will no longer be a trace to retrieve. Human episodic memory likewise exhibits recency effects due to interference.

7.8   Performance: Paraphrasing Stories and Answering Questions

7.8.1   Training and testing DISCERN

DISCERN is obviously a very complex system and the above description has only sketched how its component networks operate. On the basis of this sketch, however, we can examine some of the performance of DISCERN. For training purposes, Miikkulainen detached the processing modules from the loops shown in figure 7.1 and directly connected each to a proto-lexicon (which stored the most recent semantic representation of each word but had not yet formed feature maps). He trained each module separately (but simultaneously with the others) to perform its task on each of 96 story instantiations generated from the scripts and tracks identified above. For the question-answering modules, script specific questions with appropriate words for each story were also used for training.

Initially each module received arbitrary representations of the words in the input/ desired output pairs, but they were bound to the correct roles. Each representation consisted of two ID units plus 10 content units. Each time a word passed through a processing module, its content units were adjusted slightly and the adjusted values replaced the former values in the lexicon. Eventually the content units for the two fancy restaurants should be similar, meaningful, and adapted to all six processing modules (i.e., reflecting the history and distributional contexts in which they were bound to roles – the location role in the case representations and the restaurant role in the script representations). A trained semantic representation is composed of two ID units plus 10 trained content units.

When this training was complete, a different kind of training produced internal structure in the two memory modules (unsupervised learning organized the feature maps, and in the Lexicon Hebbian learning associated its two feature maps). Then the modules were reconnected for normal operation and testing (i.e., the output of one network was copied on to the appropriate input units of the next network in the loop).

Overall DISCERN performed very accurately on tests. In producing complete paraphrases of incomplete input stories, for example, 98 percent of the (ortho-graphic) words ultimately output by the lexicon were correct. The percentage fell as low as 93 percent within particular modules (especially the feature maps), but later modules were able to clean up and recover from most of the errors made by earlier modules in the loop. However, restricting attention to those words with the ID + content format (by disregarding words like *the* and *to*) lowers these percentages to 93 percent correct on final output and as low as 83 percent within modules. This was due primarily to difficulties with the ID values which distinguished pairs of other-wise identical words; only the Story Parser had some ability to recover from an ID error rather than passing it to the next module.

One can gain a sense of DISCERN's performance by examining what happened when it read the following five incomplete stories. Having parsed and laid down a memory trace for each, DISCERN was then asked to paraphrase one and ask questions about others.

1   John went to Denny's. John asked the waiter for fish. John ate a bad fish.
2   Mary went to Leone's. Mary asked the waiter for steak. Mary left a small tip.
3   Mary went to CircuitCity. Mary looked for a good TV. Mary took the best TV.
4   John went to RadioShack. John looked for a good TV. John took the best TV.
5   Mary went to DFW. Mary checked in for a flight to SFO. The plane arrived at SFO.

7.8.2   Watching DISCERN paraphrase a story

The first story was used for a paraphrase task, in which DISCERN was expected to produce the complete story after reading the incomplete one. This would indicate that the system had captured the statistical regularities implicit in the complete versions of all 96 stories during training and could use its knowledge to identify the appropriate story and infer the missing information. In fact, parsing the first story resulted in the following script representation being output from the Story Parser and submitted to Episodic Memory:

Script	Track	Customer	Food	Restaurant	Taste	Tip
|$restaurant	$coffee	*John*	*fish*	*Denny's*	*bad*	*small*|

Note that though the story was incomplete, the Story Parser created a complete script representation. For example, it supplied the value *small* for tip because bad food was correlated with small tips in the restaurant stories. To paraphrase the story, this script representation had to be retrieved from Episodic Memory and fed to the Script Generator, which had learned during training to chunk the script information into six different (though overlapping) sentence-length "packages," each of which was output one word at a time and retained by building a complete case-role representation on the input units of the Sentence Generator. That module rejuggled each case-role representation and produced an appropriate sentence one word at a time. The Lexicon translated the semantically represented words in each sentence into the orthographic representations needed to communicate with the outside world. The result was this full story (which was identical to one in the system's training corpus):

> John went to Denny's. John seated John. John asked the waiter for fish. John ate a bad fish. John left a small tip. John paid the cashier. John left Denny's.

7.8.3   Watching DISCERN answer questions

The other basic activity that DISCERN performs is answering questions. As a simple illustration of its ability, consider its response when the question *WHAT DID MARY EAT AT LEONE'S?* was posed after it had read all five of the above stories and created traces in the Episodic Memory. Receiving a case-role representation of the question from the Sentence Parser, the Cue Former used the knowledge embedded in its simple (nonrecurrent) FGREP network to create the following probe:

Script	Track	Customer	Food	Restaurant	Taste	Tip
|$restaurant	$fancy	Mary	steak	Leone's	good	*from(small)*|

The Cue Former has approximately the same knowledge of scripts as the Story Parser, differing mainly in its use of a nonrecurrent FGREP architecture (the case roles are filled simultaneously using assemblies of input units rather than sequential input) and in its knowledge of wh-words (*who*, *what*, *where*, etc.). Like the Story Parser, it can fill most of the script slots correctly after reading just one sentence (which now is a question rather than the first sentence of a story).

But why is the tip slot filled by *from(small)*? Miikkulainen used this awkward notation to remind us that it is actually semantic vectors (patterns of activation across units) that fill the slots. Usually these are close enough to the vector of an actual word that it is reasonable to use the word to indicate how a slot was filled. (Miikkulainen arrived at these words by feeding the vectors to the Lexicon's semantic map, noting what word, if any, had its corresponding map unit in the activation bubble, and using that word to indicate in English what sort of vector filled each slot.) In this example, a small tip and big tip were about equally likely and therefore a semantic vector intermediate between those for *small* and *big* was generated for the tip slot. The vectors activate units on the semantic map, only some of which correspond to words. It happened that the active unit, though between the units for *small* and *big*, was closest to that for *from*. Miikkulainen therefore put *from* in the tip slot, but also noted the correct word in parentheses and set these off by asterisks to signal the difficulty: *from(small)*.

Interestingly, the cue already includes the answer to the question posed: what Mary ate was steak. This was partly due to luck, however. Because steak and lobster are about equally likely in a fancy restaurant, an intermediate semantic vector filled the food slot. This time the map unit activated by the vector corresponded to one of the two competing words, and it happened (by a hair) to be *steak* rather than *lobster*. However, this is not the system's final answer and it is not crucial that it be correct. The cue (assemblies for script, track, and script roles, each filled by a semantic vector) is submitted to the Episodic Memory, which has traces of all five stories. The story that best matches the cue is retrieved from the part of the role-binding map shown in figure 7.7 (MSLS: Mary Steak Leone's Small). It is converted into the same script format as the cue (assemblies filled by semantic vectors), but again we use the closest word to each vector for purposes of exposition:

Script	Track	Customer	Food	Restaurant	Taste	Tip
|$restaurant	$fancy	Mary	steak	Leone's	good	small|

Roles that could not be filled with confidence from the cue alone now have clear bindings (those of the original story): the vector for tip now is very close to the canonical vector for *small* and the vector for food is now very close to the canonical vector for *steak*. Because the system has retrieved the complete story from memory, questions can be answered with confidence. To make this happen, the script representation of the story is supplied along with the case-role representation of the question to the Answer Producer. Using its nonrecurrent FGREP architecture, this module outputs a case-role representation of the answer, and it is further processed through the Sentence Generator and the Lexicon so that DISCERN can output the correct answer: *MARY ATE A GOOD STEAK*. It answers this question even though the original story (see above) never said that Mary ate the steak. The script representation does not distinguish what Mary ordered from what she ate, and so DISCERN uses the information about what she ordered to also supply the information about what she ate. It would also respond to other questions about information that was not specified as long as the script representation supplied values for these slots based upon what was most frequent in the training set.

Amongst many other examples of DISCERN's performance that Miikkulainen offers, it will be useful to look at one case in which the question, *WHO BOUGHT TV?* was ambiguous, since two stories involved the buying of a TV. The Sentence Parser constructed the case-role representation:

Script	Track	Customer	Item	Store
|who	bought	—	TV	RadioShack|

guessing that the TV was bought at RadioShack because of the statistics in the training data. The Cue Former, though, created the following script representation:

Script	Track	Customer	Item	Store
|$shopping	$electronics	John	TV	*CircuitCity (RadioShack)*|

proposing, again on the basis of statistical regularities, that John bought the TV, but now combining this with the inappropriate store information (given the stories). While this probe could activate the memory of either story, the story about John was most recent, and so it won the competition and resulted in the output script representation:

Script	Track	Customer	Item	Store
|$shopping	$electronics	John	TV	RadioShack|

which in turn caused the Answer Producer, Sentence Generator, and Lexicon to combine in producing the answer *JOHN DID*.

7.9   Evaluating DISCERN

In many respects, DISCERN is an impressive demonstration of how connectionist tools might be employed to model higher cognitive tasks. More specifically, it illustrates how multiple connectionist networks can collaborate to accomplish simplified versions of such tasks as reading stories and questions, paraphrasing stories, and answering questions about them. It shows the efficiencies achieved by a sequential modular organization, in which the output of each network becomes the input of the next network (in fact, Miikkulainen created and ran a nonmodular version of his system to demonstrate it was less efficient than the modular one). The structure-sensitive representations developed by the FGREP architecture play a major role in this efficient collaboration. The networks each individually introduce errors, but frequently these errors are corrected as processing proceeds through later networks in the loop.

There are also clear limitations to DISCERN, among which are the following. First, once trained, the network does not handle novelty well. Despite capacity for limited kinds of generalization within each module, in the end any new story will be treated as an instance of the scripts it has already learned. Second, there are severe limitations in the representations the network can use. For example, only a small subset of actual sentences have the word order and case roles required by DIS-CERN, and even those have considerably more structure than is recovered by DISCERN. Third, the scripts cannot be combined nor employ recursion. (Neither can DISCERN process sentences with embedded clauses, but a subsequent simulation of Miikkulainen's indicates how one might overcome this difficulty.) Fourth, there are several unrealistic technical requirements. To cite just two: (a) the modules must be hooked up in a special way while the Lexicon self-organizes (but people acquire new words seamlessly during acts of comprehension); (b) a parameter governing the contribution of the lateral connections must be reset whenever the Episodic Memory module switches between storage and retrieval. Miikkulainen explicitly notes these and other limitations, and his book should be consulted for intriguing suggestions as to how some might be overcome.

Beyond these more specific limitations, though, DISCERN raises a more general question about the use of connectionist networks in modeling higher cognitive processes: what is (or should be) the relation of connectionist models to traditional symbolic models in the same domain? In the case of DISCERN, there were several points of contact between the network model and traditional approaches to cognitive modeling.

First, and most obviously, the script framework had been developed within the traditional symbolic tradition and was then given a connectionist implementation in DISCERN. The implementation added some desirable characteristics. For example, the task-relevant representations developed by the FGREP architecture supported the system in making plausible inferences and in cleaning up errors that arose, overcoming to some extent the brittleness that is characteristic of symbolic models. On the negative side, it took herculean effort to produce a model that implemented only the simplest version of a script approach at a time when Schank (pursuing his own distinctive variety of traditional AI) had progressed considerably beyond it.

Second, the ideas that words should be stored in a lexicon and that stories should be stored in an episodic memory has traditional roots as well. Again, DISCERN implemented these ideas using nonsymbolic means that carry attractive advantages. In addition to achieving content-addressable memory storage, Kohonen feature maps display the capacity for self-organization that is an essential aspect of human cognition. Some compromises were needed to get the system built, such as Miikkulainen's role in crafting the hierarchical map structure in DISCERN's Episodic Memory.

Third, the traditional nature of the tasks performed by each module was no accident. The idea of modular organization as well as the method of determining the number of modules and their division of labor were borrowed from traditional cognitive science. The method involves an *a priori* task analysis. Miikkulainen complied by carrying out a rather high-level cognitive decomposition to determine subtasks of his two overall tasks (paraphrasing and question-answering) and designed one module for each of the eight subtasks identified. Cooper (1994) leaned especially on this aspect of DISCERN in suggesting that Miikkulainen had not realized his professed desire to perform all operations within a subsymbolic framework. Instead, Cooper pointed out, by predefining the modules and using assemblies of units to obtain compositional representations Miikkulainen may have provided much or all of what Fodor (1975, 1987) requires for a language of thought.

Miikkulainen's book was the focus of multiple reviews in issues of *Psycoloquy* between 5(46) and 7(34).

This is not the first time we have encountered some tension in the connectionist enterprise between its revolutionary aspirations and traditional roots. DISCERN is a relatively well developed example of what connectionists were able to achieve in their first decade while tolerating this tension. Having now completed our discussion of DISCERN we find ourselves at a major transition point, where we must ask what path or paths different researchers pursued during connectionism's second decade (the 1990s). The major ones are outlined in the next section. In keeping with the broad introductory goals of the book, the first three paths are not pursued further, but each of the next three paths is discussed in its own chapter.

7.10   Paths Beyond the First Decade of Connectionism

Classic connectionism.   Existing designs, such as multi-layered networks with featural input representations, provide the familiar advantages of connectionism and are relatively simple to build. For many cognitive scientists, connectionism has already paid its way by contributing useful architectures to the toolkit. Those focused on problems rather than tools choose network designs when their characteristics are needed and more traditional designs when those are sufficient. Others take seriously a theoretical commitment to connectionism and focus on exploring the capabilities and applications of existing network designs.

A more connectionist connectionism.   Some investigators view the traditional, symbolic roots of connectionism as a fact about its history, while putting current energy into designing more flexible, adaptable, thoroughly connectionist models with the potential to scale up to larger, more realistic problem domains. This path overlaps somewhat with the first one but emphasizes new developments. If a successor to DISCERN could itself decide what work each module should perform, and could revise the modular structure when necessary, it might out-perform a human designer at dealing with fluctuating task requirements. For example, if daughter-of-DISCERN had developed modules adequate for answering questions about familiar stories and then was presented with the new task of making inferences under counterfactual conditions, it might add this capability by adapting existing modules, or it might add one or more new modules to work with the existing ones, or it might reorganize its modules more extensively. It is hard for a human designer to know which approach would work best. At this point networks cannot achieve this either, but some preliminary efforts have been made towards building networks that can define their own modules (see Jacobs, Jordan, and Barto, 1991, in section 10.2.1 for one example). In the same spirit, others have specified ways that single-module networks can develop in a task environment so as to end up with an appropriate number and arrangement of units (see Nolfi, Miglino, and Parisi, 1994, in section 9.4). Although there have been some intriguing developments in network design along these and other lines, the task is difficult and there are no dramatic breakthroughs to report yet.

Hybrid networks.   Some connectionists, while equally interested in advancing design, hold no brief against the traditional symbolic approach and prefer to *increase* rather than decrease its influence. They deliberately design *hybrid systems* that use connectionist means to implement traditional ideas, designs, and systems. An early example, Touretzky's (1986) connectionist implementation of a production system, was discussed in detail in the first edition of this book. More recent exemplars include Barnden (1995), Sun and Alexandre (1997), and Touretzky (1990).

Dynamical networks. A major new development in the 1990s was the application of *dynamical systems theory* to cognitive modeling. One way of doing this brings together connectionist networks and dynamical tools and concepts. Chapter 8 provides an introduction.

Network robot controllers. Another field that attracted increasing attention across the 1990s is *artificial life*. One approach involves using a connectionist network (usually evolved using a genetic algorithm) as the "brains" of a robot. The advantages of connectionist over symbolic models is especially apparent in sensorimotor domains, making this a very natural and promising step to take. Chapter 9 focuses on this development.

Network models in neuroscience. Advances in neuroscience, especially neuroimaging, have brought cognitive science and neuroscience into much closer alignment during the 1990s than in the previous two decades. As part of this overall trend, connectionists have shown an increased interest in designing network models of particular brain areas or functions. Chapter 10 addresses this convergence, and is the final chapter of the book.

NOTES

1   Miikkulainen does not explicitly refer to input/output buffers or place them within the Lexicon. Though they would seem to be needed at least during the self-organizing process, thereafter the Lexicon may simply store weight vectors and use them to move representations in or out of the assemblies that are located within processing modules.
2   If, however, a cue activates a unit that is outside of any basin, the network will oscillate due to the inhibitory connections around that unit; such oscillation is interpreted as indicating that the network has no memory of hearing a story of this sort.

SOURCES AND SUGGESTED READINGS

Fodor, J. A. (1983) *The Modularity of Mind.* Cambridge, MA: MIT Press.
Kohonen, T. (1989) *Self-organization and Associative Memory*, 3rd edn. Berlin: Springer-Verlag.
Kohonen, T. (2001) *Self-organizing Maps*, 3rd edn. Berlin: Springer-Verlag.
Miikkulainen, R. (1993) *Subsymbolic Natural Language Processing: An Integrated Model of Scripts, Lexicon, and Memory.* Cambridge, MA: MIT Press.
Schank, R. C. and Abelson, R. (1977) *Scripts, Plans, Goals, and Understanding.* Hillsdale, NJ: Lawrence Erlbaum.

8

CONNECTIONISM AND THE DYNAMICAL APPROACH TO COGNITION

8.1 Are We on the Road to a Dynamical Revolution?

We saw in chapter 1 that connectionism has its roots in the 1940s, when ideas about the nervous system, computation, and intelligence came together synergistically. We briefly traced the path from *formal neurons* to *perceptrons* and noted that events in the 1960s led to a period in which these neural network models became overshadowed by symbolic models of intelligence. With the rise of connectionism in the 1980s neural networks regained prominence, and for two decades the two approaches have each sought to dominate cognitive science.

This is part of a larger story. The energetic collaborations of the 1940s had multiple, sometimes intertwined strands, of which the best known is an emphasis on feedback and control in the *cybernetics* of Norbert Wiener and others. This required attention to the dynamics of change in time, an aspect of the functioning of systems which has often been ignored by connectionists (though not by Stephen Grossberg and his group, who continued to advance network research during the period when symbolic models were dominant; see Grossberg, 1982). In an even broader context, the dynamics of complex physical systems have been mathematically describable at least since Newton (building on work by Galileo) formulated his three laws of motion and developed the calculus to gain the ability to predict specific planetary configurations. New geometrical approaches to dynamics by Poincaré in the late nineteenth century prepared the way for the rise of Dynamical Systems Theory (DST) in the twentieth century. Initially applied primarily to physical phenomena such as eddies in a stream (Landau, 1944), by the 1980s DST was being extended to motor coordination by Michael Turvey, Peter Kugler, and J. A. Scott Kelso (see Kelso, 1995) and by the 1990s to the development not only of coordinated activity but also more cognitive capacities (see the 1994 book by Esther Thelen and Linda Smith). Although the mathematics of nonlinear dynamical systems can be daunting, DST has spawned compelling graphics that help to provide an intuitive grasp of key concepts (among the suggested readings at the end of the chapter, see especially the copiously illustrated introduction by Abraham and Shaw, 1992).

The idea that cognition is dynamic and can best be understood using the tools of DST attracted increasing attention across the 1990s but is still somewhat of a frontier outpost in cognitive science. Much of the excitement was conveyed in *Mind as Motion*, a 1995 book originating in a 1991 conference which brought together many of the pioneering modelers. The editors, Robert Port and Timothy van Gelder, wanted to convince a broad audience that DST has revolutionary implications for cognitive science. In an introductory chapter they characterized cognitive science as wedded to what they call the computational approach (i.e., symbolic modeling) and called for a change, contending that "dynamical and computational systems are fundamentally different *kinds* of systems, and hence the dynamical and computational approaches to cognition are fundamentally different in their deepest foundations" (van Gelder and Port, 1995, p. 10). Further, they portrayed the emergence of the dynamical approach in cognitive science as a Kuhnian revolution:

> The computational approach is nothing less than a research paradigm in Kuhn's classic sense. It defines a range of questions and the form of answers to those questions (i.e., computational models). It provides an array of exemplars – classic pieces of research which define how cognition is to be thought about and what counts as a successful model. . . . [T]he dynamical approach is more than just powerful tools; like the computational approach, it is a worldview. The cognitive system is not a computer, it is a dynamical system. It is not the brain, inner and encapsulated; rather, it is the whole system comprised of nervous system, body, and environment. The cognitive system is not a discrete sequential manipulator of static representational structures; rather, it is a structure of mutually and simultaneously influencing *change*. Its processes do not take place in the arbitrary, discrete time of computer steps; rather, they unfold in the *real* time of ongoing change. . . . The cognitive system does not interact with other aspects of the world by passing messages or commands; rather, it continuously coevolves with them. . . . [T]o see that there is a dynamical approach is to see a new way of conceptually reorganizing cognitive science as it is currently practiced.   (van Gelder and Port, 1995, pp. 2–4)

If computational and dynamical worldviews are poles apart, connectionism occupies a somewhat more ambiguous territory in between. Highly interactive networks, such as Boltzmann machines, are dynamical systems of considerable interest in principle. In practice, they are hard to use and hard to analyze even with the availability of DST tools. Feedforward networks have made the greatest inroads into cognitive science, in part due to their tractability, but the only aspect of this architecture that is dynamical is the adaptation of weights during learning. Most connectionist models, even interactive ones, carry some symbolic/computational baggage and therefore are not the best poster children for van Gelder and Port's revolution. We see a somewhat different future, in which connectionist modeling can benefit from both computational and dynamical approaches and can sometimes even combine them within the analysis of a single network.

In what follows we will introduce some basic dynamical concepts and tools in section 8.2; describe how the simplest concepts have been utilized in four areas of network research in 8.3; and describe how the concept of chaos has been utilized in two network models in 8.4. Then in 8.5 we return to philosophical issues raised by van Gelder and Port. From their overall claim that classic connectionism occupies an untenable halfway position between the computational and dynamical approaches, we move to more specific arguments concerning explanation (countered by Bechtel) and representation (countered by Clark and Wheeler). The counter-arguments lead towards a more inclusive cognitive science, and in 8.6 we discuss a controversial version offered by philosophers Terrence Horgan and John Tienson. Let us start, then, by introducing some concepts and tools from the mathematical core of the dynamical approach: dynamical systems theory (DST).

8.2   Basic Concepts of DST: The Geometry of Change

8.2.1   Trajectories in state space: Predators and prey

If a picture is generally worth a thousand words, in the case of dynamical systems theory each picture is worth at least ten times that many: among DST's innovations is the adroit use of geometrical representations to help conceptualize how systems change. The simplest picture is a plot of the states traversed by a system through time, that is, the system's *trajectory* through *state space*. The trajectory is a continuous curve if the system is defined in real time, or a sequence of points in discrete time. Each dimension of state space corresponds to one variable of the system, and each point in the space corresponds to one of the possible states of the system. For systems with one continuous variable, the state space is a range of values on one dimension (e.g., the frequency of a tone; the height of a person; the firing rate of a neuron; the population size of a species in its habitat). The trajectory of a pure tone is a regular oscillation between two values (if a time dimension is added to the plot, a sine wave is obtained). A trajectory for height starts with an infant's height at birth and rises (irregularly) over time.

To move up to a two-dimensional state space, the most obvious way is to consider an additional variable; for example, you can visualize your child's growth by graphing height and weight on orthogonal axes and plotting a point each week; connecting the points approximates the child's trajectory through height-weight space in real time. Another way of moving up to a two-dimensional state space is to examine the same variable for two different individuals (or neurons, populations, network units, etc.). Keep adding more, and you end up with a high-dimensional system. For example, the activation values across a 90-unit output layer in a feedforward connectionist network can be represented as a single point in a 90-dimensional state space – each unit's activation is treated as a separate variable of the system. If the network is feedforward, its response to an input is one point in the space. If it is interactive, the changing activation values are represented as a sequence of points – that is, as a trajectory through activation state space – but the outcome may be similar since some trajectories simply converge on a point and remain there.

A two-dimensional state space is much easier to visualize than a 90-dimensional one, so we will use the case of two species in a predator–prey relationship to illustrate some key concepts (the case is described by Ralph Abraham and Christopher Shaw, 1992, pp. 82–5). The classic account was proposed independently by Alfred James Lotka (1925) and Vita Volterra (1926). Our first picture, figure 8.1(a), shows several variations on an idealized *cyclic trajectory* (also called a *periodic trajectory*) in the state space for number of prey (horizontal axis) and number of predators (vertical axis); it was inspired by periodicity in the population sizes of different species of fish in the Adriatic Sea. To understand the cyclic changes in population size, four parts of the outermost curve (labeled I–IV) can be considered separately. (See below for discussion of the whole family of curves.) When there are relatively few of both predators and prey, the number of predators declines for lack of food while the number of prey increases for lack of predators (region I). The increase in prey, though, provides a more ample food source for the predators, and beyond a transition point, the number of predators will begin to increase along with the number of prey (region II). But the increase in predators results in increased consumption of

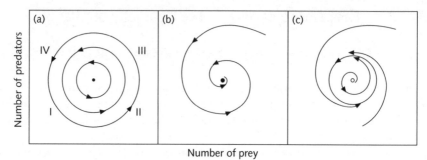

Figure 8.1   Possible trajectories through state space for interacting predator and prey populations: (a) cyclic trajectories (no attractor); (b) point attractor with spiraling transient; (c) cyclic attractor with spiraling transients beginning at points inside and outside of it.

prey, so after another transition point the number of prey declines while predators continue to increase (region III). But eventually the shrinking prey population leads to starvation for predators and both predators and prey decline in population (region IV). When the number of predators becomes sufficiently low, the number of prey will begin to increase again (region I). And so forth: in principle, each population's size is predicted to *oscillate* (move between two extremes) forever, with the same *period* (elapsed time) on each cycle. The prediction derives from the Lotka–Volterra equations, in which the rate of change of each population depends on the current number of prey (x) and predators (y) as well as the values of the *control parameters* (A, B, C, and D):

$$\frac{\partial x}{\partial t} = (A - By)x \qquad (1)$$

$$\frac{\partial y}{\partial t} = (Cx - D)y \qquad (2)$$

To obtain a cyclic trajectory using these equations, an appropriate set of parameter values must be identified (not all values will produce such a trajectory).[1] As shown in figure 8.1(a) for one such set of values, the equations then yield a family of concentric closed curves around a central equilibrium point. Within that family, the particular curve – ranging from no oscillation at the center to the extreme population swings of the largest-diameter circle – depends upon the initial values of x and y. Once the system embarks on one of these trajectories, it will repeat it indefinitely – unless perturbed by some change outside the system. For example, unusually high temperatures may increase the predators' mortality rate, D, and also affect reproduction and predation rates, reflected in A–C.

Another way to get different trajectories is to change the equations. In fact, later researchers found that the Lotka–Volterra equations alone are unrealistic (e.g., they make no provision for competition among prey or predators for limited resources). One kind of revision to the system of equations adds "ecological friction" (by analogy to the physical friction that brings a pendulum asymptotically to rest by damping its oscillations). Figure 8.1(b) shows how this produces a very characteristic DST state space plot. The illustrative trajectory now has two parts. The *point attractor* at the center (also called the *limit point*) is stable – if exactly these predator and prey population sizes are attained, the system is in equilibrium and will remain in that state. Thus, the attractor is the stable part of the trajectory, and can be viewed as describing the long-term behavior of the system. The curve that leads to the attractor is a *transient*, the part of the trajectory that the system traverses as it moves from its initial state towards equilibrium. The spiraling transients in this system reflect a story similar to the one we told for sections I–IV of the outer cycle in figure 8.1(a), except that here the system approaches the equilibrium point as the oscillations in population size diminish in amplitude. When the transient spirals towards a point like this, the system is a *damped oscillator* and the point attractor is also called a *focal point*.

Crucially, trajectories from many different initial states will converge on the same focal point: for various initial numbers of predators and prey, the populations will approach this point of equilibrium along an appropriate, spiraling transient. In fact, it is primarily the convergence of nearby trajectories to this equilibrium point that qualifies it as an attractor (cf. the equilibrium point in figure 8.1(a), which is not an attractor); and it is specifically a point attractor (limit point) because the subset of state space to which the trajectories converge (the *limit set*) consists of just one point. The set of all initial states whose trajectories converge on this attractor is its *basin of attraction* (generally a region of state space but possibly the entire space). The state space – also called *phase space* – filled with the possible trajectories of this system is its *phase portrait*. In figure 8.1(b) this was reduced, for display purposes, to a representation of the point attractor (by convention, a small solid circle) and one typical trajectory. For systems with multiple attractors (and perhaps other special features, such as *repellors*, *saddle nodes*, and the *separatrices* that may form boundaries between basins), a larger number of trajectories or special display conventions are needed to convey the essentials of the phase portrait.

This is a good place to pause and note that considerable idealization is involved in using even the modified system of equations to model changes in the population sizes of two species in a predator–prey relationship. First, the real-life populations are not a closed system; as already mentioned, external factors such as ocean temperature can affect parameter values. Second, here as in many other dynamical systems (those classified as *dissipative*), convergence is asymptotic – the state of the system approaches the attractor as time approaches infinity. Beyond the formal nature of this characterization, it also assumes a continuity that cannot be attained in population dynamics. Each birth or death brings a discrete change in the value of x or y. At best these values will jiggle around in the vicinity of the equilibrium point as individuals are born and die. This leads to another notion that is worth making explicit: even if the system could reach true equilibrium, what is stable is the value of two collective variables. Out in the Adriatic Sea, individual fish are still giving birth and dying, eating or being eaten. Trajectories of change in the lives of individual fish are not inconsistent with lack of change in the size of their two populations.

A phase portrait that is somewhat more realistic for the Adriatic case (though still idealized) can be obtained by making one more revision to the system of equations. Figure 8.1(c) shows a *cyclic attractor* (also called a *periodic attractor* or *limit cycle*) along with a few of the possible transients. This is a form of stable behavior that at least involves movement – the state of the system endlessly cycles around in state space rather than remaining at a single point as in (b). But the comparison to portrait (a) is even more informative. The circle in the middle of (c) looks the same as one of the circles in (a), but the dynamics producing it are quite different. As a cyclic attractor, it is the stable part of a variety of trajectories rather than a single trajectory.

That is, in (c) many different starting points all converge on the same circle (that is why it is called an attractor), whereas in (a) the starting point is already part of the circle and determines its diameter.[2] (Note that although both of these cycles are circles, in other systems they might be any sort of closed curve; we will see much odder-shaped limit cycles in figure 8.3(a).) Examining (c) more closely, it can be seen that a trajectory that begins with many predators and many prey and another that begins with very few predators but almost as many prey both have transients that converge on the limit cycle; that is, the long-term behavior of both trajectories is the same. Trajectories with transients inside the limit cycle also converge on it; in the one exemplar shown in (c), the trajectory begins near a *point repellor* (a point from which trajectories diverge – the opposite of an attractor – shown conventionally as a small hollow circle) and spirals out to converge on the limit cycle. Thus, the basin of attraction is extensive.

8.2.2   Bifurcation diagrams and chaos

Some systems exhibit behavior that is more complex than in figure 8.1. In addition to the possibility of multiple attractors and other special features, there exist unstable trajectories which appear random despite following a deterministic path (i.e., the trajectory never repeats itself, but from any given point in the state space there is an algorithm that determines the next point). Perhaps more dramatically than necessary, this is called a *chaotic trajectory*. When the (infinite number of) possible chaotic trajectories of a system exhibit the characteristics of an attractor, the system is said to have a *chaotic attractor*. In particular, trajectories that begin near each other in the (infinitely large) limit set of the attractor will tend to diverge (a characteristic known as *sensitive dependence on initial conditions*), while trajectories that begin in the limit set's basin of attraction will converge on it. Chaotic attractors tend to be topologically complex. One of the simpler examples starts with the doughnut-shaped torus, which can be thought of as offering an infinite number of cyclic trajectories. A system with a torus attractor in its phase portrait will exhibit quasi-periodic behavior (continuously circling the torus but not repeating any particular cycle). However, the behavior becomes unstable for a torus in a very high-dimensional space: the system samples various cyclic trajectories along the surface of the torus, jumping from one to the next at irregular intervals. This unstable sampling of cycles is a chaotic trajectory. And this glimpse of a complex field of mathematics will have to suffice here.

Chaotic behavior is one innovative concept of DST; another is the importance of parameter values in whether a system exhibits that behavior. Even simple nonlinear systems may exhibit *phase transitions* (rapid shifts from one phase portrait to another) when the value of one or more control parameters changes slightly. For example, a single difference equation may produce a single point attractor, a cyclic attractor (limit cycle), or a chaotic attractor for x depending on the value of one control parameter A. The rapid transition in dynamics, brought about by a small but critical change in the parameter, is referred to mathematically as a *bifurcation*. The simplest example (from which the general term derives) is a *pitchfork bifurcation*, wherein a single point attractor splits in two. To explain and illustrate this concept, we will use a *bifurcation diagram* to display the varied behavior of a well-studied type of system defined in discrete time. It is specified by the logistic equation (which should not be confused with the logistic activation function introduced in chapter 2):

$$x_{t+1} = Ax_t \, (1 - x_t) \tag{3}$$

where x is a variable with range $0<x<1$ and A is a control parameter from the range $0<A<4$. The subscripts t and $t + 1$ index successive time-steps t_0, t_1, t_2, t_3, and so forth; any value x_{t+1} depends in part on the value x_t on the previous time-step. We can begin by simply examining the sequence of values taken by x (its trajectory) when A is fixed, as it is generally assumed to be for a given system. Here is the calculation of the first five points of the trajectory when A = 3 and the initial state $x_0 = 0.5$:

$x_1 = 3 \times 0.5 \times 0.5 = 0.75$
$x_2 = 3 \times 0.75 \times 0.25 = 0.5625$
$x_3 = 3 \times 0.5625 \times 0.4375 = 0.7383$
$x_4 = 3 \times 0.7383 \times 0.2617 = 0.5796$
$x_5 = 3 \times 0.5796 \times 0.4204 = 0.7310$

It can be seen even from these few points that the system is behaving as a damped oscillator (its behavior through much but not all of the stated range). It is converging on a point attractor at 0.6667 and the transient is a discrete version of the continuous spiral in figure 8.1(b). That is, it alternates between high and low values rather than spiraling between them. (In both cases, since the oscillation is damped, the high and low values themselves keep changing as the system converges on the attractor.) If a different initial value of x is used, the high and low values may begin further apart or closer together but will converge on the same attractor value of 0.6667.

From all this detail about the trajectories of x when A = 3, the only information needed for the bifurcation diagram is the value of the point attractor, 0.6667. In general the bifurcation diagram for the logistic equation shows, for values of A within some range, the stable (long-term) values that x may attain. The transients one would obtain from different initial values of x are ignored; only the stable value or values to which they converge are plotted. A single stable value is the simplest outcome, and that is how this equation behaves when A is between 0 and 3.

Figure 8.2 shows the bifurcation diagram for values of A between 2.6 and 4.0. This catches some of the simple part of the range. The first bifurcation (a pitchfork) appears just beyond A = 3 where x's stable long-term behavior suddenly switches to an alternation between two values (that is, the point attractor is replaced by a periodic attractor with periodicity of 2). These values (the prongs of the fork) drift further apart as A increases, but what matters most is that the dynamics are qualitatively different before vs. after the point of transition, which is called a *bifurcation point*. Just beyond 3.4 another bifurcation point is reached, and the system's periodicity increases to 4.

At a value of A beyond 3.6 a different kind of bifurcation begins to develop, one in which the attractor ceases to be periodic and becomes chaotic. The darkened region is a rough representation of the fact that x is taking a nonrepeating sequence of values. The value at each time step is deterministic since it is generated by equation (3), but each value is a new one. The new phase portrait contains a *chaotic attractor*, which changes form as the value of A increases. Interestingly, there are even values

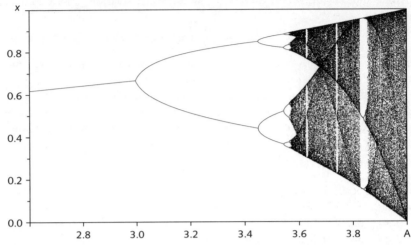

Figure 8.2   Bifurcation plot of the logistic function (1) for values of A between 2.6 and 4.0. For values of A less than 3.0 the function settles into a point attractor. Above 3.0 it bifurcates into a two-point attractor, than a four-point attractor, and so forth. Beyond 3.6 it enters a chaotic regime punctuated by periodicity within narrow ranges.

of A beyond the initial bifurcation to chaos for which x will once again exhibit simple periodicity. The values of x comprising each sequence show up in figure 8.2 as little lines within otherwise white bands near A = 3.6, 3.7, and 3.8.

8.2.3   Embodied networks as coupled dynamical systems

Now we can return to the assumption that A is a constant for a given system. This actually applies only if the system is an *autonomous dynamical system* – one that is unaffected by any other system. If so, trajectories through the state space can be specified in terms of equations (frequently nonlinear) which simply relate the variables of the system. Often, however, a system will be influenced by factors outside its boundaries (e.g., if we construe planet Earth as a system, variation in the sun's radiant energy is an external factor influencing this system). A *nonautonomous dynamical system* is one in which the values of one or more parameters vary due to external influences.

The dynamics get especially interesting if two systems are nonautonomous because they are *coupled,* with the states of each system influencing the values of parameters or variables in the other system across time. Thus, when the cognitive system is construed as a dynamical system, it may be further construed as coupled with other dynamical systems involving the organism's body and environment. In carrying out even a simple activity such as tapping a pencil, there may be reciprocal relations among three systems: the firing of neurons (brain), the movements of the fingers (body), and the tapping of the pencil against a surface (environment). This is the sort of interaction among brain, body, and environment that might best be modeled by construing them as coupled dynamical systems. (One can also construe coupled dynamical systems as a single, autonomous dynamical system, but at a cost of complexity. Considerations of tractability often dictate treating the systems as separate, with each affecting the other by determining the values of some of its parameters.)

Dynamicists often celebrate coupling as a much more powerful and useful way of thinking about the interactions between the cognitive system and its environment than is offered by traditional perspectives. Both symbolic and connectionist modelers have found it difficult to advance beyond the "boxes in the head" models which began to replace stimulus–response models in the 1960s. This legacy includes a static characterization of the environment (e.g., the fixed corpus that provides input patterns to a network) and a cognitive model that acts with no further reference to the environment once an input is received. The input is operated upon (with interim results passed from one processor to another) and the result is sent out of the system as an output. For example, the DISCERN system (chapter 7) has a sequence of processing modules, each of which performs its own transformation on the input it receives and sends output to the next module (and, when the last module has completed its work, back out to the world). Most of DISCERN's modules are simple recurrent networks, but this allows only a very limited type of interactive processing (no settling dynamics, and connections remain within the bounds of the module). None of the modules has loops out to the environment and back or a means of changing its own operations in sync with ongoing changes in the environment. Interactive network designs offer some potential as tools to implement such loops, but in the absence of correspondingly complex characterizations of the environment (e.g., in terms of coupled dynamical systems) they do not overcome the limitations of traditional input–processing–output architectures.

Dynamicists are much more inclined to focus on the multiple ongoing inter-actions between the cognitive system and its environment, and some have already begun adapting the notion of coupling and other tools of DST to this ambitious project. In so doing, they have become natural allies of a diverse community of researchers who emphasize situated and embodied cognition. Rejecting the idea that one can study cognition solely as a set of processes occurring within an agent, these theorists focus on the interactions between cognitive operations and such external structures as the instruments in an airplane cockpit (Hutchins, 1995). Cognitive science has become increasingly receptive to this view and to the use of DST as a source of sophisticated tools for modeling more fine-grained transactions amongst the brain, body, and world – a trend celebrated by Andy Clark in the subtitle of his 1997 book, *Being There: Putting Brain, Body, and World Together Again*.

8.3   Using Dynamical Systems Tools to Analyze Networks

In applying dynamical systems tools to connectionist networks, one must decide which variables of the system to represent. In the case of connectionist networks, the two most plausible choices are the weights on connections (viewing learning as a trajectory through weight space) or the activation values of units (viewing process-ing as a trajectory through activation space). We begin with some examples in which state-space plots have been used to analyze trajectories through activation space. Of particular interest are the displays of attractors in phase portraits.

8.3.1   Discovering limit cycles in network controllers
for robotic insects

Randall Beer (1995; see also Beer, 1997) has made effective use of state space plots to analyze connectionist networks designed to be coupled to a model insect in order to control its leg movements. The model insect has six legs, each with a foot at one end and a joint connecting it to the body at the other end. Each leg has three effectors: one raises or lowers the foot, and the other two apply opposing torques at the joint which combine to move the leg forward or backward. Each leg also has a single sensor that tracks the angle of the joint. The insect lives as a computer simulation, though it could also be embodied in a robot. Its walking is controlled by a 30-unit recurrent network composed of 6 subnetworks. The subnetwork controlling each leg consists of five units that are fully interconnected. Three are output units (motor neurons) which send instructions to the leg's three effectors, and two are connected only to the output units and to each other (interneurons). Each unit also receives weighted input from the leg's sensor, completing a loop between the leg and its controller network. That is, the dynamical systems of the body and the control network are coupled. Additional connections between subnetworks assure that the sensory information and motor activity of the six legs are coordinated.

With this basic architecture as a starting point, several different controller networks with task-adapted weights on their connections were created using a genetic algorithm procedure (see section 9.1). The fact that the weights were obtained by simulated evolution rather than learning is not crucial here; Beer's focus was on the dynamics of the systems once they had those weights. To contrast autonomous with nonautonomous dynamical systems, he manipulated access to sensory feedback. *Coupled networks* evolved with full access to input from the joint angle sensors (the network and the body were nonautonomous dynamical systems because each received input from the other); *autonomous networks* evolved with the sensors turned off (the body, still controlled by the network, was nonautonomous; but the network, lacking feedback, generated its own states autonomously); and *mixed networks* evolved with the sensors sometimes on and sometimes off.

All networks eventually could make the model insect walk employing the "tripod gait" characteristic of fast-moving six-legged insects: the front and back legs on one side would move in synchrony with the middle leg on the opposite side. While one set of three feet was swinging, the other set would remain on the ground, providing support. However, the three sets of networks fared differently when challenged in further testing. The coupled networks exhibited fine-tuned control of walking, but performed poorly if the sensors were turned off; they had evolved circuits that were dependent on a constant flow of sensory input and could not generate an appropriate sequence of states when forced to function autonomously. The autonomous networks produced walking in a stereotyped tripod gait regardless of whether sensory input was now made available; they autonomously cycled through the same sequence of states and had no means of incorporating a new, external variable to generate a modified sequence. The mixed networks worked as well as the coupled networks with sensory input, but could also function autonomously when input was removed.

To more closely examine these differing dynamics, Beer began with the relative simplicity of the autonomous networks and narrowed his focus to a single five-unit subnetwork controlling what he posited was a single-legged insect. Beer sought to

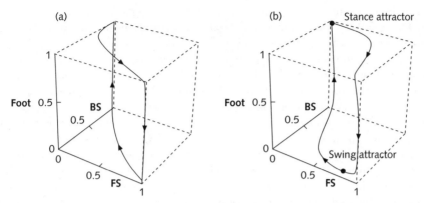

Figure 8.3   Trajectories in motor space for two of Beer's (1995) network controllers for a model insect. Successive activation values are plotted for the foot, backward swing (BS), and forward swing (FS) motor neurons in the subnetwork controlling one leg. (a) The autonomous network (sensor off) produces a limit cycle. When the activation values are in the upper back corner the foot is down and the network is in a stance phase; when activation values are in the lower front corner, the network is in a swing phase. (b) The coupled network (sensor on) exhibits a roughly similar trajectory, but it is produced by moving between two point attractors.

understand how the network controlled the leg's movement. He found that the five-dimensional state space for this simplified control system exhibited a limit cycle, which is projected into a three-dimensional motor space in figure 8.3(a). When sent to the effectors, this repetitive sequence of motor neuron activation patterns propels the leg repeatedly through a one-legged version of the tripod gait. For example, when the control network is in the state at the lower right front corner (the middle of the swing phase), the insect's foot is raised and leg is swinging forward while the torso remains still. In the state at the upper left rear corner (the middle of the stance phase), the foot is on the ground and the leg is still; the backward-swing torque is transmitted to the torso, propelling it forward. The shift from one phase to another depends upon reversing the relative dominance of the forward swing neuron (**FS**) and backward swing neuron (**BS**) as well as the activity of the foot neuron (values above 0.5 instruct the foot to be down); on each cycle there is one such shift into a swing phase and another into a stance phase. Following the trajectory from the rear to front corner, the relative dominance is shifting from the backward swing neuron (**BS**) to the forward swing neuron (**FS**); from the front to rear corner, the opposite shift occurs.

When the same kind of analysis is applied to a coupled network (one that evolved with the leg-angle sensor turned on), the results are superficially similar. Figure 8.3(b) shows that a limit cycle fairly similar to the one in figure 8.3(a) is obtained, and it produces essentially the same gait in the insect. The underlying dynamics are quite different, however. The leg angle is now variable, rather than taking a constant value of zero. Because the sensor supplies a stream of leg-angle values to the network, each point on the limit cycle has its own instantaneous trajectory. Most of these trajectories terminate in one of two point attractors, which are superimposed on the state space plot as solid circles. For example, each point on the leftmost portion of the limit cycle has a trajectory that terminates in the stance attractor (top circle). For the lowest of these points the trajectory to that attractor is relatively long, but as the network's states advance up the limit cycle the instantaneous trajectories get shorter.

Eventually the stance attractor is reached and the network remains in that state for a time. However, the state is one that produces forward motion of the body, which gradually changes the leg angle; under the leg-angle sensor's influence, the stance attractor disappears and the swing attractor appears. (Additional, unstable attractors make a brief appearance during the transition.) Now the state of the network progresses along the rightmost portion of the limit cycle in accord with a sequence of instantaneous trajectories terminating in the swing attractor.

While more interesting than the dynamics of the autonomous network, the reliance on sensory feedback to make the appropriate attractor appear has a price. If the coupling is broken by turning the sensor off, the network will get stuck on one trajectory leading to the stance attractor and, once it reaches that state, will have no way to move out of it. The insect will stand forever. The mixed network avoids this fate because its instantaneous trajectories are based on limit cycle attractors rather than point attractors. Not only does it not get stuck if input is removed; it exhibits an adaptive "functional plasticity" as its trajectories dynamically adjust to the flow of sensory feedback. For example, when Beer intervened by making the sensory input change more slowly than normal (as would happen if the insect's legs were longer), the mixed controller network became entrained by the sensory signal, slowing its own cycle to remain in phase. Beer (1995, p. 203) remarked: "The likelihood of anyone designing such a flexible and compact leg controller by hand is probably rather low." To continuously adjust to a changing environment, he finds the "messy" design of intermittently coupled dynamic systems more promising than the modular designs of engineers.

If Beer's study had been run purely as a network simulation, without the DST analysis, there would have been no plotting of limit cycles and instantaneous trajectories, no understanding of the role of attractor dynamics, and no explanation of why the constantly coupled network fails to function properly when the sensor is turned off but the intermittently coupled (mixed) network does. In the next section we show that DST is equally important for attaining a deeper understanding of a quite different class of models: layered interactive networks trained to simulate reading aloud. This more differentiated, cognitive task elicits the development of multiple point attractors.

8.3.2   Discovering multiple attractors in network models of reading

We saw in chapters 2 through 5 that feedforward networks can be used for a variety of tasks involving pattern recognition (e.g., assignment to semantic categories) and pattern transformation (e.g., past-tense formation). A simple way to add interactivity to such networks is to add recurrent connections between pairs of output units. Lateral inhibition produces dynamical interaction, in which even a small advantage in initial activation value can become a large difference as the system settles. The disparity in activation values between two units at time t is one determinant of the disparity in their inhibitory effects on each other at time $t + 1$, with the more active unit suppressing the less active unit via its stronger inhibitory signal. We saw lateral inhibition at work in the Jets and Sharks simulation in section 2.1, McClelland and Rumelhart's 1981 word-recognition model in section 4.1.2, and (along with lateral excitation) in the lexical and episodic memory modules of DISCERN in sections 7.5 and 7.7.

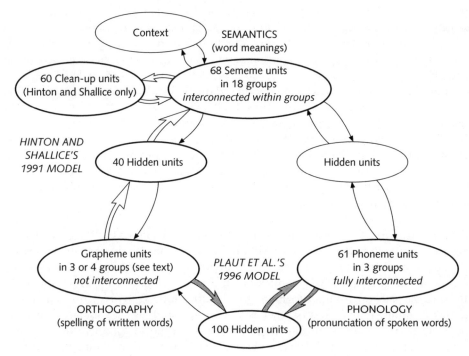

Figure 8.4 An overall framework for lexical processing adapted from Seidenberg and McClelland (1989). Those pathways that had been implemented by 1996 are in shown in boldface: the pathway from orthography to phonology (Plaut et al., 1996: filled arrows) and the pathway from orthography to semantics (Hinton and Shallice, 1991: hollow arrows). Neither model included the full set of feedforward and feedback connections of the original framework. Plaut et al. left out the hidden-to-grapheme feedback connections and Hinton and Shallice obtained interactivity by adding clean-up units rather than feedback connections. The models also differed in how they specified their grapheme units (see text).

In dynamical terms, we can say that such networks have multiple attractors and, when provided with an input, follow a trajectory in activation space that converges on the most appropriate one. In a network that learns to sort input patterns into four categories, for example, each of the four categories may develop its own point attractor in the activation state space for the output units. As long as the initial response to an exemplar is a pattern that falls into the basin of attraction for the appropriate category, the repeated revisions of each output unit's activation will gradually bring the pattern arbitrarily close to the desired pattern for that category (i.e., the system follows a trajectory that converges on the point attractor).

Interactive networks that develop multiple basins of attraction (*attractor networks*) have played a key role in a research area with a long and contentious history: accounting for how humans read. Figure 8.4 shows an overall framework for lexical processing adapted from Seidenberg and McClelland (1989), in which specialized groups of units (including groups of hidden units) interact with each other. To model reading, input is provided to the orthographic units. If the goal is to read aloud, then the system must generate a phonological output. If the goal is to under-stand the word, then it must retrieve a semantic interpretation. (Usually humans do both while reading aloud – they interpret the text as they pronounce it.) Since all of the interactions between groups of units are bidirectional in this overall framework, semantics can influence a phonological output and phonology can influence a semantic interpretation. In practice, it has been difficult to implement the full framework (but see section 10.2.3.3 for a rough approximation to the interaction between semantics and phonology that was advantageous in a model of surface dyslexia). Here we focus on more limited models in which only one of the pathways involved in reading was extracted and examined in isolation. Specifically, Hinton and Shallice (1991) modeled the pathway from orthography to meaning (large unfilled arrows) and Plaut, McClelland, Seidenberg, and Patterson (1996) modeled the pathway from orthography to phonology (large solid arrows). The number of units and other details in figure 8.4 refer to these two simulations. The units at the end of each pathway were completely or partly interconnected as indicated, with the result that multiple point attractors developed in those groups of units.

8.3.2.1   Modeling the semantic pathway

Hinton and Shallice's (1991) network runs vertically through figure 8.4. As we will discuss in chapter 10, they planned to lesion the network to simulate errors made by individuals with deep dyslexia when reading aloud (most frequently semantics-based errors such as *PEACH* → "apricot"). Because the pathway from orthography to semantics appears to play a prominent role in this disorder, Hinton and Shallice isolated it for study. (They assumed that the pathway from semantics to phonology, which is needed to complete the reading-aloud task, functioned with little error and was not crucial in simulating this particular disorder.) In their intact model of this pathway, 28 grapheme units encode a word's orthography (i.e., its spelling or visual form) and send activation through a hidden layer to 68 sememe units. As described below, there are interactive connections within this last layer and between it and a layer of *clean-up units*; aided by attractor dynamics, the semantic layer settles into the pattern corresponding to the word's meaning. There is no further interactivity, though: the connections specified in figure 8.4 from orthography to hidden units and from hidden units to meaning were unidirectional rather than bidirectional in this particular model.

Hinton and Shallice trained the network on a corpus of 40 three- and four-letter words across 1,000 epochs of backpropagation. Each written word (indicated by upper case; e.g., *MUD*) could be given a localist, position-specific encoding using binary grapheme units. Position 1 (linguists call it the *onset*) had 11 consonant units, position 2 (*vowel*) had 5 vowel units, position 3 had 10 consonant units, and position 4 had optional *E* or *K* (positions 3 and 4 are both part of the *coda* which follows the vowel in some but not all syllables of English). The word meanings (indicated by lower case; e.g., *mud*) were limited to five semantic categories (animals, foods, body parts, indoor and outdoor objects) and were represented using semantic roles appropriate to those categories. For each role a group of sememe units was designated (sometimes called an *ensemble* or *assembly* of units), and activation of one unit provided a localist encoding of how that role was filled in a particular word meaning. For example, units 9–15 formed an ensemble for encoding color, with one unit each for white, brown, green, transparent, etc. Representing the meaning of one word involved activating approximately 15 units, which could include multiple units from a given role ensemble (e.g., *lime* has two fillers for the taste role: **sweet** and **strong**).

The challenge for the model is that visually similar words (e.g., *MUD* and *MUG*) need to be mapped on to dissimilar meanings (e.g., role:filler sememes for the meaning *mud* include **hardness:soft** and **location:on-ground** and those for *mug* include **hardness:hard** and **location:indoors**), whereas visually different words (*MUD* and *BOG*) need to be mapped on to similar meanings. But their network does not treat the spelling of a word as an arbitrary pointer to its meaning, Hinton and Shallice noted, because networks most naturally develop weights that map similar inputs to similar outputs (that is why networks are good at generalization). Extra work is needed to overcome this tendency. Hinton and Shallice therefore employed interactive connections to move the initial semantic patterns towards the more distal desired patterns and to form point attractors at these locations. During learning, changes in the weights on the interactive connections created appropriate basins of attraction in semantic space. Similar-looking words initially produce similar semantic patterns in the resulting network, but if the points in the corresponding semantic space are in different attractor basins, the system should follow a trajectory to the correct meaning in each case. As shown in figure 8.5 for *MUD* and *MUG* (using points in spaces of reduced dimensionality to partly represent patterns in the network), the similarity in spelling tends to result in representations that maintain some proximity through the transformations from orthographic to hidden to semantic layers of the network. But then the interactive dynamics among sememes put the two words on to diverging trajectories (less direct than shown) towards distant attractors. The additional words shown (without their basins of attraction) indicate that attractors for other words in the same semantic category tend to be nearby.

The interactive connections that implemented this dynamic were of two kinds. First, Hinton and Shallice inserted pairwise connections between sememe units within the same semantic role ensemble, which tended to produce varying degrees of lateral inhibition within these groups. Second, they added a set of 60 *clean-up units* which received input from the sememe units and sent activation back to them. These units learned which combinations of sememes were characteristic in the corpus and guided the sememe patterns towards these combinations. For example, when the units for **size:small** and **hardness:hard** and **shape:3D** all are active, **location:indoors** also should be active. The clean-up units will notice that and boost the net input to the **location:indoors** unit over time until it crosses its activation threshold. That is, the co-occurrence of these four units is an attractor, and its dynamics enhance processing of such words as *mug, cup, can, gem,* and *bone.* Moreover, the entire sememe pattern comprising the meaning *mug* is an attractor in part due to this subregularity and in part due to idiosyncratic factors and other subregularities it shares with other words. For example, *mug* shares the cluster **use:for-eating-drinking/location:on-surface/location:indoors/shape:3D** with *can, rum, pop,* and *lime* (*cup* differs because it is placed on a saucer rather than on a surface and *gem* and *bone* are not used for eating or drinking). In effect, attractor basins for subregularities like these are assembled into word-sized attractor basins, each of which occupies a distinctive region in the full 68-dimensional semantic space. These 40 basins guide the network into the appropriate meaning for each input despite the initial tendency to keep visually similar words too close together.

8.3.2.2 Modeling the phonological pathway Whereas Hinton and Shallice introduced interactivity because they anticipated that attractors in semantic space would help solve a problem, Plaut, McClelland, Seidenberg, and Patterson (1996; hereafter, PMSP) included an interactive network as part of a long-standing commitment to interactive architectures on the part of their research team. They compared it to an otherwise identical feedforward network in part to find out whether interactivity

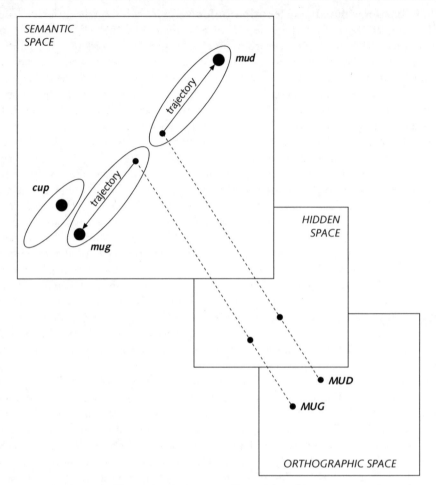

Figure 8.5   A schematic illustration in just two dimensions of how attractor dynamics overcome the tendency for visually similar words like and *MUD* and *MUG* to land near each other in semantic space (Hinton and Shallice, 1991). Each word's meaning corresponds to a point attractor (large dots, far apart for these two words) whose large basin of attraction includes the initial point of entry to the space (small dots, nearby for these two words). Via interactive processing each word follows a trajectory (less direct than shown) to the appropriate point attractor, *mud* or *mug*. Note that *mug* is close to *cup*, not to *mud*.

would be disadvantageous for this particular task, which modeled the pathway leading from orthography directly to phonology. Though ultimately they expected the entire network in figure 8.4 to be involved in the reading-aloud task, this pathway seemed most crucial for reading in general (especially somewhat mechanical or absent-minded reading) and for a form of surface dyslexia in which low-frequency exception words are especially prone to disruption. Like Hinton and Shallice, they planned to simulate one form of dyslexia by lesioning their network (this part of their project is discussed in section 10.2.3).

   Reading aloud is a task that is *quasi-regular*; that is, largely systematic, but with exceptions. For example, *MINT, HINT*, and *TINT* are regular words but *PINT* is an exception word because its vowel has an atypical pronunciation. The regularities are sometimes described using rules of grapheme–phoneme correspondence, but one of PMSP's goals was to show that both regular and exceptional pronunciations can be successfully modeled using a network rather than explicitly stated rules. PMSP trained their network to map graphemic into phonemic encodings using a corpus of 2,998 regular and exception words (restricted to onset–vowel–coda monosyllables, e.g., *TH–I–NK*). Like Hinton and Shallice they used a localist, position-specific encoding scheme, but it had to be more elaborate because their words were more complex (they could include multi-letter graphemes like *TH* and also multiple graphemes in each position). There were 105 grapheme units divided into three ensembles: 30 onset units such as *G*, *W*, *WH*, and *TH*; 27 vowel units such as *A*, *I*, *AI*, *OO*, and *OY*; and 48 coda units such as *G*, *X*, *KS*, *TH*, *SS*, and *TCH*. The hidden and phoneme layers were as shown in figure 8.4. The three groups of phoneme units were position-specific for onset, vowel, or coda. More than one unit could be active for a position; for example, to present *THINK* to the network requires activating three onset units (the primary grapheme *TH* and by convention also *T* and *H*), one vowel unit (*I*) and two coda units (*N* and *K*, which are separate graphemes). In addition to the feedforward connections, each phoneme unit sent a lateral connection to every other phoneme unit (including itself) and a feedback connection to each hidden unit; it was interactive processing across these two sets of connections that produced attractors in the network. (Note that the use of position-specific ensembles of units in the input and output layers contrasts with Seidenberg and McClelland's use of Wickelfeature representations in a 1989 model; reasons for changing their encoding system are noted in section 10.2.3.3.)

The network was trained with the *backpropagation through time* procedure (an adaptation of backpropagation for recurrent networks). After 1,900 epochs of training it had learned to pronounce all but 25 of the 2,998 regular and exception words in the corpus. The comparison network, which had the same feedforward connections but neither type of recurrent (interactive) connection, learned much more easily; it made 0 errors after just 300 epochs of training. However, given that interactive networks are more neurally plausible than purely feedforward networks, PMSP thought it important to find out whether an attractor network was able to generalize its training on words so as to attain human-like performance in pronouncing nonwords. It was by no means obvious that this would be the case, since attractor dynamics are supposed to help ensure that a network's response will be one of those already learned (e.g., the pronunciation "think," which is /θink/ in phonemic notation), not only to the inputs on which it was trained (e.g., the written word *THINK*) but also to similar inputs on which it was not trained. (e.g., the nonword *BINK*). As long as the input activates a point within some word's basin of attraction, the interactions between the units during settling should result in the activation of that word. This would seem to preclude the network correctly reading aloud nonword test items; for example, if the initial response to *BINK* fell into the attractor basin for the pronunciation of *THINK* it would be incorrectly pronounced /θink/.

In fact, though, the network performed very well. It was tested on a list of 86 nonwords created by Glushko (1979), in which half were derived from regular words and half from irregular words, and a list of 80 nonwords used by McCann and Besner (1987) for a control condition. Table 8.1 compares the performance of human participants in their studies with that of the interactive (attractor) network as well as the comparable feedforward network. The similarities are impressive, with the same pattern of difficulty in each row and the absolute percentages very close in

Table 8.1   Percentages of regular pronunciations in tests of three sets of nonwords

	Glushko (1979)		McCann and Besner (1987)
Reader	*Regular nonwords*	*Exception nonwords*	*Control nonwords*
Humans	93.8	78.3	88.6
Interactive network	93.0	62.8	86.3
Feedforward network	97.7	67.4	82.5

Note: Adapted from Plant et al. (1996), table 3.

two of the three columns. Moreover, error in the networks, used as an index of difficulty, showed the same regularity by frequency interaction as human naming latencies (i.e., infrequent exception words are slower than frequent ones, whereas regular words show little or no frequency effect). A closer analog to naming latency was available for the interactive networks (average time to a criterion of stable responding); it showed the same interaction. (However, Spieler and Balota, 1997, argued that the model should yield good predictions of relative performance by humans on individual items, not just two-way interactions involving broad categories such as high-frequency items. On their analysis, it did not.)

How was an attractor network able to respond appropriately to nonwords? PMSP proposed that the network's primary strategy was to develop, not whole-word attractors, but rather *componential attractors* – one each for the various onset, vowel, and coda clusters that make up words (a cluster contains one or more graphemes or phonemes, such as the N and K in the coda of *THINK*). That is, the network did not always treat written words as unanalyzed wholes but rather learned the usual pronunciation of each onset, vowel, and coda that recurred across the words of the corpus. It encoded them as "soft" activation-based correspondences between orthographic feature patterns and phonemes rather than "hard" grapheme–phoneme correspondence rules. Learning the regularities in this way produced attractors for particular phoneme clusters in phonemic space that were associated with the appropriate orthographic clusters via additional attractors in hidden-unit space. To pronounce a regular word, in effect, the network found the intersection in each of these spaces of the attractors for its onset, vowel, and coda. The same dynamic could work just as well for pronouncing nonwords composed of novel combinations of familiar, regular phoneme clusters. For example, the intersection of attractors for /b/ and /i/ and /nk/ would yield the correct pronunciation of *BINK* even though the entire pattern *BINK* had never been experienced.

Exception words are more complex, since they present a mixture of regular and irregular correspondences. PMSP suggested that the system takes advantage of whatever regularities do exist within the word but goes part-way to a whole-word approach to handle the more idiosyncratic aspects. In order to support this claim, they created several innovative analyses of how the onsets, vowels, and codas of various types of words were handled by the network. For example, if *MINT* were in the corpus, they could show that the orthographic encoding of the onset *M* would be responsible for the inclusion of /m/ in the network's output, the vowel *I* would be responsible for /i/, and so forth. But for the exception word *PINT*, the onset and coda in the orthographic representation actually would be more influential than the vowel. These analyses provided a window on what was happening at the hidden layer in the absence of a good way to directly examine the attractors that developed there. Even the indirect analyses were too complex to describe here, but the need for them underscores that part of the unfinished business of connectionism is to attain better tools for understanding activity in large networks. In the next section we return to a simulation by Jeffrey Elman that was discussed at some length in section 6.4. We can now view it as a discrete dynamical system and examine an additional analysis he performed which combined principal components analysis with state space plots to get a direct (though partial) look at hidden layer activity.

8.3.3   Discovering trajectories in SRNs for sentence processing

One way of examining the activity of units in a network is to plot trajectories in a state space. Each dimension represents the activation value of one unit, and a trajectory in this space displays the changing state of the network across time. As we saw above, Beer (1995) made good use of this method to unearth the reasons why his autonomous, coupled, and mixed networks behaved so differently in certain tests. By limiting his analysis to three motor neurons controlling a single leg, he was able to provide three-dimensional displays of the limit cycles that evolved and, for the networks with variable input, characterize the dynamics in terms of instantaneous trajectories and attractors.

In this section we show how Jeffrey Elman (1990, 1991) used trajectories in state space to explore the activity of simple recurrent networks (SRNs). His project is otherwise so different from that of Beer that it provides some sense of how broadly useful the tools of DST can be. One difference is that Beer had an unusually small number of units to examine. For most network models, including that of Elman, some method of collapsing the activity of numerous units into a low-dimensional plot is needed in order to visualize the state space. Another difference is that SRNs have a distinctive design that lies somewhere between interactive networks (whose recurrent connections can exhibit attractor dynamics) and feedforward networks (which have no recurrent connections and cannot develop attractors). They have recurrent connections, but they are used in a special way that enables the network to retain and re-use a (compressed) history of its own sequence of states (it recursively copies states; no attractor dynamics are involved or possible). Changes of state are discrete, in response to input, but the possible changes are constrained by the state history that forms part of the input. In DST terms, SRNs are nonautonomous systems (because they receive input) which change state at discrete time-steps (once per input) and might be viewed as composed of subsystems, two of which are coupled (because the units that store the state history and the hidden units provide input to each other).

As we discussed in section 6.4, Elman trained simple recurrent networks to predict successive words in a corpus of sentences. He was interested not merely in the network's success, but also in understanding how it accomplishes its task. In his 1990 paper he used cluster analysis to show that hidden unit patterns were similar for words with similar privileges of occurrence in sentences; that is, patterns for words in the same syntactic/semantic class, such as *human* or *transitive verb*, were clustered together in the hierarchy extracted by the analysis. This way of examining hidden-unit activity was necessarily rather coarse-grained: since patterns had to be averaged across contexts to obtain a single pattern for each word, the cluster analysis provided no insight into how the hidden-unit patterns for a given word varied according to current grammatical context. Such variations play a key role in enabling an SRN to predict the next word.

To examine the time dimension rather than averaging it away, a DST framework would suggest plotting the trajectories of the activation patterns on the hidden layer as the network moves from one word to the next in a corpus. For a network with 70 hidden units this would require a trajectory in an activation space of 70 dimensions, which can easily be computed but cannot be displayed on a page nor grasped by mere mortals. Elman (1991) turned to principal components analysis as a method for taming the surfeit of detail. This statistical procedure extracts a set of orthogonal dimensions (principal components) that captures much of the structure in the data and projects the high-dimensional vectors on to this reduced space. If the number of derived dimensions is still larger than desired, a state space plot can be limited to two or three of them (selected because they account for the most variance or are most relevant for a specific analysis). Elman views his networks as having learned constraints on possible trajectories. When a word is presented along with a record of the sentence's trajectory so far (on the input and context units, respectively), the hidden units integrate this information and propagate it to the output units so as to activate one (or more) words that meet the constraints. The plots generated using dimensions from the principal components analysis display the word-by-word trajectory of a sentence through a subspace of the overall hidden-unit activation space.

Elman (1991) used this technique to view some of the dynamics involved in processing sentences generated by a phrase structure grammar (the grammar and the "starting small" technique of training simple sentences first are the same as in Elman, 1993; see section 6.4 for details). Figure 8.6 displays plots in the two-dimensional state space obtained from principal components 1 and 11. This particular hidden-unit subspace happened to be particularly informative about the processing of relative clauses. A separate plot is provided for each of the following sentences. (To minimize other influences on the trajectories, *boy* is the only noun used throughout.)

(a) boy chases boy.
(b) boy chases boy who chases boy.
(c) boy chases boy who chases boy who chases boy.
(d) boy who chases boy chases boy.

Consider sentence (a). The first word (*boy*) is presented on the 26 input units and becomes re-encoded on the 70 hidden units. Weights on the connections leading out from the hidden layer support the network's prediction on the 26 output units (which is not a single word, but rather all words that satisfy the distributional constraints of the corpus: all of the singular verbs, including *chases*, plus the word *who*). When the 70-dimensional activation vector on the hidden layer is projected on to the subspace to give us a partial look at it, in figure 8.6(a), we see it has landed in the lower right corner (at a point high on component 1 and somewhat low on component 11). Now the network is (in effect) wiped clean except that the hidden-layer vector is copied on to the context units and the next word (*chases*) is presented on the input units. This combination produces a hidden-unit vector that projects to a middle left point in the state space. After it has been used to predict the next word

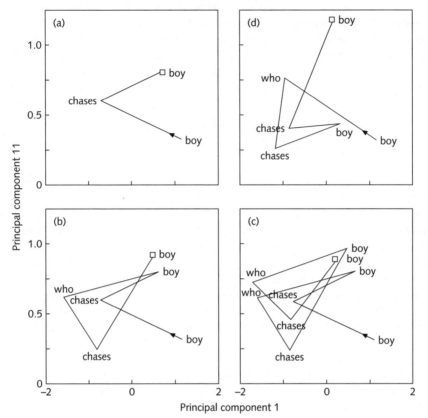

Figure 8.6   Trajectories through activation state space as Elman's (1991) simple recurrent network (SRN) predicts successive words in a corpus generated by a phrase structure grammar. Only the first and eleventh principal components of the hidden unit activations are shown. Sentences (a) through (d) are displayed counter-clockwise to facilitate comparison of (a) to the sentences obtained by adding an object relative clause (b) or subject relative clause (d). Recursion of the object relative clause is shown in (c).

on the output layer, this new hidden-layer vector (which now encodes the history of hidden-layer responses to *boy* and then *chase*) is copied on to the context units and the next word (another token of *boy*) is presented on the input units (it is another token of *boy*, and would have been among the predicted words on the previous step if the network had learned its task well). This combination (*boy* as the next word in a sequence beginning with *boy chases*) produces a hidden-unit vector different enough from the first one that it projects to a different part of the state space (it is similar on component 1 but much higher on component 11 than the first *boy*).

To make this short sentence's trajectory easy to see in figure 8.6(a), the three points in the state space are labeled and joined with lines, with an arrowhead added near the beginning and a square at the end. It is a genuine trajectory, in that each state is constrained by the previous state (e.g., the positioning of *boy* is context-dependent). However, because the state changes are discrete and input-driven, intermediate points are not actually traversed by the network. The lines merely indicate the temporal order in which the system jumps from one point to the next. Nonetheless, it will become evident as we discuss plots (b)–(d) that state-space plots combined with principal components analysis provide an extremely useful window on the sequential activity of simple recurrent networks.

Figure 8.6(b) shows what happens when an embedded clause is added to the simple sentence (a). The trajectory begins as in 8.6(a) but then reveals (for just components 1 and 11) how the network deals with a relative clause modifying the object. Though *who* is a subject, like the initial *boy*, the network takes note of its relative pronoun category and context by producing a hidden-layer encoding that yields a negative value on component 1 (i.e., the trajectory jumps to the far left of the state space). The embedded *chases boy* subtrajectory is more like that of the main clause: though displaced somewhat, it still has the object *boy* higher and further right than the verb *chases*.

When yet another relative clause is added, figure 8.6(c) shows that a triangular subtrajectory much like that of the first relative clause is produced – but displaced slightly. This small difference in states is not accidental; it reflects the fact that although each clause is linguistically identical (a relative clause modifying an object) their contexts are different. One is preceded by another relative clause; the other is followed by another relative clause. Elman states that the failure of the network to informationally encapsulate each clause contrasts with the way recursion is handled in a formal grammar or computational push-down stack. He calls the network's solution "leaky recursion" (p. 218) and argues that it is actually advantageous to encode the same kind of clause in different contexts a bit differently on the hidden layer, even though they result in the same output behavior (the network produces the same sequence of word predictions twice).

The remaining plot, figure 8.6(d), shows what happens when those same words must be predicted, but in a context with very different sequential dependencies (modifying the subject rather than the object). The fact that the words make up a relative clause is reflected in their now-familiar triangular subtrajectory; the fact that this clause modifies a subject rather than an object is reflected in its very distinctive placement in the space compared to 8.6(b).[3]

What if additional relative clauses are added? Since an increasingly long history must be compressed on to a fixed number of hidden units as they recursively track progress through a sentence, eventually the network's performance degrades. In sentence (d), for example, the first *boy* and the final *chases* must agree in number. The second principal component (not shown in figure 8.6) is especially sensitive to the subject noun's number; here, it captures that *boy* is singular, not plural.[4] The weights leading out from the hidden units know how to use this information to predict a verb that agrees in number (here, *chases* rather than *chase*), and also know how to delay exercising this knowledge when an intervening embedded clause is encountered. With additional embeddings, the hidden-layer encoding becomes too compressed and sends less usable information to the outgoing weights. In a nutshell, networks (like humans) become less dependable at dealing with long-distance dependencies as distance increases.

8.3.4 Dynamical analyses of learning in networks

The state space plots in this chapter have displayed activation spaces for networks, some (such as Elman's) focusing on individual trajectories and others (phase portraits) showing at least some of the attractors in a particular system. State space plots can also be used to display a network's weight space and the trajectory of weight changes it traverses during learning. Because error reduction plays such a key role in connectionist learning algorithms, generally a dimension is added to the weight dimensions which displays the amount of error associated with each weight state. In chapter 3 we introduced two plots of this type. Figure 3.1 was the simplest possible plot: error on the vertical axis and the range of possible weights for one unit on the horizontal axis. Its curvilinear function indicated how much error was associated with each weight within a range for a hypothetical system. The lowest point on the line is especially important; we referred to it there as a global minimum, but in dynamical terms it is an attractor. (The single local minimum in that figure is also an attractor.)

Learning rules such as the delta rule and backpropagation are gradient descent rules, which means they change weights in a network so as to follow a trajectory to a lower error. The various points in weight space from which a network will settle into a particular minimum constitutes its basin of attraction. When there are multiple attractor basins, as in figure 3.1, they are separated by repellors – points in the weight space from which the system will move away. (A successful learning procedure can escape local minima by perturbing the weights enough to get beyond repellors.) In figure 3.3 we showed how such a weight space representation can be generalized to two weights.[5] Again, the low points are attractors (now on a two-dimensional error surface rather than a line), and gradient descent will lead the network to follow a (frequently meandering) downwards trajectory. The networks used to model human performance generally have high-dimensional weight spaces, but the same general concepts apply.

8.4   Putting Chaos to Work in Networks

8.4.1   Skarda and Freeman's model of the olfactory bulb

Most of the researchers reviewed so far in this chapter are card-carrying connectionists who design and test network models in the usual way and then add DST tools to obtain a better than usual understanding of how the models work. How does the research differ when DST is the starting point, and networks are simply one of the possible mediums in which to explore the potential of DST tools and concepts? Beer's work on network controllers for model insects provides a partial answer, and in this section we will consider work from two additional groups of investigators. One characteristic of DST-driven research that quickly becomes apparent in the original papers is the extent to which mathematical considerations and analyses are front and center. For example, the paper by Beer cannot be meaningfully summarized without talking about limit cycles and attractors. In this section we go further by considering, at a very schematic level, systems that exhibit *chaos* in some phases of their behavior. Another characteristic is that DST researchers enthusiastically put genuinely novel findings on display. These are not easily assimilated by the uninitiated, and in section 8.5 we will discuss arguments for (and against) regarding dynamical approaches to cognition as a new paradigm that supersedes, rather than augments, existing paradigms.

DST researchers also exhibit a bias towards systems with *nonstationary* dynamics – those with an intrinsic ability to keep moving between states rather than getting stuck in an attractor. This contrasts with the typical connectionist view of networks as input–output devices; from that perspective, using an input to push a system's state into the appropriate point attractor is a pretty interesting way to get an output. The fact that nothing will happen next, unless an external agent zeros the activation values and supplies another input, has not been a high-priority concern. Christine A. Skarda and Walter J. Freeman (1987, p. 172) tried to raise consciousness on this issue by noting that "the neural system does not exhibit behavior that can be modeled with point attractors, except under deep anesthesia or death. Convergence to a point attractor amounts to 'death' for the system." Instead, they view the nervous system as a dynamical system that is constantly in motion, finding different opportunities not only on trajectories within a single phase portrait but also as changes in parameters reshape the phase portraits themselves.

Even the humblest aspect of nervous system functioning is re-construed by these neuroscientists: its background activity is claimed to emerge from deterministic chaos rather than random noise. Despite the drama of the term "chaos," this simply means that the system continuously changes state along a trajectory that appears random but is determined by the equations governing the system and its initial conditions (the values of its variables at t_0). Skarda and Freeman viewed chaos as a way of keeping the overall state space active and ready for more targeted action, in contrast to the usual assumption that background activity is noise that is unrelated to signals and obscures them. (Chaotic systems are famous for their sensitivity to initial conditions – that is, small differences in initial values tend to produce quite dissimilar trajectories – but the particular trajectories are unimportant for Skarda and Freeman's purposes.)

Skarda and Freeman sought to entice their readers towards this perspective by discussing Freeman's (1987) model of the olfactory bulb. The model is a network, but is connectionist only in the broadest sense of that term. Its design was motivated by considerations from DST and neuroscience: each component of the olfactory system (with subsets of excitatory and inhibitory neurons of different cell types treated as separate components) is represented by a second-order nonlinear differential equation, and these components are coupled via excitatory and inhibitory connections into an interactive network. In a painstaking series of studies, Freeman and his earlier collaborators had conditioned animals (typically rabbits) to respond to particular odors. In tracking concomitant electrical activity using EEG recordings, they had found that the olfactory bulb exhibits a pattern of disorderly firing during exhalation and more orderly firing during inhalation. The model exhibits similar alternations. During late exhalation it receives no input and behaves chaotically – engaging in "restless, but bounded, activity" (p. 165). During inhalation an odor is supplied, which usually sends the system from chaos into the basin of one of several limit cycle attractors that rather suddenly make an appearance. Each attractor is a previously learned response to a particular odor (except that one corresponds to a no-odor control condition); hence, the system can be said to have recognized an odor when the system lands in the appropriate attractor.

Note that the recognition response is not static. First, when the trajectory is pulled into a limit cycle attractor it cycles through multiple states (vs. a point attractor's single state). Second, once that cyclic attractor has done its job, other aspects of the system's dynamics (referred to as nonstationary) provide routes into other activity. One way out is that the relatively organized phase portrait for inhalation includes the low-energy *chaotic well* to which the system will retreat if a novel

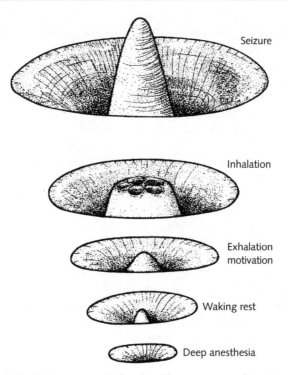

Figure 8.7   Hypothetical phase portraits for the olfactory system Reprinted with permission from Freeman (1987, p. 146), who emphasized the inhalation and exhalation phases in rabbits when motivated by presentation of previously-conditioned odors.

odor is supplied (and from which a new limit cycle can form across repeated presentations). The more usual way out is that the phase portrait itself is continuously changing. During exhalation the limit cycle attractors disappear and the system finds new opportunities in chaos. Skarda and Freeman (p. 168) "conjecture that chaotic activity provides a way of exercising neurons." On the next inhalation, chaos plays a more task-relevant role, allowing "rapid and unbiased access to every limit cycle attractor . . . so that the entire repertoire of learned discriminanda is available to the animal at all times for instantaneous access. There is no search through a memory store."

For Skarda and Freeman, then, odor recognition is achieved when the olfactory system alternates between relatively free-ranging chaotic behavior (exhalation) and odor-specific cyclic behavior (inhalation). The same system is capable of reaching extremes of anesthesia and seizure, as shown by the hypothetical "snapshots" of some of its possible phases in figure 8.7. In each phase portrait the two primary dimensions represent the overall activity of two subsets of neurons (excitatory and inhibitory). The vertical dimension represents the amount of energy when a point is active. During anesthesia a point attractor produces a temporary "death" (very low-energy state). A point repellor replaces it as the system moves to a waking rest. A chaotic well (the circular trench, whose base is a chaotic attractor) develops and deepens as the system becomes more motivated and alternates between exhalation and inhalation. The limit cycles are represented in the center of the inhalation portrait, and become latent as the system relaxes into exhalation or (exceptionally) gets repelled into the degenerate, low-dimensional chaos of seizure.

The system's ability to temporarily lose and regain its limit cycles via its own nonstationary dynamics is an intriguing solution to the problem of how to stop responding to one input and begin responding to another. To understand what moves Freeman's model between inhalation and exhalation, recall the logistic equation (equation (1)). In figure 8.2 it was seen to exhibit chaotic dynamics in a region with values of A beyond 3.6. But within this region there existed values of A for which the dynamics again became periodic. This suggests the possibility of a system moving from chaotic regimes to temporarily stable ones (and back to chaotic ones) through small changes in parameter values – an ability that would be extremely useful for a nervous system. The equations describing the functioning of the olfactory bulb are more complex, but they show this same characteristic. Importantly, changes in parameter values are not arbitrary (e.g., some reflect the influence of systems to which the olfactory bulb is connected). As Skarda and Freeman (p. 167) note in discussing the overall states captured in figure 8.7: "[T]he olfactory system and its corresponding model have a hierarchy of states. The basic neural dynamics and the equations are the same in all states but, depending on various neural conditions and model parameters, the systems behave differently. . . . Both systems display the capacity for abrupt, dramatic global jumps from one state to another. These are the bifurcations."

8.4.2   Shifting interpretations of ambiguous displays

In Freeman's model, changes in parameter values (usually due to the activities of related systems) are responsible for the system's transitions; the role of chaos is affected by, but does not effect, those changes. Chaos has been argued to play a much more prominent role in the spontaneous shifts of attention that people report when they look at such well-known ambiguous figures as the duck/rabbit, young/old woman, and the Necker cube. For example, Cees van Leeuwen and his collaborators (van Leeuwen, Steyvers, and Nooter, 1997) proposed a DST-based network model of people's shifting perceptions of the ambiguous display at the center of figure 8.8. To the left and right of it are unambiguous displays that produce relatively stable percepts. The same network model that can simulate ordinary percepts like these becomes destabilized in the presence of the ambiguous display, repeatedly switching between column and row interpretations of its organization. In their words (p. 321): "The noisy processes which help construct the pattern will revolt against it, once it becomes established." In achieving switching behavior, they made an important advance beyond the first network model of perceiving ambiguous figures, in which the network settled to one of two point attractors (chose one of the possible interpretations of a Necker cube) but then stopped (Rumelhart, Smolensky, McClelland, and Hinton, 1986).

The work of van Leeuwen et al. expanded upon three related strands of research. First, Skarda and Freeman (see section 8.4.1) had the insight that chaos may be fundamental to perception and constructed the first network model in which chaotic and stable behavior alternate.

Second, J. A. Scott Kelso showed that coupled systems with nonlinear dynamics could switch between *metastable* (not quite stable) states at irregular intervals, mim-

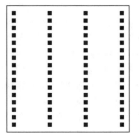 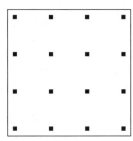 

Figure 8.8   Stimuli used in van Leeuwen, Steyvers, and Nooter (1997). If the gestalt principle of symmetry is used to group items, the black squares in the left display will be grouped vertically and those in the right display horizontally. Those in the center display, however, will be ambiguous and subjects may alternate between grouping them vertically and grouping them horizontally.

icking the switching intervals of people asked to press a button each time their interpretation of a Necker cube reversed. On Kelso's account (see Kelso, 1995), each interpretation is attractive to the system but is not quite an attractor. The system therefore exhibits *intermittency*, alternating between metastable states and chaotic bursts in which the system breaks free and moves erratically through state space. In the words of Kelso (1995, p. 200): "[T]he system dwells for varying times near attractive states where it can switch flexibly and quickly. Faced with ambiguous stimuli, the brain will be revealed as a twinkling metastable system living on the brink of instability."[6] Kelso also emphasized that the metastable states (and the flow of patterns in the brain more generally) are an outcome of *self-organization*. Patterns are generated by a large number of components interacting nonlinearly, with no supervisors or agents needed. Although Kelso gave considerable attention to the dynamics resulting when two or more self-organized systems become coupled, he characterized the systems themselves in terms of equations with a small number of variables and parameters (see section 8.5.2).

This leads to the third strand contributing to van Leeuwen et al.'s work. One way to understand how the systems became self-organized in the first place is to build a network model whose units are low-level components of the perceptual system. Kunihiko Kaneko (1990) explored the stability characteristics of a type of network called a *coupled map lattice* (CML). A *lattice* is a sparsely connected network in which the couplings (connections) can be viewed as topologically arranged such that *neighbors* are coupled and other units are not; for example, the Kohonen feature maps used for DISCERN's lexical and episodic memories in chapter 7 are lattices. A *map* is a type of function in which values are iteratively determined in discrete time; for example, the logistic equation (equation (3) in section 8.2.2) is a map and was used by Kaneko to obtain the value of each unit in a lattice at each time-step. This choice yields coupled nonlinear units which move between values within a range (*oscillate*) in discrete time either periodically (e.g., alternating between the two most extreme values) or chaotically (yielding a quasi-random sequence of values within the range). Such a network can exhibit different kinds of behavior depending on what values have been assigned to certain control parameters; among the possibilities are synchrony[7] across periodic or chaotic units (i.e., all units in a cluster have the same sequence of activation values, even if that sequence is chaotic) and chaotic behavior across chaotic units (*chaoto-chaotic emergence*).

Van Leeuwen et al. proposed that CML networks could be harnessed as lower-level, self-organizing mechanisms for achieving intermittency in models of perception. Given the ambiguous display in the center of figure 8.8 as input, an appropriate CML quickly comes to exhibit one pattern of synchronized activity for the columnar interpretation (as on the left) and a different one for the row interpretation (as on the right). These patterns are metastable states of the network, so they can suddenly reorganize (shifting the synchronization from rows to columns or vice versa, or under some conditions from global to more localized synchronization or vice versa).

Preliminary to studying a full-scale CML model of perceptual organization, van Leeuwen et al. first examined the simplest network in which synchronization can be achieved – a network of just two units. Since individual neurons probably are linear, each unit is best thought of as a micro-ensemble of excitatory (pyramidal) and inhibitory (stellate) neurons. The net input to each unit is calculated according to the following equation, in which a_x represents the value of unit x (our notation, reflecting that it is roughly comparable to an activation value in a traditional connectionist network) and C represents a coupling parameter (comparable to a connection weight) that determines how much each unit is affected by its own value versus that of the other unit:

$$netinput_x = Ca_y + (1 - C)a_x \qquad (4)$$

To obtain the value of unit x at each discrete time, they incorporated the net input calculated by equation (4) within the logistic equation (see equation (3)):

$$a_{x,t+1} = A \ netinput_{x,t} \ (1 - netinput_{x,t}) \qquad (5)$$

The net input and value of unit y were obtained in the same way. As shown earlier (in figure 8.2 for equation (3)), the values of a unit approach a point attractor at lower values of A and periodic attractors at intermediate values, but behave chaotically for most values above 3.6. This is how each unit on its own would behave. Because the units are coupled, however, the additional parameter (C) can alter these outcomes. The overall behavior of the two-unit network depends on the values of both A and C.

In this miniature network it is easy to measure synchronization: the two units are synchronized when the difference between their activation values at each time-step is zero. Generally they do not start out synchronized, but van Leeuwen et al. demonstrated that the size of the difference will decrease monotonically to zero when

$$\tfrac{1}{2}(1 - 1/A) < C < \tfrac{1}{2}(1 + 1/A).$$

That is, for appropriate values of C relative to A, after a transition period the two units will exhibit the same sequence of values – a sequence which itself (depending on A) may be chaotic. It is outside this range of guaranteed synchrony that things get interesting. The size of the difference may be a constant or may vary periodically, quasi-periodically, or even chaotically. Most relevant for a psychological model of perception, the size of the difference may vary intermittently: alternating between zero (a semi-stable state of synchronization) and a chaotic sequence of values (wandering through state space until the difference rests temporarily at zero again).

Van Leeuwen et al. then extended their analysis to the larger CML networks appropriate for perceptual tasks. For example, each unit in an array of 50 × 50 units may be sparsely coupled to just four other units – its neighbors in the array. (Note that van Leeuwen et al. usually coupled each unit to its corresponding unit in additional arrays as well, but one array is enough to get the key results.) They began by simply generalizing equations (4) and (5) to apply to more than two units, and found that small values of C relative to A tended to generate relatively small clusters within which units may synchronize their activity. What was needed to simulate shifting perceptions of the grid in figure 8.8, however, was a very specific synchronization in which the clusters were specialized to its rows and columns; for more stable perception of a large "X" pattern, two diagonal clusters (at different orientations) were needed. To obtain networks that could adapt to the input patterns of interest, they modified the way in which C and A were used. First, A became a variable controlled by input rather than a fixed parameter. Relatively high activity in the receptive field of a unit was realized by lowering the value of A for that unit. (This seems backwards, but lower values of A would tend to drive the unit to a level of chaotic activity at which it is more likely to synchronize with other units: *weak chaos*.) Second, the coupling parameter C was replaced by adaptive weights on each local connection plus a global parameter C_{max}, which scales those weights so as to produce a bias towards stability or instability (depending on the value of A). When the activation sequences of two units begin to synchronize the weight between them is increased; this favors greater synchronization in the succeeding time-steps. Thus, synchronization that initially just happened to occur between two chaotic sequences gets grabbed and used by the system to move towards more structured activity. In a sense, the weights serve as a short-term memory of recent synchronization that helps to reinstate that synchronization. With this occurring across multiple pairs of units simultaneously, the system can advance towards larger clusters within which all units are synchronized (e.g., a cluster specialized to the third column) and leave behind its chaotic behavior in favor of one of the metastable states (e.g., seeing the grid as organized in columns).

Using this adaptive CML, van Leeuwen et al. were able to simulate the behavior of a perceiver switching between metastable synchronizations when the input represents an ambiguous figure, but also attaining stably synchronized clusters when the input is an unambiguous figure. What is important is that the system has the intrinsic capacity to achieve percepts via synchronization but also the flexibility to change to a different percept via desynchronization. Ambiguous figures are useful for researchers because they can be counted upon to put the system into irregular swings between synchronization and desynchronization. This case would be only a curiosity, though, if it did not point the way to the system's overall design and capacities. That the same system can handle unambiguous figures is an initial demonstration of the generality of the design. Recently this research group has provided further demonstrations. Within perception, they have shown that CMLs can provide an especially efficient solution to Grossberg's boundary contour problem (van Leeuwen, Verver, and Brinkers, 2000). In a much bolder move, they have proposed to extend the timescale at which coupled maps are considered to operate downwards as far as iconic memory and upwards to long-term memory (van Leeuwen and Raffone, 2001). In this unified view of perception and memory, representations at a variety of timescales may be realized and maintained by the chaotic dynamics of coupled oscillators. A bold claim elicits tough questioning. Much work would be needed to show that this mechanism is adequate to account for a broad variety of perceptual and memory phenomena; and even if it works as a base, additional mechanisms may be needed as well. There is also the question of whether this is the way the brain actually does the job.

The questions raised by chaos-inspired dynamical models, exemplified here by those of Skarda and Freeman and van Leeuwen's group, will not be answered quickly. The results to date suggest that incorporating a DST perspective in the very design of networks yields distinctive properties which may be used to advantage in modeling and may also change the way cognitive scientists think about perception and cognition. However, the approach is too new to have moved much beyond individual models; for example, Freeman and van Leeuwen make very different uses of chaos. As researchers gain more experience with DST-driven network design, principles and practices will emerge and the approach will have its best chance of gaining increased visibility and impact within cognitive science. Will enough researchers be sufficiently enticed to re-situate their own work within an unfamiliar theoretical territory, bringing about a Kuhnian paradigm shift? If so, would the impact of connectionism be seen retrospectively as merely transitional? We now leave specific models behind and return to philosophical inquiry into implications.

8.5   Is Dynamicism a Competitor to Connectionism?

8.5.1   Van Gelder and Port's critique of classic connectionism

Connectionist networks are clearly complex systems and, as we have seen, certain connectionists have found DST tools to be extremely useful in analyzing the behavior of their networks and developing new kinds of networks. As exemplified in the quotation from van Gelder and Port at the beginning of the chapter, though, for some theorists the emergence of dynamical approaches offers not just a set of tools to be utilized within existing paradigms but an actual Kuhnian revolution in cognitive science. On this view, connectionism was not the real revolution:

> [C]onnectionism should not be thought of as constituting an alternative to the computational research paradigm in cognitive science. The reason is that there is a much deeper fault line running between the computational approach and the dynamical approach. In our opinion, connectionists have often been attempting, unwittingly and unsuccessfully, to straddle this line: to use dynamical machinery to implement ideas about the nature of cognitive processes which owe more to computationalism. From the perspective of a genuinely dynamical conception of cognition, classic PDP-style connectionism (as contained in, for example, the well-known volumes [of] Rumelhart and McClelland, 1986, and McClelland and Rumelhart, 1986) is little more than an ill-fated attempt to find a halfway house between the two worldviews.   (van Gelder and Port, 1995, pp. 33–4)

In support of this claim, they asserted that the classic connectionism that used networks (especially feedforward networks) as "sophisticated devices for mapping static inputs into static outputs" (p. 32) is disappearing as it splits into two distinct streams. Researchers in the relatively computational stream design networks that straightforwardly implement computational mechanisms or have hybrid architectures. Researchers in the relatively dynamical stream design networks like those discussed in the current chapter and give at least some attention to their dynamics. Van Gelder and Port allow that (p. 34): "Connectionist researchers who take the latter path are, of course, welcome participants in the dynamical approach" but also point to ways they differ from nonconnectionist dynamicists – especially those dynamicists taking the quantitative approach that van Gelder and Port regard as a standard or prototype.

One difference that tends to keep connectionists at the periphery of dynamical modeling is the type of formal model employed: massive networks targeting the "microstructure of cognition" versus equations with collective variables targeting its macrostructure. Moreover, van Gelder and Port seem concerned that connectionists are still carrying baggage from the classical computational approach that slows their progress along the road from the halfway house. This concern is elucidated in several papers in which van Gelder laid out his view of the differences between the computational and dynamical worldviews (van Gelder, 1995, 1998, 1999). In what follows we will first briefly contrast the two styles of modeling and then grapple with whether the computational baggage is a help or a hindrance by discussing issues of explanation and representation.[8]

8.5.2   Two styles of modeling

Dynamicists generally strive for compact models in which one or more (preferably differential) equations capture the overall behavior of a system in terms of a very small number of variables and parameters. Connectionists (even those taking a dynamical approach) produce models which have about the same number of equations but apply them repeatedly across the ranges of variables. Iteration of this kind yields as many activation values as there are units and as many weights as there are connections at each time-step. These differences in the type of formal model employed reflect differences in goals and desired grain-size of one's account.

For example, we have already seen that in van Leeuwen et al.'s CML account of the perception of ambiguous figures (a network-like dynamical model) a large number of coupled oscillators are governed by the same equations but do not behave identically. They interact to produce conflicting, metastable interpretations of a stimulus. Kelso's (1995) standard dynamical account also achieves metastability (pp. 218–23), but with respect to the value of a single collective variable (ϕ) that measures the synchrony of just two coupled oscillators. The two primary interpretations of the ambiguous figure are indexed by these values rather than simulated. It is a new application of Kelso's signature model of a surprisingly salient task: finger twiddling. People are asked to move both index fingers up and down either together (in-phase) or in opposition to one another (antiphase) in synchrony with a metronome. As the speed of the metronome increases it becomes impossible to maintain the antiphase movement, and subjects involuntarily switch to in-phase twiddling. This can be dynamically understood as a transition from a landscape with stable attractors for both types of movement to one with a stable attractor only for in-phase movement. Intermediate values of *relative phase* (φ) may appear during the transition (e.g., one finger just a bit ahead of the other in their up–down cycles). The attractor landscapes (V) within which in-phase, antiphase or intermediate relative phases occur can be obtained from equation (6) by providing appropriate values of the parameters:

$$V = -\varphi\delta\omega - a \cos \varphi - b \cos 2\varphi \tag{6}$$

To genuinely understand this equation and its ramifications, you must read Kelso's book. The main point here is that an equation with just a few parameters can give an account of the behavior of two coupled oscillators (here, fingers). The difference between the fingers' spontaneous frequency and the metronome's frequency is reflected in $\delta\omega$. The a and b parameters reflect (indirectly) the oscillation frequency (how fast the fingers are moving), and a/b is a crucial coupling ratio (when it is small, oscillation is fast and in-phase movement is the only attractor). Certain combinations of parameter values produce intermittency (the system fluctuates chaotically between the two kinds of movement, which now are semi-stable rather than stable). Change the realization of the equation from finger phases to competing interpretations of an ambiguous figure (by changing the interpretation of each collective variable), and *voilà* – equation (6) models a perceptual phenomenon (the distribution of switching times) at an abstract level.

Van Leeuwen et al.'s CML model is different in part because it does two jobs. Unlike Kelso's model, it simulates the percepts themselves – its units actually organize themselves into synchronized columns or rows to simulate the two interpretations of the ambiguous display. Like Kelso's model, though, it also models the more global perceptual phenomenon of semi-stable interpretation by repeatedly but irregularly switching between these percepts.

This difference in style of modeling has other consequences. Certain concepts that are part of the "computational baggage" (our metaphor) apply much more naturally to dynamical network models than to standard dynamical models. In the ambiguous figures task, van Leeuwen et al.'s explanation comes in the form of a *mechanistic model*, within which the metastable patterns can reasonably be regarded as two alternative *representations* of the stimulus (albeit distributed rather than classical). Kelso's compact system was not designed to do these jobs; it models the fluctuation between interpretations of the stimulus array but not the interpretations themselves. In taking a closer look at these computational concepts and at the dynamical alternatives, we will find that each can play a different but useful role in exploring dynamical network models.

8.5.3   Mechanistic versus covering-law explanations

The notions of mechanistic model and representation that we find useful in thinking about dynamical network models are rooted in stronger, classical notions: homuncularity and symbolic representation. Van Gelder (1995, p. 351) had the classical versions in mind when he characterized the computational approach in terms of "a mutually interdependent cluster" of properties: "representation, computation, sequential and cyclic operation, and homuncularity." A computer program with subroutines is a prototype that gives a good, quick sense of what he means. Computation involves discrete operations that manipulate representations; they apply sequentially (not in parallel); and sometimes a particular sequence of such operations will apply iteratively or recursively (cyclic operation – here a discrete notion that is not to be confused with oscillation or limit cycles in a dynamical model). When combined with these other properties, representations are sequences of manipulable elements that usually also have meaning (are symbolic) – this special case is the classical notion of representation. Before discussing representation further, we will take a look at computational versus dynamical approaches to explanation and the special case of homuncularity.

The homuncularity property derives from Daniel Dennett's (1977) characterization of the components in a mechanistic model of the mind as homunculi. By this metaphor – whimsical but making a serious claim – Dennett saw the mind as a committee of little agents, each with its own specialized subtask (e.g., discrimination, memory, evaluation), who pass messages (representations) to one another to perform the overall task. Each little agent itself can be analyzed as a committee of somewhat more specialized, less clever agents; and so forth until the lowest-level agents perform primitive calculations such as picking the larger of two numbers. Put less colorfully, such a system has a hierarchy of components, each of which performs its subtask by taking representations as input, operating on them, and sending the outputs to other components.

A mechanistic model relaxes this characterization, such that in some cases the components may function and interact continuously rather than discretely and their interactions may be better characterized as causal or information-bearing than as classically representational. One way in which scientists construct such a model is to first decompose a task into subtasks and then try to recompose it by specifying the component performing each subtask and its interactions with other components (see Bechtel and Richardson, 1993). The model is taken to provide an explanation of the system's performance of the task. In principle the decomposition could continue down to primitives (cognitive models are often assumed to "bottom out" in neurobiology), but in practice modelers usually limit themselves to going down one or two levels. When the components of a model like this can be localized in the system being modeled (e.g., identifying edge-detectors in the primary visual cortex), Bechtel and Richardson (1993) call them *complex systems* to distinguish them from *simple systems* (for which components have not been identified) and from *integrated systems* (in which the components interact by feedback loops or other reciprocal connections – the most difficult kind of model and usually not achieved until a research program reaches maturity).

Who needs mechanistic explanation? Most explanations in the mainstream of biology tend to be of this genre. Symbolic models in cognitive science generally qualify – they served as Dennett's paradigm case of homuncularity and van Gelder's prime target. (However, competence models such as Chomskian grammars have a componential structure that may not map cleanly on to the processing system modeled). Standard dynamical models are generally claimed to bypass the mechanistic style of explanation. It is network models for which the question gets most interesting, but to show why, we first need to ask: what are dynamical modelers doing if not providing mechanistic explanations?

One possibility is that dynamicists merely *describe* a system by identifying regularities in its behavior. But van Gelder (1998, p. 625) rejected this suggestion, noting that dynamical accounts of cognition are no different in form than dynamical accounts of physical phenomena such as planetary motion. Since the latter count as explanatory, so should the former. Indeed, his point is well taken; the contrast is not between explanation and description, but rather between two forms of explanation. The logical positivists identified a form of explanation, deductive-nomological or covering-law explanation, which fits the dynamicist case. In a covering-law explanation, a phenomenon is explained by showing how a description of it can be derived from a set of laws and initial conditions. The dynamical equations provide the laws for such covering-law explanations, and by supplying initial conditions (values of variables and parameters), one can predict and explain subsequent states of the system. That is the appropriate kind of explanation for van Gelder, since he proposes to regard cognition solely as a dynamical system – one that changes states in time as expressed in equations.

Now we can consider networks. The simplest thing to say is that the type of explanation attributed to them can vary with the design of the network and with the designer's leanings between classical connectionism and dynamicism. Much more interesting is the prospect that they may lead us to new kinds of explanation that combine and extend current options. Van Gelder (1995, p. 374) projected that combining ingredients of the two worldviews in connectionism "may well turn out to be an unstable mixture" and refrained from doing so; we prefer to focus on the constructive synthesis that may emerge from the energy put into such a project. (Clark, 1997b, was similarly optimistic about combining these types of explanation and provided a thoughtful discussion of explanation more generally.)

Here are some cases. Sejnowski and Rosenberg's (1986) NETtalk network can serve as an exemplar of a feedforward connectionist design, which in this case provides a mechanistic explanation of reading aloud (see section 3.2.2.3 for more details). At the first level down, it is easy to identify components (the input, hidden, and output layers) and to state they are connected by two full sets of feedforward connections. Below that there are two more levels of decomposition on the input layer (seven sets of letter units) and one more level on the output layer (one set of articulatory feature units). It is distinctive to connectionist networks that the hidden layer affords only a functional decomposition: cluster analysis reveals functional components for various grapheme–phoneme regularities, vowels vs. consonants, etc. The connectivity of the network is also highly distributed, unlike classical systems. The designers built the network as a mechanistic model, but cannot give a complete mechanistic analysis of the microfeatures and microactivities that result from its adaptive weight changes during learning. However, the incomplete mechanistic explanation is the best available; dynamical analysis has little to offer towards understanding feedforward networks.

When interactivity is added to layered networks of this type via recurrent connections, complex activity extended across time and connections becomes very important. This aspect of a network model benefits from dynamical analysis. We suggest that a connectionist dynamical approach offers the opportunity to embrace both types of explanation and use them to serve complementary purposes (see Bechtel, 1998). Most simply, the dynamical analysis can offer covering laws that characterize overall patterns of change in a system (generally in terms of aggregate or external variables), and the mechanistic one can show how those changes are effected. The connectionist researcher built the network, knows its components and how they are connected, and can use this knowledge to "go behind the scenes" and provide a (partial) mechanistic account of the phenomena captured in the dynamical covering-law explanation of the system. Dynamical tools may then be used not only to characterize the complete system, but also the interaction of the components. For example, in building the CML model of ambiguous figure perception, van Leeuwen et al. (1997) knew from Kelso's work that two coupled oscillators could produce the right kind of semi-stable behavior. They wanted to build a system at a much finer grain to model the microstructure and microactivity underlying the percepts themselves in addition to the overall semi-stable behavior. Their novel solution (using a large number of coupled oscillators as components) was informed by the prior dynamical model but extended it significantly by treating component parts as dynamically interacting oscillators. The resulting CML model is best described using a combination of dynamical and mechanistic analysis.

In another example from this chapter, a mechanistic analysis gets even further with Skarda and Freeman's (1987) model of the olfactory bulb. Built at an intermediate grain-size, the "units" were just 16 large nervous system components that were less homogeneous than the units of a connectionist network; for example, all of the excitatory (pyramidal) cells of the anterior olfactory nucleus were represented collectively in one component. However, their interactive connections produced complex behavior in the network as a whole. Dynamical concepts and analysis were crucial for understanding the chaotic and limit cycle behavior that emerged. Another example: Beer's autonomous controller network for insects' tripod gait has six replications of the same five units (a componential organization at this level). Three of the units controlling each leg have well-defined subtasks (each clearly controls its own specialized motor effector) but are dynamical in their quantitative states and interconnected activity (including influence from the other two units – the interneurons). Each leg's activity is best understood in terms of a limit cycle, but the state space is defined with respect to components of the network.

The ability of these two perspectives to complement each other becomes even more evident when dynamical analysis is applied not only to the whole network but also to some of its components. This can work even in a network with thoroughly homogeneous units within each layer. An interesting case covered above is that of Elman (1991), who knew the gross architecture of his simple recurrent network (SRN) for predicting words in sentences and could give a rough mechanistic account based on his own design work. However, he also used principal components analysis (a tool from yet another tradition, multivariate statistical analysis) to identify functional components of the system on the hidden layer and used DST tools to discover exactly what task those components were accomplishing. For example, plotting trajectories through the state space of components 1 and 11 revealed the phenomenon that relative clauses were being wrapped corkscrew-like into the space.

It is not known to what extent an orchestration of methods like this might yield insight into large networks with more complex interactions among units. Michael Wheeler (1998) considered the difficulty of explaining the activity of networks exhibiting what Clark (1997a, pp. 163–6) called "continuous reciprocal causation." An example is Beer's nonautonomous control network, in which sensor input completes a loop between the controller and the environment, but Wheeler was most concerned about larger, more homogeneous networks and especially those in evolutionary robotics (see sections 9.4 and 9.5) whose organization is minimally constrained by human preconceptions of design. He thought the explanatory stance must become more holistic as the amount of continuous reciprocal causation increases, shifting away from modular (mechanistic) explanation and towards system dynamics. "The justification for this claim is that the sheer number and complexity of the causal interactions in operation in such systems force the grain at which useful explanations are found to become coarser" (Wheeler, in press, p. 16). Clark (1997a, p. 175) had a similar concern but argued for proceeding more optimistically, "adding new tools to cognitive science's tool kit, refining and reconfiguring but not abandoning those we already possess. After all, if *the brain* were so simple that a single approach could unlock its secrets, *we* would be so simple that we couldn't do the job!"[9]

In accord with the more optimistic view of Clark, we look forward to seeing how much headway can be made, even with highly interactive networks, when mechanistic and dynamical explanation are combined and extended. However, it is so early in dynamical network research that this suggestion of complementary, even integrated, use of two kinds of explanation must be tentative. Those who wish to use an exclusively dynamical approach to cognition may find their own way to go behind the scenes, in some way parsing the system and building a hierarchy of dynamical models that cover a variety of grain-sizes from the overall phenomenon of interest on down. In his 1995 book, Kelso sketched such a vision in chapter 2 and considered modeling at neuronal levels in chapter 8. He emphasized, though, that his equations give a different parsing than does a mechanistic analysis of the biological systems that realize them. For now, networks of homogeneous units and connections, each with its own application of the equations governing the system, do a modeling job that is hard to replace by purely dynamical analyses. Can we do better than simply performing each kind of analysis separately? It would be most interesting if attempts to grapple with these problems led to new notions of explanation within the philosophy of science in addition to better models.

8.5.4   Representations: Who needs them?

We turn now to a second area of discrepancy between connectionist and dynamical approaches that places those who seek to combine them at the periphery of dynamicism (but perhaps at the leading edge of the future of cognitive modeling): the role of representations. Disagreements about representation abound. It is least troublesome within the symbolic approach, where the notion that cognition involves operations upon representations (construed as structured sequences of symbols) is central. At the other end of the road, among those dynamicists who attend to the concept of representation at all, it tends to be either denied or radically redefined. Between these extremes are the connectionists, who see part of their mission as (less radically) redefining representation. Activation patterns across the layers of a network are commonly (though not universally) regarded as "subsymbolic" (Smolensky, 1988) – a departure from symbols in their fine grain, their status as numerical vectors, and the kinds of activity that generate them (parallel processing, and for interactive networks, settling into attractors or other kinds of change across a nontrivial temporal dimension). However, van Gelder and Port (1995) worried that connectionists taking this view (especially those working with feedforward networks such as NETtalk) have insufficiently shed notions of representation rooted in the symbolic approach. On this view, an unchanging composition of subsymbols is in danger of being treated as a static symbol.

Dynamical reappraisals of representation were considered as part of an argument for the *dynamical hypothesis* by van Gelder (1998; quotes from p. 622). His starting point was to unequivocally dispense with "static configurations of symbol tokens" – a core commitment of what he calls the computational view (some of the commentators on this BBS paper, seeing computation as broader, would prefer a different term). The main alternative he noted is that dynamicists "find their representations among the kinds of entities that figure in DST, including parameter settings, system states, attractors, trajectories, or even aspects of bifurcation structures" and eventually "even more exotic forms." (See also van Gelder and Port, 1995, p. 12.) That he felt no urgency to pare down this mixed bag of possibilities reflects the fact that few if any dynamicists view representation as a core concern. Indeed, van Gelder also noted (refraining from endorsement or disapproval) the more radical view that dynamicists can develop models of cognition that "sidestep representation altogether."[10] He cited the work by Beer and by Skarda and Freeman (discussed above in sections 8.3.1 and

8.4.1) as exemplifying the ability "to imagine how any nonrepresentational system could possibly exhibit cognitive performances" and also to model such a system.

One could quibble about whether models of sensorimotor function are a sufficient basis to argue that cognition more generally can be modeled nonrepresentationally; yet, they give a toehold. Freeman and Skarda (1990) clearly endorsed the position that representation can be dispensed with (at least in dynamical models of perception grounded in brain function) in a commentary with the title "Representations: Who needs them?" They answered: "Functionalist philosophers, computer scientists, and cognitive psychologists need them, often desperately, but physiologists do not, and those who wish to find and use biological brain algorithms should also avoid them" (p. 379). Why should they be avoided? "[T]he idea of representation is seductive," giving "the illusion that we understand something that we do not" but in fact "is unnecessary to describe brain dynamics" and even "impedes progress" (pp. 375–6). In illustration they gave this remarkable reprise of their olfactory bulb work (note that the "burst" they refer to is a spatial pattern of activity across the entire bulb under the control of one of the cyclic attractors sketched in figure 8.7):

> For more than 10 years we tried to say that . . . each burst served to represent the odor-ant with which we correlated it. . . . This was a mistake. After years of sifting through our data, we identified the problem: it was the concept of representation. . . . [They explain that the pattern for a given odor occurs only under conditioning and changes if the reinforcement contingency is altered or a new odor is added.] Our findings indicate that patterned neural activity correlates best with reliable forms of interaction in a context that is behaviorally and environmentally co-defined by what Steven Rose (1976) calls a dialectic. There is nothing intrinsically representational about this dynamic process until the observer intrudes. It is the experimenter who infers what the observed activity patterns represent to or in a subject, in order to explain his results to himself (Werner, 1988a, 1988b).   (Freeman and Skarda, 1990, p. 376)

They further stated that this insight led them to ask new questions of their data and that their dynamical network model, with its emphasis on the role of chaos, was one of the novel answers that resulted.

Skarda and Freeman's network was intended to model an actual biological system. Researchers in the field of artificial life (the topic of chapter 9) attempt a more abstract characterization of such biological constructs as evolution, sensation, and motor control, and many of them share the skepticism about representation. For example, speaking from his experience with autonomous agents (including his insect controller networks), Beer (1995, p. 144) concluded that generally "there need be no clean decomposition of an agent's dynamics into distinct functional modules and no aspect of the agent's state need be interpretable as a representation." Philosophers focusing on evolutionary robotics, including Beer's work, have launched into a major re-examination of the notion of representation. Wheeler (1998), writing about systems that exhibit high degrees of continuous reciprocal causation, assumed that his arguments against their homuncularity (and more generally, their modularity) counted as well against their having representations. (He argued elsewhere the point that makes this plausible: the claim that these properties are mutually supportive.) This was a soft rather than hard conclusion; for example, he left open the possibility that more sophisticated evolved robotic control systems of the future would be more decomposable. Clark (1997a; all quotes from pp. 174–5) agreed that such systems present the "most potent challenge" in finding a role for internal representation, but again preferred a more optimistic and inclusive stance. First, in coming to grips with such complex dynamics, "the notion of internal representation itself may be subtly transformed," losing some of its classical connotations while co-opting dynamical notions of inner events (chaotic attractors, trajectories in state space, and so forth; a list similar to van Gelder's). But Clark equally threw down the gauntlet to dynamicists:

> The recent skepticism concerning the role of computations and representation in cognitive science is, I believe, overblown. . . . The minimal conditions under which internal representation talk will be useful, I have argued, obtain whenever we can successfully unpack the complex causal web of influences so as to reveal the information-processing adaptive role of some system of states or of processes. . . . [C]ontinuous reciprocal causation between internal and external factors . . . appears unlikely to characterize the range of cases for which the representational approach is in any case most compelling–viz., cases involving reasoning about the distant, the nonexistent, or the highly abstract. In such cases, the focus shifts to the internal dynamics of the system under study. The crucial and still-unresolved question is whether these internal dynamics will themselves reward a somewhat more liberalized but still recognizably representation-based understanding. . . . no alternative understanding of genuinely representation-hungry problem solving yet exists, and . . . it is hard to see how to give crisp, general, and perspicuous explanations of much of our adaptive success without somehow reinventing the ideas of complex information processing and of content-bearing inner states." (Clark, 1997a, pp. 174–5)

So far we have looked at how the notion of representation has fared when confronted with biological systems and with their simulated counterparts, evolved robot controllers. Van Gelder added industrial machinery to the array of test cases in a 1995 article, "What might cognition be, if not computation?" His general goal was to argue that dynamical systems provide a plausible alternative to computational ones, and that such systems need not have representations. Although at some points in the paper he focused on a classical computational definition of representation, he also said that his arguments should go through using "pretty much any reasonable characterization, based around a core idea of some state of a system which, by virtue of some general representational scheme, stands in for some further state of affairs, thereby enabling the system to behave appropriately with respect to that state of affairs" (van Gelder, 1995, p. 351; he adapted this characterization from Haugeland, 1991). This definition of representation is broad enough to cover both classical symbolic and connectionist subsymbolic approaches.

The notion of "stands in for" requires some explication. One way to characterize it is in terms of carrying information: one state or event can stand in for another if it carries information about that other state or event. The notion of carrying information about something is usually explicated in terms of causal relations (Dretske, 1988). But this notion of information is both too general and too narrow for explicating representation. It is too general because any effect carries information about its cause, but not every effect constitutes a representation. It is too narrow because it fails to account for misrepresentation – the possibility that some state might falsely represent something else when it was not caused by it. Based on this and other arguments, Millikan (1993) proposed that we need to look in a different direction, specifically, at the agent or device that uses (consumes) the information. If a consumer Z is designed (e.g., by evolution or by an engineer) to use Y to carry information about X, then Y might serve as a representation of X even if Y never actually carries information about X. For example, a radiation detector (Y) may have been designed for a plant supervisor who wants to be informed if there is ever a radiation leak (X). If no leaks occur, it will in fact produce only false alarms; nonetheless, the radiation detector serves to represent radiation leaks.

In practice, we generally need to look in both directions: some state is a representation only if it is used to gain information about something else, but we identify what it represents by determining what is capable of bringing it about. For example, in Lettvin et al.'s (1959) classic identification of ganglion cells in the frog's retina as bug detectors, two kinds of findings jointly were needed to determine what the firing of these cells represented: (a) increased firing of these cells generated bug-eating behaviors in the frog; (b) bug-like shapes generated increased firing. There are, therefore, three interrelated components in a representational story: what is represented (bugs), the representation (increased firing of ganglion cells), and the user of the representation (the frog, or the frog's action system).

While this is not a complete characterization of representation, it provides a sufficient foundation to begin considering van Gelder's contention that dynamical systems need not have representations. To make his case, van Gelder reached back over two centuries to James Watt's groundbreaking design for using a steam engine to power machinery via a flywheel, and suggested that its centrifugal governor would be "preferable to the Turing machine as a landmark for models of cognition" (van Gelder, 1995, p. 381). The governor was the second of two major innovations necessary to the invention's success. Watt's first innovation was a gearing system that allowed an oscillating piston to drive a rotating flywheel. But the solution to the problem of translating one kind of motion into another raised a second problem: how to maintain a constant flywheel speed in the face of constantly fluctuating steam pressure as well as resistance due to workload on the machinery being driven by the flywheel. (For many kinds of machinery, such as industrial weaving machines, it is important that a constant speed of operation be maintained, despite fluctuations in resistance, via constant flywheel speed.) The speed at which the flywheel turns can be reduced, when necessary, by partly closing a valve to reduce the amount of steam coming through the pipe leading from the boiler to the piston. Similarly, partly opening the valve increases the amount of steam. But who or what would keep adjusting the valve?

Watt's solution borrowed a technology already employed in windmills; it is shown pictorially in figure 8.9(a) and schematically in figure 8.9(b). (The pistons and gearing system between the valve and flywheel are not shown, but complete the loop.) To create a governor, he attached a vertical spindle to the flywheel which would rotate at a speed proportionate to that of the flywheel, and attached to the spindle two arms with metal balls on their ends. The arms were free to rise and fall as a result of centrifugal force. Through a mechanical linkage, the angle of the arms would change the opening of the valve, thereby controlling the amount of steam driving the piston and hence the rotational speed of the flywheel itself.

As a first step towards establishing the plausibility of the idea that cognitive systems, construed as dynamical systems, lack representations, van Gelder argued that the Watt governor operates without representations. He called "misleading" "a common and initially quite attractive intuition to the effect that the angle at which the arms are swinging is a representation of the current speed of the engine, and it is because the arms are related in this way to engine speed that the governor is able

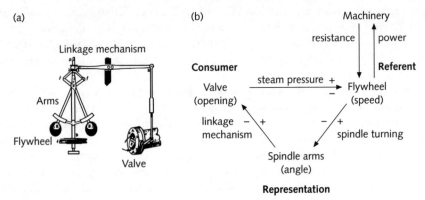

Figure 8.9 Watt's centrifugal governor for a steam engine. (a) Drawing from J. Farley, *A Treatise on the Steam Engine: Historical, Practical, and Descriptive* (London: Longman, Rees, Orme, Brown, and Green, 1927). (b) A schematic representation showing that the angle of the spindle arms carries information about the speed of the flywheel for the valve, which uses the angle to determine the opening, thereby regulating the speed of the flywheel.

to control that speed" (van Gelder, 1995, p. 351). He offered several arguments for not construing the angle of the arms as representations; here we suggest counter-arguments to two of them (for a fuller discussion of these and the other arguments, see Bechtel, 1998). Van Gelder began by contending that there is no explanatory utility in describing the angle of the arms in representational terms (that is, the dynamical analysis is sufficient). To establish explanatory utility, we must argue that (a) a mechanistic analysis is informative, and (b) that analysis includes a particular representational story about the arm angles: they *stand in for* the speed of the flywheel and can regulate the valve opening *because* they carry this information.

First, then, here is a brief mechanistic analysis of the Watt governor (see Bechtel, 1999). It has several different parts, including the flywheel, the spindle and arms, and a linkage mechanism connected to a valve. As figure 8.9(b) makes clear, each component operates on a different engineering principle and hence performs a specific subtask; each subtask contributes to the overall task of the system via the component's connection with the next component in the loop. That is, the opening of the valve gets transformed (via the piston) into the rotation of the flywheel, which gets transformed into the angle of the spindle arms, which gets transformed into the opening of the valve. In this way, we have shifted vocabularies from one describing the overall behavior of the Watt governor to one describing what its parts do. Then there is an extra step back up to the system level by connecting the task of each component to the needs of the whole system. Here it becomes clear why Watt inserted the spindle arms. It is *because* the spindle arms rise and fall in response to the speed of the flywheel that their angle can be used by the linkage mechanism to open and shut the valve. Without the spindle arms and their linkage mechanism, the valve has no access to information about the flywheel speed. They were inserted in order to encode that information in a format that could be used by the valve-opening mechanism.

This makes the spindle arm angle an instance of a more general point about representation: typically someone (a designer, or evolution, or the particular consumer produced by design or evolution) has gone to the trouble of representing a state of affairs in another medium because the representational medium is more suitable for use by the consumer. This can be due to its format, its accessibility (e.g., words are generally more accessible to our cognitive system than are their referents), the efficiency with which it can be manipulated (e.g., computer-aided design), economy (e.g., industrial prototypes), and so forth. The representation is not just one vertex of the triangle in figure 8.9(b), a part like any other part of the dynamic loop; it was inserted to play a particular (representational) role and the system functions because it was designed appropriately for that role.

Another of van Gelder's arguments "for supposing that the centrifugal governor is not representational is that, when we fully understand the relationship between engine [flywheel] speed and arm angle, we see that the notion of representation is just the wrong sort of conceptual tool to apply" (van Gelder, 1995, p. 353). Because "arm angle and engine speed are at all times both determined by, and determining, each other's behavior" the relationship is "much more subtle and complex . . . than the standard concept of representation can handle." Here is Clark's continuous reciprocal causation again, but the complexity resides only in the dynamical analysis. It is quite possible, and desirable, to undertake a complementary classical analysis. As just noted, it (a) identifies the system's components, the subtasks they perform, and their connectivity, and (b) picks out the spindle arm angle as *representing* the flywheel's speed for use by the valve. It happens in this case that something is standing in for something else by being coupled to it in a dynamical manner. This opens the way to a dynamical analysis that makes use of the identified components, but emphasizes their coupling and provides equations that provide an elegant and specific account of their state changes in time. Within the confines of this dynamical analysis the components form a loop in which no one of them is viewed as providing a starting point, let alone a differentiated role such as referent or representation. If the equations can be uncovered, this analysis yields an elegant covering-law explanation of the dynamics of that loop—no more and no less.

In analyzing the Watt governor in this way, we have taken the position that representations should be construed broadly rather than restrictively. They can be dynamic rather than static; vary continuously in time rather than discretely; and involve quantitative operations rather than sequential manipulations of symbols. The important thing is that something is standing in for something else. Generalizing the lessons learned from the Watt governor to biological or artificial agents, it would seem that they can coordinate their behavior with an environment because components of these agents vary their states in response to the environment so as to stand in for it. Without such representations, it seems difficult to explain how the system is able to take into account specific features of the environment. We should emphasize that this does not require that the system build up a complete representation of its environment. Theorists such as Ballard (1991) and Churchland, Ramachandran, and Sejnowski (1994) have argued that we only selectively, and actively, sample the environment. Whatever information we do sample, however, must ultimately be represented within the system in order to be employed in coordinating behavior.

De-emphasizing the importance of the quantitative status of a system turns out to be helpful in characterizing dynamical analysis as well. Rick Grush pointed out in a review of Port and van Gelder's 1995 book that "A large portion of the models of 'higher' cognitive processes articulated in the book have exactly the same processing-step character as the vilified computational alternatives, even though the language, mathematics, and illustrations used to present the models obscure this fact" (Grush,

1997b, p. 235). Where equations were supplied, that is, they tended to be difference equations by which the value of a variable at time $t + 1$ depends on that variable and others at time t. This is no closer to real time than the processing steps of a classical AI model. In responding to this argument, van Gelder (1999, p. 8) arrived at a more realistic way of distinguishing types of models. "In dynamical models, there are distances in state, and distances in time, and both are systematically related to the behavior of the system." It is the geometry of state spaces in relation to time (whether discrete or continuous) that best characterizes dynamical analysis. This also suggests that the suitability of dynamical analysis for a particular network has more to do with whether trajectories in state space capture something important than with the fact that their representations are quantitative vectors rather than symbol strings. That sounds just right.

8.6   Is Dynamicism Complementary to Connectionism?

Terence Horgan and John Tienson (1996) presented a very specific vision of how connectionism and DST can collaborate in providing an alternative to classicism. They unfolded it by first characterizing the classical approach in terms of David Marr's (1982) well-known three levels of description and then adding five specific assumptions of classicists regarding these levels. Essentially, this is the same starting point as van Gelder and Port's computational approach, although in the end Horgan and Tienson rejected less of it. In summarizing their framework here, we primarily use their terminology and their characterization of classicism but also (in parentheses) show Marr's way of referring to each level.

Level 1: Cognitive-state transitions (Marr: an abstract theory of the computation) A *cognitive-transition function* (CTF) maps one *total cognitive state* (TCS) to the next; that is, it specifies input–output mappings of intentional states. The choice of function depends in part on the goal of the computation. The CTF is regarded as *tractably computable* because, classically, general psychological laws reduce what would otherwise be a brute list of mappings (*see assumption 5*).

Level 2: Mathematical-state transitions (Marr: an algorithmic specification of the computation)   An *algorithm* is chosen to realize the level-1 input–output mapping (CTF) and *representations* are chosen for the input and output. Classically, formal rules (*see assumptions 2 and 3*) manipulate syntactically structured sequences of symbols (*see assumptions 1 and 4*).

Level 3: Physical implementation (Marr: implementation)   The level-2 computations are realized (implemented) in a physical system. A particular machine language program run on a particular digital computer is the best exemplar, both generally and for classicists.

Horgan and Tienson then identified the five key assumptions of classicism. Assumptions 1–3 give the basic layout of level-2 rule-governed symbol manipulation (3 is a stronger version of 2 and implies it; both imply 1). Assumption 4 makes language or language-like processing a special case (it is a stronger version of 1 and implies it, but leaves room for imagistic processing, for example, to satisfy 1 but not 4). Assumption 5 asserts the fundamentally computational worldview, which the other assumptions elaborate, and also makes a specific claim that it is realizable within available resources. Retaining the numbering and wording of the assumptions (pp. 24–5) but labeling and rearranging them for easy reference:

Fundamental computational assumption (level 1):
   (5) Human cognitive transitions conform to a *tractably computable* cognitive-transition function.

Representation (level 2):
  Weak   (1)   Intelligent cognition employs structurally complex mental representations.
  Strong   (4)   Many mental representations have *syntactic* structure.

Processing (level 2):
  Weak   (2)   Cognitive processing is sensitive to the structure of these representations (and thereby is sensitive to their content).
  Strong   (3)   Cognitive processing conforms to precise, exceptionless rules, statable over the representations themselves and articulable in the format of a computer program.

In evaluating these five assumptions for their own (nonclassicist) purposes, Horgan and Tienson made a provocative cut: in addition to retaining the weakest assumptions about representation and processing, they also argued for retaining the strong assumption that representations can be syntactically structured. They picked out "hard" rules (algorithms) and computational tractability as classicism's points of vulnerability. Hence, in arguing for an alternative to classicism, they retained assumptions 1, 2, and 4 and denied assumptions 3 and 5. Their favored alternative was a dynamically oriented connectionism, which they viewed not as a half-hearted halfway house but rather as the kind of dynamicism that is needed for the job of modeling cognition.

    These choices put Horgan and Tienson into several different fights, not just with classicists but also with most connectionists and most dynamicists. Horgan and Tienson took issue with classicists over assumptions 3 and 5 (by rejecting hard rules and expressing extreme skepticism that cognition could be computationally tractable). They stood with their fellow connectionists in rejecting hard rules (the general arguments are covered at length in chapter 5 and need not be reviewed here). But their insistence that there is indeed a language of thought, and that its syntactic structure must in some way be represented, placed them in opposition to many connectionists (see chapter 6). Finally, dynamicists should applaud Horgan and Tienson's rejection of assumption 5 but would tend to agree with van Gelder and Port that connectionist networks are a rather marginal medium for dynamical modeling (especially if they are viewed as realizing syntactically structured representations).

    Horgan and Tienson dealt with the nay-sayers in two ways: argumentatively by dissecting and debating each assumption and positively by trying to entice them into the alternative framework that they called *noncomputational dynamical cognition* (we will simply call it dynamicism). To make the contrast with classicism clear, they constructed a noncomputational dynamical reconstrual of Marr's three levels. Their claims at each level can be summarized as follows (see their pp. 63–4 for more detail):

Level 1: Cognitive-state transitions   In dynamicism the cognitive system is viewed as having general dispositions to move from one total cognitive state to another, and these dispositions are captured in psychological laws that are soft rather than general. There is no need for a tractably computable cognitive-transition function.

Level 2: Mathematical-state transitions   Total cognitive states are realized as points in the state space of a dynamical system, and transitions between states are realized in trajectories through that state space. Each representation is a point (or region), but not every point is a representation. Relations between syntactic structures (e.g., sentences with vs. without a direct object) are captured not in the presence or absence of certain steps in the algorithm generating a tree but rather in the relative positions of points. The discrete mathematics of algorithms is replaced by the continuous mathematics of dynamical systems theory. More specifically, given how the dynamical system is implemented at level 3, it is a high-dimensional activation landscape in which each dimension corresponds to the range of possible activation values of one unit in a network.

Level 3: Physical implementation   The dynamical system is implemented in a neural network of some sort (working hypothesis: a connectionist network). "Points in the state space of a dynamical system are realized by total activation patterns in the associated network" (p. 64).

Horgan and Tienson's denial of assumption 5 (the need for a tractably computable function) involves a distinction between *computable* and *tractably computable*. One could ask whether or not the cognitive transition functions that classicists attempt to realize in algorithms are actually computable (e.g., by a universal Turing machine). But to Horgan and Tienson, this was not the real issue. A cognitive system whose transitions are computable but intractable is as nonrealizable as one whose transitions are noncomputable. Any actual cognitive system must be realizable in a physical system that can implement mappings efficiently and quickly enough to be usable. They noted that tractable computation of this kind is far from guaranteed:

> [T]here are infinitely many functions [even] with *finite* domain and range that are not tractably computable. Consider, for example, any googolplex of unrelated pairings. (A googolplex is 1 followed by 10^{100} zeros.) The difference between infinite and huge-but-finite is not important for cognitive science!   (Horgan and Tienson, 1996, p. 26)

Classicists purport to get into the small-and-finite range by means of general psychological laws which reduce what would otherwise be a brute list of mappings " too gargantuan" to specify. Horgan and Tienson presented arguments that laws of the right sort for a computational system (hard laws) are not what the cognitive system consists in, nor are they implemented by hard rules at the algorithmic level. On their view, the way the cognitive system actually is built does not involve computation (the discrete mathematics of algorithms), so the tractability question does not even arise.

Instead of general laws, Horgan and Tienson claimed that cognition has an isotropic and Quinean nature that makes computation untractable if not impossible. The problem of *isotropy* is that of gaining access to the right information for solving a given task from all of the information in the system, while the *Quinean* problem concerns measuring the appropriate characteristics of the whole network of beliefs (e.g., its coherence) so as to determine how to revise beliefs. They credited Fodor with recognizing that these problems, originally identified in the context of confirming scientific hypotheses, extend to the general task of belief fixation faced regularly by cognitive systems. They did not see Fodor, or anyone else, as having shown how a classical system can overcome these challenges so as to handle a new input appropriately and efficiently: "Not only do we have no computational formalisms that show us how to do this; it is a highly credible hypothesis that a tractable computational system with these features is not possible for belief systems on the scale possessed by human beings" (p. 42). One avenue of response would be to deny that these are problems that need to be solved. Waskan and Bechtel (1997) contended that cognition is far less isotropic and Quinean than suggested by Fodor or Horgan and Tienson. A system with some degree of modularity (in the weaker sense exemplified in chapter 7, not Fodorian modularity) can concentrate its resources within a small part of the overall system. Rather than exhibiting an overall property of isotropy, for example, in such a system finding the right information quickly will depend on whether the right module is active (and in fact, humans not infrequently do fail to access relevant information that is somewhere in the system). A different avenue of response was preferred by Horgan and Tienson: they claimed that noncomputational dynamical cognition could easily be isotropic and Quinean. The problem of how to compute in such an environment (a version of the tractability problem) does not arise if the system does not compute.

In characterizing their noncomputational dynamical conception of cognition, Horgan and Tienson retained the commitment to syntactic structure that is a legacy of the symbolic approach (as stated in assumption 4). They construed as mistaken the common view that one of connectionism's contributions is to repudiate the use of syntactically structured representations in cognitive models. As Horgan pointed out, instead of improving on classical symbolic accounts this move produces "a seriously crippled cousin of classicism." He asked:

> What exactly are we supposed to be gaining, in terms of our abilities to model cognitive processes, by adopting an approach which (i) retains the assumption that cognitive processing is representation-level computation, but (ii) eschews one extremely powerful way to introduce semantic coherence into representation-level computation: viz., via the syntactic encoding of propositional content? *Qua* representation-level computation, it looks as though this amounts to trying to model semantically coherent thought processes with one hand – the *good* hand – tied behind one's back.   (Horgan, 1997, p. 17)

It quickly becomes apparent, however, that their construal of syntax is one that many connectionists – but no classicists – would find comfortable. They pointed to Pollack's RAAM networks as exemplifying how to get syntactically structured representations in a noncomputational cognitive system. These are the same representations that we characterized in section 6.3 as exhibiting only *functional* compositionality, in contrast to the *explicit* compositionality of symbolic representations. What makes RAAM representations functionally compositional is that there is usable information in them about the constituent structure of the tree from which they were generated. However, neither Pollack nor Horgan and Tienson have probed to discover how much syntactic information is represented nor for what range of linguistic performances it is adequate (beyond the passive transformation). They also have not pursued in any detail how the dynamical level of analysis contributes (though work by Elman and Christiansen suggests such a pursuit would be rewarding).

8.7   Conclusion

Cognitive scientists, including connectionist modelers, increasingly are employing dynamical concepts and the tools of DST. In this chapter we have seen how some researchers have plotted trajectories through state space and identified different types of attractors to better understand how their interactive networks did their job, and others have incorporated concepts such as chaos even at the design stage of their research. But some advocates of a dynamical approach to cognition claim that much more is at stake than the introduction of new tools. Van Gelder and Port (1995) contended that dynamics offers a paradigm for cognitive science that promises to replace both the symbolic and connectionist approaches. We examined critiques of mechanistic explanation and representation and concluded that these concepts need not be discarded (e.g., mechanistic explanation is complementary to the covering law explanations of dynamicism). Finally, we provided an overview of Horgan and Tienson's version of a dynamical approach to cognition, which was friendlier than van Gelder and Port's version with respect to both connectionist networks and the symbolic notion that representations have syntactic structure. We did not agree with all their claims, but their placement of dynamical and connectionist approaches at two different levels of a Marr-style analytic framework is a good starting point for working out how these approaches can complement each other.

NOTES

1   A simulator for running Lotka–Volterra equations developed by Hendrik J. Blok is available free at http://www.physics.ubc.ca/~blok/files.html.

2   Of course, (c) also has starting points that are already on the cycle, and it is one of the defining characteristics of an attractor that trajectories beginning at those points will remain within it. These special trajectories have no transients. Although the cycle in (a) exhibits this characteristic, it lacks another defining characteristic of attractors, the tendency to attract nearby trajectories. Thus, *none* of its trajectories have transients.

3   Interestingly, it does not much disturb encoding of the matrix (outer) clause; the three relevant points are similar to those in figure 8.6(a). This may be a leaky network analog to "popping" the push-down stack in a standard symbolic parser.

4   This sensitivity is important, because pairs of words such as *boy* and *boys* were given unrelated encodings on the input layer. The hidden layer seems to have extracted the systematic contrast between singular and plural (as well as the essentials of subject–verb agreement) purely from distributional information in the corpus. The principal components analysis not only provides evidence of the network's systematization of number but also localizes identification of subject noun number in component 2 – an impressive contribution to understanding how the network performs its task.

5   A weight space with an error dimension yields a very detailed display of its attractors – not just their locations but also their relative depths along the error surface. Occasionally activation spaces are plotted with an energy dimension included to obtain the same effect, as in figure 8.7 in section 8.4.1 (reprinted from Freeman, 1987).

6   Understanding why the system behaves in this way requires considerably more depth in DST than our brief introduction can provide. To pursue this elsewhere, a reader should pay particular attention to the tangency of stable (attracting) and unstable (repelling) directions at saddle nodes; to obtain intermittency, the system must be nudged to near-tangency. "When the saddle nodes vanish, indicating loss of entrainment, the coordination system tends to stay near the previously stable fixed point. It's as though the fixed point leaves behind a remnant or a phantom of itself that still affects the overall dynamical behavior. . . . Motion hovers around the ghost of the previously stable fixed point most of the time, but occasionally escapes along the repelling direction (phase wandering)" (Kelso, 1995, p. 109).

7   In section 6.2 we discussed simulations of Shastri and Ajjanagadde (1993) that made use of synchrony to effect variable binding. In their simulation synchrony did not emerge spontaneously, but was created by the way in which connections were engineered. An important feature of the van Leeuwen et al. simulation is that synchrony emerges from the local activities of the components.

8   As the commentaries to van Gelder's (1998) paper make clear, there is considerable disagreement about the scope and definition of such terms as *computational, dynamical,* and *representation.* To keep the discussion manageable, we will focus on van Gelder's version.

9   Clark included a footnote to this last sentence beginning: "The phrase is memorable, but its authorship rather elusive."

10   In the words of van Gelder and Port (footnote 8, p. 40): "A more radical possibility is that dynamical systems can behave in a way that depends on knowledge without actually *representing* that knowledge by means of any particular, identifiable aspect of the system."

Sources and Suggested Readings

Abraham, R. H. and Shaw, C. D. (1992) *Dynamics: The Geometry of Behavior.* New York: Addison-Wesley.

Beer, R. D. (2000) Dynamical approaches to cognitive science. *Trends in Cognitive Sciences,* 4, 91–9.

Devaney, R. (1986) *An Introduction to Chaotic Dynamical Systems.* New York: Addison-Wesley.

Gleick, J. (1987) *Chaos: Making a New Science.* New York: Viking Penguin.

Horgan, T. and Tienson, J. (1996) *Connectionism and the Philosophy of Psychology.* Cambridge, MA: MIT Press.

Kellert, S. H. (1993) *In the Wake of Chaos.* Chicago: University of Chicago Press.

Kelso, J. A. S. (1995) *Dynamic Patterns: The Self-organization of Brain and Behavior.* Cambridge, MA: MIT Press.

Port, R. and van Gelder, T. (eds) (1995) *Mind as Motion.* Cambridge, MA: MIT Press. (See especially chapter 1 by van Gelder and Port, and chapter 2 by Norton.)

Waldrop, M. M. (1992) *Complexity: The Emerging Science at the Edge of Order and Chaos.* New York: Simon and Schuster.

9

NETWORKS, ROBOTS, AND ARTIFICIAL LIFE

9.1 Robots and the Genetic Algorithm

9.1.1 The robot as an artificial lifeform

In previous chapters we have seen that connectionist networks are adept at recognizing patterns and satisfying soft constraints. The pattern-recognition capability is useful for a variety of tasks, including visual perception, categorization, language, and even logical reasoning. The constraint-satisfaction capability can serve an equally diverse range of functions, such as controlling motor behavior, making decisions, and solving such classic problems as finding optimal routes for a traveling salesperson. A single network can combine both capabilities. For example, sensory information presented on an input layer can be interpreted on hidden layers as indicating the location of an object in a room. This information can then be used to generate appropriate motor commands on an output layer. A network like this knows how to locate and move to an object in a room – a simple but essential sensorimotor achievement. If yoked to a mechanical body and provided with a learning procedure, this sensorimotor network yields a very interesting device: a robot that can use experience to improve its own functioning. We have already encountered some elements of such a device in section 8.3.1, where the robot controllers designed by Beer (1995) were our first encounter with a newly emerging research area known as *artificial life* or *A-Life*. In the current chapter we will sample other exemplars of this line of research and consider benefits, limitations, and implications.

For connectionist modelers, embodying networks in robots can be envisioned as bringing some appealing benefits:

- If learning can be made to rely on consequences produced in the environment by the robot's actions, these embodied networks will learn much more naturally than the usual stand-alone networks provided with predetermined input–output pairings by a teacher.
- Placing networks in robots can be viewed as distributing the tasks of cognition beyond the internal cognitive systems (the networks) by coupling them to an environment. Sharing the cognitive burden in this way ought to reduce the load on the networks themselves (Clark, 1997a).

- Confronting the practical problems involved in making a robot perceive and act in an environment reminds us that these sensorimotor abilities are foundational to other cognitive performance. In real organisms, perception and action are major foci of early development and become effective, though still primitive, relatively quickly. In both phylogeny and ontogeny, systems seem to redeploy already-existing systems rather than building completely new ones, so it seems plausible that basic perceptual and motor systems provide computational frameworks which can be re-utilized in the evolution and development of higher cognitive capacities. (This essentially Piagetian point is modified, but not necessarily abandoned, by more recent investigators who would add certain conceptual, mnemonic, and other abilities to the inventory of foundational systems.)

This attractive picture has not yet been realized in its entirety. First, as always, advantages must be weighed against disadvantages. Building robots and training networks in them is expensive, in terms of both hardware and training time. Moreover, the fledgling attempts of a network to control the movements of a robot may produce serious damage to the physical robot. Some researchers sidestep these disadvantages, at the cost of weakening the advantages as well, by creating computer models in which simulated robots receive input and feedback from a simulated environment. Beer (1995) went even further by using the simulated robot body itself as the only environment in which the controller network functioned. (Recall that he used the simulated body's leg angle as the only source of sensory input to the network.) A second variation on the above picture pursued by many robot researchers, including Beer, is using simulated evolution as a method of developing networks in addition to (or in place of) learning.

One obvious advantage of the simulated evolution strategy is that it overcomes an unrealistic feature of most connectionist simulations: the networks start with random weights and must learn everything from scratch. Evolution can produce networks whose weights are fairly well adapted to their tasks prior to any experience. A second advantage is that the network architecture itself (not just the weights) can be allowed to evolve. Simulated evolution may even produce useful network configurations that would not be discovered by human designers (Harvey, Husbands, and Cliff, 1993).

9.1.2   The genetic algorithm for simulated evolution

Studies of simulated evolution generally rely on some version of the *genetic algorithm*, which was developed by John Holland (1975/1992) to explore the nature of adaptive systems (also see the textbook by Goldberg, 1989). Holland sought to simulate three processes that are critical to biological evolution: an inheritance mechanism that can produce offspring that resemble their parents, a procedure for introducing variability into the reproductive process, and differential reproduction. In the standard picture of biological evolution, the inheritance mechanism involves chromosomes (composed of genes), variability is achieved when genes recombine (an advantage of sexual reproduction) or mutate, and differential reproduction is caused by natural selection. (Alternatives to this standard picture have been proposed; for example, Gould and Lewontin, 1979, claim that differential reproduction sometimes is due to developmental constraints rather than external selection forces operating on the organism.)

In the genetic algorithm, strings of symbols play the role of chromosomes, operations such as recombination and mutation of these symbols are employed to introduce variation when the strings reproduce, and the fitness function governs selective reproduction by determining which strings are successful enough to be allowed to reproduce. The genetic algorithm applies recursively to produce a succession of generations. In each generation the most successful strings are selected to be parents, a new generation of strings is created by copying them (recombining or mutating the copies to introduce new variability), the offspring in turn undergo appraisal of their fitness, and those selected become parents of yet another generation. For example, in simulated evolution of an immune system (Forrest, Javornik, Smith, and Perelson, 1993), the evolving strings encode antibodies, and the fitness function evaluates how well each such string matches a specific antigen (represented by a string that does not evolve). In the case of connectionist networks (e.g., Belew, McInerney, and Schraudolph, 1991), a simple choice is to evolve strings of connection weights, but more interesting simulations are discussed below.

The new research area of artificial life is not limited to explorations of real and simulated robots and the evolution of networks to control them. Its general goal is to understand biological systems and processes. Its method is simulation, usually by means of computer programs. It can be carried out at a variety of levels (from individual cells or neural circuits to organisms to populations) and timescales (from that of metabolic processes to ontogenesis to phylogenesis). Robots are artificial organisms that operate at the timescale of individual actions or action sequences; networks are artificial nervous systems within these organisms and operate at the timescale of propagation of activation across connections or layers of connections. Artificial life researchers have investigated these plus much more. Before presenting a few specific studies of network controllers for robots, we will take a brief look at other research strategies in artificial life and how they have been applied in exploring very simple abstract organisms.

9.2   Cellular Automata and the Synthetic Strategy

Artificial life is related to biology somewhat as artificial intelligence (AI) is related to psychology. Psychology focuses on cognitive processes and behavior exhibited by actual organisms, whereas AI separates cognitive processes from their realization in living organisms. AI researchers have done this by constructing computer systems that function intelligently. Likewise, biology focuses on carbon-based life on earth, whereas artificial life separates the processes of life from their carbon-based realization. Like AI, artificial life relies on computers, but this time to simulate living systems and their evolution. Since behavior and cognitive processes are among the activities of living systems, the boundary between artificial life and AI is not rigid.

9.2.1   Langton's vision: The synthetic strategy

Christopher Langton is perhaps the person most responsible for having brought a body of research together under the label "artificial life" (partly by organizing a five-day Artificial Life Workshop at Los Alamos in 1987). He emphasizes the idea that artificial life, like AI, adopts a synthetic approach to understanding the evolution and operation of living systems: researchers build simulated systems out of already-identified components and see what emerges from their operation. In contrast, biologists (and psychologists) primarily take the analytic approach of decomposition and localization in their investigations of naturally occurring systems: starting with a real organism, they figure out what component processes are involved in its functioning and where in the system each process is carried out. Langton writes:

> *Artificial Life is simply the synthetic approach to biology: rather than take living things apart, Artificial Life attempts to put things together....* Thus, for example, Artificial Life involves attempts to (1) synthesize the process of evolution (2) in computers, and (3) will be interested in whatever emerges from the process, even if the results have no analogues in the natural world. (Langton, 1996, p. 40)

Langton's third point follows from what it means to adopt a synthetic strategy. Elementary processes, characteristics, rules, or constraints are first identified by following an analytic strategy in particular species or bodily systems. Once identified, however, they can be put together strategically. For example, an artificial life researcher may build abstract organisms – hypothetical beings that are intended to simulate life at a certain level (the organism) and degree of complexity (usually low) but are not necessarily intended to represent any particular species. The designer can experiment with these abstract organisms by subjecting them to simulated evolution, placing them in a variety of simulated environments, changing certain rules or processes, varying values of parameters, and so forth.

As useful as the synthetic strategy has been in both AI and artificial life, not all investigators would agree with Langton that it is defining of their field. Some view their artificial systems first and foremost as models of some actual system. In AI, for example, the competing pulls between analysis and synthesis can be seen in the fact that some computer programs are constructed to play chess like a human and others are constructed to play chess well. Currently, the programs that play chess well enough to sometimes defeat grand masters do so by following search trees much more deeply than is possible for their human opponents. The computer and human are fairly well matched in skill, but differ in their means. At what point is the difference so great that the program no longer qualifies as an exemplar of a synthetic investigation into intelligence and instead should be viewed simply as a feat of engineering? And how can good use be made of both the (relatively analytic) program that seeks to closely simulate human processes and the (relatively synthetic) program that is only loosely inspired by them?

We can see how the same tension between analysis and synthesis appears in artificial life research by considering Reynolds (1987). To simulate flocking behavior, he constructed a simple model environment and a number of simple, identical artificial organisms (*boids*). In a given simulation run, the boids were placed at different random starting locations in the environment. All moved at the same time but each boid individually applied the same simple rules: match your neighbors' velocities; move towards their apparent center of mass; and maintain a minimum distance from neighbors and obstacles. Viewing the boids' movements in the aggregate, they exhibited flocking behavior – an emergent behavior in which, for example, the group would divide into subgroups to flow around both sides of an obstacle and then regroup. Note that boids are so sketchily drawn that they can stand in for fish as well as birds. Reynolds's work is probably best viewed as a rather abstract investigation into achieving global behavior from simultaneously acting local rules (synthetic strategy), but it could arguably be viewed instead as an initial step towards obtaining a realistic simulation of behaviors observed in several actual species (analytic strategy).

Despite this tension, the synthetic and analytic strategies share the same ultimate goal: to understand the processes of life. This goal imposes its own constraint that the abstract beings must have some grounding in important characteristics of real beings, a grounding that is provided by biologists who have observed the behavior of particular species. The results of synthetic research, in turn, will sometimes suggest new avenues for analytic research. For example, a study like that of Reynolds (relatively synthetic) could suggest particular variables to measure in real birds (purely analytic), and the results might contribute to a more detailed, realistic computer model (relatively analytic). The same interplay of research strategies can be observed in investigations of such activities as perception, food-finding, mating, predation, and communication, all of which have been studied by artificial life researchers as well as biologists in the field. (For an overview of such studies as well as many other kinds of research and issues in artificial life, see the volume edited by Langton, 1995.)

9.2.2   Emergent structures from simple beings: Cellular automata

Perhaps the most abstract studies in artificial life are those involving *cellular automata* – formal systems that were conceived by the Polish mathematician Stanislas Ulam. A cellular automaton (CA) consists of a lattice (a network of cells in which only neighbors are connected) for which each cell is a finite automaton – a simple formal machine that has a finite number of discrete states and changes state on each time-step in accord with a *rule table* (sometimes called a *state transition table*). A CA is defined in part by the size of its neighborhoods. For example, in a one-dimensional CA (a row of cells) the neighborhood of each cell might be the cell itself plus two cells on each side. For each possible configuration of states in a neighborhood there is a rule stipulating the updated state of the target cell on the next time-step. (This should sound familiar: the CA is the same kind of device as a coupled map lattice, used in van Leeuwen et al.'s model of shifting perceptions in section 8.4.2, except that each unit in a CML takes continuous states via the logistic equation rather than the discrete states of a finite automaton.)

The operation of a CA can be illustrated using a one-dimensional array of ten cells, each of which can take just two states: *off* or *on*. We can stipulate that a neighborhood includes only the cell itself and one cell to each side, and that the leftmost and rightmost cells count as neighbors to each other. Then there will be just eight possible kinds of neighborhoods (eight different configurations of states for a cell and its neighbors). For each of them we enter a rule in the table to show which state its target cell should enter on the next time-step. Using the numerals *0* for *off* and *1* for *on*, here is one rule table:

cell and neighbors at t	111	110	101	100	011	010	001	000
cell at $t+1$	0	1	1	0	1	0	0	1

The behavior of any CA is determined solely by the initial pattern of states across its cells and its rule table. For our example, suppose that at time-step 0 the states

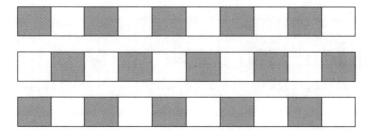

Figure 9.1 A simple outcome of using the rule table in the text. A one-dimensional cellular automaton with ten cells is shown at time-step 1 (top) and at two successive time-steps. Empty cells are on; shaded cells are off.

(a)   (b)

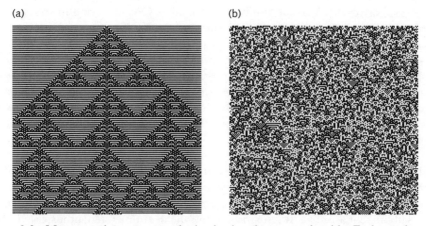

Figure 9.2 More complex outcomes obtained using the same rule table. Each panel shows a one-dimensional cellular automaton with 200 cells at 200 time-steps; each row displays the state of each cell on one time-step. In panel (a) the initial pattern had just one cell *on*, whereas in panel (b) the initial pattern had half of the cells *on* (randomly selected). Figures 9.1 and 9.2 were generated using the cellular automata simulator at http://alife.santafe.edu/alife/topics/ca/caweb/.

happen to form an alternating pattern in which every other cell is *on*, as shown in figure 9.1. Just two of the eight rules will be relevant for this simple case. Each *on* cell (shaded) is flanked by neighbors that are *off* (empty), so at time-step 1 it will turn *off* (*010 → 0*); and each *off* cell is flanked by neighbors that are *on*, so at time-step 1 it will turn *on* (*101 → 1*). The first three time-steps are displayed; clearly this array will keep switching between the *on–off–on–off–* . . . and the *off–on–off–on–* . . . patterns indefinitely.

   A great variety of patterns across time can be obtained – many of which are more complex than this repeated switching between two alternating patterns – even without changing to a new rule table. For example, trying two different initial patterns with a larger CA (one row of 200 cells) yields two quite different patterns through time as shown in figure 9.2. (Starting with time-step 0 at the top, each line represents the pattern at the next time-step; the displays were made square by ending at time-step 200.) An initial pattern with just one cell *on* generates the interesting display on the left; one with half the cells *on* generates the more chaotic display on

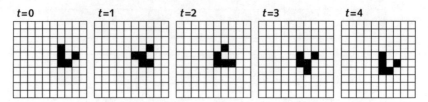

Figure 9.3 A glider in the Game of Life (see text for the rules used to generate it). On every fourth time-step the original shape is restored, but has moved one square left and one square down.

the right. These results were obtained using the CA simulator at <u>http://alife.santafe. edu/ alife/topics/ca/caweb/</u>. You can use it to create other CAs (differing in size and rule tables) and explore how different initial patterns change through time.

Cellular automata need not be limited to a single dimension. One of the best-known exemplars is the Game of Life, developed by John Conway (see Gardner, 1970) and used in many screensaver programs. In the Game of Life a computer screen is divided into a large grid of squares. Initially, some squares are shaded (alive) and the rest are empty (dead). Each square has eight neighbors (including those on the diagonals). As time proceeds different squares come alive or die depending on two simple rules:

- If a square is dead on one time-step but has exactly three immediate neighbors that are alive, it comes alive on the next time-step; otherwise, it stays dead.
- If a square is alive on one time-step and has exactly two or three immediate neighbors that are alive, it remains alive on the next time-step; otherwise, it dies.

(Stating these rules in English efficiently summarizes the formal rule table for the 512 configurations that are possible for this size of neighborhood.) The Game of Life attracts attention due to the variety of shapes that can develop. For example, gliders are patterns which move across the screen. Figure 9.3 exhibits a glider which, after every fourth time-step, has moved one square down and one square left; in the intervening steps it transmogrifies into a variety of other forms. Since these shapes and movements are not prespecified in setting up the CA, they are generally construed as emergent structures (as were the movements of flocks of boids in the Reynolds study).

9.2.3　Wolfram's four classes of cellular automata

Different rule tables can yield very different activity, leading Stephen Wolfram (1984) to develop a general classification of cellular automata. Using CAs slightly more complex than those above (by increasing neighborhood size to two rather than one cell per side), exemplars of all four Wolfram classes can be found.

- *Class I automata* enter the same state (e.g., all dead or all alive) from almost any starting configuration, usually in just a few time-steps. If the second line of the rule table in 9.2.2 contained only *0*s, then no matter how many squares were initially alive, they would all become dead on time-step 1 and remain dead. In DST terms, the system settles on a *point attractor* (limit point).

- *Class II automata* form at least one nonhomogeneous pattern (e.g., some squares are alive and others are dead). Typically the system, once beyond any transient patterns, exhibits periodic behavior. That is, it repeatedly cycles through the same sequence of patterns (if the cycle length is zero it will settle to a single static pattern). In DST terms, the system has a *periodic attractor* (limit cycle). Figure 9.1 provides a simple example.

- *Class III automata* are disordered rather than orderly. They exhibit quasi-random sequences of patterns which (were it not for their finiteness) correspond to what is known as *chaos* in DST. The display on the right side of figure 9.2 appears chaotic or near-chaotic.

- *Class IV automata* are the most interesting. They exhibit complex behaviors (e.g., expanding, splitting, recombining) that may be interpreted as realizations of self-organization or computation. Some dynamicists call this *complexity* in contrast to *chaos*. The Game of Life exemplifies this class (see figure 9.3), and van Leeuwen et al.'s coupled map lattice (section 8.4.2), though not a CA, shows comparable behavior when parameter values are chosen so as to produce intermittency.

9.2.4   Langton and λ at the edge of chaos

Christopher Langton (1990) proposed that different values of a parameter, λ, would tend to correspond to different Wolfram classes. Although he explored two-dimensional CAs with 8 states, in our simpler examples λ is simply the proportion of rules in the rule table that have a *1* in the second row; it indicates the potential for cells to be *on* at the next time-step. Langton identified key ranges of values by conducting a Monte Carlo exploration (that is, he generated and ran a large number of CAs varying in λ and initial patterns). There was a great deal of variability in the results, but he sought to capture "average behavior" by calculating several statistics across the CAs tested at each λ. With very small λ, Class I automata tend to occur; when raised towards 0.2, Class II automata emerge. With λ in a range of approximately 0.2 to 0.4, the complex Class IV automata predominate, but as it is raised to values surrounding 0.5 order breaks down and chaotic Class III automata become predominant. Langton referred to the range in which λ tends to produce Class IV automata as *critical values* that are at *the edge of chaos* and proposed that these CAs could be used to perform interesting computations. Since the distributions in fact overlap considerably, a value of λ in the critical range can only suggest that a particular CA is likely to exhibit Class IV behavior; independent evidence would be needed to actually classify it.

    The interest in Class IV CAs goes beyond the fact that they can create interesting novel patterns; Langton inspired other researchers to explore their usefulness for computation and problem solving. Norman Packard (1988) focused on a rule table that had earlier been found to perform a useful (though approximate) computation. If more than half of the automaton's cells were *on* initially, usually all of its cells turned *on* eventually (requiring many time-steps, in which the configurations used to determine state updates included three neighbors on each side). If more than half were *off* initially, usually all of its cells turned *off* eventually. If about half were *on* and half *off*, its eventual configuration was less predictable. Hence, it acted as a fairly reliable detector of which state predominated in its own initial pattern – a global property captured via local computations. Packard's innovation was to use a genetic algorithm to evolve additional rule tables that could perform this task. Since the first row of the table has a fixed ordering of neighborhoods for a given number of states (he used 2) and neighbors (he used 3 on each side), CAs could be evolved using genotypes that explicitly represented only the states on the next time-step (the $2^7 =$ 128 binary digits in the second row of the the the table). A simpler example of a genotype can be obtained from the rule table in section 9.2.2, which has just 8 binary digits due to the smaller neighborhood size:

$$0\ 1\ 1\ 0\ 1\ 0\ 0\ 1$$

The fitness function was provided by the success of the many CAs that evolved (i.e., whether they correctly determined that the initial proportion of active cells was greater than or less than 0.5). Packard was especially interested in the fitness of rule tables with λ in Langton's region of complexity (centered around 0.25 or, on the other side of the chaotic region, around 0.80). He found that they indeed (on average) were best suited to perform the computation.

Packard interpreted his findings as supporting Langton's proposal that interesting computations (class IV automata) emerge in the critical region he identified for λ. However, there is more to the story. A research team at the Santa Fe Institute (Melanie Mitchell, James Crutchfield, and Peter Hraber, 1994) later evolved CAs to perform the same computation, but used a more standard implementation of the genetic algorithm. Contrary to Packard, they found that rule tables with λ values not far from 0.5 performed best and provided a theoretical argument as to why this would have to be the case. While granting that some interesting CAs such as the Game of Life do have λ values in the range Langton identified, they offered their findings as an existence proof against "a generic relationship between λ and computational ability in CA" and concluded there was "no evidence that an evolutionary process with computational capability as a fitness goal will preferentially select CAs at a special λ_c [critical λ] region." They did not, however, deny that relatively simple CAs are characteristic at the extremes of the λ range nor did they evaluate rule tables for other kinds of computation in that paper. In their more recent work (e.g., Crutchfield, Mitchell, and Das, 1998), this team has continued simulated evolution studies of CAs but have focused on applying a computational mechanics framework and a variety of refined quantitative analyses to obtaining "a high-level description of the computationally relevant parts of the system's behavior" (p. 40). This leaves Langton's intriguing proposal about λ as a possible evolutionary dead-end in understanding CAs.

We will end our brief discussion of cellular automata here; it should have given the flavor of the more abstract end of artificial life research. We must skip over a great deal of work in the mid-range of biological realism and complexity, leaving Reynolds's boids as our one example. The rest of the chapter will focus on the evolution of connectionist networks rather than CAs, beginning in section 9.3 with networks that simulate simple food-seeking organisms (which learn as well as evolve) and progressing in 9.4 to network controllers for robots (which develop phenotypes as well as evolve). Robot controllers were our entry point to the science of artificial life in sections 8.3.1 and 9.1, and we look at one additional robot project in 9.5. Finally we return to philosophical issues and implications in 9.6.

9.3   Evolution and Learning in Food-seekers

9.3.1   Overview and study 1: Evolution without learning

If you wish to use networks to control sensorimotor behavior in artificial organisms more complex than cellular automata, how do you get a network that does a good job? A talented designer may quickly arrive at a network that works well for a particular environment and task, but what if some aspect changes? Including a learning procedure has been the traditional way to make networks adaptive. Artificial life research using the genetic algorithm suggests that simulated evolution is another route to adaptivity that is worth exploring. We have already been introduced to the intersection between connectionist networks and artificial life techniques in the work of Beer (section 8.3.1). Here we see how including both kinds of adaptivity in networks simulating simple food-seeking organisms has produced a better understanding of how learning across the lives of organisms can actually have an impact on the evolutionary process. This line of research began with Hinton and Nowlan (1987) and was further pursued by Ackley and Littman (1992) and by Stefano Nolfi and his collaborators. We will sample it in this section by presenting two simulation studies on abstract organisms (Nolfi, Elman, and Parisi, 1994), and then in section 9.4 we will track Nolfi's move to related work with robot controllers (Nolfi, Miglino, and Parisi, 1994).

Nolfi, Elman, and Parisi (hereafter called NolfiEP) invented simple abstract organisms that evolved and learned to traverse a landscape with scattered food sites. Each of these food-seekers was simulated using a very simple connectionist network which encoded and linked a limited repetoire of sensations and motor behaviors. Each network's architecture was fixed but its connection weights were adjusted in the course of learning and evolution. It had four input units: two sensory units encoded the angle and distance of the nearest food site, and two proprioceptive units specified which action the organism had just performed. These two kinds of information were sent through the network's seven hidden units in order to determine which action would be performed next, and the decision was encoded on two output units. After applying a threshold, there were just four possible actions: turn right (01), turn left (10), move forward one cell (11), or stay still (00). NolfiEP's first simulation (study 1) used this architecture for all of its networks. In a second simulation (study 2; see section 9.3.2), two additional output units were added whose task was to predict the next sensory input. The expanded version of the network is shown in figure 9.4, but we will begin with study 1 and the network without the prediction units.

There is another difference between the two studies. In study 1, improvements in food-finding behavior were achieved exclusively by simulated evolution. The main goal was to show that purposive behavior could be sculpted from initially random behavior by applying a genetic algorithm across generations. In study 2, there was another source of change in addition to evolution: learning was used across the lifespan of each organism to modify three of the four sets of connection weights. Here the main goal was to explore how learning and evolution might interact.

An initial population of 100 organisms was created for study 1 by randomly assigning weights to the connections in 100 otherwise identical networks (four input

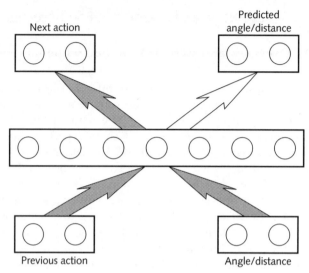

Figure 9.4   The network used by Nolfi, Elman, and Parisi (1994) to simulate abstract food-seeking organisms. Each large arrow is a complete set of connections between units. The three shaded arrows indicate which layers and connections made up the network used in study 1: based on sensory information and the organism's previous action, the next action is determined. The additional output units for predicting the next sensory inputs were added to the network in study 2.

units, seven hidden units, two output units). Each organism lived for 20 epochs, during which it navigated its own copy of a 10 cell × 10 cell environment in which 10 of the 100 cells contained food. In each epoch it performed 50 actions in each of 5 environments (differing in which cells were randomly assigned to contain food); at the end of its life the number of food squares it had encountered was summed. Organisms in this initial generation tended to perform poorly. For example, a typical trajectory in one of these environments, as indicated by the dotted line in figure 9.5, included just one food encounter. Nonetheless, the 20 organisms who happened to acquire the most food were allowed to reproduce. Reproduction was asexual (five copies were made of each organism), and variation was introduced by mutation (in each copy, five randomly chosen weights were altered by a randomly chosen amount). By the tenth generation, the organisms had evolved sufficiently to find many more food squares, with more gradual improvement thereafter. The solid line in figure 9.5 shows a typical path traversed by an organism in the fiftieth (last) generation. In contrast to the earlier path, this one looks purposive. NolfiEP emphasized the importance of achieving lifelike, goal-directed behavior by means of a lifelike, evolutionary process. While acknowledging certain simplifications in their method (e.g., asexual copying of complete networks rather than sexual reproduction with crossover of the genetic codes governing the construction of networks), they found simulated evolution to be a successful and biologically plausible tool for developing networks. They particularly appreciated the biological plausibility of this technique compared to the standard network development technique of supervised learning. Nature provides variation and selection but no explicit teachers.

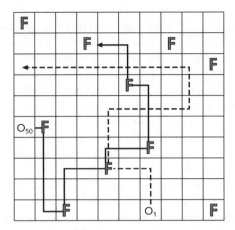

Figure 9.5 Typical trajectories through the 10 × 10 environments of the model organism in Nolfi, Elman, and Parisi's (1994) study 1. The dotted line is a trajectory for a model organism in the first generation; it encountered just one food site. The solid line is a trajectory for a model organism in the fiftieth generation, which encountered six food sites.

9.3.2 The Baldwin effect and study 2: Evolution with learning

Are any roles left, then, for learning? Nolfi and Parisi (1997) discussed three. At the very least, learning augments evolution by permitting adaptations to environmental changes that occur too quickly for an evolutionary response. Learning also enables flexibility, because behavior can be determined by more information than could be encoded in the genome. However, in both of these roles, learning is essentially an add-on that enhances individual performance but does not interact with the evolutionary process. More intriguing is the possibility of a third role for learning: to *guide* evolution. This idea was given its most direct and extreme interpretation in Lamarckian evolution – the discredited nineteenth-century claim that acquired characteristics become directly incorporated in the genome and can be inherited in the next generation. A more indirect way for learning to have an impact on evolution was first suggested by James Mark Baldwin (1896). The basic idea is that successful learners will also be successful breeders, and this source of selection will subtly push evolution in an appropriate direction; across many generations, the genome itself will move towards variations that originally relied on learning. This *Baldwin effect* has been accepted for decades as consistent with a contemporary Darwinian framework, but was often overlooked or misinterpreted. However, Hinton and Nowlan (1987) revived interest by achieving the effect in connectionist networks undergoing simulated evolution and sketching a neat computational interpretation of this heretofore obscure corner of evolutionary theory. They limited their investigation to an extreme case in which only one specific set of weights could render the organism adapted, and all others were maladaptive.

Study 2 in NolfiEP explored how learning could guide evolution by expanding on both the simulations and the computational interpretation pioneered by Hinton and Nowlan. They first added two output units to the original network architecture, as we already have seen in figure 9.4. These units were designed to *predict* the sensory outcome of making the movement encoded on the other two output units – that is, the new angle and distance of the nearest food site. The other major design decision was to make the weights of the connections leading into these new units modifiable by backpropagation. If learning has been successful, the predicted angle/distance should be the same as the actual angle/distance presented to the input units on the next time-step. This allowed for a learning scheme in which the desired or target output pattern need not be supplied by an external teacher, because it is available from the environment as soon as the organism makes its intended movement. That is, the difference between the predicted and actual angle/distance of the nearest food is used as the error signal for learning. Because backpropagation allocates error back through the network, this scheme modifies the weights for all connections except those linking the hidden units to the two original output units for the next action (which have no way of getting a desired action for comparison). Nolfi et al. applied this learning procedure during the life cycle of each organism, and organisms were selected for reproduction in the same manner as in study 1: at the end of each generation's lifespan, the 20 organisms who found the most food were allowed to reproduce. The offspring were created by copying and mutating the *original* weights of the parents, not those acquired by learning. Hence, there was no Lamarckian inheritance of acquired characteristics.

NolfiEP were investigating whether learning might play a useful role in guiding evolution, and their results indicated that it could. Learning during the lifetime of the organisms led to much better performance in later generations – by a factor of two compared with non-learning lineages – even though the descendants could not benefit directly from that learning. NolfiEP's explanation of how selective reproduction and learning interact to produce better organisms in this situation is that learning provides a means for determining which organisms would most likely benefit from random mutations on their weights. An organism that gains from learning is one with a set of initial weights which, if changed somewhat, produce even better results. That would tend to put the good learners into the group selected (based on good performance) to reproduce. By comparison, an organism that does not gain from learning is one whose weights are such that small changes will not produce any benefits. That organism may have found a local minimum in weight space (see figures 3.1 and 3.3). If so, small changes in weights – whether produced by learning or evolutionary changes – will not bring further benefits. Hence, including learning in the life histories of the organisms yields information that permits the evolutionary devices of variation and selection to operate more effectively. NolfiEP's work provides a novel explanation of the Baldwin effect by obtaining it in networks that evolve.

There is another aspect of the interaction between learning and evolution that is noteworthy. Evolution imposes needs on the organism, and learning has improved the organism's ability to satisfy those needs. While labeling the task *food searching* is simply an interpretation, since the organism gains nothing from the food squares in this simplified simulation, nonetheless, the task of visiting certain squares is imposed on the organism by the selection procedure. The fact that learning to predict the environment serves to promote this end is behavioral evidence that visiting food squares has become the goal for the organisms. The activation patterns on the hidden units can be viewed as providing representations of the environment. In the learning task these representations enable the organism to better predict its future sensory input; in the evolutionary task, they permit it to better secure food. Since learning one task (predicting the future appearance of the environment) enhances performance on the other (finding and acquiring food), the representations must carry information that is relevant to both tasks.

We can understand how this might be possible by considering a situation in which the nearest food location is at an angle of 90°. This is information that should lead both to a decision to turn right and to an expectation that after one does, the food will be at approximately 0°. Both the outputs specifying actions and those predicting future angle/distance of food depend upon grouping the input patterns into similarity groups. This is a function served by the hidden units, so the same similarity groups will be available to subserve both tasks. It is in this way that learning to perform one task can facilitate an organism's performance of another task.

9.4   Evolution and Development in Khepera

9.4.1   Introducing Khepera

Ideally, the interaction of evolution and learning would be studied in a less abstract organism than the food-seekers just discussed. Two of the above investigators joined with another collaborator to take a step forward in complexity by developing networks to control a tiny mobile robot called Khepera (Nolfi, Miglino, and Parisi, 1994; hereafter called NolfiMP). As shown in figure 9.6, it was equipped with physical sensors and motor mechanisms and hence could navigate an actual environment (a 60 × 35 cm arena with walls and a small circular target area). For practical reasons, though, NolfiMP developed the control networks using a simulation of the robot in its environment. (In other studies they addressed the question of how such simulations could be applied to developing controllers for real robots; see below.)

Khepera has a diameter of 55 mm (about 2 inches) and is supported by two wheels and two teflon balls. Each wheel is driven by a small motor that allows it to rotate forwards or backwards. Khepera also has eight pairs of sensors. The light sensors can detect lit-up areas at a range of distances, and the infrared sensors can detect obstacles (objects or walls) in close proximity by bouncing their own light off them. As diagrammed in figure 9.6, there are six front and two rear pairs of sensors. They influence Khepera's movements by means of whatever internal control network is provided. An engineer could quickly design such a network, but then Khepera would be just another robot (one with little practical skill) rather than a simulated lifeform. The real interest is in watching the control networks emerge via lifelike processes of simulated evolution and learning, in pursuit of an ultimate goal of better understanding real evolution and learning. NolfiMP's decision to use a simulated rather than physical robot added another degree of removal from this ultimate goal, but it allowed them the freedom to make some other aspects of their study more complex than would otherwise be practicable.

NolfiMP prepared for their simulation by using the physical robot to generate a pool of sensory inputs and a pool of motor outputs. That is, first they placed Khepera in different orientations and locations in the physical arena, producing a systematic sample of states on its sensors in which the walls and target area would be seen from different angles and distances. Then they gave Khepera's two motors different combinations of commands and recorded its movements. The resulting pools of information were used in constructing a simulated world in which the task was to move towards the small target area in the arena. Simulated evolution and learning

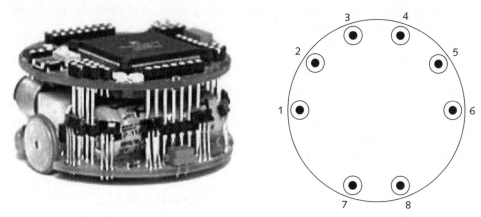

Figure 9.6   The Khepera robot and a diagram showing the locations of its sensors. The filled circles represent the infrared sensors used to detect objects, while the open circles represent light sensors.

interacted to develop networks which adaptively linked the sensory and motor patterns so as to perform this target-seeking task. (Given a different task, the same sensory inputs would get linked differently, though still systematically, to motor outputs – the robot might avoid the target area rather than seek it, for example.)

9.4.2   The development of phenotypes from genotypes

NolfiMP's primary innovation in this particular study was to develop a more biologically realistic model of how a genotype (the design specifications inherited in the genes) figures in the development of a phenotype (the actual organism that results from applying those specifications). In previous studies using networks as artificial organisms, the genotype specified a single phenotypic network. If the network then changed its architecture or weights due to learning in its environment, the genotype played no further role in guiding the resulting series of phenotypes. NolfiMP, in contrast, made the genotype active throughout the life of the organism. Because both genotype and environment influenced the developing network (a series of phenotypes), the same genotype could manifest itself differently in different environments.

In order to create this more biologically realistic genotype–phenotype relationship, NolfiMP used "genes" (structure-building instructions) to produce "neurons" (units) with "axons" (potential connections) that gradually grew into a "nervous system" (neural network). Key points in this process are illustrated in figure 9.7 and described below. The full set of genes – the genotype – ensures that each nervous system is limited to feedforward connections and has a maximum of 17 internal neurons (hidden units, which may be arranged in a maximum of 7 layers), 10 sensory neurons, and 5 motor neurons. Whether a given neuron becomes part of the mature nervous system (i.e., becomes functionally connected within a path from sensory to motor neurons) is determined by the interaction of the robot's genotype and its experiences.

The genotype contains a separate block of genes for each of the 32 possible neurons. Some of the genes specify basic information about the neuron: its location

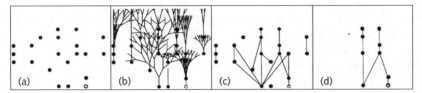

Figure 9.7   An evolved network controller for the Khepera robot at four stages of development: (a) the initial 21 neurons; (b) the growth of branching axons; (c) the network after it has been pruned to leave only the connections where the axon had made contact with another neuron; (d) the functional network. Adapted from Nolfi, Miglino, and Parisi (1994).

in a two-dimensional Euclidean space (suggestive of a vertical slice through a cortical column in a real brain), the weight on any connections to units above it, and its threshold or bias. Additionally, each sensory neuron has a gene specifying to which sensor it is to be connected and whether it detects ambient light or obstacles, and each motor neuron has a gene specifying whether it should be connected to the motor for the left or right wheel. (If more than one motor unit is connected to a given motor, the behavior of the motor is determined by averaging the activations of these units.) Finally, the most interesting genes code for the growth of axons that may connect to other neurons.

Carrying out the basic instructions produces up to nine layers of neurons; the nascent network in figure 9.7(a) has 21 neurons in eight layers. Those in the outer layers are connected to the robot's sensors (at bottom; not shown) or motors (at top; not shown), but initially none of the neurons are connected to other neurons. The genes that encode growth give each neuron the potential to send out an axon which may branch up to four times. One gene specifies the length of each branch and another specifies the angle at which it branches. Realizing this potential depends on experience. The rest of figure 9.7 shows the consequences of applying these instructions and experiential constraints:

Figure 9.7(b):   Depending upon the genetic instructions, the branching can yield a sweeping arborization extending up through several layers (e.g., that of the leftmost sensory neuron) or instead can yield arborizations that are narrower and/or shorter. Not all neurons send out an axon, however; this is governed by the expression threshold gene in interaction with experience. If this gene's value is 0, an axon will sprout immediately (maturation with no need for learning). Otherwise, it specifies a threshold value for the variability of the neuron's last ten activation values, which must be exceeded for an axon to sprout. Once axonal growth has begun, a new uncertainty arises: whether any of the branches will contact another neuron. If so, a connection is established.

Figure 9.7(c):   The details of axonal branching are omitted and each connection is indicated by a straight line. Some of the connections are nonfunctional, however, because they do not lie on a path extending all the way from the sensory to the motor layer.

Figure 9.7(d):   The isolated connections and neurons are omitted, leaving the functional part of the neural network. In this example, it includes just two sensory neurons (one of each type), four internal neurons in three different layers, and two motor neurons. It is the outcome of the joint activity of genes and environment in a single organism within a single generation. We refer to this as "learning" to distinguish it from evolution, but the word is a crude shorthand for a complex process by which a genotype in an environment creates a developmental series of phenotypes in which maturation and learning are intertwined.

9.4.3 The evolution of genotypes

Along with NolfiMP, we next turn our attention to evolution. To cultivate a population of simulated robots, they employed a strategy very similar to that used to cultivate food-seekers in the previous simulation. They began with 100 randomly generated genotypes, each of which was used to obtain one simulated Khepera. Each such robot lived for 10 epochs of 500 actions each; in each epoch, both the robot and the target area were placed in random locations in the arena and the robot produced actions that moved it through the arena. Under the joint influence of its genotype and the inputs it received through its sensors, the robot developed a specific network architecture and assignment of connection weights. The robot's fitness was determined in each epoch by its ability to reach the target area; it was calculated by summing the value of $500-N$ across all 10 epochs, where N is the number of actions the robot needed to reach the target the first time in an epoch. The 20 robots who achieved the greatest fitness in a given generation reproduced, creating 5 copies of their genotype (varied by random mutations). NolfiMP also alternated between "light" and "dark" environments. In even generations the robots were placed in an environment in which a light illuminated the target area; in odd generations the light was left off, thus reducing the usefulness of the light sensors.

By examining the best 20 individuals in each generation, NolfiMP were able to show that the robots exhibited considerable increases in fitness (between three- and four-fold) over the first 50 to 100 generations if analysis was limited to the even-numbered generations (light environment). Odd-numbered generations (dark environment) showed a much shallower fitness function (only a two-fold increase). NolfiMP then set out to evaluate the distinctive effects of learning in the two kinds of environment by examining mature phenotypes of the control network. To do this they allowed two clones with the same highly evolved genotype to develop in light and dark environments and compared the two networks that resulted (see figure 9.8). While there are some clear similarities between the networks produced by the same genotype, there are also impressive differences. The network that developed in the light environment came to rely on three infrared sensors and two light sensors, while the network that developed in the unlighted environment relied only on (the same) three obstacle sensors. There were also quite different patterns of connection from sensory neuron 2 to the motor neurons.

9.4.4 Embodied networks: Controlling real robots

We have been speaking of evolution and learning in many generations of robots, but recall that this was actually a simulation study that did not use the actual environment and physical robot after obtaining samples of its sensory and motor events.

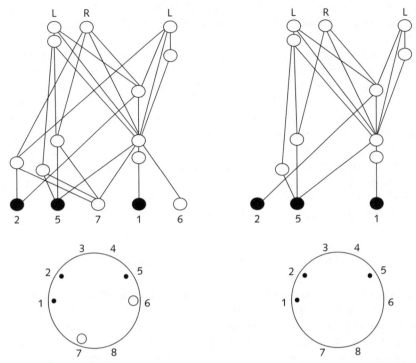

Figure 9.8   Two evolved network controllers cloned from the same genotype. The
controller on the left is from a robot that developed in a light environment, whereas
the controller on the right is from a robot that developed in a dark environment. Beneath
each controller is a depiction of the sensors that were active in each case.

Could a network developed by such simulation techniques be inserted into the
physical robot and succeed in controlling it? Nolfi, Floreano, Miglino, and Mondada
(1994) explored this question by evolving controllers using (a) real robots and environment, (b) simulated robots and environment, and (c) a hybrid strategy in which
controllers developed for simulated robots were inserted into real robots for the last
30 of a total of 330 generations. The robots again were Khepera, but the environment and tasks were a little different than those of Nolfi, Miglino, and Parisi and the
networks were simpler and did not learn. In the hybrid study, performance temporarily declined immediately after the network was transferred into a real robot, but
then quickly recovered. They noted several ways in which the simulation procedure
differed from the real one, and recommended the hybrid strategy as offering an
efficient way to get effective controllers.

   This last study brings us a step closer to reality. Unlike many artificial organisms,
Khepera is embodied. Though its controllers exist as computer code, the robot itself
has a physical body that registers light and takes actions in an actual arena. Sampling
these physical events lent a degree of realism to NolfiMP's computer simulation of
Khepera, but only by hooking the controller network into an actual robot would
completely realistic connections between particular sensory and motor patterns get
made. When a real Khepera makes a move, it will vary slightly from the planned
movement and what is seen next will depend upon the actual movement. By evolving networks in real robots and environments, we assure that they must cope with

constraints and variation that cannot be perfectly simulated. Work of this kind provides grounding for those studies that use simulated or hybrid strategies for evolving controllers.

Nonetheless, many aspects of life are still merely simulated in the studies using actual robots. The robot is itself a silicon model of a hypothetical organic being. Its controller simulates a real nervous system, the evolution of its controller simulates a simplified version of biological evolution, and its learning procedures are intended to simulate key properties of learning in real organisms. Langton's synthetic approach to understanding life brings tradeoffs between realism and the degree to which the investigator can manipulate the components of interest and interpret the results. The various studies by Nolfi and his colleagues make different choices about those tradeoffs, and the investigations of cellular automata are even more extreme in their preference for manipulability over realism. There is something to be learned from each of them, and more to be learned from comparing them.

9.5   The Computational Neuroethology of Robots

We have not yet discussed one of the major benefits of using artificial neural networks as robot controllers: investigators can analyze the behavior of their components in much the same manner as neuroscientists use cellular recordings to analyze the activities of individual neurons in real brains. This enables researchers to discover the mechanisms that determine the behavior of the robot in its environment. Such robot studies are part of the field of *computational neuroethology*, a term coined by Dave Cliff (1991). The corresponding studies of living organisms are situated in the parent field of *neuroethology*. (A complete account of the nomenclature and range of studies comprising computational neuroethology would be much more complex; for example, Randall Beer independently coined the term in presenting his studies of artificial insects, as did Walter Heiligenberg for his computer models of real animals.)

To exhibit the potential of this approach, Cliff, Harvey, and Husbands (1997) reported on studies they conducted on networks evolved to control robots moving about in rooms. The robot, the room, and for that matter the network (as usual) were simulated. The robot specifications include a cylindrical shape and three wheels – two in the front which drive it and one in the rear to provide stability. Each of the wheels can turn at five different speeds: full forward, half forward, off, half reverse, and full reverse. The robot has six tactile sensors: bumpers in front and rear and whiskers positioned partway forward and partway back on each side. It is also equipped with two photoreceptors, whose direction of view and angle of receptivity are under evolutionary control. The architecture of the controller networks was evolved through a variation on the genetic algorithm, with an evaluation procedure based on the ability of the robot to move rapidly to a predesignated part of its environment. This placed an emphasis on evolution of the photoreceptors to guide behavior. (No learning procedure was incorporated in these simulations.)

The networks that Cliff et al. evolved in this manner are rather complex, with many backward as well as forward connections. They noted that the networks were very different (better) than what would be created by a human engineer. To simplify the networks for purposes of analysis they removed from consideration all redundant connections and units with no outputs. (The genome itself determined which connections were actually present, in contrast to Nolfi et al.'s inclusion of developmental processes for that purpose as described in section 9.4.2.) They then performed the equivalent of multi-cell recording in real animals – that is, they recorded the activation level of a number of units (in fact, all of them) while the robot performed the activity of interest. To further simplify analysis, they eliminated from consideration those units that were largely inactive during the behavior. This still left a relatively complex network, but one much reduced from the original and in which it was possible to provide a (still complex) description of the flow of activation. To give the flavor, we quote just one portion of the analysis of one robot controller: "Initially, relatively high visual input to unit 6 excites unit 2, which inhibits unit 12, so units 12 and 13 stay inactive. Meanwhile, the effects of visual input arriving at unit 11 give a low-radius turn. Eventually, the robot turns towards the (dark) wall and the visual input falls, so unit 2 no longer inhibits units 12" (Cliff, Harvey, and Husbands, 1997, p. 140). They then commented on how such analysis is similar in character to the analysis one would give of a biological nervous system:

> The task of analysing an evolved neural-network robot controller is similar to the task of analysing a neuronal network in a real animal. The techniques we have employed bear some resemblance to those used in neuroethology, and they give broadly similar results: a causal mechanistic account of the processes by which perturbations in the system's inputs give rise to alteration in the system's outputs. That is, the internal mechanisms of the agent are not treated as a black box, and so it is possible to understand how the observed behaviour is generated.   (pp. 149–50)

In addition to a mechanistic analysis focusing on individual units, Cliff et al. also developed a quantitative dynamical analysis that revealed how one controller network, which turned out to be successful in many environments other than the one in which it was evolved, developed dynamical attractors which governed the network's behavior. Like Beer's analysis, this combination of mechanistic and dynamical analysis has the kinds of advantages we discussed in section 8.5.3. Because the analysis involved a much larger network, though, it is harder to extract a higher-level description of the mechanism.

9.6   When Philosophers Encounter Robots

The various research programs that we have surveyed in this chapter – most of which used the genetic algorithm to evolve cellular automata or network controllers for robots – fall broadly under the rubric of *artificial life*. Like the more established sciences, artificial life has attracted the attention of philosophers. Most see it as *raising* new philosophical questions (or new variations on traditional philosophical questions), but at least one (Daniel Dennett) sees it as offering a new method for *addressing* philosophical questions.

9.6.1   No Cartesian split in embodied agents?

For many who have cast a philosophical eye on work in artificial life, one of the most notable features is the emphasis placed on embodying cognitive agents and locating them in environments. For Wheeler (1996), this challenges one of the fundamental Cartesian splits – that between mind and world – that modern cognitivists have tended to accept. The other Cartesian split – Descartes' radical mind–body dualism – is rejected by both artificial-life and cognitive researchers, who generally agree that the mind is simply the activity of the brain. Thus, the axis on which the two clusters differ is that the mind is isolated from the world in cognitivism but coupled to the world in artificial life.

To pursue this distinction, cognitivists view the mind as involving operations over internal representations and develop models of this abstract kind of thinking without giving serious consideration to the ongoing activities of the host organism in its environment. They assume that some sort of interface to sensory transducers and motor effectors will provide links to the environment, but that incorporating these links is not crucial to developing a good cognitive model. In contrast, artificial-life researchers take as their starting point an organism situated in an environment. The primary function of internal processes is to use sensation to control action, so the Cartesian separation of mental processes from worldly events is avoided. If more abstract processes develop, it is assumed that their form and functioning would be influenced by the more basic sensorimotor processes; they would not be studied in isolation. Moreover, insofar as the internal control systems constantly engage with the physical body and environment (e.g., by receiving new sensory input as a result of moving the body), the last vestiges of the Cartesian scheme are overcome. Instead of a Cartesian scheme, Wheeler suggests that such artificial life embodies a Heideggerian perspective wherein agents begin by being actively engaged with their world through skills and practices; whatever cognitive reflection occurs, it is grounded in this activity.

9.6.2   No representations in subsumption architectures?

For roboticist Rodney Brooks (1991), pursuing this program has generated some fresh ways of thinking about the mind's architecture. He builds a separate control system for each task a robot must perform; each is a hard-wired finite state machine which Brooks calls a *layer* (a very different use of the term than in connectionism). For example, in his simplest robot the first layer specializes in avoiding obstacles, the second layer generates wandering (randomly determined movements), and the third layer generates exploration (moving towards a particular location). Each layer is a complete system extending all the way from sensation to action and is capable of acting alone. Typically, however, they can be active simultaneously; minimal circuitry between layers manages when one layer will suppress another, or sometimes calculates a compromise direction of movement. Brooks calls this a *subsumption architecture*, and it follows from deciding to decompose activities horizontally by task rather than vertically by function. A function such as visual perception may be carried out separately and differently within several layers of the system; there is no overall, shared vision module in the sense either of Fodor or of traditional AI. This means there are no central representations. Even within a layer, information is accessed from the real world as needed, obviating the need to construct and keep updating an internal model of the world. Brooks argues, moreover, that the states of the various registers of the finite state machine constituting each layer do not even qualify as local representations: they do not involve variables or rules, and individual states do not have semantic interpretations (rather, the whole layer is grounded in the world it moves in).

Critics, however, are dubious of the ability of such a system to simulate all or even most forms of intelligent behavior (Brooks himself suggested that it will suffice for 97 percent). Kirsh (1991), for example, allowed that it could suffice for an activity such as solving a jigsaw puzzle. A person might look at the shape required at a particular gap and compare it to the shapes of available pieces, and might attempt to physically position each of the pieces in the gap if necessary; the task requires minimal cognitive activity and no complex models. But he argued that a host of important activities cannot be accomplished through such direct linkages to the environment – activities that require: (1) predicting the behavior of other agents; (2) taking into account information not presently available (e.g., precautionary activities to produce or avoid future outcomes); (3) taking an objective, not an egocentric point of view (e.g., obtaining advice from other agents); (4) problem-solving prior to action; and (5) creative activities (e.g., writing poetry).

The objections raised by Kirsh (and similarly by Clark and Toribio, 1994) seem telling against extreme antirepresentationalist positions such as that of Brooks and some others engaged in the artificial life movement. But what if a Brooks-style architecture were used as the starting point for a new system responsive to Kirsh's objections? Its designers could build sensorimotor controllers specialized for various activities in the world as a foundation, but then add the capacity to reason and solve problems in ways that partially decouple the internal system from the environment. Such a system could develop plans and strategies that enabled it to respond more effectively to situations that arose, and thereby enhance its evolutionary prospects (for a suggestion along these lines, see Grush, 1997a).

9.6.3   No intentionality in robots and Chinese rooms?

One attractive consequence of starting with an embodied system acting in the world is that whatever cognitive, representational processes are built on top of that will have their representations grounded in the world. Researchers taking this kind of hybrid approach might thereby hope to overcome the problem of accounting for intentionality in AI systems that was posed by John Searle (1980). The term *intentionality* refers to the character of linguistic utterances or thoughts as being about something and in that respect having meaning (e.g., the thought that John Searle teaches at Berkeley is about the actual person John Searle). Searle makes his case against AI systems by offering his Chinese Room thought experiment, in which a person or machine simulates the behavior of a speaker of Chinese using Chinese characters to engage in a written interaction. The simulation is accomplished by repeatedly consulting a handbook of rules for manipulating the Chinese characters as formal symbols (i.e., shapes with no meaning). Searle contends that the person or machine engaging in such symbol manipulation, because they do not understand the Chinese characters they are responding to or producing, does not have the (intentional) thoughts of the real Chinese speaker being simulated. If embodied artificial life systems are elaborated so as to develop representations that stand in for aspects of the environment with which they are interacting, then, unlike the purely formal system operating in Searle's Chinese room, these representations might be credited as exhibiting intentionality.

Beyond those projects using actual robots as embodied artificial organisms, much of the research in artificial life relies on simulation techniques. Even Nolfi, Miglino, and Parisi's (1994) work on evolving network controllers for Khepera relied upon off-line samples of the actual robot's experiences (a kind of simulation). If controllers for simulated robots are viewed as employing representations in their hidden layers (which Brooks might deny but many others would assert), Searle's objection would seem to arise again – the representations are completely formal and lack content. If indeed the network controllers evolved in such simulations turn out to be virtually equivalent to those evolved in real robots, on one view, this draws into question the intentionality of the representations in the real robots as well. This is likely the view Searle would adopt, since he uses the Chinese Room thought experiment to demonstrate, by contrast, the causal powers of real brains in producing intentional states. But an alternative interpretive stance on the simulated controllers would regard their internal states as representations insofar as they evolved in response to the evolutionary and learning conditions imposed by their simulated environment (the similarity to controllers evolved for real robots would be due to similarities in those conditions). We cannot hope to settle here the issues concerning the intentionality of representational states that develop in simulated and real robot controllers. However, this aspect of robotics clearly exemplifies how artificial life research can engage long-standing philosophical concerns.

9.6.4 No armchair when Dennett does philosophy?

Perhaps the most radical suggestion about artificial life is Daniel Dennett's (1995) proposal that it offers not just a new domain that philosophers can pounce upon and subject to their usual methods of analysis and criticism; more interestingly, it can provide a new method for doing philosophy itself. One of the traditional methods, as just illustrated by Searle's Chinese Room, is to pose thought experiments. The philosopher generates interesting circumstances (often fanciful or contrary-to-fact, but regarded as diagnostic) and reasons about their likely consequences. The results generally are far from definitive; philosophers with different intuitions, biases, and other limitations arrive at different consequences. Dennett suggests that building artificial life simulations offers an improvement upon this method, because it offers a way for elaborate thought experiments to be not merely created but also rigorously tested. If what the philosopher imagines can be realized (implemented) in the design of an artificial life simulation, then running the simulation will reveal the consequences. Philosophers inspired to add this technique to their toolkit will be able to break new ground in posing and testing ideas. As one example, Dennett points to the question of how a complex phenomenon like cooperation might emerge. If a philosopher's tentative answer can be realized in an artificial life simulation which indeed produces cooperative behavior (e.g., that of Ackley and Littman, 1994), this should be a more convincing way to evaluate the proposal than to reason about why the tentative answer might or might not succeed (the time-honored, perhaps time-worn, armchair method of doing philosophy). A similar issue that Dennett indicates might lend itself to investigation through artificial life modeling is whether highly purposive intentional systems with beliefs and desires might evolve gradually from simpler automata. The further the method is stretched beyond its biological roots, the wider is the range of traditional philosophical issues that can be opened to new insights.

We have touched on several ways in which successful simulations are likely to help advance philosophical inquiry; of these, Dennett's rethinking of thought experiments probably has the greatest implications for philosophy as a discipline. However, it can be expected that many philosophers will respond to simulation results by questioning whether the apparent cooperative behavior or intentionality are real instantiations of these constructs, or are pale imitations of uncertain consequence. Do the simplifications and abstractions involved in any simulation compromise the epistemic status of its outcome? Many rounds of argument could emerge from a skeptical comment of this kind, and they would remind us that simulation or any other new method would only augment, not replace, reasoning and debate as a way of doing philosophy.

9.7   Conclusion

The networks we discussed in previous chapters had been hand-crafted by humans and employed to solve problems that had been encoded by human designers on their input units. In this chapter we have explored early efforts to expand the scope of connectionist research so as to avoid these two constraints. By installing networks into robots as controllers, they are not restricted to what the researcher wants them to learn; they incorporate the regularities in an actual environment whatever those turn out to be. The genetic algorithm provides a way of evolving network designs; these evolved designs may turn out to be far more brain-like than those created by human designers if their early promise is realized. The final point considered here was that the lines of research discussed in this chapter are also ripe for philosophical analysis, both by raising philosophical questions such as whether the representations developed in embodied robot controllers achieve genuine intentionality and by offering a vehicle for carrying out philosophical thought experiments.

SOURCES AND SUGGESTED READINGS

Adami, C. (1998) *Introduction to Artificial Life*. New York: Springer-Verlag.
Boden, M. A. (ed.) (1996) *Artificial Life*. Oxford: Oxford University Press.
Clark, A. (1997) *Being There: Putting Brain, Body, and World Together Again*. Cambridge, MA: MIT Press.
Langton, C. G. (ed.) (1995) *Artificial Life: An Overview*. Cambridge, MA: MIT Press.
Morris, R. (1999) *Artificial Worlds: Computers, Complexity, and the Riddle of Life*. New York: Plenum Trade.
Nolfi, S. and Florano, D. (2000) *Evolutionary Robotics: The Biology, Intelligence, and Technology of Self-organizing Machines*. Cambridge, MA: MIT Press.
Steels, L. and Brooks, R. (1995) *The Artificial Life Route to Artificial Intelligence: Building Embodied, Situated Agents*. Mahwah, NJ: Lawrence Erlbaum.

10

CONNECTIONISM AND THE BRAIN

10.1   Connectionism Meets Cognitive Neuroscience

It is clear from the last few chapters that connectionist networks have had a broad impact in the cognitive sciences, often on their own as models of cognitive systems but increasingly in combination with other new approaches. We have seen, in particular, that artificial life researchers have evolved networks to control robots, and dynamicists have analyzed state changes in networks as trajectories to stable attractors or chaos. Not everyone engaged in these enterprises likes the term *connectionism* and the entire package of commitments it tends to suggest. Some prefer the terms *neural network* or *artificial neural network* (ANN), which are more neutral in some respects but do carry a strong reminder that the oldest and most prominent roots of network modeling lie in the neuroscience of the mid-twentieth century. As we saw in chapter 1, McCulloch and Pitts (1943) added simplifying assumptions to the neurophysiology of their day in order to define simplified, abstract "neurons" and connected them at "synapses" to obtain networks that, they demonstrated, amounted to logic circuits capable of computing propositional functions. But that presses the issue that is the focus of this final chapter: what is or should be the relation between connectionism and studies of the brain? We begin by quickly reviewing the trajectories of these two enterprises and their intersections.

McCulloch and Pitts's idea of regarding the nervous system as a computational system gave rise to a field that is now known as *computational neuroscience*. Its investigators have employed a variety of mathematical, engineering, and simulation techniques, of which the best-known products are the first wave of neural network models. Their designers generally shared an ultimate goal of a better understanding of the brain, but they differed in shorter-term strategy and emphasis. Those trained in neurophysiology aspired to biological realism – sometimes focusing their models on specific brain areas such as the hippocampus (Marr, 1971) or primary visual cortex (Bienenstock, Cooper, and Munro, 1982; von der Malsburg, 1973) – but they had to make idealizations and compromises in order to achieve computationally tractable models and to bridge gaps in biological knowledge. Those whose background was in computation or formal systems, in contrast, put their emphasis on demonstrating or improving the computational capabilities of networks. First-wave designers of either orientation were modest in the types of tasks for which they designed networks: sensorimotor functions, simple memory functions, pattern completion, and the like (e.g., J. A. Anderson, 1972; Grossberg, 1982, 1988; Kohonen, 1972, 1989; Little and Shaw, 1975; Rosenblatt, 1958; see section 1.2).

As empirical knowledge in biology as well as computational modeling techniques advanced, computational neuroscientists turned much of their attention to precise models of neural mechanisms. The most microscopic models targeted structure, functioning, or learning within an individual neuron or at synapses (e.g., Abbott and LeMasson, 1993; Bower, 1992; Collingridge and Bliss, 1987; Koch, 1990; Shepherd, 1990); others explored how networks of neurons function (e.g., Amari and Maginu, 1988) or develop and learn (e.g., Miller, Keller, and Stryker, 1989). Bugmann (1996) argued that fairly abstract models of networks of neurons can be useful if they respect the properties of individual neurons. Some investigators ventured into even less familiar territory, adding surmises and extrapolations to existing knowledge to make very general, provocative proposals concerning how brain circuits work. Among these were neural Darwinism (Edelman, 1987; Reeke and Edelman, 1988); the concept of routing circuits (van Essen, Anderson, and Olshausen, 1994); and the idea that synchrony in neural firing might solve the binding problem (Singer, 1994; von der Malsburg, 1996). Other investigators continued to make advances in modeling specific brain areas (e.g., prefrontal cortex: Braver, Cohen, and Servan-Schreiber, 1995; motor cortex: Lukashin and Georgopoulos, 1994). Work emphasizing computation rather than biology also took some new directions, including Bayesian-based approaches to learning (e.g., Dayan, Hinton, Neal, and Zemel, 1995) as an alternative to more biologically based Hebbian learning. Recently, Eliasmith and Anderson (forthcoming) proposed a general framework for neural modeling in which multiple functions (e.g., vector functions and probability density functions), transformations (linear combinations of sets of functions), and levels (e.g., neurons and neural groups) can be combined. Overall, the field has become much more diverse and its models much more targeted and biologically realistic than during the first wave of neural network models.

At the same time that computational neuroscience was moving beyond its roots in the first wave of neural network models, a second wave of researchers from cognitive psychology and artificial intelligence adopted neural networks as a medium for modeling human cognition. This intersection of two previously distinct trajectories in the early 1980s produced the distinctive approach to network modeling known as connectionism. The primary goal was to achieve a deeper, more complete account of cognition than had been obtained from the rules and symbolic representations of the information processing framework. Both neural plausibility and computational power were attractive to connectionists, but primarily as means to the end of modeling and understanding cognition. Connectionist networks were "neurally inspired" but did not need to resemble any particular parts of the nervous system. Backpropagation increased computational power, but that would have been of limited interest to connectionists if it resulted in learning outcomes unlike those of humans. When these researchers evaluated a network, the first priority was that it mimic human performance in tasks ranging from past-tense formation to story-schema extraction – tasks for which neither the biological substrates nor the optimal computational machinery are well understood, but for which human data exist to be compared to the performance of network models.[1]

Across the 1980s and well into the 1990s, most cognitive scientists (including connectionist modelers) and neuroscientists (including computational neuroscientists) pursued their own paths. Connectionists tended to hold neuroscience at arm's length, in part because the grain size of cognitive models had very limited potential for dovetailing with available knowledge in neuroscience. Biological findings concerning subcellular mechanisms and neurochemical accounts of neural transmission were too fine-grained for connectionists to use. Simple localizations of global functions in brain areas, such as neuropsychological findings regarding language processing in Broca's area, were too coarse-grained to guide modeling. Hubel and Wiesel's (1962, 1968) simple and complex cells in primary visual cortex caught the attention of cognitive scientists working on vision, but few empirical results from neuroscience were "just right" for those focused on higher cognition. (Goldilocks would understand this dilemma.) The most fruitful contacts were between researchers in both camps who shared an interest in computational aspects of networks.

During this period, though, certain neuroscientists were making other advances that drew increased attention from cognitive scientists in the early 1990s. Most notable was the idea of obtaining PET scans from individuals performing cognitive tasks (Petersen, Fox, Posner, Mintun, and Raichle, 1988). By comparing blood flow patterns for related tasks, researchers could produce color-coded images that were taken to indicate which brain areas were most active in performing particular kinds of cognitive operations. For example, Petersen et al. subtracted the pattern obtained while simply reading a word from the pattern obtained while performing a semantic operation on that word. Color-coding a brain image so that the areas with the largest differences were red, the most prominent "hot spots" were inferred to be involved in operations on word meanings. More recently, developments in fMRI technology have enabled progress towards identifying the circuits in which these areas play a prominent but not exclusive role. Such neuroimaging techniques were at the right grain size to propel cognitive psychologists and neuroscientists into collaboration, and some of the new teams learned to take better advantage of neuroscience's other technologies (e.g., Neville and Lawson's 1987 use of evoked-response potentials (ERP) to study visual attention) and constructs (e.g., Cohen and Servan-Schreiber's incorporation of a parameter representing dopamine level in their 1992 simulation of schizophrenia). By the second half of the 1990s *cognitive neuroscience* was a thriving interdisciplinary research area that was attracting increased funding, students, and attention, trends that are continuing in the twenty-first century.

One last trend is of particular importance: the boundaries between these already-interdisciplinary fields are beginning to blur. Established researchers in cognitive science and neuroscience, especially those engaged in connectionist modeling, computational neuroscience, or cognitive neuroscience, are collaborating and reading each other's work. Younger scientists are emerging who have competencies in more than one of these three specialized areas and interests that span them. Two of them recently produced the first textbook that seamlessly covers all three areas (O'Reilly and Munakata, 2000). In large measure, we have regained the synergistic energy of the 1940s and 1950s, when the first neural network models were among the products of collaborative work on intelligent systems by physiologists, logicians, engineers, psychologists, and computer scientists. Connectionists have contributed to this renewed cooperation by developing network models that answer to both behavioral and neural evidence. In section 10.2 we examine several exemplars of that work. However, there also is at least one ongoing source of division: neuroscientists tend to be concerned about the extent to which connectionist models, even those targeting brain processes, are biologically unrealistic. In section 10.3 we consider this complaint and how connectionists respond to it.

10.2 Four Connectionist Models of Brain Processes

In this section we will describe four different endeavors by connectionists to incorporate specific findings from neuroscience in the design of a network model. The researchers are rooted in the connectionist tradition, but each has made a particular effort to incorporate certain aspects of what is known about neural structure and function or neuropsychological data. None of these networks should be viewed as simply implementing an accepted theory, because in each case there is considerable debate about theory. This has given network modelers an opening to contribute their own explanations and predictions, some of which have already had some uptake. As such models become more numerous and more specific, it will be interesting to observe whether neuroscience changes network models more than the models change neuroscience.

10.2.1 *What/Where* streams in visual processing

Our first example involves modeling an aspect of the neurobiology of vision. By the end of the nineteenth century, studies of lesions in dogs, monkeys, and humans had yielded sufficient evidence to conclude that the occipital lobe of cerebral cortex (at the back of the brain) played a major role in visual processing – especially the area which later became known as striate cortex or Brodmann's area 17 and more recently as primary visual cortex or V1. By the 1960s, David Hubel and Torsten Wiesel were recording the activity of individual neurons in cats and monkeys to determine how V1 produced a low-level analysis of visual input, and they and other researchers were tracing projections to extrastriate areas (anterior to V1). By the 1970s, researchers such as Semir Zeki were uncovering the functions of these areas by recording neurons in monkeys. Evidence of specialization accumulated; for example, Zeki found that the area now known as V4 had cells responsive to color and area MT in the superior temporal sulcus had cells responsive to motion (see Zeki, 1993, and Bechtel, 2001, for historical overviews).

A major theoretical proposal regarding the organization of the brain's visual processing system was advanced by Leslie Ungerleider and Mortimer Mishkin (1982). As illustrated in figure 10.1, visual processing beyond V1 and V2 (OC and OB in the mapping system they used) was divided into two pathways, one proceeding ventrally (downwards) into the temporal lobe and the other proceeding dorsally (upwards) into the parietal lobe. Based on studies of visual deficits in monkeys with lesions in either the ventral or dorsal pathway, Ungerleider and Mishkin proposed that the ventral pathway analyzed an object's properties and used this information to identify it, whereas the dorsal pathway was concerned with spatial relations and could encode the location of the same object. A substantial body of literature based on recording from cells in these two pathways supported the basic division in visual processing. These have come to be known as the *what* and *where* pathways.

Subsequent research complicated this neat picture. Livingston and Hubel (1988) identified a bifurcation of processing beginning even at the retina and continuing through the lateral geniculate nucleus of the thalamus to V1; they proposed this bifurcation connected into the ventral and dorsal pathways. A more serious revision of the original proposal came from researchers whose detailed neuroanatomical

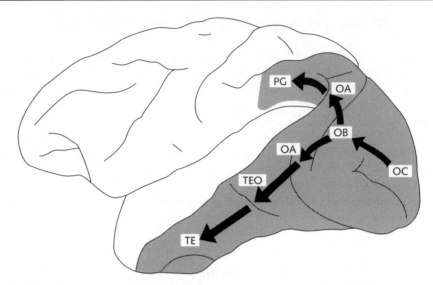

Figure 10.1 Two visual pathways in the rhesus monkey proposed by Mishkin and Ungerleider. Each begins in area OC (primary visual cortex, now called V1) and projects into prestriate areas OB (V2) and OA (V3, V4, and MT). The *what* pathway projects ventrally into inferior temporal cortex (areas TEO and TE), and the *where* pathway projects dorsally into inferior parietal cortex area (PG). Illustration from Mishkin, Ungerleider, and Macko (1983). Reprinted with permission.

studies revealed that extensive interconnections existed not only within the two pathways but also between them. The crosstalk between the *what* and *where* pathways makes them more like *processing streams* (Felleman and van Essen, 1991) than like Fodor's (1983) encapsulated modules. Other researchers have questioned the interpretation of the function of the two pathways. In particular, David Milner and Melvyn A. Goodale (1995) proposed that the division is based on the cognitive function for which the information is used rather than types of information and also made tentative suggestions regarding an additional stream. On this account, the ventral stream is primarily concerned with analyzing information required for perception and higher cognitive processes, including object recognition; the previously identified dorsal stream (through the superior parietal lobe) is primarily concerned with visual guidance of action, including eye movements; and a third stream (through the inferior parietal lobe) is used for a variety of visuospatial purposes, including the encoding of location but also the transformation of images (e.g., Turnbull, 1999, suggests this stream's capacity for mental rotation may sometimes contribute to object recognition).

Even these revisions to the original *what/where* proposal leave intact the intriguing question it raises: why would the brain largely segregate the processing of information when it all is derived from the same source and appears unified in our phenomenal experience? The development of connectionist modeling provided a way to address this question. Specifically, one line of connectionist simulation research has explored the consequences of partitioning the flow of processing in networks that are presented with visual patterns on an artificial retina. In a first effort, Jay G. Rueckl, Kyle R. Cave, and Stephen Kosslyn (1989) designed three-layer networks with a 5 × 5 array of input units (their artificial retina) and two sets of output units (*what* units and *where* units). The networks were trained to perform a dual task when presented with an input pattern: they had to identify its shape on their *what* units and its location (a 3 × 3 subarea of the retina) on their *where* units. Rueckl and colleagues compared the success of two network designs. In the more distributed design, activation was sent through a single set of hidden units; potentially, every hidden unit could contribute to both the *what* and *where* responses. In the more modular design, the connectivity pattern partitioned the hidden units into two sets: one set sent activation only to the *what* units, and the other set sent activation only to the *where* units. They demonstrated that the dual task was learned more readily by the modular networks. If there is a computational advantage to segregated processing in a connectionist network, at least during learning and possibly thereafter, the same could be true in the brain as well. Hence, Rueckl and colleagues pointed the way towards a rationale not only for the original proposal of separate *what/where* pathways, but also for the refined versions that followed and for instances of segregated neural processing elsewhere in the brain.

But how does segregated processing arise? In the study by Rueckl and colleagues, the designers themselves did most of the work: they decomposed the task and designated certain output units (as well as hidden units in the modular network) as specialists in *what* vs. *where*. Robert Jacobs, Michael Jordan, and Andrew Barto (1991) took a different approach, as shown in figure 10.2. Their design was modular, but the system itself had to determine how to use each module. The modules were three *expert networks*, each of which received activation from the same input units (a 5 × 5 retina and a task-specifier unit) but had its own array of 9 output units. Two of the expert networks also had a hidden layer of 18 or 36 units. The system's task on each trial was set to *what* or *where* via the task-specifier unit, and one of Rueckl et al.'s shapes was presented within a 3 × 3 area of the retina.

Jacobs and colleagues expected that the network with no hidden layer would come to specialize in the *where* task (because it is linearly separable) and that one of the networks with hidden layers would come to specialize in the *what* task. The system had to produce a single overall response on a final set of output units, however, and this was obtained by adding a gating network that allocated influence among the three expert networks. (The small squares in figure 10.2 indicate that the values in each expert network's output vector are multipled by a number between 0 and 1, as determined by the gating network; each number tends towards 0 or 1 across training.) As part of the training of the whole system, the gating network induced a competition between the expert networks in which only the winning expert network would be further trained by backpropagation (enabling it to become an even better expert on similar problems). As a result of its own training, the gating network learned which of the expert networks was most likely to provide the best answer on a given type of problem; it could then selectively pass the output vector of just that network to the final output units. The system performed as expected. By the end of training, the network with no hidden units had become expert in the *where* task and the network with 36 hidden units had become expert in the *what* task.

To appraise what benefits the modular design offered, Jacobs and colleagues compared its performance to that of a single network trained to perform both tasks. The modular system learned to perform the task faster and more accurately than the nonmodular system. Moreover, the nonmodular system's learning was impaired if the *what* and *where* trials were blocked (that is, grouped together rather than intermixed within each epoch). This is a consequence of *catastrophic interference* – the

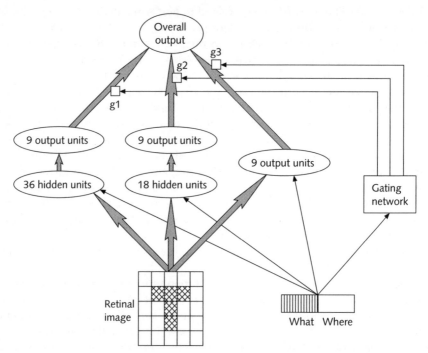

Figure 10.2 A modular system in which three networks compete to respond to images on a 5 × 5 retina (Jacobs, Jordan, and Barto, 1991). Large shaded arrows indicate a full set of connections between the units in two layers; each regular arrow indicates a single connection. The desired response is the identity or location of the image, depending whether the task-specifier unit is set to *what* or *where*. The task specification is also sent to the gating network, which develops three gating weights (g1–g3) which regulate how much each expert network influences the system's overall response. In the simulation they reported, the network with 36 hidden units became expert in the *what* task and the network with no hidden units became expert in the *where* task; the third network acquired little influence.

troublesome phenomenon that learning subsequent items can change weights sufficiently that the network loses the ability to respond correctly to previously learned items (see section 2.2.4). In contrast, the modular system showed no deficits when trials were blocked. In their introduction, Jacobs and colleagues suggested additional advantages of modular design: more appropriate generalization (because each expert will be responsible for generalization only within its own task), development of more intelligible and useful representations (because the representations will be task-specific), and more efficient use of computational hardware (because each expert network will have to represent only a limited set of dimensions).

Although they are very small and simple in comparison to the brain's own networks, modular connectionist networks have proven to be useful tools for exploring segregated processing as one design feature of the brain's architecture. The simulations discussed here showed that networks are capable of developing appropriate assignments of tasks to modules and pinpointed such advantages as rapid learning and avoidance of catastrophic interference. Perhaps the brain itself evolved the *what/where* design to gain these same advantages. Confirming and expanding upon this suggestion will require that neuroscientists gain more detailed information about the brain's pathways and that modelers incorporate these details in networks and compare them with alternative designs that nature rejected or used elsewhere. In this way, network models can contribute to the development of explanatory theoretical accounts that are responsive to discoveries about the brain.

10.2.2   The role of the hippocampus in memory

10.2.2.1   The basic design and functions of the hippocampal system   The hippocampus is a limbic structure located along the ventral medial surface of each temporal lobe, an area reached by starting at the bottom of the temporal lobe and following its surface inwards and upwards as it disappears from sight deep in the middle of the brain. It interconnects with nearby neocortical areas to form a *hippocampal system* whose functioning has defied simple characterization. On the one hand, humans with lesions to the hippocampal system exhibit profound amnesia that is primarily of the less commonly known anterograde variety; that is, they remember most of their lives before their injury but forget the new events of their post-injury lives. This has led some investigators to focus on the contributions of the hippocampus to forming new memories and transferring them to longer-term storage elsewhere. On the other hand, rats with hippocampal lesions exhibit serious navigational deficits. This has inspired proposals that the hippocampus provides an *allocentric* representation of space, a maplike representation in which locations have the same relation to each other regardless of the location and orientation of one's own body (in contrast to egocentric representations that are anchored by one's own body). Some advocates of each of these construals have turned to connectionist-style modeling. A major reason is that the hippocampus is anatomically very different from cerebral cortex, and modeling has helped elucidate how its structure might support the particular functions assigned to it. We will provide a quick overview of that anatomical structure before looking at some of the models.

The architecture of the hippocampus is basically a loop. Major components and connections are shown schematically in the bottom half of figure 10.3. The connectionist models we will discuss have emphasized the two-way street between the hippocampus proper and neocortex, as indicated in the top half of figure 10.3. The key to this interaction is three closely communicating areas of neocortex that comprise what we call the "gateway" to the hippocampus, or more properly, the parahippocampal region (parahippocampal gyrus, perirhinal cortex, and entorhinal cortex or EC). Inputs from widespread areas of the brain (including the amygdala and other limbic structures in addition to various sensory and other areas of neocortex) converge on this gateway to get integrated, compressed, and funneled into the hippocampus, which performs its own transformations and then returns outputs to the same areas. Though we are focusing here on the gateway function, parts of the parahippocampal region also have been credited with such functions as integrating information from different sensory modalities, representing facts, and remembering visually presented objects long enough to recognize them after a delay.

In interpreting studies of "hippocampal" function, variations in definition and inclusiveness have been troublesome and should not be ignored. The core of the hippocampus is Ammon's horn (CA1, CA2, and CA3). We also include the dentate gyrus (DG) when referring to the "hippocampus proper" (though some exclude it).

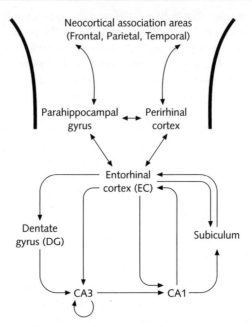

Figure 10.3 Schematic diagram of the hippocampal system. Information from widespread areas of neocortex converge on the parahippocampal region (parahippocampal gyrus, perirhinal cortex, and entorhinal cortex, EC) to be funneled into the processing loops of the hippocampal formation. The tightest loop runs from EC into the core areas of the hippocampus (CA1 and CA3) and back; the loop through the dentate gyrus and the recurrent connections in CA3 are also important; and the subiculum, which is not part of the hippocampus proper, provides an alternative return to EC. Not shown are a number of subcortical inputs and details of pathways and their synapses.

The "hippocampal formation" adds the subiculum (sometimes also the fornix), and we add the three gateway structures as well when we refer to the "hippocampal system." The term "medial temporal lobe" is used similarly but sometimes is taken to include the amygdala as well (either way, it refers to a region that encompasses both neocortical and subcortical structures). Even the term "gateway" has multiple uses: the week we sent this book to the publisher, Gluck and Myers (2001) arrived, offering a guided tour of computational models of the hippocampal system, the *Gateway to Memory*. It makes especially salient a cautionary note that our anatomical overview omits a number of direct and indirect pathways (e.g., via the fornix) by which certain more distant areas connect with the hippocampus proper and the subiculum. But enough is included to suggest that the hippocampal system receives input from and sends output to so much of the brain that it is well equipped to play a key role. The challenge is to reach some consensus on the exact nature of that role.

Three areas of the hippocampus have received the most attention: the dentate gyrus (DG), CA3, and CA1. The final gateway encodings received from EC are re-encoded in the granule cells of DG (which has ten times as many neurons as EC, but fewer firing for a given input). These sparse encodings are compressed into re-encodings (even sparser and more distinctive than those in DG) in the CA3 pyramidal cells. CA3 also receives some inputs directly from EC, and is similar to DG (and to CA1) in its number of excitatory neurons; all areas also have smaller numbers of inhibitory interneurons. CA3's pyramidal cells are highly interconnected via recurrent connections (indicated by a small looping arrow), and the same cells also send activation forward to the pyramidal cells in CA1 via the small CA2 area. CA1 forwards its own translation of the input back to EC, where a high level of more distributed activity completes the loop. (Alternatively, the loop can be completed by a less direct route through the subiculum.) Of particular interest for modelers, whether they emphasize spatial or episodic memory functions, is the overall loop structure of the hippocampus, the sparse encodings sent from DG to CA3, and the extensive recurrent connections in CA3.

10.2.2.2   Spatial navigation in rats   The classic presentation of the view that the hippocampus is dedicated to allocentric spatial representation was offered by John O'Keefe and Lynn Nadel in their 1978 book, *The Hippocampus as a Cognitive Map*: "the hippocampus is the core of a neural memory system providing an objective spatial framework within which the items and events of an organism's experience are located and interrelated" (p. 1). This interpretation was inspired by outcomes they observed after removing the hippocampus bilaterally from rats. The lesioned rats exhibited severe deficits on a type of maze problem that was easy for intact rats: navigating from a novel starting point to a previously rewarded location. To do this, the rat must use visual cues or landmarks in the room to orient itself in allocentric space. Most studies use an eight-arm radial maze or a Morris water maze. In the latter the target is a platform submerged in milky water. A normal rat released from a different location from where it first found the platform will orient itself using room cues and swim directly towards the platform. A lesioned rat instead swims in stereotyped circles (Morris, Garrud, Rawlins, and O'Keefe, 1982). These findings were explained in part by single-cell recording studies of CA3 which found *place cells* – cells that fire only when the rat is in a particular location in a familiar environment (O'Keefe and Dostrovsky, 1971). Though each place cell is itself fairly specific, from the mosaic of place cells the hippocampus seems to achieve an overall maplike representation of a particular environment. Later it was found that an individual rat has a different map for each environment and that place cells have different response properties for different maps.

   Those network modelers who have taken their lead from this array of findings on spatial tasks typically have designed models of how place cells develop and how they figure in navigation. Sharp (1991) and Zipser (1985), among others, emphasized that place cells in the hippocampus depend upon neocortical encodings of the animal's relation to landmarks in its environment (its *local view*). McNaughton and colleagues (e.g., McNaughton and Nadel, 1990) added to this the idea that the hippocampus implements a recurrent associative memory network in CA3. Via a feedback loop with parietal cortex, this network could associate local views with movements to compute trajectories through space (cf. Shapiro and Hetherington, 1993). David Touretzky and A. David Redish (1996; see also Redish, 1999) developed a detailed network model in which the parietal encodings of a rodent's local view as well as a vector representation of its position are combined in DG. The sparse connections from DG to CA3 give each new location a distinctive encoding, and the recurrent connections in CA3 produce attractors in CA3 for these locations. They proposed that the direct pathway from EC to CA3 plays its role later by directing activity to the appropriate attractor basin in CA3 when the rodent re-enters one of the now-familiar locations. Redish and Touretzky (1997) implemented parts of this model in a navigating robot, and Redish and Touretzky (1998) simulated a mechanism for using the CA3 attractors to replay spatial memories later in the absence of external input. Also, O'Keefe (1989) offered a computational model in which matrix operations are used to manipulate an animal's location with respect to its environment, and suggested plausible localizations of operations within the hippocampal system.

10.2.2.3 Spatial versus declarative memory accounts In their classic account of findings on rat navigation and other tasks, O'Keefe and Nadel (1978) viewed hippocampal lesions as impairing a *locale* system (for allocentric spatial functions) and preserving various non-hippocampally-based *taxon* systems (for taxonomic functions). There are different taxon systems in different domains, but each seeks clusters of similar items in support of categorization and generalization within its domain. Examples can be as diverse as Hullian stimulus–response learning, specialized systems for face recognition and language, and the *what* and *where* systems in parietal and temporal cortex respectively (for which there is preliminary evidence even in rats). Nadel (1994) discussed several dimensions on which the locale/taxon systems differ: learning (rapid/slow), use (flexible/rigid), context (encoded/not encoded), representational principle (separation based on differences / generalization based on similarity), and motivation (exploration/reinforcement). However, he insisted that the hippocampus is fundamentally a Fodorian spatial module that evolved to store and use its particular kind of content, and that the abstract characteristics merely reflect the demands of that specialized task. To build theory around the abstractions rather than each content-specific system is to "put the cart before the horse" (p. 54).

This raises an issue regarding the primary basis on which brain areas are organized. Do different brain areas handle different kinds of *contents* (a domain-based modular view) or different kinds of global *functions* (consistent with many information-processing models)? In hippocampal research, the latter approach has its foundation in Neal Cohen and Larry Squire's (1980) distinction between declarative and procedural memory (knowing that vs. knowing how, now often referred to as explicit versus implicit memory). Declarative memory encompasses Tulving's (1972) episodic memory (memory for specific events including where/when/what, often said to be bound together in a "snapshot" encoding) and semantic memory (knowledge of the world that has been derived from one or more specific events but is no longer bound to spatiotemporal context: what without the where and when). Procedural memory involves skills that are used rather than explicitly recalled, such as how to kayak or play the saxophone. Applying these definitions has been troublesome; for example, Tulving would restrict episodic memory to humans, but researchers relating spatial navigation to claims about memory (e.g., Nadel, Redish) tend to view their tasks as episodic. Most researchers with a primary emphasis on animal models of declarative memory and amnesia produce lesions in animals who are learning objects, locations, or associations and do not try to distinguish episodic from semantic tasks.

Further developing his construal of the hippocampal system in terms of functions, Cohen wrote a book with Howard Eichenbaum (Cohen and Eichenbaum, 1993; see also Eichenbaum, Otto, and Cohen, 1994) in which declarative memory was viewed as comprising two anatomically distinct but coordinated processing stages: (1) intermediate-term storage of representations of individual items in the parahippocampal (gateway) region, which enables (2) comparing them to other representations and thereby creating relational representations that can be flexibly

accessed and manipulated; this second stage was assigned to the hippocampal formation. They viewed O'Keefe and Nadel's cognitive maps as excellent exemplars of
relational representations, but rejected the idea of limiting them to the spatial domain.
For example, they did rat studies in which forming relational encodings of odors
(same or different odor) was localized in the hippocampal formation. In yet another
variation, Sutherland and Rudy (1989) proposed a "configural association theory" in
which the hippocampal system is involved in forming representations of combinations of cues. (Note that if the cues include an event's time and place, the combination is an episodic memory.) Nadel (1994) accepted the idea that areas connected to
the hippocampus proper (the subiculum and what we have called the gateway structures) represent individual items or facts. However, he rejected characterizations of
the role of the hippocampus proper as involving domain-independent relational or
configural encodings. Depending how you read him, the "bits and pieces" represented
in nearby areas are bound with spatiotemporal context to create episodic encodings
in the hippocampus (p. 54), or the hippocampus specializes in the maplike spatial part
of episodic encodings (p. 53). O'Keefe (1989) adopted the first of these interpretations.

Some investigators who have emphasized function over content have the goal of
reconciling the spatial and declarative memory approaches. Episodic memory can be
viewed as exhibiting the abstract characteristics of the locale system and in that respect
as a superordinate of spatial memory. The encoding of an episode – including
nonspatial as well as spatial elements – is fast, flexible, and context-specific. Likewise,
procedural memory can be viewed as exhibiting the abstract characteristics of the
taxon system – slow, rigid, and not bound to context. Redish (1999) classified various
aspects of rodent navigation as involving episodic memory (e.g., using maps consisting of place cells) or procedural memory (e.g., the nonallocentric spatial navigation
strategy of moving directly towards a visible landmark). Seeing the benefits of an
animal model for human memory, he was especially concerned to identify what
aspects of the hippocampal locale system might suit it to episodic memory more
generally. He settled on two (p. 216): (1) the key step of reinstantiating an appropriate previous context when needed, whether it is a rat's map of a particular room in a
laboratory to which it is being returned, or a human's encoding of a conversation
that must be recounted to another person or re-entered after an interruption; (2)
"replaying" memories that are in intermediate-term storage in the hippocampus
(especially during sleep, according to work from McNaughton's laboratory). For a
rat the replays would include recent routes traversed, and hence also the map by
which the rat oriented itself to plot those routes.

More speculatively, Redish notes that replaying recent memories may be crucial
to their gradual incorporation into existing long-term memories in neocortex, a
process called *consolidation*. Otherwise they may be lost, because of the generally
time-limited nature of hippocampal storage.[2] This proposal integrates numerous
studies of the hippocampus's role in navigation by rats with the separate, longer-
standing literature on memory and amnesia in humans. Recently Gluck and Myers
(2001) have sought to integrate and provide computational models of a variety of
human and animal findings, including studies of the role of the hippocampus in
unsupervised associative learning and in certain uses of context, with an understanding of memory and amnesia in humans as one goal. In the next section we
briefly describe the best-known case in the amnesia literature and then consider
some models that seek to show why and how the hippocampus would play a role in
consolidation.

10.2.2.4 Declarative memory in humans and monkeys The discovery that the hippocampus plays a crucial role in human long-term memory is credited to William B. Scoville and Brenda Milner (1957) and is a byproduct of surgeries Scoville performed on several patients in the 1950s. The clearest case was that of HM, who had large portions of his medial temporal lobes removed bilaterally in a successful attempt to relieve his intractable epilepsy. An unanticipated result was profound *anterograde amnesia* – a disorder of episodic (and possibly semantic) memory in which he could no longer form long-term memories of new events in his life. For example, he could not remember meeting someone if the person left and returned a few minutes later, and he has never learned to recognize even his regular medical caregivers. There appeared to be a disconnection between his short-term memory, which was normal, and his long-term memory.

However, further investigation of HM and similar patients painted a more com-plex picture. On the positive side, HM's ability to form new procedural memories was normal. He could, for example, learn to solve Tower of Hanoi problems and then utilize this skill later (procedural memory) even while failing to remember ever having solved such a problem in the past (episodic memory). Hence, there was no global inability to form and retain new long-term encodings. On the negative side, it became apparent that HM's anterograde amnesia was accompanied by *retrograde amnesia*, an additional type of long-term memory problem in which retrieval was compromised for events that had already occurred prior to his surgery. Moreover, the retrograde amnesia was *graded*: the probability of retrieval was essentially zero for events just prior to surgery but improved further back, approaching the normal range for events which had occurred more than three years earlier. Animal models of this intriguing combination of profound anterograde amnesia and graded retrograde amnesia have been achieved (with tasks and timeframes appropriate to the species), but in both animals and humans there are difficulties identifying which structures of the medial temporal lobe are responsible. Overall, as noted in the preceding section, it appears that some part of the hippocampal system serves as an intermediate-term storage area whose contents can gradually become consolidated into more per-manent storage in neocortex. Variations on this proposal can be found in Buzsaki (1989), Marr (1971), Rolls (1990), Squire, Cohen, and Nadel (1984), and Wilson and McNaughton (1993).

A number of researchers have investigated *how* the design of the hippocampus enables it to play this role, and we will summarize just two papers from that literature below. First, though, we will discuss a paper that focuses on *why* the hippocampus is involved. James McClelland, Bruce McNaughton, and Randall O'Reilly (1995) integrated and built upon the already-extensive literature on the hippocampus in addressing two questions:

1 Why is the hippocampus involved in consolidation at all, rather than sending inputs directly to the neocortical areas in which they will eventually be retained as long-term memories?
2 Why does this process of consolidation take as long as it does?

They proposed that the key to answering both questions was to posit different architectures for the hippocampus and neocortex, which separately have their own limitations but together can form a viable memory system. They found it plausible that neocortical storage would employ many of the same design principles as feedforward connectionist networks. As we have seen, such networks develop appropriate weight matrices only after many epochs of training. Also, they find the general structure in a repeatedly presented corpus, maintaining no record of individual training trials. Most important, if the original training regimen is supplanted with a new one, they become subject to catastrophic interference. McClelland and colleagues suggested that learning directly from experience would be so risky for a feedforward design that a different kind of network has been interposed in the processing stream. Specifically, the hippocampus could use a sparse network to achieve a rapid but distinctive encoding of new items and then hold them in intermediate-term storage along with somewhat older ones. By interleaving new with old items in replaying them as a training regimen for neocortex, the hippocampus could direct a gradual change of weights in neocortex. Crucially, it would learn the new items in a way that incorporated them into the structure already discovered in the old items rather than destroying that structure. In their terms, the hippocampus repeatedly *retrieves* the items for use in training trials that *reinstate* them in neocortex, with each reinstatement resulting in a small change of weights in neocortex. The hippocampal encodings could be allowed to decay with time, since their important features would be getting firmly established in neocortex in the course of consolidation. Thus, the answers to the two questions are:

1 The hippocampus is involved "to provide a medium for the initial storage of memories in a form that avoids interference with the knowledge already acquired in the neocortical system."
2 The process of consolidation takes so long because new items must be repeatedly interleaved with older items. "If the changes were made rapidly, they would interfere with the system of structured knowledge built up" already from related items.

(McClelland, McNaughton, and O'Reilly, 1995, p. 435)

Although this was largely a theoretical paper, McClelland and colleagues included three simulations, They did not need to be precise about which kind of declarative memory or which areas of the hippocampal system were involved. They first investigated catastrophic interference (McCloskey and Cohen, 1989; Ratcliff, 1990), but instead of using arbitrary pairings they used Rumelhart's (1990) semantically structured materials to train a multilayer network. Once it had learned a number of facts (e.g., robins can fly) it was repeatedly trained on three new, inconsistent facts (penguins are birds and can swim but not fly). When the new facts were presented as a repeated block, they were learned rapidly but interfered with related older facts (though less abruptly than in studies using arbitrary materials). When the new facts were *interleaved* with the older facts, they were learned slowly but without interference. This latter result showed why consolidation must take so long.

Next they simulated two experiments on consolidation in which animals were trained on arbitrary materials and then lesioned to produce retrograde amnesia. Again the internal workings of neocortex were simulated by a feedforward network but the hippocampus (by which they meant the hippocampal system) was treated as a black box. That is, the investigators themselves played the role of the hippocampus by manipulating the content of training sessions in accord with their assumptions about its activity. They were seeking to approximate the following division of labor between brain areas. First, a variety of repetitive background events were already consolidated in neocortex before the experiment begins and continued to be experienced. Then both neocortex and the hippocampus experienced items presented by an experimenter, but the hippocampus also repeatedly retrieved its encodings of those items on subsequent days and presented them to neocortex (interleaving them with that day's external events). Finally the hippocampus was lesioned, leaving neocortex to be tested on its own (control animals had access to both areas when tested).

One of these simulations was based on a rat experiment by Kim and Fanselow (1992). We will focus on the other, which was a rough analog to Zola-Morgan and Squire's (1990) finding of graded retrograde amnesia in monkeys performing a discrimination task in which numerous pairs of "junk objects" were repeatedly presented. One object in each pair was consistently reinforced, and the monkey had to learn to choose the reinforced object each time. McClelland and colleagues represented each object as a random bit pattern across 25 input units (50 total input units) and each choice as the state of a single output unit (*on* to choose object 1 and *off* to choose object 2). Adding a 15-unit hidden layer completed their feedforward network model of neocortical encoding of this task. The network was trained by backpropagation, with each epoch corresponding to one day of the experiment.

- In phase 1, a batch of existing memories was created by training the network on random subsets of 250 "background" items across 100 epochs (days). Though the hippocampus presumably would play a role in the initial consolidation and ongoing maintenance of such memories, the simulation was simplified by presenting the items directly to the feedforward network. They were never tested but mimicked the stable encoding in the monkey's neocortex of familiar ongoing events.
- In phase 2, background trials continued but 100 "direct experience" items were added on a sequential schedule mimicking that of the actual experiment. Specifically, on a given day the external training focused on just 2 of the 100 direct experience items (14 trials per item), with one epoch of review and then a break from training after each subset of 20 items. However, the hippocampus was also presumed to be encoding these items and delivering its own "reinstated experience" trials to neocortex (the feedforward network). Its role was mimicked by including in each day's training some repeats of trials that had previously been directly experienced. (Probability of reinstatement declined over time, simulating decay of encodings in the hippocampus.)
- Phase 3 occurred after all 100 items had been trained (directly, and most via repeated reinstatements as well). At this point in the actual experiment, training stopped, the investigators removed parahippocampal cortex, EC, and the hippocampus itself from the lesion subjects (controls had sham lesions), and two weeks later all were tested. These events were simulated by discontinuing both direct and reinstated training but continuing training on background items (for the control network, reinstated experience items continued during these two weeks). At the time of the lesion, the five subsets of 20 items differed in how long they had been in the pool of items eligible to be randomly selected each day for reinstatement training (i.e., in the length of their consolidation period). Items in the five subsets (from first to last trained) averaged 15, 11, 7, 3, and 1 weeks of consolidation in both monkeys and network if lesioned, and 2 weeks longer for controls. The simulation had 200 "subjects" (runs) for each condition. For the lesion condition the final test was based only on performance of the feedforward

network, but for the control condition retrieval was first attempted from the hippocampus (by a simple calculation based on overall retrieval probability and decay) and only if that failed from the feedforward network.

Performance on the final test was plotted as a function of the consolidation period for the monkeys and also the best-fitting simulation runs. Results were generally similar: lesioned monkeys and networks (relying only on cortical/feedforward encodings) performed poorly on items with the shortest consolidation period (1 week) and showed modest improvement across the five sets (ending at 15 weeks). Controls (initially boosted by their access to hippocampal encodings, which decayed over time) started well and showed modest decline. The two conditions had converged by 15 weeks (about 70 percent correct). A mathematical model produced functions fitting the simulation data and (to the extent possible) the somewhat noisier animal data. McClelland and colleagues noted that the training schedules and rapid decay limited the extent of consolidation in the simulation, but it was sufficient to reveal graded retrograde amnesia.

These simulations by McClelland, McNaughton, and O'Reilly made assumptions about the output of the hippocampus in order to explore *why* it would be involved in training neocortex. The next step was to ask *how* the internal operations of the hippocampal system equipped it for that role. This question was addressed using mathematical modeling by O'Reilly and McClelland (1994) and Treves and Rolls (1994) with similar results, and using network models by Alvarez and Squire (1994), Gluck and Myers (1993), and Rolls (1995). We will present O'Reilly and McClelland's version of the mathematical analysis and then the network model by Rolls.

O'Reilly and McClelland focused on two requirements the hippocampus must satisfy but which initially appear inconsistent. On one hand, to ensure that new memories are formed for new events, the hippocampus needs to separate incoming items by giving each a distinctive encoding. On the other hand, to retrieve existing memories from imperfect cues (for current use and/or to reinstate them in neocortex), the hippocampus needs to be able to perform pattern completion. Their goal was to show how the hippocampus can mimimize the tradeoff between these requirements and perform both memory encoding and memory retrieval functions adequately.

The ability of connectionist networks to complete patterns is one we have emphasized in earlier chapters, and now we see the hippocampus has that ability as well. In particular, the attractor basins created by the recurrent connections in CA3 seem ideally suited to complete the partial patterns entering the hippocampus via EC (see McNaughton and Nadel, 1990). This architecture would seem to undercut the capacity for pattern separation, however, since new patterns similar to incomplete old patterns could land in the old attractor basins rather than get a new encoding. To avoid this, some provision for increasing the separation between representations of similar events is needed. O'Reilly and McClelland proposed that the less direct pathway from EC to CA3 via DG can play precisely that role and offered a mathematical analysis of each pathway's suitability for its function.

Some of the major findings were that a network with high variance in its input signal, limited random connectivity, sparse activity (few neurons firing at any given time), and multiple layers (as found in the path from EC to CA3 via DG) would be well designed for the separation function. Hebbian learning (increasing the weight between an input and output unit if both are active) facilitates the opposing function of pattern completion. O'Reilly and McClelland found that separation could be increased without reducing completion by also decreasing the weight on any connection between an inactive input unit and active output unit. As applied to actual neural processes in the hippocampus, this suggests that Long-Term Potentiation (LTP), a rapidly induced and long-lasting strengthening of excitatory synaptic activity, should be complemented by Long-Term Depression (LTD). (On LTP, see Brown, Kairiss, and Keenan, 1990; on evidence for the more controversial LTD, see Levy, Colbert, and Desmond, 1990.) O'Reilly and McClelland also proposed another way to minimize tradeoffs between conflicting goals: designing pathways such that one is optimized for separation and another for completion. Their analysis of how to achieve this focused on two-layer networks in which there are limited random connections from the input layer to the output layer and a simple k-Winners-Take-All activation function. This means that the k output units with the greatest number of active input units connected to them on a given trial will themselves become active (the outcome is comparable to combining feedforward propagation of activation with lateral inhibition). The sparse activity of DG can be simulated by using a small value of k. They showed that with a smaller k there is more separation of outputs for similar inputs, and that additional separation can be obtained on the connections from DG to CA3 (depending on parameter values). Thus, they proposed that the direct pathway from EC to CA3 facilitates pattern completion, while the indirect pathway via DG facilitates pattern separation. A given input can be processed via both routes, thus achieving distinctive encodings as well as excellent retrieval.

As mentioned above, Alessandro Treves and Edmund Rolls (1994) provided a similar mathematical analysis of the conflicting demands of separation and completion and how they could be reconciled, and Rolls (1995) designed a network model to see if it could be made to work in practice. Both papers were put in a broader context in their recent book (Rolls and Treves, 1998). The challenge for Rolls (1995) was to make a model hippocampus that could store a large number of patterns (via distinctive encodings) and then find the right one when needed (via pattern completion). His design included every component in the bottom part of figure 10.3 except the subiculum (that is, EC, DG, CA3, and CA1). Rolls used neuroanatomical information about the number of cells, synapses per cell, and proportion of cells typically firing in each part of the rat's hippocampal system (sparseness) as a rough guide in building his scaled-down model. For example, whereas the rat has approximately 10^6 granule cells in DG, Rolls employed 1,000 units in his model DG. Each granule cell in the rat's DG sends projections to at least 15 of the approximately 300,000 CA3 pyramidal cells. In the model, each DG unit sent connections to 4 of the 1,000 CA3 units. In all other pathways, each unit sent connections to either 60 or 200 units in the next component, and the number of units was 1,000 except in EC (which had just 600 units). Further, the sparseness of activity in each component was regulated by allowing only the units with the greatest net input to fire (5 percent of units, except in CA1 only 1 percent were allowed to fire).

The network had the task of storing 100 random patterns presented just once each as inputs to EC; storage was accomplished by adjusting weights in the various components of the system by means of Hebbian learning. The architectural differences just noted affected how each part of the network functioned. Thus, after training, competitive learning in the pathways from EC to DG and from EC and CA3 to CA1 determined the activation patterns in DG and CA1; the pathways from EC to CA3 and from CA1 to EC functioned as pattern associators, and activation also passed along the very sparse connections from DG to CA3. After getting initial activation directly from EC and from EC via DG, CA3 ran 15 cycles on its recurrent connections to function as an autoassociative network. Activation then passed from CA3 to CA1 and from there back to EC, completing the processing loop.

Rolls measured the success of the model by its ability, when just part of each pattern was presented as input to the EC units, to regenerate the whole pattern on the same units (now as an output pattern). When the partial pattern was similar enough to the complete pattern – a correlation of just 0.40 was sufficient – the network could regenerate the complete pattern perfectly. In addition to obtaining this impressive overall result, Rolls was able to pin down some crucial design decisions. He already expected from the mathematical analysis and from the example of the rat hippocampus that varying the number of connections and sparseness would provide both separation and completion capacities. He also expected the recurrent connections in CA3 to be important, and demonstrated that turning them off eliminated CA3's ability to complete patterns (the pathways beyond it could partially but not completely compensate). Finally, he was surprised to discover that another way to eliminate CA3's pattern completion ability was to use an activation function that made the response of CA3 units binary rather than graded. On this basis, he suggested that neurophysiologists look for a bimodal distribution of firing rates in pyramidal cells of the hippocampus.

The hippocampus has clearly provided a provocative arena for connectionist modeling in the 1990s. Both its spatial and declarative memory functions have been simulated in networks, but the more abstract accounts that might bring them closer (such as that of Eichenbaum) have not been implemented. It is still unclear to what extent the two functions *should* be separated, and exactly what role each part of the hippocampal system plays. Given the difficulty of obtaining precise lesions limited to one functional or anatomical component in animals (and the impossibility in humans), network models can provide a valuable medium for exploring various ways of designing components, assigning tasks to them, and then assembling them into overall performances on spatial and nonspatial tasks. Sometimes, as with the suggestion from Rolls to seek neurons with bimodal firing patterns, the models can suggest possibilities to be checked out in the laboratory. Thus, modeling should both contribute to and benefit from progress in biological studies as cognitive neuroscience continues its rapid maturation.

10.2.3 Simulating dyslexia in network models of reading

10.2.3.1 Double dissociations in dyslexia There is a long tradition in neuroscience of lesioning specific brain areas to determine which functions are subserved by each area. As we saw in the previous section, this method runs into limitations as investigators try to zoom down to very specific components, such as those within the hippocampal system, giving connectionist modelers an opportunity to help sort things out. We now move to human functions – such as reading aloud – that cannot be studied using animal models. Instead of investigator-induced lesions, information about dysfunction comes from "experiments of nature" in which the brain fails to develop as expected (thereby producing developmental disabilities) or is damaged later in life (producing acquired disabilities). The interpretation of such disabilities is generally the province of neuropsychologists armed with test batteries rather than biologists bearing surgical instruments.

Even when the sites of damage can be localized in the brain (sometimes they cannot), mechanistic accounts of the systems involved in distinctively human functions traditionally have been constructed at the cognitive level, with mapping to the brain deferred to the future. As noted in section 7.3, neuropsychologists have contributed a method of constraining these accounts based on the behavioral profiles of two different disabilities. The goal is to find a *double dissociation*, in which two functions have opposite patterns of impairment vs. preservation. A classic example is the dissociation between syntactic and semantic processing in Broca's aphasia (syntax impaired, semantics preserved) versus Wernicke's aphasia (semantics impaired, syntax preserved). The traditional interpretation of a double dissociation is that it "cuts nature at its joints" and thus the dissociated functions are subserved by independent mechanisms – modules whose operations are effectively encapsulated, as Fodor would have it.

This strong interpretation has been challenged recently, making it evident that finding a double dissociation is just the beginning of the search for an explanation. Even if two mechanisms are inferred, what is the internal structure of each? Are they quite dissimilar, or is each a task-appropriate variation on the same basic architecture? Does a double dissociation really provide sufficient evidence that the mechanisms operate in relative isolation, or might this result be obtained even from mechanisms that interact as each performs its task? What additional kinds of evidence must a successful model address? In this section we will discuss how connectionists have sought answers for such questions by confronting the neuropsychological literature on *acquired dyslexia*. This is a family of reading impairments that adults may exhibit when certain brain areas are lesioned due to head injury or stroke or are impacted by a progressive neurological condition. No two cases are identical and, especially when damage is extensive, dyslexia may be associated with other disorders of varying severity. However, researchers have been able to identify major types of acquired dyslexia and their characteristic symptom complexes, three of which are relevant here.

First, individuals with *surface dyslexia* make numerous *regularization errors* when they attempt to read aloud written words that have exceptional pronunciation. For example, they may incorrectly pronounce the exception word *PINT* to rhyme with the regular words *HINT* and *MINT* rather than accessing the irregular but correct pronunciation; another example would be pronouncing *BROAD* to rhyme with *ROAD*. The lower the word's frequency of use, the more likely it is to get regularized. Such responses seem to involve overreliance on typical letter–sound correspondences in preference to knowledge about the spelling and sound of the specific word as a whole (its *surface* form). This yields the wrong vowel in these examples but works very well on regular words and even on nonwords. In *phonological dyslexia*, on the other hand, both exception words and regular words are pronounced correctly, but nonwords like *ZAT* often draw a blank (about half cannot be pronounced in mild cases, and none in the most severe cases). Individuals with this disorder have robust knowledge about specific words, but appear to be impaired in accessing typical letter–sound correspondences to construct a phoneme-by-phoneme *phonological* encoding of an unfamiliar written word or nonword. Surface dyslexia and phonological dyslexia present us with a double dissociation between exception words and nonwords that must be considered in evaluating any model of reading aloud. (Note that each disorder is named by what is impaired, as indicated here by italics.)

Deep dyslexia is more complicated. As in phonological dyslexia, individuals with deep dyslexia generally are impaired in reading nonwords, but additional symptoms suggest that the damage also goes *deeper* into the system. The most salient characteristic is a high frequency of semantic errors (e.g., reading *PEACH* as "apricot" or *MOUSE* as "rat"). This usually is taken to suggest that reading in deep dyslexia is mediated by a processing route through semantics which, though damaged, is more functional than the highly impaired knowledge of typical letter–sound correspondences. However, for many years no one could satisfactorily explain why certain other errors always accompany the semantic ones: visual errors (*MAT* → "rat"), mixed errors (*CAT* → "rat"), and derivational errors (*BAKE* → "baker"). It is particularly puzzling that mixed errors – the co-occurrence of semantic and visual errors – are far more frequent than expected by chance. This suggests that the mechanisms underlying these errors are not independent, but it was hard to imagine why. Another symptom of this complex disorder is that abstract words (e.g., *FACT, DEED*) and especially function words (e.g., *THE, WAS*) show even greater impairment than concrete words, sometimes resulting in errors (*WAS* → "and") but often just silence.

The distinctive error patterns in different types of dyslexia have been invaluable in developing and testing general models of how people read aloud. We first encountered connectionist models of reading aloud in section 8.3.2. As was illustrated in figure 8.4, two different teams of researchers each implemented just one of the three interactive networks that comprised the overall lexical processing system envisaged by Seidenberg and McClelland (1989). In the context of chapter 8, "Connectionism and the Dynamical Approach to Cognition," the development of attractors in these networks was of greatest interest: attractors for word meanings in Hinton and Shallice (1991) and for word pronunciations in Plaut, McClelland, Seidenberg, and Patterson (1996). In the current chapter, interest shifts to what happened next. Each team "lesioned" its chapter 8 network model in hopes of simulating one type of dyslexia; built on what was learned to create an expanded model (and, for Plaut et al., a revised account); and then lesioned the new model in a variety of ways to press towards a more refined account.

Figure 10.4 provides an overview of the connectionist account of dyslexia that emerges when the full set of simulations is pieced together. It seeks to capture the double dissociation between exception words and nonwords as well as the distinctive errors of deep dyslexia. Three networks and three types of dyslexia are shown, but they are not associated one-to-one. Two of the networks are viewed as working together to comprise a *semantic pathway* and the third is a more direct *phonological pathway* from written to spoken words. Here are the types of damage that connectionists have proposed for different forms of dyslexia:

- Phonological dyslexia is identified with damage to the phonological pathway (but perhaps just the phoneme units themselves in some cases). The rationale is that this pathway is the part of the system that uses componential attractors to construct pronunciations – a "soft" way to implement letter–sound correspondences.[3]
- Surface dyslexia is identified with damage to the semantic pathway, contrary to the McClelland group's earlier proposals, but tentatively supported by their final 1996 simulation.
- Deep dyslexia is identified with damage to the phonological pathway (impairing nonword reading) plus additional damage to the semantic pathway (causing the word substitution errors that are distinctive to deep dyslexia).

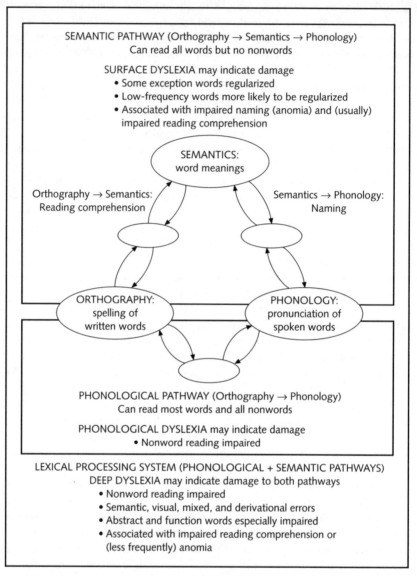

Figure 10.4 A connectionist framework for modeling the lexical processing system. The intact system has two pathways between spelling (orthography) and sound (phonology), shown using the overall network design suggested by McClelland and Seidenberg (1989). Most words can be read aloud using either pathway, but some words are encoded only in the semantic pathway (composed of two networks, as shown in the upper box) and nonwords rely on the phonological pathway (one network, as shown in the lower box). Different types of dyslexia produce symptoms that suggest damage to one or both pathways.

The claim that there is damage to the semantic pathway in both surface and deep dyslexia is further supported by the occurrence of collateral disorders (see Patterson and Lambon Ralph, 1999). Anomia (impaired naming, usually assessed by presenting pictures of objects) suggests damage in semantics → phonology or perhaps earlier in that pathway. Anomia is severe in "pure" surface dyslexia (sometimes called *semantic dyslexia*), and may occur in milder form in deep dyslexia. Impaired reading comprehension suggests damage earlier in the pathway – in the orthography → semantics network – and tends to accompany both surface dyslexia (most severely) and deep dyslexia (less severely). In surface dyslexia, the spared phonological pathway enables patients to correctly read aloud many words that are impaired in comprehension and naming. In deep dyslexia, abstract and function words (usually a particular subset for a given patient) are misread, miscomprehended, and (not as well documented) omitted from spontaneous speech.

One overall lesson from the simulations should be stated up-front: omitting any of the constituent networks has serious consequences. Precisely because it has been denied that the networks act as isolated mechanisms, implementing just one of the three networks carries the implicit assumption that the others have been damaged beyond use. Unfortunately, training the full system shown in figure 10.4 was too computation-intensive to be practicable on laboratory computers in the last decade of the twentieth century. (Plaut, 1997, estimated that approximately six months of run time would be required on a Silicon Graphics R4400 processor at 150Mhz.) Accordingly, phonological dyslexia had not been simulated within this framework as of the completion of this chapter in mid-2000. Surface dyslexia was simulated with increasing success; the last and most complete model added a black-box abstraction of the semantic pathway to a completely simulated phonological pathway (section 10.2.3.3). Deep dyslexia, though the most complex disorder, was computationally the easiest to simulate: severe damage to the phonological pathway could be approximated by simply excluding it from the implementation, and less severe damage to the semantic pathway could be achieved by building network models of it and lesioning them.

These connectionist models developed in the course of competition with the long-standing *dual-route theory* which they aspire to replace. According to that theory, one route uses a lexical look-up mechanism for whole words and the other uses correspondence rules to determine each sound separately; these two dissimilar mechanisms race against each other to supply the system's output. We will present the key connectionist simulations of deep and surface dyslexia before comparing them to dual-route theory. Specifically, we examine the progress made by Geoffrey Hinton, Tim Shallice, and David Plaut in simulating deep dyslexia and by James McClelland, Mark Seidenberg, Karalyn Patterson, and David Plaut in simulating surface dyslexia.

10.2.3.2 Modeling deep dyslexia   The simulations discussed in this section have their roots in *PDP:3*, where Hinton, McClelland, and Rumelhart (1986) fortuitously picked the mapping from written words (orthography) to meanings (semantics) to illustrate the claim that arbitrary mappings between two domains can be learned by a three-layer network with distributed representations. Hinton and Sejnowski (1986) in *PDP:7* did the actual implementation to test their Boltzmann machine learning procedure, and ensured cleaned-up semantic representations (attractors) by adding complete interconnections at that level. As a by-product of showing that the network was tolerant of damage, they obtained semantic errors that Hinton, McClelland, and Rumelhart recognized as akin to those in deep dyslexia. Hinton subsequently teamed up with neuropsychologist Tim Shallice to do a more purposeful simulation, and the result was a 1991 paper (part of which was discussed in section 8.3.2) that offered a non-obvious, but elegant, explanation for the puzzling co-occurrence of

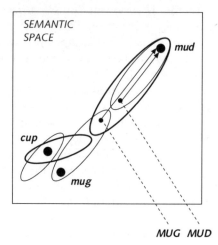

Figure 10.5 Changes in the basins of attraction when Hinton and Shallice's network is lesioned (see text).

certain errors in deep dyslexia. This was actually more than they had expected: they targeted semantic errors (reading *MOUSE* as "rat") and were surprised to also obtain visual errors (reading *CAT* as "mat") and above-chance occurrence of mixed errors (reading *CAT* as "rat").

Hinton and Shallice began by implementing the first half of the semantic pathway (orthography → semantics), resulting in the network schematized on the left side of figure 8.4. To simulate dyslexia they lesioned each part of the network in turn, using one of two methods: removing a proportion of connections (or units) or adding noise to the connections. After each lesion they tested the network on the 40 words on which it had been trained, recording for each word the pattern on the sememe units after the network had settled. Rather than implementing the second half of the semantics pathway (semantics → phonology), they assumed that the network would "read aloud" the word whose semantic representation came closest to the obtained pattern and thus simply looked up and recorded that word themselves. Since the majority of individuals with deep dyslexia are impaired in reading comprehension but not in naming, this was a reasonable simplification. (They also cannot read nonwords, and Hinton and Shallice cited this nonfunctionality of the phonological pathway as justification for leaving it unimplemented.)

Almost every lesion condition yielded all three characteristic types of error, in varying proportion. Hinton and Shallice noted: "Such a mixture of error types may be as much a sign of the operation of a layered connectionist system with attractors as dissociations are of modular systems" (p. 89). To see why, first look back to figure 8.5. The possible patterns on each layer of units are represented there as points in a space in which each unit corresponds to one dimension (though only two are shown). This facilitates thinking in terms of attractor dynamics. Diverging trajectories in semantic space lead to the point attractors labeled *mug* and *mud* (which actually denote two different patterns across the sememe units, not lexical items as such). The trajectories begin close together in semantic space due to lingering effects of the proximity of the written words *MUG* and *MUD* in orthographic space. The locations of the attractors themselves are based entirely on meaning, not visual similarity of the written words. Thus, the attractor labeled *mug* is located near *cup*, not near *mud*. Long, narrow attractor basins around these point attractors assure that words initially landing in one part of the semantic space (as a legacy of their visual form) will follow a trajectory to the part of the space most appropriate to their meanings. At the network level of analysis, this is assured by the weights on the connections involved in interactive processing. Damaging those connections can change the shape or location of the basins.

As a hypothetical example, removing 20 percent of the connections between sememes and clean-up units might have effects like those shown in figure 10.5. The original attractor basins are outlined with light lines and the distorted ones with darker ones. First, the basin around *mud* has been stretched enough that not only *MUD*, but also the visually similar *MUG*, now land in it. That is, interactive processing involving the damaged weights will send both words on trajectories to the attractor point labeled *mud*. For *MUD* this is the appropriate clean-up function, but for *MUG* it is a trajectory in the wrong direction and produces a visual error when the word is read aloud (*MUG* → *mud* → "mud"). The basin around *mug* has also changed; smaller and knocked upwards, it has not only lost the initial point of entry from *MUG* but also the attractor point *mug* that had been at its tip. Now any word landing within this basin – perhaps a carelessly written *MUG* that looks less like *MUD* than usual – will end up activating *cup*, resulting in a semantic error (*MUG* → *cup* → "cup"). Although not illustrated, a system like this would also be very prone to make mixed errors (*MUG* → *jug* → "jug") since the relevant basins would be close together at both ends. This elegant, motivated explanation for what had previously been a mysterious error profile has been widely accepted by dyslexia researchers.

Plaut and Shallice (1993) used Hinton and Shallice's model as the foundation for creating a family of five models so that the importance of various architectural variations could be assessed. All of them were trained and tested on their own, and then were attached to a newly implemented semantics → phonology network for further exploration (rather than simply assuming it was in working order, as above). The expanded model most similar to the original is shown in figure 10.6. In the orthography layer, distributed representations over four groups of eight orthographic feature units replaced the original localist representations on grapheme units; with this new design, the visual similarity of letters like M and N would influence processing. The phonology layer was localist, however, with one unit for each of 13 onset, 11 vowel, and 9 coda phonemes (a total of 33 phoneme units). In the semantics layer the original interconnections between sememe units within the same group were removed, but the recurrent connections with clean-up units were retained. The semantic activation patterns produced by the resulting interactive processing now had a double function: they were the outputs of the orthography → semantics network but also the inputs for the semantics → phonology network.

The two linked networks in figure 10.6 were very similar. Both had feedforward designs except for their clean-up units, which were sufficient to produce attractors at each output layer. As an implementation of the semantic pathway, they differed from Seidenberg and McClelland's (1989) overall framework (figure 8.4, shown more schematically within figure 10.4) in that clean-up units rather than feedback connections were the means of achieving interactive processing and attractor dynamics. However, this was just one of Plaut and Shallice's designs. In their other variations they experimented with feedback connections, within-layer interconnections at various layers, different numbers of units, and different densities of connectivity (100

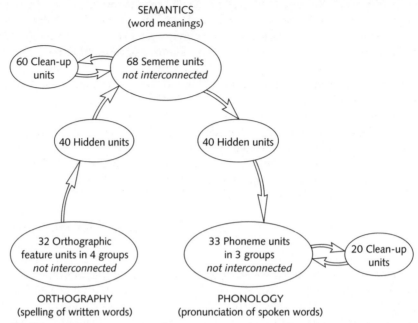

SEMANTICS
(word meanings)

Figure 10.6   One of the network models used by Plaut and Shallice (1993) to simulate
deep dyslexia. Their design differs slightly from the semantic pathway shown in the
upper half of figure 10.4, in that clean-up units rather than feedback connections are used
to implement interactivity. Damage to almost any part of the system results in the semantic,
visual, and mixed errors characteristic of deep dyslexia. This confirms and extends the
findings obtained by Hinton and Shallice (1991) when they lesioned the network shown on
the left side of figure 8.4. Note that the lack of a phonological pathway is part of the model,
capturing the fact that nonword reading is severely impaired in deep dyslexia.

percent of possible connections implemented vs. the original density of 25 percent).
All of the designs worked, and when lesioned, all except one produced the various
error types characteristic of dyslexia. This was because all of the networks had
sources of interactivity that produced attractor dynamics. Different designs and
different lesion locations merely affected the relative frequencies with which the
error types were produced. These findings were not what would have been expected
based on traditional approaches within neuropsychology in which the number and
location of damage sites are emphasized, and provided an almost irresistible demonstration of the benefits of computational modeling.

   In another simulation, Plaut and Shallice expanded their corpus by adding
abstract words, whose meanings involve fewer active sememe units than those of
concrete words. They used this corpus to train a network that included every possible kind of interactive connection and hence produced very strong attractors. When
some of the feedforward connections between orthography and semantics were
lesioned, abstract words showed the greatest decrements in performance. However,
when some of the connections between the semantic and clean-up units were lesioned,
it was concrete words that showed the greatest decrement. Although unusual, this
relative sparing of abstract words has been observed in at least one deep dyslexic,
CAV. Combined with the more typical pattern obtained from feedforward lesioning,

this counts as a double dissociation between concrete and abstract words. By the usual logic for interpreting double associations, it might be inferred that these two kinds of words are stored in separate components of the system. Plaut and Shallice proposed an alternative. With numerous sememe units involved in their semantic representations, concrete words can still be identified if the connections into a few of these units are lost; however, damaging the clean-up part of the network can leave some of these words with no attractors in the semantic layer. The sparser patterns for abstract words have less need of the clean-up units but also are less robust under damage to the feedforward connections. In short, the same system works differently for patterns with different characteristics; there is no need to posit separate systems for concrete and abstract words.

10.2.3.3 Modeling surface dyslexia Like the models of deep dyslexia, connectionist models of surface dyslexia have their computational roots in one of the 1986 volumes, in this case the chapter on past-tense formation by Rumelhart and McClelland in *PDP:18*. The mappings from base verb to past-tense verb and from spelling to sound are both *quasi-regular* (largely systematic, but with exceptions), and both tasks require some sort of representation of spoken words. Thus, Seidenberg and McClelland (1989) were able to use *Wickelfeature* phonological representations (originally developed for the past-tense model) in their model of reading aloud via the phonological pathway (orthography → phonology). They developed context-sensitive, coarse-coded representations for orthography as well. From these they built a feedforward network with 400 orthographic units, 200 hidden units, and 460 phonological units.[4] Presumably it could learn words of any length, because context-sensitive units need not be position-specific, but Seidenberg and McClelland limited themselves to monosyllables like *log* and *clasp*. In a direct challenge to dual-route theories, they succeeded in showing that a single mechanism could "read aloud" both regular and exception words. But a serious shortcoming became apparent: the mapping from spelling to sound was so dispersed and context-specific that the network was poor at reading nonwords.

Further problems emerged in the initial attempts to model dyslexia. Surface dyslexia has been characterized as "reading without semantics" (Shallice, Warrington, and McCarthy, 1983). The 1989 network, as an implemention of the phonological pathway in isolation from the semantic pathway, did just that – but did it too successfully to serve as a simulation of surface dyslexia. Patterson, Seidenberg, and McClelland (1989) therefore lesioned it, and the resulting modest impairment on exception words, mainly those of low frequency, matched the primary symptoms of a patient denoted MP. Unlike MP, though, the network's errors did not tend to be regularizations and its nonword reading was poor. (MP made reading errors on 7 percent of high-frequency and 27 percent of low-frequency exception words but less than 5 percent of nonwords and regular words; 90 percent of errors were regularizations.) A more serious problem was the failure to approximate the more severe surface dyslexic pattern of another patient, KT, by making a larger lesion in the network. (KT made reading errors on 74 percent of low-frequency and 53 percent of high-frequency exception words, but none on nonwords or high-frequency regular words and 11 percent on low-frequency regular words; 85 percent of errors were regularizations.) Because MP and KT present unusually pure cases of surface dyslexia, they are a touchstone in the field and any successful model must account for both of them.

Retaining their commitment to the general network architecture in figure 8.4 (shown more schematically in figure 10.4), McClelland's group designed two new network models of the phonological pathway and used each in multiple simulations (Plaut, McClelland, Seidenberg, and Patterson, 1996; hereafter, PMSP). In the PMSP model, Wickelfeatures were replaced by position-specific grapheme and phoneme units. One network was feedforward (with connections from grapheme to hidden units and hidden to phoneme units) and the other was made interactive by adding feedback connections from phoneme to hidden units and a full set of collateral connections between phoneme units. Also, the new training corpus was much larger. As discussed in section 8.3.2, both new networks, even the interactive one which developed attractors, succeeded in reading nonwords in addition to regular and exception words and exhibited a frequency by regularity interaction.[5]

PMSP used their new networks to test two very different ideas about what kind of damage produces surface dyslexia. First they retested their original idea of damaging the phonological pathway by removing connections or hidden units or adding noise to the new interactive network (simulation 4, part 1). The approximation to MP was now closer, with sparing of nonword reading and more (still not enough) regularizations in the errors on high-frequency exception words. However, larger lesions still did not reproduce KT's pattern of severe impairment on exception words but sparing of nonwords and most regular words. Therefore, PMSP developed a different idea about implementing "reading without semantics" within the overall framework of figure 10.4. As shown in figure 10.7, they proposed that the semantic pathway should be included in the simulation during training, just as individuals with acquired surface dyslexia previously had access to semantics for many years. The damage producing surface dyslexia would then be simulated by disconnecting the semantic pathway and requiring the phonological pathway to read on its own (simulation 4, part 2). Thus, surface dyslexia could be simulated without damaging the phonological pathway, but *it had to have been linked to the semantic pathway while it learned to read*. That enabled the system to conserve its resources by encoding certain exception words (especially those of low frequency) only in the semantic pathway. In the resulting division of labor between the two pathways, the phonological pathway would be fully competent on regular words and nonwords but spotty in its encodings of exception words. The semantic pathway would encode all known words but have no nonword capabilities. If this idea is right, damaging the semantic pathway would reveal which exception words the phonological pathway had not bothered to encode, revealing the extent of its dependency on the semantic pathway.

A full exploration of this revised account would involve adding an implementation of the semantic pathway – perhaps from Plaut and Shallice (1993) – and running the simulation with both pathways in operation. Because this would be too computation-intensive, PMSP instead approximated the full system by adding a black-box semantic pathway to their feedforward version of the phonological pathway.[6] That is, they assumed that the input to phonology from semantics would activate the appropriate pattern for the current word, and directly fed that pattern of activation to the phoneme units. The phoneme units combined that influence with activation flowing in from orthography via the hidden units. This interim step towards modeling a collaboration between different networks is illustrated in figure 10.7. Importantly, PMSP assumed that the strength of the influence from semantics (S) would increase asymptotically over the training period (simulating the effects of extensive practice with reading) and would be greater for high-frequency words (simulating the quicker

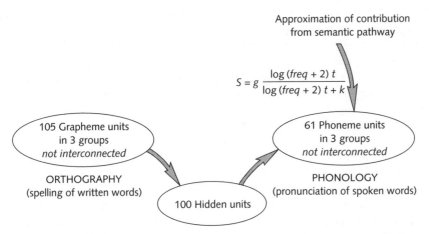

Figure 10.7 The final model used by Plaut, McClelland, Seidenberg, and Patterson (1996) to simulate surface dyslexia (simulation 4, part 2). Beginning with a feedforward network version of the phonological pathway, they added a black-box semantic pathway by specifying that the strength of the input from semantics (*S*) was greatest for words of higher frequency (*freq*) and increased across epochs (*t*) at a rate determined by the time to asymptote (*k*) and asymptotic level of input from semantics (*g*). This minimal implementation of the two pathways in figure 10.4 was chosen so that a division of labor between them could be approximated without exceeding computational capacity. After training the phonological pathway under the influence of the semantic pathway, a severe lesion of the semantic pathway was simulated by disconnecting it. The phonological network, undamaged but now on its own, exhibited the key symptoms of surface dyslexia; that is, it regularized low-frequency exception words without losing the ability to pronounce nonwords.

retrieval of their semantic representations). This produced a complicated learning trajectory that can be roughly divided into four stages (percentages are based on a subset of the training corpus from Taraban and McClelland, 1987):

- Epochs 1–200:   The system as a whole gained the ability to activate the correct pronunciation for all 2,998 words in the training corpus. Error at individual phoneme units (discrepancy between desired and actual activation values) was within tolerances for each word. Tested on its own, the feedforward network was 95.4 percent correct on nonword reading but was unable to handle some of the words in the corpus (almost half of the low-frequency and almost 10 percent of the high-frequency exception words).
- Epochs 200–400:   The feedforward network continued to adapt its weights, reducing its contributions to error at the unit level when the system was tested as a whole and reducing the number of words read incorrectly when tested on its own (30 percent of low-frequency exception words and very few others). A comparison network trained without semantic influence had reached this level by epoch 200 rather than 400, demonstrating that even the relatively small amount of semantic influence on the main network in early epochs made it less attentive to exception words.
- Epochs 400–800:   Although the system as a whole continued to read flawlessly (overt behavior), very interesting events were transpiring within the feedforward

network (covert behavior). It actually lost a substantial part of of the knowledge of exception words that it already had gained: when tested on its own at epoch 800, the feedforward network was *incorrect* on about 63 percent of low-frequency and 25 percent of high-frequency exception words.

- Epochs 800–2000: The feedforward network continued to give up knowledge, but at a much reduced pace. It may have stabilized by epoch 2000, when it was incorrect on slightly more than 70 percent of low-frequency and 45 percent of high-frequency exception words.

How can the network's loss of knowledge of exception words beginning around epoch 400 be explained? First, PMSP had included in the design of the network a weight decay process that produced a bias towards small weights. The main impact would fall on exception words, which need a few extreme weights to override typical spelling–sound correspondences, and these effects would accumulate over time. In early epochs the pressures to reduce error were stronger than the effects of decay, and the network had a net gain in knowledge. However, the increasing influence of semantics served to reverse this imbalance. By epoch 400 input from semantics had already attained much of its asymptotic maximum value (about half for low-frequency words and over two-thirds for high-frequency words). What error remained in the input to the phoneme units from the feedforward network became a smaller share of their total input, so their output patterns came much closer to the desired ones. This left less opportunity for the feedforward network (the phonological pathway) to fine-tune itself via backpropagation, and decay towards smaller weights became the predominant kind of change. The more extreme weights already developed for exception words were gradually forfeited. In short, the semantic pathway pre-empted what would have been the natural course of learning, had the phonological pathway been left to its own devices.[7] Although not exactly comparable, this is reminiscent of the nonautonomous network in Beer (1995); coupled to a sensor, it became dependent on sensory feedback rather than fully incorporating other available information in its weights (section 8.3.1).

The method that PMSP used to determine what the phonological pathway (feedforward network) knew at each epoch was to test it while detached from the black-box semantic pathway (the equation in figure 10.7). This method of probing the system also counts as a test of the idea that surface dyslexia results from severe damage to the semantic pathway after the phonological pathway has become somewhat dependent on it. Left alone to read aloud as best it can, the intact but only partly competent phonological pathway is viewed as simulating the brain of a patient with surface dyslexia. In fact, the performance pattern obtained by removing the semantic pathway after extensive training (epochs 800–2000 above) was very similar to that of KT, the patient who could not read most exception words. If the semantic pathway was removed earlier (epochs 200–400 above), a pattern like MP's was found instead. Contrary to the usual assumption that such patients differ in the extent of their brain damage, PMSP suggested that "differences among patients in their ability to read exception words . . . may reflect differences in their premorbid division of labor between pathways, with the patients exhibiting the more severe impairment being those who had relied to a greater extent on semantic support" (p. 98). Although differing amounts of reading experience (as roughly indexed by epochs in the model) could affect the division of labor in humans, so could reading instruction methods, computational resources, and many other factors.

Plaut (1997, simulation 1) further pursued individual differences by varying the strength of each pathway in figure 10.7 during training. Strength was positively related to g in the equation standing in for the semantic pathway and negatively related to the weight-decay parameter for the phonological pathway. He found that certain combinations assumed to be infrequent in people (e.g., both strong or both weak) produced the same atypical performance pattern in which patients exhibit severe semantic impairments but little or no surface dyslexia. This addressed a criticism of the 1996 model that it could not account for two atypical patients, DRN and DC. The more typical finding of impaired reading of exception words and an interaction with frequency resulted from the parameter combination that had been assumed for experienced readers in the 1996 paper (semantic pathway stronger than phonological pathway). Of course, what counts as a strong parameter value in the model is not predetermined, and emerges from plausible guesses and perhaps trying different values. By allowing these values to vary widely to capture different individual patterns, Plaut wrote a promissory note that someday will need to be paid by showing that patients matching the various predicted patterns indeed had premorbid differences for which these values are good surrogates. Meanwhile, just the possibility that the proposal is correct is an exciting development in the often frustrating enterprise of finding insightful explanations for individual differences in both intact and dyslexic individuals.

10.2.3.4   Two pathways versus dual routes   We have told only half of a very complex story (and only some highlights of that half). Connectionist models of reading aloud and dyslexia developed in the context of a vigorous competition with more traditional *dual-route theories*. These had roots in Marshall and Newcombe's (1973) paper on dyslexia, and had matured into the dominant framework for studying lexical processing and disorders by the 1980s. Competition with connectionist accounts was under way by the end of that decade; the ensuing rapid change and development within both camps brought them closer together in some respects while leaving their fundamental differences intact. Here we will briefly look at the initial conflict and then consider the current version in which the two connectionist *pathways* in figure 10.4 compete with two or three *routes*. (The two terms have little intrinsic difference in meaning, but make it clear which account is being discussed.)

In the classic form of dual-route theory (e.g., Coltheart, 1985; Morton and Patterson, 1980), spellings are linked with pronunciations in two different ways. The *nonlexical* route offers general rules on how to pronounce each part of the word. These are called grapheme–phoneme correspondence (GPC) rules, and they can be used to assemble a pronunciation for nonwords as well as regular words – but will produce errors on exception words, since these violate the rules. For example, the GPC rule *I*→/i/ yields the correct vowel sound for pronouncing the written word *MINT* but a regularization error for *PINT*. The *lexical* route passes through a lexicon that has an entry for every written word – but no nonwords. Looking up a word leads to its specific pronunciation, whether exceptional or not. For example, looking up *PINT* yields the correct /pInt/, not the erroneous /pint/. (In the notational convention used here, upper-case vowels represent different phonemes than lower-case ones.) One virtue of this account is that it provides a very simple account of the double dissociation between nonwords and exception words. If the nonlexical route is damaged, nonwords will be impaired (phonological dyslexia); if the lexical route is damaged, exception words will be impaired (surface dyslexia). Regular words can be pronounced using whichever route is undamaged.

A major goal of Seidenberg and McClelland's (1989) model of reading aloud was to show that (1) a single mechanism is sufficient to handle both regular and exception words; and (2) this mechanism involves propagating activation through a network, not looking up whole words in a lexicon or applying rules to parts of words. Their model usually produced accurate pronunciations for both kinds of words, demonstrating the feasibility of the overall approach, but its poor reading of nonwords suggested that some of the functionality of GPC rules was missing from its solution. This was one target of Coltheart, Curtis, Atkins, and Haller's (1993) spirited critique, and was remedied in the 1996 PMSP networks primarily by replacing the Wickelfeature representations.

As noted above, the long debate triggered by this model of reading aloud was a variant of the debate over Rumelhart and McClelland's (1986a) model of past-tense formation in English (see chapter 5). Both of these are quasi-regular domains for which a classic account specified two dissimilar mechanisms. In the past-tense case, classically there was a rule "add -*ed*" for regular verbs, and a look-up procedure involving a lexicon for irregular verbs. The connectionist alternative was good enough to demonstrate the feasibility of using a single network, but the Wickelfeature representations (a common element of both models) were replaced by position-specific phonemes in later work.

The representational and other changes in the 1996 PMSP simulations produced an even stronger demonstration that a single network could handle both regular and exception words, and this time the network exhibited the functionality of both routes of the dual-route theory. The first three simulations all did an excellent job of reading nonwords, and the interactive network (simulation 3) was shown to have done this via componential attractors. These were similar to GPC rules in their scope and effect but were dynamic, flexible, and adaptive. Moreover, the same network automatically developed attractors of greater scope to get the right pronunciations for exception words – a function handled by the lexicon in dual-route models.

Having demonstrated the feasibility of a single network handling a quasi-regular domain, PMSP decided that this particular task nonetheless required more than one network. The impetus was the first part of simulation 4: when damaged, the interactive network came closer to surface dyslexia than had the 1989 network, but not close enough. PMSP's response was not to add a different kind of mechanism (the dual-route approach), but rather to take steps towards including the whole group of three interacting networks envisaged in 1989 (figure 10.4). Superficially this looks like a dual-route model. The phonological pathway, like the nonlexical route, can handle nonwords and most words; when it is damaged, the system as a whole is predicted to show symptoms of phonological dyslexia (not implemented). The semantic pathway, like the lexical route, can handle all words but no nonwords; when it is damaged, the system as a whole shows symptoms of surface dyslexia (tentatively supported by the partial implementation in simulation 4, part 2). But note the importance of the phrase "most words" – in the previous model it was "all words," and using the influence of semantics to take away from the phonological pathway some of the words it was capable of encoding was the key change for better simulating surface dyslexia. It was exactly those exception words that the phonological pathway never learned or forgot that were predicted to be vulnerable. These tended to be low-frequency, but it was a soft boundary and (also to fit existing data) was proposed to show large individual differences.

Meanwhile, dual-route theory itself was changing. The DRC (Dual-Route Cascaded) model of Coltheart, Rastle, Perry, Langdon, and Ziegler (2001) differs from classic dual-route theory in several ways. First and most important, parts of it have been implemented in a computional model. The lexical and nonlexical routes both operate in discrete time at rates set by parameters. Each sends its interim outputs across time to the same set of phoneme units, and generally the route that is fastest for a particular word will have the most influence on the resulting pronunciation. Latencies from the model are similar to latencies from people for lexical decision and reading aloud tasks. Second, the front end of the lexical route (mapping visual features to letters and letters to words) has been implemented using an adaptation of McClelland and Rumelhart's (1981) Interactive Activation and Competition (IAC) model – that is, a localist connectionist network rather than a look-up procedure. This signifies that Coltheart and his colleagues do not reject networks in the same way that connectionists reject rules. As dual-route theorists they seek different mechanisms for different tasks, and do not mind if one is a network. Third, dual-route theory actually has become a three-route theory (without changing its name). The lexical route was initially conceived as involving semantics, but in rare cases patients seem to have lost that route while retaining one that directly links whole written words to pronunciations. It is this lexical-nonsemantic route that has in fact been implemented, due to its relative simplicity. (There is a lexical unit for each spelling and also one for each pronunciation; activation is channeled from a spelling unit to the appropriate pronunciation unit via excitatory and inhibitory connections, and the rate of increase in activation is scaled by relative word frequency.) Fourth, the GPC rules have existed in some form for many years, but a different method for determining the precise rules was used in this new implementation.

The differences that remain between the dual-route and connectionist accounts may seem subtle but in fact reflect fundamental differences between the two approaches. First, and most obviously, the pathways of the connectionist account are networks (assumed to be interactive and often implemented that way) whereas the DRC account uses at least two different kinds of mechanisms. Methods of damaging the systems also differ: connectionists remove or add noise to microcomponents whereas Coltheart and colleagues primarily change the values of parameters in the DRC account.

Second, the two approaches differ in which parts of the system and therefore which forms of dyslexia they have made greatest progress in simulating. *Deep dyslexia* has an elegant connectionist account by Hinton, Shallice, and Plaut. Coltheart and colleagues have declined to simulate it on the grounds that it reflects atypical right-hemisphere processing rather than a damaged left hemisphere (a localization that is in dispute; e.g., see Price et al., 1998, for evidence from PET of significant left-hemisphere activation in two patients). Hence, they have been able to defer implementing DRC's lexical-semantic route. One type of *phonological dyslexia* has been well simulated in DRC; both groups have plausible but unimplemented proposals about other types. Finally, *surface dyslexia* was simulated earlier and more parsimoniously in DRC, but now has been simulated by PMSP and Plaut (1997) as well.

The simulations of surface dyslexia currently are the main locus of competition. Both approaches predict that some proportion of exception words will be impaired, but the sources of the predictions differ in interesting ways. For dual-route theorists exception words are encoded exclusively in the lexical route, so extent of damage would be the main determinant of which words become impaired in surface dyslexia.

In the final PMSP model, the reason that some exception words escape impairment is that they have a back-up encoding in the phonological pathway. Those that do not are vulnerable when the semantic pathway is damaged. The membership of the impaired subset gets determined at the time of damage in one model and over years of reading experience in the other model. Direct evidence on these claims would be quite relevant, since currently they cannot be well discriminated empirically.

In this section we have focused on models that can simulate unimpaired cognitive performance when intact but mimic the damage underlying dyslexia when lesioned. Considering such a broad range of data has been advantageous in several ways. First, models of the intact system are better than they otherwise would have been; most recently, PMSP's difficulties in simulating surface dyslexia convinced them that the phonological pathway should not be trained in isolation – an important, if still tentative, claim. Second, models of the damaged system occasionally yield nonobvious clinical implications. For example, Plaut (1996) found that relearning in damaged networks is better when a disproportionate number of atypical items are included in the training set, a result that may carry over to human interventions. Third, such models make evident the need for a more nuanced way of interpreting double dissociations. Plaut and Shallice showed that a double dissociation between concrete and abstract words could be obtained by damaging different sets of connections to and from a single layer of semantic units. PMSP ultimately found nonwords and certain exception words to be handled by different pathways, but argued this resulted from how the pathways interacted; the double dissociation would not have been obtained if the pathways had been trained in isolation. These are existence proofs that double dissociations need not imply independently operating modules (also see Cohen et al., 1994; Farah, 1994; Plaut, 1995; and Van Orden, Pennington, and Stone, 1990). But neither do they exclude them; a simple modular network like that of Rueckl, Cave, and Kosslyn (1989) for *what/where* (section 10.2.1) presumably would produce double dissociations if different modules were damaged.

10.2.4   The computational power of modular structure in neocortex

A general feature of neural organization in the cerebral cortex is the presence of columns of neurons which share certain response properties. These columns were first identified in somatosensory cortex by Mountcastle (1957) and in primary visual cortex by Hubel and Wiesel (1963). For example, when Hubel and Wiesel inserted an electrode to record cells at different depths, if they kept it perpendicular to the surface (i.e., remaining within a column) they encountered numerous cells that were responsive to lines of a particular orientation (e.g., 35 degrees). But if they inserted the electrode at an angle, the orientation to which cells were responsive rotated as they went deeper (e.g., 35 degrees might be followed by 25 degrees, 17 degrees, etc.); this was taken as evidence that the electrode was crossing from one orientation-specific column to another. Columnar organization also was found for eye preference (left vs. right) and directional preference. This semi-systematic assignment of different sensitivities to different columns now is known to be characteristic of neocortex more generally, but is especially well described for visual cortex. Along with retinotopic mapping (information from adjacent retinal positions is mapped to adjacent areas of cortex, preserving the 2D layout of the visual field), columnar organization cross-cuts the long-recognized organization of cortex into layers of varying depth. Thus, within a column that is sensitive to a particular orientation, neurons in different layers (conventionally numbered I–VI) tend to differ in the type and size of receptive field and binocularity (and some are unresponsive to orientation). Short-distance connections, such as the synapses made by a basket cell axon in an adjacent layer of the same column, tend to be inhibitory. Long-distance connections, like those connecting a pyramidal cell to cells in other columns, tend to be excitatory.

The discovery of columnar organization brought the realization that the generally modular design of the nervous system continues down to impressively small-scale structures. Inspired by this, a group of researchers at Leiden University and the University of Amsterdam designed modular networks to perform a task – unsupervised categorization of patterns – for which the fine-grained neural underpinnings are not yet known. They ventured the idea that the general design principles of columnar structure would apply to areas of cortex performing this task. Jacob Murre, R. Hans Phaf, and Gezinus Wolters (1992) called their networks CALM modules (Categorizing And Learning Modules). They viewed each module as roughly comparable to a cortical column, and intended that they work together as specialized components of a larger system. In emulation of cortical columns, they placed excitatory connections between modules and predominantly inhibitory connections within modules. However, they did not make any more detailed attempt to simulate the six layers of cells within each cortical column.

We will illustrate the internal structure and connections using just two CALM modules and one input module (figure 10.8). Modules are built from three types of *nodes* (their term for units): Representational (R), Veto (V), and Arousal (A). Within a module, each R-node has an excitatory connection to a corresponding V-node and to the single A-node for that module (heavy lines terminating in arrowheads). The V-nodes have inhibitory connections to each other, to each of the R-nodes, and to the A-node (light lines terminating in solid circles). All have predetermined, fixed weights (e.g., the negative weight from a V-node to its corresponding R-node is much weaker than those to the other R-nodes). In contrast, connections into a module from outside are excitatory, restricted to the R-nodes, and modifiable by unsupervised learning. Each large arrow indicates a full set of such connections to a layer of R-nodes:

- It is the R-nodes that receive activation from the input units.
- If a module is linked to external nodes (E-nodes), it is the R-nodes that receive activation from them.
- Interaction between modules occurs via the R-nodes: the large bidirectional arrow at the center of figure 10.8 indicates that each R-node in the left module both sends output to and receives output from each R-node in the right module.

As we noted in discussing competitive learning in section 3.2.4, internal inhibitory connections serve to create a winner-take-all competition. Within CALM modules, V-nodes provide an indirect implementation of lateral inhibition between the R-nodes: as one R-node begins to win the competition its corresponding V-node suppresses the other R-nodes (and their V-nodes). The winning R-node is the module's categorization of the current input. In addition, a loop through the R-, A-, and E-nodes provides a mechanism for modulating this competition. When competition between R-nodes is intense, the A-node becomes more active and propagates that activation to the E-node (whose external status roughly simulates nonspecific

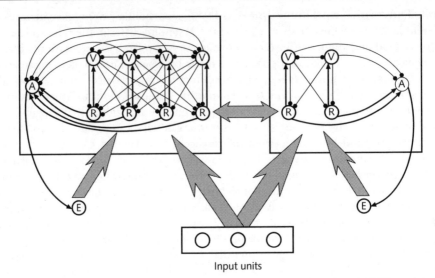

Input units

Figure 10.8   Two interconnected Categorizing and Learning Modules (CALM modules), which illustrate the basic design of the larger modular systems investigated by Murre, Phaf, and Wolters (1992). Within each module, representational nodes (R) engage in a winner-take-all competition to categorize input patterns. Competition is implemented by inhibitory connections from separate veto nodes (V) rather than direct lateral inhibition between R-nodes. It is modulated by the response of external nodes (E), which send random excitation to each R-node in response to arousal nodes (A). The large shaded arrows indicate full sets of modifiable connections to the R-nodes from the input units, E-nodes, and the R-nodes in other modules. Via unsupervised learning, each module comes to specialize in its own way of categorizing the same input.

subcortical activation). When the E-node becomes more active it (a) increases the learning rate and (b) sends random excitations to each R-node. This R–A–E–R loop provides a *state-dependent noise mechanism* which, by modifying the patterns on the R-nodes, serves to break deadlocks and (much like the temperature parameter in the Boltzmann machine) enables the system to escape local minima. As one R-node begins to win the competition, the rising activity in its V-node will send inhibition to the A-node at the same time as the losing R-nodes are sending it less excitation. The CALM module gets calmer as it settles into its response.

Each CALM module is thus a dynamical system in which each R-node that has come to represent a category during learning functions as an attractor. The shape of each basin of attraction is adaptively determined by the weights on the modifiable connections (large arrows). These weights are adjusted during the ongoing activity of a module using a version of Hebbian learning. (No learning occurs within a module, since those weights are fixed.) To gain an appreciation of this process, consider a single module with two R-nodes which receive input from three input units and an E-node (the CALM module on the right in figure 10.8). A number of different patterns are presented in turn on the three input nodes. They can be continuously valued, but sometimes are binary (e.g., the first four patterns may be 101 010 100 001). When the first pattern is presented, the random excitation delivered from the E-node to the R-nodes assures that one of them will happen to win the competition. As it begins to win, the weights of its connections to the active input nodes will gradually strengthen via Hebbian learning. When the next pattern is presented (after all activations in the network have been reset to zero), a new competition ensues and generally the other R-node will win the competition, leading to an increase in the connection weights between it and those input nodes that are now active. When either of these two inputs is again presented, the R-node that won the initial competition should now win more easily. As well, these two rounds of learning will have created two attractor basins such that a new input pattern similar to one of the originals will tend to activate the same R-node. Continued Hebbian learning serves to refine the shape of the basins.

In the brain, even though neurons in individual columns have few connections to adjacent columns, they do send and receive connections from columns elsewhere in cortex. In those columns a different categorization of the same input may be realized. This type of long-distance coupling is what is simulated by the excitatory connections between R-nodes (the large arrow at the center of figure 10.8). Bart Happel and Jacob Murre (1994) suggested that these coupled networks are comparable to the neural assemblies that Hebb proposed would arise spontaneously in the nervous system. In an initial study, they explored how coupled CALM modules might jointly carry out more accurate categorization than a single module. They found that the coarse-grained categorization made by a smaller module (one with fewer R-nodes) would constrain the categorization arrived at by a larger module to which it was coupled. Applying an invented example to figure 10.8, this would ensure that if the module on the right came to distinguish plants from animals, the module on the left would respect that division; that is, none of its four categories would mix animals and plants. In Happel and Murre's simulations, multi-module systems were more likely than single-module systems to generate categorizations in which the *a priori* similarity structure of the inputs was respected. These investigators went on to explore how larger numbers of CALM modules might be linked to perform more complex tasks; for example, they used a genetic algorithm to evolve a system of five CALM modules for reading handwritten digits. The pattern of connectivity between modules was partly unidirectional and ordered, but some modules had bidirectional connections that produced interesting dynamics (including chaotic behavior).

The work on CALM modules illustrates how researchers can make good use of neurally inspired architectural principles like columnar structure, and also employs notions we have developed in the last two chapters: processing in dynamical attractor networks and the design of networks through simulated evolution. What they have not done, however, is to show that the processing done by different CALM modules corresponds to the distinctive activities of particular areas of cortex, a task that remains for the future.

10.3   The Neural Implausibility of Many Connectionist Models

In this chapter we have emphasized the points of contact between connectionist modeling and studies of brain systems. But in previous chapters we saw that classical connectionist modeling is only loosely inspired by general characteristics of the nervous system. Even within the projects just described in section 10.2 as targeting specific neural structures, the architectures and the extent of their biological realism varied considerably. In this last section of the book, we first review some ways in which classical connectionist networks differ from real neural networks. Then we

discuss attitudes towards such differences, ranging from the functionalism of classical symbolic modeling (the differences are of no concern) to the biological realism
of computational neuroscience (the differences should be minimized), with connectionists tending to fall between these extremes.

10.3.1   Biologically implausible aspects of connectionist networks

A number of practitioners and observers of connectionist modeling have been drawn
to the question of how connectionist networks stack up against the real neural
networks of the brain (e.g., Crick 1989). The original neural inspiration of the
networks guaranteed some obvious similarities: the emphasis on numerous units
(analogous to neurons) with different and changing degrees of activity; propagation
of activity across connections between units (whose weights are analogous to synaptic
efficiency); adaptive plasticity; graded responsivity; and tolerance to damage and
noise. If the metaphor is pushed much further, though, it breaks down in a number
of ways.

   First, there are substantial differences between units and neurons, of which three
are particularly salient.

- Units are assigned activation values, while neurons emit a spike train.
- Connectionist networks use the single device of summing weighted activations
  to obtain net input, whereas connectivity in real brains is implemented chemic-
  ally via various neurotransmitters with different properties
- In connectionist networks the inputs to a unit (each $weight_{ui} \, a_i$) are simply summed
  to obtain a net input, whereas neurons seem to use a more intricate mechanism
  which relies in part on the specific location at which an axon synapses with a
  dendrite or cell body.

Second, there are differences in overall architecture.

- In a classical connectionist network every unit in one layer is connected to every
  unit in the next layer, but in the nervous system patterns of connectivity differ
  depending on cell type and location. For example, within the hippocampus some
  pathways are more sparsely connected than others.

Third, there are differences in learning principles.

- While backpropagation is one of the most widely utilized connectionist learning
  algorithms, there is no evidence of a mechanism for backwards propagation of
  error in the nervous system. Instead, learning relies upon a much more local
  signal.

The neural implausibility of backpropagation has provoked the most comment and
involves several dimensions of difference (Crick, 1989; Phillips, 1997; chapter 5 of
Rolls and Treves, 1998). First, there is no evidence that a neuron computes an error
signal that takes into account the contribution of all other neurons that synapse with
it and weights them as in backpropagation. Second, even if a neuron did make this
computation, it stretches credibility to suggest that it would send the result back-

wards through the neurons that synapse with it and then further back through the neurons that synapse with those and so on. Third, backpropagation works as well as it does in part because the number of hidden units is kept low to force generalization, but neural architectures do not lend themselves to implementing informational bottlenecks. Fourth, as an algorithm for supervised learning, backpropagation requires that a target output pattern be specified on every trial, information that usually is not available inside the system itself. One solution to this problem, which we noted in section 9.3.2, has been to have networks predict their next input as part of their output. When the next input arrives, it can be employed as the target against which to assess the prediction (that is, the discrepancy between predicted and actual input would be used as an error signal for training). While this is a promising idea that might bear empirical investigation, currently there is no evidence that real brains employ this strategy.

Given all these considerations, there has been no real dispute that the connections between neurons do not directly implement backpropagation. Disagreements arise in what to make of this, and to some extent reflect what goals have been considered most salient at different points in the short history of connectionism. When the specifically connectionist approach to network modeling began taking shape in the early 1980s, the new networks were regarded as cognitive models, not brain models. What excited people was that they had advantages of flexibility and adaptivity over classical symbolic models of cognition – advantages gained by incorporating some very general characteristics of the nervous system within some very general, all-purpose architectures. However, the early networks suffered from rather severe computational limitations: they could be multi-layered or could learn, but not both. Then backpropagation was discovered – more than once independently, in fact, but it was the formulation by Rumelhart, Hinton and Williams (1986b) that had immediate and enormous impact. With this learning algorithm for multi-layered networks at hand, *what* connectionist models could learn was suddenly much closer to human abilities and made them serious competitors to symbolic models. However, this advance in computational efficiency and psychological reality came at the expense of biological reality. As neuroscience and especially cognitive neuroscience flourished across the 1990s, the question of *how* connectionist networks accomplished their tasks became more of an issue. Is biological implausibility a fatal flaw, or is there a valid role for connectionist networks which employ biologically implausible mechanisms?

10.3.2 How important is neurophysiological plausibility?

In the eyes of biologically oriented researchers, any differences between mechanisms found in the brain and those used in connectionist models point to shortcomings in the models. From this perspective, although compromises may be necessary in the short term, cognitive models ultimately rest upon or constitute neural models; that is, they should specify the structure and activity of just those neural pathways that carry out the specific cognitive task being modeled. Accordingly, facts about the brain's operation are relevant in evaluating models, and neural plausibility is a mark of progress. Whether implicitly or explicitly, this position rests on a theoretical commitment known in philosophy as *mind–brain identity theory*. In the most common version of this theory, type identity theory, particular types of mental states are identical to particular types of brain states (Smart, 1959). Such an identity of mental and neural states permits an alignment between accounts – at the limit, a reduction of cognitive theories to biological ones.

At the other end of the philosophical spectrum, *functionalism* holds that cognitive models generally should be autonomous from brain models (Putnam, 1975b; Fodor, 1974). For functionalists, mental states are characterized in terms of their inter-action with other mental states and their relation to inputs and outputs. Although mental states can be implemented in the human brain, they can also be implemented in computers or other mediums. There is no systematic or necessary relationship between mental states and brain states, and no point in trying to align cognitive and biological accounts. Functionalists typically have created and defended classical symbolic accounts in which rules are used to manipulate representations. Though functionalism potentially could coexist with a variety of cognitive accounts, there is less flexibility in the other direction: symbolic models do not have much affinity with brain models and it makes more sense to keep them at their own levels (the functionalist approach) than to try to translate between them (the identity approach).

Most cognitive scientists have assumed some version of identity theory in theory but have been more or less functionalist in practice. That is, they assume that some day the neural underpinnings of cognition will all be worked out, but in the mean-time there are cognitive models to build and it would be a hindrance to try to make them biologically realistic. Connectionists have tended to be more concerned than other cognitive scientists about questions of biological realism, but vary consider-ably in their answers.[8] Paul Smolensky (1988) argued for a *proper treatment of connectionism* (PTC) that leaned towards the functionalist end of the spectrum. For him, connectionist models are subsymbolic – just a step below the symbolic level – and are evaluated by their ability to generate appropriate behavior, not their neurophysiological plausibility:

> it is better *not* to construe the principles of cognition being explored in the connectionist approach as the principles of the neural level. . . . To be sure, the level of analysis adopted by PTC is lower than that of the traditional, symbolic paradigm; but, at least for the present, the level of PTC is more explicitly related to the level of the symbolic paradigm than it is to the neural level.   (1988, p. 3)

Among the connectionists at this end of the spectrum, network models are generally regarded as abstract simulations of the processing that occurs in the nervous system. Those who come closest to a functionalist position are primarily concerned with developing the computational power and techniques that will best produce human-like intelligence, that is, they emphasize *what* result is achieved rather than *how*. Thus, enhancements to network designs can make them less brain-like if that is what does the job. For example, there is no prohibition against building in specific kinds of structure so as to account for rule-based reasoning involving variables (Shastri and Ajjanagadde, 1993). Other connectionists, though, lean towards the other end of the spectrum, biological realism. At a minimum they try to keep the *how* from conflicting with current knowledge of the nervous system, but increasingly they seek to incorporate some of that knowledge in connectionist networks.

The differences between these leanings are evident in treatments of backpropaga-tion. (a) A relatively abstract, functionalist construal of back-propagation emphasizes that it is a gradient descent (error-reduction) procedure, and it does not matter which method of gradient descent is used to set the weights in a network. Once trained, the network can be independently assessed as a cognitive model. That is, even if such a simulation is completely wrong about how a task is learned, it may be right about how the task is performed once learned. In choosing among implementations of gradient descent, computational considerations are more salient than biological ones. These relatively functionalist connectionists might incorporate a more efficient procedure in their models, but would not adopt one that is more biologically realistic but less efficient. (b) A connectionist taking a more moderate position between functionalism and mind–brain identity might use backpropagation as an interim implementation of gradient descent, but prefer to find an alternative which comes closer to mimicking the brain's own procedure. On this view, the legitimacy of using backpropagation to show *what* gradient descent might achieve rests on the expectation that biological research will uncover *how* the nervous system implements gradient descent. It matters whether the nervous system has such a mechanism. (c) Among those network modelers (including some connectionists) who place the highest priority on neurological plausibility, backpropagation has been abandoned in at least some of their modeling endeavors. Instead, they generally prefer working with variations on the Hebbian learning rule, which relies only on locally available information and is consistent with other known characteristics of long-term potentiation. (For thoughtful discussions of the relation between Hebbian learning and LTP as well as other points of contact between networks and brains, see McNaughton, 1989; Rolls and Treves, 1998.)

An approach that tries to satisfy goals at both ends of the spectrum has been proposed by O'Reilly (1996), building on Hinton and McClelland's (1988) recirculation algorithm. In O'Reilly's *generalized recirculation algorithm* (GeneRec), an approximation to backpropagation is achieved using essentially Hebbian local computations as components. To do this, he takes advantage of the fact that brain areas linked by feedforward connections also tend to have plentiful feedback connections and divides the use of this bidirectional circuitry into two phases. Focusing on the hidden units in a network of three layers with connections in both directions, during the first phase an input initiates interactive processing. The system retains the eventual activation value of each hidden unit after settling, which reflects not just the pattern supplied to the input units but also is influenced by the response of the output units over time. In the second phase both an input and a desired output pattern are supplied to the network and again interactive processing ensues. The eventual activation value of a given hidden unit after settling is compared to its value at the end of the first phase. Taking the difference is a local computation, and approximates the difference in net input to the hidden unit over the feedback connections from the output units. To change the weight on each connection from an input unit to the hidden unit, the difference is multiplied by the activation of the input unit and the learning rate, which again is a local computation. In contrast to backpropagation, as derived in box 3.2, net input and the derivative of the activation function need not be calculated, and error need not be passed back through the layers of the network. Although this procedure gains the advantage of local computation, making it generally more neurologically plausible than backpropagation, there is no specific evidence that the nervous system uses its feedforward and feedback connections in this particular way. The challenge of getting sufficient computational power while assuring biological reality will remain with us for some time.

Another moderate construal of backpropagation was offered by David Zipser (1990), who was concerned with biological reality but found that it was more achievable for

what than *how* questions in his study. Providing a three-layer network with information about retinal location and eye position, he used backpropagation to train it to
compute the location of an object using head-centered coordinates. Zipser discovered
that the hidden units developed response properties very similar to those that Richard
Andersen had found for neurons in Brodmann's area 7a in parietal cortex of the
monkey (Andersen, Essick, and Siegel, 1985). About half of the neurons in this area
employ a coding scheme that represents both retinal location and eye position. Despite
wide variation in a number of parameters such as number of hidden units or learning
rate, the network developed very similar coding schemes as the neurons that represent
both retinal and eye position. Yet there was an intriguing difference: the artificial
network achieved these biologically realistic hidden unit encodings in the course of
being trained to produce head-centered representations on its output layer. However, there was no evidence of neural encodings of head-centered representations in
the monkey. Attempting an explanation, Zipser suggested that it may actually be the
hidden layer patterns, not the output patterns, that get passed forward to networks
carrying out further computations (in the brain's own network and hence in any
model of that network). He was willing to leave unanswered the question of what
other procedure, either evolutionary or developmental, could generate the same
hidden encodings as he achieved using backpropagation: "The justification for the
learning paradigm rests on the empirical observation that the internal representation
generated by training actually resembles that found in the brain" (1990, p. 357).

Eventual answers to the *how* question may include some that lie beyond the reach
of current learning algorithms. Cognitive neuroscientists of the future may find that
we have been endowed with much more efficient ways of learning which often
replace gradient descent, and network modelers may learn to capture those alternatives. For example, existing networks might be copied and adapted (as suggested by
Bechtel and Abrahamsen, 1991, p. 270), or might first be redescribed in a more
skeletonized form and then copied and adapted (as suggested by Clark and Karmiloff-
Smith, 1993). Abrahamsen (1993) and Bechtel (1993) pointed out problems in making this work in practice, and currently such dramatic alternatives to backpropagation
lie closer to the realm of philosophy and functionalism than of biology.

10.4   Whither Connectionism?

Connectionists occupy a broad swath of a spectrum from functionalism (autonomous cognitive models) to mind–brain identity (biologically realistic cognitive models),
typically avoiding the extremes. Neither traditional cognitive scientists nor cognitive neuroscientists are fully pleased with connectionist models or their placement on
this spectrum. The disagreements are reminiscent of the controversy over the place of
connectionism in the dynamical systems approach that we discussed in section 8.5.
Some advocates of a dynamical approach argue that interactive networks are a half-
hearted kind of dynamical system, and see little to recommend them over the real
thing. Similarly, strong advocates of biologically realistic models tend to view connectionist networks as transitional at best.

Connectionists have defended their stance as uniquely useful not only against
dynamicists and neuroscientists but also against the symbolic theorists who occupy
the other end of both of these dimensions of disagreement – the original competitors
of connectionists. The best argument is not that connectionism can do a better job

than alternative approaches but rather that it can act as an honest broker between them. On a research landscape in which different methods, goals, and theoretical commitments pull researchers in different directions, connectionists can help create some special zones of confluence in which competition is subordinated to genuine integrations of knowledge. One example is the convergence of robotics, network models, simulated evolution, and the philosophical position of embodied cognition in the work on robot controllers discussed in sections 9.4 and 9.5. Even in the current chapter, the mere existence of the models in section 10.2 permits some optimism that the common formalism of neural network modeling will foster closer ties between neuroscientists and connectionists despite differences in commitment to neurobiological realism. Crucially, connectionists bring to those interactions an emphasis on cognitive function and familiarity with the very different formalisms of cognitive science. As the science of the mind of the early twenty-first century unfolds, who will bring together aspects of symbolic, dynamical, and biological approaches in multiply motivated models if not connectionists?

NOTES

1 Of course, any brief history like this oversimplifies. Connectionists, like computational neuroscientists, had a range of priorities. Some thought biological plausibility was an important goal whereas others viewed networks as models at a cognitive rather than biological level. Some focused on extending the range and computational power of network architectures and learning procedures while others were more concerned with whether these advances provided better fits to human data. Overall, though, the desire to account for cognition was a unifying theme.

2 There is evidence for some exceptions to this characterization, but most of the models we will discuss include a decay parameter.

3 The phonological pathway also develops attractors of larger scope, giving it a capacity for whole-word mappings from orthography to phonology that distinguishes it from the nonlexical route in the competing dual-route theory; see section 10.2.3.4.

4 In fact, there was also one layer of feedback connections from the hidden to orthographic units, but these did not affect the phonological output.

5 PMSP emphasized that consistency with neighboring words rather than conformance to general rules (regularity) is the key dimension. Even within regular words, those with inconsistent neighbors (e.g., -*INT* words such as *MINT* have the exceptional neighbor *PINT*) are named more slowly than those in consistent neighborhoods (e.g., -*ODE* words such as *CODE* and *NODE* have no exceptional neighbors). Like regularity, consistency interacts with frequency (its effects occur mainly in lower-frequency words). Unlike regularity, consistency can be varied in nonwords and has effects like those in words, a finding hard to account for in dual-route models.

6 PMSP had found in their first two simulations that the feedforward network better approximated human data on consistency effects when trained with actual word frequencies (simulation 2) rather than logarithmically compressed frequencies (simulation 1). Since actual frequencies required more than four times as many training trials, here they compromised by using a square-root compression (simulation 4, part 2). The resulting pre-lesion behavior was similar to that of the simulation they regarded as most realistic, that is, the interactive network with actual frequencies (simulation 3).

7 This simulation can be viewed as a feasibility study assessing the relevance of a collaboration between different networks, as more fully envisaged in figure 10.4. Plaut (1997, simulation 2) built an alternative implementation in which all three parts of the system

were represented, though only by feedforward networks producing semantic outputs: orthography → semantics and orthography → phonology → semantics. A single hidden layer feeding into semantics was shared. Even this minimal feedforward architecture required almost 10 days of CPU time for training. At that point, it could distinguish words from nonwords "without recourse to word-specific structural representations" (p. 14) – that is, it could perform a lexical decision task without a lexicon. It did so by computing a measure of the familiarity of each test item, which turned out to exhibit little overlap between words and nonwords.

8   For a philosopher's-eye view of varieties of connectionism with respect to functionalism, see Lycan (1991).

SOURCES AND SUGGESTED READINGS

Abbott, L. and Sejnowski, T. J. (eds) (1999) *Neural Codes and Distributed Representations.* Cambridge, MA: MIT Press.

Arbib, M. (ed.) (1995) *The Handbook of Brain Theory and Neural Networks.* Cambridge, MA: MIT Press.

Churchland, P. S. and Sejnowski, T. J. (1996) *The Computational Brain.* Cambridge, MA: MIT Press.

Gazzaniga, M. (ed.) (2000) *The New Cognitive Neurosciences.* Cambridge, MA: MIT Press.

Gluck, M. A. and Myers, C. E. (2000) *Gateway to Memory: An Introduction to Neural Network Modeling of the Hippocampus and Learning.* Cambridge, MA: MIT Press.

Gluck, M. A. and Rumelhart, D. E. (eds) (1990) *Neuroscience and Connectionist Theory.* Hillsdale, NJ: Lawrence Erlbaum.

Hanson, S. J. and Olson, C. R. (eds) (1990) *Connectionist Modeling and Brain Function: The Developing Interface.* Cambridge, MA: MIT Press.

O'Reilly, R. C. and Munakata, Y. (2000) *Computational Explorations in Cognitive Neuroscience: Understanding the Mind by Simulating the Brain.* Cambridge, MA: MIT Press. (Keyed to **PDP++** software.)

Rolls, E. T. and Treves, A. (1998) *Neural Networks and Brain Function.* New York: Oxford University Press.

Sejnowski, T. J. and Churchland, P. S. (1989) Brain and cognition. In M. I. Posner (ed.), *Foundations of Cognitive Science.* Cambridge, MA: MIT Press, 301–56.

APPENDIX A: NOTATION

The following diagram compares three notations for frequently used equations. They are shown with respect to input unit i and output unit u in a two-layer network that is being trained using the delta rule for changing weights and the logistic function for computing activation.

Notation used in this book (index for time or input–output pattern is suppressed)	PDP:2 (t indexes time)	PDP:8 (p indexes input–output pattern)
$$a_u = \frac{1}{1 + e^{-netinput_u}}$$	$$a_i(t+1) = \frac{1}{1 + e^{-net_i(t)}}$$	$$o_{pj} = \frac{1}{1 + e^{+net_{pj}}}$$
$$netinput_u = \sum_i weight_{ui}\,output_i + bias_u$$	$$net_i(t) = \sum_j w_{ij}\,o_j(t) - \theta_i$$	$$net_{pj} = \sum_i w_{ji}\,i_{pi} + \theta_j$$
FAN-IN FROM ALL INPUT UNITS $$input_{ui} = weight_{ui}\,output_i$$ $$\Delta weight_{ui} = lrate\,(d_u - a_u)\,a_i$$	$$\Delta w_{ij} = \eta(t_i(t) - a_i(t))\,o_j(t)$$	$$\Delta w_{ji} = \eta(t_{pj} - o_{pj})\,i_{pi}$$
FAN-OUT TO ALL OUTPUT UNITS $$output_i = a_i$$	$$o_j(t) = a_j(t)$$	i_{pi} (or o_{pi} in a more general version of the notation)
PROVIDED: a_i (input) and d_u (desired output)	PROVIDED: a_j (input) and t_i (target output)	PROVIDED: i_{pi} (input) and t_{pj} (target output)

Diagram (left column): $a_u \leftarrow$ (unit u) $\Leftarrow$ [$weight_{ui}$] $\Leftarrow$ (unit i)

Appendix B: Glossary

Note: Terms appearing in definitions which are defined elsewhere in this glossary are indicated in SMALL CAPITAL LETTERS.

activation, activation function, activation rule: The activation of a UNIT is a value that indicates its current level of activity. It is calculated by an activation function (activation rule) from the NET INPUT to the unit, and for some functions, also from the DECAY RATE, previous activation, and/or other factors. Typically nonlinear functions are used, e.g., a threshold or logistic function, and activations are binary (0 or 1) or continuous. Activations are calculated once for each presentation of and INPUT PATTERN in a FEEDFORWARD NETWORK, or once per CYCLE in an INTERACTIVE NETWORK (i.e., many times per input pattern). They are calculated regardless of whether the network is in TRAINING MODE or TEST MODE (in contrast to WEIGHTS, which are changed only in training mode). The pattern of activations across the HIDDEN and OUTPUT UNITS indicates the network's construal of the input pattern. (See sections 2.1.1 and 2.2.2).

attractor: An object in STATE SPACE (e.g., a point, cycle, or CHAOTIC TRAJECTORY) to which nearby TRAJECTORIES converge. (See section 8.2 for an introduction to different types of attractors.)

attractor network: An INTERACTIVE NETWORK with multiple BASINS OF ATTRACTION in its STATE SPACE.

autonomous dynamical system: A DYNAMICAL SYSTEM that is unaffected by any other system. The control parameters in the set of equations specifying the system will be constants, whereas those in nonautonomous systems vary due to the external influence of other systems.

backpropagation, generalized delta rule: A LEARNING RULE that can be applied to MULTI-LAYERED NETWORKS by utilizing a generalization of the DELTA RULE. The ERROR measure, which is calculated at the output units, is propagated back through the network layer by layer. At each layer, WEIGHTS are adjusted according to the equation: $\Delta weight_{jk} = lrate\ delta_j\ a_k$. The $delta_j$ itself is calculated recursively by a function that utilizes the delta values and weights on the next-higher layer as well as the activation of unit j. (See section 3.2.2).

basin of attraction: The set of all initial states whose TRAJECTORIES converge on an ATTRACTOR. In a STATE SPACE PLOT (phase portrait), one or more basins may be indicated by showing sample TRAJECTORIES or by enclosing a region around each ATTRACTOR with a closed curve (2D) or surface (3D).

bias: A constant input to a unit which is provided regardless of the amount of activation propagated from other units. It is sometimes simulated by introducing an additional unit with a constant activation of 1.0 that has a CONNECTION only to the biased unit. Optionally, the WEIGHT of this connection can be adjusted during learning. The negation of bias can be used as a threshold which the input to a binary unit must exceed in order for it to become active.

bifurcation: A rapid transition in the values that are taken by a variable in a system due to a small but critical change in the value of a control parameter. See section 8.2.2 for an explanation and for an illustration using a bifurcation diagram.

Boltzmann machine: A type of INTERACTIVE NETWORK proposed by Hinton and Sejnowski (1983, 1986). It has (a) UNITS that take binary ACTIVATION values; (b) an asynchronous update procedure; (c) a stochastic ACTIVATION RULE which is a probabilistic version of the logistic function; (d) a TEMPERATURE parameter that is typically lowered across time by a procedure called *simulated annealing*, by analogy with cooling schedules used to avoid faults in the formation of crystals. Characteristics (c) and (d) help to avoid the local minima to which Hopfield nets are subject. Harmony theory (Smolensky, 1986) specifies a similar type of interactive network. (See sections 2.2.2.2 and 3.2.3).

case: The term we have used to refer to a particular pairing of an INPUT PATTERN with an OUTPUT PATTERN (which may be a DESIRED OUTPUT pattern); for clarity, we often use the term *input–output* case. A network is trained by presenting it with a series of cases, usually with many trials for each case (one per EPOCH). Its performance can be tested using the same cases, or its ability to generalize can be tested using a new set of cases from the same universe of cases.

cellular automaton: A lattice (a network of cells in which only neighbors are connected) for which each cell is a finite automation that changes state on each timestep in accord with a rule table specifying allowable transitions in state. Artificial life researchers use cellular automata as simple abstract organisms.

chaotic trajectory: A TRAJECTORY through STATE SPACE which appears random (it never repeats itself) but is deterministic (from each point, the next point is determined by an algorithm).

clean-up units: A layer of units which is connected in both directions with another layer and serves to sharpen its output patterns. Adding such a layer is one way of modifying a FEEDFORWARD NETWORK to obtain an INTERACTIVE NETWORK.

cluster analysis: A method of analysis that is increasingly being used to characterize globally what information the HIDDEN UNITS have become sensitive to in a learning paradigm; it is often more tractable than trying to characterize each hidden unit separately. The method extracts regularities in the ACTIVATION patterns across the hidden units across various input–output CASES, and uses them to construct a tree structure representation that clusters together those cases with similar hidden unit patterns. (See section 6.4.3).

coarse coding: An innovative means of achieving DISTRIBUTED REPRESENTATIONS. Each individual UNIT (called a *receptor* in this context) is designed to have many different INPUTS in its receptive field, and each input is in the receptive field of many different units. The coding scheme can be set up such that no two units have exactly the same receptive field. The presence of a particular input is inferred if there is a high level of activity across many of the units that are receptive to it. (See section 2.2.4.2).

competitive learning: An UNSUPERVISED LEARNING PROCEDURE in which a network is presented with a series of INPUT PATTERNS and must discover regularities in those patterns that can be used to divide them into clusters of similar patterns. In the simplest case, there is a set of input units and a set of what we refer to as *detector units* (which combine some of the properties of HIDDEN UNITS and of OUTPUT UNITS); there are INHIBITORY CONNECTIONS among the detector units to assure that just one unit will "win" the competition for a particular input pattern. The effect is to classify the inputs into *n* categories when there are *n* detector units. In more complex systems there may be multiple sets of detector units, or intermediate layers of units. (See section 3.2.4).

connection: The UNITS in a network are linked by connections, which may be either unidirectional or bidirectional and either EXCITATORY or INHIBITORY. Each connection has a WEIGHT which indicates its importance and modulates the propagation of ACTIVATION along that connection. (See sections 2.1.1 and 2.2.1).

connectionism: An approach to cognitive modeling that has rather deep historical roots, but that in contemporary usage refers to particular classes of computer-implemented models of human or artificial intelligence. Most narrowly, it refers to LOCALIST NETWORKS such as those of Feldman and his colleagues at the University of Rochester. More broadly, it also refers to PARALLEL DISTRIBUTED PROCESSING networks such as those of Rumelhart, McClelland, and their colleagues at University of California, San Diego; Stanford University; and Carnegie-Mellon University. SPREADING ACTIVATION models such as those of Anderson at Carnegie-Mellon University could also be regarded as connectionist, but the term is not typically used in that context (primarily for reasons of sociology of science). Similarly, connectionist-style models by individuals with a neuroscience focus, such as Grossberg, are often referred to by such terms as *neural networks*. Usage is not consistent; for example, some cognitive modelers prefer the term *neural networks*. We have limited our use of the term *connectionism* to refer to localist networks in the Rochester tradition and to PDP networks, distinguishing between these when relevant. Most of our general material also applies to neural networks in neuroscience, but we do not specify those links.

coupled networks: Networks that function as nonautonomous dynamical systems because each receives input from the other continuously or repeatedly across time; cf. AUTONOMOUS NETWORK.

cycle: The updating loop in a synchronous INTERACTIVE NETWORK. One presentation of an INPUT PATTERN results in multiple cycles of processing during which the ACTIVATIONS dynamically interact until the network relaxes into a stable state (a state in which the INPUT to any unit does not change the probability of ACTIVATION of the unit). The complete set of cycles is needed to yield a response (solution, stable state) to a single input pattern; in contrast, in a FEEDFORWARD NETWORK a single pass of activation updates yields the network's response to the input. Cycles (which involve computation of activations) should not be confused with training EPOCHS (which involve computation of WEIGHTS). (See sections 2.1.2, 2.2.2.2 and 3.2.3).

decay: A decrease in ACTIVATION that occurs as a function of time or number of events. For example, in an INTERACTIVE NETWORK with a synchronous update procedure, each UNIT can be set to decay once per timing CYCLE by including a decay term in the equation to calculate change in activation (Δa). (Feedforward networks typically do not include a decay term, as activations are computed in a single forward sweep across layers of units.) Often the decay term is obtained by multiplying a decay rate (a constant between 0 and 1) by some other value. For example, in equations 3 and 4 of chapter 2, the decay rate of 0.1 is multiplied by the difference between the current activation and the resting activation. (See sections 2.1.2.2 and 2.2.2.2).

deep dyslexia: An acquired reading disorder characterized by difficulty reading nonwords and semantic, visual, and mixed errors when reading some words.

delta rule: A LEARNING RULE that utilizes the discrepancy between the DESIRED and actual OUTPUT of each OUTPUT UNIT to change the WEIGHTS feeding into it. Specifically, $\Delta weight_{ui} = lrate\,(d_u - a_u)\,a_i$. The delta rule's incorporation of an error correction procedure makes it a prototypical example of SUPERVISED LEARNING. The delta rule is guaranteed to find a solution if the input ppatterns form a linearly independent set and the input–output mappings are linearly separable, but it also works well at detecting regularities in input–output mappings for nonindependent inputs. It is also known as the Widrow–Hoff rule and as the least mean squares (LMS) rule. (See section 3.2.1.3).

desired output: The ACTIVATION value for an OUTPUT UNIT that has been designated as correct in certain SUPERVISED LEARNING procedures, such as those utilizing the DELTA RULE or the GENERALIZED DELTA RULE. The pattern of designated values across all output units is the desired output pattern. Often the terms *target output* and *target output pattern* are used instead.

distributed network, distributed representation: A distributed network is one in which each item of interest is encoded across multiple UNITS in the network (cf. a LOCALIST NETWORK, in which each item of interest is encoded by a single unit in the network). There are a variety of ways to obtain a distributed encoding. The least extreme approach is to distribute the representation across meaningful, context-free units at a lower level of analysis (e.g., phonemic distinctive features if recognition of spoken words is the task). Two ways of further distributing the encoding are (a) to make units like these context-sensitive (e.g., Wickelfeatures) or (b) to use a learning paradigm to obtain HIDDEN UNITS whose behavior is not defined by the designer. Finally, COARSE CODING is an innovative means of obtaining highly distributed representations. (See section 2.2.4.2).

Dynamical Systems Theory (DST):   A transdisciplinary field concerned with systems that can be specified by a set of equations in which one variable is time. One contribution of DST is the development of conventions for visually representing a system's possible states (its values on other variables) and changes in state (its values on other variables as a function of time) in STATE SPACE PLOTS.

enthymeme: A logic problem in which some parts of a complete pattern or string representing an argument are left unspecified; when the incomplete pattern is presented on the INPUT UNITS of a network, the task is to respond with the complete pattern on the OUTPUT UNITS.

epoch: The training loop, usually with regard to FEEDFORWARD NETWORKS. When a network is in learning or TRAINING MODE, one way to schedule training is to present repeatedly the same set of training cases (input–output patterns) to the network. One run through the set of training patterns is one epoch of training; that is, the epoch includes one trial per training case. WEIGHTS may be altered either after each case within the epoch, or just one time at the end of the epoch (with almost equivalent results). Generally, a large number of epochs is needed to arrive at weights that cannot be further improved. Note that an alternative way to schedule training is to present a large number of cases that are randomly selected from the universe of cases of interest; weights are changed after each case has been processed, and there is no organization of training trials into epochs. Variations on either method may be used in training INTERACTIVE NETWORKS, but if the TEMPERATURE parameter is altered (by simulated annealing) this additional factor yields a more complex training schedule in which the unit relevant to weight-changes is sometimes called a *sweep*.

error: The discrepancy between the DESIRED OUTPUT and ACTUAL OUTPUT of a UNIT in a SUPERVISED LEARNING paradigm. In McClelland and Rumelhart's (1998) exposition of error correction procedures, the errors are squared and summed across all output units to obtain the *pattern sum of squares* (*pss*). Further, the *pss* values are summed across all input–output cases to obtain the *total sum of squares* (*tss*). The *tss* value is a measure of the network's current performance; alternative versions of *pss* and *tss* are obtained by dividing by 2 (see boxes 3.1 and 3.2). The goal is to drive error as low as possible (to a global, rather than local, minimum). (See section 3.2.1.3).

excitatory connection: A CONNECTION that tends to increase the activity of the UNIT into which it feeds INPUT, typically by means of a positive WEIGHT. Excitatory connections are the means by which activation is propagated through a network. Many connectionist networks have INHIBITORY CONNECTIONS as well as excitatory connections.

feature map: See Kohonen feature map.

feedforward network: A network in which the UNITS are organized into separate layers, including at least an input layer and output layer and optionally one or more intermediate layers of HIDDEN UNITS, and activations feed forward from the input to the output layer. In the most typical version, each unit of a given layer has a unidirectional CONNECTION to each unit of the next (adjacent) layer. When an INPUT PATTERN is presented, units in one layer feed their ACTIVATION forward to the units in the next layer until the output layer is reached; there are no iterative cycles of change in activation as in an INTERACTIVE NETWORK. Variations include: the addition of INHIBITORY CONNECTIONS within a layer; the addition of connections between nonadjacent layers; sequential networks; recurrent networks; and networks with downwards connections in order to achieve top-down constraints on activation. Note that the number of layers in a feedforward network can be expressed either in terms of the number of layers of connections (the most usual practice) or units (the practice in this book). (See section 2.2.1.1).

generalized delta rule: See BACKPROPAGATION.

genetic algorithm: An algorithm used to evolve successive generations of artificial organisms that become adapted to a specified task or tasks. As applied in chapter 9, it is used to obtain a network that can serve as the "brain" of an abstract or embodied artificial organism (e.g., a robot). The genetic algorithm may replace learning or be combined with learning as a means of obtaining a network adapted to its task.

graceful degradation: The property of gradual decline of function when a system is overloaded or damaged. Nervous systems exhibit this property, and so do connectionist networks (particularly those using DISTRIBUTED REPRESENTATIONS). (See section 2.3.3).

harmony theory: See BOLTZMANN MACHINE.

Hebbian learning rule: A LEARNING RULE that specifies how much the WEIGHT of the CONNECTION between two UNITS should be increased or decreased in proportion to the products of their ACTIVATIONS: $weight_{ui} = lrate\ a_u\ a_i$. It builds on Donald Hebb's suggestion that the connection between two neurons might be strengthened whenever they fire at the same time. The Hebbian rule works well if the INPUT PATTERNS are uncorrelated (orthogonal), but this and other limitations are so severe that contemporary connectionist models often use different rules, or additional rules. One of the Hebbian rule's most important roles is as an ancestor of the DELTA RULE. (See sections 2.2.3 and 3.2.1.2).

hidden units: The UNITS in a network which cannot be accessed externally; their operations are "hidden" from the environment. There are no hidden units in the simplest networks, such as a typical PERCEPTRON. In a multi-layered FEEDFORWARD NETWORK, the units in all layers except the INPUT and OUTPUT layers are the hidden units; in an INTERACTIVE NETWORK, units that do not function to receive input and deliver output are the hidden units. Units that are not hidden units are called VISIBLE UNITS. (See section 3.2.2.1).

Hopfield net: A type of INTERACTIVE NETWORK developed by physicist John Hopfield by analogy with a physical system known as a *spin glass*. It has (a) UNITS that take binary ACTIVATION values (0 or 1); (b) an asynchronous update procedure; (c) an ACTIVATION RULE that yields an activation of 1 if the net input is greater than zero. Hopfield showed that such networks can reach a stable state by tending towards an energy minimum. (See section 2.2.2.2).

inhibitory connection: A CONNECTION that tends to reduce the activity of the UNIT into which it feeds INPUT, typically by means of a negative WEIGHT. Inhibitory connections are often used to assure that just one unit of a set or layer of units will achieve a high degree of activation, as in COMPETITIVE LEARNING. They are inspired by the phenomenon of lateral inhibition in the nervous system. Many connectionist networks have EXCITATORY CONNECTIONS but no inhibitory connections.

input: The $input_{ui}$ to a UNIT u is the product of the $output_i$ of unit i and the WEIGHT of the CONNECTION from i to u. That is, it is the propagated ACTIVATION from i to u, as scaled by the strength of the connection. All of the inputs to u are summed to obtain the *net input* to u. Inputs can be fed *from* INPUT UNITS or HIDDEN UNITS, and are fed *to* hidden units or OUTPUT UNITS.

input units, input layer, input pattern: Input units are those UNITS that can receive ACTIVATION from the external environment (or from another part of the network), initiating the propagation of activation to other units. In a FEEDFORWARD NETWORK, units are organized into layers; the first layer is the input layer (which may itself be subdivided into sets of units that receive specialized types of input). In an INTERACTIVE NETWORK, the input units may perform double duty as OUTPUT UNITS and may simply be referred to as *visible units*. The input pattern is the pattern of activation across the n input units (which can be treated mathematically as a vector in n-dimensional space). Note that the term *input* alone is sometimes a short form for *input pattern*, but it properly (and distinctively) refers to the value being fed to a unit u along each incoming CONNECTION.

input–output case: See CASE.

interactive network: A network in which UNITS are bidirectionally connected to one another, and ACTIVATIONS change dynamically across a large number of CYCLES. A distinction is made between VISIBLE UNITS and HIDDEN UNITS. INPUT PATTERNS are typically presented to the visible units (or a subset of those units); OUTPUT PATTERNS are the activation patterns across the visible units after processing. Sometimes the input pattern is "clamped" on to a subset of visible units, and the output of interest is the pattern attained across the remaining visible units (i.e., pattern completion). Exemplars include HOPFIELD NETS, BOLTZMANN MACHINES, and HARMONY THEORY; also, the Jets and Sharks simulations in chapter 2 involve a LOCALIST interactive network. (See sections 2.2.1.2 and 2.2.2.2).

Kohonen feature map: A self-organizing system in which a set of high-dimensional vectors (e.g., the patterns obtained on a layer of a connectionist network) are gradually mapped to a lower-dimensional space (the feature map) such that similar vectors tend to get mapped to neighboring units of the map.

language of thought: Jerry Fodor's (1975) term for the innate language-like medium in which, he claims, thought is carried out. Like external language or any other means of symbolic representation, the language of thought has a compositional syntax and semantics. Connectionists typically would deny these claims. (See section 1.3.2).

learning rule: An algorithm or equation which governs changes in the WEIGHTS of the CONNECTIONS in a network. A good learning rule is adaptive; that is, it increases the appropriateness of the network's responses to a class of INPUTS. Many learning rules incorporate an error-reduction procedure, by which the weight changes tend to minimize the difference between the actual and DESIRED OUTPUT pattern across a set of training inputs. A learning rule is typically applied repeatedly to the same set of training inputs across a large number of training EPOCHS; error is gradually reduced across epochs as the weights are fine-tuned. (See sections 2.2.3 and 3.2).

linear associator: A learning device obtained by applying the HEBBIAN LEARNING RULE in a two-layer FEEDFORWARD NETWORK with a linear ACTIVATION RULE.

linear threshold unit: A UNIT that takes binary ACTIVATION values; if its NET INPUT exceeds a threshold (usually 0) the activation is set to 1; otherwise its activation is set to 0.

localist network: A network in which each item of interest is encoded by assigning it to one UNIT in the network (cf. a DISTRIBUTED NETWORK, in which each item of interest is encoded across multiple units in the network). Generally, each individual unit of a localist network can be semantically interpreted. (See section 2.2.4.1).

microfeature, microstructure: See SUBSYMBOL.

modular connectionist architecture: A system in which a division of labor is achieved by specifying multiple specialized networks (modules) and connecting them such that some modules send their outputs to others. Sometimes the term "modular" is restricted to systems that satisfy stringent criteria specified by Fodor (1983), including informational encapsulation.

multi-layered network: A FEEDFORWARD NETWORK that has three or more layers of UNITS (and hence, two or more layers of CONNECTIONS). We describe networks in terms of the number of layers of units; more frequently, networks are described in terms of the number of layers of connections.

net input: The sum of all of the inputs to a UNIT u. The sum may be scaled by a constant, and separate sums and constants may be used if the same unit receives external inputs as well as internal inputs (from other units). Most simply: $\sum_i input_{ui}$. There is one internal input for each CONNECTION from another unit i. In the simplest case $activation_i = output_i$. In all cases $weight_{ui}$ multiplied by $output_{ui}$ yields $input_{ui}$. By combining these inputs from all units i feeding into unit u, ACTIVATIONS propagate through the network. In some (*interactive*) networks, the net input to u is the major (sometimes the only) value that determines the activation of u (in accord with the ACTIVATION FUNCTION). Calculating net input is analogous to a neuron pooling the influences of all the dendrites from other neurons that contact that neuron. (See sections 2.1.2.2 and 2.2.2.1).

nodes: See UNITS.

output: The *output*$_i$ of a unit *i* is a function of the *activation*$_i$ of UNIT *i*. In the simplest case it is the identity function: *output*$_i$ = *activation*$_i$. One alternative is to set a threshold at zero so that outputs will never be negative. Unit *i* sends the same output value to every unit *u* to which it is connected, but the outputs are modified by WEIGHTS before they reach the units *u*; hence, some units will be more affected by the activity of *i* than others. The CONNECTIONS feeding out of *i* are sometimes called the *fan-out* of *i*. Each output is analogous to the activity sent along one dendrite leading out of a neuron. (See section 2.1.2.2).

output units, output layer, output pattern: Output units are those UNITS that deliver the network's response to an INPUT PATTERN, culminating the propagation of activation through the network. In a FEEDFORWARD NETWORK, units are organized into layers; the final (highest) layer is the output layer. In an INTERACTIVE NETWORK, the output units may perform double duty as input units and may simply be referred to as *visible units*. The output pattern is the pattern of activation across the *n* output units (which can be treated mathematically as a vector in *n*-dimensional space). Note that the term *output* alone is sometimes a short form for *output pattern*, but it properly (and distinctively) refers to the value being fed from a unit *i* along each outgoing connection.

overregularization: See REGULARIZATION.

parallel distributed processing (PDP):   See PARALLEL PROCESSING.

parallel proessing: An approach to cognitive or computer system design in which computations are carried out in parallel, rather than serially as in the von Neumann architecture that characterizes contemporary digital computers. Although early advances are being made in parallel hardware, most cognitive models that specify parallel processing are actually implemented on serial computers presently (at considerable cost in processing speed). All connectionist models, including LOCALIST models, specify that processing is carried out in parallel. The parallel distributed processing (PDP) type of connectionist model achieves extreme parallelism by combining parallel processing with DISTRIBUTED REPRESENTATIONS. It has been pointed out that certain rule models can also exhibit some degree of parallel processing (e.g., parallel matching of the conditions of production rules).

pattern associator: A FEEDFORWARD NETWORK that has just two layers of UNITS: INPUT UNITS and OUTPUT UNITS. When is WEIGHTS are properly set, this type of network can respond to each of a variety of input patterns with its own distinctive output pattern; therefore it is sometimes referred to as a *pattern associator*. The best-known variety of pattern associator is the *perceptron*. (See section 2.2.1.1).

perceptron: In its narrowest sense, a two-layer network for which both the INPUT and OUTPUT UNITS take binary ACTIVATIONS, and the output units act as linear threshold units. Rosenblatt (1962) did much of the early research on these devices, and contributed the important *perceptron covergence theorem*. (See section 1.2).

recurrent network: A variation on the FEEDFORWARD NETWORK architecture, in which the pattern obtained on a HIDDEN layer is copied on to special units in a lower layer which feed back into the hidden layer. Typically the input is a string that is presented sequentially rather than as a simultaneous pattern, and the OUTPUT UNITS are used to predict the next element in the sequence. For example, after processing the first element, the network has copied the pattern on the hidden units on to the special units. When the network then processes the second element, the hidden units will receive INPUT both from the regular INPUT UNITS and the special units. Hence, this kind of network is able to gather and utilize information about a sequence. (See sections 2.2.1.1 and 6.4.2).

regularization, overregularization: The application of a general rule to a variety of items. When the scope of application is appropriate, the items have been regularized (e.g., forming a regular past tense for the set of regular verbs). When the scope of application is overly broad, the items have been overregularized (e.g., forming a regular past tense for irregular as well as regular verbs). (See section 5.2.3).

relaxation, settling: Terms for the process by which an INTERACTIVE NETWORK approaches a stable state that maximizes constraint satisfaction and minimizes ERROR. A network has fully relaxed, or settled, when it reaches a global energy minimum. (See section 2.2.2.2).

soft constraints: Refers to a situation in which multiple constraints compete, and the best overall solution is found by satisfying as many of them as possible. Connectionist networks are well suited to this task. A set of hard constraints, in contrast, must be completely satisfied; for example, in a traditional production system if no rule has all of its conditions met, no rule will fire. (See section 2.3.2).

spreading activation: A term that, in its most narrow usage, designates the theory of activation embodied in a class of LOCALIST NETWORKS derived from semantic networks beginning in the 1970s. The most prominent examples are found in John Anderson's (1976, 1983) ACT and ACT* theories. The ACTIVATION RULE in ACT* achieves nonlinearity by incorporating a negative exponential function, and shows other similarities to the propagation of activation within some connectionist networks. The activation functions differ in several respects, however, and ACT* is further distinguished by its hybrid architecture (a production system utilizes the network) and by its localist (rather than distributed) approach to encoding. In its broadest usage, the term *spreading activation* is used interchangeably with the connectionist term *propagation of activation*. The terminology and theory of spreading activation are antecedent to the 1980s era of connectionist models, and can be regarded as an early subclass of the localist variety of connectionist modeling. (See section 2.2.3).

state space: An *n*-dimensional space in which each dimension corresponds to one of the variables in a system. Each possible state of the system has a corresponding point in the space.

state space plot (phase portrait):   A geometrical diagram in which ATTRACTORS and their basins of attraction in a STATE SPACE can be indicated. In more complex plots, separatrices (indicated by closed curves or surfaces) may partition the state space into multiple basins of attraction. Other kinds of objects, such as repellors, saddle nodes, or CHAOTIC ATTRACTORS, may be indicated using special display conventions.

subsymbol, subsymbolic paradigm: One way of characterizing PDP (PARALLEL DISTRIBUTED PROCESSING) models is to point out that they are subsymbolic rather than symbolic, and that PDP research adheres to a subsymbolic paradigm rather than the symbolic paradigm of the traditional rules and representations approach to cognition. Smolensky (1987) distinguishes between *conceptual* and *subconceptual* levels of analysis, and argues that subsymbolic models can capture either level exactly, whereas symbolic models can capture only the conceptual level exactly. Further, a number of competencies traditionally regarded as conceptual are claimed to require a subconceptual level of analysis. Subsymbols are also called *microfeatures* (see Rumelhart and McClelland, 1986), and refer to encodings that are small-grained rather than large-grained; often they are designed to be context-sensitive as well. For example, Rumelhart and McClelland's (1986) Wickelfeatures are context-sensitive adaptations of phonological distinctive features (the smallest grain of traditional linguistic analysis). Subsymbols need not be derived from theories, however, some COARSE CODING schemes for INPUT UNITS have rather arbitrary receptive fields (e.g., Touretzky and Hinton, 1988), and individual HIDDEN UNITS in trained networks are often difficult to interpret or label. Also, note that one way of thinking about subsymbols would use grain size as a relative notion; whether the UNITS are subsymbols would depend upon whether they are at a smaller grain than usual for modeling performance on the task. (See section C.1.2).

supervised learning: The class of LEARNING procedures in which the network is provided with explicit feedback as to what OUTPUT PATTERN was desired for a particular INPUT PATTERN (and must compare that to its actual output); the DELTA RULE is one example. UNSUPERVISED LEARNING, in contrast, refers to the class of learning procedures in which the network gradually achieves, without feedback, a weight matrix that allows it to classify a set of inputs (by discovering the regularities exhibited by subsets of the input patterns). COMPETITIVE LEARNING is one example.

surface dyslexia: An acquired reading disorder characterized by difficulty reading exception words (they tend to get regularized) but preserved ability to read regular words and nonwords.

target output: See DESIRED OUTPUT.

temperature (T):   A parameter in certain ACTIVATION RULES for INTERACTIVE NETWORKS (e.g., BOLTZMANN MACHINES); lower values of T generally make activation patterns change more slowly. When a *simulated annealing* schedule is used, temperature is slowly reduced to avoid settling into local minima.

test mode, test trial: Relevant to a network in a LEARNING paradigm. When the network is in test mode, typically following a period in training mode, it is presented with a series of INPUT PATTERNS in order to observe its response to those patterns. They can be the same input patterns used in training, or may be a new set from the universe of input patterns in order to assess generalization. The purpose of test trials is limited to assessment of the performance achievable with the current WEIGHTS; no changes are made in the weights. (See section 3.2.2.1).

training mode, training trial: Relevant to a network in a LEARNING paradigm. When the network is in training mode, it is presented with a series of training trials.

Each trial consists of one presentation of one INPUT–OUTPUT CASE; at the end of the trial (or at the end of the set of training trials constituting an EPOCH), the WEIGHTS of the CONNECTIONS in the network are altered in accord with a LEARNING RULE. (See section 2.2.2.1).

trajectory: A path through STATE SPACE traversed by a DYNAMICAL SYSTEM through time. Each state of the system (the current values of its n variables) is indicated by a point in an n-dimensional space. In real time, a trajectory (or part of a trajectory) is a continuous curve; in discrete time, a sequence of points. If the trajectory takes the system from an initial state to equilibrium, the nonequilibrium part of the trajectory is called the "transient".

units, nodes: The elements of a network. Units receive INPUTS from other units (or from the environment) and compute a function that determines what OUTPUT they send to other units. In some models they are intended to function as a simplified neuron; in other models they are regarded as higher-level elements that do not correspond to neurons but are neuron-like or neurally inspired. (See section 2.1.1).

unsupervised learning: See SUPERVISED LEARNING.

variable binding: A capacity of certain systems of symbolic representation that is challenging to achieve in connectionist networks. When a rule (or other symbolic expression) includes variables, in order to apply the rule each variable must be bound to (linked to, or replaced by) a constant. If there are multiple instances of the same variable, each instance must be bound to the same constant. (See section 2.2.2).

visible units: The UNITS in a network which can be accessed externally (e.g., from the environment). In a FEEDFORWARD NETWORK, the units of the INPUT and OUTPUT LAYERS are the visible units; in an INTERACTIVE NETWORK, the same units may function both to receive input and to deliver output. Units that are not visible are called *HIDDEN UNITS*.

weight: Weight is a variable that indicates the strength (importance) of the CONNECTION between two UNITS. The OUTPUT of unit i ($output_i$) is multiplied by the weight of its connection to unit u ($weight_{ui}$) to obtain the input to unit u ($input_u$). Typically weights range between -1 and $+1$, or between 0 and 1, but they may also be unbounded. The weights between two layers can be displayed in a weight matrix using rows for the units in one layer and columns for the units in the other layer. Weights can either be set by the network designer and left unchanged, or can be changed in TRAINING MODE according to a function that is computed each EPOCH. The weights (and optionally, the BIASES) are the means by which knowledge about a domain is retained in a network. Along with the more transitory activation values, they determine the network's responses (OUTPUT PATTERNS) to a variety of INPUT PATTERNS. (See section 2.1.1).

Wickelphones, Wickelfeatures: Elements of a system for phonological representation. Wickelphones, proposed by Wickelgren (1969), are phonemic segments that have been made context-sensitive by indicating the immediately preceding and immediately following phoneme as well as the phoneme of interest, e.g., $_kA_m$.

Wickelfeatures, an extension proposed by Rumelhart and McClelland (1986) in *PDP:18*, provide a lower level of representation. A Wickelfeature includes just one distinctive feature for each of the three phonemes comprising a Wickelphone. For example, (Back, Low, Front) is one Wickelfeature for the Wickelphone ${}_kA_m$. Wickelfeatures are used to provide a DISTRIBUTED REPRESENTATION of the segmental phonology of a word. Their context sensitivity is a device for constraining the order of phonemic segments, since connectionist networks do not straightforwardly encode serial order. (See section 5.2.1).

XOR, exclusive or: A logical operation (propositional connective) of disjunction, meaning "one or the other but not both." That is , *A XOR B* is true if *A* is true and *B* is false, or if *B* is true and *A* is false; it is false if *A* and *B* are both true, or if *A* and *B* are both false. These truth conditions are distinct from those for *inclusive or* (often written v), which means "one or the other and possibly both" and therefore is false only if both *A* and *B* are false. *Inclusive or* is the connective commonly used in propositional logic (along with *and, not, if . . . then*, and *if and only if*). *Exclusive or* has been of particular interest to connectionists because it cannot be computed by a two-layer network; this was one of the limitations of PERCEPTRONS that were pointed out in the critique by Minsky and Papert (1969). The problem is that both-true and both-false are maximally dissimilar but must yield the same output (i.e., false). Inclusion of a HIDDEN layer solves this problem by permitting intermediate computations that produce a pattern with a more tractable similarity structure for use by the OUTPUT LAYER. (See section 3.2.1.5).

BIBLIOGRAPHY

Abbott, L. F. and LeMasson, G. (1993) Analysis of neuron models with dynamically regulated conductances. *Neural Computation*, 5, 823–42.

Abraham, R. H. and Shaw, C. D. (1992) *Dynamics: The Geometry of Behavior*. New York: Addison-Wesley.

Abrahamsen, A. A. (1987) Bridging boundaries versus breaking boundaries: Psycholinguistics in perspective. *Synthese*, 72, 355–88.

Abrahamsen, A. A. (1991) Bridging interdisciplinary boundaries: The case of kin terms. In C. Georgopoulons and R. Ishihara (eds), *Interdisciplinary Approaches to Language: Essays in Honor of S.-Y. Kuroda*. Dordrecht: Kluwer, 1–24.

Abrahamsen, A. A. (1993) Cognizer's innards and connectionist nets: A holy alliance? *Mind and Language*, 8, 520–30.

Ackley, D. H., Hinton, G. E., and Sejnowski, T. J. (1985) A learning algorithm for Boltzmann machines. *Cognitive Science*, 9, 147–69.

Ackley, D. H. and Littman, M. L. (1992) Interactions between learning and evolution. In C. G. Langton, J. D. Farmer, S. Rasmussen, and C. E. Taylor (eds), *Proceedings of the Second Artificial Life Conference*. New York: Addison-Wesley, 487–509.

Ackley, D. H. and Littman, M. L. (1994) Altruism in the evolution of communication. In R. A. Brooks and P. Maes (eds), *Artificial Life IV (Proceedings of the Fourth International Workshop on the Synthesis and Simulation of Living Systems)*. Cambridge, MA: MIT Press, 40–8.

Acredolo, L. and Goodwyn, S. (1990) Sign language in babies: The significance of symbolic gesturing for understanding language development. In R. Vasta (ed.), *Annals of Child Development*, vol. 7. Greenwich, CT: JAB Press.

Adami, C. (1998) *Introduction to Artificial Life*. New York: Springer-Verlag.

Aizawa, K. (1997) Explaining systematicity. *Mind and Language*, 12, 115–36.

Allen, R. B. (1988) Sequential connectionist networks for answering simple questions about a microworld. *Proceedings of the Tenth Annual Conference of the Cognitive Science Society*, 489–95.

Alvarez, P. and Squire, L. (1994) Memory consolidation and the medial temporal lobe: a simple network model. *Proceedings of the National Academy of Sciences*, 91, 7041–5.

Amari, S. I. (1983) Field theory of self-organizing neural nets. *IEEE Transactions on Electronic Computers*, EC-16, 741–8.

Amari, S. and Maginu, K. (1988) Statistical neurodynamics of associative memory. *Neural Networks*, 1, 63–73.

Andersen, R. A., Essick, G. K., and Siegel, R. M. (1985) Encoding of spatial location by posterior parietal neurons. *Science*, 230, 546–8.

Anderson, J. A. (1972) A simple neural network generating an interactive memory. *Mathematical Biosciences*, 14, 197–220. Reprinted in Anderson and Rosenfeld (1988), 181–92.

Anderson, J. A. (1995) *An Introduction to Neural Networks*. Cambridge, MA: MIT Press.

Anderson, J. A., Pellionisz, A., and Rosenfeld, E. (1990) *Neurocomputing 2: Directions for Research*. Cambridge, MA: MIT Press.

Anderson, J. A. and Rosenfeld, E. (eds) (1988) *Neurocomputing: Foundations of Research*. Cambridge, MA: MIT Press.

Anderson, J. R. (1974) Retrieval of propositional information from long-term memory. *Cognitive Psychology*, 6, 451–74.

Anderson, J. R. (1976) *Language, Memory, and Thought*. Hillsdale, NJ: Lawrence Erlbaum.

Anderson, J. R. (ed.) (1981) *Cognitive Skills and their Acquisition*. Hillsdale, NJ: Lawrence Erlbaum.

Anderson, J. R. (1983) *The Architecture of Cognition*. Cambridge, MA: Harvard University Press.

Anderson, J. R. (1989) A theory of the origins of human knowledge. *Artificial Intelligence*, 40, 313–51.

Anderson, J. R. (1990) *The Adaptive Character of Thought*. Hillsdale, NJ: Erlbaum.

Anderson, J. R. (1993) *Rules of the Mind*. Hillsdale, NJ: Erlbaum.

Anderson, J. R. and Bower, G. (1973) *Human Associative Memory*. Washington, DC: V. H. Winston.

Anderson, J. R. and Lebière, C. (1998) *The Atomic Components of Thought*. Mahwah, NJ: Erlbaum.

Anderson, J. R. and Thompson, R. (1989) Use of analogy in a production system architecture. In S. Vosniadou and A. Ortony (eds), *Similarity and Analogical Reasoning*. Cambridge: Cambridge University Press.

Baars, B. J. (1986) *The Cognitive Revolution in Psychology*. New York: Guilford Press.

Baldwin, J. M. (1896) A new factor in evolution. *American Naturalist*, 30, 441–51.

Ballard, D. H. (1991) Animate vision. *Artificial Intelligence*, 48, 57–86.

Ballard, D. H. (1997) *An Introduction to Natural Computation*. Cambridge, MA: MIT Press.

Barnden, J. A. (1988) CONPOSIT, a neural net system for high-level symbolic processing: Overview of research and description of register-machine level. MCCS-88-145. Memoranda in Computer and Cognitive Science, Computing Research Laboratory, New Mexico State University Las Cruces, NM.

Barnden, J. A. (1989) Neural-net implementation of complex symbol-processing in a mental model approach to syllogistic reasoning. In *Proceedings of the International Joint Conference on Artificial Intelligence – 1989*. San Mateo, CA: Morgan Kaufmann.

Barnden, J. A. (1995) High-level reasoning, computational challenges for connectionism, and the Conposit solution. *Applied Intelligence*, 5, 103–35.

Barto, A. G. and Anandan, P. (1985) Pattern recognizing stochastic learning automata. *IEEE Transactions on Systems, Man, and Cybernetics*, 15, 360–75.

Bates, E., Bretherton, I., and Snyder, L. (1988) *From First Words to Grammar: Individual Differences and Dissociable Mechanisms*. Cambridge: Cambridge University Press.

Bechtel, W. (1988) *Philosophy of Science: An Overview for Cognitive Science*. Hillsdale, NJ: Lawrence Erlbaum.

Bechtel, W. (1993) The path beyond first-order connectionism. *Mind and Language*, 8, 531–9.

Bechtel, W. (1994a) Levels of description and explanation in cognitive science. *Minds and Machines*, 4, 1–25.

Bechtel, W. (1994b) Natural deduction in connectionist systems. *Synthese*, 101, 433–63.

Bechtel, W. (1998) Representations and cognitive explanations: Assessing the dynamicist's challenge in cognitive science. *Cognitive Science*, 22, 295–318.

Bechtel, W. (1999) Dynamics and decomposition: Are they compatible? In R. Heath, B. Hayes, A. Heathcote, and C. Hooker (eds), *Dynamical Cognitive Science: Proceedings of the Fourth Australasian Cognitive Science Conference*. Newcastle, NSW: University of Newcastle.

Bechtel, W. (2001) Decomposing and localizing vision: An exemplar for cognitive neuroscience. In W. Bechtel, P. Mandik, J. Mundale, and R. S. Stufflebeam (eds), *Philosophy and the Neurosciences: A Reader*. Oxford: Blackwell.

Bechtel, W. and Abrahamsen, A. A. (1991) *Connectionism and the Mind: An Introduction to Parallel Distributed Processing in Networks*. Oxford: Blackwell.

Bechtel, W., Abrahamsen, A., and Graham, G. (1998) The life of cognitive science. In W. Bechtel and G. Graham (eds), *A Companion to Cognitive Science*. Oxford: Blackwell, 1–104.

Bechtel, W. and Richardson, R. C. (1993) *Discovering Complexity: Decomposition and Localization as Strategies in Scientific Research*. Princeton, NJ: Princeton University Press.

Beer, R. D. (1995) A dynamical systems perspective on agent–environment interaction. *Artificial Intelligence*, 72, 173–215.

Beer, R. D. (1997) The dynamics of adaptive behavior: A research program. *Robotics and Autonomous Systems*, 20, 257–89.

Belew, R. K., McInerney, J., and Schraudolph, N. (1991) Evolving networks: Using the genetic algorithm with connectionist learning. In *Proceedings of the Second Artificial Life Conference*, Reading, MA: Addison-Wesley, 511–47.

Berkeley, I. S. N., Dawson, M. R. W., Medler, D. A., Schopflocher, D. P., and Hornsby, L. (1995) Density plots of hidden value activations reveal interpretable bands. *Connection Science*, 7, 167–86.

Berko, J. (1958) The child's learning of English morphology. *Word*, 14, 150–77.

Bever, T. G. (1991) The demons and the beast – modular and nodular kinds of knowledge. In C. Georgopoulos and R. Ishihara (eds), *Interdisciplinary Approaches to Language: Essays in Honor of S.-Y. Kuroda*. Dordrecht: Kluwer.

Biederman, I. (1995) Visual object recognition. In S. M. Kosslyn and D. N. Osherson (eds), *Visual Cognition*. Cambridge, MA: MIT Press, 121–65.

Bienenstock, E. L., Cooper, L. N., and Munro, P. W. (1982) Theory for development of neuron selectivity: orientation specificity and binocular interaction in visual cortex. *Journal of Neuroscience*, 2, 32–48. Reprinted in Anderson and Rosenfeld (1988), 439–55.

Blank, D. S., Meeden, L., and Marshall, J. B. (1992) Exploring the symbolic/subsymbolic continuum: A case study of RAAM. In J. Dinsmore (ed.), *Closing the Gap: Symbolism vs. Connectionism*. Hillsdale, NJ: Lawrence Erlbaum.

Block, H. D. (1962) The perceptron: A model for brain functioning. I. *Reviews of Modern Physics*, 43, 123–35.

Bloom, L. (1970) *Language Development: Form and Function in Emerging Grammars*. Cambridge, MA: MIT Press.

Bobrow, D. G. and Winograd, T. (1977) An overview of KRL, a knowledge representation language. *Cognitive Science*, 1, 3–46.

Boden, M. A. (ed.) (1996) *Artificial Life*. Oxford: Oxford University Press.

Bohannon, J. N. and Stanowicz, L. (1988) The issue of negative evidence: Adult responses to children's language errors. *Developmental Psychology*, 24, 684–9.

Bower, J. M. (1992) Modeling the nervous system. *Trends in Neurosciences*, 15, 411–12.

Braine, M. D. S., Reiser, B. J., and Rumain, B. (1984) Some empirical justification for a theory of natural propositional logic. In G. H. Bower (ed.), *The Psychology of Learning and Motivation*, vol. 18. Orlando: Academic Press.

Braver, T. S., Cohen, J. D., and Servan-Schreiber, D. (1995) A computational model of prefrontal cortex function. In D. S. Touretzky, G. Tesauro, and T. K. Leen (eds), *Advances in Neural Information Processing Systems*. Cambridge, MA: MIT Press, 141–8.

Brooks, R. (1991) Intelligence without representation. *Artificial Intelligence*, 47, 139–59.

Brown, R. (1973) *A First Language*. Cambridge, MA: Harvard University Press.

Brown, T. H., Kairiss, E. W., and Keenan, C. L. (1990) Hebbian synapses: Biophysical mechanisms and algorithms. *Annual Review of Neuroscience*, 13, 475–511.

Bugmann, G. (1996) Biologically plausible neural computation. *Biosystems*, 40, 11–19.

Buzsaki, G. (1989) Two-stage model of memory trace formation: A role for "noisy" brain states. *Neuroscience*, 31, 551–70.

Bybee, J. L. and Slobin, D. I. (1982) Rules and schemas in the development and use of the English past tense. *Language*, 58, 265–89.

Chalmers, D. J. (1990) Syntactic transformations on distributed representations. *Connection Science*, 2, 53–62.

Chauvin, Y. and Rumelhart, D. E. (1995) *Backpropagation: Theory, Architecture, and Applications*. Hillsdale, NJ: Erlbaum.

Chomsky, N. (1957) *Syntactic Structures*. The Hague: Mouton.

Chomsky, N. (1959) Review of Skinner's Verbal Behavior. *Language*, 35, 26–58.

Chomsky, N. (1965) *Aspects of a Theory of Syntax*. Cambridge, MA: MIT Press.

Chomsky, N. (1968) *Language and Mind*. New York: Harcourt, Brace, and World.

Christiansen, M. H. (1992) The (non) necessity of recursion in natural language processing. *Proceedings of the 14th Annual Conference of the Cognitive Science Society*. Hillsdale, NJ: Erlbaum, 665–70.

Christiansen, M. H. (1994) *Infinite Languages, Finite Minds: Connectionism, Learning and Linguistic Structure*. Unpublished PhD dissertation, University of Edinburgh.

Christiansen, M. H., Allen, J., and Seidenberg, M. S. (1998) Learning to segment speech using multiple cues: A connectionist model. *Language and Cognitive Processes*, 13, 221–68.

Christiansen, M. H. and Chater, N. (1994) Generalization and connectionist language learning. *Mind and Language*, 9, 273–87.

Christiansen, M. H. and Chater, N. (1999) Toward a connectionist model of recursion in human linguistic performance. *Cognitive Science*, 23, 157–205.

Churchland, P. M. (1995) *The Engine of Reason, the Seat of the Soul*. Cambridge, MA: MIT Press.

Churchland, P. S. (1986) *Neurophilosophy: Toward a Unified Science of the Mind-Brain*. Cambridge, MA: MIT Press.

Churchland, P. S., Ramachandran, V. S., and Sejnowski, T. J. (1994) A critique of pure vision. In C. Koch and J. L. Davis, *Large-scale Neuronal Theories of the Brain*. Cambridge, MA: MIT Press.

Churchland, P. S. and Sejnowski, T. J. (1996) *The Computational Brain*. Cambridge, MA: MIT Press.

Cipra, B. A. (1989) Do mathematicians still do math? *Science*, 244, 769.

Clark, A. (1993) *Associative Engines: Connectionism, Concepts, and Representational Change*. Cambridge, MA: MIT Press.

Clark, A. (1997a) *Being There: Putting Brain, Body and World Together Again*. Cambridge, MA: MIT Press.

Clark, A. (1997b) The dynamical challenge. *Cognitive Science*, 21, 461–81.

Clark, A. and Karmiloff-Smith, A. (1993) The cognizer's innards: A psychological and philosophical perspective on the development of thought. *Mind and Language*, 8, 487–519.

Clark, A. and Toribio, J. (1994) Doing without representing? *Synthese*, 101, 401–31.

Cliff, D. (1991) Computational neuroethology: A provisional manifesto. In J.-A. Meyer and S. W. Wilson (eds), *From Animals to Animats: Proceedings of the First International Conference on Simulation of Adaptive Behavior*, Cambridge, MA: MIT Press, 29–39.

Cliff, D., Harvey, I., and Husbands, P. (1997) Artificial evolution of visual control systems for robots. In M. Srinivisan and S. Verkatesh (eds), *From Living Eyes to Seeing Machines*. Oxford: Oxford University Press, 126–57.

Cohen, J. D., Romero, R. D., Servan-Schreiber, D., and Farah, M. J. (1994) Mechanisms of spatial attention: The relation of macrostructure to microstructure in parietal neglect. *Journal of Cognitive Neuroscience*, 6, 377–87.

Cohen, J. D. and Servan-Schreiber, D. (1992) Context, cortex, and dopamine: A connectionist approach to behavior and biology in schizophrenia. *Psychological Review*, 99, 45–77.

Cohen, N. J. and Eichenbaum, H. (1993) *Memory, Amnesia, and the Hippocampal System*. Cambridge, MA: MIT Press.

Cohen, N. J. and Squire, L. R. (1980) Preserved learning and retention of pattern-analyzing skill in amnesia: dissociation of "know how" and "knowing that." *Science*, 210, 207–10.

Collingridge, G. L. and Bliss, T. V. P. (1987). NMDA receptors – their role in long-term potentiation. *Trends in Neurosciences*, 10, 288–93.

Coltheart, M. (1985) Cognitive neuropsychology and the study of reading. In M. I. Posner and O. S. M. Marin (eds), *Attention and Performance XI*. Hillsdale, NJ: Lawrence Erlbaum, 3–37.

Coltheart, M. (1998) Modeling visual word recognition and reading aloud. Colloquium presentation at Washington University, June 24.

Coltheart, M., Curtis, B., Atkins, P., and Haller, M. (1993) Models of reading aloud: Dual-route and parallel-distributed-processing approaches. *Psychological Review*, 100, 589–608.

Coltheart, M., Rastle, K., Perry, C., Langdon, R., and Ziegler, J. (2001) DRC: A Dual Route Cascaded model of visual word recognition and reading aloud. *Psychological Review*, 108, 204–56.

Cooper, R. (1994) Representation in modular networks: Book review of Miikkulainen on language network. *Psycoloquy*, 5, 88.

Cottrell, G. W., Munro, P., and Zipser, D. (1989) Image compression by back propagation: An example of extensional programming. In N. E. Sharkey (ed.), *Models of Cognition: A Review of Cognitive Science*, vol. 1. Norwood, NJ: Ablex, 208–40.

Cottrell, G. W. and Tsung, F.-S. (1989) Learning simple arithmetic procedures. *Proceedings of the Eleventh Annual Conference of the Cognitive Science Society*. Hillsdale, NJ: Lawrence Erlbaum, 58–65.

Cowan, J. D. and Sharp, D. H. (1988) Neural nets and artificial intelligence. *Daedalus*, 117, 85–121.

Crick, F. H. C. (1989) The recent excitement about neural networks. *Nature*, 337, 129–32.

Crutchfield, J. P., Mitchell, M., and Das, R. (1998) The evolutionary design of collective computation in cellular automata, Technical Report 98-09-080. Santa Fe Institute, Santa Fe, New Mexico.

Cummins, R. and Cummins, D. D. (eds) (2000) *Minds, Brains, and Computers: The Foundations of Cognitive Science: An Anthology*, Oxford: Blackwell.

Dawson, M. R. W., Medler, D. A., and Berkeley, I. S. N. (1997) PDP models can provide models that are not mere implementations of classical theories. *Philosophical Psychology*, 10, 25–40.

Dayan, P., Hinton, G. E., Neal, R. N., and Zemel, R. S. (1995) The Helmholtz machine. *Neural Computation*, 7, 889–904.

Dennett, D. C. (1977) *Brainstorms*. Cambridge, MA: MIT Press.

Dennett, D. C. (1978) Toward a cognitive theory of consciousness. In C. W. Savage (ed.), *Perception and Cognition: Issues in the Foundations of Psychology. Minnesota Studies in the Philosophy of Science*, vol. 9. Minneapolis, MN: University of Minnesota Press. Reprinted in D. C. Dennett (ed.), *Brainstorms*, Montgomery, VT: Bradford Books (1978), 149–73.

Dennett, D. C. (1995) Artificial life as philosophy. In C. G. Langton (ed.), *Artificial Life: An Overview*. Cambridge, MA: MIT Press, 291–2.

Dretske, F. (1988) *Explaining Behavior: Reasons in a World of Causes*. Cambridge, MA: MIT Press.

Dreyfus, H. L. and Dreyfus, S. E. (1986) *Mind over Machine: The Power of Human Intuition and Expertise in the Era of the Computer*. New York: Free Press.

Durbin, R. and Willshaw, D. J. (1987) An analogue approach to the traveling salesman problem using an elastic net method. *Nature*, 326, 689–91.

Dyer, M. G. (1991) Symbolic NeuroEngineering for natural language processing: A multilevel research approach. In J. Barnden and J. Pollack (eds), *Advances in Connectionist and Neural Computation Theory*. Norwood, NJ: Ablex, 32–86.

Edelman, G. (1987) *Neural Darwinism: The Theory of Neuronal Group Selection*. New York: Basic Books.

Eichenbaum, H., Otto, T., and Cohen, N. J. (1994) Two component functions of the hippocampal memory systems. *Behavioral and Brain Sciences*, 17, 449–72.

Eliasmith, C. and Anderson, C. H. (forthcoming) *Neural Engineering: The Principles of Neurobiological Simulation*, Cambridge, MA: MIT Press.

Ellis, R. and Humphreys, G. (1999) *Connectionist Psychology: A Text with Readings*. East Sussex: Psychology Press.

Elman, J. L. (1990) Finding structure in time. *Cognitive Science*, 14, 179–212.

Elman, J. (1991) Distributed representations, simple recurrent networks, and grammatical structure. *Machine Learning*, 7, 195–225.

Elman, J. L. (1993) Learning and development in neural networks: The importance of starting small. *Cognition*, 48, 71–99.

Elman, J. L. (1995) Language as a dynamical system. In R. F. Port and T. van Gelder (eds), *Mind as Motion*. Cambridge, MA: MIT Press, 195–225.

Elman, J. L., Bates, E. A., Johnson, M. H., Karmiloff-Smith, A., Parisi, D., and Plunkett, K. (1996) *Rethinking Innateness: A Connectionist Perspective on Development*. Cambridge, MA: MIT Press.

Engel, A. K., König, P., and Singer, W. (1991) Direct physiological evidence for scene segmentation by temporal coding. *Proceedings of the National Academy of Sciences, USA*, 88, 9136–40.

Ervin, S. (1964) Imitation and structural change in children's language. In E. Lenneberg (ed.), *New Directions in the Study of Language*. Cambridge, MA: MIT Press.

Fahlman, S. E. (1979) *NETL, A System for Representing and Using Real-World Knowledge*. Cambridge, MA: MIT Press.

Farah, M. J. (1994) Neuropsychological inference with an interactive brain: A critique of the "locality" assumption. *Behavioral and Brain Sciences*, 17, 43–104.

Feldman, J. A. and Ballard, D. H. (1982) Connectionist models and their properties. *Cognitive Science*, 6, 205–54. Reprinted in Anderson and Rosenfeld (1988), 484–507.

Felleman, D. J. and van Essen, D. C. (1991) Distributed hierarchical processing in the primate cerebral cortex. *Cerebral Cortex*, 1, 1–47.

Fenson, L., Dale, P. S., Reznick, J. S., Bates, E., Thal, D., and Pethick, S. J. (1994) Variability in early communicative development. *Monographs of the Society for Research in Child Development*, 59.

Fodor, J. A. (1974) Special sciences (Or: Disunity of science as a working hypothesis). *Synthese*, 28, 97–115.

Fodor, J. A. (1975) *The Language of Thought*. New York: Crowell.

Fodor, J. A. (1980) Methodological solipsism considered as a research strategy in cognitive psychology. *Behavioral and Brain Sciences*, 3, 63–109.

Fodor, J. A. (1983) *The Modularity of Mind*. Cambridge, MA: MIT Press.

Fodor, J. A. (1984) Semantics, Wisconsin style. *Synthese*, 59, 231–50.

Fodor, J. A. (1987) *Psychosemantics: The Problem of Meaning in the Philosophy of Mind*. Cambridge, MA: MIT Press.

Fodor, J. A. and McLaughlin, B. (1990) Connectionism and the problem of systematicity: Why Smolensky's solution doesn't work. *Cognition*, 35, 183–204.

Fodor, J. A. and Pylyshyn, Z. W. (1988) Connectionism and cognitive architecture: A critical analysis. *Cognition*, 28, 3–71.

Forrest, S., Javornik, B., Smith, R., and Perelson, A. (1993) Using genetic algorithms to explore pattern recognition in the immune system. *Evolutionary Computation*, 1, 191–211.

Freeman, W. J. (1987) Simulation of chaotic EEG patterns with a dynamic model of the olfactory system. *Biological Cybernetics*, 56, 139–50.

Freeman, W. J. and Skarda, C. A. (1990) Representations: Who needs them? In J. L. McGaugh, N. M. Weinberger, and G. Lynch (eds), *Brain Organization and Memory: Cells, Systems, and Circuits*. Oxford: Oxford University Press, 375–80.

French, R. M. (1992) Semi-distributed representations and catastrophic forgetting in connectionist networks. *Connection Science*, 4, 365–77.

Fukushima, K. (1980) Neocognitron: A self-organizing multilayered neural network model for a mechanism of pattern recognition unaffected by shift in position. *Biological Cybernetics*, 36, 193–202.

Gardner, H. (1970) The fantastic combinations of John Conway's new solitaire game "Life." *Scientific American*, 223, 120–3.

Gibson, J. J. (1966) *The Senses Considered as Perceptual Systems*. Boston, MA: Houghton Mifflin.

Gigerenzer, G. (1991) How to make cognitive illusions disappear: Beyond "heuristics and biases." In W. Stroebe and M. Hewstone (eds), *European Review of Social Psychology*, vol. 2, New York: John Wiley and Sons, 83–115.

Gigerenzer, G., Hell, W., and Blank, H. (1988) Presentation and content: The use of base rates as a continuous variable. *Journal of Experimental Psychology: Human Perception and Performance*, 14, 513–25.

Gluck, M. A. and Bower, G. H. (1988) Evaluating an adaptive network model of human learning. *Journal of Memory and Language*, 27, 166–95.

Gluck, M. and Myers, C. (1993) Hippocampal mediation of stimulus representation: a computational theory. *Hippocampus*, 3, 491–516.

Gluck, M. A. and Myers, C. E. (2001) *Gateway to Memory: An Introduction to Neural Network Modeling of the Hippocampus and Learning*. Cambridge, MA: MIT Press.

Glushko, R. J. (1979) The organization act activation of orthographic knowledge in reading aloud. *Journal of Experimental Psychology: Human Perception and Performance*, 5, 674–91.

Goldberg, D. E. (1989) *Genetic Algorithms in Search, Optimization, and Machine Learning*. New York: Addison Wesley.

Goodman, N. (1955) *Fact, Fiction, and Forecast*. Cambridge, MA: Harvard University Press.

Gorman, R. P. and Sejnowski, T. J. (1988) *Learned classification of sonar targets using a massively-parallel network*, IEEE Transactions: Acoustics, Speech, and Signal Processing.

Gould, S. J. and Lewontin, R. C. (1979) The spandrels of San Marco and the panglossian paradigm: A critique of the adaptationist programme. *Proceedings of the Royal Society of London*, B205, 581–98.

Gray, C. M. and Singer, W. (1989) Stimulus-specific neuronal oscillations in orientation columns of cat visual cortex. *Proceedings of the National Academy of Sciences, USA*, 86, 1698–1702.

Grodzinsky, Y. (2000) The neurology of syntax: Language use without Broca's area. *Behavioral and Brain Sciences*, 23, 1–20.

Grossberg, S. (1976) Adaptive pattern classification and universal recoding: I. Parallel development and coding of neural feature detectors. *Biological Cybernetics*, 23, 121–34. Reprinted in Anderson and Rosenfeld (1988), 245–58.

Grossberg, S. (1982) *Studies of Mind and Brain: Neural Principles of Learning, Perception, Development, Cognition, and Motor Control*. Dordrecht: Reidel.

Grossberg, S. (ed.) (1988) *Neural Networks and Natural Intelligence*. Cambridge, MA: MIT Press.

Grush, R. (1997a) The architecture of representation. *Philosophical Psychology*, 10, 5–23.

Grush, R. (1997b) Review of *Mind as Motion: Explorations in the Dynamics of Cognition*. *Philosophical Psychology*, 10, 233–42.

Hadley, R. F. (1994a) Systematicity in connectionist language learning. *Mind and Language*, 9, 247–72.

Hadley, R. F. (1994b) Systematicity revisited: Reply to Christiansen and Chater and Niklasson and van Gelder. *Mind and Language*, 9, 431–44.

Hadley, R. F. (1997) Cognition, systematicity, and nomic necessity. *Mind and Language*, 12, 137–53.

Hadley, R. F. and Hayward, M. B. (1997) Strong semantic systematicity from Hebbian connectionist learning. *Minds and Machines*, 7, 1–37.

Hampshire, J. B. and Waibel, A. H. (1989) A novel objective function for improved phoneme recognition using time-delay neural networks, Technical Report CMU-CS-89-118, Computer Science Department, Carnegie Mellon University, Pittsburgh, PA.

Hanson, N. R. (1958) *Patterns of Discovery*. Cambridge: Cambridge University Press.

Happel, B. L. M. and Murre, J. M. J. (1994) The design and evolution of modular neural network architectures. *Neural Networks*, 7, 985–1004.

Hart, Jr., J., Berndt, R. S., and Caramazza, A. (1985) Category-specific naming deficit following cerebral infarction. *Nature*, 316, 439–40.

Harvey, I., Husbands, P., and Cliff, D. (1993) Issues in evolutionary robotics. In J.-A. Meyer, H. L. Roitblat, and S. W. Wilson (eds), *From Animals to Animats 2*, Cambridge, MA: MIT Press.

Haselager, W. F. G. and van Rappard, J. F. H. (1998) Connectionism, the frame problem, and systematicity. *Minds and Machines*, 8, 161–79.

Haugeland, J. (1981) Semantic engines: An introduction to mind design. In J. Haugeland (ed.), *Mind Design*, Cambridge, MA: MIT Press.

Haugeland, J. (1985) *Artificial Intelligence: The Very Idea*. Cambridge, MA: MIT Press.

Haugeland, J. (1991) Representational genera. In W. Ramsey, S. P. Stich, and D. E. Rumelhart (eds), *Philosophy and Connectionist Theory*, Hillsdale, NJ: Lawrence Erlbaum, 61–89.

Hebb, D. O. (1949) *The Organization of Behavior*. New York: John Wiley and Sons.

Henley, N. M. (1969) A psychological study of the semantics of animal terms. *Journal of Verbal Learning and Verbal Behavior*, 8, 176–84.

Hertz, J., Krogh, A., and Palmer, R. (1991) *Introduction to the Theory of Neural Computation*. Redwood, CA: Addison-Wesley.

Hetherington, P. A. and Seidenberg, M. S. (1989) Is there "catastrophic" interference in connectionist networks? *Proceedings of the Eleventh Annual Conference of the Cognitive Science Society*, Hillsdale, NJ: Lawrence Erlbaum, 26–33.

Hinton, G. E. (1986) Learning distributed representations of concepts. *Proceedings of the Eighth Annual Conference of the Cognitive Science Society*, Hillsdale, NJ: Lawrence Erlbaum, 1–12.

Hinton, G. E. (1987) Learning translation invariant recognition in a massively parallel network. In *PARLE Parallel Architectures and Languages Europe*, vol. 1. Berlin: Springer-Verlag, 1–14.

Hinton, G. E. (1989) Connectionist learning systems. *Artificial Intelligence*, 40, 185–234.

Hinton, G. E. (1990) Mapping part–whole hierarchies into connectionist networks. *Artificial Intelligence*, 46, 47–75.

Hinton, G. E. and Anderson, J. A. (eds) (1981) *Parallel Models of Associative Memory*. Hillsdale, NJ: Lawrence Erlbaum.

Hinton, G. E. and McClelland, J. L. (1988) Learning representations by recirculation. In D. Z. Anderson (ed.), *Neural Information Processing Systems: Denver, CO, 1987*, New York: American Institute of Physics, 358–66.

Hinton, G. E., McClelland, J. L., and Rumelhart, D. E. (1986) Distributed representations. In Rumelhart, McClelland, and the PDP Research Group (1986), chapter 3, 77–109.

Hinton, G. E. and Nowlan, S. J. (1987) How learning guides evolution. *Complex Systems*, 1, 495–502.

Hinton, G. E. and Sejnowski, T. J. (1983) Optimal perceptual inference. In *Proceedings of the Institute of Electronic and Electrical Engineers Computer Society Conference on Computer Vision and Pattern Recognition*, Washington, DC: IEEE, 448–53.

Hinton, G. E. and Sejnowski, T. J. (1986) Learning and relearning in Boltzmann machines. In Rumelhart, McClelland, and the PDP Research Group (1986), chapter 7, 282–317.

Hinton, G. E. and Shallice, T. (1991) Lesioning an attractor network: Investigations of acquired dyslexia. *Psychological Review*, 98, 74–95.

Hirsh-Pasek, K. and Golinkoff, R. M. (1996) *The Origins of Grammar: Evidence from Early Language Comprehension*. Cambridge, MA: MIT Press.

Hobbes, T. (1651/1962) *Leviathan: Or the Matter, Forme and Power of a Commonwealth Ecclesiastical and Civil*. London: Collier Books.

Holland, J. H. (1975/1992) *Adaptation in Natural and Artificial Systems*. Cambridge, MA: MIT Press.

Holland, J. H., Holyoak, K. J., Nisbett, R. E., and Thagard, P. R. (1986) *Induction: Processes of Inference, Learning, and Discovery*. Cambridge, MA: MIT Press.

Holyoak, K. J. and Thagard, P. R. (1989) Analogical mapping by constraint satisfaction. *Cognitive Science* 13, 295–355.

Holyoak, K. J. and Thagard, P. (1995) *Mental Leaps: Analogy in Creative Thought*. Cambridge, MA: MIT Press.

Honavar, V. and Vhr, L. (1988) A network of neuron-like units that learns to perceive by generation as well as reweighing of its links. In D. Touretzky, G. Hinton, and T. Sejnowski (eds), *The Proceedings of the 1988 Connectionist Models Summer School*. San Mateo, CA: Morgan Kaufmann, 472–84.

Hopfield, J. J. (1982) Neural networks and physical systems with emergent collective computational abilities. *Proceedings of the National Academy of Sciences*, 79, 2554–8. Reprinted in Anderson and Rosenfeld (1988), 460–4.

Hopfield, J. J. (1984) Neurons with graded response have collective computational properties like those of two state-neurons. *Proceedings of the National Academy of Sciences*, 81, 3088–92. Reprinted in Anderson and Rosenfeld (1988), 579–83.

Hopfield, J. J. and Tank, D. W. (1985) "Neural" computation and constraint satisfaction and the traveling salesman. *Biological Cybernetics*, 55, 141–52.

Horgan, T. (1997) Connectionism and the philosophical foundations of cognitive science. *Metaphilosophy*, 28, 1–30.

Horgan, T. and Tienson, J. (1996) *Connectionism and the Philosophy of Psychology*. Cambridge, MA: MIT Press.

Hubel, D. H. and Wiesel, T. N. (1962) Receptive fields, binocular interaction and functional architecture in the cat's visual cortex. *Journal of Physiology (London)*, 160, 106–54.

Hubel, D. H. and Wiesel, T. N. (1963) Receptive fields of cells in striate cortex of very young, visually inexperienced kittens. *Journal of Neurophysiology*, 26, 994–1002.

Hubel, D. H. and Wiesel, T. N. (1968) Receptive fields and functional architecture of monkey striate cortex. *Journal of Physiology (London)*, 195, 215–43.

Hummel, J. E. and Biederman, I. (1992) Dynamic binding in a neural network for shape recognition. *Psychological Review*, 99, 480–517.

Hutchins, E. (1995) *Cognition in the Wild*. Cambridge, MA: MIT Press.

Hyams, N. (1986) *Language Acquisition and the Theory of Parameters*. Dordrecht: Reidel.

Jacobs, R. A., Jordan, M. I., and Barto, A. G. (1991) Task decomposition through competition in a modular connectionist architecture: The what and where vision tasks. *Cognitive Science*, 15, 219–50.

Jaeger, J. J., Lockwood, A. H., Kemmerer, D. L., Van Valin, R. D., Murphy, B. W., and Khalak, H. G. (1996) A positron emission tomographic study of regular and irregular verb morphology in English. *Language*, 72, 451–97.

Johnson, J. S. and Newport, M. (1989) Critical period effects in second language learning: The influence of maturational state on the acquisition of English as a second language. *Cognitive Psychology*, 21, 60–99.

Jordan, M. I. (1986a) An introduction to linear algebra in parallel distributed processing. In Rumelhart, McClelland, and the PDP Research Group (1986), chapter 9, 365–422.

Jordan, M. I. (1986b) Attractor dynamics and parallelism in a connectionist sequential machine. In *Proceedings of the Eighth Annual Conference of the Cognitive Science Society*, Hillsdale, NJ: Lawrence Erlbaum, 10–17.

Kaneko, K. (1990) Clustering, coding, switching, hierarchical ordering, and control in a network of chaotic elements. *Physica D*, 41, 137–72.

Karmiloff-Smith, A. (1992) *Beyond Modularity: A Developmental Perspective on Cognitive Science*. Cambridge, MA: MIT Press.

Kelso, J. A. S. (1995) *Dynamic Patterns: The Self-organization of Brain and Behavior*. Cambridge, MA: MIT Press.

Kim, J. J. and Faneslow, M. S. (1992) Modality-specific retrograde amnesia of fear. *Science*, 256, 675–7.

Kim, J. J., Pinker, S., Prince, A., and Prasada, S. (1991) Why no mere mortal has ever flown out to center field. *Cognitive Science*, 15, 173–218.

Kirsh, D. (1991) Today the earwig, tomorrow man? *Artificial Intelligence*, 47, 161–84.

Koch, C. (1990) Biophysics of computation: towards the mechanisms underlying information processing in single neurons. In E. L. Schwartz, *Computational Neuroscience*. Cambridge, MA: MIT Press, 97–113.

Kohonen, T. (1972) Correlation matrix memories. *IEEE Transactions on Computers C-21*, 353–9. Reprinted in Anderson and Rosenfeld (1988), 174–80.

Kohonen, T. (1981) Automatic formation of topological maps of patterns in a self-organizing system. In *Proceedings of the 2nd Scandinavian Conference on Image Analysis*, Espoo, Finland: Pattern Recognition Society of Finland, 214–20.

Kohonen, T. (1982) Clustering, taxonomy, and topological maps of patterns. In M. Lang (ed.), *Proceedings of the Sixth International Conference on Pattern Recognition*, Silver Spring, MD: IEEE Computer Society Press, 114–25.

Kohonen, T. (1989) *Self-organization and Associative Memory*, 3rd edn. Berlin: Springer-Verlag.

Kohonen, T. (2001) *Self-organizing Maps*, 3rd edn. Berlin: Springer-Verlag.

Kuczaj, S. A. (1977) The acquisition of regular and irregular past tense forms. *Journal of Verbal Learning and Verbal Behavior*, 16, 589–600.

Kuczaj, S. A. (1978) Children's judgments of grammatical and ungrammatical irregular past tense verbs. *Child Development*, 49, 319–26.

Kuhn, T. S. (1962/1970) *Structure of Scientific Revolutions*. Chicago: University of Chicago Press.

Lachter, J. and Bever, T. G. (1988) The relation between linguistic structure and associative theories of language learning – a constructive critique of some connectionist learning models. *Cognition*, 28, 195–247.

Laird, J. E., Newell, A., and Rosenbloom, P. S. (1987) SOAR: An architecture for general intelligence. *Artificial Intelligence*, 33, 1–64.

Lakoff, G. (1970) *Irregularity in Syntax*. New York: Holt, Rinehart, and Winston.

Landau, L. (1944) On the problem of turbulence. *C. R. Academy of Science, URSS*, 44, 311–16.

Langton, C. G. (1990) Computation at the edge of chaos: Phase transitions and emergent computation. *Physica D*, 42, 12–37.

Langton, C. G. (ed.) (1995) *Artificial Life: An Overview*. Cambridge, MA: MIT Press.

Langton, C. G. (1996) Artificial life. In M. A. Boden (ed.), *Artificial Life*, Oxford: Oxford University Press, 39–94.

Larkin, W. and Burns, D. (1977) Sentence comprehension and memory for embedded structure. *Memory and Cognition*, 5, 17–22.

Lashley, K. S. (1951) The problem of serial order in behavior. In L. A. Jeffres (ed.), *Cerebral Mechanisms in Behavior – The Hixon Symposium*, New York: Wiley.

Lawson, E. T. and McCauley, R. N. (1990) *Rethinking Religion: Connecting Cognition and Culture*. Cambridge: Cambridge University Press.

Le Cun, Y. (1986) Learning processes in an asymmetric threshold network. In E. Bienenstock, F. Fogelman-Soulie, and G. Weisbuch (eds), *Disordered Systems and Biological Organization*. Berlin: Springer.

Lettvin, J. Y., Maturana, H. R., McCulloch, W. S., and Pitts, W. H. (1959) What the frog's eye tells the frog's brain. *Proceedings of the IRE*, 47, 1940–51.

Levine, D. S. (1991) *Introduction to Neural and Cognitive Modeling*. Hillsdale, NJ: Erlbaum.

Levy, W. B., Colbert, C. M., and Desmond, N. L. (1990) Elemental adaptive processes of neurons and synapses: a statistical/computational perspective. In M. A. Gluck and D. E. Rumelhart (eds), *Neuroscience and Connectionist Theory*, Hillsdale, NJ: Erlbaum, 187–235.

Lin, S. and Kernighan, B. W. (1973) An algorithm for the TSP problem. *Operations Research*, 21, 498.

Lindsay, P. H. and Norman, D. A. (1972) *Human Information Processing: An Introduction to Psychology*. New York: Academic Press.

Little, W. A. and Shaw, G. L. (1975) A statistical theory of short and long term memory. *Behavioral Biology*, 14, 115–33. Reprinted in Anderson and Rosenfeld (1988), 231–41.

Livingstone, M. and Hubel, D. (1988) Segregation of form, color, movement, and depth: Anatomy, physiology, and perception. *Science*, 240, 740–9.

Lotka, A. J. (1925) *Elements of Mathematical Biology*. Baltimore: Williams and Wilkins.

Lukashin, A. V. and Georgopoulos, A. P. (1994) Directional operations in the motor cortex modeled by a neural network of spiking neurons. *Biological Cybernetics*, 71, 79–85.

Lycan, W. (1991) Homuncular functionalism meets PDP. In W. Ramsey, S. P. Stich, and D. E. Rumelhart (eds), *Philosophy and Connectionist Theory*, Hillsdale, NJ: Erlbaum, 259–86.

MacDonald, M. C. and Christiansen, M. H. (in press) Reassessing working memory: A comment on Just and Carpenter (1992) and Waters and Caplan (1996). *Psychological Review*.

MacWhinney, B. and Bates, E. (eds) (1989) *The Crosslinguistic Study of Sentence Processing*. Cambridge: Cambridge University Press.

Marchman, V. A. and Bates, E. (1994) Continuity in Lexical and morphological development: a test of the critical mass hypothesis. *Journal of Child Language*, 21, 339–66.

Marchman, V. A., Plunkett, K., and Goodman, J. (1997) Overregularization in English plural and past tense inflectional morphology: a response to Marcus (1995). *Journal of Child Language*, 24, 767–79.

Marcus, G. F. (1995) The acquisition of the English past tense in children and multilayered connectionist networks. *Cognition*, 56, 271–9.

Marcus, G. F., Pinker, S., Ullman, M., Hollander, M., Rosen, T. J., and Xu, F. (1992) Overregularization in language acquisition. *Monographs of the Society for Research in Child Development*, 57 (4, Serial no. 228).

Marcus, G. F., Vijayan, S., Bandi Rao, S., and Vishton, P. M. (1999) Rule learning by seven-month-old infants. *Science*, 283, 77–80.

Mareschal, D., Plunkett, K. and Harris, P. (1995) Developing object permanence: A connectionist model. *Proceedings of the Seventeenth Annual Conference of the Cognitive Science Society*, Hillsdale, NJ: Erlbaum.

Margolis, H. (1987) *Patterns, Thinking, and Cognition. A Theory of Judgment*. Chicago: University of Chicago Press.

Marks, L. E. (1968) Scaling of grammaticalness of self-embedded English sentences. *Journal of Verbal Learning and Verbal Behavior*, 7, 965–7.

Marr, D. (1969) A theory of cerebellar cortex. *Journal of Physiology*, 202, 437–70.

Marr, D. (1970) A theory for cerebral cortex. *Proceedings of the Royal Society of London, Series B*, 176, 161–234.

Marr, D. (1971) Simple memory: A theory for archicortex. *Philosophical Transactions of the Royal Society of London, B*, 262, 23–90.

Marr, D. (1982) *Vision*. San Francisco: Freeman.

Marshall, J. C. and Newcombe, F. (1973) Patterns of paralexia: a psycholinguistic approach. *Journal of Psycholinguistic Research*, 2, 175–99.

Matthews, R. J. (1997) Can connectionists explain systematicity? *Mind and Language*, 12, 154–77.

McCann, R. S. and Besner, D. (1987) Reading pseudohomophones: Implications for models of pronunciation and the locus of the word frequency effects in word naming. *Journal of Experimental Psychology: Human Perception and Performance*, 13, 14–24.

McClelland, J. L. (1981) Retrieving general and specific information from stored knowledge of specifics. *Proceedings of the Third Annual Conference of the Cognitive Science Society*, 170–2.

McClelland, J. L. (1987) The case of interactionism in language processing. In M. Coltheart (ed.), *Attention and Performance XII: The Psychology of Reading*, London: Erlbaum, 3–36.

McClelland, J. L. (1989) Parallel distributed processing: Implications for cognition and development. In R. Morris (ed.), *Parallel Distributed Processing: Implications for Psychology and Neurobiology*, Oxford: Clarendon Press.

McClelland, J. L. (1996) Integration of information: Reflections on the Theme of Attention and Performance XVI. In T. Inui and J. L. McClelland (eds), *Attention and Performance XVI: Information Integration in Perception and Communication*, Cambridge, MA: MIT Press, 633–48.

McClelland, J. L. and Kawamoto, A. H. (1986) Mechanisms of sentence processing: Assigning roles to constituents. In J. L. McClelland, D. E. Rumelhart, and the PDP Research Group (eds), *Parallel Distributed Processing: Explorations in the Microstructure of Cognition*, vol. 2: *Psychological and Biological Models*, Cambridge, MA: MIT Press, 272–325.

McClelland, J. L., McNaughton, B. L., and O'Reilly, R. C. (1995) Why there are complementary learning systems in the hippocampus and neocortex: Insights from the successes and failures of connectionist models of learning and memory. *Psychological Review*, 102, 419–57.

McClelland, J. L. and Rumelhart, D. E. (1981) An interactive activation model of context effects in letter perception: Part 1. An account of basic findings. *Psychological Review*, 88, 375–407.

McClelland, J. L. and Rumelhart, D. E. (1988) *Explorations in Parallel Distributed Processing: A Handbook of Models, Programs, and Exercises*. Cambridge, MA: MIT Press.

McClelland, J. L., Rumelhart, D. E., and the PDP Research Group (1986) *Parallel Distributed Processing: Explorations in the Microstructure of Cognition*, vol. 2: *Psychological and Biological Models*. Cambridge, MA: MIT Press.

McCloskey, M. and Cohen, N. J. (1989) Catastrophic interference in connectionist networks: The sequential learning problem. In G. H. Bower (ed.), *The Psychology of Learning and Motivation*, vol. 24. New York: Academic Press, 109–65.

McCulloch, W. S. and Pitts, W. (1943) A logical calculus of the ideas immanent in nervous activity. *Bulletin of Mathematical Biophysics*, 5, 115–33. Reprinted in Anderson and Rosenfeld (1988), 18–27.

McKoon, G. and Ratcliff, R. (1979) Priming in episodic and semantic memory. *Journal of Verbal Learning and Verbal Behavior*, 18, 463–80.

McLaughlin, B. (1993) Systematicity, conceptual truth, and evolution. In C. Hookway and D. Peterson (eds), *Philosophy and Cognitive Science*, Cambridge: Cambridge University Press, 217–34.

McLeod, P., Plunkett, K., and Rolls, E. (1998) *Introduction to Connectionist Modelling of Cognitive Processes*. Oxford: Oxford University Press.

McNaughton, B. L. (1989) Neuronal mechanisms for spatial computation and information storage. In L. Nadel, L. A. Cooper, P. Culicover, and R. M. Harnish (eds), *Neural Connections, Mental Computation*, Cambridge, MA: MIT Press, 285–350.

McNaughton, B. L. and Nadel, L. (1990) Hebb–Marr networks and the neurobiology representation of action in space. In M. A. Gluck and D. E. Rumelhart (eds), *Neuroscience and Connectionist Theory*, Hillsdale, NJ: Erlbaum, 1–63.

McNeill, D. (1975) Semiotic extension. In R. L. Solso (ed.), *Information Processing and Cognition: The Loyola Symposium*, Hillsdale, NJ: Lawrence Erlbaum.

Medin, D. L. (1989) Concepts and conceptual structure. *American Psychologist*, 44, 1469–81.

Medin, D. L. and Schaffer, M. M. (1978) A context theory of classification learning. *Psychological Review*, 85, 207–38.

Miikkulainen, R. (1993) *Subsymbolic Natural Language Processing: An Integrated Model of Scripts, Lexicon, and Memory*. Cambridge, MA: MIT Press.

Miikkulainen, R. and Dyer, M. (1991) Natural language processing with modular PDP networks and distributed lexicon. *Cognitive Science*, 15, 343–99.

Miller, G. A. and Chomsky, N. (1963) Finitary models of language users. In R. D. Luce, R. R. Bush, and E. Galanter (eds), *Handbook of Mathematical Psychology*, vol. 2. New York: Wiley.

Miller, G. A. and Isard, S. (1964) Free recall of self-embedded English sentences. *Information and Control*, 7, 292–303.

Miller, K. D., Keller, J. B., and Stryker, M. P. (1989) Ocular dominance column development: Analysis and simulation. *Science*, 245, 605–15.

Millikan, R. (1993) *White Queen Psychology and Other Essays for Alice*. Cambridge, MA: MIT Press.

Milner, A. D. and Goodale, M. A. (1995) *The Visual Brain in Action*. Oxford: Oxford University Press.

Minsky, M. (ed.) (1968) *Semantic Information Processing*. Cambridge, MA: MIT Press.

Minsky, M. A. and Papert, S. (1969) *Perceptrons*. Cambridge, MA: MIT Press.

Mishkin, M., Ungerleider, L. G., and Macko, K. A. (1983) Object vision and spatial vision: Two cortical pathways. *Trends in Neuroscience*, 6, 414–17.

Mitchell, M., Crutchfield, J. P., and Hraber, P. T. (1994) Dynamics, computation, and the "edge of chaos": A re-examination. In G. Cowan, D. Pines, and D. Melzner (eds), *Complexity: Metaphors, Models, and Reality*. Santa Fe Institute Studies in the Sciences of Complexity, 19, Reading MA: Addison-Wesley, 497–513.

Mitchell, T. (1997) *Machine Learning*. New York: McGraw Hill.

Morris, R. G. M., Garrud, P., Rawlins, J. N. P., and O'Keefe, J. (1982) Place navigation impaired in rats with hippocampal lesions. *Nature*, 297, 681–3.

Morris, R. (1999) *Artificial Worlds: Computers, Complexity, and the Riddle of Life*. New York: Plenum Trade.

Morton, J. and Patterson, K. (1980) A new attempt at an interpretation, or, an attempt at a new interpretation. In M. Coltheart, K. Patterson, and J. C. Marshall (eds), *Deep Dyslexia*. London: Routledge and Kegan Paul, 91–118.

Mountcastle, V. B. (1957) Modality and topographic properties of single neurons of cat's somatic sensory cortex. *Journal of Neurophysiology*, 20, 408–34.

Murre, J. M. J., Phaf, R. H., and Wolters, G. (1992) CALM: Categorizing and learning module. *Neural Networks*, 5, 55–82.

Nadel, L. (1994) Multiple memory systems: What and why, an update. In D. L. Schacter and E. Tulving (eds), *Memory Systems 1994*. Cambridge, MA: MIT Press, 39–63.

Neisser, U. (1967) *Cognitive Psychology*. New York: Appleton-Century-Crofts.

Neisser, U. (1983) Toward a skillful psychology. In D. R. Rogers and J. A. Sloboda (eds), *The Acquisition of Symbolic Skills*. New York: Plenum.

Nelson, K. (1973) Structure and strategy in learning to talk. *Monographs of the Society for Research in Child Development*, 38 (1–2, Serial no. 149).

Nelson, K. E. and Bonvillian, J. D. (1978) Early language development: Conceptual growth and related processes between 2 and 4 1/2 years of age. In K. E. Nelson (ed.), *Children's Language*, vol. 1. New York: Gardner Press, 467–556.

Neville, H. J. and Lawson, D. (1987) Attention to central and peripheral visual space in a movement detection task: An event related potential and behavioral study. I: Normal hearing adults. *Brain Research*, 405, 253–67.

Newell, A. (1989) *Unified Theories of Cognition*. Cambridge, MA: Harvard.

Newell, A. (1990) *Unified Theories of Cognition*. Cambridge, MA: Harvard University Press.

Newell, A. and Simon, H. A. (1956) The logic theory machine. *IRE Transactions on Information Theory*, 3, 61–79.

Newell, A. and Simon, H. A. (1972) *Human Problem Solving*. Englewood Cliffs, NJ: Prentice Hall.

Newell, A. and Simon, H. (1981) Computer science as empirical inquiry. In J. Haugeland (ed.), *Mind Design*. Montgomery, VT: Bradford Books, 35–66.

Nolfi, S., Elman, J. L., and Parisi, D. (1994) Learning and evolution in neural networks. *Adaptive Behavior*, 3, 5–28.

Nolfi, S. and Floreano, D. (2000) *Evolutionary Robotics: The Biology, Intelligence, and Technology of Self-organizing Machines*. Cambridge, MA: MIT Press.

Nolfi, S., Florano, D., Miglino, O. and Mondada, F. (1994) How to evolve autonomous robots: Different approaches in evolutionary robotics. In R. Brooks and P. Maes (eds), *Proceedings of the International Conference on Artificial Life IV*. Cambridge, MA: MIT Press, 190–7.

Nolfi, S., Miglino, O., and Parisi, D. (1994) Phenotypic plasticity in evolving neural networks. In D. P. Gaussier and J.-D. Nicoud (eds), *Proceedings of the International Conference From Perception to Action*. Los Alamitos, CA: IEEE Press, 146–57.

Nolfi, S. and Parisi, D. (1997) Learning to adapt to changing environments in evolving neural networks. *Adaptive Behavior*, 5, 75–98.

Norman, D. A. (ed.) (1970) *Models of Human Memory*. New York: Academic Press.

Norman, D. A., Rumelhart, D. E., and the LNR Research Group (1975) *Explorations in Cognition*. San Francisco: Freeman.

O'Keefe, J. (1989) Computations the hippocampus might perform. In L. Nadel, L. A. Cooper, P. Culicover, and R. M. Harnish (eds), *Neural Connections, Mental Computation*, Cambridge, MA: MIT Press, 225–84.

O'Keefe, J. and Dostrovsky, J. (1971) The hippocampus as a spatial map: Preliminary evidence from unit activity in the freely moving rat. *Brain Research*, 34, 171–5.

O'Keefe, J. A. and Nadel, L. (1978) *The Hippocampus as a Cognitive Map*. Oxford: Oxford University Press.

O'Reilly, R. C. (1996) Biologically plausible error-driven learning using local activation differences: The generalized recirculation algorithm. *Neural Computation*, 8, 895–938.

O'Reilly, R. C. and McClelland, J. L. (1994) Hippocampal conjunctive encoding, storage, and recall: Avoiding a tradeoff. *Hippocampus*, 4, 661–82.

O'Reilly, R. C. and Munakata, Y. (2000) *Computational Explorations in Cognitive Neuroscience: Understanding the Mind by Simulating the Brain*. Cambridge, MA: MIT Press.

Packard, N. H. (1988) Adaptation toward the edge of chaos. In J. A. S. Kelso, A. J. Mandell, and M. F. Shlesinger (eds), *Dynamic Patterns in Complex Systems*. Singapore: World Scientific, 293–301.

Papert, S. (1988) One AI or many? *Daedalus*, 117, 1–14.

Parker, D. B. (1985) Learning logic. Technical Report TR-87, Center for Computational Research in Economics and Management Science, MIT. Cambridge, MA.

Patterson, K. and Lambon Ralph, M. A. (1999) Selective disorders of reading? *Current Opinion in Neurobiology*, 9, 235–9.

Patterson, K., Seidenberg, M. S., and McClelland, J. L. (1989) Connections and disconnections: Acquired dyslexia in a computational model of reading processes. In R. G. M. Morris (ed.), *Parallel Distributed Processing: Implications for Psychology and Neurobiology*. Oxford: Oxford University Press, 131–81.

Pavel, M., Gluck, M. A., and Henkle, V. (1988) Generalization by humans and multi-layer adaptive networks. *Proceedings of the Tenth Annual Conference of the Cognitive Science Society*. Hillsdale, NJ: Lawrence Erlbaum, 680–7.

Petersen, S. E., Fox, P. T., Posner, M. I., Mintun, M., and Raichle, M. E. (1988) Positron emission tomographic studies of the cortical anatomy of single-word processing. *Nature*, 331, 585–8.

Phillips, W. A. (1997) Theories of cortical computation. In M. D. Rugg (ed.), *Cognitive Neuroscience*. Cambridge, MA: MIT Press, 11–46.

Pinker, S. (1999) *Words and Rules: The Ingredients of Language*. New York: Basic Books.

Pinker, S. and Prince, A. (1988) On language and connectionism: Analysis of a parallel distributed processing model of language acquisition. *Cognition*, 28, 73–193.

Pitts, W. and McCulloch, W. S. (1947) How we know universals: The perception of auditory and visual forms. *Bulletin of Mathematical Biophysics*, 9, 127–47. Reprinted in Anderson and Rosenfeld (1988), 32–41.

Plaut, D. C. (1995) Double dissociation without modularity: Evidence from neuropsychology. *Journal of Clinical and Experimental Neuropsychology*, 17, 291–321.

Plaut, D. C. (1996) Relearning after damage in connectionist networks: Toward a theory of rehabilitation. *Brain and Language*, 52, 25–82.

Plaut, D. C. (1997) Structure and function in the lexical system: Insights from distributed models of word reading and lexical decision. *Language and Cognitive Processes*, 12, 765–805.

Plaut, D. C., McClelland, J. L., Seidenberg, M. S., and Patterson, K. E. (1996) Understanding normal and impaired word reading: Computational principles in quasi-regular domains. *Psychological Review*, 103, 56–115.

Plaut, D. C. and Shallice, T. (1991) Effects of word abstractness in a connectionist model of deep dyslexia. *Proceedings of the Thirteenth Annual Meeting of the Cognitive Science Society.* Hillsdale, NJ: Lawrence Erlbaum.

Plaut, D. C. and Shallice, T. (1993) Deep dyslexia: A case study of connectionist neuropsychology. *Cognitive Neuropsychology*, 10, 377–500.

Plunkett, K. (1995) Connectionist approaches to language acquisition. In *Handbook of Child Language*, eds P. Fletcher and B. McWhinney, Oxford: Blackwell, 36–72.

Plunkett, K. and Elman, J. L. (1997) *Exercises in Rethinking Innateness: A Handbook for Connectionist Simulations.* Cambridge, MA: MIT Press/Bradford Books.

Plunkett, K. and Marchman, V. (1991) U-shaped learning and frequency effects in a multilayered perceptron: Implications for child language acquisition. *Cognition*, 38, 43–102.

Plunkett, K. and Marchman, V. A. (1993) From rote learning to system building: Acquiring verb morphology in children and connectionist nets. *Cognition*, 48, 21–69.

Plunkett, K. and Marchman, V. A. (1996) Learning from a connectionist model of the acquisition of the English past tense. *Cognition*, 61, 299–308.

Plunkett, K. and Nakisa, R. C. (1997) A connectionist model of the Arabic plural system. *Language and Cognitive Processes*, 12, 807–38.

Pollack, J. (1990) Recursive distributed representations. *Artificial Intelligence*, 46, 77–105.

Port, R. and van Gelder, T. (eds) (1995) *Mind as Motion: Explorations in the Dynamics of Cognition.* Cambridge, MA: MIT Press.

Posner, M. I. and Keele, S. W. (1968) On the genesis of abstract ideas. *Journal of Experimental Psychology*, 77, 353–63.

Price, C. J., Howard, D., Patterson, K., Warburton, E. A., Friston, K. J., and Frackowiak, R. S. J. (1998) A functional neuroimaging description of two deep dyslexic patients. *Journal of Cognitive Neuroscience*, 10, 303–15.

Prince, A. and Smolensky, P. (1993) *Optimality Theory: Constraint Interaction in Generative Grammar.* Technical report, TR-2, Rutgers University Center for Cognitive Science, and CU-CS-696-93, Department of Computer Science, University of Colorado, Boulder. To appear in the Linguistic Inquiry Monograph Series, MIT Press.

Prince, A. and Smolensky, P. (1997) Optimality: From neural networks to universal grammar. *Science*, 275, 1604–10.

Putnam, H. (1975a) Philosophy and our mental life. In H. Putnam (ed.), *Mind, Language, and Reality. Philosophical Papers of Hilary Putnam*, vol. 2. Cambridge: Cambridge University Press, 291–303.

Putnam, H. (1975b) The meaning of "meaning." In H. Putnam (ed.), *Mind, Language, and Reality: Philosophical Papers of Hilary Putnam*, vol. 2. Cambridge: Cambridge University Press, 215–71.

Pylyshyn, Z. W. (1984) *Computation and Cognition: Toward a Foundation for Cognitive Science.* Cambridge, MA: MIT Press.

Quillian, M. R. (1968) Semantic memory. In M. Minsky (ed.), *Semantic Information Processing*. Cambridge, MA: MIT Press, 227–70.

Quine, W. V. (1969a) Natural kinds. In W. V. Quine, *Ontological Relativity and Other Essays*. New York: Columbia University Press, 114–38.

Quinlan, P. (1991) *Connectionism and Psychology*. Chicago: University of Chicago Press.

Ramsey, W., Stich, S. P., and Rumelhart, D. E. (eds) (1991) *Philosophy and Connectionist Theory*. Hillsdale, NJ: Erlbaum.

Ratcliff, R. (1990) Connectionist models of recognition memory: Constraints imposed by learning and forgetting functions. *Psychological Review*, 97, 285–308.

Redish, A. D. (1999) *Beyond the Cognitive Map*. Cambridge, MA: MIT Press.

Redish, A. D. and Touretzky, D. S. (1997) Navigating with landmarks: Computing goal locations from place codes. In K. Ikeuchi and M. Veloso (eds), *Symbolic Visual Learning*. Oxford: Oxford University Press.

Redish, A. D. and Touretzky, D. S. (1998) The role of the hippocampus in solving the Morris water maze. *Neural Computation*, 10, 73–111.

Reeke, G. N. and Edelman, G. M. (1988) Real brains and artificial intelligence. *Daedalus*, 117, 142–73.

Reicher, G. M. (1969) Perceptual recognition as a function of meaningfulness of stimulus material. *Journal of Experimental Psychology*, 81, 274–80.

Reynolds, C. W. (1987) Flocks, herds, and schools: A distributed behavioral model. *Computer Graphics*, 21, 25–34.

Rips, L. J. (1994) *The Psychology of Proof: Deductive Reasoning in Human Thinking*. Cambridge, MA: MIT Press.

Rolls, E. T. (1990) Principles underlying the representation and storage of information in neuronal networks in the primate hippocampus and cerebral cortex. In S. F. Zornetzer, J. L. Davis, and C. Lau (eds), *An Introduction to Neural and Electronic Networks*, San Diego, CA: Academic Press, 73–90.

Rolls, E. T. (1995) A model of the operation of the hippocampus and entorhinal cortex in memory. *International Journal of Neural Systems*, 6, suppl.: 51–70.

Rolls, E. T. and Treves, A. (1998) *Neural Networks and Brain Function*. Oxford: Oxford University Press.

Rosch, E. (1975) Cognitive representations of semantic categories. *Journal of Experimental Psychology: General*, 104, 192–233.

Rose, S. P. R. (1976) *The Conscious Brain*. New York: Vintage Books.

Rosenblatt, F. (1958) The perceptron: A probabilistic model for information storage and organization in the brain. *Psychological Review*, 65, 368–408. Reprinted in Anderson and Rosenfeld (1988), 92–114.

Rosenblatt, F. (1959) Two theorems of separability in the perceptron. In *Mechanisation of Thought Processes: Proceedings of a Symposium Held at the National Physical Laboratory, November, 1958*, vol. 1. London: HMSO, 421–56.

Rosenblatt, F. (1962) *The Principles of Neurodynamics*. New York: Spartan.

Rueckl, J. G., Cave, K. R., and Kosslyn, S. M. (1989) Why are "what" and "where" processed by separate cortical visual systems? A computational investigation. *Journal of Cognitive Neuroscience*, 1, 171–86.

Rumelhart, D. E. (1975) Notes on a schema for stories. In D. G. Bobrow and A. M. Collins (eds), *Representation and Understanding*. New York: Academic Press.

Rumelhart, D. E. (1990) Brain style computation: Learning and generalization. In S. F. Zornetzer, J. L. Davis, and C. Lau (eds), *An Introduction to Neural and Electronic Networks*, San Diego, CA: Academic Press, 405–20.

Rumelhart, D. E., Hinton, G. E., and McClelland, J. L. (1986) A general framework for parallel distributed processing. In Rumelhart, McClelland, and the PDP Research Group (1986), chapter 2, 45–76.

Rumelhart, D. E., Hinton, G. E., and Williams, R. J. (1986a) Learning internal representations by error propagation. In Rumelhart, McClelland, and the PDP Research Group (1986), chapter 8, 318–62.

Rumelhart, D. E., Hinton, G. E., and Williams, R. J. (1986b) Learning representations by back-propagating errors. *Nature*, 323, 533–6.

Rumelhart, D. E. and McClelland, J. L. (1982) An interactive activation model of context effects in letter perception: Part 2. The contextual enhancement effect and some tests and extensions of the model. *Psychological Review*, 89, 60–94.

Rumelhart, D. E. and McClelland, J. L. (1985) Levels indeed! A response to Broadbent. *Journal of Experimental Psychology: General*, 114, 193–7.

Rumelhart, D. E. and McClelland, J. L. (1986a) On learning the past tense of English verbs. In McClelland, Rumelhart, and the PDP Research Group (1986), chapter 18, 216–71.

Rumelhart, D. E. and McClelland, J. L. (1986b) PDP models and general issues in cognitive science. In Rumelhart, McClelland, and the PDP Research Group (1986), chapter 4, 110–46.

Rumelhart, D. E., McClelland, J. L., and the PDP Research Group (1986) *Parallel Distributed Processing: Explorations in the Microstructure of Cognition*, vol. 1: *Foundations*. Cambridge, MA: MIT Press.

Rumelhart, D. E. and Siple, P. (1974) Process of recognizing tachistoscopically presented words. *Psychological Review*, 81, 99–118.

Rumelhart, D. E., Smolensky, P., McClelland, J. L. and Hinton, G. E. (1986) Schemata and sequential thought processes in PDP models. In McClelland, Rumelhart, and the PDP Research Group (1986), chapter 14, 7–57.

Rumelhart, D. E. and Zipser, D. (1985) Feature discovery by competitive learning. *Cognitive Science*, 9, 75–112. Reprinted in Rumelhart and McClelland (1986), chapter 5, 151–93.

Ryle, G. (1949) *The Concept of Mind*. New York: Barnes and Noble.

Saffran, J. R., Aslin, R. N., and Newport, E. L. (1996) Statistical learning by 8-month-old infants. *Science*, 274, 1926–8.

Schank, R. C. (1972) Conceptual dependency: A theory of natural language understanding. *Cognitive Psychology*, 3, 552–631.

Schank, R. C. (1975) *Conceptual Information Processing*. Amsterdam: North Holland.

Schank, R. C. (1982) *Dynamic Memory: A Theory of Reminding and Learning in Computers and People*. Cambridge: Cambridge University Press.

Schank, R. C. and Abelson, R. (1977) *Scripts, Plans, Goals, and Understanding*. Hillsdale, NJ: Lawrence Erlbaum.

Schneider, W. (1987) Connectionism: Is it a paradigm shift for psychology? *Behavior Research Methods, Instruments, and Computers*, 19, 73–83.

Scoville, W. B. and Milner, B. (1957) Loss of recent memory after bilateral hippocampal lesions. *Journal of Neurology, Neurosurgery, and Psychiatry*, 20, 11–21.

Searle, J. (1980) Minds, brains, programs. *Behavioral and Brain Sciences*, 3, 417–24.

Seidenberg, M. S. and McClelland, J. L. (1989) A distributed, developmental model of word recognition and naming. *Psychological Review*, 96, 523–68.

Sejnowski, T. J. and Rosenberg, C. R. (1986) NETtalk: a parallel network that learns to read aloud. Electrical Engineering and Computer Science Technical Report JHU1EECS-86101, Johns Hopkins University, Baltimore, MD. Reprinted in Anderson and Rosenfeld (1988), 663–72.

Sejnowski, T. J. and Rosenberg, C. R. (1987) Parallel networks that learn to pronounce English text. *Complex Systems*, 1, 145–68.

Selfridge, O. G. (1959) Pandemonium: A paradigm for learning. In *Symposium on the Mechanization of Thought Processes*. London: HMSO.

Selfridge, O. G. and Neisser, U. (1960) Pattern recognition by machine. *Scientific American*, 203, 60–8.

Shallice, T. (1988) *From Neuropsychology to Mental Structure*. Cambridge: Cambridge University Press.

Shallice, T., Warrington, E. K., and McCarthy, R. (1983) Reading without semantics. *Quarterly Journal of Experimental Psychology*, 35A, 111–38.

Shapiro, M. L. and Hetherington, P. A. (1993) A simple network model simulates hippocampal place fields: Parametric analyses and physiological predictions. *Behavioral Neuroscience*, 107, 34–50.

Sharp, P. E. (1991) Computer simulation of hippocampal place cells. *Psychobiology*, 19(2), 103–115.

Shastri, L. and Ajjanagadde, V. (1993) From simple associations to systematic reasoning: A connectionist representation of rules, variables and dynamic bindings using temporal synchrony. *Behavioral and Brain Sciences*, 16, 417–94.

Shepard, R. N. (1989) Internal representation of universal regularities: A challenge for connectionism. In L. Nadel, L. A. Cooper, P. Culicover, and R. M. Harnish (eds), *Neural Connections, Mental Computation*. Cambridge, MA: MIT Press, 104–34.

Shepherd, G. M. (1990) The significance of real neuron architectures for neural network simulations. In E. L. Schwartz, *Computational Neuroscience*, Cambridge, MA: MIT Press, 82–96.

Shipley, E. F. (1988) Two types of hierarchies: Class inclusion hierarchies and kind hierarchies. Paper presented at the annual meeting of the Jean Piaget Society, Philadelphia, PA, June.

Siegler, R. S. (1976) Three aspects of cognitive development. *Cognitive Psychology*, 8, 481–520.

Siegler, R. S. (1996) *Emerging Minds: The Process of Change in Children's Thinking*. Oxford: Oxford University Press.

Simon, H. A. (1967) The logic of heuristic decision making. In N. Rescher (ed.), *The Logic of Decision and Action*. Pittsburgh, PA: University of Pittsburgh Press, 1–20.

Simon, H. A. (1969) *The Sciences of the Artificial*. Cambridge, MA: MIT Press.

Singer, W. (1994) Putative functions of temporal correlations in neocortical processing. In C. Koch and J. L. Davis (eds), *Large-scale Neuronal Theories of the Brain*. Cambridge, MA: MIT Press, 201–37.

Skarda, C. A. and Freeman, W. J. (1987) How brains make chaos to make sense of the world. *Behavioral and Brain Sciences*, 10, 161–95.

Skrzypek, J. and Hoffman, J. (1989) Visual recognition of script characters: Neural network architectures. Technical Report UCLA-MPL-TR-89-10, Machine Perception Laboratory, University of California, Los Angeles.

Slobin, D. I. (1971) On the learning of morphological rules. A reply to Palermo and Eberhart. In D. I. Slobin (ed.), *The Ontogenesis of Grammar: A Theoretical Symposium*, New York: Academic Press.

Smart, J. J. C. (1959) Sensations and brain processes. *Philosophical Review*, 68, 141–56.

Smith, B. C. (1996) *On the Origin of Objects*. Cambridge, MA: MIT Press.

Smith, E. E. (1988) Concepts and thought. In R. J. Sternberg and E. E. Smith (eds), *The Psychology of Human Thought*. Cambridge: Cambridge University Press, 19–49.

Smith, E. E. and Medin, D. L. (1981) *Categories and Concepts*. Cambridge, MA: Harvard University Press.

Smolensky, P. (1986) Information processing in dynamical systems: Foundations of harmony theory. In Rumelhart, McClelland, and the PDP Research Group (1986), chapter 6, 194–281.

Smolensky, P. (1987) The constituent structure of connectionist mental states: A reply to Fodor and Pylyshyn. *The Southern Journal of Philosophy*, Supplement, 26, 137–61.

Smolensky, P. (1988) On the proper treatment of connectionism. *Behavioral and Brain Sciences*, 11, 1–74.

Smolensky, P. (1990) Tensor product variable binding and the representation of symbolic structures in connectionist systems. *Artificial Intelligence*, 46, 159–216.

Spieler D. H. and Balota, D. A. (1997) Bringing computational models of word naming down to the item level. *Psychological Science*, 8, 411–16.

Squire, L. R., Cohen, N. J., and Nadel, L. (1984) The medial temporal region and memory consolidation: A new hypothesis. In H. Weingartner and E. Parker (eds), *Memory Consolidation*. Hillsdale, NJ: Erlbaum, 185–210.

Stich, S. (1983) *From Folk Psychology to Cognitive Science*. Cambridge, MA: MIT Press.

Sun, R. and Alexandre, F. (1997) *Connectionist-Symbolic Integration: From Unified to Hybrid Approaches*. Mahwah, NJ: Lawrence Erlbaum Associates.

Sutherland, R. W. and Rudy, J. W. (1989) Configural association theory: The role of the hippocampal formation in learning, memory and amnesia. *Psychobiology*, 17, 129–44.

Suppes, P. (1970) Probabilistic grammars for natural languages, *Synthese*, 22, 95–116. Reprinted in D. Davidson and G. Harman (eds), *Semantics of Natural Languages*. Dordrecht: Reidel.

Sutton, R. S. and Barto, A. G. (1998) *Reinforcement Learning: An Introduction*. Cambridge, MA: MIT Press.

Taraban, R. and McClelland, J. L. (1987) Conspiracy effects in word recognition. *Journal of Memory and Language*, 26, 608–31.

Taylor, W. (1956) Electrical simulation of some nervous system functional activities. In E. C. Cherry (ed.), *Information Theory*. London: Butterworths.

Tesar, B., Grimshaw, J., and Prince, A. (1999) Linguistic and cognitive explanation in Optimality Theory. In E. Lepore and Z. Pylyshyn (eds), *What is Cognitive Science?* Malden, MA: Blackwell, 295–326.

Thagard, P. (1988) *Computational Philosophy of Science*. Cambridge, MA: MIT Press.

Thagard, P. (1998) Machine learning. In W. Bechtel and G. Graham (eds), *A Companion to Cognitive Science*, Oxford: Blackwell, 245–9.

Thelen, E. and Smith, L. B. (1994) *A Dynamical Systems Approach to the Development of Cognition and Action*. Cambridge, MA: MIT Press.

Thibadeau, R., Just, M. A., and Carpenter, P. A. (1982) A model of the time course and content of reading. *Cognitive Science*, 6, 157–204.

Touretzky, D. S. (1986) BoltzCONS: Reconciling connectionism with the recursive nature of stacks and trees. *Proceedings of the Eighth Annual Conference of the Cognitive Science Society*. London: Lawrence Erlbaum, 522–30.

Touretzky, D. S. (1990) BoltzCONS: Dynamic symbol structures in a connectionist network. *Artificial Intelligence*, 46, 5–46.

Touretzky, D. S. and Hinton, G. E. (1988) A distributed connectionist production system. *Cognitive Science*, 12, 423–66.

Touretzky, D. S. and Redish, A. D. (1996) A theory of rodent navigation based on interacting representations of space. *Hippocampus*, 6, 247–70.

Treves, A. and Rolls, E. T. (1994) A computational analysis of the role of the hippocampus in memory. *Hippocampus*, 4, 374–91.

Tulving, E. (1972) Episodic and semantic memory. In E. Tulving and W. Donaldson (eds), *Organization of Memory*. New York: Academic Press, 381–403.

Turnbull, O. H. (1999) Of two minds about two visual systems. *Psyche*, 5(8).

Tversky, A. and Kahneman, D. (1982) Judgments of and by representativeness. In D. Kahneman, P. Slovic, and A. Tversky (eds), *Judgment under Uncertainty: Heuristics and Biases*. Cambridge: Cambridge University Press, 84–98.

Ungerleider, L. G. and Mishkin, M. (1982) Two cortical visual systems. In D. J. Ingle, M. A. Goodale, and R. J. W. Mansfield (eds), *Analysis of Visual Behavior*. Cambridge, MA: MIT Press, 549–86.

van Essen, D. C., Anderson, C. H., and Olshausen, B. A. (1994) Dynamic routing strategies in sensory, motor, and cognitive processing. In C. Koch and J. L. Davis (eds), *Large-scale Neuronal Theories of the Brain*. Cambridge, MA: MIT Press, 271–99.

van Gelder, T. (1990) Compositionality: A connectionist variation on a classical theme. *Cognitive Science*, 14, 355–84.

van Gelder, T. (1995) What might cognition be, if not computation? *The Journal of Philosophy*, 92, 345–81.

van Gelder, T. (1998) The dynamical hypothesis in cognitive science. *Behavioral and Brain Sciences*, 21, 615–28.

van Gelder, T. J. (1999) Bait and switch? Real time, ersatz time and dynamical models. In R. Heath, B. Hayes, A. Heathcote, and C. Hooker (eds), *Dynamical Cognitive Science: Proceedings of the Fourth Australasian Cognitive Science Conference*. Newcastle, NSW: University of Newcastle.

van Gelder, T. and Port, R. (1995) It's about time: An overview of the dynamical approach to cognition. In R. Port and T. van Gelder (eds), *Mind as Motion*. Cambridge, MA: MIT Press, 1–43.

van Leeuwen, C. and Raffone, A. (2001) Coupled nonlinear maps as models of perceptual pattern and memory trace dynamics. *Cognitive Processing*, 2.

van Leeuwen, C., Steyvers, M., and Nooter, M. (1997) Stability and intermittency in large-scale coupled oscillator models for perceptual segmentation. *Journal of Mathematical Psychology*, 41, 319–44.

van Leeuwen, C., Verver, S., and Brinkers, M. (2000) Visual illusions and outline-invariance in nonstationary activity patterns. *Connection Science*, 12, 279–98.

Van Orden, G. C., Pennington, B. F. and Stone, G. O. (1990) Word identification in reading and the promise of subsymbolic psycholinguistics. *Psychological Review*, 97, 488–522.

Volterra, V. (1926) Fluctuations in the abundance of a species considered mathematically. *Nature* 118, 558–60.

von der Malsburg, C. (1973) Self-organizing of orientation sensitive cells in the striate cortex. *Kybernetik*, 14, 85–100.

von der Malsburg, C. (1981) The correlation theory of brain function. *Internal Report 81–2*. Department of Neurobiology, Max-Planck-Institute for Biophysical Chemistry, Göttingen, Germany.

von der Malsburg, C. (1996) The binding problem of neural networks. In R. Llinás and P. S. Churchland (eds), *The Mind–Brain Continuum*. Cambridge, MA: MIT Press, 131–46.

von Neumann, J. (1956) Probabilistic logics and the synthesis of reliable organisms from unreliable components. In C. E. Shannon and J. McCarthy (eds), *Automata Studies*. Princeton, NJ: Princeton University Press.

Vygotsky, L. S. (1962) *Thought and Language*. Cambridge, MA: MIT Press. (Originally published in Russian, 1934.)

Waddington, C. H. (1975) *The Evolution of an Evolutionist*. Ithaca, NY: Cornell University Press.

Waskan, J. and Bechtel, W. (1997) Directions in connectionist research: Tractable computations without syntactically structured representations. *Metaphilosophy*, 28, 31–62.

Wasserman, P. D. (1989) *Neural Computing: Theory and Practice*. New York: Van Nostrand Reinhold.

Watson, J. B. (1930) *Behaviorism*. Chicago: University of Chicago Press.

Werbos, P. J. (1974) *Beyond Regression: New Tools for Prediction and Analysis in the Behavioral Sciences*. Unpublished Ph.D. dissertation, Harvard University, Cambridge, MA.

Werner, G. (1988a) Five decades on the path to naturalizing epistemology. In J. S. Lund (ed.), *Sensory Processing in the Mammalian Brain*. New York: Oxford University Press, 345–59.

Werner, G. (1988b) The many faces of neuroreductionism. In E. Basar (ed.), *Dynamics of Sensory and Cognitive Processing by the Brain*. Berlin: Springer-Verlag, 241–57.

Wheeler, D. D. (1970) Processes in word recognition. *Cognitive Psychology*, 1, 59–85.

Wheeler, M. (1996) From robots to Rothko: The bringing forth of worlds. In M. A. Boden (ed.), *Artificial Life*. Oxford: Oxford University Press, 206–36.

Wheeler, M. (1998) Explaining the evolved: Homunculi, modules, and internal representation. In P. Husbands and J.-A. Meyer (eds), *Evolutionary Robotics: Proceedings of the First European Workshop*. New York: Springer-Verlag (1998) 87–107.

Wickelgren, W. A. (1969) Auditory or articulatory coding in verbal short-term memory. *Psychological Review*, 76, 232–5.

Widrow, B. and Hoff, M. E. (1960) Adaptive switching circuits. *1960 IRE WESCON Convention Record*. New York: IRE, 96–104. Reprinted in Anderson and Rosenfeld (1988), 126–34.

Wilson, M. A. and McNaughton, B. L. (1993) Dynamics of the hippocampal ensemble code for space. *Science*, 261, 1055–8.

Wimsatt, W. C. (1986) Developmental constraints, generative entrenchment, and the innate–acquired distinction. In W. Bechtel (ed.), *Integrating Scientific Disciplines*. Dordrecht: Martinus Nijhoff, 105–208.

Winograd, S. and Cowan, J. (1963) *Reliable Computation in the Presence of Noise*. Cambridge, MA: MIT Press.

Wittgenstein, L. (1953) *Philosophical Investigations*. New York: Macmillan.

Wolfram, S. (1984) Computer software in science and mathematics. *Scientific American* (September), 188–203.

Worden, R. (1992) Navigation by fragment fitting: A theory of hippocampal function. *Hippocampus*, 2, 165–87.

Zadeh, L. A. (1965) Fuzzy sets. *Information and Control*, 8, 338–53.

Zeki, S. (1993) *A Vision of the Brain*. Oxford: Blackwell Scientific.

Zemel, R. S., Mozer, M. C., and Hinton, G. E. (1988) Traffic: A model of object recognition based on transformations of feature instances. In D. S. Touretzky, G. E. Hinton, and T. J. Sejnowski (eds), *Proceedings of the 1988 Connectionist Models Summer School*. San Mateo: Morgan Kaufmann.

Zipser, D. (1985) A computational model of hippocampal place fields. *Behavioral Neuroscience*, 99, 1006–18.

Zipser, D. (1990) Modeling cortical computation with backpropagation. In M. A. Gluck and D. E. Rumelhart (eds), *Neuroscience and Connectionist Theory*. Hillsdale, NJ: Lawrence Erlbaum.

Zipser, D. and Andersen, R. A. (1988) A backpropagation programmed network that simulates response properties of a subset of posterior parietal neurons. *Nature*, 331, 679–84.

Zola-Morgan, S. and Squire, L. R. (1990) The primate hippocampal formation: Evidence for a time-limited role in memory storage. *Science*, 250, 288–90.

Zurif, E. B. (1980) Language mechanisms: A neuropsychological perspective. *American Scientist*, May.

Name Index

SUBJECT INDEX

Boldface numbers indicate entries in Appendix B: Glossary. The Glossary entries are a good place to obtain a quick introduction to a term or concept and so are listed first

λ, 289, 290

accommodation and assimilation, 117
acquired disabilities, 323
ACT, ACT*, and ACT-R, 15, 37, 41, 105, 108
activation, **350**, 2, 3, 20–41, 45–6, 57–70, 78–81
  and learning, 51
  continuous function, 92
  interactive, 19, 93–100; and competition, 19, 337
  linear rule, 33–4, 58, 91–2
  logistic function, 70, 74, 76, 111, 123, 126, 241
  nonlinear rule, 37, 70, 83
  parallel propagation, 38, 168
  probabilistic rule, 32
  rule, 24, 30, 32–4
  spreading, **359**, 15, 37, 38, 41
  stochastic function, 127, 147
  values, 20–5, 30, 32–5
  see also bias; clamping; learning; threshold
affirming the consequent, 107, 108
alternative syllogism, 107, 112
ambiguous figures, 260, 263–5
amnesia, 313, 316–21
  retrograde, 318–21
analysis
  by hidden units, 77
  cluster, 78, 176, 182, 253–4, 268
  dynamic, 268, 269, 274–6, 301
  featural, 41–2

levels of, 160, 162, 198, 344
  linguistic, 136, 156
  mathematical, 321–3
  mechanistic, 268, 270, 274, 301
  of hidden units, 112
  principal components, 254, 256
  symbolic level of, 16
annealing see simulated annealing
anomia, 326, 327
aphasia, 48, 217, 324
architecture
  classical, 194
  connectionist, 15, 19–20, 29, 86, 140, 160, 165, 194
  feature map, 217
  FGREP see FGREP architecture
  functional, 161
  hippocampal, 313
  localist, 315
  modular see modular network architecture
  multilayer, 31
  neural, 45, 312, 343
  production system, 15, 38
  recurrent, 221, 223
  SOAR, 15
  subsumption see subsumption architecture
  symbolic, 45
artificial intelligence (AI), 1–2, 10–11, 56–7, 102, 106, 162, 201, 284–5, 303, 307
artificial life (A-life), 15, 17, 271, 282–306
associationism, 13, 54–5, 82–4, 87